Clinical Neuropsychology

Clinical Neuropsychology

Edited by

KENNETH M. HEILMAN, M.D.
PROFESSOR OF NEUROLOGY AND CLINICAL PSYCHOLOGY
UNIVERSITY OF FLORIDA COLLEGE OF MEDICINE

EDWARD VALENSTEIN, M.D.
ASSOCIATE PROFESSOR OF NEUROLOGY
UNIVERSITY OF FLORIDA COLLEGE OF MEDICINE

New York / Oxford
OXFORD UNIVERSITY PRESS
1979

Copyright © 1979 by Oxford University Press, Inc.

Library of Congress Cataloging in Publication Data

Main entry under title:
Clinical neuropsychology.

   Bibliography: p.
   Includes index.
   1. Neuropsychiatry. 2. Neuropsychology.
I. Heilman, Kenneth M., 1938- II. Valenstein, Edward.
[DNLM: 1. Neurologic manifestations. 2. Behavior.
3. Psychophysiology. 4. Nervous system diseases.
WL340.3.C641] RC341.C693 616.8'5 78-16059
ISBN 0-19-502477-X

Printed in the United States of America

Foreword

The term *neuropsychology,* which seems to be a relatively recent invention, has two closely related meanings. The first is simply the empirical correlation of behavioral change with site and type of damage in the nervous system. The second is the attempt to elucidate neural mechanisms underlying behavior. It may at first appear that this separation is artificial, but a careful reading of the literature will reveal two distinctive styles in the pursuit of neuropsychology, and distinguished contributors will be found in both camps. Indeed, the delicately balanced tension between emphases on either psychological description or neurological mechanism is one of the sources of the distinctive intellectual atmosphere of this field.

Neuropsychology, as a field of study, can be traced back to the beginnings of modern clinical neurology in the last half of the nineteenth century. The phrenologists had made the attempt to correlate the prominence of different mental functions with individual variations in the structure of the brain, but their effort failed because, as Wernicke pointed out, "They assigned psychic functions, arbitrarily differentiated on the basis of linguistic usage . . . to areas of the cerebral cortex designated in an equally arbitrary way." It was probably Meynert who initiated the methodical attempt to link mental function to the growing knowledge of neuroanatomy, and he had an influence on Wernicke, whose pioneer work of 1874, *The Symptom-Complex of Aphasia,* explicitly emphasized the need for sophisticated functional analysis. The subtitle of this publication, *A psychological study on an anatomical basis,* reflected this new emphasis. Wernicke pointed out that it had already been demonstrated many times in the few years since Broca's first writings on aphasia that not all patients with aphasic speech had lesions in the lower frontal lobe. One of his astute observations was that the speech of frontal and temporal aphasic patients different in its *linguistic* features. This observation, repeatedly confirmed over the past hundred years, may perhaps be regarded as the birth of neurolinguistics.

Systematic neuropsychology—the application of the full array of modern psychological methods (including carefully selected controls) to patients known to have brain lesions, the creation of new measuring techniques, and the use of advanced statistics—grew slowly. One can see some beginnings of this in Liepmann's studies on apraxia; comparing groups of right hemiplegics with aphasia, right hemiplegics without aphasia, left hemiplegics, and demented patients, he found that apraxic disorders occurred overwhelmingly in the first group. The use of such methods in the years between the wars became increasingly sophisticated as neurologists like Kurt Goldstein formed close ties with professional psychologists. Neuropsychology's major growth, however, came after World War II, spurred by such investigators as Luria, Hécaen, Milner, Benton, Goodglass, and Teuber, until today it is a large field with all the paraphernalia of an academic discipline including its own journals and pre- and post-doctoral training programs.

Dr. Heilman and Dr. Valenstein have brought together for this book a group of authors representing a wide variety of disciplines but all converging on the problems of brain-behavior relationships. This reflects one of the major needs of the field—to share knowledge gained by a multiplicity of techniques. The fact that humans cannot, and must not, be subjected to possibly dangerous experimental studies whose purpose is entirely investigative has been a powerful stimulus to the ingenuity of neuropsychological scientists to extract information from all possible sources. This book is a fitting testimonial to that ingenuity. It will serve as an excellent introduction to the new era in which computerized X-rays, evoked potentials, and noninvasive methods for studying local cerebral metabolic changes will enhance our ability to traverse the narrowing abyss between behavior and neural events.

Norman Geschwind, M.D.
James Jackson Putnam Professor of Neurology
Harvard Medical School, Boston

Preface

The growth of interest in brain-behavior relationships has generated a literature that is both impressive and bewildering. In teaching neuropsychology, we have found that the reading lists necessary for adequate coverage of the subject have been unwieldy, and the information provided in the reading has been difficult to integrate. We therefore set out to provide a text that comprehensively covers the major clinical syndromes. The focus of the text is the *clinical* presentation of human brain dysfunction. The authors who have contributed to this volume have provided clinical descriptions of the major neuropsychological disorders. They have discussed methods of diagnosis, and have described specific tests, often of use at the bedside. They have also commented upon therapy. Since the study of pathophysiological and neuropsychological mechanisms underlying these disorders is inextricably intertwined with the definition and treatment of these disorders, considerable space has been devoted to a discussion of these mechanisms, and to the clinical and experimental evidence which bears on them.

A multi-authored text has the advantage of allowing authorities to write about areas in which they have special expertise. This also exposes the reader to several different approaches to the study of brain-behavior relationships, an advantage in a field in which a variety of theoretical and methodological positions have been fruitful. We therefore have not attempted to impose our own views on the contributing authors, but where there were conflicts in terminology, we have provided synonyms and cross-references. Much of brain activity is integrative, and isolated neuropsychological disturbances are rare. Discussions of alexia or agraphia must necessarily include more than a passing reference to aphasia, and so on. Since we wanted each chapter to stand on its own, with its author's viewpoint intact, we have generally allowed some overlap between chapters.

We wish to thank all of the persons who devoted their time and effort to this book. Professor Arthur Benton not only contributed two outstanding chapters, but was instrumental in advising us about authors and content, and in leading us to Oxford University Press. We are grateful to all the other contributing authors, who promptly provided high quality manuscripts; to our secretary, Ann Tison, who typed our manuscripts so many times; and to the editors at Oxford University Press, who helped to improve our grammar and syntax, and, not infrequently, the clarity of our thought. Not least, we are grateful to our families, who have endured many evenings of work with this volume with patience and understanding.

Gainesville, Florida   K.M.H.
March 1979   E.V.

Contributors

Martin L. Albert, M.D., Ph.D.
Associate Professor of Neurology, Boston University Medical School,
Chief, Clinical Neurology Section, Boston Veterans Administration
Medical Center, Boston

D. Frank Benson, M.D.
Professor of Neurology, Boston University Medical School,
Director, Neurobehavioral Center, Boston Veterans Administration
Medical Center, Boston

Arthur Benton, Ph.D., D.Sc.
Professor Emeritus of Neurology and Psychology, University of Iowa, Iowa City

Joseph E. Bogen, M.D.
Clinical Professor of Neurosurgery, University of Southern California
School of Medicine,
Senior Neurosurgeon, Ross Loos Medical Group, Los Angeles

Nelson Butters, Ph.D.
Professor of Neurology (Neuropsychology), Boston University School of Medicine,
Research Psychologist, Boston Veterans Administration Medical Center, Boston

Antonio R. Damasio, M.D., D.Med.Sci.
Associate Professor of Neurology,
Director, Division of Behavioral Neurology, University of Iowa
College of Medicine, Iowa City

Martha Bridge Denckla, M.D.
Assistant Professor of Neurology, Harvard Medical School,
Director, Learning Disabilities Clinic, Children's Hospital Medical Center, Boston

Henry Hécaen, M.D.
Professor of Neuropsychology and Neurolinguistics, École des Hautes Études
en Sciences Sociales, Paris

Kenneth M. Heilman, M.D.
Professor of Neurology and Clinical Psychology, University of Florida
College of Medicine, Gainesville

Robert J. Joynt, M.D., Ph.D.
Professor and Chairman, Department of Neurology, University of Rochester
School of Medicine and Dentistry and Strong Memorial Hospital, Rochester

Andrew Kertesz, M.D., F.R.C.P.(C.)
Associate Professor of Neurology, University of Western Ontario,
Chief, Department of
Clinical Neurological Sciences and Director, Aphasia Research Laboratory,
St. Joseph's Hospital, London, Ontario

Harvey S. Levin, Ph.D.
Assistant Professor, Division of Neurosurgery and Departments of Neurology
and Psychiatry, University of Texas Medical Branch, Galveston

Pierre Marcie
Research associate, Institut National de la Santé et de la Recherche Médicale,
Paris

Alan R. Rubens, M.D.
Associate Professor of Neurology, University of Minnesota,
Chief, Neurobehavioral Unit, Hennepin County Medical Center, Minneapolis

Ira Shoulson, M.D.
Assistant Professor of Neurology, Medicine and Pharmacology, and Toxicology,
University of Rochester School of Medicine and Dentistry and Strong Memorial
Hospital, Rochester

Edward Valenstein, M.D.
Associate Professor of Neurology, University of Florida College of Medicine,
Gainesville

Contents

xiii

3

4

8
Visuoperceptive, Visuospatial, and Visuoconstructive Disorders, 186
ARTHUR BENTON

9
Agnosia, 233
ALAN B. RUBENS

10

Neglect and Related Disorders, 268
KENNETH M. HEILMAN

11

The Callosal Syndrome, 308
JOSEPH E. BOGEN

12

The Frontal Lobes, 360
ANTONIO DAMASIO

13

Emotional Disorders Resulting from Lesions of the Central Nervous System, 413
EDWARD VALENSTEIN AND KENNETH M. HEILMAN

17

Childhood Learning Disabilities, 535
MARTHA BRIDGE DENCKLA

18

The Syndrome of Hyperactivity, 574
MARTHA BRIDGE DENCKLA AND KENNETH M. HEILMAN

Clinical Neuropsychology

1
Introduction

KENNETH M. HEILMAN AND
EDWARD VALENSTEIN

BRIEF HISTORICAL REVIEW

Aristotle thought that the mind, with the function of thinking, had
no relation to the body or the senses and could not be destroyed.
The first attempts to localize mental processes to the brain may
nevertheless be traced back to antiquity. In the fifth century B.C.,
Hippocrates of Croton claimed that the brain was the organ of intellect, and the heart the organ of the senses. Herophilus, in the
third century B.C., studied the structure of the brain and regarded
it as the site of intelligence. He believed that the middle ventricle
was responsible for the faculty of cognition and the posterior ventricle was the seat of memory. Galen, in the second century B.C.,
thought that the activities of the mind were performed by the substance of the brain rather than the ventricles, but it was not until
the anatomical work of Vesalius in the sixteenth century A.D. that
this thesis was accepted. Vesalius, however, thought that the brains
of most mammals and birds had similar structures in almost every
respect except for size, and that the brain attained its greatest dimensions in man. In the seventeenth century, Descartes suggested
that the soul resided in the pineal. He chose the pineal because of
its central location: all things must emanate from the soul.

3

At the end of the eighteenth century, Franz Joseph Gall postulated that various human faculties were localized in different organs or centers of the brain. He thought that these centers were expansions of lower nervous mechanisms and that, although independent, they were able to interact with one another. Unlike Descartes, Gall conceived brain structures to have successive development, with no central point where all nerves unite. He proposed that the vital forces resided in the brainstem and that intellectual qualities were situated in various parts of the two cerebral hemispheres. The hemispheres were united by the commissures, the largest being the corpus callosum.

Unfortunately, Gall also postulated that measurements of the skull may allow one to deduce moral and intellectual characteristics, since the shape of the skull is modified by the underlying brain. This hypothesis was the foundation of phrenology. When phrenology fell into disrepute, many of Gall's original contributions were blighted. His teaching, however, was the foundation of modern neuropsychology.

Noting that students with good verbal memory had prominent eyes, Gall suggested that memory for words was situated in the frontal lobes. He studied two patients who lost their memory for words and attributed their disorder to frontal-lobe lesions. In 1825, Bouillaud wrote that he also believed cerebral function to be localized. He demonstrated that discrete lesions could produce paralysis in one limb and not others, and cited this as proof of localized function. He also believed that the anterior lobe was the center of speech. He observed that the tongue had many functions other than speech and that one function could be disordered (e.g., speech) while others remained intact (e.g., mastication). This observation suggested to him that an effector can have more than one center which controls its actions.

In 1861, Broca heard Bouillaud's pupil, Auburtin, speak about the importance of the anterior lobe in speech and subsequently asked Auburtin to see a patient suffering from right hemiplegia and loss of speech and writing. He was able to understand speech, but could articulate only one word, "tan." This patient died, and postmortem inspection of the brain revealed that there was a cavity filled with fluid on the lateral aspect of the left hemisphere. When the fluid was drained, a large left-hemisphere lesion could be seen which included the first temporal gyrus, the insula and corpus striatum, and the frontal lobe, including the second and third frontal convolutions as well as the inferior portion of the transverse convolution. In 1861, Broca saw another patient who had lost the power of speech and writing but who could comprehend spoken language. Autopsy again revealed a left-hemisphere lesion involving the second and third frontal convolutions.

Broca later saw eight patients who had suffered a loss of speech (which he called *aphemia*, but which Trousseau later called *aphasia*). All eight had left-hemisphere lesions. This was the first demonstration of left-hemisphere dominance for language (Broca, 1861).

Broca's observations produced great excitement in the medical world. Despite his clear demonstration of left-hemisphere dominance, medical opinion appeared to split into two camps, one favoring the view that different functions were exercised by the various portions of the cerebral hemisphere and the other denying that psychic functions were or could be localized.

Following Broca's initial observations, there was a flurry of activity. In 1868, Hughlings Jackson noted that there were two types of aphasic patients—fluent and nonfluent—and, in 1869, Bastian argued that there were patients who had deficits not only in the articulation of words but also in the memory for words. Bastian also postulated the presence of a visual and auditory word center and a kinesthetic center for the hand and the tongue. He proposed that these centers were connected and that information, such as language, was processed by the brain in different ways by each of these centers. Lesions in these centers would thus produce distinct syndromes, depending upon which aspect of the processing was disturbed. Bastian thus viewed the brain as a processor. He was the first to describe word deafness and word blindness.

In 1874, Wernicke published his famous *Der Aphasische Symptomenkomplex*. He was familiar with Meynert's work which demonstrated that sensory systems project to the posterior portions of the hemispheres whereas the anterior portions appear to be efferent. Wernicke noted that lesions of the posterior portion of the superior temporal region produced an aphasia in which comprehension was poor. He thought that this auditory center contained sound images

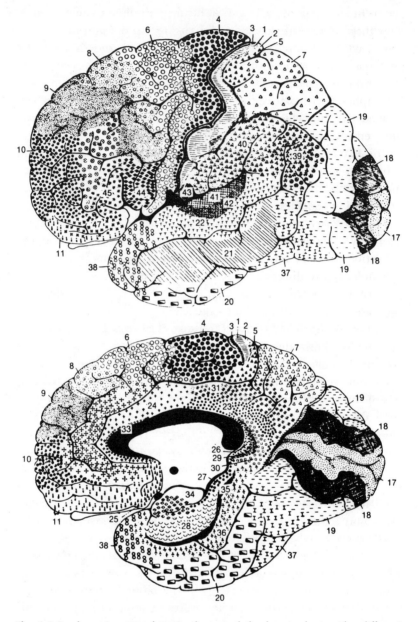

Fig. 1-1 Brodmann's cytoarchitectural map of the human brain. The different areas are defined on the basis of subtle differences in cortical cell structure and organization. Broca's area corresponds roughly to areas 44 and 45; and Wernicke's area to the posterior part of area 22.

while Broca's area contained images for movement. He also thought that these areas were connected by a commissure and that a lesion of this commissure would disconnect the area for sound images from the area for images of movement.

Wernicke's scheme could account for motor, conduction, and sensory aphasia with poor repetition. Lichtheim (1885), however, described patients who were nonfluent but who repeated normally, and sensory aphasics who could not comprehend but could repeat words. Elaborating on Wernicke's ideas, he devised a complex schema intended to explain the mechanisms underlying seven types of speech and language disorders.

Following the First World War the localizationist and connectionist approach was abandoned in favor of a holistic approach. Probably there were many factors underlying this change. The localizationist theory was built on the foundation laid by Gall. When phrenology was discredited, other localizationist theories became suspect. Lashley (1938), using experimental methods (as opposed to the case reports of the classical neurologists), found that engrams were not localized in the brain but rather appeared to be diffusely represented. From these observations, he proposed a theory of mass action: the behavioral result of a lesion depends on the amount of brain removed more than on the location of the lesion. Henry Head (1926) studied aphasics' linguistic performance and was not satisfied with the classical neurologists' attempts to deduce schemas from clinical observations. Discussing one of Wernicke's case reports, he wrote, "No better example could be chosen of the manner in which the writers of this period were compelled to lop and twist their cases to fit the Procrustean bed of their hypothetical conceptions." Although Freud, early in his career, studied the relationships between brain and behavior, he later provided the scientific world with psychodynamic theories of behavior which did not rely on an understanding of brain–behavior relationships. The Gestalt psychologists abandoned localizationism and connectionism in favor of the holistic approach.

Social and political influences, however, were perhaps more important in changing neuropsychological thought than the newer scientific theories. The continental European scientific community was strongly influenced by Immanuel Kant's *Critique of Pure Reason* which held that, although knowledge cannot transcend experience, it is nevertheless in part a priori. According to Kant, the outer world produces only the matter of sensation, while the mental apparatus (the brain) orders this matter and supplies the concepts by means of which we understand experience. After the First World War, the influence of science on the continent waned, while in English-speaking countries it bloomed. The American and English political and social systems were strongly influenced by John Locke, the seventeenth-century liberal philosopher who, unlike Kant, believed that behavior and ideas were not innate but rather were derived from experience.

In the second half of the twentieth century, there has been a reawakening of interest in brain–behavior relationships. Many different developments contributed to this. The classical neurologists were rediscovered and their findings were replicated. Electronic technology provided researchers with new instruments for observing physiological processes. New statistical procedures enabled them to distinguish random results from significant behavior. New behavioral paradigms such as dichotic listening and bilateral visual half-field viewing permitted psychologists to explore brain mechanisms in normal individuals as well as in pathological cases. Anatomical studies using new staining methods permitted more detailed mapping of connections, and advances in neurochemistry and neuropharmacology ushered in a new form of neuropsychology where, in addition to studying behavioral–structural relationships, investigators can study behavioral–chemical relationships.

METHODS AND CONCEPTS

Numerous problems, both philosophical and practical, are encountered in the study of brain–behavior relationships. A full discussion of the philosophical problems is beyond the scope of this introduction, but it is important to consider some of the assumptions which underlie the attempt to relate behavior to the brain.

The basic assumption is that all behavior is mediated by physical processes, and that the complex behavior of higher animals depends upon physical processes in the central nervous system. We assume that certain aspects of behavior are "hard-wired" into the nervous system: this is doubtless true of reflex and instinctual behavior. In addition, it appears that the capability of acquiring even very complex behavior such as language is "hard-wired" in the nervous system. Other species, lacking this genetic imprinting, do not spontaneously acquire language and cannot be taught a language in the true sense of the word. It is true that chimpanzees can be taught a complex symbolic code, but many do not consider this the equivalent of language acquisition. Just as the capacity for certain species-specific behaviors is imprinted in the nervous system, so are numerous other intellectual and emotional capabilities such as memory, emotional responsiveness, and the like. Brain lesions that destroy some of this "hard-wiring" may permanently disrupt certain aspects of behavior. Naturally occurring ablative lesions in humans have provided numerous examples of such selective disturbance of higher intellectual functions. The permanent language deficits that follow lesions of the left hemisphere and the severe loss of certain memory functions that follows bilateral hippocampal destruction in man are particularly dramatic examples of this.

This is not to deny that experience is important in determining aspects of behavior. The task of the neuropsychologist is to "read through" the aspects of behavior governed by variations in experience to learn in what ways behavior is changed by alterations in brain structure, physiology, and chemistry. For example, a patient with a frontal-lobe tumor may appear apathetic and disheveled. It might plausibly be explained that the patient, realizing he has a fatal illness, becomes depressed and that his apathy and poor grooming are the result of depression. If we accept this explanation, however, we learn nothing about the way in which frontal-lobe lesions affect behavior. Psychodynamic explanations, which do not treat the physical state of the brain as a relevant variable, are of no use in studying brain–behavior relationships except insofar as they exclude from consideration behavior that is psychodynamically determined. When it becomes clear that apathy and loss of grooming are not "normal" reactions to illness, they can be treated as behavioral features to be correlated with specific abnormalities of the brain.

It is not to be denied that experience may physically affect the brain. Indeed, all learning can be so construed. The "hard-wiring" of the brain, however, imposes limits on what can be learned (as in the example of language acquisition), but it may not prevent functions from being assumed by structures that normally would not perform them. This plasticity of the central nervous system clearly complicates the study of brain–behavior relationships and accounts, in part, for the greater difficulty of studying behavioral disorders in children (since plasticity is greater in the immature nervous system). (See Chapter 16, p. 507.) However, many behavioral deficits following brain lesions are sufficiently stable to permit meaningful study, even in children.

Methods
There are many valid approaches to the study of brain–behavior relationships, and no morally and intellectually sound approach should be neglected. We will briefly consider the major approaches, emphasizing those which have been used to greatest advantage.

THE BLACK BOX APPROACH
Behavior can be studied without any knowledge of the nervous system itself. Just as the electrical engineer can study the function of an electronic apparatus without taking it apart (by applying different inputs and studying the outputs), the brain can also be approached as a "black box." The object of the black box approach is to determine laws of behavior. These laws can be used to predict behavior, which of course is one expressed aim of the study of psychology.

To the extent that laws of behavior are determined by the "hardwiring" of the brain, the black box approach also yields information about brain function. In this regard, the systematic study of any behavior or set of behaviors is relevant to the study of brain function. Psychology, linguistics, sociology, aesthetics, and related disciplines may all reveal a priori principles of behavior. The study of linguistics, for example, has revealed a basic structure that is common to all languages (Chomsky, 1967). Since there is no logical constraint that would give language this structure, and since its generality makes environmental influences unlikely, one can assume that the basic structure of language is "hard-wired" in the brain. However, although the black box approach yields useful behavioral information about brain function, such information is limited because the brain itself is not studied. This approach is therefore peripheral to the study of neuropsychology, which reflects its origins in nineteenth century medical science by emphasizing brain anatomy, chemistry, and physiology as relevant variables.

BRAIN ABLATION PARADIGMS

Lesions in specific areas of the brain change behavior in specific ways. Studies correlating these behavioral changes with the site of lesions will yield information that can be used to predict from a given behavioral disturbance the site of the lesions, and vice versa. Such information has great clinical utility.

It is another matter, however, to try to deduce from the behavioral effects of an ablative lesion the normal mechanisms of brain function. As Hughlings Jackson pointed out nearly a century ago, the abnormal behavior observed after a brain lesion reflects the functioning of the remaining brain tissue. This remaining brain may react adversely to, or compensate for, the loss of function caused by the lesion, and thus either add to or minimize the behavioral deficit. Acute lesions often disturb function in other brain areas (termed *diaschisis*); these metabolic and physiological changes may not be detectable by neuropathological methods and may thus contribute to an overestimate of the function of the lesioned area (see Chapter 16, pp. 504–506). Lesions may also produce changes in behavior by releasing other brain areas from facilitation or inhibition. Thus it may be difficult to distinguish behavioral effects caused by an interruption of processing normally occurring in the damaged area from effects due to less specific alterations of function in other areas of the brain.

Possible nonspecific effects of a lesion, such as diaschisis, "mass action" effects, and reactions to disability or discomfort, can be excluded as major determinants of abnormal behavior by the use of "control" lesions. If lesions of comparable size in other brain areas do not produce similar behavioral effects, one cannot ascribe these effects to nonspecific causes. It is especially elegant to be able to demonstrate that such a "control" lesion has a different behavioral effect. This has been termed the "double dissociation" effect: lesion *A* produces behavioral change *a* but not *b*, while lesion *B* produces behavioral change *b* but not *a* (Teuber, 1955).

Once nonspecific effects have been excluded, one must take into account the various ways in which a lesion may specifically affect behavior. If a lesion in a particular region results in the loss of a behavior, one must not simply ascribe to that region the normal function of performing that behavior. The first step toward making a meaningful statement about brain–behavior relationships is a scrupulous analysis of the behavior in question. If a lesion in a particular area of the brain interferes with writing, that does not mean that the area is the "writing center" of the brain. Writing is a complex process which requires many other functions: sensory and motor control over the limb must be excellent; there must be no praxic disturbances; language function must be intact; the subject must be mentally alert and able to attend to the task, and so on. One must study every aspect of behavior that is directly related to the task of writing in order to define as closely as possible which aspect of the process of writing is disturbed. It may then be possible to make a correlation between the damaged portion of the brain and the aspect of the writing process that has been disrupted. It is important to distinguish between lesions that destroy areas of the brain involved in processing and lesions that disconnect such areas from one another, disrupting processes which require coordination between two or more such areas (Geschwind, 1965). When a person is writing, for example, the language and motor areas must be coordinated. Lesions that disconnect these areas will produce agraphia even though there may be no other language or motor deficit. A lesion in the corpus callosum, for example, may disconnect the language areas in the left hemisphere from the right-hemisphere motor area, thus producing agraphia in the left hand.

In addition to these difficulties in interpretation, gross ablations have a further disadvantage in the investigation of brain function. Natural lesions, such as strokes or tumors, do not necessarily respect anatomical boundaries. Ischemic strokes occur in the distribution of particular vessels and the vascular territory often overlaps various anatomical boundaries. The association of two behavioral deficits may thereby result not from a functional relationship, but rather from the fact that two brain regions with little anatomical or physiological relation are nevertheless supplied by the same vessel. The association of a memory disturbance with pure word blindness (alexia without agraphia) merely indicates that the mesial temporal lobe is in the distribution of the posterior cerebral artery. Experimental lesions in animals can avoid this problem; however, even within a specific anatomical region, there may be many systems operating, often with contrasting behavioral functions. Experimental lesions in the lateral hypothalamus, for example, can be shown to affect several neurotransmitter pathways, which may have different functions.

Despite all of these problems, the study of brain ablations in humans and animals has yielded more information about brain–behavior relationships than other approaches, and it continues to be an important method of investigation.

BRAIN STIMULATION PARADIGMS

Brain stimulation has been used to map connections in the brain and to elicit changes in behavior. One attraction of this method has been that stimulation, as opposed to ablation, is reversible. (Reversible methods of ablation such as cooling have been used, however.) The additional claim that stimulation is more like normal physiological function is open to question: it is highly unlikely that gross electrical stimulation of the brain reproduces any normally occurring physiological state. The stimulation techniques that are usually employed cannot selectively affect only one class of neurons. Furthermore, stimulation disrupts ongoing activity, frequently inhibiting it in a way that resembles the effects of ablation. Some of these objections may be overcome by the use of neurotransmitters or drugs with similar properties to stimulate (or inhibit) specific neurotransmitter systems.

NEUROCHEMICAL MANIPULATIONS

Neurochemical and immunological methods have identified groups of neurons in the central nervous system which use specific neurotransmitters. The number of neurotransmitters identified continues to increase: in addition to norepinephrine, dopamine, acetylcholine, and serotonin, amino acids such as glycine and gamma-aminobutyric acid (GABA) have been identified as transmitters. Most recently, polypeptide neurotransmitters have been found (the endorphins and enkephalins) which act at receptors that are also stimulated

by opiates. Some of these systems can be selectively stimulated by
the ontophoresis of neurotransmitters or of drugs with similar properties. Some can be selectively depressed by drugs that block the action of the transmitter (or inhibit its release), and some can be selectively destroyed by drugs that damage the neurons containing a
specific transmitter. Brain sections can be analyzed to determine the
concentration of transmitters, and the concentrations can be correlated with behavioral data. These and related techniques are just
beginning to be used in the study of animal and (to a limited extent) human behavior. They hold great promise, especially because
of their ability to correlate the behavioral effects of pharmacological
agents with dysfunction in anatomical areas "redefined" by chemical
criteria.

ELECTROPHYSIOLOGICAL STUDIES

   The Electroencephalogram (EEG). Electrophysiological studies of
human behavior have been attempted during brain surgery, but
most studies rely on the surface-recorded electroencephalogram
(EEG). The raw EEG, however, demonstrates changes in amplitude
and frequency which are generally nonspecific and poorly localizing. Computer analysis of EEG frequency and amplitude (power
spectra) in different behavioral situations (and from different brain
regions) has demonstrated correlations between EEG activity and
behavior, but only for certain aspects of behavior (such as arousal)
or for broad anatomical fields (e.g., between hemispheres). The use
of computer averaging has increased our ability to detect electrical
events which are time-locked to stimuli and responses. Thus, cortical evoked potentials to visual, auditory, and somesthetic stimuli
have been recorded, as have potentials which precede a response.
Certain potentials appear to correlate with expectancy or arousal
(the contingent negative variation and the P300 potential). The use
of these techniques in behavioral research has been limited by our
ignorance of the meaning of the various components of averaged responses and by technical difficulties. The conditions of the experiment must insure that the stimulus (or the signal to respond) is
temporally discrete and reproducible and that extraneous activity
does not interfere with the recording of the response.

   Single-Unit Recording. Discrete activity of individual neurons can be recorded by inserting microelectrodes into the brain. Obviously, this is largely limited to animal experiments. Much has been learned (and remains to be learned) from the use of this technique in alert, responding animals. Responses to well-controlled stimuli can be recorded with precision and can be analyzed quantitatively. Interpretation of single-unit recording presents its own difficulties. The brain activity related to a behavioral event may occur simultaneously in many cells spatially dispersed over a considerable area. Recording from only one cell may not yield a meaningful pattern. In addition, single-unit recording may be difficult to analyze in relation to complex behaviors.

INTROSPECTION

At times, a patient's observations of his own mental state may be not only helpful but necessary. How else can one learn of many sensory abnormalities, hallucinations, or emotional changes? It is conceivable that insights of persons into their own mental processes may be of importance in delineating brain mechanisms. For example, persons with "photographic" memory not surprisingly report that they rely on visual rather than verbal memory, and experiments suggest that visual memory has a greater capacity than verbal memory. Patients may have similarly useful insights, and the clinician would do well to listen carefully to what his patients say. This does not mean, however, that he must believe it all. In normal persons, introspection is not always trustworthy. In brain-damaged patients, it may be even less reliable. This is particularly true when the language centers have been disconnected from the region of the brain that is processing the information the patient is asked about (Geschwind, 1965). For example, a patient with a callosal lesion (separating the left language-dominant hemisphere from the right hemisphere) will not be able to name correctly an object placed in his left hand. Curiously, the patient does not say that he cannot name it nor does he explain that his left hand can feel it but he cannot find the right word. Instead, in every such case recorded, the patient confabulates a name. It is clear that in this situation the patient's language area, which is providing the spoken "insight," cannot even appreciate the presence of a deficit (until it is later brought to its attention), let alone explain the nature of the difficulty. In other situations, it is apparent that patients make incorrect assumptions about their deficits. The patient with pure word deafness (who can understand no spoken language but who nevertheless can speak well and can hear) often assumes that people are deliberately being obscure; the result of this introspection is often paranoia. Thus, although the patient's introspection at times can provide useful clues for the clinician, this information must always be treated critically and used with caution.

Animal versus human experimentation

Many of the techniques mentioned above are either not applicable to humans or can be applied only with great difficulty. In detailed anatomical studies, for instance, discrete brain lesions are made and the whole brain is studied meticulously soon after the operation. Other anatomical methods entail the injection of substances into the brain. Advances in neurochemistry and neurophysiology, like those in neuroanatomy, rely heavily on animal work. Despite major differences in anatomy between even the subhuman primates and man (Fig. 1-2), much of this basic research is of direct relevance to human neurobiology. Behavioral studies in animals have also yielded a great deal of information, but the applicability of this information to the study of complex human behavior is not clear-cut. Nothing in the literature on temporal-lobe lesions in animals would have led to the prediction that bilateral temporal lobectomy in man would result in permanent impairment of memory. Studies of the limbic system and hypothalamus in animals have contributed important information about the relevance of these structures to emotional behavior; however, the emotional content of behavior is difficult to study in animals that cannot report how they feel. Most obviously, animals cannot be used to study behavior which is uniquely human, such as language. The relevance of studies of nonlinguistic communication in animals to language organization in humans is not at all clear.

PROBLEMS OF HUMAN EXPERIMENTATION

Human experimentation is therefore necessary, but it presents many problems. The ablation paradigm must rely upon lesions occurring naturally or upon lesions made by neurosurgeons for medical rea-

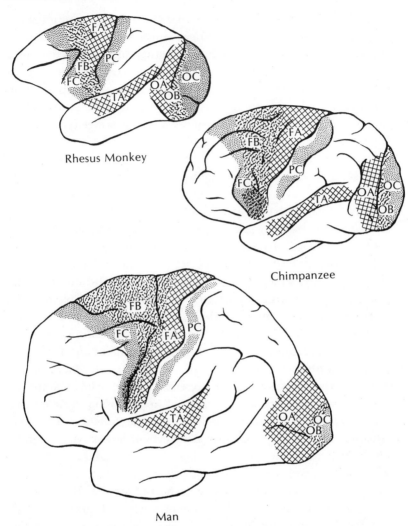

Fig. 1-2 The primary motor (FA) and visual (OC) areas, and the association areas of the motor, visual, somatosensory (PC), and auditory (TA) systems are compared in these lateral views of the hemispheres of the monkey, chimpanzee, and man. Note the expansion of the unshaded areas of cortex, particularly in the frontal lobe and in the area between TA and OA, as one progresses from monkey to man. The latter area is important for language development (see Chapter 2). The significance of the frontal lobes is discussed in Chapter 12.

sons. Obviously, such lesions often are not ideally situated for study of the problem at hand. In addition, considerable labor and some luck are required to collect a series of comparable patients for study. Unlike experimental animals which are often comparable in both genetic and environmental terms, patients vary widely in premorbid capabilities and backgrounds. Finally, experiments must be designed to avoid putting the patient at any additional risk. Even if the experimental manipulations themselves are harmless, the researcher must always be sure that he is not interfering with expeditious medical evaluation and treatment.

FORMS OF HUMAN EXPERIMENTATION

Studies of normals. A few of the techniques mentioned above can yield physiological data in normal individuals. EEG studies have revealed hemisphere asymmetries associated with cognitive mode. Evoked response studies have also been fruitful. Dichotic listening (and binocular viewing) techniques have revealed hemisphere asymmetries in the processing of verbal, visuospatial, and musical information. (In this approach, competing [dissimilar] auditory or visual stimuli are presented to the two half-fields simultaneously. The subject identifies what he has heard or seen. Usually more correct responses are made for stimuli presented to the field opposite the hemisphere which is primarily involved in processing the stimulus.)

Case reports. The careful study of a single patient can provide valuable clues to the mechanisms underlying a behavioral deficit. The advantage of the case report is that an individual patient can be studied in depth and an effort can be made to relate all the manifestations of the patient's illness to each other and to the pathology which has been identified. The famous studies of Dejerine (1892) and of Liepmann and Maas (1907) were of single patients. The problem with case reports is that it is difficult to generalize from one patient.

Series of patients. The study of a group of patients increases one's ability to generalize from the data presented. In 1861, finding a single patient with aphasia and a lesion in the left frontal lobe would have been of interest as a case report, but the finding of eight such cases enabled Broca to state that language deficits appeared to be associated specifically with *left* frontal opercular lesions. Precise statistical methods now permit the simultaneous analysis of several variables. The problem with the statistical analysis of a group of patients is that potentially significant data from an individual patient may be lost when averaged with data from the group. For example, a study of a group of patients might demonstrate that language disability is correlated with impairment on nonverbal tests of intelligence. In such a study, the finding of one patient with severe language disability but normal performance on nonverbal cognitive tasks might be neglected; however, it could be argued that the data on this single patient would be more important than all the rest. For this patient would indicate that the abilities to make verbal and nonverbal generalizations were likely to be functionally and anatomically discrete. The statistical analysis of the whole group of patients, however, might support the opposite conclusion.

Conceptual analysis

We often hear that science proceeds by way of careful observation, followed by analysis and then hypothesis on the basis of the observed data (a posteriori hypothesis). In fact, meaningful observations frequently cannot be made without some sort of a priori hypothesis. How else can one decide which observations to make? An observation can only be significant in terms of a conceptual framework.

Some investigators are loathe to put either their a priori or a posteriori hypotheses in print, feeling that they are too tentative. They report observations with a minimum of interpretation. This may be unfortunate because tentative hypotheses are the seeds of further observations and hypotheses. Other investigators speculate extensively on the basis of only a few observations. These speculations may lead to clearly stated hypotheses which generate further observations, but there is a risk that observations may be honestly and inadvertently distorted to fit the hypotheses. For example, investigators always discard "irrelevant" information either intentionally or not; however, an investigator with an alternative hypothesis may find observations presumed irrelevant by others to be of critical importance. It is important to deal with all hypotheses as though they were tentative so that, as Head (1926) warned, we do not invite observations to sleep in the Procrustean bed of our hypotheses.

We are too far from understanding brain–behavior relationships
to be able to state hypotheses entirely without the use of metaphorical terms. Metaphor is not to be taken literally. Diagrams, for example, may be used in a metaphorical way to present a hypothesis.
The diagrams found in this book are offered in this spirit: they are
not meant to be pictures of the brain but are sketches of hypotheses.

Similarly, when we speak of the function of different areas of the
brain, it often appears that we assume that the area under discussion operates entirely independently from others. Clearly, this is
true only to a limited extent. For the purposes of analysis, however,
we must often ignore interactions between brain regions in order to
discuss the distinguishing features of these areas. We do not deny
that consideration of the brain as a functioning whole may at times
be of equal value in explaining behavioral data, as it is in explaining the concept of diaschisis.

Thus, we support a flexible approach to the study of brain–
behavior relationships. We know too little about the subject to
limit our methods of investigation. We must be prepared to analyze
data from many sources, and make new hypotheses, and test them
with the best methods available for that purpose. Similarly, behavioral testing and methods of treatment must be tailored to the individual situation. Inflexible test batteries, although necessary for obtaining normative data, limit our view of the nervous system if used
exclusively. Rigid formulations of therapy similarly limit progress.
Changes in testing and therapy, however, should not be made capri-
ciously, but rather according to our current understanding of brain–
behavior relationships. In this book, therefore, we do not emphasize
standardized tests or treatment batteries, but we hope to present the
existing knowledge of brain–behavior relationships which should
form the basis of diagnosis and treatment.

References

Bastian, H. C. (1869). On the various forms of loss of speech in cerebral
    disease, *British and Foreign Medico-surgical review 43*:470–492.
Bouillaud, J. B. (1825). Recherches cliniques propres a demontrer que la
    perte de la parole correspond a la lesion de lobules anterieurs du
    cerveau, et a confirmer l'opinion de M. Gall sur le siege de l'organe du
    langage articule, *Archives Generales de Medecine 8*:25–45.

Broca, P. (1861). Nouvelle observation d'aphemie produite par une lesion de la moite posterieure des deuxieme et troisieme circonvolutions frontales. *Bulletin de la Society Anatomique de Paris 36*:398–407.

Chomsky, N. (1967). The General Properties of Language. In *Brain Mechanisms Underlying Speech and Language,* C. H. Millikan and F. L. Darley (eds.). New York: Grune & Stratton.

Dejerine, J. (1892). Contribution a l'etude anatomo-pathologique et clinique des differentes varietes de cecite verbale. *Memoires de la Societe de Biologie 4*:61–90.

Dejerine, J. (1914). *Semiologie des Affections du Systeme Nerveaux.* Paris: Masson.

Geschwind, N. (1965). Disconnexion syndrome in animals and men. I & II. *Brain 88*:237–294 & 585–644.

Head, H. (1926). *Aphasia and Kindred Disorders of Speech.* Cambridge: Cambridge University Press.

Kussmaul, A. (1877). *Die Storungen der Sprache.* Leipzig: Vogel.

Lashley, K. S. (1938). Factors limiting recovery after central nervous lesions. *J. Nervous Mental Dis. 88*:733–755.

Lichtheim, L. (1885). On aphasia. *Brain 7*:433–484.

Liepmann, H. and Maas, O. (1907). Fall von linksseitiger Agraphie und Apraxie bei rechtsseitiger Lahmung. *Z. f. Psychol. u. Neurol. 10*:214–227.

Teuber, H. L. (1955). Physiological psychology. *Ann. Rev. Psychol. 6*:267–296.

Wernicke, C. (1874). *Des Aphasische Symptomenkomplex.* Breslau: Cohn and Weigart.

2
Aphasia

D. FRANK BENSON

INTRODUCTION

Aphasia is a clinical term that denotes the loss or impairment of language following brain damage and therefore, by definition, aphasia is a neurological disorder. Over 50 years ago the British neurologist, Kinnear Wilson (1926), stated that aphasia was unique among neurological disorders in that it demanded understanding from anatomical, physiological, and psychological viewpoints. At present an understanding from several other viewpoints must be brought to bear on the study of aphasia, most prominently linguistics, the development of language, and the response to aphasia therapy.

Neuropsychology is a comparatively recent subspecialty that takes a psychological approach to neurological, particularly brain, disorders. The methods used for neuropsychological investigation vary widely (see Chapter 1). Many studies are done on animals and on normal human subjects. The most direct, but also most difficult neuropsychological approach, is to observe and test patients with neurological disorders, including aphasia. This chapter will ap-

Supported in part by grant NS 06209 to the Aphasia Research Center, Boston University School of Medicine from the National Institutes of Health and by research funds provided by the Veterans Administration.

proach aphasia from the latter combination of neurological and psychological viewpoints. While a complete review of the neuropsychological investigations of aphasia cannot possibly be presented, an attempt will be made to correlate current neurological and neuropsychological thinking on aphasia and to draw upon other specialized approaches when they offer information pertinent to the discussion.

HISTORICAL BACKGROUND

The work and thought on aphasia over the past 150 years are both controversial and fascinating and many excellent historical reviews, invariably slanted in the direction of the author's bias, have been published. Only selected highlights can be presented here; for more complete historical background, the reader is referred to the following books and papers: Freud, 1953; Head, 1926; Weisenburg and McBride, 1964; Benton and Joynt, 1960; Brain, 1961; Hécaen and Albert, 1977.

While reports describing most of the recognized varieties of aphasia, alexia, and agraphia existed centuries ago, aphasia as it is currently recognized dates from 1861. After several centuries of debate two different views of the brain's function in language production had formed. One group, taking their lead from the early phrenologists, maintained that specific mental functions were subserved by separate areas of the brain. Opponents of this "localizationist" viewpoint, on the other hand, believed that mental capability reflected total brain volume. In 1861, a primitive skull was demonstrated to the French anthropological society and used to support a direct relationship between mental competence and brain volume. A series of lively debates followed and during this period a patient of one physician-member became "speechless" and then died. Postmortem studies revealed a large frontal lesion and the physician, Paul Broca (1861), submitted this case as evidence favoring the localizationist viewpoint. Much further debate followed and other cases of speechlessness (aphasia) were presented which both supported and failed to support the localizationist viewpoint. This introduction of case material into the controversy between the localizationist and holistic views of brain function raised great interest in the clinical aspects of language impairment and led to much of the current thinking about aphasia.

A second major advance for the localizationist viewpoint followed publication of Wernicke's doctoral thesis (1874) in which two distinct types of aphasia, motor and sensory, were outlined and supported by clinical-pathological correlations; a third variety, conduction aphasia, was postulated on the basis of a hypothetical diagram of language function in the brain. Following Wernicke's initial presentation, both the clinical-pathological localization of varieties of aphasia and the use of diagrams became popular. Within a few years, many similar schemes of aphasia appeared and most subsequent work supporting localization of language functions in designated areas of the brain has followed the same format. The localizationists claimed that specific areas of the brain were of particular importance for specific language functions and that this was confirmed by the correlation of different language disturbances (aphasias) with postmortem findings of pathology at specific brain sites. Among the major contributors to this approach to aphasia were Lichtheim (1885), Charcot (1889), Bastian (1898), Dejerine (1914), Henschen (1922), Kleist (1962), and Nielsen (1962). Much of the localizationists' work was performed late in the nineteenth and early in the twentieth centuries and corresponded to the flowering of the clinical-pathological approach to medicine in Europe. Excesses in the claims of this group are now obvious, and many of the functions which they correlated with pathology would not be accepted as language functions at present. The localizationist viewpoint eventually received considerable criticism and lost credibility.

During the same period there were many who advocated a more holistic view of language disturbances. One of the earliest and most powerful proponents of this view was John Hughlings Jackson (1968), the great English neurologist. Jackson's opinions were neither well understood nor accepted for many years but eventually they attained considerable influence. Sigmund Freud, in a monograph on aphasia published in 1894, strongly criticized the "diagram makers" but received scant attention. It was only with Pierre Marie (1906) that the holistic point of view reached a wide audience. Another debate, not dissimilar to the 1861 argument, occurred in Paris between Dejerine, a proponent of the classic localizationist view, and

Marie. From this time, the influence of the holistic approach steadily increased and has included such significant advocates as Head (1926), Pick (1973), Isserlin (1929, 1931, 1932), Kinnear Wilson (1926), and more recently Weisenburg and McBride (1964), Critchley (1970), Bay (1964), Wepman (1951) and Schuell (1964).

Despite these differences, almost every serious student of aphasia made observations supportive of both viewpoints; only in the overview was there a clash. Indeed, any number of influential workers are linked, theoretically, with one approach but produced meaningful work in the other. In particular, Kurt Goldstein (1948) is best recognized as a staunch proponent of a holistic (organismic) approach to aphasia, but in his writings one finds some of the best descriptions of localized varieties of aphasia available in contemporary literature. Similarly, the Russian psychologists headed by Luria (1970), are often considered to have an anti-localizationist bias and yet their work features superb descriptions of aphasic syndromes with distinct localizing features. Thus, while it is accurate to divide prevailing philosophies into the anatomically based localizing and the more psychologically based holistic camps, almost all investigators utilize both approaches to a greater or lesser degree.

One additional historical note is relevant. Interest in aphasia waned considerably before and immediately after World War II but the work of many contemporary investigators has altered this situation, both by reviving older localizationist ideas and by developing a better integrated, neuropsychological approach to aphasia. Geschwind (1965) emphasized cortical–cortical disconnection as a source of language disorder. The Italians, DeRenzi and Vignolo (1962), the French investigators, Lhermitte (1969) and Hécaen (1965), the Russians headed by Luria (1966), the Germans Leischner (1959), Bay (1964) and Poeck (1972), and the Americans Goodglass (1972) and Benton (1964), have all contributed to the resurgence of interest. Research into aphasia continues and while the opposing theoretical stances outlined by the Paris Debates of 1861 remain, it would appear within the reach of the neuropsychological approach to bridge them.

In his book *Aphasia and Kindred Disorders,* Henry Head (1926) described the field of aphasia study as "chaos." He then added his own novel ideas, which seriously compounded the chaos. But Head also introduced a new method in the study of aphasia: the use of a standard series of tests. Weisenburg and McBride (1964) borrowed the idea and designed a battery of language function tests for use with their aphasic subjects. Testing with a standardized battery has now become a major tool for the study of aphasia.

CLASSIFICATIONS OF APHASIA

There has been a strong tendency for individual investigators to subdivide aphasia into a number of separate syndromes, and as a result many classifications of aphasia have been produced. Probably more than any other factor this proliferation of classification schemes has led to the difficulty that most new students experience in this area. The same name (e.g., semantic aphasia) may be used in two classifications to represent strikingly different clinical syndromes. In recent years, the confusion has been increased by non-physicians (linguists, speech pathologists, psychologists) who have introduced classifications expressed in their own specialized jargon. A careful study of the classifications of aphasia is almost mandatory.

One long-standing problem has been the attempt to describe the aphasias in simple dichotomies. Probably the most widely used is the expressive–receptive division of Weisenberg and McBride (1964). Adequate only as a rough description, this concept is inherently misleading. There is almost no aphasia that does not involve some expressive abnormality and, similarly, a purely receptive aphasia, one without any expressive problem, must be extremely rare. Thus, the expressive–receptive dichotomy is inadequate for clinical classification.

Another commonly used description of the aphasias is the division into motor and sensory varieties suggested by Wernicke. This dichotomy attempts to link language problems with cortical localization; most sensory activities are carried out in the posterior cortex and most motor activities are controlled by the anterior or frontal regions. A division of aphasia into two types, anterior-motor and posterior-sensory can claim some utility, but fails to encompass the significant clinical differences that distinguish the varieties of aphasia.

The most complete lumping of categories was made by Marie

(1906), who suggested that there was only one type of aphasia, the "sensory" aphasia originally described by Wernicke. In this "classification" all variations consist of aphasia as defined above plus involvement of neighboring motor or sensory functions, the combination producing the rich variation of symptomatology seen in aphasia. The fully holistic view probably reached its zenith in the studies of Schuell (1964), whose extensive writings emphasized the "one aphasia" concept. The work of the linguist Jakobson (1964) strongly refuted this holistic approach and subsequent neuropsychological studies have supported the view that there is greater diversity in aphasia.

Beyond all the babel, however, there is, as Davis Howes noted a number of years ago (1964), considerable agreement on most salient points among those experienced in the field. In many ways it would appear that the academic effort to classify the aphasic disturbances has been a major roadblock to their understanding. The same few basic clinical disorders appear in most classifications, the number of these disorders is finite, and most types of aphasia in one classification can be correlated with types in other classifications.

A review of classification systems for the aphasias reveals an apparently overwhelming variation in the types and terminologies proposed. Nonetheless, by focusing on clusters of symptoms (a syndrome) for each variety of aphasia in a given classification and by noting, when available, the suggested location of pathology, obvious correlations between the various classifications can be seen. The clusters of clinical findings represented in the different classifications have a definite consistency. Table 2-1 presents a number of well-known classifications beginning with the earlier continental writers and moving to the contemporary literature. For each variety of aphasia listed, either the clinical syndrome or the location of pathology (or both) is sufficiently well described by the author to allow correlation with other classifications. Note that four or five types of aphasia are present in most classifications; syndromes such as those often called Broca's aphasia and Wernicke's aphasia occur in all, and several other syndromes appear in most. Table 2-1 includes the classification of the aphasias currently in use at the Aphasia Research Center of the Boston Veterans Administration Hospital and later in the chapter descriptions of each aphasic syn-

TABLE 2-1 *Classifications of Aphasia*

WERNICKE-LICHTHEIM (1885)	HEAD (1926)	KLEIST (1934)	NIELSEN (1948)	GOLDSTEIN (1948)	BRAIN (1962)	GLONING (1963)	BAY (1964)	WEPMAN (1964)	LURIA (1966)	BVAH (1971)	HÉCAEN ALBERT (1977)
Cortical motor	Verbal	Word muteness	Broca's	Central motor	Broca's	Motor	Cortical dysarthria	Syntactic	Efferent motor	Broca's	Motor
Cortical sensory	Syntactic	Word deafness	Wernicke's	Wernicke's sensory	Central	Sensory	Sensory	Jargon pragmatic	Sensory	Wernicke	Sensory
Conduction		Repetition		Central	Central	Conduction	Sensory		Afferent motor	Conduction	Conduction
				Isolation of speech area						Mixed transcortical	
Transcortical motor			Transcortical motor	Transcortical motor			Echolalia		Dynamic	Transcortical motor	Transcortical motor
Transcortical sensory	Nominal		Transcortical sensory	Transcortical sensory					Acoustic-mnestic	Transcortical sensory	Transcortical sensory
	Semantic	Amnestic	Amnesic	Amnesic	Nominal	Amnestic	Pure	Semantic	Semantic	Anomic	Amnesic
Subcortical motor		Anarthric	Subcortical motor	Peripheral motor	Pure word dumbness					Aphemia	Pure motor
Subcortical sensory		Word sound deafness		Peripheral sensory	Pure word deafness	Pure word deafness				Pure word deafness	Pure word deafness

drome in this classification will be presented and can be correlated with the other classifications. In no way should it be construed that this scheme is considered superior to the others. The table emphasizes that much of the confusion in classifying aphasia is artificial and that some agreement on nomenclature is essential to the future understanding of aphasia.

EXAMINATION FOR APHASIA

Another reflection of the differences in opinion on aphasia is seen in the methods of evaluation. Each school of thought on language disturbance has its own set of test methods, yet another source of chaos in the field. In this section three different approaches to language evaluation will be discussed. The first is that of the clinician evaluating language as part of an overall physical and mental status examination. Next, some of the more widely used standardized aphasia test batteries will be described. And, finally, some of the myriad experimental tests devised in recent years by psychologists, linguists, speech pathologists, and others, to probe language function will be presented.

Clinical testing for aphasia

Clinical testing for aphasia is the oldest, although not necessarily the best established of the testing methods. It is neither exacting nor thorough and is usually performed by evaluating fixed language functions (e.g., naming, reading). Unfortunately, most of these functions were selected over a century ago and, in many cases, reflect obsolete concepts. The traditional approach is widely used, however, and will be presented here.

CONVERSATIONAL SPEECH

Evaluation of aphasia traditionally begins with a description of the spontaneous or conversational verbalization of the patient. Some clinicians have attempted to classify the verbal output as fluent or nonfluent. This division is recorded at least as early as 1868 (Jackson) and the terms fluent and nonfluent were used by Wernicke in 1874. In recent years several studies have been performed to probe the validity of this dichotomy and, in general, have supported it

(Benson, 1967; Wagenaar, Snow, and Prins, 1975). A number of specific output criteria were outlined in these studies. Nonfluent speech was described as having the following characteristics: sparse output (under 50 words per minute), considerable effort, poor articulation, short phrase length (often only a single word), notable dysprosody, and preferential use of substantive, meaningful words. Fluent aphasia was described as almost the direct opposite: plentiful output (100–200 words per minute), easy production, good articulation, normal phrase length (averaging 5–8 words per phrase), normal prosidic quality but a tendency to omit words (usually the meaningful, semantically significant words), and an excessive occurrence of paraphasia.

Using these criteria, the studies demonstrated that a majority of aphasics clearly fall into one of the two subtypes and that an anatomical correlation is possible. Fluent paraphasic aphasia almost invariably indicates pathology located posterior to the major central sulcus (fissure of Rolando) while, with a few well established exceptions (Benson, 1967), nonfluent aphasia is associated with pathology anterior to this sulcus.

REPETITION

The ability to repeat, exactly, words presented by the examiner is a significant language function that has received insufficient emphasis until recent years. Repetition is readily tested, starting with simple tasks such as repeating digits or single-syllable words and building to repetition of multisyllabic words, complex sentences and phrases, verbal sequences, etc. Many aphasic patients have inordinate difficulty repeating words. Often this is correlated with problems of verbal output or poor comprehension of spoken language but in some cases repetition difficulty is more pronounced than either of these problems. On the other hand, some aphasics are remarkably competent at repetition, despite poor spontaneous output and/or poor comprehension.

Both disturbed repetition and normal repetition have important anatomic correlations. In general, individuals with aphasia who have serious problems in repetition have pathology involving the perisylvian region, either the posterior-superior temporal lobe (Wernicke's area), the posterior-inferior frontal area (Broca's area), or the superior perisylvian region between these two areas (arcuate fasciculus, parietal operculum). In aphasia with preserved ability to repeat (sometimes the only remaining language function), the perisylvian area is free of pathology. The pathology in such cases is located in the cortex surrounding the perisylvian area (the border between the middle cerebral and the anterior and posterior cerebral artery circulations). A strong, often mandatory, tendency to repeat what is said by the examiner (called *echolalia*) usually indicates such a border zone location of pathology.

COMPREHENSION OF SPOKEN LANGUAGE

Comprehension is difficult to test. Both clinical evaluations and standardized tests of language comprehension are likely to be inadequate and can produce downright misleading results. One classic method for probing comprehension is through response to commands. Maintained ability to carry out complex commands, particularly when presented in multiples, is a fair indication of intact comprehension. Unfortunately, failure to carry out commands does not necessarily indicate serious comprehension difficulties and is easily misinterpreted. Both *apraxia* (disturbance in carrying out motor activities on verbal command—see Chapter 6) and difficulty in maintaining sequences can cause serious interference without proving that the patient has language comprehension difficulties. To obviate these problems, tests, such as yes–no questions, which require decreased amounts of motor activity in responding are needed. Unfortunately, some aphasics cannot handle yes and no, giving incomprehensible, perseverative or combination responses, and the examiner cannot be certain that the response is either right or wrong. Another approach is to ask the patient to point to objects about the room or in an array when the examiner gives the name. If the patient can accomplish the pointing task, the requests can be made increasingly complex by offering vague, functional descriptions of the specific objects. However, even the simple task of pointing cannot be accurately performed by some apraxic individuals and thus this test may also fail to reflect their true ability to comprehend language.

Comprehension is not an all-or-none phenomenon. Many aphasic patients comprehend frequently used words but fail to understand words used less often. Other aphasics comprehend concrete real-world names, but do not understand relational or syntactical structures which contain components such as prepositions, possessives, verb tenses, etc. There is much to be learned about comprehension testing but it is almost never correct to state flatly that comprehension is either present or absent. Most aphasics understand some language and almost all have at least some degree of deficiency. Comprehension abnormality should be described in qualitative as well as quantitative terms.

Recently reported clinical studies have demonstrated several different types of comprehension problems and have suggested a correlation of these variations with localization of pathology (Luria, 1966; Benson, 1978). These clinical observations are enticing and are now being evaluated by more stringent neuropsychological techniques.

WORD FINDING

Almost without exception, every aphasic has some difficulty in word finding (*anomia*), although the degree and circumstances vary considerably. Testing for word-finding difficulty is comparatively easy. Objects, parts of objects, body parts, colors, geometrical figures, actions, and so forth are demonstrated and the patient is asked for the name. Failure to produce the name indicates a word-finding defect. Many examiners follow such a failure by offering a multiple-choice list of names including the correct one; this is a test of comprehension, not of naming, but is frequently misinterpreted by the naive observer as proof that the patient actually does "know" the name. It is much better to follow a patient's failure to produce a name with prompting (offering a cue). An initial phoneme (phonetic prompting) or an open-ended statement in which the missing word would be appropriate (contextual prompting) can be presented.

Recent studies have demonstrated distinct variations in word-finding problems and have suggested a correlation between these variations and the site of aphasia-producing pathology (Benson, 1979). It must be noted that many "nonaphasic" disorders, such as dementia and confusional states, also cause problems in word finding. Word-finding difficulty, thus, is not necessarily an indication of aphasia. When anomia is present, however, aphasia must be considered.

READING

Disturbances of reading ability (*alexia*) either with or without aphasia, have long been recognized (see Chapter 3). Reading is relatively easy to evaluate and specific test materials must be used only if quantified results are required. Simply offering the written name of a body part or a room object for the patient to identify is one way to begin. Success at this level can be followed by phrases or sentences composed of high- or low-frequency words and by phrases depending on relational words for interpretation. A more challenging test of reading ability might require understanding of a paragraph from a newspaper or magazine. The most common mistake in testing reading ability is to equate the ability to read aloud with the ability to comprehend written material. Many aphasics with output disturbances fail to read aloud but comprehend written material adequately. Others, conversely, may read aloud sentences which they cannot comprehend. The ability to comprehend written language must be tested.

Distinct varieties of alexia with discrete anatomical correlations have been accepted for nearly a century and will be discussed in Chapter 3.

WRITING

Almost without exception, everyone with aphasia suffers some degree of *agraphia*. It must be recognized, however, that the ability to sign one's name is so ubiquitous that many aphasics with severe writing disturbances produce their signature without difficulty. Therefore testing of writing ability cannot stop here and should include dictated words and sentences plus sentences produced to command (i.e., "Describe your job."). There is qualitative variation in agraphia and four aspects of writing disorder deserve study: defects of handwriting (orthography), of written syntax, of semantic content, and of spelling. Disorders of writing are discussed in Chapter 4.

The clinical testing of aphasia is inexact, nonstandardized, and constantly changing. Therein lies both the weakness and the strength of the clinical approach. Many of the techniques used in clinical and research testing have developed from the experiences of the clinical examiner at the bedside. An experienced examiner can evaluate an aphasic patient in minutes and, by focusing on the primary problems, obtain an in-depth view of the aphasia. Even in the best of hands, however, test results are subject to the theoretical bias of the examiner, and in the hands of an inexperienced examiner clinical evaluation methods can be quite untrustworthy. The need for exact, standardized testing methods is obvious.

Formal tests of aphasia

In the past 25 years many formal tests of aphasia have been devised, standardized to a greater or lesser degree, and widely utilized. While these tests tend to be similar, there are significant differences. There is no consensus as to which tests are best, and all of the tests to be mentioned are in use somewhere. Nearly all aphasics entering a formal therapy program are given part or all of one or more of these tests. In this section we can only list some of the currently popular tests and mention some of their characteristics.

One of the earliest tests still in use is Eisenson's *Examining for Aphasia* (1954). This is of medium length and is divided into two sections, expressive and receptive. Many of its techniques for language evaluation are found in later tests. A somewhat similar test is the *Aphasia Evaluation Summary* of Sklar (1966), which covers a broad inventory of language functions. While not so widely used, it is the major testing implement in some centers.

Subsequently, two long and rationally formulated tests came into general use, the *Language Modalities Test for Aphasia* of Wepman (1961) and the *Minnesota Test for the Differential Diagnosis of Aphasia* of Schuell (1957). These are significantly different in composition. The Schuell test is designed to divide aphasic patients into five types related to prognosis for language recovery, and it is a fairly inclusive evaluation of language functions. The full test is long and somewhat difficult to present but provides considerable information about the aphasic individual's language dysfunction. The Wepman test, on the other hand, was designed along psychological parameters with emphasis on stimulus and response functions. It is interesting to note that although the Schuell test was devised by an aphasia therapist to guide aphasia therapy and the Wepman test was devised by a psychologist and utilizes psychological characteristics, findings from the Wepman test have proved very helpful to the aphasia therapist planning a language therapy program.

More recently a highly quantified test of language disability, the *Porch Index of Communicative Ability* (PICA) (1967), has become popular. This relatively short test (approximately one hour for administration) is easily repeated with good reliability. While easy to administer, the scoring system is rigid and exacting and demands thorough training. The PICA gives excellent quantitative results but comparatively little qualitative information and its greatest usefulness lies in recording language recovery. Unfortunately, therapy directed toward tasks on the PICA can improve the score without significantly altering the functional use of language. When this trap is avoided the PICA has an important place among current testing methods.

Several other tests have become popular in recent years. The most widely used is the *Boston Diagnostic Aphasia Evaluation* (BDAE) (1972), which provides the broadest range of evaluation but is so lengthy that it must be administered in separate sessions over several days. The results are difficult to interpret from a manual as they demand knowledge of the system of classifying aphasic disturbances used at the Boston Veterans Administration Hospital Aphasic Research Center (see below). The test is far more inclusive than any of its predecessors, however, and when properly interpreted offers much more diagnostic information. A shorter test based on the BDAE, the *Western Aphasia Battery* (1974), is used at several Canadian centers. A somewhat similar test that has not yet been as widely adopted is the *Neurosensory Center Test for Aphasia* (NSCTA) (1969). Excellent normal values (percentiles) are available for each subtest of the NSCTA and each language function can be rated separately or the disturbance can be rated as a whole. Both the BDAE and the NSCTA are superior to previous tests for diagnostic purposes and as research tools but, to date, have not proved superior in helping the therapist plan a rehabilitation program.

Finally, there are several tests that measure the ability to communicate rather than the specific language dysfunction. The original and most widely used of these is the *Functional Communication Profile* devised by Sarno (1965). Though not a standardized test, this is a helpful guide for making qualitative judgments and for evaluating rapid changes in communication. There is comparatively little quantification and the test relies on comparative observations by the evaluator. The observations are easily classified even by untrained personnel, and formal evaluations have demonstrated good inter-observer reliability. A more complete evaluation of communication ability is under study at present: the *Assessment of Communicative Activities Relevant to Daily Living* devised by Holland and colleagues (1977) under a contract from the National Institutes of Health. This communication scale has not yet been offered for general use.

Each test mentioned above has some usefulness and none has proved clearly superior to all others.

Research testing procedures

The most striking change in the approach to aphasia evaluation of the past several decades has been the introduction of psychological experimentation techniques. Since the work of Weisenburg and McBride in the 1930's, the use of these techniques has been expanding geometrically. Activity has been so intense that it has stimulated the publication of three journals either exclusively or primarily devoted to neuropsychological studies of language, plus innumerable articles in other journals and a number of books. Even a cursory review of this plethora of information would reach far beyond the scope of this chapter and only a few of the more prominent studies can be highlighted.

Among the outstanding investigators in this field are Luria, Hécaen, and Zangwill and their respective co-workers who have made many advances in the understanding of language through the study of language impairment. DeRenzi and Vignolo of Italy are best known for the *Token Test,* considered an excellent probe for subtle comprehension difficulties. In America the leaders in the neuropsychological study of language are Arthur Benton, Hans-Lucas Teuber, and Harold Goodglass, whose investigations have been performed with careful, fully replicable designs. The number of psychologists and linguists currently studying language disorders is enormous and the field is advancing rapidly.

After the initial neuropsychological studies, investigations of aphasia were begun by linguists and by psychologists with training and experience in linguistics. As one might anticipate, their approach has been distinguished by the combination of linguistic knowledge and theory with the scientific design of experimental psychology. Some psycholinguists have specialized in phonological problems, others have studied syntactical or grammatical problems, and still others have investigated semantic disturbances. Most early work by linguists centered on normal language and only recently have these specialists discovered the wealth of information available from aphasia studies. Most psycholinguistic studies are still designed to probe normal language by studying aphasic disabilities, but the potential for a reciprocal understanding of aphasia is obvious. Both neuropsychological and psycholinguistic studies have produced significant results, which will be given very cursory review here.

Abnormalities of syntax have been investigated in aphasics. Goodglass and Berko (1960) demonstrated consistent defects in the syntactical structure of the output of certain aphasics, a condition that has been called agrammatism. Agrammatic output is characterized by omission of the relational words of language—the articles, prepositions, conjunctions, and minor modifiers—and is a feature of nonfluent aphasia. More recent studies (Zurif, Caramazza, and Myerson, 1972; Samuels and Benson, 1979) demonstrate that a comparable comprehension defect, an inability to "understand" these same relational words, co-exists with agrammatic output. Agrammatic individuals handle (verbalize and comprehend) substantive, semantically significant words far better than the relational, syntactically significant words. All of these studies correlate this syntactic disability with Broca's or other anterior aphasia, suggesting that grammatical performance depends primarily on frontal language function.

The question of intelligence in aphasia (whether retained or lost) has been widely and rather futilely argued. Disturbed language function invalidates most of the recognized intelligence assessment techniques. To some observers this alone is evidence of decreased intelligence (Goldstein, 1948; Bay, 1962), but many others believe that some aphasics retain essentially normal intelligence, locked in by the language problem (Kennedy and Wolf, 1936; Orgass et al.,

1972). Nonverbal tests such as the Ravens Matrices (Ravens, 1952)
and the performance section of the WAIS (Wechsler, 1958) have
been used as substitute techniques but demand rather unsatisfactory
interpolation. The major problem in this debate, of course, is the
difficulty of defining intelligence. It is safe to say that most aphasics
have more understanding and more intelligence than can be demonstrated by our present evaluation techniques (Zangwill, 1969). It can
be anticipated that future neuropsychological techniques will overcome at least part of the testing problem and provide a better gauge
of the aphasic patient's underlying intelligence.

The relationship of language loss to cerebral dominance, handedness, and functional laterality of the hemispheres has been under
study for a long time. The unique role of the left hemisphere in
language was recognized early (Broca, 1864) and clinical observations have suggested asymmetry of hemispheric influence on a number of higher activities (Gloning et al., 1969; Warrington, 1969;
Bogen and Bogen, 1969; Gainotti, 1972; Galin, 1974). Studies of
language dysfunction following section of the corpus callosum
(Geschwind and Kaplan, 1962; Gazzaniga and Sperry, 1967) and
following hemispherectomy (Smith and Sugar, 1975); of language
loss after intracarotid barbiturate injection (Wada and Rasmussen,
1960); of asymmetrical interference with language by dichotic auditory stimulation (Broadbent, 1971; Sparks and Geschwind, 1968);
and of neuroanatomical asymmetries of the hemispheres (Yakovlev
and Rakic, 1966; Geschwind and Levitsky, 1969) have all improved
knowledge of the two hemispheres' roles in language.

In recent years there have been extensive studies of language function and malfunction through the use of dichotic listening techniques, the simultaneous presentation of different verbal (and nonverbal) messages to each ear (hypothetically to the contralateral
hemisphere). After Broadbent's original report (1971), Kimura and
co-workers studied language dominance (1967) and many others
have studied linguistic functions by this method (Bryden, 1963;
Shankweiler and Studdert-Kennedy, 1967; Spellacy, 1970).

Finally, linguists have made elegant studies of the characteristics
of aphasic output. These include studies of the phonology of aphasic
output, particularly the articulatory disturbances of the anterior
aphasias (Lecours and Lhermitte, 1969; Blumstein, 1973), or seman-

tic disturbances (Osgood, 1960; Goodglass and Baker, 1976) and of syntactical abnormalities (Zurif, Caramazza, and Myerson, 1972; Goodglass et al., 1972). The field of linguistic research in aphasia is wide and very active. Several recent books (Goodglass and Blumstein, 1973; Whitaker and Whitaker, 1977) and the journal *Brain and Language* are good sources of information in this field.

VARIETIES OF APHASIA

Earlier in this chapter it was noted that despite a proliferation of classifications of aphasia, the actual number of different aphasias is limited. In this section we will describe a number of aphasic syndromes utilizing the terminology proposed at the Aphasia Research Center, Boston Veterans Administration Hospital (Table 2-2). For comparison of this nomenclature with other systems, readers are referred to Table 2-1. The division in Table 2-2 between aphasias in which repetition is seriously disturbed and those in which this ability remains intact is dramatic and clinically useful.

Broca's aphasia

This syndrome has been given many names but is almost universally recognized as Broca's aphasia. Clinically, the patient has a nonfluent aphasic output, relatively intact comprehension (almost never fully intact, however), and a serious difficulty in repetition similar to, but often not as severe as the disorder of conversational expression.

TABLE 2-2   *Varieties of Aphasia*

Aphasia with Abnormal Repetition
  Broca's aphasia
  Wernicke's aphasia
  Conduction aphasia

Aphasia with Preserved Repetition
  Mixed transcortical aphasia
  Transcortical motor aphasia
  Transcortical sensory aphasia
  Anomic aphasia

Total Aphasia
  Global aphasia

Naming is usually poor but characteristically can be aided by contextual or phonetic prompting. Reading comprehension may be intact but much more often is not (see Chapter 3). Reading aloud is invariably disturbed and so is writing, usually severely. Along with the characteristic language syndrome, several other features are noteworthy. Most patients with Broca's aphasia have a right hemiplegia and while they may have some degree of sensory loss or even of visual field disturbance, these two findings are less common and less severe than the motor disturbance. In addition, a significant motor apraxia affecting the "good" left side is common (Benson and Geschwind, 1971). Thus, simple actions that can be carried out spontaneously and are easily imitated by the left extremities will be performed clumsily or not at all on verbal command (see Chapter 7). The syndrome named after Broca is the first variety of aphasia to have been recognized; it is common and is widely accepted as a specific type.

There is genral agreement that individuals with the clinical symptoms of Broca's aphasia will have pathology involving the posterior,

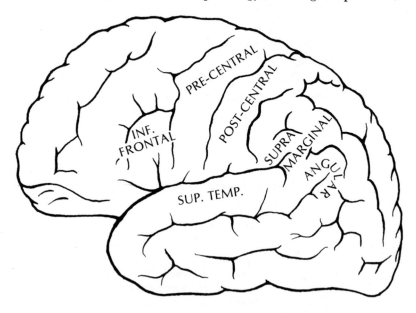

Fig. 2-1 Lateral aspect of the left cerebral hemisphere. Broca's area is in the inferior frontal gyrus. Wernicke's area is in the posterior portion of the superior temporal gyrus.

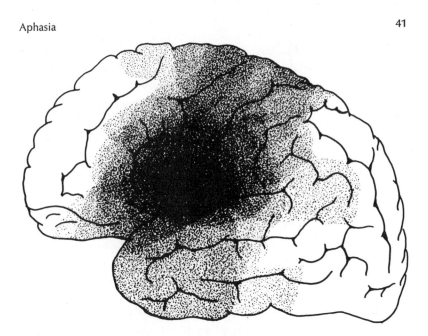

Fig. 2-2 Composite diagram: the areas of abnormality in the brain scans of 14 patients with Broca's aphasia are superimposed. Note the overlapping of lesions in the region of Broca's area. (From Kertesz, Lesk, and McCabe, 1977.)

inferior portion of the dominant (usually left) hemisphere (the frontal operculum, often called Broca's area, Fig. 2-2). There may be a considerable variation in the amount of cerebral tissue damaged and there is evidence suggesting that variations in the clinical picture and the degree of recovery in Broca's aphasia reflect this quantitative aspect (Mohr, 1973). However, it has also been contended that at least some of the variation seen in this syndrome depends upon which of the neighboring frontal anatomical structures is involved in the pathology. This difference of opinion resembles the original localizationist–holist argument.

Wernicke's aphasia

The second type of disorder in Table 2-2, Wernicke's aphasia, is dramatically different from Broca's aphasia. The verbal output is fluent but almost invariably contaminated with paraphasia, consisting mostly of semantic substitutions (verbal paraphasia). The key language finding in Wernicke's aphasia, however, is a striking disturbance of comprehension and a matching disturbance of repetition. The abilities to repeat and to comprehend often run parallel, so that comprehension of a few words is likely to be accompanied by a similar degree of repetition. Naming ability is almost always severely disturbed in Wernicke's aphasia and, in contrast to Broca's aphasia, prompting rarely helps. Reading is seriously disturbed: again, this usually runs parallel to the disturbance of auditory language comprehension. But some investigators (Hécaen and Albert, 1978) suggest that there are two variations of Wernicke's aphasia, one in which reading ability is poorer than ability to comprehend spoken language (predominantly word-blind) and another in which the opposite is true (predominantly word-deaf). If reading ability is relatively intact in the face of a serious auditory comprehension defect, then the term "pure word deafness" (see below) is appropriate. Writing ability is routinely compromised in Wernicke's aphasia and often consists of real letters in combinations which have the appearance of words but make little or no sense. Unlike patients with Broca's aphasia, those with Wernicke's aphasia often have no apparent physical or elementary neurological disability. Not infrequently, the individual who suddenly fails to comprehend spoken language and whose output is contaminated with jargon is diagnosed as psychotic and the neurological etiology is overlooked. Patients with Wernicke's aphasia certainly inhabited some of the old lunatic asylums and probably are still being misplaced in contemporary no-diagnosis, no-return mental health services.

The pathology in most cases of Wernicke's aphasia involves the dominant temporal lobe, particularly the auditory association cortex located in the posterior-superior portion of the first temporal gyrus (Wernicke's area, Fig. 2-3). In those cases in which word-deafness overshadows the reading disturbance, there is probably a greater degree of pathology deep in the first temporal gyrus involving the fibers approaching the primary auditory cortex. On the other hand, in those cases in which word-blindness is greater, the pathology is probably more posterior, involving the junction area of the angular gyrus and the dominant temporal lobe.

Conduction aphasia

The third variety of aphasia with abnormal repetition is considerably more controversial, but has gained fairly wide acceptance as a

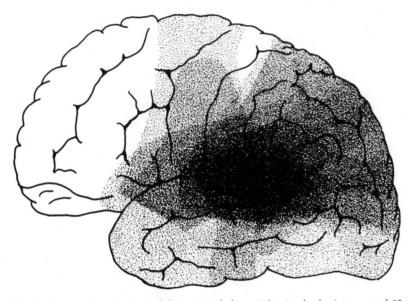

Fig. 2-3 Composite diagram of the areas of abnormality in the brain scans of 13 patients with Wernicke's aphasia. The area of greatest involvement is inferior to the Sylvian fissure, in Wernicke's area. (From Kertesz, Lesk, and McCabe, 1977.)

specific variety. As Table 2-3 indicates, the speech characteristics of conduction aphasia include fluent paraphasic output (primarily phonetic substitutions, often called literal paraphasia), relatively normal comprehension of spoken language, and severe disability in repetition. Most individuals with conduction aphasia have difficulty naming things but not infrequently this is caused by contamination of the name with incorrect phonemes, producing a literal paraphasia or a totally unrecognizable word (neologism). Classically, individuals with conduction aphasia cannot read out loud (again because of paraphasic contamination) but can comprehend written material. Problems with writing are common but relatively mild, generally involving insertion of incorrect letters or reversal of letters or words in a sentence (See Chapter 4, pp. 104–105).

It has been suggested that pathology in conduction aphasia involves the white matter beneath the supramarginal gyrus. A lesion here could separate the intact language comprehension area in the temporal lobe from an equally intact language output area in the

TABLE 2-3   *Language Symptomatology in Aphasia*

TYPE OF APHASIA	SPONTANEOUS SPEECH	COMPRE-HENSION	PARAPHASIA	REPETITION	NAMING
Broca's aphasia	Nonfluent	Good	Uncommon	Poor	Poor
Wernicke's aphasia	Fluent	Poor	Common (verbal)	Poor	Poor
Conduction aphasia	Fluent	Good	Common (literal)	Poor	Poor
Mixed transcortical	Nonfluent	Poor	Uncommon	Good-echolalia	Poor
Transcortical motor	Nonfluent	Good	Uncommon	Good-echolalia	Poor
Transcortical sensory	Fluent	Poor	Common	Good-echolalia	Poor
Anomic	Fluent	Good	Absent	Good	Poor
Global	Nonfluent	Poor	Variable	Poor	Poor

frontal lobe (Geschwind, 1965; Benson et al., 1973). Not all reported cases of conduction aphasia have had lesions in this area, however. In fact, conduction aphasia has been reported following damage to a variety of areas in the posterior perisylvian region, including both supra- and sub-sylvian sites and combinations of the two (see Fig. 2-4). While conduction aphasia has been reported with purely temporal lesions and with purely supra-sylvian lesions, the language characteristics remain consistent and always indicate pathology in the posterior perisylvian region of the dominant hemisphere.

Mixed transcortical aphasia (Isolation of the Speech Area)

The outstanding characteristic of the transcortical aphasias is an intact or at least good ability to repeat spoken language despite serious aphasia. The most dramatic example is the patient with mixed transcortical aphasia who is nonfluent (in fact, does not speak at all unless spoken to), does not comprehend spoken language, cannot name, cannot read or write, but can repeat what is said by the examiner. A characteristic finding is *echolalia,* a strong, sometimes mandatory, tendency to repeat what has just been said. As Stengel (1947) demonstrated, such individuals have a remarkable ability to complete sentences. When given an overlearned phrase such as "roses are ———," the patient will complete the phrase and

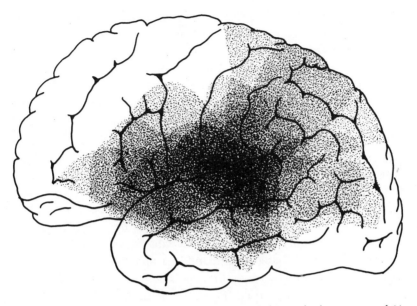

Fig. 2-4 Composite diagram of the areas of abnormality in the brain scans of 11 patients with conduction aphasia. Note that there are both supra- and infra-Sylvian lesions. (From Kertesz, Lesk, and McCabe, 1977.)

may well carry on with the next line. Fully developed cases of mixed transcortical aphasia are rare. An excellent case has been published under the title of "Isolation of the Speech Area" (Geschwind, Quadfasel, and Segarra, 1968); the pathology spared the perisylvian area (Broca's area, Wernicke's area, and the white matter connecting them) but involved the surrounding area, often called the border zone or watershed area. The most common etiology in mixed transcortical aphasia is carotid artery occlusion which produces an inadequate blood flow that is most pronounced in the distal tributaries of the middle cerebral artery. The syndrome has also been reported following hypoxic episodes and severe cerebral edema. Here again, it is surmised that the distribution of pathology reflects poor oxygen supply in the outer vascular tributaries.

Transcortical motor aphasia
A partial transcortical aphasia in which motor disturbance is predominant is considerably more common. Verbal output is nonfluent except for the ability to echo. Comprehension is relatively well

preserved and repetition is excellent. Most such patients have difficulty naming but accept and benefit from cues. Reading comprehension is often preserved but writing is almost invariably abnormal.
In cases of transcortical motor aphasia, the pathology is located in
the dominant frontal lobe, either superior or anterior to Broca's
area. The etiology may be vascular disease, but trauma and postoperative brain tumor are also common causes of this distinctive
type of aphasia.

Transcortical sensory aphasia

A somewhat less common variety of aphasia with intact repetition
involves the sensory modalities. The classic description of transcortical sensory aphasia includes fluent output, frequently utilizing
repetition (echoing) of what has been said by the examiner and
occasionally contaminated by semantic paraphasia. Comprehension
of spoken language is severely limited. There are serious problems
in both reading and writing. The exact location of the pathology
underlying transcortical sensory aphasia is not well defined but
primarily involves the border zones of the parietal or temporal regions or, more likely, the junction of these areas.

Anomic aphasia

Anomic (amnesic, nominal) aphasia is very common and yet it is
the most difficult variety to localize. After recovery from any type
of aphasia, some residual anomia is almost always present (see
Chapter 16). Almost all aphasics have some degree of word-finding
difficulty and there is little agreement as to which variation deserves
the title of anomic aphasia. Certain language characteristics, however, suggest the diagnosis. These include a fluent output with little
or no paraphasia, relatively normal ability to comprehend spoken
language, and excellent ability to repeat words coupled with a
notable deficiency in the ability to produce names. Word-finding
problems may be apparent on evaluation of conversational speech:
the patient may produce a wordy, lengthy output lacking specificity
and often called "empty speech." Such a patient may try to substitute when he needs a word he can't immediately produce. If the
phrase used in substitution also demands a specific word which is
unavailable, the patient may be forced into yet another substitute

phrase, a convoluted output that has been called *circumlocution*. Empty speech almost always has many pauses while the patient searches for words. While not necessarily involved, reading and writing are frequently abnormal in cases of anomic aphasia. In fact, the combination of alexia with agraphia (see Chapter 3) and anomic aphasia (and often the Gerstmann syndrome) is common and strongly suggests pathology involving the dominant angular gyrus. It must be realized, however, that anomia alone does not necessarily indicate angular gyrus pathology. In fact, pathology involving almost any part of the language area, and even any part of the non-dominant hemisphere can cause word-finding problems. Anomia alone is not a useful indication of the site of pathology, and localization of anomic aphasia is treacherous unless there are clear neighborhood signs.

Global aphasia

Aphasia in which language loss is nearly complete is usually called total or global aphasia. The exact definition of this disorder is rather difficult. In the view of most investigators, global aphasia indicates a severe output disturbance (nonfluent), equally severe disturbance of comprehension, and little or no ability to repeat, read, or write. A more rigid quantitative basis is sometimes used in defining global aphasia. Thus, patients who score lower than 6.0 on the PICA or 1.5 standard deviations or more below normal on the major subtests of the BDAE have been diagnosed as global aphasics. The degree and localization of pathology varies considerably, however, and both the scores and description given fail to reflect the significant variations of global aphasia seen in the clinic. In general, both Wernicke's and Broca's areas and, to a greater or lesser extent, the remainder of the language territory of the dominant hemisphere are involved in global aphasia (Fig. 2-5).

Disturbances of a single language modality

There are three conditions in which only a single modality of language input or output is disrupted. Legitimately, these should not be called aphasia since basic language function is intact. Nonetheless, they are so closely related to the varieties of aphasia just mentioned that they must be considered when examining for aphasia.

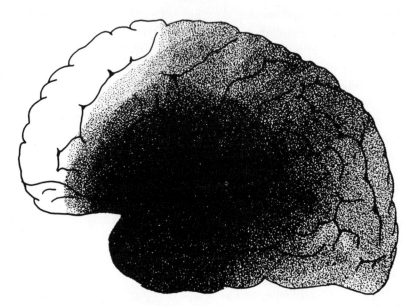

Fig. 2-5 Composite diagram of the areas of abnormality in the brain scans of 12 patients with global aphasia. Note the extensive involvement, which usually involves both Broca's and Wernicke's areas. (From Kertesz, Lesk, and McCabe, 1977.)

The first of these has been given a number of different names, none of which has gained general acceptance. These include aphemia, pure word dumbness, anarthria, and subcortical motor aphasia. The patient becomes acutely mute. With recovery there is a severe hypophonia that gradually improves to a soft, slow but grammatically intact verbal output. During the entire period comprehension of spoken language and the ability to read and to write are preserved. Of particular note, in neither verbal nor written output does the patient show signs of agrammatism or anomia. Aphemia involves only speech output and is not truly an impairment of language (aphasia), but it has a place in the differential diagnosis of the aphasias. In the few cases of aphemia that have come to autopsy, lesions have been found either in Broca's area or in the area immediately under it (Bastian, 1898; Mohr et al., 1975). A nearly identical syndrome, however, can result from pathology in other locations. In particular, acute involvement of the dominant supplementary motor area produces mutism followed by hypophonic but grammatically correct language, and a somewhat similar set of language disturbances is associated with dominant thalamic pathology and surgical thalamotomy.

Abnormalities involving only reception of spoken language are traditionally called *pure word deafness*. Clinically, the individual with pure word deafness does not understand spoken language although he has adequate hearing and can identify nonverbal sounds (e.g., whistle, telephone ring). His verbal output may be entirely normal although some paraphasia is usually present in the acute stage. In long-standing cases of pure word deafness, quite normal verbal output may be present though there is almost no comprehension of spoken language. These patients cannot repeat spoken language but read without difficulty and write adequately. Pathology in autopsied cases of pure word deafness has been found in two different locations (Weisenburg and McBride, 1933). About half of the cases reported have had subcortical lesions of the dominant superior temporal region, in particular involving the primary auditory cortex or the auditory pathways from the medical geniculate nucleus. Other cases, however, have had bilateral pathology involving the superior temporal gyrus, particularly the mid-portion of the first temporal gyrus on both sides. Again, pure word deafness should not be considered a true aphasia since language production is not disturbed, only the ability to receive spoken language. (See Chapter 9, pp. 252–254.)

A similar disorder involving reading will be discussed in Chapter 3. This has been called *alexia without agraphia* or pure word blindness, a condition in which the patient is unable to read but has no other language disturbances. As in pure word deafness, the pathology involves a primary sensory modality and separates this area from the intact language area.

Mention should be made of a controversial syndrome called "thalamic aphasia." A number of authorities have suggested that thalamic pathology, particularly that which involves the posterior thalamus, should produce some language disturbance because of the rich connections between this area and the cortical structures of the language area (Ojemann, 1971). Until recently there has been little evidence of a true thalamic aphasia (Brown, 1974). With the advent of the CAT scan as a diagnostic tool, the ability to diagnose thalamic hemorrhage has improved considerably and a number of independent investigators have reported a fairly characteristic apha-sic picture in these cases (Mohr, 1975; Rubens, 1977). They describe a fluent but paraphasic output and mild disturbance in the compre-hension of spoken language but relatively good ability to repeat. Disturbance of reading and writing has also been present in most reported cases. The combination of fluent paraphasic verbal output, normal repetition, and relatively normal comprehension is not typical of other aphasic syndromes and appears to represent a dis-tinct disturbance. However, similar findings have been noted in cases without thalamic involvement, particularly intracranial mass lesions. That this distinct language syndrome is actually caused by increased pressure affecting the language area is a possibility. Cer-tainly, thalamic hemorrhage initially produces a considerable in-crease in intracranial pressure.

Finally, a note of caution must be voiced concerning the cor-relation of language symptoms with neuropathology. Most of the syndromes discussed above were described long ago and the clinical-pathological correlations outlined here have been confirmed con-sistently through the years. In the past decade several studies have demonstrated good correlations between these syndromes and the location of pathology as demonstrated by radioisotope scan (Benson, 1967; Kertesz, Lesk, and McCabe, 1977) and CAT scan (Naeser, 1976). It cannot be stated, however, that pathology involving a spe-cific area will always produce a given syndrome, much less a specific language dysfunction. There have been many reports of destructive pathology involving Broca's area, Wernicke's area, and other regions that did not produce the anticipated language disturbances. It can only be stated that although pathology in a specific area does not guarantee a specific language dysfunction, a group of characteristic language problems (a syndrome) strongly suggests pathology in a specific area. This is valuable information for both clinicians and for investigators attempting to understand the brain's function in the language process.

THERAPY FOR APHASIA

The first attempts to treat aphasia were made by neurologists, who usually reported single case studies in detail (Helm, unpublished).

Formal aphasia therapy dates only from the time of World War II. At first performed by psychologists or educators, formal therapy is currently performed largely by specially trained speech pathologists.

Since spontaneous recovery does occur in many aphasic patients, the assessment of the efficacy of speech therapy is difficult. Although recent studies suggest a benefit from therapy (Basso, Faglioni, and Vignolo, 1975), the benefit might well accrue from the emotional support of therapy, rather than the specific therapeutic methods. Recovery of function and therapy for aphasia are considered in more detail in Chapter 16.

Most "traditional" aphasia therapy represents variations on techniques used in speech training and education, particularly rote practice (Darley, 1975). A number of innovations in aphasia therapy have been made in the past few years, and it would appear that many more are due. Melodic intonation therapy (MIT) (Albert, Sparks and Helm, 1973) has met with some success in the treatment of aphasics with severe expressive difficulty, poor repetition, and good comprehension. In this program patients are first taught to maintain a rhythm for a spoken phrase as the phrase is intoned by the therapist, and then, while maintaining the rhythm, the patient also intones the phrase. As the patient's intonation becomes successful, the therapist ceases intonation and the patient eventually ceases rhythm tapping but continues with intonation.

The attempt to use sign language as a substitute for verbal means of communication has met with only minimal success (Chen, 1971; Skelly et al., 1974). It appears that sign language demands as much language competency as spoken language. A variety of speaking machines have been devised to aid the aphasic in communication, but to little avail. Even those aphasics who do master the operation of the apparatus almost invariably report that they can communicate better without the machine. The successful teaching of a symbol system for communication to chimpanzees (Gardner and Gardner, 1969; Premack, 1971) has been followed by an attempt to use a similar system with aphasic adults (Gardner et al., 1976). While improvement has not been striking, some encouraging preliminary results have been seen in the treatment of global aphasics. Another system of symbols—a visual communication system (VIC)—has been shown to help some global aphasics (Baker et al., 1975).

While traditional therapy has been rather broad and has not offered a specific type of treatment for a specific type of aphasia, some of the newer methods of therapy appear to be more specific. MIT has proved effective for a limited group of aphasics: nonfluent aphasics who improve little with repetition but who have relatively good comprehension of spoken language. VIC and other new symbol systems appear particularly suited to patients with poor comprehension. It seems likely that therapies will be designed for specific types of aphasia.

Finally, some attention should be given to the important part played by emotional support in aphasia therapy. The loss of language is a severe blow at any age and aphasics often suffer language loss when they are at their prime. Both employment and economic status are often drastically altered and, in addition, position as family leader, regular recreation activities, and even sexual activities are threatened. Frustration and depression often complicate the picture of aphasia. Careful attention to these emotional factors is a mandatory part of any aphasia therapy program.

The loss, real or threatened, of position in the family must be faced, particularly if the individual has been the breadwinner and leader in the family. Careful counseling of the family, helping them to understand the situation and to aid the patient in maintaining as much of his or her prior status as possible, is important. Similarly, many aphasics have serious physical problems such as hemiplegia and visual disturbance. Full-scale rehabilitation programs should be carried out in conjunction with language therapy. Success in a physical rehabilitation program is often reflected by improvement in language therapy programs and vice versa. The aphasic gets considerable support from working with someone who understands aphasia and is dedicated to the improvement of his language function. Thus, the therapist, as a person, becomes an important factor in the patient's improvement. Similarly, many aphasics benefit from group interaction. Either observing or actively participating with others who share the disorder offers a form of psychic support. Watching other individuals improve and realizing that they themselves have improved in comparison to others entering the program is another source of support.

References

Albert, M. L., Sparks, R. W., and Helm, N. A. (1973). Melodic intonation therapy for aphasia. *Arch. Neurol. 29*:130–131.

Baker, E., Berry, T., Gardner, H., Zurif, E., Davis, L., and Veroff, A. (1975). Can linguistic competence be dissociated from natural language functions? *Nature, 254*:509–510.

Basso, A., Faglioni, P., and Vignolo, L. A. (1975). Etude controlle de la reeducation du langage dous l'aphasie: comparison entre aphasiques traites et nontraites. *Rev. Neurol. 131*:607–614.

Bastian, H. C. (1898). *Aphasia and Other Speech Defects.* London: H. K. Lewis.

Bay, E. (1962). Aphasia and non verbal disorders of language. *Brain 85*: 411–426.

Bay, E. (1964). Principles of classification and their influence on our concepts of aphasia, in *Disorders of Language,* A. V. S. DeReuk and M. O'Connor (Ciba eds). Boston: Little, Brown.

Benson, D. F. and Patten, D. H. (1967). The use of radioactive isotopes in the localization of aphasia-producing lesions. *Cortex 3*:258–271.

Benson, D. F. (1967). Fluency in aphasia correlation with radioactive scan localization. *Cortex 3*:373–394.

Benson, D. F. (1978). Neurologic correlates of aphasia and apraxia, in *Recent Advances in Neurology,* W. B. Matthews and G. Glaser (eds). London: Churchill Livingstone.

Benson, D. F. (1979). Neurologic correlates of anomia, in *Studies in Neurolinguistics,* Vol. 4, H. Whitaker and H. Whitaker (eds). New York: Academic Press.

Benson, D. F. and Geschwind, N. (1971). Aphasia and related cortical disturbances, in *Clinical Neurology,* A. B. Baker and L. H. Baker (eds). New York: Harper & Row.

Benson, D. F., Sheremata, W. A., Buchard, R., Segarra, J., Price, D., and Geschwind, N. (1973). Conduction aphasia. *Arch. Neurol. 28*:339–346.

Benton, A. L. (1964). Developmental aphasia and brain damage. *Cortex 1*: 40–52.

Benton, A. L. and Joynt, R. J. (1960). Early descriptions of aphasia. *Arch. Neurol. 3*:205–222.

Blumstein, S. E. (1973). *A Phonological Investigation of Aphasic Speech.* The Hague: Mouton.

Bogen, J. E. (1969). The other side of the brain. I: Dysgraphia and dyscopia following cerebral commissurotomy. *Bull. Los Angeles Neurol. Soc. 34*: 73–105.

Bogen, J. E. (1969). The other side of the brain. II: An appositional mind. *Bull. Los Angeles Neurol. Soc. 34*:135–162.

Bogen, J. E. and Bogen, G. M. (1969). The other side of the brain. III: The corpus callosum and creativity. *Bull. Los Angeles Neurol. Soc. 34*: 191–220.

Brain, R. (1961). *Speech Disorders—Aphasia, Apraxia and Agnosia.* London: Butterworths.

Broadbent, D. E. (1971). *Decision and Stress.* New York: Academic Press.

Broca, P. (1861). Remarques sur le siege de la faculte du langage articule, suives d'une observation d'aphemie. *Bull. Soc. Anat. 36*:330–357.

Broca, P. (1864). Deux cas c'aphemie tramatique, produite par des lesions de la troisieme circonvolution frontale gauche. *Bull. d.l. Soc. d. Chiurg. V*:51–54.

Brown, J. W. (1974). Language, cognition and the thalamus. *Confin. Neurol. 36*:33–60.

Bryden, M. P. (1963). Ear preferences in auditory perception. *J. Exp. Psychol. 65*:103–105.

Charcot, J. M. (1889). *Clinical Lectures on Diseases of the Nervous System,* Vol. 3. London: New Sydenham Society.

Chen, L. C. (1971). Manual communication by combined alphabet and gestures. *Arch. Phys. Med. Rehab. 52*:381–384.

Critchley, M. (1970). *Aphasiology.* London: Edward Arnold Ltd.

Darley, F. L. (1975). Treatment of acquired aphasia, in *Advances in Neurology,* Vol. 7, W. J. Friedlander (ed). New York: Raven.

Dejerine, J. (1914). *Semiologie des Affections du Systeme Nerveaux.* Paris: Masson.

DeRenzi, E. and Vignolo, L. A. (1962). The token test: a sensitive test to detect receptive disturbances in aphasics. *Brain 85*:665–678.

Eisenson, J. (1954). *Examining for Aphasia.* New York: Psychological Corp.

Freud, S. (1953). *On Aphasia,* Trans. E. Stengl. New York: Int. Univ. Press.

Gainotti, G. (1972). Emotional behavior and hemispheric side of the lesion. *Cortex 8*:41–55.

Galin, D. (1974). Implications for psychiatry of left and right cerebral specialization. *Arch. Gen. Psychol. 31*:572–583.

Gardner, H., Zurif, E., Berry, T., and Baker, E. (1976). Visual communication in aphasia. *Neuropsychologia 14*:275–292.

Gardner, R. A. and Gardner, B. (1969). Teaching sign language to a chimpanzee. *Science 165*:664–672.

Gazzaniga, M. S., and Sperry, R. W. (1967). Language after section of the cerebral commissures. *Brain 90*:131–148.

Geschwind, N. (1965). Disconnexion syndromes in animals and man. *Brain 88*: Part II, 237–294; Part III, 585–644.

Geschwind, N. and Kaplan, E. F. (1962). A human cerebral deconnection syndrome. *Neurology 12*:675–685.

Geschwind, N., Quadfasel, F. A., and Segarra, J. (1968). Isolation of the speech area. *Neuropsychologia 6*:327–340.

Geschwind, N. and Levitsky, W. (1968). Human brain: left-right assymmetries in temporal speech region. *Science 161*:186–187.

Gloning, I., Gloning, K., Haub, C., and Quatember, R. (1969). Comparison of verbal behavior in right-handed and non-right-handed patients with anatomically verified lesion of one hemisphere. *Cortex 5*:43–52.

Goldstein, K. (1948). *Language and Language Disturbances*. New York: Grune & Stratton.

Goodglass, H. and Berko, J. (1960). Agrammatism and inflectional morphology in English. *J. Speech Hearing Res. 3*:257–267.

Goodglass, H. and Kaplan, E. (1972). *The Assessment of Aphasia and Related Disorders*. Philadelphia: Lea & Febiger.

Goodglass, H., Gleason, J. B., Bernholtz, N. A., and Hyde, M. (1972). Some linguistic structures in the speech of Broca's aphasia. *Cortex 8*:191–192.

Goodglass, H. and Blumstein, S. (1973). *Psycholinguistics and Aphasia*. Baltimore: Johns Hopkins.

Goodglass, H. and Baker, E. (1976). Semantic field naming and auditory comprehension in aphasia. *Brain and Language 3*:359–374.

Head, H. (1926). *Aphasia and Kindred Disorders* (2 volumes). London: Cambridge University Press.

Hécaen, H. and Angelergues, R. (1965). *Pathologie du Langage*. Paris: Larousse.

Hécaen, H. and Albert, M. (1978). *Human Neuropsychology*. New York: Wiley.

Helm, N. A. (unpublished). A history of aphasia rehabilitation, 1904–1950.

Henschen, S. E. (1922). *Klinische und Anatomische Bertrage zur Pathologie der Gehirns*. Stockholm: Almquist and Wiksell.

Holland, A. L. (unpublished). Assessment of communicative activities relevant to daily living. Research project sponsored by NIH.

Howes, D. (1964). Application of the word frequency concept to aphasia, in *Disorders of Language: A Ciba Foundation Symposium*, A. V. S. DeReuk and M. O'Connor (eds). London: Churchill.

Isserlin, M. (1929, 1931, 1932). Die pathologische Physiologie der Sprache. *Eigebn. Physiol. 29*:129–249; *33*:1–202; *34*:1065–1144.

Jackson, J. H. (1968). On the physiology of language. *Medical Times and Gazette 2*:275 (1915). Reprinted in *Brain 38*:59–64.

Jakobson, R. (1964). Towards a linguistic typology of aphasic impairments, in *Disorders of Language*, A. V. S. DeReuk and M. O'Connor (eds). Boston: Little, Brown.

Kennedy, F. and Wolf, A. (1936). The relationship of intellect to speech defect in aphasic patients. *J. Nervous Mental Dis. 84*:125–145, 293–311.

Kertesz, A., Lesk, D., and McCabe, P. (1977). Isotope localization of infarcts in aphasia. *Arch. Neurol. 34*:590–601.

Kertesz, A. and Poole, E. (1974). The aphasia quotient: the taxonomic approach to measurement of aphasic disability. *Can. J. Neurol. Sci. 1*: 7–16.

Kimura, D. (1967). Functional asymmetry of the brain in dichotic listening. *Cortex 3*:163–178.

Kleist, K. (1962). *Sensory Alphasia and Amusia—The Myeloarchitectunic Basis*. London: Pergamon Press.

Lecours, A. R. and Lhermitte, F. (1969). Phonemic paraphasias: linguistic structures and tentative hypotheses. *Cortex 5*:193–228.

Leischner, A. (1957). *Die Storungen der Schriftsprache (Agraphie und Alexie)*. Stuttgart: Georg Thieme Verlag.

Lhermitte, F. and Gautier, J. C. (1969). Aphasia, in *Handbook of Clinical Neurology*, Vol. 4, P. J. Vinken and G. W. Bruyn (eds). Amsterdam: North Holland.

Lichtheim, L. (1885). On aphasia. *Brain 7*:433–484.

Luria, A. R. (1966). *Higher Cortical Functions in Man*. New York: Basic Books.

Luria, A. R. (1970). *Traumatic Aphasia*. The Hague: Mouton.

Marie, Pierre (1906). *Semaine Medicale XXVI*:241–247, 493–500, 565–571.

Mohr, J. P. (1973). Rapid amelioration of motor aphasia. *Arch. Neurol. 28*:77–82.

Mohr, J. P., Wattes, W. C., and Duncan, G. W. (1975). Thalamic hemorrhage and aphasia. *Brain and Language 2*:3–18.

Mohr, J. P., Finklestein, S., Pessin, M. S., Duncan, G. W., and Davis, K. (1975). Broca's area infarction versus Broca's aphasia. Presentation to 27th Annual Meeting of American Academy of Neurology, Bal Harbor, Florida.

Naeser, M. A. and Hayward, R. W. (1976). The evolving stroke and aphasia: a case study with computed tomography. Presented Academy of Aphasia Meeting, Miami, Florida.

Nielsen, J. M. (1962). *Agnosia, Apraxia and Aphasia: Their Value in Cerebral Localization*, 2nd ed. New York: Hafner.

Ojemann, G. and Ward, A. (1971). Speech representation in ventrolateral thalamus. *Brain 94*:669–680.

Orgass, B., Hartje, W., Kerschensteiner, M., and Poeck, K. (1972). Aphasie und nichtsprachliche Intelligenz. *Nervenartz 43*:623–627.

Osgood, C. E. (1960). *Method and Theory in Experimental Psychology*. New York: Oxford.

Pick, A. (1973). *Aphasia*. Springfield, Ill.: C. C. Thomas.

Poeck, K., Kerschensteiner, M., and Hartje, W. (1972). A quantitative study on language understanding in fluent and nonfluent aphasia. *Cortex 8*:299–305.

Porch, B. (1967). *Porch Index of Communicative Ability*. Palo Alto: Consulting Psychologists.

Premack, D. (1971). Language in the chimpanzee. *Science 172*:808–822.

Ravens, J. C. (1952). *Human Nature: Its Development, Variations and Assessment*. London: H. K. Lewis.

Rubens, A. B. (1977). The role of changes within the central nervous system during recovery from aphasia, in *Rationale for Adult Aphasia Therapy*. Omaha: University of Nebraska Press.

Samuels, J. and Benson, D. F. Observations on anterior alexia. *Brain and Language* (in press).

Sarno, M. T., Silverman, M., and Sands, E. (1970). Speech therapy and language recovery in severe aphasia. *J. Speech Hearing Res. 13*:607–623.

Schuell, H. (1957). *Minnesota Test for the Differential Diagnosis of Aphasia*. Minneapolis: University of Minnesota Press.

Schuell, H., Jenkins, J., and Jimenez-Pabon, E. (1964). *Aphasia in Adults—Diagnosis, Prognosis and Treatment*. New York: Harper & Row.

Shankweiler, D. and Studdert-Kennedy, M. (1967). Identification of consonants and vowels presented to the left and right ears. *Quart. J. Exp. Psychol. 19*:59–63.

Skelly, M., Schinsky, L., Smith, R., and Fust, R. (1974). American Indian sign (Amerind) as a facilitator of verbalization for the oral verbal apraxic. *J. Speech Hearing Disorders 39*:445–446.

Sklar, M. (1966). *Sklar Aphasia Scale*. Los Angeles: Western Psychological Services.

Smith, A. and Sugar, O. (1975). Development of above-normal language and intelligence 21 years after left hemispherectomy. *Neurology 25*:813–818.

Sparks, R. and Geschwind, N. (1968). Dichotic listening in man after section of neocortical commissures. *Cortex 4*:3–16.

Spellacy, F. (1970). Lateral preferences in the identification of patterned stimuli. *J. Acoust. Soc. Am. 47*:574–578.

Spreen, O. and Benton, A. (1969). *Neurosensory Center Comprehensive Examination for Aphasia*. Victoria: Neuropsychology Laboratory, University of Victoria.

Stengel, E. (1947). A clinical and psychological study of echo reactions. *J. Mental Sci. 93*:598–612.

Taylor, M. L. (1965). A measurement of functional communication in aphasia. *Arch. Phys. Med. Rehab. 46*:101–107.

Wada, J. and Rasmussen, T. (1960). Intracarotid injection of sodium amytal for the lateralization of cerebral speech dominance: experimental and clinical observations. *J. Neurosurg. 17*:266–282.

Wagenaar, E., Snow, C., and Prins, R. (1975). Spontaneous speech of aphasic patients: a psycholinguistic analysis. *Brain and Language 3*: 281–303.

Warrington, E. W. (1969). Constructional apraxia, in *Handbook of Clinical Neurology*, Vol. 4, P. J. Vinken and G. W. Bruyn (eds). Amsterdam: North Holland.

Wechsler, D. (1958). *The Measurement and Appraisal of Adult Intelligence*. Baltimore: Williams and Wilkins.

Weisenburg, T. S. and McBride, K. L. (1964). *Aphasia*. New York: Hafner.

Wepman, J. (1961). *Language Modalities Test for Aphasia.* Chicago: Education Industry Service.

Wepman, J. (1951). *Recovery from Aphasia.* New York: Ronald.

Wernicke, C. (1874). *Der Aphasiche Symptomencomplex.* Breslau: Cohn & Weigart.

Whitaker, H. and Whitaker, H. A. (1977). *Studies in Neurolinguistics,* Vol. 3. New York: Academic Press.

Wilson, S. A. K. (1926). *Aphasia.* London: Kegan Paul.

Yakovlev, P. I. and Rakic, P. (1966). Patterns of decussation of bulbar pyramids and distribution of pyramidal tracts on two sides of the spinal cord. *Trans. Am. Neurol. Assoc. 91:*366–367.

Zangwill, O. (1946). Some qualitative observations on verbal memory in cases of cerebral lesion. *Br. J. Psychol. 37:*8–19.

Zangwill, O. (1969). Intellectual status in aphasia, in *Handbook of Clinical Neurology,* Vol. 4, P. J. Vinken and G. W. Bruyn (eds). Amsterdam: North Holland.

Zurif, E. B., Caramazza, A., and Myerson, R. (1972). Grammatical judgments of agrammatic asphasics. *Neuropsychologia 10:*405–417.

3
Alexia

MARTIN L. ALBERT

DEFINITIONS AND HISTORICAL BACKGROUND

Definitions

Alexia may be defined as an acquired inability to comprehend written language, as a consequence of brain damage. The term *acquired dyslexia* is used by some authors synonymously with alexia. Acquired dyslexia, in contrast to developmental dyslexia, occurs in the individual who has already learned to read in a normal fashion; developmental dyslexia refers to an inability to learn to read normally from childhood. In the definition of alexia, emphasis is placed on the impairment of comprehension. Inability to read aloud may, as we shall see, form part of an alexic syndrome, but this defect is neither necessary nor sufficient for the diagnosis of alexia. The term "word blindness" is a classical expression for alexia, and is still in use, especially in continental Europe.

Historical background

The history of studies on alexia may be roughly divided into four periods: the clinical, the clinico-anatomical (this period may be loosely subdivided into localizationist and connectionist or associationist), the anti-localizationist, and the neuropsychological-neurolinguistic. There is considerable overlap among these periods, prin-

cipally because new ideas—representing new approaches to the study
of alexia—were added to older notions and did not displace them.

CLINICAL PERIOD

The clinical period refers to those scattered, often anecdotal, clinical descriptions of impaired reading due to brain damage that have
appeared in diverse reports for the past two thousand years. Benton
(1964) credits the earliest observation of alexia to Valerius Maximus
who in 30 A.D. described a man who was struck on his head by an
axe and lost his memory for letters, but had no other cognitive defects. Sporadic case reports appear from the 1500's to the mid-1800's
(Mercuriale, 1588, Schmidt, 1673; Gesner, 1770; Gendrin, 1838;
Trousseau, 1865; Broadbent, 1872); and these are cited in the historical reviews by Benton and Joynt (1960) and Benton (1964) and
in the excellent review of the alexias by Benson and Geschwind
(1969). Mercuriale (1588) had noted "a truly astonishing thing; this
man [following a seizure] would write but could not read what he
had written."

In all cases, reading difficulties were found in relative isolation
from other cognitive impairments. Little or no attempt was made
to provide an anatomical explanation for the reading disorders.

CLINICO-ANATOMICAL PERIOD

Toward the end of the 1800's, and continuing to the present, clinico-
anatomical correlations of the alexias have been reported and debated. In 1872 Broadbent discussed the "cerebral mechanism of
speech and thought," describing a patient with a severe reading
deficit, and with mild aphasia and agraphia. His patient had a large
hemorrhage into the substance of the left hemisphere, plus an old
infarction beneath the parieto-occipital junction. Broadbent suggested that this old infarction was so placed as to interfere with the
connections of verbal and visual material.

A major step forward was made by Kussmaul (1877). He proposed an associationist model for language in which alexia, or word
blindness, represented one of the six possible forms of aphasia, and
resulted from a lesion of the center for verbal visual images. Many
subsequent interpretations of alexia were based on this theory.

Charcot (1890) attempted to synthesize his own observations and those of Kussmaul and others. He described the clinical features: inability to read printed or handwritten material, often in the absence of significant disorders of spoken language, although naming defects may be present, and often with preserved ability to write. A right homonymous hemianopia was usually present; and the clinical findings, together with reports from the few published cases with anatomical correlation, suggested that lesions in the inferior parietal lobule and superior temporal gyrus produced the syndrome.

The main contribution to the clinico-anatomical understanding of alexia in the 1880's was that of Dejerine. In separate reports in 1891 and 1892 he described two different varieties of alexia which he attributed to lesions interfering with the normal reading process at different stages. One type, which he called "pure word blindness" was associated with preserved capacity to write and resulted from a lesion in the visual (occipital) cortex of the language-dominant hemisphere coupled with a lesion in the splenium of the corpus callosum (Dejerine, 1892). Another type, alexia associated with agraphia, was shown to be due to a lesion of the dominant angular gyrus (Dejerine, 1891). Dejerine considered the alexia in this case to be a variety of sensory aphasia in which "word blindness was more marked than word deafness." The distinction between these two basic types of alexia has been confirmed repeatedly, although sometimes with different labels (see, e.g. Benson and Geschwind, 1969; Hécaen, 1967; Hécaen and Kremin, 1977).

Although Dejerine's concepts fell within the category of associationist theory, he emphasized the role of the angular gyrus as the center for verbal visual images. Wernicke (1885) proposed a distinction between cortical alexia and subcortical alexia; for both of these a disconnection between two critical areas would be the mechanism underlying the deficit. Summarizing reports in the literature and adding six of his own, Hinshelwood brought up to date, as of 1900, the subject of alexia for readers of English. His conclusions tended to support the connectionist theory.

Another approach to alexia was to consider it a form of visual agnosia. A close relationship was found between agnosias for pictures, objects, and colors and pure alexia (Lissauer, 1889; Nodet, 1889). Here, the anatomical theory of associative visual agnosia was applied, i.e., pure alexia was a syndrome caused by the combination of lesions in the left occipital cortex and splenium of the corpus callosum. The perceptual nature of the alexia was stressed by Jack (1900) and Poetzl (1928), with the principal lesion being in the left occipital cortex. Others, even until the contemporary period, have considered alexia without agraphia to be a form of agnosia (e.g., Quensel, 1931; Stengel, 1948).

A series of studies in the past two decades has rejuvenated the theory of disconnection syndromes as a basis for pure alexia (e.g., Geschwind, 1962, 1965; Gazzaniga, Bogen, and Sperry, 1965).

ANTI-LOCALIZATIONIST PERIOD

For the subject of aphasia, the holist, gestaltist, antilocalizationist school of Marie (1906), Head (1926), and Goldstein (1948) has had a powerful and continuing impact. The same cannot be said, however, for the subject of alexia.

According to Gestalt theory, reading is not an autonomous function. A single lesion cannot, therefore, cause a pure alexia; rather, there is a breakdown in the capacity to use symbols or to differentiate a figure from its background. Marie (1906) maintained at first that a strictly subcortical lesion could not cause a pure alexia—that the syndrome simply did not exist, except to the extent that the lesion extended toward Wernicke's area and that the clinical syndrome included features of sensory aphasia, however mild. In a subsequent study, however, he admitted that alexia without agraphia could exist, and could result from a deeply placed occipital lesion (Marie and Foix, 1917). These cases, he concluded, were variants of visual agnosia.

The gestaltist school (e.g., Goldstein, 1948; Conrad, 1948; Leischner, 1957), while making important theoretical contributions concerning the nature of reading disorders, has had difficulty maintaining its credibility concerning the nonspecificity of particular anatomical lesions. Goldstein (1948) divided alexias into primary and secondary. Primary alexia was a manifestation of visual agnosia in reading, resulting from a loss of abstract attitude and an inability to distinguish a form from its context. Secondary alexia was a reading disorder within a syndrome including other aphasic problems. Goldstein did not deny that specifically located lesions could be responsible for the different forms of alexia.

Conrad (1948) argued that reading disorders never appeared in isolation, but were elements of a more general defect—an impairment in the "structuration of forms." This defect is a gnostic disorder and when caused by a lesion in the parieto-occipital region may be more marked in the visual and verbal spheres. In a similar vein Leischer (1957) denied the clinical reality of pure alexia. Alexia, for him, is a deterioration of the ability to grasp a gestalt— an inability to understand or manipulate isolated symbols.

Despite the extensive and often lucid discussions of apparently isolated reading disorders in relation to global cognitive functioning, proponents of the holist approach rarely went so far as to deny that specific and different lesions could cause specific and different forms of alexia.

NEUROPSYCHOLOGICAL-NEUROLINGUISTIC PERIOD

Following the Second World War, dramatic technical advances were made in the fields of neuroanatomy and neurophysiology. Behavioral scientists were quick to adopt the appealing new methods and adapt them for their own purposes. Conditioning techniques, more precise observations, the tools of experimental psychology, quantitative and systematic study of large series of humans with war-induced brain injuries—all produced an explosive advance in the field of neuropsychology. General cognitive theories, including theories of alexia, were rendered suspect if not supported by experimental verification.

Neuropsychologists and behavioral neurologists began to analyze performances of large groups of brain-damaged subjects selected because of the presence of some type of reading problem (e.g., Hoff et al., 1954; Hécaen et al., 1952, 1957). Forms of pure alexia were functionally dissected, related to clusters of associated cognitive deficits, and correlated with anatomical locus of lesion. Arguments for and against the existence of pure alexia were offered. Syndromes of alexia were classified and reclassified.

For example, the study by Alajouanine et al. (1960) was based on evaluation of 22 brain-damaged patients who had reading difficulty as the prominent behavioral deficit. They found 12 subjects to have pure alexia, which they called optic or agnosic alexia, and 10 subjects to have alexia with agraphia, which they called aphasic alexia.

They were able to confirm anatomically that two different lesion sites were correlated with the two different neuropsychological syndromes. The agnosic alexia resulted from a combined lesion in the left occipital lobe and splenium of the corpus callosum. The aphasic alexia resulted from a parieto-occipito-temporal junction lesion. Agnosic alexia was characterized clinically by an inability to read words and phrases, with relative sparing of the ability to read individual letters. Aphasic alexia had a different clinical picture: some degree of aphasia was always present; agraphia was marked; and reading of letters was more severely impaired than reading of words.

Other neuropsychological studies of alexia, with similar findings, but occasionally with differing interpretations, have been published (e.g., Casey and Ettlinger, 1960; Hécaen and Angelergues, 1964; Hécaen, 1967).

The neurolinguistic approach distinguishes research on alexia during the past ten years from that which preceded it. As Hécaen and Kremin (1977) indicate in their thorough treatment of alexia, reference to linguistic models was not lacking even in the earliest studies. However, truly detailed linguistic analyses of breakdowns in the reading process as they relate to cerebral dysfunction, and serious attempts to structure, classify, and categorize the alexias from a linguistic perspective did not appear until the mid-sixties (see, for example, Marshall and Newcombe, 1966, 1973; Newcombe and Marshall, 1973; Hécaen, 1967; Dubois-Charlier, 1971, 1972).

This period is characterized by quantitative and qualitative analyses of linguistic errors which occur in the course of alexic syndromes. Paralexias, linguistic levels, grammatical categories, etc. are described and counted and placed in the context of contemporary models of theoretical linguistics. The result is an attempt to understand the alexias in terms of the rules of grammar which may exist for normal reading and to use breakdowns in these rules as tools for clarifying normal processes of reading.

CLASSIFICATION OF THE ALEXIAS

Classification of the alexias has differed among various authors depending on the emphasis each wanted to attribute to description or interpretation.

One standard practice has been to divide the alexias into major clinical types with respect to the reading deficit: literal alexia, inability to read letters, with relative preservation of ability to read words, versus verbal alexia, inability to read words, with relative preservation of ability to read letters, versus global alexia, inability to read letters or words (see, for example Benson et al., 1971, for a contemporary statement of this position). Using neuropsychological and neurolinguistic evidence from his own laboratory, Hécaen has extended this typology to literal, verbal, sentential (alexia for sentences), and global (Dubois-Charlier, 1971; Hécaen and Kremin, 1977).

Another approach has been to speak of the alexias with reference to the presence or absence of writing disorders. Thus we have alexia without agraphia (pure alexia, pure word blindness) versus alexia with agraphia (Dejerine, 1891, 1892). This dichotomy has anatomical implications, and, accepting the same clinical distinctions, Wernicke (1874) and Kleist (1934) spoke of cortical alexia (alexia with agraphia) versus subcortical alexia (pure alexia); Hermann and Poetzl (1926) spoke of parietal alexia-agraphia versus pure word blindness.

A third approach has been to consider the reading disorder in terms of the mechanism which may have produced it. According to this formulation we have agnosic alexia versus aphasic alexia (e.g., Misch and Frankl, 1929; Alajouanine et al., 1960). It should be stressed that regardless of interpretations and labels used to explain the phenomena, these two syndromes are identical to the clinical syndromes of pure alexia (agnosic alexia) and alexia with agraphia (aphasic alexia). Using different terminology, Goldstein (1948), Brain (1961), and Luria (1966) spoke of the same two clinical syndromes: for agnosic versus aphasic alexia respectively, Goldstein spoke of primary versus secondary alexias; Brain, of agnosic alexia versus visual asymbolia; and Luria, of visual alexia versus aphasic alexia. Each of the two clinical varieties may have subtypes, and the subtypes may be characterized in terms of nature of reading deficit: literal, verbal, or global.

Thus, for all the words that have been written on the subject, virtually all authors agree that there are two principal varieties of alexia: alexia without agraphia versus alexia with agraphia. Each of these varieties is clinically distinctive, each has subtypes, each may have a different anatomical basis, and each has a different theoretical explanation. In the section on clinical syndromes of alexia which follows, I shall use this major clinical dichotomy: alexia without agraphia versus alexia with agraphia.

CLINICAL SYNDROMES OF ALEXIA

Alexia without agraphia

Pure alexia is an accepted clinical syndrome, although the underlying mechanisms which cause the syndrome are still disputed. For Dejerine (1891, 1892) and many of his followers, it represented a specialized form of aphasia. For Marie (1906), Poetzl (1928), Alajouanine et al. (1960), and others, it represented a specialized form of visual agnosia. For Goldstein (1948) and Conrad (1948) it represented the clinical expression of a more general disturbance: the loss of "structuration of forms" and the loss of abstract attitude. Hécaen and Kremin (1977) considered it an incorrect application of the rules of recoding from the written to the spoken language.

Clinically, in addition to the impaired comprehension of written language, one often finds (1) impairment of ability to copy and (2) acalculia. By contrast, oral language is normal or nearly normal—there may be a mild anomia. Writing and spelling are normal. Occasionally one finds visual agnosia for objects and/or colors. Right homonymous hemianopia is almost always present. Hemiplegias are rare and, if they occur at all, are mild.

Detailed evaluation of the reading disorder has demonstrated different subtypes within the main syndrome. These varieties of alexia have often been considered to be variations in intensity of the basic disorder. However, neurolinguistic analyses of alexia without agraphia have shown that the different forms do not represent different degrees of severity of the same basic disorder; rather they represent distinctive disorders (Hécaen, 1967; Dubois-Charlier, 1971, 1972; Hécaen and Kremin, 1977). These subtypes of pure alexia are literal, verbal, sentential (alexia for sentences), and global.

LITERAL ALEXIA

In literal alexia the brain-damaged subject is unable to read letters despite a relative preservation of the ability to read words. These patients can usually read some letters some of the time. In fact, in one testing session a subject may be unable to read certain letters and in another testing session that subject may be able to read those same letters but unable to read others. Grammatical-function words and nonsense words are more difficult to read than words with high semantic content. Visual and semantic paralexias are common (Beringer and Stein, 1930; Marshall and Newcombe, 1973). Word length does not seem to be a critical factor. Short, one-step commands may be read and carried out, but longer or more complex commands are only partially understood. Reading of numbers and musical notation is usually impaired.

Together with the reading disorder, other deficits commonly occur. Writing is not entirely normal; paragraphias are frequent. Copying is virtually impossible. Disorders of color recognition are common. Mild apraxias and asomatognosias may be seen. Right homonymous hemianopia is the rule, but exceptions may occur (whereas in verbal alexias, right homonymous hemianopias are virtually always present).

In this form of alexia the subject is unable to read by spelling a word aloud, although some words may be captured globally. Marshall and Newcombe (1966) found nouns to be easiest to read, then verbs, then adjectives, and finally grammatical-function words. With nouns, the paralexic errors tend to be of a semantic type; with verbs and adjectives they are visual, e.g., "next" instead of "exit." Hécaen and Kremin (1977) noted that the individual letters might be discriminated and "recognized but not read."

VERBAL ALEXIA

In verbal alexia the subject is unable to read or grasp words globally, but the ability to read and identify letters is preserved. Thus, the subject can spell out the word and come to understand it. Neither the ability to read letters, nor the inability to read words is complete. Word length is critical; the longer the word, the more difficult it is to read. Both nonsense words and meaningful words may be read by the spelling-out process. Reading of single digits and short multidigit numbers is preserved.

Associated findings are common. Minor spelling mistakes may occur in spontaneous writing. Copying is moderately impaired, but transposition from block print to cursive writing is possible, unlike the situation in literal alexia. Written calculations usually have errors. Oral spelling is intact. A mild anomia is usually present; especially common are problems with color naming. Right homonymous hemianopia is virtually constant.

ALEXIA FOR SENTENCES
Based on a series of neurolinguistic studies of brain-damaged patients with reading disorders, Hécaen and his co-workers have proposed a separate category which they call "alexia for sentences" (Hécaen, 1967; Dubois-Charlier, 1971, 1972; Hécaen and Kremin, 1977). The existence of this form of pure alexia has not yet been confirmed in other laboratories. This alexia is characterized mainly by a deficit in reading sentences and paragraphs. The ability to read letters and words is largely preserved, along with the ability to read single- and multidigit numbers. Recognition of nonsense syllables is poor. Paralexias occur in reading individual words due to an incorrect rendering of word endings. Individual words and their meanings may be grasped, but when presented as groups or strings, the words are not easily recognized. Errors increase as the length of a command or sentence or as grammatical complexity increases. The nature of the errors implies an incorrect application of the proper syntactic rules for written language. Writing is more impaired in this form of alexia than in the others.

GLOBAL ALEXIA
Global alexia refers to a total inability to read letters and words despite the relatively preserved ability to read single digits and multidigit numbers and the ability to recognize letters by kinesthetic feedback (Charcot, 1890; Dejerine, 1892). These subjects can "read" words by actively tracing the letters with their fingers. Writing is normal. Recognition of musical notes is impaired. Acalculia is present. Impaired recognition of objects, pictures, and especially colors (Poetzl, 1928) is found. Right homonymous hemianopia is almost always present (except in the single case described by Peron and Goutner, 1944).

Alexia with agraphia
It seems reasonable on the basis of clinical, anatomical, and neuropsychological data to subdivide this condition into two separate syn-

dromes: one, consisting of alexia with agraphia in relative isolation from disorders of oral language; the other, a form of alexia which accompanies sensory aphasia.

ALEXIA-AGRAPHIA

The syndrome of alexia with agraphia in the absence of obvious or significant aphasia has been called "parietal alexia" by some authors (e.g., Hermann and Poetzl, 1926; Quensel, 1931; Hoff, Gloning, and Gloning, 1954). Clinically, the reading disorder is primarily of the verbal alexia type. Letters can be read, and short commands can be carried out. Long words or long sentences cannot be read with complete understanding. Disorders of writing are severe, and appear in all aspects of writing (spontaneous, to dictation, etc.).

Associated findings are as follows. Apraxia is often present. Disorders of spoken language are either absent or quite mild, although an anomia is usually found. The ability to spell is always affected. Often, but not always, one may see elements of the Gerstmann syndrome: agraphia, acalculia, right-left spatial disorientation, and impairment in the ability to identify fingers. One of these, acalculia, is almost always found. Hemianopia is not necessarily present. Kinesthetic feedback does not benefit these patients. Of significance in this variety of alexia is the loss of the perceptual strategies for reading as defined for normals (Haselrud and Clark, 1957), which tend to be intact in the pure alexias.

APHASIC ALEXIA

The syndrome of sensory aphasia frequently has an associated reading disorder. DeMassary (1932) argued that a major aphasic disturbance caused enough problems in language to involve reading secondarily. When the reading disorder is a prominent feature of the total aphasic picture, one may speak of aphasic alexia (Dejerine, 1891; Wolpert, 1930; Nielsen and Raney, 1938; Alajouanine et al., 1960; Luria, 1966; Hécaen, 1967).

Clinically, the reading disorder may have different characteristics, depending on lesion localization. According to Alajouanine et al. (1960) the defect resembles literal alexia more than verbal alexia: The subjects read words globally and do not attempt letter-by-letter analysis. For Hécaen and Kremin (1977), however, when alexia is part of a syndrome of sensory aphasia, reading of letters is less affected than reading of words. My own observations suggest that when aphasic alexia follows a lesion involving angular gyrus, reading of letters is markedly impaired, and reading of words is variably affected. When the lesion is located more posteriorly or inferiorly in the hemisphere, reading of letters is less impaired, and the verbal alexia appears more prominent.

In either case, writing is defective in all of its forms. Associated deficits include acalculia and a variety of disturbances of oral language, especially anomia and defective auditory comprehension. Paralexias in oral reading are striking. Kinesthetic feedback does not facilitate reading.

NEUROANATOMICAL ASPECTS OF ALEXIA

The two major clinical syndromes, alexia without agraphia and alexia with agraphia, have traditionally been thought to have two different sets of underlying lesions. I shall consider each syndrome separately. The anatomical evidence comes primarily from clinico-pathological correlations of alexic patients with some kind of cerebral lesion (usually stroke or tumor) and from neurosurgical procedures (e.g., occipital lobectomies, section of corpus callosum, etc.) in patients with cerebral pathology.

The anatomy of alexia without agraphia
A DISCONNECTION SYNDROME

Dejerine (1891, 1892) described two different varieties of alexia for which he proposed two different anatomical lesions. One type, pure word blindness, resulted from destruction of fibers connecting the calcarine region to the angular gyrus, with the central site of damage being in the white matter of the lingual lobule. Poetzl (1928), who disagreed with Dejerine's interpretation of the mechanism of pure alexia, agreed with the anatomical localization. Dejerine referred to a lesion of the corpus callosum in his report of 1892, but did not ascribe any role to it in the pathogenesis of alexia. Brissaud (1900) and Redlich (1895) pointed out that two lesions, one involving the left primary visual area and the other destroying the corpus callosum, might prevent the arrival of visual impulses from the intact hemisphere. It was Quensel (1931) who stressed the necessity of the callosal lesion, and emphasized the "disconnection" aspect of the syndrome.

According to this theory, the lesion in the left visual area prevents visual stimuli entering the left hemisphere from reaching the angular gyrus, which is necessary for reading, while visual stimuli which enter the intact right hemisphere are prevented from reaching the left hemisphere because of the destroyed splenium of the corpus callosum. This theory—that the significant factors in pure alexia are a combination of lesions in the lingual and fusiform gyri of the dominant occipital lobe and in the splenium of the corpus callosum—has been stressed by most authors (Vincent et al., 1930; Geschwind, 1962, 1965; Geschwind and Fusillo, 1966; Sperry and Gazzaniga, 1967; Mouren et al., 1967; Cumming, 1970), Credit for renewing current interest in the disconnection theory has been given to Geschwind (1965).

Most cases of pure alexia, but not all, result from cerebrovascular lesions. Foix and Hillemand (1925) indicated that pure alexia followed disturbances in the territory of the posterior cerebral artery, rather than of the middle cerebral artery, which had been found to be the territory responsible for oral language disorders. Subsequent studies have confirmed these observations.

ARGUMENTS FOR AND AGAINST THE DISCONNECTION THEORY
At the same time that contemporary research has provided more detailed observations confirming the disconnection theory as an explanation for pure alexia, some authors have argued that the corpus callosum may be intact in certain cases. For these cases, some other theory must be provided.

According to the disconnection theory of pure alexia, several factors must be considered: (1) pure alexia represents a deficit only in the verbalization of graphic symbols; (2) a right homonymous hemianopia is implicit in the syndrome. As to the first factor, Hécaen and Kremin (1977) ask how can *objects* be named, and words not named, if there is a posterior callosal disconnection? As to the second factor, they ask, how can one explain those cases of pure alexia with no right homonymous hemianopia? (e.g., Hinshelwood, 1900; Peron and Goutner, 1944; Alajouanine et al., 1960; Ajax, 1967; Goldstein et al., 1971; Greenblatt, 1973).

Finally, there is a third factor. In some cases of pure alexia the splenium may be intact (e.g., Hécaen and Gruner, 1975). How can these cases be explained?

Geschwind (1965) tried to overcome the first problem by suggesting that the visual input relating to objects can evoke sensory associations other than visual ones, and this nonvisual information may cross the corpus callosum in the intact anterior portions. Oxbury et al. (1969) proposed, alternatively, that the posterior callosal lesion may not be complete, and that degraded visual information may traverse the corpus callosum sufficiently to allow gross visual recognition (e.g., for objects) but not fine visual recognition (e.g., for reading).

Recent studies by Greenblatt (1973, 1976), Ajax et al. (1977), and Vincent et al. (1977) deal directly with the second and third problems. In two cases of alexia without agraphia and without hemianopia Greenblatt described and interpreted the anatomical findings. His interpretation is consistent with Dejerine's hypothesis of a lesion deep in the white matter of the left occipitoparietal region disconnecting visual cortex from angular gyrus. Greenblatt proposed four types of pure alexia and the anatomical lesions causing them: splenio-occipital alexia with and without hemianopia; and subangular alexia with and without hemianopia.

Splenio-occipital alexia is the usual type of pure alexia and is caused by a combination of lesions in the left lingual and fusiform gyrus of the occipital lobe and in the posterior third (splenium) of the corpus callosum. Splenio-occipital alexia without hemianopia (Ajax, 1967; Greenblatt, 1973) is rare, and is caused by a combination of lesions in the splenium and in the afferent pathways from the left calcarine cortex. In this situation, both calcarine areas are intact, but are disconnected from the left angular gyrus. Alexia but no hemianopia occurs.

The subangular alexias, according to Greenblatt, are caused by lesions located in the white matter beneath the angular gyrus, undercutting the angular gyrus and isolating it from visual stimuli. Subangular alexia with hemianopia (Wechsler et al., 1972; Sroka et al., 1973) would result from a subangular lesion located more dorsally and medially, affecting the optic radiations. Subangular alexia without hemianopia would occur if the lesion were more ventrally located, sparing the optic radiations.

The case reports by Vincent et al. (1977) and Ajax et al. (1977) support Greenblatt's suggestions. They indicate that the angular gyrus receives dorsal and ventral inputs from the splenium of the corpus callosum as well as medial and lateral inputs from the visual cortex. Selective lesions in corpus callosum or occipital lobe or both may interrupt different sets of inputs to the angular gyrus, thereby producing pure alexia, with or without hemianopia, with or without a callosal lesion. Some form of disconnection theory thus seems to explain all forms of pure alexia.

LITERAL VERSUS VERBAL ALEXIA

Many authors have considered literal and verbal alexia to be different degrees of severity of the same process. Hécaen and his collaborators have shown them to be qualitatively different syndromes (Hécaen, 1967; Hécaen and Kremin, 1977). If they are different syndromes, do they have a different pathological anatomy? Benson et al. (1971) presented evidence that verbal alexia resulted from dominant medial occipital pathology, and literal alexia followed dominant frontal-lobe lesions in Broca's area. It is difficult to be certain if these authors (Benson et al., 1971) were comparing the same types of problems in their two anatomic situations, since their verbal alexics had pure alexia, while their literal alexics had alexia as part of a syndrome of Broca's aphasia.

Basing their analyses on neurolinguistic and neuropsychological evaluations of 41 subjects with reading disorders associated with left hemispheric lesions, Hécaen and Kremin (1977) concluded that in literal alexia the lesion would be located inferomedially in the occipital temporal region, without the corpus callosum necessarily being involved, while in verbal alexia a medial occipital lesion (fusiform and lingual gyri) is implicated. They added that sentence alexia relates to lesions extending from the medial occipital lesion either to temporal or to parietal lobes; and global alexia follows the double lesion of occipital lobe and splenium of corpus callosum.

The anatomy of alexia with agraphia

Much less controversy surrounds the anatomical basis of alexia with agraphia. In 1891 Dejerine discussed the anatomy of a syndrome of impaired ability to read and write with minimal disturbances in oral language. He found a cortical-subcortical lesion affecting the left angular gyrus. Since then, most authors have agreed that a dominant angular gyrus lesion is the anatomical correlate of this syndrome (Wolpert, 1930; Nielsen and Raney, 1938; Alajouanine et al., 1960; Hécaen, 1967; Benson and Geschwind, 1969; Hécaen and Kremin, 1977). The syndrome is even called "parietal alexia" by some investigators (e.g., Poetzl, 1928; Quensel, 1931; Hoff et al., 1954).

In the clinical section above, I divided alexia with agraphia into two syndromes: one (alexia-agraphia), in which the alexic disturbances occurred in relative isolation from aphasic disturbances; the other (aphasic alexia), in which the alexia was part of a more general disturbance of language including sensory aphasia. This is in keeping with traditional clinical observations (e.g., Nielsen, 1947; Leischner, 1957). The anatomical correlates of these two syndromes are as follows. Alexia-agraphia is associated with lesions of the dominant angular gyrus. In aphasic alexia the lesion extends to involve the posterior temporal region.

The "Third" Alexia

Benson (1977) has argued that a variety of alexia can be demonstrated which may be distinguished clinically and anatomically from the two classically recognized types. This variety is associated with lesions in the dominant frontal lobe and is found as part of a syndrome of Broca's aphasia. Patients with this form of alexia can read and understand words which have a high semantic value better than relational words or words which serve as grammatical markers. The reading disorder would thus parallel, to a certain extent, the oral language disorder. The predominant deficit in reading resembles the clinical picture of literal alexia. Agraphia accompanies this form of alexia.

With this form as the "third" alexia, Benson (1977) proposed the following clinico-anatomical scheme: posterior versus central versus anterior alexias. Posterior alexia (also called occipital alexia, agnosic alexia, or pure word blindness) represents the classical alexia without agraphia, and is primarily a verbal alexia. Central alexia (also called parietal alexia, aphasic alexia, or word-and-letter blindness) represents the classical alexia with agraphia, and is a mixture of literal and verbal alexias. Anterior alexia (also called frontal alexia, motor alexia, or pure letter blindness) would be primarily a literal alexia.

One problem with this study is that the presence of posterior lesions, while not likely on clinical grounds, was not unequivocally excluded. It would be useful to follow-up this clinical study with anatomical verification.

NEUROPSYCHOLOGICAL AND NEUROLINGUISTIC ASPECTS OF ALEXIA

Neuropsychological studies

With alexia, as with all aspects of behavioral neurology and neuropsychology, the theoretical bias of the researcher determines not only the methodology in a given study, but also the interpretation of results. For the Gestalt theorist, the process of reading does not represent an independent behavioral function. Goldstein (1948) considered pure alexia to be a variety of visual agnosia. Knowledge of the meaning and significance of simple or complex forms may deteriorate in brain damage and be seen clinically in a variety of syndromes including the inability to read. More basic is the abstract attitude. Expression of abstract attitude in the normal individual is the ability to discriminate figure from background, and the differentiation of abstract attitude into specific functional abilities. Brain damage causes a loss of abstract attitude, the inability to discriminate figures from their backgrounds, and a "dedifferentiation" of function.

Conrad (1948) and Leischner (1957) are representatives of this school. Reading problems are never completely pure but are always associated with other deficits in the "structuration" of forms. A cerebral lesion may impair the ability to read by preventing the ability to structure the form (i.e., identify individual letters) or integrate the whole from its parts (i.e., put the letters together to make a word). The notion of centers for specific higher cortical functions is to be discarded.

It should be noted that even the gestaltists accepted the clinical reality of different types of alexia, and the fact that the alexias were more likely to occur with lesions in one hemisphere, and in certain locations within that hemisphere.

The 1960 study by Alajouanine et al. and the early studies on alexia by Hécaen and Ajuriaguerra and their colleagues (Hécaen et al., 1952, 1957) introduced a different approach. Based on examinations of large groups of brain-damaged patients selected either because of reading difficulties or because of lesion localization, these studies systematically documented the clusters of clinical features commonly associated with specific lesion localizations. Alajouanine et al. (1960) spoke of the syndrome of agnosic alexia resulting from splenio-occipital lesions, and aphasic alexia resulting from parieto-temporal lesions.

Casey and Ettlinger (1960) reviewed 700 unselected neurological cases and found 35 with some degree of language disorder. Of this group of 35 they found 4 in whom the degree of reading or writing impairment was more severe than the degree of impairment of spoken language. They tentatively proposed that reading and writing may function to some extent independently of spoken language, and that despite extensive overlap of anatomical systems for written and spoken language, there might be some degree of anatomical independence.

Two subsequent studies (by Hécaen and Angelergues, 1964; and Hécaen, 1967) were based on performances of large numbers of subjects with anatomically verified hemispheric lesions. Results demonstrated different types of reading disturbances following temporal versus parietal versus occipital lesions. With purely temporal lesions, frequency of reading impairment was greater than with parietal or occipital lesions, and the severity of the deficit was directly proportional to task complexity. With occipital lesions, reading of isolated words or short sentences was more impaired than reading of letters or paragraphs.

As discussed in the previous section on anatomy, the 1960's witnessed the rebirth of the disconnection theory approach to alexia, due primarily to the work of Geschwind (1962, 1965; Geschwind and Fusillo, 1966) and Gazzaniga, Bogen, and Sperry (1965). The argument presented was that damage to the left calcarine cortex and the splenium of the corpus callosum would produce a pure alexia together with an inability to match seen colors to their spoken names.

Neuropsychological studies in the 1970's have attempted to dissect with more precision the cognitive deficit associated with alexic syndromes. The detailed case study by Denckla and Bowen (1973) of a 30-year-old man with a left occipitotemporal lobectomy is an example. In addition to residual deficits of right homonymous hemianopia, slow color naming, and verbal memory impairment, the patient also had a variety of alexia resembling one form of developmental dyslexia. His psychometric profile on the Wechsler Adult Intelligence Scale was identical to that reported as the most common profile for children with "pure" developmental dyslexia on the Wechsler Intelligence Scale for children.

The study by Shallice and Warrington (1977) concerned two patients with literal alexia. The reading impairment was found not to be specific to letters but to stimuli in which more than one item of the same category was simultaneously present in the visual field. The authors suggested that the alexia was a result of impaired selective attention.

The report by Gardner and Zurif (1975) considered oral reading abilities of language-impaired patients. The main findings were that part of speech and picturability contribute to the readability of a word, and that words whose referents can be easily manipulated (operative nouns) proved easier to read than words whose referents were difficult to manipulate (figurative words).

Two recent studies have emphasized preserved reading capacities, rather than defective reading, in alexia. Albert et al. (1973) described a patient who had alexia with agraphia and mild anomic aphasia but a preserved ability to spell words presented to him orally and to recognize words from their letters spelled aloud to him. The patient could neither read aloud nor carry out written commands. However, by a series of matching and forced-choice tests, the authors were able to show that the patient could discriminate words on the basis of their meaning, i.e., word perception was intact and semantic understanding was preserved. This case raises the possibility that one mechanism underlying some alexias is a specific naming deficit for written material. Caplan and Hedley-Whyte (1974) found that a patient who had alexia without agraphia could respond to written stimuli when a variety of cues was used; they suggested that faulty visual exploration of a written word symbol might explain some alexias.

These cases highlight the need for clinical neuroscientists to de-

velop instruments for systematically evaluating preserved capacities
in the brain-damaged patient which are as sensitive and as sophisticated as those used for evaluating defects.

Perceptuomotor problems in alexia

Throughout the history of studies on alexia, arguments have been
provided that one or another form of alexia may result from disorders of visual perception, or disorders of oculomotor function, or
some combination of the two.

Right-hemisphere lesions may be associated with reading disorders which form part of the syndrome of unilateral spatial agnosia;
these may be called "spatial dyslexia." Examples have been provided for many years (e.g., Kleist, 1934; Paterson and Zangwill,
1944). Paralexias may occur (Kinsbourne and Warrington, 1962).

Since no disorders of oral language are seen in these cases, it has
been thought that perceptual factors may contribute to the disorder.
Martin (1954) provided a review of concepts whereby pure word
blindness might be the result of disturbances of visual space perception, ranging from impairments of visual-geometric appreciation to
optical refractive errors.

In considering the possibility that visual space perception is a
relevant variable in alexia, one should take into account those reports in which paralexias cluster at the ends of words (the paralexias of "visual completion," Marshall and Newcombe, 1973). In
many alexics with left hemispheric lesions, these disorders cluster at
the right end of the word. In some patients with spatial alexia and
right hemispheric lesions, the defect has been shown at the left end
of the word. In an Israeli alexic, the impairment was most marked
on the left (Sroka et al., 1973); and in a Japanese patient, on the
lower part of the word (Sasanuma, 1974).

In some instances the alexia was felt to be caused by a difficulty in
simultaneous visual-form perception, or simultanagnosia (Wolpert,
1924; Kinsbourne and Warrington, 1962, 1963). This concept has
been presented by certain authors as a problem in oculomotor function or visual scanning (Holmes, 1918; Warrington and Zangwill,
1957; Botez et al., 1964, 1967; Hartje, 1972). (See Chapter 8, pp.
195–197.)

Factors which may influence normal reading have also been found to influence reading ability in alexics. Howes (1962), for example, found that in a patient with pure alexia, higher luminance and longer exposure time facilitated reading; and that shorter words were generally easier to read than longer words. Woods and Pöppel (1974) noted an effect of print size on the recognition of words, but not pictures, letters, or objects in their patient with verbal alexia without agraphia. In addition to this material-specific size effect, they also found an effect of exposure time.

Studies of Japanese alexics

The Japanese writing system uses ideograms, called "kanji" (derived from Chinese characters) and two types of phonograms, called "kana" (kata-kana and hiragana). (See Sasanuma and Fujimura, 1971 and Yamadori, 1975, for detailed elaboration of the origins and current usage of kanji and kana in Japan.) Those who study alexia have had a particular interest in Japanese alexics because of the possibility that cerebral lesions might produce selective impairments in the ideographic or phonographic system.

In a series of studies of Japanese aphasics and alexics, Sasanuma and her colleagues described the independent functioning of the kana system (phonetic symbols used for syllable-sized units) and kanji system (nonphonetic, ideographic, semantic symbols) (Sasanuma et al., 1971, 1975). The alexic patient had a syndrome of alexia without agraphia accompanied at first by agnosia for pictures, colors, and spatial relations. Copying was impaired equally for kana and kanji, but otherwise writing was intact. Reading was severely impaired for words written in kana, but much less so for words written in kanji. A variety of tests showed differential reading performances for the two writing systems. Taking her various studies together, Sasanuma concluded that selective impairment of kana and kanji "represents dysfunction at two different levels of linguistic behavior, i.e. semantic vs. phonologic processing respectively." She ascribed to each of these conditions a different anatomical locus of lesion.

Yamadori has also provided contemporary reviews and personally studied case reports on this topic (Yamadori, 1975; Yamadori and Ikumura, 1975). His alexic patient had a reading difficulty which was severe in words composed of phonograms and mild in words composed of ideograms. Writing was impaired with both types of characters. Occlusion of the angular branch of the left middle cerebral artery was considered responsible for the syndrome.

Yamadori reviewed other cases of Japanese alexics and found them similar to his own. He concluded that studies of Japanese alexics supported the hypothesis of Albert et al. (1973) that a functional disconnection existed between intact visual and intact auditory-oral systems. What is impaired in these cases of selective alexia in kana is not the ability to discriminate one grapheme from another but the dynamic process of integrating a grapheme with its auditory counterpart.

Neurolinguistic studies

Concern with the linguistic aspects of alexia is not a new phenomenon. However, the systematic attempt to evaluate breakdowns of the reading process in terms of models of normal language, and efforts to relate these categorized patterns of linguistic breakdown to a neurological substratum are relatively recent (since the early 1960's these attempts have been increasing). Dubois-Charlier (1972) summarized earlier models proposed as explanations for the alexias. She defined three pairs of contrasting models: one pair had written language derived from spoken language versus written language being independent of spoken language (this is seen clinically as aphasic alexia versus pure alexia); a second had a word being comprised of a combination of letters versus the word being an ideogram or semantic unit (this is seen clinically as literal and verbal alexia representing different degrees of severity of the same basic deficit versus literal and verbal alexia representing different, independent syndromes); the third had reading disorders represent breakdowns in symbolic language function versus reading disorders resulting from nonlanguage factors (e.g., perceptuomotor problems).

Neuropsychologists and neurolinguists have attempted to describe the language characteristics of alexic patients. In a series of studies Marshall and Newcombe (1966, 1973) described syntactic and semantic patterns of paralexia in language-impaired patients. Presenting neurological, psychological, and linguistic details, they proposed three types of impairment. "Visual dyslexia" resulted when paralexias were caused by confusions of words or letters which were graphically similar. The general pattern of visual dyslexia showed striking similarities to patterns of errors seen in normal readers. "Surface dyslexia" or "grapheme-phoneme dyslexia" resulted when paralexias were caused by breakdowns in the application of grapheme-phoneme conversion rules. "Deep dyslexia" or "syntactico-semantic dyslexia" resulted from an instability of the "central language component." The authors made tentative steps toward the proposal of a model for word recognition and retrieval.

Shallice and Warrington (1975), accepting the general approach of Marshall and Newcombe, studied word recognition performance in a patient with "phonemic dyslexia." Reading performance was related to parts of speech, word frequency, and word concreteness; and reading errors were analyzed. The authors concluded that the findings were consistent with a dual encoding model of word recognition. Their patient illustrated that a phonemic route may be impaired, while a direct graphemic-semantic route may be relatively spared. Their conclusion supports a similar conclusion previously presented by Albert et al. (1973). The importance of the phonemic versus semantic-syntactic aspects of reading in alexia has also been stressed by Bottcher (1974).

The concrete–abstract distinction was studied in alexics by Richardson (1975a,b). He found that the reading performance of an alexic correlated with the imageability of the reading material, but not with its concreteness. Errors were more likely to be semantically related to the correct responses when the reading material was imageable.

Hécaen and his collaborators have been studying linguistic aspects of alexia for many years. In 1967, Hécaen summarized his findings and suggested three clinical types of alexia: pure alexia, caused by an occipital lesion; alexia with agraphia without aphasia, caused by a posterior parietal lesion; and alexia as part of sensory aphasia, caused by a temporal lesion. With respect to the pure alexias, he was able to distinguish three subtypes, based on the nature of the reading disorder and the type of paralexic error: verbal, literal, and global alexia.

Working on the basis of Hécaen's classification of the alexias, Dubois-Charlier (1971, 1972) studied the linguistic performances of alexic patients with a new battery of tests. This battery incorporated tests of naming, discrimination, and comprehension of items at the graphemic, semantic, and syntactic levels. She was able to confirm the clinical reality of the syndromes as described by Hécaen, and in addition, she added a new variety: sentence alexia. On the basis of her analysis she concluded that alexias may result from defective functioning at three different linguistic levels. Defects at the graphemic level could produce literal alexia. Defects at the morphological level could produce verbal alexia. Defects at the syntactic level could produce sentence alexia.

More recently, Hécaen and Kremin (1977) completed a new study. A battery of reading tests and other tests of cognitive function was administered to 41 right-handed subjects with left hemispheric lesions. The reading test included items at the grapheme, word, sentence, and paragraph levels. Their conclusions were consistent with their previous observations. In addition, they suggested that a good approach to the understanding of the alexias would take into account three sets of contrasting techniques: recognition versus reading, meaningfulness versus nonmeaningfulness, and combinatory versus global comprehension. Such an approach, they concluded, demonstrates that different factors may influence the different stages of the reading process.

In a broad sense, one might conclude that all neurolinguistic studies support the notion that the alexias may be dissociated according to linguistic characteristics into several distinctive syndromes, and that these syndromes, each reflecting a disruption of the reading process at a different linguistic level, are caused by different sets of pathophysiological mechanisms.

TREATMENT, RECOVERY PATTERNS, AND PROGNOSIS

In their review of the alexias, Benson and Geschwind (1969) were pessimistic about treatment and prognosis. "The therapy of alexia," they stated, "must be individualized, demands arduous labor on the part of both the patient and the therapist plus considerable ingenuity on the part of the therapist and in many cases an end result far below normal levels must be accepted." With respect to current therapy, little has changed since that statement in 1969. And yet, the contemporary work of behavioral neurologists and neuropsychologists has provided insights into the direction which the needed therapeutic ingenuity might take.

Alexia is not a single deficit in reading comprehension. There are several alexias, each with its own clinical features and pathophysiological basis. The approach to therapy should take into account qualitative neuropsychological and neurolinguistic differences. If phonemic alexia may be distinguished from semantic alexia, for example, attempts should be made to apply to therapy our knowledge of this fact.

The study by Saffran et al. (1976) suggests that such attempts are being made. These authors explored the effects of semantic constraints on the occurrence of paralexic responses in two patients who produced semantic errors in reading aloud. The tendency to make semantic paralexic errors was controlled by limiting the associations evoked by the stimulus word.

A variety of cuing, deblocking, or facilitating devices or techniques has been introduced to aid the alexic. Goldstein (1948) and others have spoken of kinesthetic facilitation. The patient moves his finger (or hand or arm) in the pattern of a letter, and slowly spells out a word by means of kinesthetic sensations. Kreindler and Ionasescu (1961) successfully used auditory and visual "unblocking" techniques to allow a patient who apparently had pure word blindness to express his preserved reading ability. Stachowiak and Poeck (1976) elaborated this technique in a patient with pure alexia. Using the facilitating effect of unblocking methods in the tactile, somesthetic, auditory, and visual modalities, they demonstrated preserved reading ability which had previously been hidden. They argued that in the unblocking situation, other pathways than the one impaired by the brain lesion are used. It seems that information other than visually presented graphemes improved their patient's visual reading. Other authors have also applied facilitating techniques in alexia with success (e.g., Botez et al., 1964, 1967; Luria et al., 1970; Albert et al., 1973; Caplan and Hedley-White, 1974).

Evidence from split-brain studies (e.g., Sperry and Gazzaniga, 1967), from patients with left hemispherectomy (e.g., Smith, 1966), and from studies of normal and brain-damaged bilinguals (Albert and Obler, 1978) suggests that the language capacity of the right hemisphere may be greater than is commonly taught. Efforts might be made with the alexic to retrain language skills by emphasizing the so-called "right-hemisphere strategies."

In attempting to evaluate new therapy modalities in alexia, we are confronted with the question: what is the natural history of alexia? Geschwind (1965) and Hécaen and Kremin (1977) have spoken of cases of occipital alexia in which the reading disorder almost completely disappeared, even after occipital lobectomy. Others (e.g., Ajax, 1967) described occipital alexias which cleared minimally, although the major difficulties could be circumvented by extensive retraining. Sroka et al. (1973) described a patient with pure alexia (from splenio-occipital involvement, presumably) who made a total recovery; these authors spoke of a "functional disconnection syndrome" in which there was no permanent anatomical damage.

What are we to do with single published case reports and anecdotal descriptions? An interesting and valuable approach to this problem is that of Newcombe and Marshall (1973). They analyzed the stages in recovery from alexia in a patient with a left occipital abscess. They wanted to see if a "lawful" description of stages in recovery could be determined. A pattern of recovery did emerge during the three-month period of evaluation. They found a parallel between language reacquisition and the initial stages of language acquisition.

Newcombe and Marshall (1973) suggested, and I agree, that longitudinal studies may clarify the nature of spontaneous recovery patterns in alexia and indicate directions for development of rational therapy programs.

References

Ajax, E. T. (1964). Acquired dyslexia. *Arch. Neurol. 11*:66–72.

Ajax, E. T. (1967). Dyslexia without agraphia. *Arch. Neurol. 17*:645–652.

Ajax, E. T., Schenkenberg, T., and Kasteljanetz, M. (1977). Alexia without agraphia and the inferior splenium. *Neurology 27*:685–688.

Alajouanine, T., Lhermitte, F., and Ribaucourt-Ducarne, B. (1960). Les alexies agnosiques et aphasiques, in *Les Grandes Activites du Lobe Occipital*, T. Alajouanine (ed)., pp. 235–265, Paris: Masson.

Albert, M. L. and Obler, L. K. (1978). *The Bilingual Brain: Neuropsychological and Neurolinguistic Aspects of Bilingualism*. New York: Academic Press.

Albert, M. L., Yamadori, A., Gardner, H., and Howes, D. (1973). Comprehension in alexia. *Brain 96*:317–328.

Benson, D. F. (1977). The third alexia. *Arch. Neurol. 34*:327–331.

Benson, D. F., Brown, J., and Tomlinson, E. B. (1971). Varieties of alexia. *Neurology 21*:951–957.

Benson, D. F. and Geschwind, N. (1969). The alexias, in: *Handbook of Clinical Neurology: Disorders of Speech, Perception, and Symbolic Behavior*, pp. 112–140, P. J. Vinken and G. W. Bruyn (eds). New York: American Elsevier.

Benton, A. L. (1964). Contributions to aphasia before Broca. *Cortex 1*:314–327.

Benton, A. L. (1975). Developmental dyslexia: neurological aspects. *Advan. Neurol. 7*:1–47.

Benton, A. L. and Joynt, R. J. (1960). Early descriptions of aphasia. *Arch. Neurol. 3*:205–222.

Beringer, K. and Stein, J. (1930). Analyse eines falles von "reiner" Alexie. *Zeitsch f. gesamte Neurol. u. Psychiat. 123*:472–478.

Botez, M. I. and Serbanescu, T. (1967). Course and outcome of visual static agnosia. *J. Neurol. Sci. 4*:289–297.

Botez, M. I., Serbanescu, T., and Vernea, I. (1964). Visual static agnosia with special reference to literal agnosic alexia. *Neurology 14*:1101–1111.

Bottcher, R. (1974). Role of graphic and semantic-syntactic factors in reading: a neuro-psycholinguistic study. *J. Psychol. 182*:40–67.

Boudouresques, J., Pocet, M., Sebahoun, M., and Alicherif, A. (1972). Deux cas d'alexie sans agraphie avec troubles de la denomination des couleurs et des images. *Oto-Neuro-Opht. 44*:297–304.

Brain, R. (1941). Visual-object-agnosia with special reference to the gestalt theory. *Brain 64*:43–62.

Brain, R. (1954). Loss of visualization. *Proc. Roy. Soc. Med. 47*:288–290.

Brain, R. (1961). *Speech Disorders*. London: Butterworths.

Brissaud, E. (1900). Cecite verbale sans aphasie ni agraphie. *Rev. Neurol. 8*:757.

Broadbent, W. (1872). Cerebral mechanisms of speech and thought. *Med. and Chirug. Transactions (London) 55*:145–194.

Caplan, L. and Hedley-Whyte, T. (1974). Cuing and memory dysfunction in alexia without agraphia: a case report. *Brain 97*:251–262.

Casey, T. and Ettlinger, G. (1960). The occasional 'independence' of dyslexia and dysgraphia from dysphasia. *J. Neurol. Neurosurg. Psychiat. 23*:228–236.

Charcot, J. M. (1890). Maladies du système nerveux. Paris: Lecrosnier et Babé.

Conrad, K. (1948). Beitrag zum Problem der parietalen Alexie. *Arch. Psychol. 181*:398–420.

Cumming, W. J. (1970). Anatomical findings in a case of alexia without agraphia. *J. Anat. 106*:170.

Cumming, W. J. K., Hurwitz, L. J., and Perl, N. T. (1970). A study of a patient who had alexia without agraphia. *J. Neurol. Neurosurg. Psychiat. 33*:34–39.

Dejerine, J. (1891). Sur un cas de cecite verbal avec agraphie suivi d'autopsie. *Memoires de la Societe de Biologie 3*:197–201.

Dejerine, J. (1892). Contribution a l'etude anatomo-pathologique et clinique des differentes varietes de cecite verbale. *Memoires de la Societe de Biologie 4*:61–90.

Dejerine, J. (1914). *Semeiologie des Affections du Systeme Nerveux.* Paris: Masson.

DeMassary, J. (1932). L'alexie. *Encephale 27*:134–164.

Denckla, M. and Bowen, F. (1973). Dyslexia after left occipito-temporal lobectomy: a case report. *Cortex 9*:321–328.

Dide, M. and Botcazo (1902). Amnesie continue, cecite verbale pure, perte du sens topographique, ramoillissement double du lobe lingual. *Rev. Neurol. 10*:676–680.

Dubois-Charlier, F. (1971). Approche neurolinguistique du probleme de l'alexie pure. *J. de Psychologie Normale et Pathologique 68*:39–67.

Dubois-Charlier, F. (1972). A propos de l'alexie pure. *Langages 25*:76–94.

Ettlinger, G. and Hurwitz, L. (1962). Dyslexia and its associated disturbances. *Neurology* (Minneapolis) *12*:477–480.

Fincham, R. W., Nibbelink, D. W., and Aschenbrener, C. A. (1975). Alexia with left homonymous hemianopia without agraphia. *Neurology 25*: 1164–1168.

Foix, C. and Hillemand, P. (1925). Role vraisemblable du splenium dans la pathologenie de l'alexie pure par lesion de la cerebrale posterieure. *Bull. et Memoires de la Soc. Med. des Hopitaux de Paris 49*:393–395.

Gardner, H. (1974). The naming and recognition of written symbols in aphasic and alexic patients. *J. Commun. Disord. (England)* 7:141–153.

Gardner, H., Denes, G., and Zurif, E. (1975). Critical reading at the sentence level. *Cortex 11*:60–72.

Gardner, H. and Zurif, T. (1975). Bee but not be: oral reading of single words in aphasia and alexia. *Neuropsychologia 13*, 2:181–190.

Gazzaniga, M. S., Bogen, J. E., and Sperry, R. W. (1965). Observations on visual perception after disconnection of the cerebral hemisphere in man. *Brain 88*:221–236.

Gazzaniga, M. S. and Sperry, R. W. (1967). Language after section of the cerebral commissures. *Brain 90*:131–148.

Geschwind, N. (1962). The anatomy of acquired disorders of reading, in *Reading Disability*, pp. 115–128, John Money (ed). Baltimore: Johns Hopkins Press.

Geschwind, N. (1965). Disconnexion syndromes in animals and man. *Brain 88*:237–294, 585–644.

Geschwind, N. and Fusillo, M. (1966). Color naming defects in association with alexia. *Arch. Neurol. (Chicago) 15*:137–146.

Goldstein, K. (1948). *Language and Language Disturbances.* New York: Grune & Stratton.

Goldstein, J., Joynt, R., and Goldblatt, D. (1971). Word blindness with intact central visual fields. *Neurology 21*:873–876.

Goodglass, H., Hyde, M. R., and Blumstein, S. (1969). Frequency picturability, and the availability of nouns in aphasia. *Cortex, 5*:104–119.

Greenblatt, S. (1973). Alexia without agraphia or hemianopia: Anatomical analysis of an autopsied case. *Brain 96*:307–316.

Greenblatt, S. (1976). Subangular alexia without agraphia or hemianopia. *Brain and Language 3*:229–245.

Hartje, W. (1972). Reading disturbances in the presence of oculomotor disorders. *Europ. Neurol. 7*:249–264.

Haselrud, G. H. and Clark, R. E. (1957). On the reintegrative perception of words. *Am. J. Psychol. 70*:97–101.

Head, H. (1926). *Aphasia and Kindred Disorders of Speech.* London: Cambridge University Press.

Hécaen, H. (1967). Aspects des troubles de la lecture (alexie) au cours des lesions cerebrales en foyer. In homage a Andre Martinet *Word 23*: 265–287.

Hécaen, H., DeAjuriaguerra, J., David, M., and Talairach, J. (1949). Etude des phenomenes de recuperation apres lobectomie occipitale, en function de l'etudue de l'ablation. *Rev. Neurol. 81*:427–430.

Hécaen, H., DeAjuriaguerra, J., and David, M. (1952). Les deficits fonctionnels apres lobectomie occipitale. *Mschr. Psychiat. Neurol. 123*:239–290.

Hécaen, H. J., DeAjuriaguerra, J., and Angelergues, R. (1957). Les troubles de la lecture dans le cadre des modifications des fonctions symboliques. *Psychiat. Neurol. (Basel), 134*:97–129.

Hécaen, H. and Angelergues, R. (1964). Localization of symptoms in aphasia, in *Disorders of Language,* A. deReuck and M. O'Connor (eds). London: Churchill.

Hécaen, H., Goldblum, M. C., Masure, M. C., and Ramier, A. M. (1974). Une nouvelle observation d'agnosie d'objet deficit de l'association ou de la categorisation, specifique de la modalite visuelle. *Neuropsychologia 12*:447–464.

Hécaen, H., and Gruner, J. (1975). Alexie "pure" avec integrite du corps calleux, in *Les Syndromes de Disconnexion Calleuse Chez L'homme,* pp. 347–361, F. Michel and B. Schott (eds). Lyon: Hospital Neurologique.

Hécaen, H. and Kremin, H. (1977). Reading disorders resulting from left hemisphere lesions: aphasic and 'pure' alexias, in *Studies in Neurolinguistics,* Vol. 2, H. Whitaker and H. Whitaker (eds). New York: Academic Press.

Heilman, K. M. (1975). Reading and writing disorders caused by central nervous system defects. *Geriatrics 30*:115–118.

Hermann, G., and Poetzl, O. (1926). *Uber die Agraphie und ihre Lokaldiagnostischen Beziehungen.* Berlin: Karger.

Hinshelwood, J. (1900). *Letter, Word, and Mind-Blindness.* London: H. K. Lewis.

Hoff, H., Gloning, I., and Gloning, K. (1954). Ueber Alexie. *Wiener Zeitschr. f. Nervenheilkunde 10*:149–162.

Holmes, G. (1918). Disturbances of visual orientation. *Br. J. Ophthal.* 2: 449–468.

Holmes, G. (1950). Pure word blindness. *Folia Psychiat. Neerl. 53*:279–288.

Howes, D. (1962). An approach to the quantitative analysis of word blindness, in *Reading Disability,* pp. 131–159, John Money (ed). Baltimore: Johns Hopkins Press.

Imura, T. (1943). Aphasia: characteristic symptoms in Japanese. *J. Psychiat. Neurol. 47*:196–218.

Jack, E. (1900). A case of alexia. *Boston Med. Surg. J. 143*:577–579.

Kinsbourne, M. and Rosenfield, D. (1974). Agraphia selective for written spelling. *Brain and Language 1*:215–225.

Kinsbourne, M. and Warrington, E. K. (1962). A variety of reading disability associated with right hemisphere lesions. *J. Neurol. Neurosurg. Psychiat. 25*:339–344.

Kinsbourne, M. and Warrington, E. K. (1963). The localizing significance of limited simultaneous visual form perception. *Brain 86*:502–697.

Kinsbourne, M. and Warrington, E. K. (1965). A case showing selectively impaired oral spelling. *J. Neurol. Neurosurg. Psychiat. 28*:563–566.

Klein, R. and Attlee, J. H. (1948). Syndrome of alexia and amnesic aphasia: subarachnoidal haemorrhage with symptoms of partial occlusion of spinal subarachnoidal space. *Br. J. Psychiat. 94*:59.

Kleist, K. (1934). *Gehirnpathologie.* Leipzig: Barth.

Kreindler, A. and Ionasescu, V. (1961). A case of "pure" word blindness. *J. Neurol. Neurosurg. Psychiat. 24*:275–280.

Kussmaul, A. (1877). Die Störungen der Sprache. *Vogel:* Leipzig (see also Kussmaul, 1884).

Kussmaul, A. (1884). *Les Troubles de la Parole,* A. Rueff (trans). Paris: Bailliere.

Leischner, A. (1957). *Die Storungen der Schriftsprache (Agraphie und Alexie).* Stuttgart: Georg Thieme Verlag.

Lhermitte, F. and Beauvois, M. F. (1973). A visual-speech disconnexion syndrome. *Brain 96*:695–714.

Lhermitte, F., Chedru, F., and Chain, F. (1973). A case of visual agnosia. *Rev. Neurol. (Paris) 128*:301–322.

Lissauer, H. (1889). Ein Fall von Seelenblindheit nebst einen Beitrage zur Theorie derselben. *Arch. f. Psychiat. u. Nerrenkr. 21*:2–50.

Luria, A. (1966). *Higher Cortical Functions in Man.* New York: Basic Books.

Luria, A. R., Simernitskaya, E., and Tubylevich, B. (1970). The structure of psychological processes in relation to cerebral organization. *Neurol. Psychologia 8*:9–13.

Lyman, R. S., Kwan, S. T., and Chao, W. H. (1938). Left occipital-parietal brain tumor with observations on alexia and agraphia in Chinese and English. *Chinese Med. J. 54*:411–516.

Marie, P. (1906). Revision de la question de l'aphasie. *Sem. Med. (Paris) 42*:493–500.

Marie, P. and Foix, C. (1917). Aphasie par lesion de la region du pli courbe, les aphasies de guerre. *Rev. Neurol. 2*:331–335.

Marshall, J. C. and Newcombe, F. (1966). Syntactic and semantic errors in paralexia. *Neuropsychologia 4*:169–176.

Marshall, J. C. and Newcombe, F. (1973). Patterns of paralexia: a psycholinguistic approach. *J. Psycholinguistic Res. 2*:175–199.

Martin, J. P. (1954). Pure word blindness considered as disturbance of visual space perception. *Proc. Roy. Soc. Med. 47*:293–295.

Misch, W. and Frankl, K. (1929). Beitrag zur Alexielehre. *Monatssch. f. Psychiat. u. Neurol. 71*:1–47.

Mohr, J. P. (1976). An unusual case of dyslexia with dysgraphia, *Brain and Language 3*:324–334.

Mouren, P., Tatossian, A., Trupheme, R., Giudicelli, S., and Fresco, R. (1967). Alexia due to visual-verbal disconnection (Geschwind). Apropros of a case of pure verbal blindness without agraphia but with disorders of designation of colors, or names and of images. *Encephale 56*:112–137.

Newcombe, F. and Marshall, J. C. (1973). Stages in recovery from dyslexia following a left cerebral abscess. *Cortex 9*:329–332.

Nielsen, J. (1937). Unilateral cerebral dominance as related to mind blindness. *Arch. Neurol. Psychiat. 38*:108–135.

Nielsen, J. (1947). *Agnosia, Apraxia, Aphasia*. New York: Hoeber.

Nielsen, J., and Raney, R. (1938). Symptoms following surgical removal of major (left) angular gyrus. *Bull. Los Angeles Neurol. Soc. 3*:42–46.

Nodet, V. (1889). *Les Agnosies*. Paris: Fayard.

Oxbury, J. M., Oxbury, S., and Humphrey, N. K. (1969). Varieties of colour anomia. *Brain 92*:847–860.

Papadakis, N. (1974). Subdural hemotoma complicated by homonymous hemianopia and alexia. *Surg. Neurol. 2*:131–132.

Paterson, J. and Bramwell, E. (1905). Two cases of word blindness. *Med. Press 79*:507–508.

Paterson, A. and Zangwill, O. (1944). Disorders of visual space perception associated with lesions of the right cerebral hemisphere. *Brain 67*:331–358.

Peron, N. and Goutner, V. (1944). Alexie pure sans hemianopsie. *Rev. Neurol. 76*:81–82.

Poetzl, O. (1928). *Die Optisch-Agnostischen Storungen*. Vienna: Deuticke.

Quensel, F. (1931). Die Alexie, in *Kurzes Handbuch der Ophtalmologie.* Berlin: Springer.

Redlich, E. (1895). Ueber die sogenannte subcorticale Alexie. *Jahrbucher f. Psychiat. Neurol. 13*:1–60.

Richardson, J. (1975a). The effect of word imageability in acquired dyslexia. *Neuropsychologia 13*:281–288.

Richardson, J. (1975b). Further evidence on the effect of word imageability in dyslexia. *Quart. J. Exp. Psychol. 27*:445–449.

Roche-Le Cours, A., Dordain, G., and Lhermitte, F. (1970). Neurolinguistic terminology. *Encephale 59*:520–546.

Rubens, A. and Benson, D. F. (1971). Associative visual agnosia. *Arch. Neurol. 24*:305–316.

Saffran, E., Schwartz, M. F., and Marin, O. S. M. (1976). Semantic mechanisms in paralexia. *Cortex 3*:255–265.

Sasanuma, S. (1974). Kanji versus kana processing in alexia with transient agraphia: a case report. *Cortex 10*:88–97.

Sasanuma, S. (1975). Kana and kanji processing in Japanese aphasics. *Brain and Language 2*:369–383.

Sasanuma, S. and Fujimura, O. (1971). Selective impairment of phonetic and nonphonetic transcription of words in Japanese aphasic patients: kana vs. kanji in visual recognition and writing. *Cortex 7*:1–18.

Sasanuma, S. and Fujimura, O. (1972). An analysis of writing errors in Japanese aphasic patients: kanji vs. kana words. *Cortex 8*:265–282.

Sasanuma, S. and Monoi, H. (1975). The syndrome of gogi (word-meaning) aphasia: selective impairment of kanji processing. *Neurology 25*:627–632.

Shallice, T. and Warrington, E. K. (1975). Word recognition in a phonemic dyslexic patient. *Quart. J. Exp. Psychol. 27*:187–199.

Shallice, T. and Warrington, E. K. (1977). The possible role of selective attention in acquired dyslexia. *Neuropsychologia 15*:31–42.

Smith, A. (1966). Speech and other functions after left dominant hemispherectomy. *J. Neurol. Neurosurg. Psychiat. 29*:467–471.

Sperry, R. W. and Gazzaniga, M. C. (1967). Language following surgical disconnection of the hemispheres, in *Brain Mechanisms Underlying Speech and Language,* pp. 108–118, C. Millikan and F. Darley (eds). New York: Grune & Stratton.

Spreen, O., Benton, A. L., and Van Allen, M. W. (1966). Dissociation of visual and tactile naming in amnesic aphasia. *Neurology 16*:807–814.

Sroka, H., Solsi, P., and Bornstein, B. (1973). Alexia without agraphia with complete recovery. *Confin. Neurol. 35*:167–176.

Stachowiak, F. J. and Poeck, K. (1976). Functional disconnection in pure alexia and color naming deficit demonstrated by facilitation methods. *Brain and Language 3*:135–143.

Stengel, E. (1948). The syndrome of visual alexia with colour agnosia. *J. Mental Sci. 94*:46–58.

Thiebault, F., Philippides, D., Helle, J., and Ruch, M. R. (1954). Alexie occipitale. *Rev. Oto-Neuro-Opthalmologic 3*:153–157.

Tzavaras, A. and Hécaen, H. (1970). Colour vision disturbances in subjects with unilateral cortical lesions. *Brain Res. 24*:541–559.

Vincent, C., David, M., and Puech, P. (1930). Sur l'alexie. Production du phenomene a la suite de l'extirpation de la corne occipitale du ventricule lateral gauche. *Rev. Neurol. 1*:262–272.

Vincent, F. M., Sadowsky, C. H., Saunders, R. L., and Reeves, A. G. (1977). Alexia without agraphia, hemianopia, or color-naming defect: a disconnection syndrome. *Neurology 27*:689–691.

Warrington, E. K. and James, M. (1967). Disorders of visual perception in patients with localised cerebral lesions. *Neuropsychologia 5*:253–266.

Warrington, E. K. and Zangwill, O. (1957). A study of dyslexia. *J. Neurol. Neurosurg. Psychiat. 20*:208–215.

Wechsler, A. F., Weinstein, E. A., and Antin, S. P. (1972). Alexia without agraphia. *Bull. Los Angeles Neurol. Soc. 37*:1–11.

Wernicke, C. (1874). *Der Aphasische Symptomencomplex*. Breslau: Frank and Weigert.

Wernicke, C. (1885). Cited by Dejerine (1914).

Wolpert, I. (1924). Die Simultanagnosie. *Z. ges. Neurol. Psychiat. 93*:397–415.

Wolpert, I. (1930). Ueber das Wesen der literalen Alexie. *Monatsschr. f. Psychiat. Neurol. 75*:207–266.

Woods, B. T., and Pöppel, E. (1974). Effect of print size on reading time in a patient with verbal alexia. *Neuropsychologia 12*:31–41.

Yamadori, A. (1975). Ideogram reading in alexia. *Brain 98*:231–238.

Yamadori, A. and Ikumura, G. (1975). Central (or conduction) aphasia in a Japanese patient. *Cortex 11*:73–82.

4

Agraphia: Writing Disorders Associated with Unilateral Cortical Lesions

PIERRE MARCIE AND HENRY HÉCAEN

HISTORICAL INTRODUCTION

In neurology, the study of writing disorders has always been linked to the study of aphasia: spoken language has always been considered primary. In studying the history of linguistics, one also finds that writing is usually considered a derived and secondary activity, a purely technical transformation of sounds into their written correlates. F. de Saussure (1916), for example, claimed, in the associationist terminology, that it is the "signifiant" of the graphic sign which is the distinctive element of language sounds: "In language only the acoustic image remains, which can be translated into a visual image." The graphic symbol is thus a derived representation of the sound. Nevertheless (and perhaps somewhat inconsistently), F. de Saussure admits that "language" and writing are "two distinct sign systems." Hjelmslev (1935) had in mind a purely "formal" analysis, stating that "there is no necessary connection between

This work was done at the Neuropsychological and Neurolinguistic Unit (U-111) of the Institut National de la Santé et de la Récherche Médicale, the Language Pathology Laboratory of the École des Hautes Etudes en Sciences Sociales and the research team associated with the Centre National de la Récherche Scientifique (E.R.A. No. 274).

92

sounds and language." Uldall (1944) argued that speech and writing were different ways of expressing language: "If either of those substances, air flow or ink flow, was a constituent part of language itself, then it wouldn't be possible to switch from one form to the other without changing language." Writing could therefore be studied independently of speech. J. Vachek (1973) agreed with such a claim; he advocated a "functional" approach to the study of written language, stating that writing, like speech, is not a mere "system" but the realization of a specific function.

Chomsky (1970) analyzes writing in the framework of generative grammar grounded on hypotheses which are, in fact, the same as Saussure's. Writing (or, to use his terminology, "orthography") is a direct point-to-point transcription of lexical representation. The lexical representation of an item is a unique sequence of phonological "segments"; in fact, lexical representation is simply the "spelling" of the word. The lexical representation provides a kind of primary "natural orthography." "What accounts then for the distortion that rapidly takes place between the spoken form and the written form of the lexical representation? Simply the fact that the spoken form, in addition to the lexical representation, also bears other elements which modify it. The written form, on the other hand, can remain the same, apart from minor variations. It seems fairly well established that the level of lexical representation is highly resistant to change and persists over long historical periods." Positing that orthography is a direct and accurate transcription of the phonemic structure, Chomsky then states that, from this point of view, the question of phoneme–grapheme correspondence may be "something of a pseudo issue . . . by and large they are very close to one-one, given certain notational conventions and disregarding a class of true exceptions and a set of oddities."

Early research on writing disorders following cortical lesions was carried out without any reference to linguistics. In addition to the importance of agraphia as a localizing neurological sign, its study became central to two basic questions about writing: can it be impaired independently from oral language and does that impairment depend on a separate anatomical lesion?

Marcé (1856) was the first author to write specifically on this topic. His purpose was "to demonstrate the existence of a coordi-

nating principle of writing," as Bouillaud (1825, 1848) had advocated the existence of a "legislative principle of language." Marcé's
position was eclectic and represented a compromise between two
views: one that considered writing an autonomous function regulated by its own coordinating principle; the other that considered
writing an activity derived from spoken language since "writing is
a much simpler function than speaking and is entirely subordinated
to language."

Benedikt (1868) thought that writing disorders could be produced by the same mechanism responsible for paraphasias in oral
language, i.e., a loss of voluntary motor association between the idea
of a word and its graphic or oral representation.

J. W. Ogle (1869) introduced the term *agraphia* for writing disorders which follow cortical lesions. He distinguished two forms of
agraphia, which were parallel to the two forms of aphasia he had
described. "In amnemonic agraphia the patient can form letters and
words with sufficient distinctness, but he either substitutes one word
for another, or writes a confused series of letters which have apparently no connection with the words intended. In ataxic agraphia
the power of writing even separate letters is lost, sometimes entirely.
Here all attempts to write result in a mere succession of up and
down strokes, bearing no kind of resemblance to letters." Like
Marcé, Ogle defined the relationship between spoken and written
language in a manner often repeated in further research: that is, by
stressing the link between agraphia and aphasia.

As will be seen, these early papers introduced the general framework in which writing disorders were later considered.

Dejerine (1891) reported the case of a left-handed patient who
wrote with his right hand and had complete motor aphasia following a right hemispheric lesion. He stated that the writing disorder
was a consequence of the language impairment. "For four years
this patient who had intact motor functions of his right hand except
for the act of writing, had a total agraphia (spontaneous writing,
writing to dictation, copying) . . . (This man) was therefore
agraphic because, since his third frontal convolution was destroyed,
he no longer had the notion of words and could no longer write
any more than he could speak."

In his *Sémiologie* (1914), Dejerine further explained his views.
He considered writing disorders simply the result of the alteration

of inner language present in aphasia. Writing is affected or completely lost precisely because inner language is altered. "In order to write one needs an intact notion of words, and normal functioning of inner language; all verbal images—images the integrity of which is indispensable to the notion of word and to inner language—must be preserved. In other words, any lesion which destroys a group of verbal images will necessarily be followed by agraphia. Any lesion sparing those images will produce no agraphia."

Dejerine thought that writing consisted of the physical translation of visual images of letters and words. He denied the existence of a "graphic center" and of any "graphic motor image." Disorders which do not alter inner language do not affect writing ability except when a particular modality is involved, and writing is tested so as to require that modality: copying is impaired in verbal blindness; writing to dictation is impaired in verbal deafness; writing is intact in aphemia or pure motor aphasia.

As a further argument against the possibility that writing could be independent from oral language, Dejerine argued that writing is not necessarily connected to the hand or to the fingers, but that it could, with only a little practice, be produced by any part of the body with enough mobility.

Within the framework of associationism, Wernicke had already expressed the opinion that writing could not be independent from language. In his main work on sensory aphasia (1874) Wernicke stated that language involved only one category of "motor images," i.e., "auditory images," which activated the movements necessary for the production of speech. The only way one can acquire writing is through the association of sound images to visual images of the corresponding letters. The mediation of sound images is indispensable for the activation of the motor zone involved in writing movements. Learning to write involves this association. But, once the ability to write has been acquired, a direct association between sound images and graphic movements allows a correct and efficient execution in the majority of writing acts without involvement of visual images. "There is in no way a direct path from the concept formed by sensory images to the motor writing center, a path by which writing movements could be activated avoiding the mediation of sound images."

P. Marie (1897), before breaking with associationism, thought that the agraphia seen in motor aphasia was "due to an impairment of the phonetic element of inner language." Later, however, after he had formulated the notion of anarthria and expelled it from the domain of aphasic disorders of phonetic articulation, he considered that anarthria, by its own definition, was free of any writing deficit. Only aphasia, as a global intellectual deterioration, was accompanied by a parallel deficit of writing. He argued (1906) that writing is subordinated to oral language and emphasized the impossibility of a cortical center specialized for writing. For the majority of people, in fact, writing is a very recent acquisition that would not be likely to have an independent cerebral organization.

But the opposite view was also argued. "Motor graphic images" of letters and words are necessary for writing, and they depend on a specialized center just as verbal motor images depend on Broca's area. Exner (1881) had reached this conclusion after analyzing a series of 169 patients, from the literature and from personal observations. On a map of the brain subdivided into 367 parts of similar area, he indicated the relative severity of the functional deficits which followed each lesion. In this manner, based on only five cases, he identified a particular zone, the foot of the second left frontal convolution, where lesions were accompanied by writing disorders.

Bastian (1894) thought that a "keiro-kinesthetic center" was responsible for the execution of writing movements just as a "glosso-kinesthetic center" was responsible for the performance of movements necessary for the production of speech. However, he did not accept the localization to the foot of the second left frontal convolution postulated by Exner, because he realized how weak Exner's anatomical arguments were.

In order to demonstrate the existence of a "center for motor graphic images," Pitres (1884) had presented the report of a case of "pure motor agraphia." The patient had neither impairment of spoken language, nor significant right-sided motor deficits; he showed, however, a total agraphia with the right hand for spontaneous writing; he had kept his ability to copy correctly, because only the "motor graphic images" were destroyed.

Pitres (1894) accepted Exner's localization of motor agraphia, although he recognized the paucity of arguments in favor of this localization. Similarly, Bastian explained the frequent association between writing disorders and disorders of spoken language by the anatomical proximity of the two centers (glosso-kinesthetic and keiro-kinesthetic) and their almost constant simultaneous involvement by the same lesion. He thought that the writing center was a functional organization made of different structural elements rather than a differentiated anatomical center.

Pitres (1894) explained sensory agraphia by implicating the destruction of the center of visual graphic images which he, like Dejerine, localized to the angular gyrus. Destruction or impairment of these images would impair writing performance in all its modalities.

In subsequent years, as more anatomical and clinical data became available, it became apparent that the systems of classification used by different authors overlapped generously, once the theoretical background peculiar to each author was recognized.

Von Monakow (1914) distinguished four varieties of agraphia: keiro-kinesthetic agraphia of apraxic nature; an agraphia found in sensory aphasia; an agraphia found in motor aphasia; and finally an agraphia associated with visual agnosia and hemianopia. Henschen (1922) proposed a systematic classification of the various forms of aphasia based on the localization of the lesion. He described an occipital agraphia associated with a lesion in the vicinity of "the first gyrus" approximately O1) and characterized by an impairment of the representation of letters as shapes; an angular agraphia due to destruction of graphic visual images; a temporal agraphia; a parietal agraphia with apraxic components; a frontal agraphia; and a conduction agraphia.

Kleist (1934) separated three types of agraphia: the agraphias associated with each variety of aphasia; the "constructive agraphias" due to destruction of optic engrams for words and letters; and the "ideokinetic agraphias" due to destruction of kinesthetic engrams necessary for the composition of written language.

Goldstein (1948) recognized two stages in the act of writing: praxic and linguistic. He therefore placed writing disorders in two major categories: the "primary agraphias" where the motor agraphic act is primarily affected, and the "secondary agraphias" associated with various types of aphasia in which the writing disorder is analogous to the deficit found in oral language. Goldstein included in the group of primary agraphias "motor" or "pure" agraphia in which the hand, independent of any other gestural impairment, could no longer be ordered to perform the necessary graphic gestures. He argued that in order for this agraphia to appear there must be a lesion in the foot of the second left frontal convolution.

Leischner (1957) concluded that agraphia is associated at least with a reading deficit and also generally with impairments of various aspects of spoken language. Therefore he argued that writing, as a secondary cerebral function, had no specialized nervous substrate. The association of agraphia with lesions in the dominant inferior parietal lobe only reflected the fact that such lesions produce deficits in the primary functions underlying reading and speaking.

NEUROLINGUISTIC STUDIES OF AGRAPHIAS

Writing disorders are almost invariably associated with oral language disorders; however, the two frequently differ in type and intensity. The features peculiar to written language as opposed to spoken language (motor features and structural differences) account for the partial autonomy of the former. Disorders of the two modes of expression may even be completely separated.

Two aspects of writing may be clearly distinguished even though they are closely linked: a primary motor function which allows the execution of gestures needed for written expression; and a linguistic function which encodes the information into its different structural levels (lexical, syntactic, and graphemic).

The graphic code cannot be considered a simple transcription of the oral code. Graphic expression provides a spatial system of symbols derived from a distinct set of linguistic rules. These rules govern the production and linkage of graphemes so as to preserve the individuality of graphemic signs within a broad range of idiolectic variants. At the syntactic level, these rules provide the structure within which graphic output can indicate segmentation. Redundancy is characteristic of writing and aids in comprehension.

Writing is an autonomous linguistic performance having close links with oral performance. Aside from their specific functioning in phonetic written languages, graphemic signs have articulatory referents, with respect to the phonemic system of the language under consideration. In addition, written sentences have the same structure of meaning as spoken sentences.

From the foregoing considerations, it may be concluded that separable varieties of agraphia may occur, each resulting from breakdown at a different level within one of the several neuropsychological systems upon which graphic symbolic expressions depend—motor, perceptual, linguistic, etc. . . . Disorders of written expression may be categorized into clinical subgroups.

One can therefore distinguish the agraphias associated with aphasias, the agraphia associated with alexia, "pure" agraphia without any other language impairment, apraxic agraphia where the deficit seems to affect the performance of the gestures necessary for writing, and, finally, disorders affecting spatial components of writing performance in patients with lesions of the minor hemisphere.

Agraphias associated with aphasias

Although the classification of aphasia used in this chapter differs from that presented in Chapter 2, it has many points of correspondence, and when possible the names used in Chapter 2 have been indicated. The subdivision of Broca's ("motor") aphasia into a type with predominant phonemic disturbance and a type with predominant grammatical disturbance is not included in Chapter 2. The term "Wernicke's aphasia" is used in this chapter to refer to all aphasias with poor comprehension, whereas in Chapter 2 it is used to denote specifically the aphasia in which comprehension and repetition are both impaired, and not also transcortical sensory aphasia, in which repetition is spared.

AGRAPHIA IN MOTOR (NON-FLUENT) APHASIAS

Agraphia in aphasia of phonemic production. This variety of aphasia corresponds to motor aphasia of the classical literature, to the "anarthria" of P. Marie (1906), to the "verbal aphasia" of Head (1926), and to the "syndrome of phonetic disintegration" of Alajouanine et al. (1939).

According to classical associationistic theory, writing remains intact in motor aphasia. Wernicke (1874) stated that a lesion in Broca's area interferes with direct activation of graphic movements by motor-center images. The movements, however, always remain available since the pathway connecting the center of visual images to the motor area for the hand and the fingers is not destroyed. This pathway is the way through which one learns to write and, in normal subjects, it is still used in the exceptional cases of writing some difficult words. In motor aphasia, this pathway resumes its function, thus allowing normal writing to be performed by these patients.

This theoretical position, strongly defended by Wernicke, was largely contradicted by clinical experience. Dejerine, whose general perspective is similar to that of Wernicke, recognized (1914) that motor aphasia, like all other forms of disorders of oral language, is accompanied by a more-or-less marked impairment of writing, a viewpoint that became generally accepted.

In this form of aphasia, writing disorders are, in fact, practically constant, however, often the character and intensity of the agraphia does not parallel the perturbations in speech and, in the extreme case, a pure motor aphasia may exist without any graphic disorders.

In many cases, the examination of writing can only be done by using alphabetical cubes because of motor deficits affecting the right upper limb. Patients are generally able to write their complete name and address. Deficits appear quite rapidly, however, as soon as they try to write spontaneously (e.g., give the written account of their illness or describe their job). In these cases, one finds either a complete refusal even to attempt to write anything or, as soon as the patient has started to write the first words of a sentence, a refusal to continue, often accompanied by manifestations of frustration.

The main characteristic of these graphic disorders is literal paragraphia; individual graphemes generally can be drawn, but at the word level there are omissions, distortions, additions, and substitutions of graphemes.

One of our motor aphasic patients who had no impairment of verbal comprehension wrote the following text to dictation:

C'est un professeur de prof (philosophie) dans le (de) Dijon qu'il (qui) a mes (fait) arrêter l'aujourd'hui ("l'" mistakenly added) dans le enfants d'un ensu (l'un de ses anciens) collègue (s) mais l'enclos (devenu escroc)

(In case of errors, the correct words or letters are cited in parentheses).

The structure of the words maintains a certain graphic relationship either with the model in case of dictation or with given actual words of the language in case of spontaneous writing. The sentence

bol   *valise*   *lavé*   *bobeau*

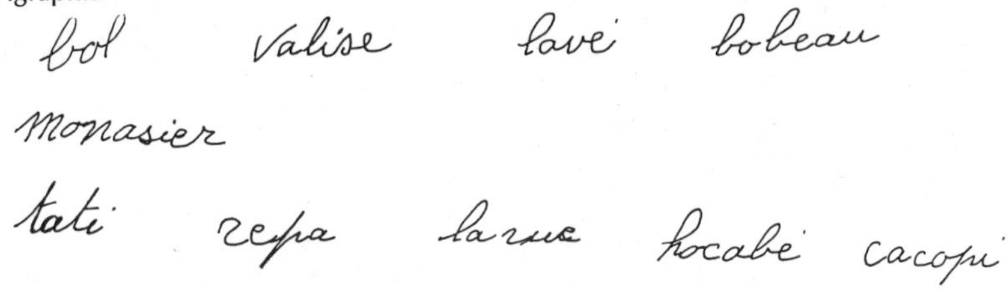

monasier

tati   *repa*   *larue*   *hocabé*   *cacopi*

Fig. 4-1 Agraphia in a patient with motor aphasia (two weeks after surgery).

Writing to dictation of five words (the first two lines): *bol, valise, lavé, Bordeaux, monarchie*.

Writing to dictation of five nonsense syllables (the last line): *tati, ropa, loru, chocabé, tacopi*.

level is hardly ever reached. Spelling, moreover, is severely impaired.

The agraphia of expressive aphasia has three characteristic features: the disorder affects spontaneous writing to dictation, while copying remains unimpaired; writing to dictation is much better for words than for nonsense syllables; and figures and numbers are generally well written.

Shankweiller and Harris (1966), among others, have emphasized the variability of the types of impairment which patients with motor aphasia show in the use of the phonetic code. Similarly, the dysorthographias shown by these patients do not seem to be in any way systematic. The use of graphic syllables, as well as the use of separations between consecutive words, remains intact.

Motor agraphia has usually been studied in patients who speak Indo-European languages. Since it is possible that the characteristics of the agraphia might depend on the structure of these languages, the study of agraphia in other languages is of interest.

Sasanuma et al. (1972, 1975) have noticed that writing disorders in Japanese patients are fundamentally similar to those observed in patients speaking Indo-European languages, despite the fact that Japanese has two separate sets of symbols for writing. These are "kana," a finite set of phonetic symbols with syllabic value, which can be used to transcribe any lexeme in the language, but which is generally used to express grammatical relationships, and "kanji," a set of ideograms which is usually used to transcribe substantive nouns. In motor aphasics, kana signs are principally affected. Graphic performances involve mainly substitutions, which are of

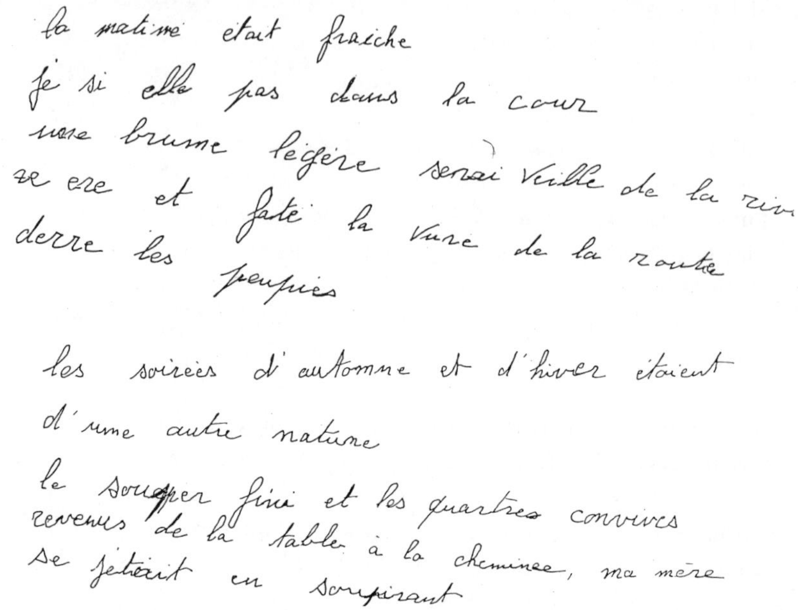

Fig. 4-2 Agraphia in a patient with motor aphasia (two weeks after surgery).

Writing to dictation (5 top lines). Dictated text: "La matinée était fraîche. Je fis quelques pas dans la cour; une brume légère se levait de la rivière et masquait la vue de la route derrière les peupliers."

Copying (5 bottom lines). Copied text: "Les soirées d'automne et d'hiver étaient d'une autre nature. Le souper fini et les quatre convives revenus de la table à la cheminée, ma mère se jettait en soupirant sur un vieux lit de jour de siamoise flambée; on mettait devant elle un guéridon avec une bougie. Je m'asseyais auprès du feu avec Lucile; les domestiques enlevaient le couvert et se retiraient."

two types: kanji lexemes are transcribed in their kana form, with or without transformations peculiar to the kana code; or, kana morphemes are substituted for other kana morphemes without affecting the kanji texture of the text. The writing deficits, therefore, mainly affect the manipulation of units belonging to the kana system. The errors reflect different permutations or substitutions within units of this code. Utilization of kanji signs is more intact. Sasanuma and Fujimura (1972) suggested that the two categories of graphic signs are treated at the cortical level by different processors: phonological and lexical (i.e., without mediation of the phonological component) for kana and kanji, respectively.

It could be argued that this dissociation between the processing of kana and kanji systems may be similar to the dissociation found in the European motor aphasics who write meaningless syllables with more difficulty than meaningful words. The former can only be received and reproduced as a result of an analysis of the sequential phonological units; they may depend on a phonological processor. The latter may be treated like the kanji items (i.e., globally) as long as this treatment is performed on the basis of meaning; they may depend on a lexical processor.

Agraphia in agrammatic aphasia (disorder of syntactic production). This type of aphasia is more a variant of the previous form than a distinct form. Expression is characterized by a discourse of isolated words, substantives, and verbs in nominal form, with reduction of grammatical words, even when well pronounced. The writing of these patients also shows a reduction of grammatical patterns. It tends to be limited to the use of lexemes or lexical verbal forms, the relative syntactic value being indicated by the order of appearance within the sentence. One of our patients thus described his job in writing: "adjoint, services économiques, pensions, marché." The punctuation was put in by the patient to emphasize the various stages of his discourse. Graphic performances are generally brief. Items are often written with only a few orthographic errors. The parallel, however, between the disorganization of oral and written expression is not as rigorous and constant as has been argued, principally by Mirallié (1895, 1896). For instance, the patient mentioned above orally described his job in the following manner: "adjoint économat alors je vais les . . . non . . . le même. . . ." Agrammatism is less systematic because one finds some functional words even if the entire message is conveyed by the two first words. There are even occasions where the impairment or the accumulation of disorders in oral expression may favor communication in the written modality. For example, a patient of ours, a primary school teacher, unable to describe orally in any intelligible fashion the history of her disease, could do it in writing, in a style which, although "telegraphic," clearly allowed one to get the message:

29 août 1954 le matin la fièvre 39°5 3 jours et parler la tête l'électricité à la tête les 3 mois et pourrais la tête j'ai pu parler. 6 septembre 1962, le 2 heures de l'aprèsmidi j'étais en hôtel la Hutte Coulombiers (Sarthe) par terre couché docteur, mon mari à Paris téléphoné qu'il vienne le soir.

AGRAPHIA IN CONDUCTION (PHRASTIC) APHASIA

The existence of this clinical form was first postulated by Wernicke (1874), and subsequently confirmed. In the framework of his associationistic views, Wernicke thought this deficit might result from a defect in conduction between the receptive and expressive zones of language. The temporal area loses control over spoken language.

Conduction aphasia is defined by the presence of paraphasias in spontaneous language and in verbal repetition, in the absence of prominent disorders of language comprehension. Paraphasias are based on telescoping words or confusing words which are phonetically close, rendering communication difficult. The patient, conscious of his errors, tries to correct them by successive approximations ("conduites d'approche"). Sentences are limited to aborted attempts or to simple clauses not related to one another, with stops and intercalations of adverbs such as *then* and *later*. With each change of enunciation, fluency of speech is lessened. Automatic series are, on the other hand, better expressed.

Writing disorders are always found, although a total agraphia is never observed (Hécaen et al., 1967). Graphic production always shows some awareness of error with frequent crossing out, overwriting, and stopping. Graphemes are correctly formed, but there are disturbances in the structure of words similar to the literal paragraphias seen in motor aphasia but with some telescoping or even substitutions or omissions of lexemes. The patient is generally able to write correctly more automatized sequences such as his name, address, or date of birth. The writing of dictated single words is better than that of nonsense syllables. At the sentence level, there is usually some impairment. Subordinate and coordinate clauses may be formed, but at the same time, function words are left out and there are slight syntactic deficiencies. Copying remains unimpaired and figures and numbers are correctly written, but oral spelling is always faulty.

The same kind of deficit is encountered in Japanese conduction aphasics. Yamadori and Ikumura (1975) note that the best writing performance is obtained in the kanji mode rather than in the kana mode. In kanji writing, an exact syllabic sequence is, in fact, not absolutely necessary.

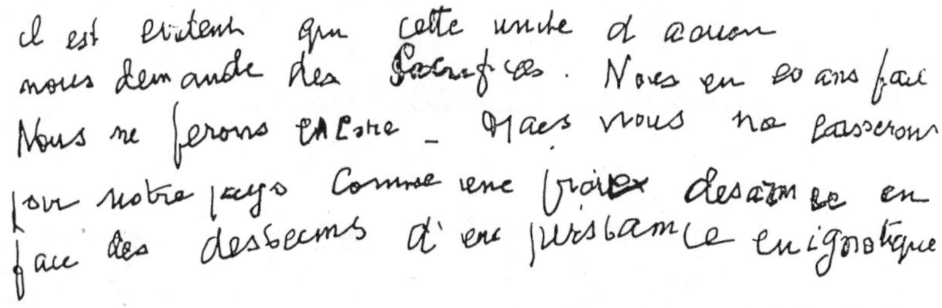

Fig. 4-3 Copying by a patient with conduction aphasia (one week following the stroke).

Copied text: "Il est évident que cette unité d'action nous demande des sacrifices. Nous en avons faits. Nous en ferons encore. Mais nous ne laisserons pas notre pays comme une proie désarmée en face des desseins d'une puissance énigmatique." (This was a statement pronounced by M. R. Pleven, French prime minister, just when he left for the States.)

There are the following errors: (second line) "avons" written "avans"; (third line) "en" written "ne"; (fourth line) "pas" written "par"; (fifth line) "desseins" written "desseims"; (fifth line) "puissance énigmatique" written "puissamce énignatique."

AGRAPHIA IN THE COURSE OF SENSORY (WERNICKE'S) APHASIA

Sensory aphasia (also called syntactic aphasia by Head (1926); receptive aphasia by Weisenburg and McBride (1935); acoustic aphasia by Luria (1969); and, more generally Wernicke's aphasia) is characterized primarily by a disorder in verbal reception and comprehension, although other associated defects are the rule. Since the original description by Bastian (1869) and Wernicke (1874), the clinical features have been frequently commented on. Spontaneous speech is fluent, or indeed hyperfluent, with an increased rate of word production and an inability to bring a sentence to a close. Intonational contours and gestural and facial expression remain normal, even while the meaning of utterances is incomprehensible. This unintelligibility of verbal output is not due to a transformation of the word in its articulatory components, but rather to an incorrect paradigmatic lexical choice. Multiple paraphasias added to the circumlocutory speech due to word-finding difficulty result in a verbal output called jargon aphasia, which permits virtually no meaningful communication. Repetition is impaired, but to varying degrees, depending on the type of sensory aphasia. Naming is also defective.

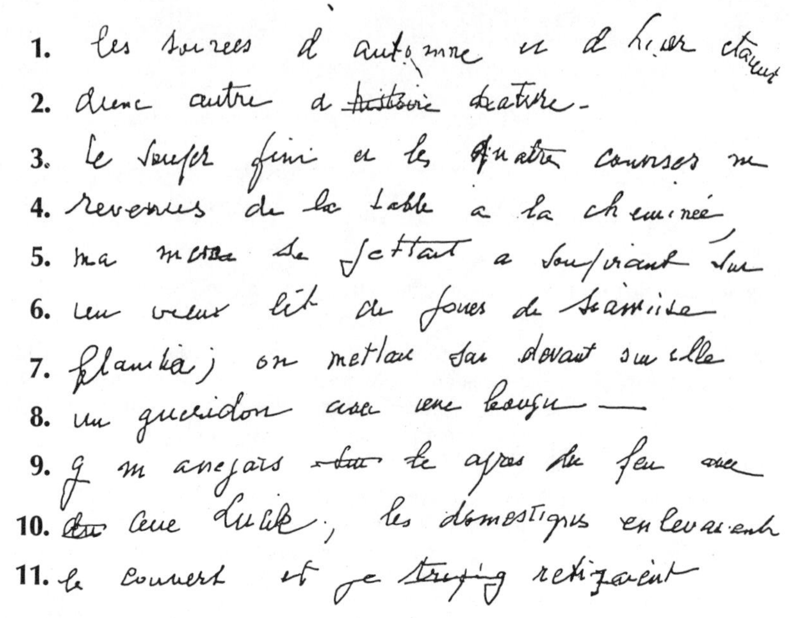

Fig. 4-4 Writing to dictation by a patient with conduction aphasia (performance one week after the stroke).

Dictated text: "Les soirées d'automne et d'hiver étaient d'une autre nature. Le souper fini et les quatre convives revenus de la table à la cheminée, ma mère se jettait en soupirant sur un vieux lit de jour de siamoise flambée; on mettait devant elle un guéridon avec une bougie. Je m'asseyais auprès du feu avec Lucile; les domestiques enlevaient le couvert et se retiraient."

Errors are as follows: "d'une" (line 2) written "diene"; "convives" (line 3) written "convises"; "ne" added at the end of the third line; "en" (line 4) written "a"; "de jour" (line 6) written "de joues"; "on mettait devant elle" (line 7) is well written, but "sur" is added twice; "auprès" (line 9) written "après"; at the beginning of the 10th line the first word is an unachieved duplication of "avec" used correctly at the end of the previous line.

Comprehension defects are the hallmark of the syndrome. They may vary from mild to total, and they are seen in both spoken and written language.

Agraphia is practically always part of the clinical picture of Wernicke's aphasia. Dejerine (1914) thought that a patient with sensory aphasia would only be able to write his own name and even that would have to be done in the form of a signature. In the majority of cases, the agraphia is less severe. The patient can write his own name and address. He may even attempt spontaneous writing, for example, describing his own illness. His performance in these cases is characterized by more-or-less severe dysorthographias. Writing tends to be abundant and unintelligible, and sometimes one can even observe jargon agraphia. Copying written material is generally possible, even though characterized by numerous and severe paragraphias. Spelling is also severely impaired in a manner consistent with the writing disorder. The patient is generally more aware of his graphic deficit than of his jargon aphasia. He, therefore, frequently discontinues his attempt and signifies his inability to write.

Although this schematic, clinical description of sensory aphasia appears simple, the complexity of the symptomatology and also its variability should be emphasized. This complexity makes it likely that different factors are involved to different degrees in different types of sensory aphasias and even in different patients with the same type.

The existence of a "pure" form of verbal deafness has been known for a long time. Here the deficit is strictly limited to the recognition of sounds of language, at least after the initial phase. In the chronic stage, the patient doesn't understand anything spoken to him aloud, nor can he write to dictation; but spontaneous writing is largely intact with the exception of several missing letters, syllables, or words. Spelling is rarely intact. Copied writing is perfect in the majority of cases.

Writing in sensory aphasia with predominance of word-deafness. Word-deafness is manifested in spontaneous language, in tests of repetition, and in writing, by certain characteristics which clearly specify this variety of sensory aphasia. Spontaneous language is logorrheic, but it maintains an idea and the transmitted information is coherent despite anomalies within the sentences. Paraphasias, which are relatively infrequent, are usually closely related to the context. They are usually either of the telescopic type or phonic approximations.

In verbal repetition, the patients do not treat words and nonsense syllables differently. The quantity of errors is considerable since no item is repeated correctly. Isolated units of syntax are repeated as unique items, without interruption of sound flow; repetition of simple sentences considerably accentuates this trait.

Fig. 4-5 Agraphia in a patient with sensory aphasia (performances three weeks after surgery).

Writing to dictation.

Dictated text: "La matinée était fraîche. Je fis quelques pas dans la cour; une brume légère se levait de la rivière et masquait la vue de la route derrière les peupliers."

Performance of the patient: "La matine était fraiché. Je fus celque pas danss dans la la court—une brume est baigné cebai lié the revuré riqueride et la la lave de la lura raguge rougede deolaiinant deviamp leur leur la riguodora."

Dictated words (bottom left) and performances within parentheses: *bol* (*buale*); *valise* (*valisa*); *laver* (*lavéa*); *Bordeaux* (*brdeaux*); *monarchie* (*mamariébris*).

Dictated nonsense syllables (bottom right) and performances within parentheses: *tati* (*tatue*); *ropa* (*Rapa*): *loru* (*babue*); *chocabé* (*chacabua*); *takopi* (*Tocaquiita*).

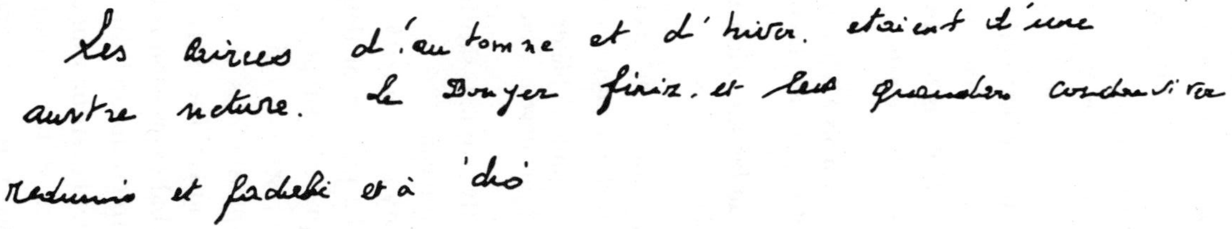

Fig. 4-6 Agraphia in a patient with sensory aphasia (three weeks after surgery): copying.

Copied text: "Les soirées d'automne et d'hiver étaient d'une autre nature. Le souper fini et les quatres convives revenus de la table à la cheminée, ma mère se jettait en soupirant sur un vieux lit de jour de siamoise flambée; on mettait devant elle un guéridon avec une bougie. Je b'asseyais auprès du feu avec Lucile; les domestiques enlevaient le couvert et se retiraient."

There are many errors: "soirées" written "cairees"; "autre nature" 2nd line) written "autre neture"; "le souper fini" written "le douper finie"; "les quatre convives revenus" written "les quandara condouviver redumis."

109

Oral verbal comprehension is nil as a result of a disorder of verbal reception. Written verbal comprehension is mostly correct or at least clearly better than oral comprehension.

The discordance is clear between spontaneous writing and writing to dictation. In essence, spontaneous writing, though always disturbed, remains possible. Thematic coherence is relatively conserved and paragraphias are relatively less abundant. On the other hand, writing to dictation most often gives rise to a true jargon agraphia, strictly incomprehensible, even if some graphic aspects maintain a link with the words of the model. The following example shows the extent of the discrepancy between spontaneous writing and writing to dictation in a patient affected by sensory aphasia with predominant verbal deafness. In his attempt to describe the history of his illness, he wrote the following text:

Je suis parti pour deux mois à Vivonne dans le château pour les pour se remettre et le 5 juillet je suis à ne plus passer sans savoir pourquoi.

The performance under dictation was the following (the model is given in parentheses):

J'ai un pasuteur de pasuteur de phyloserie de Sauge qui a fait arreter aujourd'jui un des ancien sangnier des erect.

(C'est un professeur de philosophie de Dijon qui a fait arrêter aujourd'hui un de ses anciens collègues devenu escroc).

Writing is generally copied satisfactorily by patients with this variety of sensory aphasia.

Writing in sensory aphasia with predominance of verbal comprehension deficit. The pattern of deficits in this disorder is distinct from that in the preceding type. For example, reception of verbal signs is relatively preserved. This variety corresponds to the "transcortical sensory aphasia," as it was called by Lichtheim (1885), Wernicke (1903), and Goldstein (1948).

Spontaneous verbal expression is extremely dysfluent and is characterized by incompletions and unfinished embedding of successive sequences. Paraphasias can be numerous, often in the form of substitutions leading to shifts in meaning. Speech is ungrammatical and it is interspersed with stereotyped sentences, even more than in the previous type of aphasia.

Oral repetition varies with the linguistic nature of the item to be repeated. It is better for meaningful words than for nonsense syllables. For words, length is a facilitating factor, whereas the converse holds for nonsense syllables. In contrast to word-deafness, repetition of elementary sentences remains possible.

The comprehension of commands, given in writing as well as orally, is very disturbed, while phonemic discrimination is altered relatively little.

The writing of meaningful words to dictation is performed better than the writing of nonsense syllables. With the latter type of item, graphemic substitutions are frequent, but the graphic identity of the proposed item remains recognizable. For instance, nonsense syllable "tati" is rendered by "tali," or "ropa" becomes "rempa."

The distinction between spontaneous and dictated writing presents a picture quite opposite to the one found in patients with sensory aphasia with predominant word-deafness. Spontaneous writing contains many paragraphias, while writing of a connected text to dictation may produce good results. For example, a patient with this variety of sensory aphasia was able to write to dictation the short text mentioned above in a way which was almost correct:

C'est un professeur de philosophie de Dijeon qui a fait arrêter aujourd'hui l'un de ses anciens collègues devenu echos.

On the other hand, this same patient in spontaneous writing, produced this almost unintelligible text in attempting to describe the meal he had just eaten:

un imparmier m'a descendu de la verricate, la gruluque était si agréable que j'ai réussi a exeder mon plat de rerevite que j'ai reussi ente au my du garde.

Actually, this dissociation is not constant, and the deficit is often as severe in writing to dictation as in spontaneous writing.

Writing in sensory aphasia with predominant attentional disorganization. By this term (Hécaen et al., 1967), we mean to designate a factor which particularly bears on linguistic performance, though it belongs to a much more general disorder, as is shown by accompanying disturbances in other aspects of behavior.

As long as there is no serious comprehension deficit or verbal deafness, the patient is able to repeat words, nonsense syllables, and sentences without difficulty.

The impairment manifests itself clearly in spontaneous language and in tasks of sentence production and transformation. It has two aspects: distractibility and perseveration. These result in ungrammatical utterances which contrast with a general conformity to grammatical patterns of language. Perseveration is manifested by severe echolalia—at least at the onset of illness—and by numerous iterations of sentence patterns. Distractibility results in an inability to complete sentences. Utterances thus consist of open-ended embedded sentences. The asemanticism of the utterances can be ascribed to the violation of selectional constraints such as those between the subject-noun phrase and the verb phrase, between a noun and its expansions, and the constraints involving subcategorization rules such as the distinction between animate and inanimate.

Writing to dictation and copying are performed well, apart from a few slips and iterations. Spontaneous writing shows the same features of asemanticism with dysfluency, extraneous additions, and "filler" phrases. For instance, a patient subjected to left anterotemporal resection for a ruptured aneurysm wrote the history of his illness:

Le comportement certains de ma maladie réside en un fait ayant accompli toute circonstance atténuantes. Je dois observer un comportement de la façon la plus originale; c'est-à-dire.

This performance only shows two dysorthographies (an "s" added to "certain," and "s" missing in "toutes circonstances"). Sentences are formally correct, but they only express the opening statement for an idea which should have been completed.

Apraxic agraphia

Disturbance of gestural capacity has long been recognized as a causative factor in many cases of agraphia. These agraphias have been linked primarily to parietal apraxia. Numerous authors have studied both the motor and the kinesthetic aspects of this praxic activity. As early as 1867, Ogle referred to "ataxic agraphia," a term which Kussmaul (1884) borrowed in describing disorders of writing due to damage of the centers of coordination between spoken and written language. Henschen (1922) emphasized the relationship of agraphia and apraxia to each other and to parietal lesions. Kleist (1934) distinguished three varieties of apraxic agraphia: an agraphia due to disturbance in the ability to manipulate writing implements, such as paper and pencil, but independent of general ideomotor apraxia; an apraxia for written discourse, with preservation of the ability to write letters and words, due to a loss of optico-kinesthetic associations; and a constructional agraphia due to a loss of the ability to form letters correctly. Goldstein (1948) accepted two major forms of writing disorder: those which he called apracto-amnesic agraphias; and the aphaso-amnesic agraphias.

Apraxia produces agraphia by impairing the ability to form normal graphemes, with inversions and distortions appearing in their stead. The disorder is seen in all modalities of writing (spontaneous, to dictation, and by copying), although infrequently the ability to spell or compose words with alphabet blocks is retained.

In certain cases, in fact, the writing deficit may be identical to the

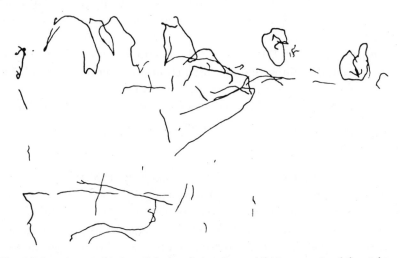

Fig. 4-7 Apraxic agraphia in a right-handed patient exhibiting paresis of the right upper limb due to a tumor of the left parietal region (two weeks after the onset of trouble; prior to surgery).

Attempt to write the name of the examiner (HÉCAEN). The patient used his left hand and explained his difficulty while writing: "I can't get my hand straight, it is not the hand."

Fig. 4-8 Apraxic agraphia in a patient exhibiting paresis of the right upper limb due to a tumor of the left parietal region (two weeks after onset of troubles; prior to surgery).

Attempt to copy the numbers 6, 18, and 15 (from left to right) with the left hand.

praxic disorder found in drawing or construction, while spelling and the composition of a word with block letters may remain intact. But these findings are exceptional and, with the exception of the case presented by Pitres (1884) where agraphia was limited to the right hand, spelling and reconstruction with block letters almost constantly show disorders of graphic encoding.

In addition to the disorders described above, the combination of writing deficit and praxic disorder may appear in the two syndromes that follow:

AGRAPHIA AND UNILATERAL LEFT IDEOMOTOR APRAXIA

In this disorder (Hécaen and Angelergues, 1966) agraphia is present in both hands, however it is accompanied by different motor abnormalities in each hand. The agraphia of the right hand is not associated with apraxia, nor is there any disorder of oral expression or reading. There is no impairment of graphic encoding despite difficulties with spelling and with composition of words with block letters. The impairment of graphic gesture appears to be related to tonic disorders (grasp reflex or avoiding reaction). The left hand demonstrates agraphia as well, but this is associated with a unilateral left ideomotor apraxia, and with difficulty in holding the pencil. The left hand also cannot arrange block letters. The lesion in this variety of agraphia is found in the left medial frontal region (Hécaen and Angelergues, 1966). (Also see Chapter 7 on apraxia.)

APRAXIC AGRAPHIA WITH ALEXIA

The more common variety of apraxic agraphia represents a combination of elements from the syndrome of parietal apraxia and that of alexia with agraphia, and is sometimes called parietal agraphia. A disturbance in both encoding and decoding of written language is found, although the severity of the defect is not necessarily parallel in the two. Frequently associated with this syndrome are disorders of spoken language, especially amnesic aphasia and mild comprehension difficulty (see also Chapter 3, pp. 68–70).

The characteristics of this agraphia reflect the influence of apraxia: distortions and inversions of graphemes are prominent. The use of alphabet blocks often improves the situation, but never completely. Spelling errors are numerous, with abundant iterations. When there is only a moderately severe agraphia, a short sentence may be reasonably well written, although paragraphic errors are still found. Agrammatism is not seen, as it is in the written production of anterior aphasics. Unlike the writing of patients with the sensory aphasia, writing in this syndrome has recognizable semantic value. The ability to copy is always disturbed. Writing of numbers is impaired, except for occasional single digits or small, multidigit numbers. Spelling is always defective, usually to a marked degree.

Certain features thus clearly distinguish these writing disorders from the agraphias found in motor or sensory aphasia: impairment in the drawing of graphemes; relative preservation of the syntactic structure of sentences; parallel impairment of all writing modalities (spontaneous, to dictation, copying). This agraphia cannot be explained entirely on the basis of apraxia, since one always finds impairment of spelling and the writing disorder does not disappear with the use of block letters, although it does improve.

The association of this type of agraphia with alexia is nearly constant, but in different cases, the severity of the two may vary independently. Recognition of letters is generally better than that of words, while context often facilitates the understanding of a sentence. Nonetheless, with longer or more complex sentences, comprehension fails. The way words are read seems to show that the normal perceptual strategy used in reading is lost (Haslerud and Clark, 1957). Kinesthetic feedback does not benefit these patients. Associated disorders include, almost invariably, a mild to moderate anomia. Often, but not always, one may see elements of the Gerstmann syndrome (finger agnosia, dyscalculia, right–left disorientation).

A lesion of the posterior portion of the left parietal lobe, especially the angular gyrus, is generally accepted as the anatomical locus underlying this syndrome. It corresponds to the area proposed by Dejerine (1891) as the center of verbal-visual images. As stated by Wernicke (1903), whether or not agraphia is found in association with alexia depends on whether the connection between the center of visual images and the motor area of language (the arcuate fasciculus) is preserved by the lesion. In a comparative study of a large number of patients, Hécaen and Angelergues (1964) noted that the relative severity of agraphia and alexia varied with the location of the lesion: in temporo-occipital lesions, alexia predominated; in parieto-occipital lesions agraphia was more marked than alexia.

"Pure" agraphia

"Pure" agraphia indicates a disorder of written language in the absence of disorders of oral language, reading, or praxis.

Few detailed reports of the clinical and neurolinguistic aspects of isolated disorders of writing have been published (Hécaen et al., 1963; Dubois et al., 1969; Assal et al., 1970; Chedru and Geschwind, 1972). Dubois, Hécaen, and Marcie (1969) studied six patients with this syndrome. They found no disorder of oral language or of constructional ability. All of their patients had acalculia and four had general intellectual deterioration. Analysis of graphic output revealed the following features. Formation of letters was normal, although dysorthographia was marked. Even though they misspelled words when writing, the patients were able to spell the same words aloud correctly. No significant differences in total errors were noted between single digits and letters as compared to multidigit numbers and words. Ability to copy was essentially intact, although errors crept in when the patient had to change from one expressive code to another (e.g., from cursive script to block print). Morphographemic rules of expression were normally maintained; and the correspondence of letter-to-sound (morphographemic-to-morphophonologic relationship) was preserved. Perseverative errors were found in only one patient.

Writing in script by hand and writing by the use of anagram letters were compared. In half the group, writing in manuscript was worse; in two patients errors were equivalent with either method. Spelling errors were further analyzed. Error types, aside from the perseverative errors of one patient, were errors of combination and of selection, with the central portion of the item accounting for the most errors.

From these observations, the authors concluded that pure agraphia consists of two forms of graphic defect: one is a spatiotemporal disorganization specific to graphic activity, and not associated with constructional apraxia; the other is a disorder of grapheme selection, even in the absence of impaired ability to name letters.

If these observations are combined with those of Gordinier (1899) and Penfield and Roberts (1959), the reality of a pure agraphia dissociated from disorders of oral language seems to be proven. But the observations of Gordinier (1899), and Penfield and Roberts (1959) differ notably from those already described. With the exception of one of the six cases, the writing disorders presented by Dubois et al. (1969) can be grouped into a homogeneous set, with characteristics similar to the writing disorders associated with the expressive aphasias. There are cases which appear intermediate between pure agraphia and the agraphia of expressive aphasia, in which severe agraphia is accompanied by a mild disorder of oral expression.

A novel form of agraphia, in which written spelling is selectively affected, was described by Kinsbourne and Rosenfield (1974). There was a dissociation between the patient's ability to spell by writing and manual sorting (which was impaired) and his ability to spell orally (which was relatively spared). The authors postulated that the programs which translate letter choice into visual terms for purposes of written (as distinct from oral) spelling may be related to a specific cerebral location (left posterior parasagittal parietal area).

There has always been an intense controversy about the localization of the lesion responsible for pure agraphia. In 1881, Exner pre-

Ma

Maison

N

Saison

Soleil

Poir

Pora

Pine

Au al

demain il fera beau.

ps

REMAIN IP· REAN

sented evidence in favor of the anatomical localization of an independent graphic center in the foot of the second left frontal gyrus, separate from Broca's area. Henschen (1922) accepted Exner's area, and suggested a sensory graphic center in the angular gyrus. In fact, precise anatomical data only exist in the cases of Gordinier (1899) (in which there was a tumor 2 cm in diameter lying on the cortex at the foot of the second left frontal convolution and affecting the underlying white matter; the third frontal convolution was perfectly intact) and Penfield and Roberts (1959) (transitory agraphia after an excision in areas F2 and F3). Of the six cases of Dubois et al. (1969), four were due to frontal lesions, although a more precise locus could not be adduced. But several observations of Russell and Espir (1961), one of the six cases of Dubois et al.; and an observation of Kinsbourne and Rosenfield (1974) describe pure agraphia in association with isolated lesions in the left posterior parietal area.

Other factors are likely to contribute to the explanation of this syndrome: the degree of mastering written language in the premorbid state, differences of cerebral functional organization in relation to manual preference, and general intellectual impairment. Chedru and Geschwind (1972) particularly emphasized this last factor, and questioned the role of focal lesions in isolated disorders of writing.

Writing disorders due to lesions of the minor hemisphere

Lastly, mention should be made of the disorders of writing resulting from right-hemisphere lesions. In these instances, the disturbance is not related to the faculty of encoding and decoding written entities but rather to difficulty in dealing with spatial factors in-

---

Fig. 4-9 Writing of a patient exhibiting pure agraphia, examined two weeks after the stroke.

Writing to dictation: (the first three lines) 3 trials to write the word "maison" (house); (the next two lines) 2 trials to write "fauteuil" (arm-chair); (the next three lines) 3 trials to write "rue" (street); (line 9) an attempt to write the sentence "Il fait beau aujourd'hui." This performance is limited to 4 letters "au ab" which have no link with the stimulus.

Copying: The sentence to be copied ("demain il fera beau") had been written in small letters and the patient was asked to write it in capital letters; he was able to read and understand this sentence quite well.

volved in these skills, or to perseveration. It is one of the features of
the minor-hemisphere syndrome (Hécaen et al., 1956), and usually
results from a lesion involving the right parieto-temporo-occipital
region.

This disturbance also occurs in reading texts, and in calculation
and consists mainly in neglect of the left side of the text or of digits
situated at the left end of the line. Also, the patient often has difficulty going from the right end of a line to the beginning of the next
line and is unable to locate precisely which is the next line. (Also
see Chapter 10 on neglect.)

Characteristic features clearly distinguish this type of agraphia
from those types related to dominant hemispheric pathology. Graphemes are well formed and morphosyntactic components of written
expression are preserved. Four major features define this clinical
syndrome: (1) Some graphemes are produced frequently with one,
two, or even more extra strokes, the letters m, n, and u especially
being duplicated. (2) The lines of writing are not horizontal, but
slant at variable angles of inclination to the top or bottom of the
page. (3) The writing occupies only the right side of the paper.
(4) There are blank spaces inserted between graphemes which dis-
organize the word and destroy its unity.

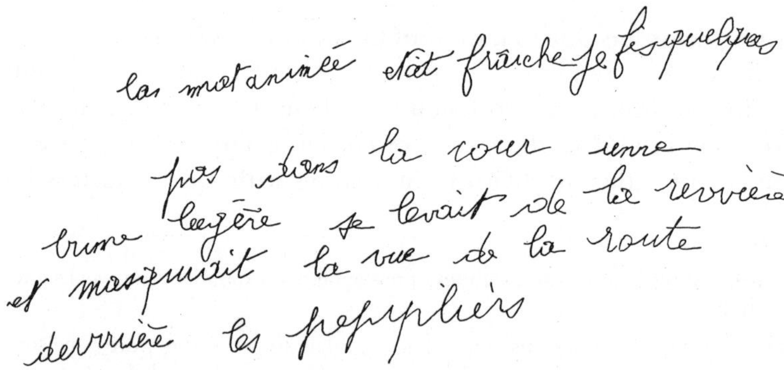

Fig. 4-10 Writing disorders in a right-handed patient with a right lesion (6 weeks
after surgery for a sylvian aneurysm).

Writing to dictation. Dictated text: "La matinée était fraîche. Je fis quelques pas
dans la cour; une brume légère se levait de la rivière et masquait la vue de la
route derrière les peupliers."

In a quantitative study of the graphic performances of 82 right-handed patients with unilateral cerebral lesions, Hécaen and Marcie (1974) made the following observations. Only the iteration of strokes and letters and enlargement of the left-hand margin were significantly associated with right-hemisphere lesions. On the other hand, the loss of continuity in the writing of words was related to left-hemisphere lesions. The spatial origin of enlargement of the left-hand margin seems clear and directly related to the presence of unilateral spatial neglect, and the repetition of both pothooks and letters is considered to be a perseverative phenomenon which is evident specifically in the spatial aspects of writing.

CONCLUSIONS

As can be seen from this review, writing disorders following left-hemispheric lesions are both very frequent and quite varied.

The variety of writing disorders is probably due to the variety of factors which contributes to the performance of writing. The "information transcodings" (Weigl, 1974; Luria, 1966) which operate in writing are diverse, as they depend on the particular task involved: spontaneous writing, writing on command, copying, writing to dictation of meaningful items (either isolated or syntagmatically connected), or writing to dictation of meaningless items. Cortical lesions produce different deficits in writing since various components need not be equally affected. Therefore, one finds different symptom complexes, each due to the alteration of one or the other of the linguistic components of writing and also to the alteration of general factors, the impairment of which affects writing performance.

It should be noted that writing disorders most often accompany disorders of oral language, and that the disorder of writing is similar in form to the disorder of oral expression. Yet the intensities of the disorders observed in writing and in speaking are often far from equal. One can see such a difference in motor aphasia and to a lesser degree in sensory aphasia. Similarly, disorders of writing and reading may be comparable in form, but may differ in intensity, as in patients with the syndrome of alexia with agraphia.

This dissociation is total in cases of pure agraphia. These cases are certainly exceptional, but their existence is now beyond dispute.

The nature of the deficit could not be reduced, at least for some of the cases, only to a praxic component. Pure agraphia is similar in many respects to the agraphia associated with motor aphasia. Such cases, however rare, argue in favor of a functional autonomy, at least a relative one, between written and oral codes. Another argument in favor of this dissociation is that in most cases one finds no parallel between the intensity of the disorders affecting written and oral expression. While the possibility of a pure motor aphasia is highly controversial, many cases are known where the disorders of oral expression are much more severe than are those of written expression. The reverse is also true.

One must emphasize, however, that in case of posterior lesions, there does not seem to be a similar clear-cut dissociation between disorders of writing and disorders of oral language. On the contrary, in patients with left temporal lesions and Wernicke's aphasia, the degree and type of impairment is strikingly similar in written and oral language. Exceptions to this rule have been noted, however. Lhermitte and Derouesne (1974) presented two interesting patients in whom writing was practically normal, whereas oral expression was severely impaired (paraphasias and semantic jargon) and verbal comprehension was only mildly disturbed. Dubois (1977) studied a group of sensory aphasics, and concluded that different types of sensory aphasia could be distinguished purely on the basis of the distribution of the types of paragraphia which they made.

One must also note that although there exists a syndrome of impairment of both encoding and decoding written language, there are well-known cases of pure alexia in which spontaneous writing and writing to dictation remain intact or at least are only slightly impaired. (See Chapter 3, pp. 66–68.)

Finally, there are some cases of agraphia following left-posterior lesions which are not accompanied by disorders of oral language. Writing deficits seem to depend more on an apraxic component, since they affect particularly the process of letter formation. Perseveration also affects writing in these patients.

Agraphias are therefore frequently, if not constantly, found in aphasias and there tends to be a marked similarity between writing disorders and the forms of aphasia in which they appear. These points favor the opinion put forth by Wernicke and Dejerine. Yet one cannot at the present time deny the existence of one or more forms of agraphia dissociated from oral language impairment.

Does such a dissociation imply a particular localization for writing, a specialized cortical center as postulated by Exner, Henschen, and others? Certainly, we have seen that frontal lesions appear to be responsible for most cases of agraphia—those with features similar to the writing disorders found in patients with aphasia due to lesions of Broca's area. It is obviously tempting to consider a "center" responsible for the organization of writing movements which would have a relation to the area of the precentral gyrus similar to the relation between Broca's area and the area representing the face and the buccophonatory organs. Let us remember, however, that there is no clinico-anatomical argument which clearly supports such a hypothesis.

In addition to anatomical factors, other factors may also explain the appearance of writing disorders isolated from oral language disturbances found after cortical lesions.

The role of confusion and/or intellectual deterioration seems well established in some cases. Writing may represent an activity so fragile that it may be disturbed in isolation when there are acute and diffuse central lesions (Chedru and Geschwind, 1972). This fragility might be due to the diversity of components involved in writing.

Another possible explanation for the fragility of writing in patients with cortical lesions is that writing may not have been mastered adequately prior to the lesion. If this activity is little automatized, a cortical lesion which is not sufficient to break down the nervous mechanism of oral language would suffice to interfere with the transcoding between oral language and written language.

The particular organization of functional cortical representations in left-handed subjects could favor the appearance of this dissociation between the functioning of the two linguistic systems. In studying a series of patients, Hécaen and Angelergues (1963) emphasized that writing disorders were, in left-handed patients, less frequently associated with a deficit or oral language than they were in right-handed patients. Heilman et al. (1973) studied agraphia and apraxia in a left-handed patient and suggested that dominance for language and dominance for handedness could be represented separately in the two hemispheres in some individuals, language in the left, and handedness in the right. Since the acquired graphemic motor skills and language may be represented separately in the two hemispheres, dissociation of the skills may induce an agraphia. (See Chapter 7 for details.)

References

Alajouanine, T. H., Ombredane, A., and Durand, M. (1939). Le syndrome de désintégration phonétique dans l'aphasie, vol. 1. Paris: Masson.

Alajouanine, T. H., Lhermitte, F., and Ribaucourt-Ducarne, B. de (1960). Les alexies agnosiques et aphasiques, in *Les Grandes activités du lobe occipital*, pp. 235–265, T. H. Alajouanine (ed). Paris: Masson.

Assal, G., Chapuis, G., and Zander, E. (1970). Isolated writing disorders in a patient with stenosis of the left internal carotid artery. *Cortex 6*: 241–248.

Bastian, H. C. (1869). On the various forms of loss of speech in cerebral disease. *British and Foreign Medico-Surgical Review 43*:470–492.

Bastian, H. C. (1894). *A Treatise on Aphasia and Other Speech Defects*. London: H. K. Lewis.

Benedikt, M. (1865). *Über aphasie, Agraphie und Verwandte Pathologische Austände*. Vienna: Wiener Medizinische Presse. 6, 897–899; 923–926; 945–948; 997–999; 1020–1022; 1067–1070; 1094–1097; 1139–1142; 1167–1169; 1189–1190; 1264–1265.

Bouillaud, J. B. (1825). Recherches cliniques propres à démontrer que la perte de la parole correspond à la lésion des lobules antérieurs du cerveau, et à confirmer l'opinion de M. Gall sur le siège de l'organe du langage articulé. *Archives Générales de Médecine 8*:25–45.

Bouillaud, J. B. (1848). Recherches cliniques propres à démontrer que le sens du langage articulé et le principe coordinateur des mouvements de la parole résident dans les lobules antérieurs du cerveau. *Bulletin de l'Académie Royale de Médecine* 1er trimestre, 699–719.

Chedru, F. and Geschwind, N. (1972). Writing disturbances in acute confusional states. *Neuropsychologia 10*:343–354.

Chomsky, N. (1970). Phonology and reading, in *Basic Studies on Reading*. H. Levin et J. P. Williams (eds). New York, London: Basic Books.

Dejerine, J. (1891). De l'agraphie. *Annales de Médecine scientifique et Pratique. 1*:5–14.

Dejerine, J. (1892). Contribution à l'étude anatomo-pathologique et clinique des différentes variétés de cécité verbale. *Mémoires de la Société de Biologie 4*:61–90.

Dejerine, J. (1926). *Sémiologie des Affections du Système Nerveux*. Deuxième tirage conforme à l'édition de 1914. Paris: Masson.

Dubois, J., Hécaen, H., and Marcie, P. (1969). L'agraphie "pure". *Neuropsychologia 7*:271–286.

Dubois, J. (1977). L'agraphie des aphasiques sensoriels. Les troubles à la dictée des mots et des logatomes. *Languages 47*:86–119.

Exner, S. (1881). Untersuchungen über die lokalisation der funktionen, in *Des Grosshirnrinde des Menschen*. Wien: Wilhelm Braumuller.

Foix, Ch. (1928). Aphasies, in *Nouveau Traité de Médecine* L. G. Roger, F. Widal, P. J. Teissier (eds.). Paris: Masson 18, 135–213.

Geschwind, N. and Kaplan, E. (1962). A human cerebral deconnection syndrome. *Neurology 12*:675–685.

Goldstein, K. (1948). *Language and Language Disturbances*. New-York: Grune & Stratton.

Gordinier, H. C. (1899). A case of brain tumor at the base of the second left frontal convolution. *Am. J. Med. Sci. 117*:526–535.

Haslerud, G. H. and Clark, R. E. (1957). On the reintegrative perception of words. *Am. J. Psychol. 70*:97–101.

Head, H. (1926). *Aphasia and Kindred Disorders of Speech*. Cambridge: Cambridge University Press.

Hécaen, H., Penfield, W., Bertrand, C., and Malmo, R. (1956). The syndrome of Apractognosia due to lesions of the minor cerebral hemisphere. *Arch. Neurol. Psychiat. 75*:400–434.

Hécaen, H., Angelergues, R., and Douzenis, J. A. (1963). Les agraphies. *Neuropsychologia 1*:179–208.

Hécaen, H. and Angelergues, R. (1966). L'agraphie secondaire aux lésions du lobe frontal. *Intern. J. Neurol. 5*:381–394.

Hécaen, H. (1969). Essai de dissociation du syndrome de l'aphasie sensorielle. *Rev. Neurol. 120*:229–237.

Hécaen, H., Dubois, J., and Marcie, P. (1967). Aspects linguistiques des troubles de la réception des signes verbaux au cours des lésions temporales antéro-internes droite et gauche. *Neuropsychologia 5*:311–328.

Hécaen, H., Dubois, J., and Marcie, P. (1968). Les désorganisations de la réception des signes verbaux dans l'aphasie sensorielle. *Rev. d'Acoustique 1*:287–305.

Hécaen, H. and Marcie, P. (1967). L'agraphie au cours de l'aphasie de conduction. *Wiener Zeitschr. f. Nervenheilkunde 2–4*:193–203.

Hécaen, H. and Marcie, P. (1974). Disorders of written language following right hemisphere lesions: spatial dysgraphia, in *Hemisphere Function in the Human Brain*. S. J. Diamond and J. G. Beaumont (eds). London: P. Elek.

Heilman, K. M., Coyle, J. M., Gonyea, E. F., and Geschwind, N. (1973). Apraxia and Agraphia in a Left-hander. *Brain 96*:21–28.

Henschen, S. E. (1922). Klinische und pathologische Beiträge zur Pathologie des Gehirns. VII, Über motorische Aphasie und Agraphie. Stockholm: Nordiske Bokhandeln.

Hjelmslev, L. (1935). On the principles of phonematics. *Proceedings of the Second International Congress of Phonetic Sciences.*

Kinsbourne, M. and Rosenfield, D. B. (1974). Agraphia selective for written spelling. An experimental case study. *Brain and Language 1*:215–226.

Kleist, K. (1934). *Gehirnpathologie.* Leipzig: J. Barth.

Kussmaul, A. (1884). *Les Troubles de la Parole.* A. Rue (trans). Paris: J.–B. Baillière et Fils.

Leischner, A. (1957). *Die Störungen der Schriftsprache (Agraphie und Alexie).* Stuttgart: Georg Thieme Verlag.

Lhermitte, F. and Derouesne, J. (1974). Paraphasies et jargonaphasie dans le langage oral avec conservation du langage écrit. Genèse des néologismes. *Rev. Neurol. 130*:21–38.

Lichtheim, L. (1885). On aphasia. *Brain 7*:433–484.

Luria, A. R. (1966). *Higher Cortical Functions in Man.* London: Tavistock Publications.

Luria, A. R. (1969). *Traumatic Aphasias.* The Hague: Mouton.

Marcé (1856). Mémoire sur quelques observations de physiologie pathologique tendant à démontrer l'existence d'un principe coordinateur de l'écriture. *Compte-rendu de la Société de Biologie* (Paris) *3*:93–115.

Marie, P. (1897). L'évolution du langage considérée du point de vue de l'Aphasie. *La Presse Médicale 109*:397–399.

Marie, P. (1926). Révision de la question de l'aphasie (Semaine Médicale, 23 mai 1906), in *Travaux et Mémoires.* Paris: Masson *1*:3–30.

Mirallié, C. (1895). Sur le mécanisme de l'agraphie motrice corticale. *Bulletin de la Société de Biologie de Paris.*

Mirallié, C. (1896). *De l'aphasie Sensorielle.* Paris: G. Steinheil.

Monakow, C. von (1914). Die lokalisation, im *Grosshirn und der Abbau der Funktion durch Corticale Herde.* Wiesbaden: J. F. Bergmann.

Nielsen, J. M. (1947). *Agnosia, Apraxia, Aphasia: Their Value in Cerebral Localization.* New-York: Hoeber.

Ogle, J. W. (1867). Aphasia and agraphia. *Saint-George's Hospital Reports 2*:83–122.

Penfield, W. and Roberts, L. (1959). *Speech and Brain Mechanisms.* Princeton: Princeton University Press.

Pitres, A. (1884). Considération sur l'agraphie à propos d'une observation nouvelle d'agraphie motrice pure. *Revue de Médecine 4*:855–873.

Pitres, A. (1894). Rapport sur la question des agraphies. *Congrès Français de Médecine Interne, Bordeaux.*

Russell, R. and Espir, M. L. E. (1961). *Traumatic Aphasia.* Oxford: Oxford University Press.

Sasanuma, S. (1975). Kana and kanji processing in Japanese aphasics. *Brain and Language 2*:369–383.

Sasanuma, S. and Fujimura, O. (1972). An analysis of writing errors in Japanese aphasic patients: kanji versus kana words. *Cortex 8*:265–282.

Saussure, F. de (1972), *Cours de Linguistique Générale, réédition.* Paris: Payot.

Shankweiler, D. and Harris, K. S. (1966). An experimental approach to the articulation in aphasia. *Cortex* 2:277–292.

Uldall, A. J. (1944). Speech and writing. *Acta Linguistica* 4:11–26.

Vachek, J. (1973). *Written Language—General Problems and Problems of English.* The Hague: Mouton.

Weigl, E. (1974). Neuropsychological experiments on transcoding between spoken and written language. *Brain and Language* 1:227–240.

Weisenburg, T. and McBride, K. E. (1935). *Aphasia: A Clinical and Psychological Study.* New-York: Commonwealth Fund.

Wernicke, C. (1874). Der aphasische Symptomencomplex. Breslau: Cohn und Weigert.

Werknicke, C. (1903). Der aphasische Symptomencomplex. *Die Deutsche Klinik* 6:487–566.

Yamadori, A. and Ikumura, G. (1975). Central (or conduction) aphasia in a Japanese patient. *Cortex* 11:73–82.

5
The Acalculias
HARVEY S. LEVIN

HISTORICAL BACKGROUND AND CLASSIFICATION OF THE ACALCULIAS

Aphasiologists in the latter half of the nineteenth century recognized that their patients often suffered impaired ability to perform numerical operations and they interpreted this as an expression of a pervasive linguistic disorder. Henschen (1919) introduced the term *acalculia* to designate an acquired disorder of calculation which he distinguished from disturbance in reading and writing numbers, "cipher alexia" and "cipher agraphia," respectively. Upon reviewing 305 cases of calculation disturbance reported in the literature and 67 of his own patients, Henschen identified a subgroup of nonaphasic or mildly aphasic patients in whom calculation disorder was the predominant deficit. He inferred the existence of a cerebral substrate for arithmetic operations that is anatomically distinct from but proximal to the neural organization of speech and musical capacity.

Preparation of this manuscript was supported by USPHS Grant NS 07377–07, Center for the Study of Nervous System Injury.

The author is indebted to Professor A. L. Benton for providing valuable advice and reviewing the manuscript.

128

Hans Berger (1926) proposed the distinction between primary and secondary acalculia on the basis of his observations that certain abilities such as short-term memory and capacity for sustained attention are necessary to perform calculation problems. He concluded that primary acalculia cannot be attributed to a more pervasive impairment, though it may occur in association with other deficits which are not sufficiently severe to disrupt calculation. Secondary acalculia, as he defined it, is an expression of a severe general disturbance of memory, language, attention, or cognition. Berger reported that the secondary type is the more frequent of the acalculias, and is often among the neuropsychological defects found in patients with diffuse cerebral disease and in left-hemisphere-damaged patients with receptive aphasia. Mild word-finding difficulty and paraphasic errors were the principal concomitant neuropsychological symptoms in the patients Berger described as manifesting primary acalculia. More recently, Hécaen, Angelergues, and Houillier (1961) proposed a classification of acquired calculation disorder which is based upon the mechanisms presumed to be responsible for the acalculia. Although Hécaen et al. elucidated the neuropsychological deficits which frequently accompany but do not necessarily produce the various types of acalculia, it is important to recognize that there is considerable overlap with respect to the associated symptoms. Their classification includes:

1. Acalculia associated with alexia and agraphia for numbers which may or may not be accompanied by verbal alexia and agraphia or other aphasic defects.
2. Impaired spatial organization of numbers frequently reflected by misalignment of digits, visual neglect, inversion (e.g., 12 and 6), and reversal errors (e.g., 12 interpreted as 21), and inability to maintain the decimal place. Hécaen et al. designated this disorder as "acalculia of the spatial type."
3. Anarithmetria, i.e., impairment of calculation per se. Of the three types of acalculia, this category corresponds most closely to Berger's primary acalculia. The concept of anarithmetria does not imply an isolated deficit but requires that the acalculia not be a manifestation of alexia and agraphia for numbers or spatial disorganization.

Nonspecific acalculia contributing to the symptom complex of dementia and developmental disturbance of calculation are not encompassed by this scheme, nor is reduced rate of calculation as a
consequence of closed head trauma (Gronwall and Wrightson, 1974).

VARIETIES OF ACALCULIA

Alexia and/or Agraphia for Numbers

Although the acalculia arising from alexia and agraphia for numbers has been referred to as "aphasic acalculia" (Benson and Weir,
1972), Hécaen et al. (1961) found that an aphasic disorder was
neither a necessary nor sufficient condition for this type of acalculia.
The relationship between alexia for numbers and impaired reading
of words was systematically investigated by Henschen (1919) who
found a dissociation in more than 50% of his cases (Table 5-1). Hécaen et al. later confirmed this dissociation and observed a greater
frequency of number-specific alexia than in Henschen's material.
Table 5-1 shows that agraphia confined to words or numbers was
also common to both series of patients, though agraphia for numbers with preserved ability to write words was more frequent in
Henschen's study. The explanation for the disparity between the
Henschen and Hécaen findings remains unclear.

The chief neuropsychological correlates of alexia for numbers

TABLE 5-1   *The Relationship Between Alexia and Agraphia for Numbers
and Impaired Reading and Writing of Words*

TYPE OF DISORDER	HENSCHEN (1919) ($n = 132$)		HÉCAEN ET AL. (1961) ($n = 101$)	
	Number	*%*	*Number*	*%*
Verbal alexia	71	54	23	23
Number alexia	4	3	20	20
Mixed alexia	57	43	58	57
	($n=105$)		($n=108$)	
Verbal agraphia	33	31	24	22
Number agraphia	21	20	13	12
Mixed agraphia	51	49	71	66

($n = 63$) found by Hécaen et al. (1961) were aphasia (in 84% of the patients), verbal alexia (79%), ideational or ideomotor apraxia (36.5%), visuoconstructive deficit (68%), and general somatognosia (26%). The latter deficit refers to a basic impairment in appreciation of body schema. It should be noted that aphasia was not confined to the alexic type of acalculia. Visual-field and oculomotor defect and somatosensory impairment were frequent neurological abnormalities though these often accompanied all three types of acalculia. Hécaen et al. characterized the aphasic disorder associated with alexia for numbers as a general disturbance in verbal formulation though other authors have emphasized the receptive impairment in patients with acalculia (Head, 1926). Paraphasic or paragraphic substitution of numbers may contaminate the calculations by patients with fluent aphasia (Benson and Denckla, 1969) and obscure their relatively preserved capacity for arithmetic operations. Benson and Denckla described a patient with suspected left parietal disease who responded orally to the written problem "4 + 5" with the answer "8"; his written answer was 5, and he chose the correct answer when given a multiple-choice format. Clinicopathological correlation has established that either a lesion of the left hemisphere or bilateral cerebral disease is responsible for number alexia and agraphia (Hécaen, 1962).

The association between alexia/agraphia for numbers and left-hemisphere disease received ample confirmation in a study of patients manifesting this type of acalculia (Hécaen et al., 1961). In a subsequent study, Hécaen (1962) reported that in a series of unselected cases of left-hemisphere damage, 37% were alexic and agraphic for numbers as compared to 2% of patients with right-hemisphere disease. Figure alexia and aphasia were often found to co-exist in patients with bilateral cerebral disease. Acquired aphasia and acalculia were also closely associated in children with left-hemisphere damage (Hécaen, 1976). In a series of 17 left-hemisphere-damaged children of whom 15 were aphasic, 11 patients had a definite acalculia while equivocal acalculia was noted in 3 other aphasic children. Although Hécaen emphasized the persistence of acalculia in these children, he did not elaborate on its qualitative aspects. No child with right-hemisphere damage ($n = 6$) in Hécaen's study showed acalculia.

Acalculia of the Spatial Type

Manifestations of the "spatial" type of acalculia include improper arrangement of numbers during the initial stage of computation or while summing the partial products of multiplication. However, the principle of calculation is retained as reflected by the relatively preserved calculation of numbers presented orally (Benton, 1963, 1966). Of the 48 cases of spatial acalculia studied by Hécaen et al. (1961), visuoconstructive impairment was present in 94% of the patients, directional confusion in 78%, oculomotor disturbance in 70%, unilateral spatial agnosia in 69%, general spatial agnosia in 62.5%, reading deficit arising from spatial problems in 58%, general cognitive deterioration in 46%, apraxia for dressing in 41.5%, and visual-field defect in 56%. These correlates of the spatial type of acalculia were corroborated in a smaller series of patients described by Cohn (1961). Selecting patients with the spatial type of acalculia, Hécaen et al. implicated the role of right-hemisphere disease, since this disorder was shown to be rare in patients with lesions confined to the left hemisphere. Bilateral brain disease produced the spatial type of acalculia with a frequency comparable to that of right-hemisphere lesions.

Acalculia of the spatial type in a patient with bilateral encephalitic disease was extensively studied by Singer and Low (1933). Despite six months of remediation and generally well-preserved speech and reading, the patient was persistently agraphic for all written material and could not perform oral calculations other than addition of single-digit numbers and rote retrieval of multiplication-table values. Subtraction and division were totally impaired, as the patient failed to enter the digits in proper columnar arrangement. The authors analyzed the pattern of errors in this patient and inferred the presence of several mechanisms contributing to the acalculia:

1. Substitution of one operation for another, e.g., $2 + 3 = 6$, $4 + 2 = 8$. The converse error, i.e., substitution of addition for multiplication was also observed. Subtraction was spontaneously substituted for addition (e.g., $8 + 2 = 6$), whereas the patient could not perform substraction on request.

2. Substitution of counting for calculation as shown by $15 + 6 = 16$ and $4 + 7 = 8$.

3. Perseveration of the last digit presented, as in $5 \times 4 = 24$.

4. Giving a reversal of a presented number as an answer, e.g., $13 + 6 = 31$.

5. Impaired immediate retention of components of the problem was inferred when the patient failed to repeat it, i.e., "2 + 6" was reported as "2 × 6." Further testing indicated that defective repetition could not be attributed entirely to decreased digit span; the context of a calculation problem appeared to accentuate repetition errors. Memory for words exceeded that for numbers.

The patient of Singer and Low could count in forward sequence, whereas backward counting was defective. Counting objects arranged in equal groups (e.g., 5 groups of 4 pills) surpassed counting objects in a discontinuous series (e.g., groups of 3, 6, 6, and 5 pills of different color) where the sum exceeded 10 objects. However, the patient was unable to utilize multiplication (e.g., 5×4) instead of counting objects in the continuous series. Reading and writing figures were limited to two-digit numbers. Number concept was relatively preserved, i.e., the patient could correctly state which of two numbers was greater, 304 or 403. However, he could not integrate orally presented single digits (e.g., 1, 4, 3 into 143) because of spatial errors in "place value."

Anarithmetria

Hécaen's definition of anarithmetria excludes impairments in calculation secondary to alexia and agraphia for numbers or spatial disorganization of numbers. Anarithmetria is compatible, however, with other associated neuropsychological deficits which may directly affect calculation. Hécaen et al. (1961) studied 72 cases of anarithmetria and found a pattern similar to that of patients with acalculia secondary to alexia and agraphia for numbers. The correlates and the corresponding percent of patients affected were: aphasia (62.5%), visuoconstructive impairment (61%), general cognitive deterioration (50%), verbal alexia (39%), and directional confusion (37%). Deficits found on neurological examination included visual-field defect (54.5%), oculomotor disturbance (33%), and sensory impairment (37%). Left-sided lesions and bilateral brain disease predominated in the cases of anarithmetria; for every patient with a lesion confined to the minor hemisphere, there were four patients with unilateral left-hemisphere damage. This pattern of hemispheric involvement is compatible with the principal concomitant deficits found in patients with anarithmetria.

Consistent with the findings of Hécaen et al. demonstrating the presence of general cognitive deterioration in half of their patients with anarithmetria, Cohn (1961) and Grewel (1952) implicated the role of memory impairment in rendering patients unable to carry numbers or retrieve previously learned multiplication-table values. Although Benson and Weir (1972) considered the possibility that disruption of memory was responsible for the post-traumatic anarithmetria which they described in a case report, there was no quantitative assessment of memory other than digit span (which was intact). The patient of Benson and Weir was mildly alexic and agraphic for words, but neither numbers nor calculation symbols (e.g., "+") were affected. Conversational speech was nonaphasic, though naming of visually presented objects was hesitant. Counting both forward and backward was preserved as was counting in series (e.g., by 3's) and in discontinuous groups. Judgment of quantities was mildly impaired (e.g., "36 ft. in a yard"). Both oral and written presentation of computational problems disclosed preservation of addition and subtraction, but the patient was unable to perform multiplication or division regardless of the format used for presentation or the mode of response. Although the patient of Benson and Weir produced individual errors at various points of the multiplication process, the most impressive deficit was observed when he attempted to "carry over" from one column to the other in multidigit multiplication. This aspect of calculation was impaired despite intact spatial organization of the numbers in their appropriate columns. Neurological findings included a right homonymous visual-field cut confined to the temporal area; subtle sensory and motor deficits were present over the right extremities and face. Serial radioisotope brain scans indicated focal left-parietal brain damage.

LOCALIZATION OF LESION IN THE ACALCULIAS

Clinico-anatomical correlations by Henschen (1919) disclosed that acalculia associated with alexia and agraphia for numbers frequently accompanied global aphasia in patients with extensive left-hemisphere disease. Henschen implicated left angular gyrus lesions in patients with alexia and agraphia for numbers who were not globally aphasic. Consistent with the evidence for behavioral dissociation of alexia and agraphia for numbers as opposed to words, Hécaen et al. found that left parietal lesions predominated in the former while left temporal and occipital lesions were primarily involved in the latter. Of the patients with alexia and agraphia for numbers studied by Hécaen, bilateral parietal lobe disease was present nearly as often as lesions confined to the dominant hemisphere. Consequently, inability to read and/or write numbers that is not an artifact of presenting figures to the neglected visual field strongly suggests a left parietal lesion but does not exclude involvement of the right hemisphere. Although the localization of lesions in patients with anarithmetria resembles that of alexia and agraphia for numbers, an important distinction may be drawn. Parietal disease confined to the right hemisphere is a definite, albeit improbable, etiology of anarithmetria, whereas this circumstance is extremely unlikely to produce figure alexia or agraphia (Hécaen et al. 1961). Hécaen et al. found that focal temporal or occipital lesions of the dominant hemisphere were sufficient to cause anarithmetria, whereas this disorder was not present in patients with right-hemisphere disease unless the parietal lobe was involved.

The spatial type of acalculia suggests a post-Rolandic lesion of the right hemisphere but does not exclude the possibility of bilateral disease (Hécean et al., 1961). However, spatial acalculia in a patient without evidence of linguistic defect or general cognitive deterioration most likely indicates the presence of a lesion confined to the right hemisphere (Hécaen et al., 1961).

The aggregate of symptoms including agraphia for words, finger agnosia, and right–left disorientation in addition to acalculia was interpreted by Gerstmann (1940) as a syndrome characterized by disturbance of body schema arising from left parietal-lobe disease. The Gerstmann syndrome was subsequently recognized by neurologists as a clinical entity with localizing significance for the posterior parietal region of the dominant hemisphere. However, there has been no consensus with respect to the type of acalculia manifested by patients with the syndrome. Gerstmann (1940) claimed that anarithmetria was a component of the syndrome, whereas the spatial type of acalculia has been implicated by other authors (Critchley, 1953). The clinical features of patients with Gerstmann syndrome described by Kinsbourne and Warrington (1963) suggested that they include both patients with acalculia related to alexia and agraphia for numbers and patients with acalculia of the spatial type. That no specific form of acalculia appears to be consistently associated with the Gerstmann syndrome is understandable in view of systematic studies which have shown that the syndrome is part of a constellation of symptoms predominated by aphasia, impaired visuoconstructive capacity, and general cognitive deterioration (Benton, 1977). In view of the heterogeneity of the acalculias and the considerable overlap in their neuropsychological correlates, the designation of acalculia in general as a component of a syndrome related to a left parietal lesion must be viewed critically.

An implication of the foregoing localization studies for hemispheric functional asymmetry is that calculation is primarily subserved by the left hemisphere. This possibility was confirmed by Sperry (1968) who demonstrated in commissurotomized patients that computation of groups of pegs presented in sequence was far superior on the right hand as compared to the left hand. Calculation based on inputs to the left hand was limited to addition of sums less than five.

CLINICAL ASSESSMENT OF NUMBER OPERATIONS

The format for presentation of computational problems and mode of response used may determine whether acalculia is detected. Oral presentation may be expected to facilitate the performance of a patient with spatial acalculia, whereas utilization of a multiple-choice format would reduce the opportunity for paraphasic errors to contaminate the performance of an aphasic patient with intact computational skill. Benton (1963) found that noteworthy inferiority of written as compared to oral calculation occurred in 2% of non-brain-damaged patients with at least an eighth grade education; 4.5% of patients with left-hemisphere disease showed this discrepancy, whereas the pattern was observed in 21% of patients with right-hemisphere lesions.

Systematic comparison of oral and written modes of presentation and responding is afforded by the examination of number operations devised by Benton (1963) which consists of 12 brief tests:

1. Appreciation of number values when presented with a pair of numbers such as 23 or 31 and asked to state which is greater.
2. Appreciation of number values when presented visually and the response is either oral or pointing to the larger of the two numbers.
3. The patient is asked to read numbers aloud.
4. The patient is required to point to written numbers which are named by the examiner.
5. Writing numbers to dictation.
6. Writing numbers from copy.

The preliminary six tests serve to estimate the patient's comprehension of numbers when presented in auditory or visual form in order to evaluate the aphasic component in number operations. Two tests assess counting ability which is a prerequisite for arithmetic calculation:

7. The patient is required to count out loud from 1 to 20, from 20 to 1, and to count in 2's from 1 to 20.
8. The patient is required to estimate the number of items in a series of continuous dots and again in a discontinuous series of dots (e.g., four groups of five dots each arranged horizontally).

It is important to note on Test 8 whether the patient utilizes a multiplication strategy in the discontinuous series instead of counting all the dots. Errors on these tests may result from severe memory impairment or unilateral visual inattention in which the errors on Test 8 are lateralized to one side of the page.

9. Oral arithmetic calculation in which simple examples are given using each of the four basic operations.
10. Written arithmetic calculation in which the examples are similar to those given orally.
11. Arithmetic reasoning ability; the Arithmetic Reasoning subtest of the WAIS is given.
12. Immediate memory for calculation problems. (This test is a component of Test 9 and serves as a control to ascertain whether

a memory deficit is responsible for inability to perform calculation of problems given orally.)

Assessment of the aphasic component of acalculia is provided by
the tests which require the patient to read, aurally comprehend, and
write numbers. Spatial aspects of acalculia are reflected by reversals
in reading or pointing to numbers (e.g., "12" instead of "21"); columns of numbers are frequently misaligned. Numbers appearing in
an area of visual neglect may be omitted by the patient. Patients
with parietal disease may produce numbers which drift vertically
across the lines and they may have difficulty in writing the digits. A
suggested modification of Tests 9 and 10 is providing the patient
with a multiple-choice format for half of the questions in each test.

Individually administered tests of achievement in mathematics,
which have been standardized in children and adolescents according
to age and grade, are available. The Wide Range Achievement Test
or WRAT (Jastak and Jastak, 1946) and the Peabody Individual
Achievement Test or PIAT (Dunn and Markwardt, 1970) are useful
if the pattern of errors is examined qualitatively for indications of
a particular type of acalculia. The WRAT includes preliminary
questions which assess counting, number concept, and written calculation problems ranging in difficulty from simple addition to
college-level mathematics. In contrast, the PIAT utilizes a multiple-
choice format to evaluate number concept, counting (e.g., "point to
the number which comes just before 100"), and number operations
presented in an admixture of verbal problems and examples using
numbers. Problems on the PIAT appear in large print and may be
presented concurrently in both written and oral modalities. Although the PIAT is less likely to reflect paraphasic errors, it is important to consider any systematic neglect of answers given in one
or the other visual half-field and to concurrently obtain oral responses from nonaphasic patients. Administration of either the
WRAT or PIAT permits direct comparison of arithmetic calculation with proficiency in reading and spelling.

SUMMARY

Acquired disorders of calculation may be divided into three categories—acalculia secondary to alexia and agraphia for numbers,

acalculia resulting from spatial disorganization of numbers, and anarithmetria or impaired calculation in the strict sense. Review of the literature provides empirical confirmation of the dissociation between alexia for words as compared to numbers and shows that the three types of acalculia are often associated with distinct patterns of cerebral lesions. Further study of anarithmetria is necessary to elucidate its mechanisms and regional localization. Innovative methodologies are needed to investigate hemispheric dominance for calculation in normal persons.

References

Benson, D. F. and Denckla, M. B. (1969). Verbal paraphasia as a source of calculation disturbance. *Arch. Neurol. 21*:96–102.

Benson, D. F. and Weir, W. F. (1972). Acalculia: acquired anarithmetria *Cortex 8*:465–472.

Benton, A. L. (1963). *Assessment of Number Operations.* Iowa City: University of Iowa Hospitals, Department of Neurology.

Benton, A. L. (1966). *Problemi di Neuropsicologia.* Firenze: Editrice Universitaria.

Benton, A. L. (1977). Reflections on the Gerstmann syndrome. *Brain and Language 4*:45–62.

Benton, A. L. and Fogel, M. L. (1962). Three-dimensional constructional praxis: a clinical test. *Arch. Neurol. 7*:347.

Berger, H. (1926). Ueber rechenstorungen bei herderkrankungen des Grosshirns. *Arch. f. Psychiat. 78*:238–263.

Cohn, R. (1961). Dyscalculia. *Arch. Neurol. 4*:301–307.

Critchley, M. (1953). *The Parietal Lobes.* London: Arnold.

Dunn, L. M. and Markwardt, F. C. (1970). *Manual for the Peabody Individual Achievement Test,* Circle Pines, Minnesota: American Guidance Service.

Gerstmann, J. (1940). Syndrome of finger agnosia, disorientation for right and left, agraphia and acalculia. *Arch. Neurol. Psychiat. 44*:398–408.

Grewel, F. (1952). Acalculia. *Brain 75*:397–407.

Gronwall, D. and Wrightson, P. (1974). Delayed recovery of intellectual function after minor head injury. *Lancet 2*:7881, 606–609.

Head, H. (1926). *Aphasia and the Kindred Disorders of Speech.* Cambridge: Cambridge University Press.

Hécaen, H. (1962). Clinical symptomatology in right and left hemispheric lesions, in *Interhemispheric relations and cerebral dominance,* V. B. Mountcastle (ed). Baltimore: The Johns Hopkins Press.

Hécaen, H. (1976). Acquired aphasia in children and the ontogenesis of hemispheric functional specialization. *Brain and Language 3*:114–134.

Hécaen, H., Angelergues, R., and Houillier, S. (1961). Les variétés cliniques des acalculies au cours des lésions rétrorolandiques: approche statistique du problème. *Rev. Neurol. 105*:85–103.

Henschen, S. E. (1925). Clinical and anatomical contributions on brain pathology, in *Arch. Neurol. Psychiat.* W. F. Schaller (trans). *13*:226–249. (originally published, 1919).

Jastak, J. F. and Jastak, S. R. (1965). *Manual for the Wide Range Achievement Test.* Wilmington. Delaware: Guidance Associates of Delaware.

Kinsbourne, M. and Warrington, E. K. (1963). The developmental Gerstmann syndrome. *Arch. Neurol. 8*:490–501.

Singer, H. D. and Low, A. A. (1933). Acalculia. *Arch. Neurol. Psychiat. 29*: 467–498.

Sperry, R. W. (1968). Mental unity following surgical disconnection of the cerebral hemispheres. *The Harvey Lecture Series 62*:293–323.

6

Body Schema Disturbances: Finger Agnosia and Right-Left Disorientation

ARTHUR BENTON

INTRODUCTION

The behavioral deficits discussed in this chapter are conventionally classified as disorders of the "body schema" (or "body image"). This concept arose out of diverse neurological and psychiatric observations that seemed to be most readily explained by hypothesizing the existence of a longstanding spatially organized model of one's body that provided a framework within which perceptual, motor, and judgmental reactions directed toward one's body occur. The phantom-limb phenomenon, for example, was interpreted as reflecting the determining influence of the amputee's schema of an intact body on his perceptual responses. Conversely, impairment of the body schema resulting from brain disease was hypothesized by Pick (1908) to explain the gross errors made by some patients in pointing to parts of their body on verbal command (termed *autotopagnosia*). Head (1920) explained normal and defective somatosensory localization on the basis of organized representational models of one's body which he called "schemata."

Such schemata modify the impressions produced by incoming sensory impulses in such a way that the final sensations of position, or of locality, rise into consciousness charged with a relation to something that has happened before. Destruction of such "schemata" by a lesion of the cortex renders impossible all recognition of posture or of the locality of a stimulated spot in the affected part of the body. (Head, 1920, pp. 607–8)

Head postulated the existence of a number of different types of schemata, the main ones being (1) postural schemata that underlie position sense and appreciation of the direction of movement and (2) body surface schemata that furnished the background for tactile point localization and two-point discrimination.

The "body schema" has never been defined in a standard way; each author presents his own view of what he means by it. To some the concept represents the conscious awareness of the body but to others it is a form of unconscious memory or representation. To some authors (Pick, for example) it was essentially a visual representation, but Head thought primarily in terms of a constantly changing somatosensory organization against which the character of current stimulation was judged.

Nor is it clear that this vague concept possesses any real explanatory value. Decades ago Oldfield and Zangwill (1942–3) discussed the many points that were ambiguous and obscure in Head's formulation. Subsequently, the topic was critically evaluated by Benton (1959) and Poeck (1965, 1969; Poeck & Orgass, 1967) with the conclusion that the "body schema" is merely a label for perceptual and localizing responses related to one's body.

However, it is a convenient label. Dissociation in level of performance with respect to one's body as compared to objects in external space is often observed. For example, many patients with visuospatial defects, such as inaccurate object localization, show intact capacity to localize the parts of their own body, including the fingers. Similarly, most patients with impaired right–left discrimination or finger localization show intact orientation to objects in external space. Thus a distinction between performances relating to the body and those relating to external space is justified.

FINGER AGNOSIA

This term was coined by Gerstmann (1924) to denote impairment in the ability to identify the fingers of either one's own hand or those of another person. He regarded the disability as the behavioral expression of a partial dissolution of the body schema and he made it the core symptom in the aggregate of deficits (finger agnosia, agraphia, acalculia, right–left disorientation) that has come to be known as the Gerstmann syndrome.

There is ample evidence that finger agnosia is not a unitary disability but rather a collective term for diverse types of defective performance relating to identification of the fingers (cf. Schilder, 1931; Benton, 1959; Ettlinger, 1963; Critchley, 1966). These performances can be classified along a number of dimensions, e.g., whether the stimulus to be responded to is verbal, visual, or tactile, whether the required response is verbal or nonverbal, whether the task involves localizing fingers on one's own hand or their representation on a two-dimensional model of the hand. It is also important to differentiate between bilateral and unilateral disturbances of finger recognition. Gerstmann meant by "finger agnosia" an impairment in finger identification on both hands. However, defective localization of tactile stimulation of the fingers of one hand in association with other types of somatosensory impairment in that hand is a recognized sign of unilateral brain disease (cf. Head, 1920; Gainotti & Tiacci, 1973).

Developmental Aspects

The development of finger recognition in preschool children has been studied in detail by Lefford, Birch, and Green (1974) who demonstrated that performance level was a function of the stimulus characteristics and response requirements of the specific tasks that were presented and that, within the age range of three to five years, performance on each task showed a regular developmental course.

The easiest task was pointing to fingers that the examiner touched as the child watched him: 73% of the three-year-old children, 93% of the four-year-olds, and 99% of the five-year-olds showed successful performance. Localizing fingers which the examiner pointed to (but did not touch) was about as easy (63, 98, and 99% success at three, four, and five years, respectively). But purely tactile recognition (i.e., identifying touched fingers without the aid of vision) was more difficult for the children (24, 63, and 72% success at three, four, and five years, respectively). Still more difficult was tactile localization of touched fingers on a schematic representation of the hand instead of the child's own hand (Fig. 6-1). Only 11% of the

Fig. 6-1 Arrangement for tactile localization of fingers on a schematic representation of the hand.

three-year-old children, 28% of the four-year-olds, and 52% of the five-year-olds succeeded on this task.

Lefford, Birch, and Green analyzed the performances of the children in terms of intrasensory differentiation (tactile-visual localization), intersensory integration (tactile localization), and the capacity for representational thinking (localization on a model). Their findings made it evident that different tasks present different age-related cognitive demands.

The normative observations of Benton (1955, 1959) on school children may be viewed as an extension of those of Lefford, Birch, and Green.

Three tasks were presented to children in the age range of six to nine: (1) with the hand visible, identification of single fingers touched by the examiner; (2) with the hand hidden from view, identification of single fingers touched by the examiner; (3) with the hand hidden from view, identification of pairs of fingers simultaneously touched by the examiner. In the purely tactile tasks, an outline drawing of the right or left hand, with the thumb and fingers numbered from 1 to 5, was placed before the child who could identify the stimulated finger or fingers by naming them, pointing to them or calling out their number (Fig. 6-1).

Virtually all six-year-olds performed adequately on the tactile-visual task. The other two types of finger localization involving identification of touched fingers on a model showed a progressive development with age. The more difficult task was, of course, the identification of simultaneously stimulated pairs of fingers, a task which a substantial proportion of nine-year-old children performed inaccurately. The studies of Wake (cf. Benton, 1959) extended these normative observations with the finding that at the age of 12 years the tactile localization of simultaneously stimulated pairs of fingers had not yet reached the level of performance of adults.

Clearly there are aspects of finger recognition that call on cognitive skills which reach maturity only after the age of 12 years. One of these skills appears to be visuospatial representational thinking, as reflected in making localizations on an external schematic model in place of one's own hand. There are also indications that the verbal encoding of sensory information may play a significant role in the performances of young school children (cf. Stone and Robinson, 1968; Lindgren, 1978).

Behavioral correlates

Since different tasks having to do with the identification of the fingers make demands on different cognitive capacities, it is evident that there is no such entity as a unitary "finger agnosia." Consequently, in discussing the clinical or pathological correlates of impairment in finger recognition, it is necessary to specify the particular tasks employed to assess the capacity.

Utilizing a nonverbal task in which mentally retarded subjects identified touched fingers (with their hand hidden from view) by pointing to them with the contralateral hand, Matthews, Folk, and Zerfas (1966) found a closer association between performance level and Wechsler-Bellevue Performance Scale IQ than Verbal Scale IQ.

This relationship was confirmed in patients with brain disease by Poeck and Orgass (1969) who assessed diverse aspects of finger recognition with verbal and nonverbal tests. The correlation coefficient of nonverbal tactile localization on a schematic model with the WAIS Performance Scale IQ was .53 while the corresponding correlation coefficient for the WAIS Verbal Scale IQ was .34. On the other hand, performance on verbal tests of finger recognition (identification on verbal command, visual naming, tactile naming) correlated somewhat more closely with the WAIS Verbal Scale IQ (mean $r = .58$) than with the WAIS Performance Scale IQ (mean $r = .52$). Poeck and Orgass found further that the verbal tests of finger recognition formed a highly intercorrelated cluster (mean $r = .72$) while nonverbal test performance showed a more modest association with these verbal tests (mean $r = .47$).

Poeck and Orgass also assessed the relationship between finger recognition performance and scores on other verbal (rote memory, Token Test) and nonverbal (recognition memory for designs) tests. The mean correlation coefficient between verbal finger recognition and the verbal tests was .48, while the correlation coefficient between verbal finger recognition and the nonverbal test was .36. Nonverbal finger recognition did not show this differential relationship with verbal and nonverbal abilities, the correlation coefficient with the verbal tests being .31 and that with the visual memory test being .32.

Studying nine patients with impairment in finger recognition as assessed by nonverbal tests, Kinsbourne and Warrington (1962) found that every patient showed some degree of visuoconstructive disability. Only two patients in the group were clinically aphasic. However, eight of the nine patients were judged to show mild to severe general mental impairment.

Thus the available correlational data indicate that it is useful to distinguish between defects in finger recognition elicited by tasks requiring naming of fingers or their identification when the name is given and those elicited by tasks requiring manual localization of fingers subjected to sensory stimulation. Both types of disability show a significant association with both linguistic and visuoperceptive impairment. But the verbal disability is somewhat more closely correlated with linguistic impairment and the nonverbal disability is somewhat more closely correlated with visuoperceptive impairment.

Anatomical correlates

When Gerstmann first described finger agnosia, he placed the causative lesion for the disability at the parieto-occipital junction around the angular gyrus of the left hemisphere. It was in this area that visual and somatosensory information was integrated to provide the basis for an intact and well-integrated body image. Subsequent study indicated that this localization was much more precise than was warranted by the facts, finger agnosia, in one form or another, being encountered in cases of lesions in the temporal and frontal lobes as well as in the posterior parietal area. At the same time, Gerstmann's localization of the responsible lesion in the left hemisphere was generally supported. For example, studying diverse performances in patients with unilateral brain disease, Hécaen (1962) found that finger agnosia was shown by 20% of patients with left-hemisphere lesions, but by only 3% of those with right-hemisphere lesions.

However, more recent investigative work has cast considerable doubt on the assumption of a specific correlation between the disability and left-hemisphere disease. The association of finger agnosia with side-of-lesion seems to be dependent, first, on whether the disability is manifested in verbal or nonverbal form and, second, on the presence or absence of aphasia and general mental impairment. The findings of two studies which explored these relationships in detail will be described.

Sauguet, Benton, and Hécaen (1971) assessed both verbal and nonverbal finger recognition in patients with unilateral brain disease. The three verbal tests were naming the fingers, pointing to fingers named by the examiner, and pointing to fingers which the examiner had designated by number. The two nonverbal tests were indicating the fingers touched by the examiner and the interdigital object identification test of Kinsbourne and Warrington (1962). Three groups of right-handed patients were studied: nonaphasic with right-hemisphere lesions; nonaphasic (or only expressive speech disorder without oral comprehension difficulties) with left-hemisphere lesions, aphasic (with oral comprehension difficulties) with left-hemisphere lesions. Of an original sample of 94 patients, 14 (15%) were excluded from consideration either because they appeared confused or they showed clinical and/or psychometric evidence of significant general mental impairment.

The results of the study may be summarized as follows: (1) naming of the fingers and their identification by name were closely associated with receptive aphasic disorder; about two-thirds of the patients with receptive language impairment showed defective verbal finger recognition, as compared to about 10% of patients in the other groups; (2) impaired performance on nonverbal tests of finger recognition was shown only by patients with receptive aphasic disorder, the frequency of failure ranging from 20% to 30%. Thus the predominant influence of linguistic impairment on performance in patients who are free from general mental impairment was evident.

Gainotti, Cianchetti, and Tiacci (1972) studied nonverbal finger recognition in right-handed patients with unilateral brain disease. The relative frequency of bilateral impairment was about equal in the patients with left-hemisphere (18%) and right-hemisphere (16%) lesions. Further analysis showed that most of the left-hemisphere patients who performed defectively were aphasic and that the right-hemisphere patients who performed defectively showed clinical and/or psychometric evidence of general mental impairment (Table 6-1).

A number of conclusions emerge when the findings of these two studies are considered together. Impairment in finger recognition is

TABLE 6-1   *Finger Agnosia in Patients with Unilateral Lesions**

Left-Hemisphere Lesions (N = 88)	*16 (18%)*
Mentally deteriorated (N = 30)	10 (33%)
Not mentally deteriorated (N = 58)	6 (10%)
Aphasic (N = 34)	13 (38%)
Not aphasic (N = 54)	3 (6%)
Right-Hemisphere Lesions (N = 74)	*12 (16%)*
Mentally deteriorated (N = 22)	10 (45%)
Not mentally deteriorated (N = 52)	2 (4%)

* Adapted from Gainotti, Cianchetti, and Tiacci (1972).

closely associated with aphasic disorder or general mental impairment in patients with left-hemisphere disease. Impairment in finger recognition is closely associated with general mental impairment in patients with right-hemisphere disease. Since patients with general mental impairment were excluded from consideration in the study of Sauguet, Benton, and Hécaen, this relationship was not evident in that study but it is quite clear in the results of Gainotti, Cianchetti, and Tiacci. Finally, neither aphasic disorder nor general mental impairment can be considered to be solely responsible for the occurrence of impairment in finger recognition. Many aphasic patients showed intact finger recognition, even on the task of finger naming, as did many mentally deteriorated patients.

Summary
Thus it appears that, imbedded as it is within a setting of either aphasic disorder or general mental impairment, finger agnosia does not represent a specific cognitive deficit or have a specific localizing significance. The question remains as to why some aphasic and mentally impaired patients show the disability in one or another form and others do not. One proposed explanation is that somatosensory defect, interacting with aphasic or mental impairment, plays a role in the production of the disability (cf. Benton, 1959; Selecki and Herron, 1965; Gainotti, Cianchetti and Tiacci, 1972). This possibility deserves to be explored.

RIGHT–LEFT DISORIENTATION

Inability to identify the right and left sides of one's body or that of the confronting examiner is a familiar symptom to neurologists. First described as one aspect of the picture of general mental impairment associated with diffuse disease, the disability attracted greater interest from a diagnostic and theoretical standpoint when Head (1926), Bonhoeffer (1923), and Gerstmann (1924, 1930) showed that it could also occur as a consequence of disease of the left hemisphere.

"Right-left disorientation" is a very broad concept, even broader than "finger agnosia." It refers not to one ability, but to a number of performances on different levels of complexity, each making demands on different cognitive abilities and types of response. Naming, executing movements to verbal command, or imitation of movements may be called for. The execution of commands involving the identification of a single lateral body part or of commands involving the identification of more than one lateral body part may be required. The patient may be requested to identify his own body parts, those of the confronting examiner, or a combination of the two. Hence, meaningful assessment of "right–left orientation" requires that it be analyzed into operationally defined components or levels.

An example of such an analysis is presented in Table 6-2. Some of the types of performance listed in the table stand in a rather definite

TABLE 6-2   *Components of Right–Left Orientation*

I. ORIENTATION TOWARD ONE'S OWN BODY
   A. Naming single lateral body parts touched by examiner
   B. Pointing to single lateral body parts on verbal command
   C. Executing double *uncrossed* movements on verbal command (e.g., touching *left* ear with *left* hand)
   D. Executing double *crossed* movements on verbal command (e.g., touching *right* ear with *left* hand)

II. ORIENTATION TOWARD ONE'S OWN BODY WITHOUT VISUAL GUIDANCE (BLINDFOLDED OR EYES CLOSED)
   A. Naming single lateral body parts touched by examiner
   B. Pointing to single lateral body parts on verbal command
   C. Executing double *uncrossed* movements on verbal command (e.g., touching *left* ear with *left* hand)
   D. Executing double *crossed* movements on verbal command (e.g., touching *right* ear with *left* hand)

III. ORIENTATION TOWARD CONFRONTING EXAMINER OR PICTURE
   A. Naming single lateral body parts
   B. Pointing to single lateral body parts on verbal command
   C. Imitating uncrossed movements of examiner (e.g., *left* hand on *left* ear)
   D. Imitating crossed movements of examiner (e.g., *left* hand on *right* ear)

IV. COMBINED ORIENTATION TOWARD ONE'S OWN BODY AND CONFRONTING PERSON
   A. Placing either left or right hand on specified part of confronting person on verbal command (e.g., placing right hand on confronting person's left ear)

---

hierarchical relationship to each other. The ability to point to single lateral body parts (IB) is prerequisite for success in the execution of double commands (IC, D) and in pointing to parts of the confronting examiner (IIIB). The ability to execute double uncrossed commands (IC) is prerequisite for success on crossed commands (ID). The ability to point correctly to the body parts of the confronting examiner (IIIB) is prerequisite for successful combined orientation performance (IVA). Other performances are qualitatively different from each other and patients may show dissociation, failing in naming but not in pointing or imitation or vice versa (cf. Sauguet, Benton, and Hécaen, 1971; Dennis, 1976).

Developmental Aspects

Many five-year-old children and the majority of six-year-olds are able to identify single lateral parts of their body in terms of "right" and "left," (Terman, 1916; Benton, 1959; Belmont and Birch, 1963). However, they are likely to make errors in the execution of double commands, particularly "crossed" commands. In the latter instance, failure to cross the midline is the most frequent type of error (e.g., the child touches his left ear with his left hand in response to the command to touch his right ear with his left hand). Some children perform decidedly less well with their eyes closed than with their eyes open. Most of them fail to make the necessary 180 degrees reversal in orientation in pointing to lateral body parts of the confronting examiner.

The ability to execute double commands develops rapidly after the age of six years and it is unusual to encounter a nine-year-old who has difficulty in executing these commands. The difference in level of performance under the "eyes open" and "eyes closed" conditions also disappears with advancing age. However, some nine-year-old children evidently are not aware of the relativistic nature of the right–left concept for they fail to make the necessary 180 degrees reorientation in pointing to the lateral body parts of the confronting examiner. Moreover, a majority of them still make errors in executing tasks involving both the "own body" and "confronting persons" systems of orientation, i.e., placing their right (or left) hand on a specified lateral body part of the confronting examiner (cf. Benton and Kemble, 1960). By the age of 12 years, practically all normal children perform successfully in identifying body parts of the confronting examiner and in combined orientation tasks.

Occasionally a child who shows a *systematic reversal* in response to instructions will be encountered. Such a child will show his left hand when asked to show his right hand and touch his right ear with his left hand when asked to touch his left ear with his right hand. The consistency of his responses indicates that the child is quite capable of discriminating between the two sides of his body. At the same time, it is clear that he has attached the wrong verbal labels to the two sides. Not surprisingly, many of these children prove to be relatively deficient in the development of language skills (Benton, 1958; Benton and Kemble, 1960).

Basis of Right–Left Orientation

When one considers the nature of these right–left discrimination tasks, it is evident that they make demands on a number of cognitive abilities. There is a verbal element in performance since the child must understand the verbal labels of "right" and "left" before he can apply them to the sides of his body and he must retain these labels in mind long enough to execute double commands. Of course, right–left orientation can be assessed by nonverbal performances, such as imitation tasks, as well as verbal performance.

[Another form of nonverbal "right–left orientation" is operationally expressed in the localization of stimulation to the right or left side of the body. Disturbances in this capacity, particularly lateral mislocalization of tactile stimulation (allesthesia, allochiria), have been described and a variety of explanations have been proposed to account for them (cf. Bender, 1952; Benton, 1959). However, the relationship between these disturbances and right–left disorientation, as conventionally defined, is a tenuous one. It is true that a few brain-diseased or hysterical patients who showed both types of impairment have been described (Jones, 1907; Seidemann, 1932; Bender, 1952; Hécaen & Ajuriaguerra, 1952). But most patients who show right–left disorientation do not show allesthesia; conversely, allesthesia, particularly when it appears in the context of spinal cord or brainstem disease, is not accompanied by right–left disorientation.]

A second component is sensory in nature. The labels of "right" and "left" are applied (or misapplied, as in systematic reversal) to a distinction between the sides of the body which necessarily involves a sensory discrimination. The basis for this distinction is not immediately obvious. The supposition is that it is primarily of a somesthetic nature, consisting of a continuous asymmetric pattern of sensory excitation from the muscles and joints of the two sides of the body (Benton, 1959; Benton and Kemble, 1960). Presumably this difference in excitation between the two sides of the body provides a *right–left gradient* of excitation which forms the basis for the intuitive awareness of a difference between the sides which most (but not all) normal persons possess. This awareness is often verbalized in terms of the right side being felt as larger, heavier, and stronger than the left.

When this gradient develops in young children is not known. It is probably related to some degree to the establishment of unilateral manual preference (cf. Elze, 1924; Benton and Menefee, 1957). However, there are normal right-handed adults who admit having difficulty in the immediate discrimination between right and left and who report a lack of any intuitive feeling of a difference between the two sides of the body. The study of Wolf (1973), in which physicians and their spouses were asked how often they experienced difficulty when they had to identify right and left quickly, provides data on sex differences in "right–left blindness," as Elze (1924) called it. Two percent of the men and 5% of the women reported that they experienced such difficulty "all the time." Another 7% of the men and 13% of the women reported "frequent" difficulty.

A third component is of a conceptual nature. Correct identification of the lateral body parts of a confronting person and simultaneous manipulation of the "own body" and "confronting person" orientational systems requires thorough understanding of the relativistic nature of the right–left concept.

Finally, a fourth element is the visuospatial component which is brought into play when pointing to lateral body parts of a confronting person or to objects on the left or right. Some of the more complex tests of right–left orientation, such as the "Hands" test of Thurstone (1938), the "Pictorial Hands" test of Kao and Li (1929) and the "Road Map" test of Money (1965) make strong demands on visuospatial abilities.

Impairment in Patients with Brain Disease

Apart from the earliest observations of defective performance in demented patients, right–left disorientation has been traditionally associated with the presence of disease of the left hemisphere and
aphasic disorders. A particularly important early contribution was
that of Bonhoeffer (1923) who described a patient with a left temporoparietal lesion who showed marked right–left disorientation.
He was aphasic and showed some impairment in oral language understanding, but his disability in right–left performances was dis-
proportionally severe. However, he also showed a variety of somesthetic disturbances in the right arm and hand—impaired tactile
localization, position sense, stereognosis, barognosis, and graphes-
thesis—raising the question of whether his right–left disorientation
might be the product of an interaction between his sensory and
linguistic impairments.

Head (1926) found that defective performance was so frequent in
his aphasic patients that he incorporated both verbal and nonverbal
tests of right–left orientation as measures of "symbolic formulation
and expression" in his assessment battery. Later confirmation of the
association between left-hemisphere disease and right–left disorientation is found in the observations of Gerstmann (1930) and McFie
and Zangwill (1960). Gerstmann related the disability (along with
finger agnosia) to dysfunction of the left parieto-occipital region.
McFie and Zangwill found defective right–left orientation in five of
eight patients with left-hemisphere lesions; in contrast, not a single
patient in the group of 21 with right-hemisphere lesions showed the
disability.

Sauguet, Benton, and Hécaen (1971) investigated the relationship
of various forms of right–left disorientation to side-of-lesion and
the presence of aphasic disorder in patients with unilateral lesions.
The major findings were: (1) With respect to orientation to their
own body, nonaphasic patients with lesions in either hemisphere
performed adequately while two-thirds of those patients with left-
hemisphere disease who had impaired language understanding performed defectively, primarily in the execution of double commands.
(2) Identification of single body parts of the confronting examiner
was performed defectively by about 50% of the patients with left-

hemisphere disease who had impaired language understanding but also by 13% of the nonaphasic patients with right-hemisphere disease; all nonaphasic patients with left-hemisphere disease performed adequately. (3) The imitation of lateral movements (the head-eye-ear items of Hand's battery) was performed defectively by aphasic patients with left-hemisphere disease (48%) and by nonaphasic patients with right-hemisphere disease (32%); 14% of the nonaphasic patients with left-hemisphere disease also performed defectively.

Thus the findings indicated that the hemispheric contribution to right–left orientation depends upon what aspect of it is assessed. Impairment in "own body" performances is shown by aphasic patients with left-hemisphere disease, but is rarely seen in nonaphasic patients. On the other hand, nonaphasic patients with right-hemisphere lesions, as well as aphasic patients, may show defects both in "confronting person" performances and in imitating right–left movements.

"Right-left disorientation" in patients with the syndrome of lateral neglect also needs to be considered. Many of these patients show a unilateral disability, so to speak, in that they will consistently fail to point to body parts on the neglected side or to point to parts of the confronting examiner corresponding spatially to the neglected side of their body (see Chapter 10).

Concluding comments

It is clear that, in general, right–left disorientation is closely connected with impairment of language comprehension in patients with unilateral brain disease. This holds for nonverbal performances, such as imitation, as well as for performances that clearly demand understanding of the labels "right" and "left." Thus it appears that Head (1926) was correct in his assumption that even the imitation of lateralized movements involves verbal mediation.

It is equally clear that some forms of right–left disorientation are associated with the presence of right-hemisphere disease. The tasks on which these patients fail are the identification of the body parts of a confronting person and the imitation of lateralized movements. It seems likely that visuospatial disability is the essential basis for failing performance in these nonaphasic patients. This is best regarded as a hypothesis for empirical test.

With the exception of the most severe dements, nonaphasic patients with general mental impairment typically perform adequately when identifying their own body parts but fail on "confronting person" and "combined orientation" tasks. Here one suspects that the conceptual demands of these tasks, rather than the linguistic or visuospatial, pose particular difficulties for the patient.

There remains the question of why some aphasic patients show failure on relatively simple right–left orientation tasks while others with equally severe linguistic defects do not. As Bonhoeffer (1923) intimated and as Benton (1959) and Selecki and Herron (1965) have proposed, the observed failure perhaps reflects the outcome of aphasic disorder combined with sensory disturbances, the latter having the effect of attenuating the asymmetric pattern of somesthetic excitation that underlies the discrimination of right and left.

References

Belmont, L. and Birch, H. G. (1963). Lateral dominance and right-left awareness in normal children. *Child. Dev. 34*:257–270.

Bender, M. B. (1952). *Disorders in Perception*. Springfield, Ill.: C. C. Thomas.

Benton, A. L. (1955). Development of finger-localization capacity in school children. *Child Dev. 26*:225–230.

Benton, A. L. (1958). Significance of systematic reversal in right-left discrimination. *Acta Psychiat. Neurol. Scandinav. 33*:129–137.

Benton, A. L. (1959). *Right-Left Discrimination and Finger Localization: Development and Pathology*. New York: Hoeber-Harper.

Benton, A. L. and Kemble, J. D. (1960). Right-left orientation and reading ability. *Psychiat. Neurol. (Basel) 139*:49–60.

Benton, A. L. and Menefee, F. L. (1957). Handedness and right-left discrimination. *Child Dev. 28*:237–242.

Bonhoeffer, K. (1923). Zur Klinik und Lokalization des Agrammatismus und der Rechts-links-desorientierung. *Monatsschr. f. Psychiat. u. Neurol. 54*:11–42.

Critchley, M. (1966). The enigma of Gerstmann's syndrome. *Brain 89*: 183–198.

Dennis, M. (1976). Dissociated naming and locating of body parts after left temporal lobe resection. *Brain and Language 3*:147–163.

Elze, C. (1924). Rechtslinksempfinden und Rechtslinksblindheit. *Zeitschrift für angewandte Psychologie 24*:129–135.

Ettlinger, G. (1963). Defective identification of fingers. *Neuropsychologia 1*:39–45.

Gainotti, G., Cianchetti, C., and Tiacci, C. (1972). The influence of hemispheric side of lesion on nonverbal tests of finger localization. *Cortex* 8:364–381.

Gainotti, G. and Tiacci, C. (1973). The unilateral forms of finger agnosia. *Confinia Neurologica* 35:271–284.

Gerstmann, J. (1924). Fingeragnosie: eine umschriebene Störung der Orientierung am eigenen Körper. *Wiener Klinische Wochenschrift 37*: 1010–1012.

Gerstmann, J. (1930). Zur Symptomatologie der Hirnläsionen im Uebergangsgebiet der unteren parietal-und mittleren Occipitalwindung. *Nervenarzt 3*:691–695.

Head, H. (1920). *Studies in Neurology*. London: Oxford University Press.

Head, H. (1926). *Aphasia and Kindred Disorders of Speech*. Cambridge, England: Cambridge Univ. Press.

Hécaen, H. (1962). Clinical symptomatology in right and left hemispheric lesions, in *Interhemispheric Relations and Cerebral Dominance*, V. B. Mountcastle (ed). Baltimore: Johns Hopkins Press.

Hécaen, H. and de Ajuriaguerra, J. (1952). *Méconnaissances et Hallucinations Corporelles*. Paris: Masson.

Jones, E. (1907). The precise diagnostic value of allochiria. *Brain 30*:490–532.

Kao, C. C. and Li, M. Y. (1939). Tests of finger orientation: methods for testing right-left differentiation and finger-identification, in *Neuropsychiatry in China*, R. S. Lyman (ed). Peking: Henri Vetch.

Kinsbourne, M. and Warrington, E. K. (1962). A study of finger agnosia. *Brain 85*:47–66.

Lefford, A., Birch, H. G., and Green, G. (1974). The perceptual and cognitive bases for finger localization and selective finger movement in preschool children. *Child Dev. 45*:335–343.

Lindgren, S. (1978). Finger localization and the prediction of reading disability. *Cortex 14*:87–101.

Matthews, C. G., Folk, E. G., and Zerfas, P. G. (1966). Lateralized finger localization deficits and differential Wechsler-Bellevue results in retardates. *Am. J. Mental Deficiency 70*:695–702.

McFie, J. and Zangwill, O. L. (1960). Visual-constructive disabilities associated with lesions of the left hemisphere. *Brain 83*:243–260.

Money, J. (1965). *A Standardized Road-Map Test of Directional Sense*. Baltimore: Johns Hopkins Press.

Oldfield, R. C. and Zangwill, O. L. (1942–3). Head's concept of the schema and its application in contemporary British psychology. *Br. J. Psychol. 32*:267–286; *33*:58–64, 113–129, 143–149.

Pick, A. (1908). Ueber Störungen der Orientierung am eigenen Körper. *Arbeiten aus den Deutschen Psychiatrischen Universitäts-Klinik in Prag*. Berlin: Karger.

Poeck, K. (1963). Die Modellvorstellung des Körperschemas. *Deutsche Zeitschrift für Nervenheilkunde 187*:472–477.

Poeck, K. (1969). Modern trends in neuropsychology, in *Contributions to Clinical Neuropsychology*, A. L. Benton (ed). Chicago: Aldine.

Poeck, K. and Orgass, B. (1967). *Ueber Störungen der Rechts-Links-Orientierung. Nervenarzt 28*:285–291.

Poeck, K. and Orgass, B. (1969). An experimental investigation of finger agnosia. *Neurology 19*:801–807.

Sauguet, J., Benton, A. L., and Hécaen, H. (1971). Disturbances of the body schema in relation to language impairment and hemispheric locus of lesion. *J. Neurol. Neurosurg. Psychiat. 34*:496–501.

Schilder, P. (1931). Fingeragnosie, Fingerapraxie, Fingeraphasie. *Nervenarzt 4*:625–629.

Seidemann, H. (1932). Cerebrale Luftembolie mach Pneumothoraxfüllung (Rechts-links-störung, Fingeragnosie, Rechenstörung). *Zentralblatt für Neurologie und Psychiatrie 63*:729–731.

Selecki, B. R. and Herron, J. T. (1965). Disturbances of the verbal body image: a particular form of sensory aphasia. *J. Nervous Mental Dis. 141*:42–52.

Stone, F. B. and Robinson, D. (1968). The effect of response mode on finger localization errors. *Cortex 4*:233–244.

Terman, L. M. (1916). *The Measurement of Intelligence*. Boston: Houghton Mifflin.

Thurstone, L. L. (1938). *Primary Mental Abilities*. Chicago: University of Chicago Press.

Wolf, S. M. (1973). Difficulties in right-left discrimination in a normal population. *Arch. Neurol. 29*:128–129.

7
Apraxia

KENNETH M. HEILMAN

DEFINITION

Disorders of learned skilled movements not caused by weakness, akinesia, deafferentation, abnormality of tone or posture, abnormal movements such as tremors and chorea, intellectual deterioration, poor comprehension or uncooperativeness are termed apraxia. In this chapter we will discuss what causes apraxia.

Constructional and dressing apraxias are discussed in Chapters 8 and 10, respectively, and will be omitted from this chapter.

Examination for apraxia

Before determining whether a defect of skilled movement is apraxic, the clinician must perform a thorough neurological examination to make certain that the defect is not being caused by one of the above-mentioned disorders (such as weakness or deafferentation) Disorders of skilled movements not associated with weakness or sensory loss can be induced by diseases that affect either the basal ganglia or the cerebellum. The functions of the cerebellum and basal ganglia have not been completely elucidated. It appears, however, that the cerebral cortex alone cannot execute a coordinated skilled movement. The cerebellum and basal ganglia are reciprocally linked to the motor cortex to form a loop (Kornhuber, 1972) that may function as a servomechanism, with the subcortical structures acting as comparators. The cerebellum seems to be important in rapid movements (ballistic, phasic) and the basal ganglia in slow movements (tonic). Although cerebellar and basal ganglia disease may interfere with the performance of skilled movements, the resulting abnormalities of movement are not considered to be apraxia. In addition to interfering with skilled movements, disorders of the basal ganglia and cerebellum are manifested by changes in posture and tone, tremors, dysmetria, and by stereotypic movements. If the symptoms are limited to one side the affected patients should have their normal side tested and, if the abnormality is mild enough to permit them to use the extremity, their abnormal extremities should also be tested, allowing for their underlying disorder.

Many apraxic patients are also aphasic, and language disorders are sometimes difficult to distinguish from apraxic disorders. Patients with comprehension disorders are sometimes thought to be apraxic and occasionally apraxic patients who have good comprehension are misdiagnosed as having a comprehension disorder. In regard to the latter, it is important to test aphasic patients not only with commands (e.g., "Stick out your tongue," or "Show me how you would throw a ball."), but also with questions that can be answered by pointing or with yes/no responses (e.g., "Point to the ceiling," or "Are you in the hospital?"). If a patient performs poorly when given limb or buccofacial commands but can answer questions that require a yes/no response, the patient does not have a comprehension disturbance but may be apraxic. A patient who fails to perform buccofacial or limb commands but also cannot correctly answer yes/no questions or pointing commands probably has a comprehension disturbance. A comprehension disturbance, however, does not preclude the possibility that the patient also has an apraxic disturbance since frequently both symptoms coexist. A comprehension disturbance does, however, make apraxia testing more difficult. Typically, when apraxic patients make errors they will use body parts as objects or make clumsy movements. These movements can be recognized as being poorly performed but with the correct intent. If a patient with a mild comprehension disturbance is asked to perform a given task and uses a body part as the object or makes a clumsy but recognizable movement, then his abnormal movement should not be attributed to a comprehension disturbance. Patients' comprehension of movement commands may also be tested by (1) asking the patient to describe what he was asked to do, (2) having the patient point to the object (from an array of objects) which he would use to perform a specific action, and (3) having the examiner perform a series of actions and having the patient pick out the correct act. Not infrequently patients with severe comprehension disturbances have a defect in language decoding but still comprehend gestures and pictures and therefore may be tested in this manner.

For a variety of reasons, it is rare that patients will spontaneously complain of apraxic disturbances. Apraxic patients may be anosognostic (see Chapter 10). Patients with apraxia frequently are also aphasic and have a right hemiparesis. Clumsiness of their left hand would appear to be only a minor problem which they attribute to being right-handed (i.e., they think their left hand is clumsy because they are not accustomed to using it). Apraxia is usually mildest when a patient uses actual objects and most severe with pantomime. Since patients at home are rarely called upon to use pantomime, they and their families are often not aware of this disorder. Therefore in order to diagnose apraxia, one cannot rely on history but must test patients with central nervous system lesions to ascertain if they are apraxic.

In testing for apraxia, there are four major ways of having the patient perform: (1) pantomime ("Show me how you would ————"), (2) imitation of pantomime ("Watch how I ————, then you do it."), (3) use of an actual object ("Here is a ————, show me how you would use it.), and (4) imitation of examiner using the object. The act may be performed by either the limb (e.g., hand) or face (buccofacial). The movement may be either a gesture or the manipulation of an object. There may be an isolated act (i.e., "Blow out a match.") or a series of acts. Table 7-1 is a list of apraxia tests.

Frequently, when patients perform pantomimed tasks, they will use a body part as the object. It is possible they perform in this manner either because they do not understand that they are supposed to pantomime (i.e., they are using the body part as a symbol of the object) or because they cannot perform the task even though

TABLE 7-1

Limb gesture	Buccofacial gesture
1. Wave goodbye	1. Stick out tongue
2. Hitchhike	2. Blow a kiss
3. Salute	
4. Beckon "Come here."	Buccofacial manipulation
5. Stop	1. Blow out a match
6. Go	2. Suck on a straw
	Serial acts
Limb manipulation	1. Clean pipe, put in tobacco
1. Open a door with a key	and light pipe
2. Flip a coin	2. Fold letter, put it in the
3. Open a catsup bottle	envelope, seal it and place
4. Use a screwdriver	stamp on it
5. Use a hamer	
6. Use scissors	

they understand it. If a patient uses a body part as the object, his performance should be corrected (e.g., "Do not use your finger as a key. Make believe you are really holding a key."). If verbal instructions do not help, the examiner should demonstrate the correct pantomime. If the patient still uses body parts as the object, then he is apraxic.

Both hands should be tested, or the nonparetic hand if one hand is severely paretic, and the type of errors made by the patient should be noted (e.g., body part as object, clumsy movement).

Goodglass and Kaplan (1972) recommend testing movements with real objects only if patients failed to command (pantomime). Since some forms of apraxia are defined by an isolated difficulty with the use of actual objects, we recommend testing the use of actual objects even when pantomime is performed correctly. Normal adults should not have difficulty with any of the acts suggested in Table 7-1.

In addition to observing a patient's performance, the clinician should ascertain if a patient is disturbed by his own errors or if he even can recognize these as errors. In addition, the examiner should determine if a patient who is making apraxic errors can distinguish (when the examiner performs) incorrect from correct movements (e.g., the examiner asks, "Am I flipping a coin?," while he pantomimes opening a door with a key). The patient should also be tested to see if he can distinguish well-executed movements from poorly executed movements (e.g., the patient uses his finger as a screw driver and the examiner asks, "Is this the way to use a screw driver?").

VARIETIES OF APRAXIA: SYNDROMES AND MECHANISMS

Callosal apraxia

Although in 1866 Hughlings Jackson (cited by Taylor, 1932) described patients with normal strength who were unable to perform voluntary skilled movements, it was primarily Liepmann (Liepmann and Maas, 1907; Liepmann, 1905) who initiated interest in apraxia as disorders of skilled movement. Liepmann and Maas (1907) studied a patient with right hemiplegia. When this patient attempted to carry out verbal commands with his left hand, he performed poorly. On postmortem examination he was found to have a lesion in the left basis pontis, which accounted for his right hemiplegia, and an infarction of the corpus callosum, which spared the splenium of the corpus callosum. A lesion of the callosum similar to that which Liepmann and Maas reported could produce abnormalities of skilled movement because it disconnected the language areas in the left hemisphere (Wernicke, 1874) from the motor areas controlling fine movements of the left hand known to be in the right hemisphere. It was apparent to Liepmann and Maas, however, that their patient's deficit could not be fully explained as a disconnection of motor centers from language since their patient also failed both to imitate skilled movements and to properly manipulate actual objects. Because this patient's primary visual area, visual association area, primary somesthetic area, somesthetic association area, and premotor and motor areas were all intact in his right hemisphere, a disconnection between the language areas in the left hemisphere and motor areas in the right hemisphere should have allowed him to use an object correctly and to imitate. Since the patient could not imitate or use an object, Liepmann and Maas concluded that the left hemisphere contains not only language but also motor engrams that control all purposeful skilled movements. Lesions of the corpus callosum therefore not only disconnect the language hemisphere from the hemisphere controlling the left hand but also separate motor engrams in the left hemisphere from the motor areas in the right hemisphere. A callosal lesion in a right-handed patient who has both motor and language engrams in his left hemisphere would produce a patient who could carry out commands, imitate, and be able to use actual objects correctly with his right hand but would have difficulty with all these tasks with his left hand (see Table 7-2).

Geschwind and Kaplan (1962) also reported a patient with callosal dysfunction who was unable to carry out commands with the left hand but was able to imitate and use objects. Later, after reviewing several other cases of corpus callosum disconnection, Geschwind (1965) remarked that the independence of the right hemisphere in nonlanguage function which is manifested by his patient is unusual and may be an exception. Perhaps, unlike Liepmann's and Maas' patient who probably had language and visuokinesthetic motor engrams restricted to his left hemisphere, the patients reported by Gazzaniga, Bogen, and Sperry (1967) and Geschwind and Kaplan (1962) were left-hemisphere dominant for language but had bilateral visuokinesthetic motor engrams (see Table 7-2).

The nature of the apraxic deficit seen with callosal lesions depends on the pattern of language and motor dominance in the individual patient. For example, we have seen left-handed patients who had right-hemisphere lesions and were apraxic (Heilman et al., 1973; Valenstein and Heilman, 1978). Motor engrams in the two patients were stored in their right hemisphere and language mediated by their left hemisphere. If prior to their right-hemispheric lesion, these patients had a lesion of their corpus callosum, the right hand, deprived of visuokinesthetic motor engrams, should perform poorly to command, imitation, and with the use of the actual object. Their left hand, deprived of language, should perform poorly to command (pantomime) but perform well with imitation and with an actual object. To our knowledge, no such case has been reported.

Most of the cases of callosal apraxia which have been reported appear to be caused by infarctions in the distribution of the anterior cerebral artery or have been iatrogenic (surgical treatment of seizure disorders by callosal section). Theoretically, one may see callosal apraxias from cystic degeneration of the corpus callosum (Marchia-fava-Bignami), multiple sclerosis, callosal and peri-callosal tumors, or anything else that may cause a callosal disconnection. Patients with congenital absence of the corpus callosum do not have apraxia (Sheremata, Deonna, and Romanul, 1973). Although it is possible that language and engrams of skilled movements are transferred by the anterior commissure, these patients may have bilateral language and motor engrams.

Ideomotor Apraxia

Liepmann's callosal hypothesis can also be applied to intrahemi-spheric lesions. For example, in a right-handed patient, lesions in the left hemisphere which destroy motor engrams or which discon-nect them from both the left and right hemisphere motor cortex would produce the same defect in both hands that a callosal lesion would produce in the left hand. Since left-handers may have motor engrams in their right hemisphere, apraxia may result from right-hemisphere lesions (Hécaen and Sanguet, 1971; Heilman et al., 1973; Valenstein and Heilman, 1978). Left-handers, however, are more likely to be ambidextrous than are right-handers, so that apraxia would be expected to be less common in left-handers than in right-handers, and this is indeed the case (Hécaen and Sanguet, 1971).

In right-handed patients, almost all cases of apraxia are from left-hemisphere lesions (Geschwind, 1965; Goodglass and Kaplan, 1963; Hécaen and Ajuriaguerra, 1964; Hécaen and Sanguet, 1971). In right-handers, the left hemisphere is also dominant for language. Apraxia therefore is commonly associated with aphasia. This has led to the suggestion that apraxia and aphasia may both be mani-festations of a primary defect in symbolization (Goldstein, 1948). Whereas aphasia is a disturbance of verbal symbolization, apraxia is a defect of nonverbal symbolization (e.g., gesture and pantomime) (Goldstein, 1948). The observation that patients with apraxia per-form poorly to command and imitation but improve with the use of the actual object (Goodglass and Kaplan, 1963) lends support to Goldstein's postulate. However, several studies lend support to Liepmann's hypothesis that the left hemisphere controls skilled movements and that destruction of the engrams or separation of

TABLE 7-2

TYPE OF APRAXIA	PERFORMANCE TO COMMAND	IMITATION	USE OF ACTUAL OBJECT	SITE OF LESION	COMMENTS
Callosal					
Unilateral representation of visuokinesthetic motor engrams and language in the left hemisphere	Poor left hand Normal right hand	Poor left hand Normal right hand	Left hand abnormal but improved Right hand normal	Corpus callosum	(?) More common in people with family history of left-handedness
Bilateral representation of engrams	Poor left hand Normal right hand	Normal both hands	Normal both hands	Corpus callosum	Has never been reported. Probably more common in left-handers
Motor engrams in right hemisphere Language in left hemisphere (or vise versa)	Poor both hands	Normal left hand Poor right hand	Normal left hand Poor right hand	Corpus callosum	
Ideomotor					
Cortical	Poor both hands	Poor both hands	Improves but abnormal both hands	Dominant parietal lobe (supramarginal gyrus)	May not be able to recognize well-coordinated from clumsy movements. May have anosognosia (for poor movements)
Subcortical	Poor both hands	Poor both hands	Improves but abnormal both hands	Subcortical white matter	(?) May be able to differentiate from preceding type in that these pa-

					Location	Comments
Limb-kinetic						
Left-sided lesion		Right hand clumsy or paretic. Left hand: see *callosal apraxia*	Right hand clumsy or paretic. Left hand: see *callosal apraxia*	Right hand clumsy or paretic. Left hand: see *callosal apraxia*	Left premotor area	tients recognize abnormal movements and do not have anosognosia
Right-sided lesion		Left hand clumsy Right hand normal	Left hand clumsy Right hand normal	Left hand clumsy Right hand normal	Right premotor area	With actual object left hand performance may not improve as much as it does with ideomotor or callosal apraxia. Even simple movements may be clumsy
Ideational						
DeRenzi's	Patients have comprehension disturbances	Normal	Normal	Poor	Retro-rolandic, left sided	May be a conceptual disorder or an agnosia
Heilman's	Poor	Normal	Normal		Dominant parietal lobe (angular gyrus or subcortical)	Associated with anomic aphasia
Pick's				Difficulty with performance of a series of acts which lead to a goal	Dementia with diffuse disease	May be due to conceptual, mnemonic, or attentional defects

these engrams from the motor areas controlling the extremity causes abnormalities of skilled movement. Goodglass and Kaplan (1963) tested apraxic aphasic patients and control aphasic subjects with the Weschler Adult Intelligence Scale and used the performance-scaled score as a measure of intellectual ability. They also tested their subjects' ability to gesture and perform simple and complex pantomimes. Although the apraxic aphasics performed poorer on these motor skills than did their intellectual counterparts in the control groups, no clear relationship emerged between the severity of aphasia and the degree of gestural deficiency; the apraxic aphasic patients were also less able to imitate than were the nonapraxic controls.

Although Goodglass and Kaplan believed that their results supported Liepmann's hypothesis, they noted that their apraxic subjects did not have any difficulty in handling objects. Liepmann, however, thought apraxic patients were clumsy with objects and Geschwind (1965) noted that although such patients may improve after actually handling objects, their actions nevertheless remain clumsy. Clumsiness of the left hand on handling objects is difficult to quantify and, if apraxia is in part a disconnection from or destruction of the area containing motor memories, then brain-damaged apraxic patients should differ from nonapraxic patients. Apraxic aphasics and nonapraxic aphasics were given a rapid finger-tapping task with their left hand (Heilman, 1975). The apraxic aphasic group performed significantly worse than did the nonapraxic aphasic group. Similar results were previously reported by Wyke (1967) who did not test for apraxia but also used a repetitive nonsymbolic movement to test patients with disease of either the right or the left hemisphere. She demonstrated that patients with left-hemisphere disease performed more poorly with their ipsilateral hand than did those with right-hemisphere disease. Wyke concluded that "ipsilateral control does not exist for the right hemisphere"; however, her results also support Liepmann's hypothesis that the left hemisphere contains the motor memories that help control the right hemisphere via the corpus callosum. Kimura and Archibald (1974) studied the ability of left-hemisphere-impaired aphasics and right-hemisphere-impaired controls to copy unfamiliar, meaningless motor sequences. The performance of aphasic apraxic patients with left-hemisphere impairment was poorer than that of the controls, which again supported Liepmann's hypothesis. Pieczuro and Vignolo (1967) performed a study which tended to refute Liepmann's hypothesis that apraxia from left-hemisphere disease is a disorder of skilled movements and not a form of asymbolia. Pieczuro and Vignolo (1967) tested the manual dexterity of 35 patients with lesions of the right hemisphere and 70 patients with lesions of the left hemisphere. These patients' performance of the task was impaired by lesions in either hemisphere and the severity of the apraxia was independent of manual dexterity. I am not certain why Pieczuro and Vignolo's study is discrepant from Wyke's (1967, 1968) and mine (Heilman, 1975). Perhaps the strongest support for Liepmann's hypothesis that apraxia is a disorder of skilled movements comes from Liepmann's own observations that only 14 out of 20 apraxic patients were aphasic. Goodglass and Kaplan (1963), Heilman et al. (1973), and Heilman, Gonyea, and Geschwind (1974) also have described similar patients. In addition, aphasic patients are often not apraxic (Heilman, 1975).

In summary, because there is a poor correlation between the severity of symbolic disorders (aphasia) and disorders of skilled movements and because even nonsymbolic movements are poorly performed by apraxics, there is little evidence to support the hypothesis that apraxia is a disorder of symbolic behavior.

Movements can be initiated by stimuli such as commands, imitation, and use of an object. It is possible that within the left hemisphere, language areas can be disconnected from motor areas, producing apraxic errors on verbal command. Geschwind (1965) proposed that language elicits motor behavior by using a neural substrate similar to that proposed by Wernicke (1874) to explain language processing. Auditory stimuli travel along auditory pathways and reach Heschl's gyrus (primary auditory cortex). From Heschl's gyrus, the auditory message is relayed to the posterior superior portion of the temporal lobe (auditory association cortex). On the left side, this area is called Wernicke's area and appears to be important in language comprehension. Wernicke's area is connected to the premotor areas (motor association cortex) by the arcuate fasciculus and the motor association area on the left is connected to the primary motor area on the left. When someone is told to carry out a command with his right hand, he uses this pathway

(Wernicke's reflex arch). To carry out a verbal command with the left hand, information must be carried to the right premotor cortex (Geschwind, 1965) and, since it is rare to find fibers that run obliquely in the corpus callosum, fibers either cross from Wernicke's area to the auditory association area on the other side or cross from the premotor area on the left side to the premotor area on the right side. The information is then conveyed to the motor areas on the right side (see Fig. 7-1). Geschwind (1965) postulated that the connections between the motor association areas are the active pathway. He believed that disruptions in Wernicke's reflex arch and its connection to the right premotor area explain most of the apraxic disturbances.

It may now be worthwhile to explore whether lesions in Wernicke's schema can indeed explain the variety of apraxic disturbances seen by neurologists. Lesions in Heschl's gyrus, Wernicke's area, or the connections between Heschel's gyrus and Wernicke's

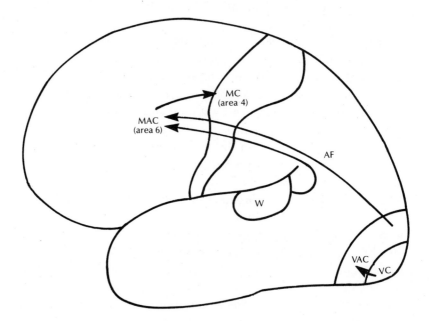

Fig. 7-1 Geschwind's schema. Lateral view of left side of brain. AF = arcuate fasciculus, MAC = motor association cortex, MC = motor cortex, VAC = visual association cortex, VC = visual cortex. The arrows indicate major connections of the areas shown.

area cause defects in comprehension. Therefore, although aphasic patients fail to carry out commands, their defect is not in the performance of skilled movements but rather in comprehending language.

We have already discussed callosal lesions which produce unilateral ideomotor apraxia. Lesions that destroy the left motor association cortex (premotor areas) would also destroy the callosal pathway from the left to the right motor association cortex. Therefore, a lesion in the left motor association cortex would induce a defect similar to that induced by a lesion in the body of the corpus callosum (sympathetic dyspraxia). Lesions of the left motor association cortex are often associated with right hemiplegia, so the right side can frequently not be tested. If, however, these patients were not hemiparetic, they would probably be apraxic on the right. According to Geschwind's (1963) schema, lesions of the arcuate fasciculus should disconnect the posterior language areas which are important in comprehension from the motor association cortex which is important in encoding motor engrams. Based on this schema, patients with parietal lesions (or arcuate fasciculus lesions) which spare motor association cortex should be able to comprehend commands but not perform skilled movements in response to command. Theoretically, however, these patients should be able to imitate—but they cannot. Geschwind attempted to explain this discrepancy by noting that fibers passing from visual association cortex to pre-motor cortex also pass anteriorly via the arcuate fasciculus. He proposed that the arcuate fasciculus of the left hemisphere is dominant for these visuomotor connections.

There is no evidence to support this hypothesis. Even if one assumes that the left arcuate fasciculus is dominant for visuomotor connections and that this dominance explains why patients cannot imitate, it could not explain why these patients are clumsy when they use objects or perform other somesthetic motor tasks (Heilman, 1975). One would have to assume that the arcuate fasciculus also carries somesthetic motor impulses and that the left fasciculus is also dominant for this function.

An alternative hypothesis that may explain why patients with a parietal lesion cannot properly imitate or use an object is that visuokinesthetic motor engrams are stored in the dominant parietal cortex. These engrams help program the motor association cortex

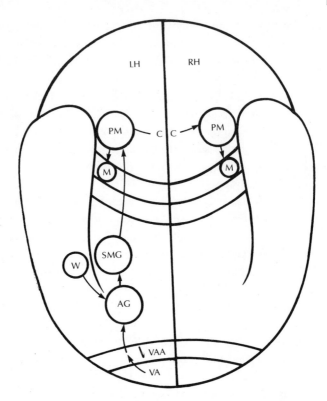

Fig. 7-2 Author's schema. View from top of brain. W = Wernicke's area, VA = primary visual area, VAA = visual association area, AG = angular gyrus, SMG = supramarginal gyrus, PM = premotor area (motor association cortex), M = motor cortex, CC = corpus callosum, LH = left hemisphere, RH = right hemisphere. The arrows indicate major connections of the areas shown.

for the necessary movements, and the motor association cortex programs the motor cortex, which innervates the specific muscle motor neuron pools needed to carry out the skilled act (Asanuma, 1975). The motor association cortex programs movements (more than one muscle) and visuokinesthetic motor engrams in the parietal cortex program sequences of movements needed to perform skilled acts (see Fig. 7-3). The schema postulated in Figures 7-2 and 7-3 explains

Fig. 7-3 Author's schema. The visuokinesthetic engrams program a sequence of movements (indicated as 1st, 2nd, 3rd) each of which, in turn, is programmed in the premotor cortex, which coordinates activation and inhibition of different motor neuron pools via the motor cortex.

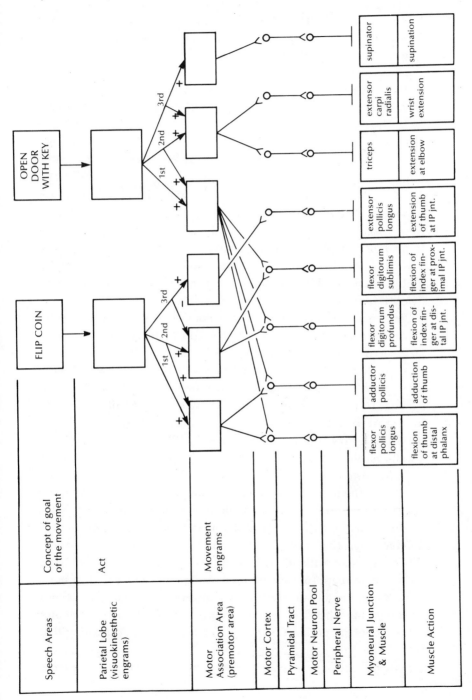

why patients with parietal lesions are unable to perform skilled acts in response to command, to imitate skilled acts, or to use objects skillfully.

Theoretically, it is possible to distinguish between dysfunction caused by destruction of parietal areas where acts are programmed (the visuokinesthetic motor engrams) and the apraxia which results from disconnection of this parietal area from motor association areas. Although patients with either disorder should experience difficulty in performing a skilled act in response to command, imitating, and using an object, patients whose engrams for skilled acts are retained but whose motor association areas are disconnected (or motor association cortex is destroyed) should be able to differentiate (recognize) a correctly performed skilled act from a poorly performed one; patients whose visuokinesthetic motor engrams are destroyed should not. In addition, patients in the latter group should not be troubled by their own poor performance because their defect is in the terminal portion of a feedback system.

Liepmann and Maas (1907) have noted that patients with ideomotor apraxia are able to distinguish correct from incorrect movement performed by the examiner. The tests usually given to these patients, however, would not be expected to distinguish between the two theoretical varieties of ideomotor apraxia predicted by our schema. In most of these recognition tests, the patient is asked to indicate if the act performed by the examiner is the target act ("Tell me if this is how you use a screwdriver."). The tester then performs a well-coordinated, skilled act (e.g., brushing hair) and will ask the patient, "Am I using a screwdriver?" Since each of the acts performed by the tester has a different semantic content, the examiner is testing the comprehension of the question, "What does this act mean?" Comprehension of pantomime may be processed by an area different from that used to process visuokinesthetic motor engrams. When a patient with ideomotor apraxia performs poorly, he does not make an inappropriate movement; that is, when asked to use a screwdriver, he does not brush his hair. His movements are correct in intent but they are clumsy. Since a patient with ideomotor apraxia does not perform inappropriate acts, it is not surprising that he can recognize inappropriate acts. As would be expected, an apraxic patient can also match an examiner's movement to a picture

(Kimura and Archibald, 1974). Matching to static pictures may not require an accurate memory of the correct movements.

To test whether patients with ideomotor apraxia have difficulty discriminating clumsy from normal movements, we (Valenstein and Heilman, in preparation) showed films of pantomimed acts (e.g., flipping a coin without the coin). Although this study has not been completed, it appears that ideomotor apraxics rarely select the inappropriate act as the correct one but will often pick the clumsy act or the act using a body part as an object. These preliminary observations suggest that some patients with ideomotor apraxia do have a defect in the comprehension of pantomimed acts. We have also noted that ideomotor apraxics seldom recognize that their poor motor performance is in error.

Unlike patients with parietal lesions, patients with destruction of motor association cortex or disconnection of motor association cortex from these visuokinesthetic engrams (callosal lesions) should be able to recognize the correct act. When they make errors, they should be able to recognize their errors. Although many apraxic patients have Broca's aphasia, Mohr et al. (1975) have demonstrated that most Broca's aphasics have lesions which extend into the parietal region and which therefore are not restricted to the motor association cortex. The ideal patient to test would be one with a lesion confined to the left premotor cortex or a patient with a callosal disconnection from an anterior cerebral artery infarction. Unfortunately, we have not tested such a patient.

The performance of a patient with ideomotor apraxia typically improves when he actually uses an object. Liepmann thought that using the actual object required somesthetic motor connections. Somesthetic motor connections are bilateral and may be intact either in both hemispheres with discrete left hemisphere posterior lesions or in the right hemisphere in large left hemispheric lesions. In addition, use of the actual objects sometimes limits the number of potential movements. For example, if a subject is asked to show how he would use a scissors (pantomime), he may move his fingers and hand in almost any direction; however, when given a scissors, he would be compelled by the object itself to open or close it.

If, as Liepmann proposed, the left hemisphere contains motor engrams and apraxia is produced by destruction of these engrams or by a disconnection of these engrams from the primary motor area, then performance of patients with ideomotor apraxia should be defective not only in pantomime (Goodglass and Kaplan, 1963), meaningful imitation (Goodglass and Kaplan, 1963), meaningless imitation (Kimura and Archibald, 1974), meaningful use of actual objects (Kimura and Archibald, 1974), and meaningless use of actual objects (Heilman, 1973), but also in acquisition and retention of new motor skills. To test acquisition and retention of motor skills, my associates and I (1975) studied nine right-handed hemiparetic patients with apraxia and aphasia and eight right-handed hemiparetic controls with aphasia but without apraxia. These subjects were given six trials on a rotary pursuit apparatus (five acquisition trials and one retention trial). All subjects used their left, nonparetic hand. The performance of the control group on the sixth trial was significantly better than on the first trial; however, there was no significant difference between the first and sixth trials in the apraxic group, suggesting that these patients had a defect in motor learning. The defect appeared to be caused by a combined impairment of both acquisition and retention. Wyke (1971) studied patients with either right- or left-hemisphere disease. Her subjects were given motor acquisition tasks that required bimanual coordination. Although patients with left-hemisphere disease demonstrated acquisition, they showed less development than those with right-hemisphere disease. Since Wyke did not separate her left hemispheric group into apraxic and nonapraxic patients, one could not be certain whether apraxic patients would have demonstrated poorer learning than the nonapraxic patients with left-hemisphere impairment. Nevertheless, these motor learning studies provide further support for Liepmann's hypothesis and support our observations that patients with ideomotor apraxia have a disturbance of the acquisition and retention of new motor skills.

Liepmann thought that lesions of the dominant parietal lobe (supramarginal gyrus) induce ideomotor apraxia. DeAjuriaguerra, Hécaen, and Angelergues (1960) confirmed that ideomotor apraxia is induced by posterior perisylvian lesions.

The most common cause of ideomotor apraxia is infarction in the distribution of the middle cerebral artery. Other diseases which produce hemispheric dysfunction (i.e., tumor, arteriovenous mal-

formations, trauma, etc.) also can produce ideomotor apraxia. Ideomotor apraxia is also commonly seen as one of the earlier signs of
Alzheimer's disease (senile dementia).

Limb-kinetic apraxia

Patients with anterior lesions have what Liepmann (1920) termed
"limb-kinetic apraxia" (see Table 7-2). Theoretically, a lesion of the
left frontal and anterior parietal lobe would destroy engrams for
movements of the right hand (see Figs 7-2 and 7-3) and disconnect
visuokinesthetic motor engrams and language from the right hemisphere. The patient with such a defect should not be able to perform with either hand in response to a command. Use of objects
would be better with the left hand than with the right and, if the
patient had visuokinesthetic motor engrams encoded in his right
hemisphere, he would be able to imitate with his left hand better
than with his right. If visuokinesthetic motor engrams were only in
his left hemisphere, as previously mentioned, both hands would
imitate poorly. Since frontal lesions are often associated with weakness, increased tone, and abnormal posture, it is not unusual to see
this array of signs. A lesion in the right frontal lobe should produce
a combination of symptoms in which the right hand performs normally in response to a command, imitates, and uses objects. The left
hand, however, should be unable to respond to a command, imitate,
or use objects. Even with more simple movements, the left hand
should be clumsy. Dr. R. T. Watson permitted me to observe such
a patient. Even with such simple movements as picking up a coin,
the patient was more clumsy than is usually seen with callosal and
ideomotor apraxia. The patient, however, had an extensor plantar
response and slightly increased reflexes on the left side, so we could
not be certain that this patient's lesion did not affect Area 4 or the
pyramidal tract. It has been demonstrated that pyramidal lesions
in monkeys may induce clumsiness which cannot be completely
accounted for by weakness, change in tone, or posture (Lawrence
and Kuypers, 1968). It is also possible that the clumsiness seen in
patients with limb-kinetic apraxia is induced by pyramidal lesions.
Like the ideomotor limb apraxias previously discussed, patients with
limb-kinetic apraxia performed poorly not only to command but
also to imitation. These patients may also improve somewhat with

use-of-object, but less so than patients with ideomotor apraxia. The same diseases which can produce ideomotor apraxia can also produce limb-kinetic apraxia.

Ideational apraxia
HEILMAN'S DEFINITION

I described three unusual patients who had neurological signs and symptoms usually associated with inferior parietal lobule dysfunction (i.e., anomia, constructional apraxia, alexia, and elements of Gerstmann's syndrome) (Heilman, 1973). Unlike the patients with ideomotor apraxia who move clumsily and use body parts as objects, these patients hesitated to make any movements and often appeared as if they did not understand the command. They could, however, demonstrate both verbally and by picking out the correct act (from several performed by the examiner) that they did understand the command. Unlike patients with ideomotor apraxia, these patients were able to imitate and use actual objects flawlessly. Because imitation and actual object use was performed well, it would seem that their engrams for motor skills were intact. What seemed to be defective in these patients was the ability to elicit the correct motor sequences in response to language. I have postulated that these patients had a disconnection between the areas decoding language and the areas containing the visuokinesthetic motor engrams for acts (see Figs. 4-2 and 4-3).

The patients with callosal lesions described by Geschwind and Kaplan (1962) and Gazzaniga et al. (1967) could not perform with their left hand in response to command, but they could imitate and use objects. Their performance with their left hand was similar to the performance with both hands of patients with left-hemisphere inferior parietal lobule lesions (Heilman, 1973). If normal performance on imitation and use-of-object suggests that visuokinesthetic motor engrams are intact and connected to premotor and primary motor areas, then those patients with callosal lesions and those with angular gyrus lesions must have a disconnection between language areas and the area where visuokinesthetic motor engrams are stored. In patients with callosal lesions, these engrams were presumed to be in both hemispheres, whereas comprehension of commands was being mediated by the left hemisphere. In patients with angular

gyrus lesions, both comprehension of the commands and the visuokinesthetic engrams were being mediated by the left hemisphere
and the angular gyrus lesion disconnected language areas from these
engrams. An alternative hypothesis is that in patients with angular
gyrus lesions the right hemisphere was mediating language comprehension, the left hemisphere contained the visuokinesthetic engrams, and the angular gyrus lesions disconnected the language
processing from these engrams.

Two of the patients we have seen with this form of ideational
apraxia had infarctions in the distribution of the middle cerebral
artery and one had a tumor; however, it is possible that other causes
of hemispheric dysfunction could also produce this picture.

DERENZI'S, PIECZURO'S, AND VIGNOLO'S DEFINITION

DeRenzi, Pieczuro, and Vignolo (1968) have described several patients who were unable to use an object. These patients, however,
could correctly perform in response to command and could imitate.
Neither we nor Geschwind (1967) have even seen this type of patient. DeRenzi, Pieczuro, and Vignolo doubted that agnosia could
be the explanation, but, unfortunately, did not test these patients
to confirm that supposition. In addition, almost all of the patients
had a defect in comprehension; therefore, possibly they did not
comprehend what was wanted by the examiner or they had other
conceptual disorders (see Table 7-2 and Figs. 7-2 and 7-3).

PICK'S DEFINITION

The inability to carry out a series of acts has also been called ideational apraxia. My colleagues and I have seen severely demented
patients similar to those described by Marcuse (1904), Pick (1905)
and Liepmann (1920) who, when given a goal that requires a series
of acts (i.e., clean the pipe, put tobacco in the pipe, light the pipe
and smoke it), have difficulty with sequencing these acts. These
demented patients seem not to know how to achieve their goal and
often forget their goal. When tested verbally (e.g., "What were you
supposed to do and how do you go about it?"), their verbal performance was just as poor as their motor performance. In addition,
these patients often have conceptual defects and may not know what
certain objects are used for; typically, they have widespread disease.

Buccofacial apraxia and apraxia of speech

Skilled movements are used not only to gesture and to manipulate objects but also to express language. With regard to speech, some authors have classified certain types of nonfluent aphasias as apraxias of speech (Johns and Darley, 1970; Deal and Darley, 1972). Buccofacial apraxia was first described by Hughlings Jackson (cited by Taylor, 1932). Patients with buccofacial apraxia have difficulty pantomiming and imitating movements such as blowing out a match, sticking out their tongue, or sucking on a straw. DeRenzi, Pieczuro, and Vignolo (1966) have noted that 90% of Broca's aphasics have buccofacial apraxia. Because there are patients with nonfluent aphasia who do not have buccofacial apraxia, it would seem unlikely that buccofacial apraxia causes this aphasic disturbance. It can be argued, however, that speech requires finer coordination than does response to a command such as "Blow out a match," and therefore the slow, badly articulated speech of the nonfluent aphasic may still be caused by an apraxic disturbance. There is evidence against this view. Buccofacial apraxia and Broca's aphasia often coexist, but they can also be completely dissociated (Heilman, Gonyea, and Geschwind, 1974) which suggests that the association cortex that mediates facial praxis is not the same as the area which mediates the organization of movements important in speech. Patients may have conduction aphasia with or without buccofacial apraxia. Buccofacial apraxia may therefore coexist with fluent speech. If one attributes the nonfluent disorders of speech in Broca's aphasics to apraxia, one cannot explain how buccofacial apraxia may be associated with the fluent speech seen in conduction aphasia. I have also examined a patient with aphemia (nonfluent speech with intact writing skills) who did not have buccofacial apraxia. Therefore, although patients with Broca's aphasia or aphemia or both may have disorders of programming movements needed for speech, buccofacial apraxia is not causing the nonfluent speech. In addition to having faulty motor programming, patients with Broca's aphasia have other language disorders, including comprehension disorders, suggesting that this aphasic disorder is more than an apraxic disturbance (Heilman and Scholes, 1976).

Apraxic agraphia

Agraphia is most commonly associated with aphasia; in most patients with agraphia, the disorder of language cannot be separated from the disorder of movement. There have been several cases, however, where disorders of writing have not been associated with language disorders. Most of these patients have been left-handed. We (Heilman et al., 1973) described a left-handed man who had been taught to write with his right hand. The patient developed a left hemiplegia. Although the patient was not aphasic, he lost the ability to write with his right (nonparetic) hand. He also had an ideomotor apraxia of his right hand. Liepmann and Maas (1907), Geschwind and Kaplan (1962), and Gazzaniga, Bogen, and Sperry (1967) have all shown that right-handed patients with callosal lesions have agraphia of their left hand but not of the right hand. In patients with callosal dysfunction, because the left hand/right hemisphere is deprived of language or motor engrams or both, we cannot be certain if the agraphia seen with left-hand performance is caused by the loss of language or a loss of motor engrams. Nielsen (1946) had a left-handed patient who probably had a callosal lesion. He could not write with his right hand but could with his left hand. I do not know which hemisphere mediated language in this patient but his agraphia may have been an example of the converse of the preceding patient who had callosal lesions. The patient we described (Heilman et al., 1973) had a large lesion in the region of the right hemisphere. Since the patient was not aphasic, language had to be mediated by the opposite (left) hemisphere. As suggested previously, Liepmann thought that manual dominance (handedness) reflected the ability of one hemisphere to learn and store motor skills more readily than the other. Because the patient we described was left-handed and language was mediated by the left hemisphere, skilled motor movements were probably mediated by the right hemisphere. Assuming that this patient was "left brained" for language and speech and "right brained" for handedness, it would follow that when he wrote with his right hand (as he was accustomed to doing), impulses must have traversed the callosum twice. Linguistic material was transferred to the right hemisphere to arouse the appropriate visuokinesthetic motor engrams. These engrams were then transferred back to the left motor region which controls the right hand. If he wrote with his left hand, impulses would have to traverse the callosum only once. A callosal section in this man would have caused (1) apraxia and agraphia of the right hand because the right hand would be disconnected from the motor engrams and (2) agraphia of the left hand because it would be disconnected from the language areas. We have reported a similar clinical picture in a right-hander (Heilman, Gonyea, and Geschwind, 1974).

Although apraxia and agraphia coexisted in our patient (Heilman et al., 1973), we were reluctant to attribute the patient's agraphia to apraxia since it was possible that the defect in writing resulted from the unavailability of linguistic input to the right hemisphere rather than from the unavailability of the engrams for forming the letters. Valenstein and Heilman (1978) described a left-handed patient who developed bilateral agraphia and apraxia following a right parietal infarction. Unlike our prior case (Heilman et al., 1973), this patient (Valenstein and Heilman, 1978) did not have a left hemiparesis. Preservation of the ability to type with the left hand demonstrated that the right hemisphere was not disconnected from language input.

RECOVERY FROM APRAXIA AND TREATMENT

Although it has been proposed that in right-handers motor engrams are stored in the left hemisphere, I have not explained why some right-handed aphasic patients are not apraxic. Possibly some of these patients have a small lesion or their lesion missed some critical area. I have, however, seen some patients with large lesions who were not apraxic but others with small lesions who were severely apraxic. Of patients who had lesions in the same area, some were apraxic and some were not. Although the size and locus of a lesion determine to a large extent the presence or absence of apraxia as well as its severity, they appear not to be the only determinants. Perhaps there are patients with large left-hemisphere lesions that are aphasic and hemiplegic but not apraxic because their right hemisphere has taken over function for the left. This hypothesis is similar to the one first proposed by Kleist (1916) to explain why certain patients with lesions of the left hemisphere recover language function. Since evidence points to familially left-handed patients having bilateral function and therefore more of a regression of functional defects (Hécaen and Sanguet, 1971), right-handers with large lesions of the left hemisphere who either recover from apraxia or never manifest symptoms of apraxia may have a higher incidence of familial left-handedness.

Therapy should be initially aimed at treating the underlying disorder. Then other therapeutic measures can be tried. Apraxic patients should be taught alternative strategies for performing tasks which pose difficulty for them. For example, one of our patients with apraxic agraphia could not write with a pen but he could type (Valenstein and Heilman, 1978). Since apraxic patients have a motor learning and retention disorder, I am not sure of the value of physical or occupational therapy. There is no well-controlled study on therapy for apraxia; however, in the absence of any evidence, I believe patients with apraxia should be given a trial of therapy.

References

Asanuma, H. (1975). Recent developments in the study of columnar arrangement of neurons within the motor cortex. *Physiol. Rev. 55*:143–156.

Broca, P. (1863). Localisation des fonctions cerebrales siege du langage articule. *Bull. Soc. Anthropology 4*:200–204.

DeAjuriaguerra, J., Hécaen, H., and Angelergues, R. (1960). Les apraxies: varietes cliniques et lateralisation lesionelle. *Rev. Neurol. 120*:566–594.

Deal, J. L. and Darley, F. L. (1972). The influence of linguistic and situational variables on phonemic accuracy in apraxia of speech. *J. Speech Hearing Res. 15*:639–653.

DeRenzi, E., Pieczuro, A., and Vignolo, L. (1966). Oral apraxia and aphasia. *Cortex 2*:50–73.

DeRenzi, E., Pieczuro, A., and Vignolo, L. (1968). Ideational apraxia: a quantitative study. *Neuropsychologia 6*:41–52.

Ettlinger, G. (1969). Apraxia considered a disorder of movements that are language dependent: evidence from a case of brain bisection. *Cortex 5*:285–289.

Gazzaniga, M., Bogen, J., and Sperry, R. (1967). Dyspraxia following division of the cerebral commissures. *Arch. Neurol. 16*:606–612.

Geschwind, N. (1965). Disconnexion syndromes in animals and man. *Brain 88*:237–294, 585–644.

Geschwind, N. (1967). The apraxias in phenomenology of will and action, in *The Second Lexington Conference on Pure and Applied Phenomenology,* E. W. Straus and R. M. Griffits (eds). Pittsburgh: Duquesne University Press.

Geschwind, N. and Kaplan, E. (1962). A human cerebral disconnection syndrome. *Neurology 12*:675–685.

Goldstein, K. (1948). *Language and Language Disturbances.* New York: Grune & Stratton.

Goodglass, H. and Kaplan, E. (1963). Disturbance of gesture and pantomime in aphasia. *Brain 86*:703–720.

Goodglass, H. and Kaplan, E. (1972). *The Assessment of Aphasia and Related Disorders.* Philadelphia: Lea and Febiger.

Hécaen, H. (1962). Clinical symptomatology in right and left hemisphere lesions, in *Interhemispheric Relations and Cerebral Dominance.* V. Mountcastle (ed). Baltimore: Johns Hopkins Press.

Hécaen, H. and de Ajuriaguerra, J. (1964). *Left-Handedness.* New York: Grune & Stratton.

Hécaen, H. and Sanguet, J. (1971). Cerebral dominance in left-handed subjects. *Cortex 7*:19–48.

Heilman, K. M. (1973). Ideational apraxia—a re-definition. *Brain 96*:861–864.

Heilman, K. M. (1975). A tapping test in apraxia. *Cortex 11*:259–263.

Heilman, K. M., Coyle, J. M., Gonyea, E. F., and Geschwind, N. (1973). Apraxia and agraphia in a left-hander. *Brain 96*:21–28.

Heilman, K. M., Gonyea, E. F., and Geschwind, N. (1974). Apraxia and agraphia in a right-hander. *Cortex, 10*:284–288.

Heilman, K. M. and Scholes, R. J. (1976). The nature of comprehension errors in Brocas, conduction and Wernicke's aphasics. *Cortex 12*:258–265.

Heilman, K. M., Schwartz, H. D., and Geschwind, N. (1975). Defective motor learning in ideomotor apraxia. *Neurology 25*:1018–1020.

Jackson, H. J. (1932). In *Selected Writings of John Hughlings Jackson,* Vol. 2, J. Taylor (ed). London: Hodder and Stoughton.

Johns, D. F. and Darley, F. L. (1970). Phonemic variability in apraxia of speech. *J. Speech Hearing Res. 13*:556–583.

Kimura, D. and Archibald, Y. (1974). Motor functions of the left hemisphere. *Brain 97*:337–350.

Kleist, K. (1916). Uber Leitungsaphasie und grammatische Storungen. *Monatsschr. f. Psychiatr. u. Neurol. 40*:118–121.

Kornhuber, H. H. (1972). Cerebral cortex, cerebellum, and basal ganglia: an introduction to their motor functions, in *The Neurosciences, Third Study Program.* F. O. Schmitt and F. G. Worden (eds). Cambridge: MIT Press.

Lawrence, D. G. and Kuypers, H. G. J. M. (1968). The functional organization of the motor system in the monkey. *Brain 91*:1–36.

Leipmann, H. (1900). Das Krankheitsbild der Apraxie. *Monatsschr. f. Psychiat. u. Neurol. 8*:15–44, 102–132, 181–197.

Liepmann, H. (1905). Du linke Hemisphare und das Handelin. *Munch. Med. Wschr. 49*:2375–2378.

Liepmann, H. (1920). Apraxia. *Ergbn. der ges. Med. 1*:516–543.

Liepmann, H. and Maas, O. (1907). Fall von linksseitiger Agraphie und Apraxie bei rechtsseitiger Lähmung. *Z. f. Psychologie u. Neurol. 10*: 214–227.

Marcuse, H. (1904). Apraktische Symptome bei einem Fall von seniler Demenz. *Zentble Mervheilk Psychiat. 27*:737–751.

Mohr, J. R., Funkenstein, H. H., Finkelstein, S., Pessin, M. S., Duncan, G. W., and Davis, K. (1975). Broca's area infarction versus Broca's aphasia. *Neurology 25*:349.

Nielsen, J. (1965). *Agnosia, Apraxia, Aphasia*. Reprint 1946 ed. New York: Hafner.

Pick, A. (1905). *Studien uber Motorische Apraxia und ihre Mahestehende Erscheinungen*. Leipzig: Deuticke.

Pieczuro, A. and Vignolo, L. A. (1967). Studio sperimentale sull'aprassia ideomotoria. *Sistema Nervoso 19*:131–143.

Sheremata, W. A., Deonna, R. W., and Romanul, F. C. (1973). Agenesis of the corpus callosum and interhemispheric transfer of information. *Neurology 23*:390.

Valenstein, E. and Heilman, K. M. (1978). Apraxia agraphia with neglect induced paragraphia. *Arch. Neurol.*

Wernicke, C. (1874). *Der Aphasische Sumptomenkomplex*. Breslau: Cohn and Weigart.

Wyke, M. (1967). Effect of brain lesions on the rapidity of arm movement. *Neurology 17*:1113–1130.

Wyke, M. (1968). The effect of brain lesions in the performance of an arm-hand precision task. *Neuropsychologia 6*:125–134.

Wyke, M. (1971). The effects of brain lesions on the learning performance of a bimanual coordination task. *Cortex 7*:59–71.

8

Visuoperceptive, Visuospatial, and Visuoconstructive Disorders

ARTHUR BENTON

INTRODUCTION

The perceptual and perceptuomotor disabilities discussed in this chapter are reflected behaviorally in a variety of performance deficits: in failure to recognize objects, pictorial representations, and faces; in defective discrimination of complex stimulus-configurations; in faulty localization of objects in space and defective topographical orientation; and in impaired capacity to organize elements in correct spatial relationships so that they form an entity, as in drawing a house or building a block model. In traditional neurological terminology, most of these deficits are described as one or another form of *visual agnosia*. The visuoconstructional deficits are usually designated as *constructional apraxia* or *apractagnosia*.

There has always been considerable controversy about the fundamental nature of the agnostic disorders. According to one point of view, they represent impairment in either perceptual-integrative or associative processes within the context of adequate sensory capacity, the assumption being that the patient cannot achieve recognition in spite of having received sufficient sensory information to do so. A competing explanation is that the agnostic disorders result from sensory defects, often coupled with general mental impairment, so that the patient has only incomplete information as a basis for achieving perceptual recognition.

Whether one considers agnosia to be a "higher-level" disorder or thinks of it in terms of sensory deficit, it is clear that the neurological mechanisms involved in the agnosic disorders are not the same as those underlying the perceptual deficits which are a direct consequence of impaired visual acuity, color blindness, or visual-field defect. Thus, in either case, these perceptual and perceptuomotor disabilities need to be considered separately from "simple" sensory or motor deficits because of their distinctive neurological implications.

Over the years, a large number of specific performance deficits indicative of visuoperceptual, visuospatial, or visuoconstructive disorder have been described. The exact nature of the relationships among these performance deficits has yet to be worked out and a definitive classification of neurologically meaningful types of disability remains an unfinished task. However, it is certain that there is a fundamental difference between defects in the identification of the formal characteristics of objects and defects in the localization of these objects in space. Many patients show dissociated impairment in this regard, i.e., they are defective in one type of performance but not in the other. An instructive study by Newcombe and Russell (1969) will be cited to illustrate both the fact of dissociation and its differential neurological implications.

Newcombe and Russell gave two visual tasks to right-handed patients with penetrating brain wounds and to control subjects. One task was the "faces" test of Mooney (1957), in which the subject is requested to identify drawings of human faces with exaggerated shadows and highlights as being that of a boy, girl, man, woman, old man, or old woman. An earlier study by Lansdell (1968) had shown that defective performance on this "closure" task, in which the subject must achieve a configurational percept from fragmentary information, is associated with right temporal-lobe injury. The second task was a visual maze test in which the subject was required to learn a 10-element path over trials. Impairment on this type of spatial learning problem has also been shown to be associated with disease of the right hemisphere (Reitan and Tarshes, 1959; Benton et al., 1963; Milner, 1965; Corkin, 1965).

Separate groups of patients with well-localized focal wounds of the left or right hemisphere, as well as control groups matched with the brain-diseased patients for age and vocabulary level, were studied. The performance of the patients with right-hemisphere lesions on both tasks was significantly inferior to that of the left-hemisphere-damaged patients, who were not different in this respect from the controls. However, although both the "closure" and "spatial" task performances proved once again to be associated with right-hemisphere disease, more detailed analysis showed that their relations to locus-of-lesion within the hemisphere and to visual field defect were quite different.

The perceptual and spatial task performances were not significantly correlated in either the right-hemisphere or the left-hemisphere group and this lack of correlation was reflected in many instances of dissociation in the right-hemisphere patients. None of the patients with markedly defective "closure" performance showed correspondingly defective "spatial" performance. They were found to have posterior temporal-lobe lesions with an associated left upper quadrantic field defect. (Curiously, the men with complete left hemianopia were not particularly severely impaired on this task.) In contrast, the patients with markedly defective spatial performances proved to have high posterior parietal injuries with an associated left hemianopia. Those with an upper quadrantic defect performed quite well, while those with a lower quadrantic defect tended to perform defectively.

This dissociation in performance level on spatial and nonspatial visual tasks on the part of patients with brain disease has been documented in a number of studies, in addition to the one by Newcombe and Russell. This fact has provided the empirical basis for a broad division of visuoperceptive performances into spatial and nonspatial types. In all probability, there are other types of defect, each with its more-or-less specific neurological implications, that need to be identified. A provisional classification of clinically differentiated forms of visuoperceptive, visuospatial, and visuoconstructive disorder is presented in Table 8-1.

HISTORICAL BACKGROUND

The first neurologist to call special attention to the occurrence of visuoperceptive and visuopractic disabilities in patients with brain

TABLE 8-1 *Classification of Visuoperceptual, Visuospatial, and Visuoconstructive Disorders*

I. VISUOPERCEPTUAL
   A. Visual object agnosia
   B. Defective visual analysis and synthesis
   C. Impairment in facial recognition
      1. Facial agnosia (prosopagnosia)
      2. Defective discrimination of unfamiliar faces
   D. Impairment in color recognition

II. VISUOSPATIAL
   A. Defective localization of points in space
   B. Defective judgment of direction and distance
   C. Defective topographical orientation
   D. Unilateral visual neglect

III. VISUOCONSTRUCTIVE
   A. Defective assembling performance
   B. Defective graphomotor performance

disease was Hughlings Jackson (1876). Advancing the idea that the posterior region of the right hemisphere played a crucial role in visual recognition and memory, he described a patient with a tumor in this area who showed what he called "imperception"—lack of recognition of familiar persons and places, losing one's way in familiar surroundings, and inability to dress oneself. Jackson's observations had little immediate influence and, rather oddly, it was the animal experimentation of Munk that made the greater impact on clinical thinking. In 1878, Munk described a condition which he designated as "mindblindness." Following limited bilateral ablation of the upper convex surface of their occipital lobes, his dogs showed a peculiar disturbance in visual behavior. Although they could ambulate freely both indoors and in the garden, avoiding or climbing over obstacles, they seemed to have lost the ability to appreciate the meaning of many visual stimuli. For example, they would merely gaze at a piece of meat instead of snapping at it as would a normal dog. If a threatening gesture was made, they would neither cringe nor bark and they showed no signs of special recognition of their master or other familiar persons as compared to strangers. Munk's explanation of the condition was that the ablation had destroyed their "memory images" of earlier visual experience. As a consequence, they could not relate current perceptions to past experience and hence failed to grasp the meaning of visually perceived stimuli.

"Mindblindness" in patients who did not recognize objects or persons despite seemingly adequate visual acuity was then the subject of many clinical reports. Wilbrand (1887) followed Munk in attributing the disability to a loss of visual memory images and he postulated the existence of a "visual memory center" in the occipital cortex. Lissauer's (1890) classic case report included a penetrating discussion of the mechanisms underlying mindblindness. According to his formulation, visual recognition involves two processes: accurate perception of an object and association of that perception with past experience. A defect in the first mechanism could lead to an "apperceptive" type of mindblindness, a defect in the second to an "associative" type of the disorder. This classification system is presented in detail in Chapter 9, pages 234–249.

But other clinicians and experimentalists, while acknowledging the empirical reality of the condition described by Munk, interpreted it as the product of visuosensory defect. Their position was well expressed by Pavlov (1927) who suggested that the classical formula for mindblindness, "the dog sees but does not understand" in fact should read "the dog understands but does not see sufficiently well."

Nomenclature in the field changed with the introduction by Freud (1891) of the concept of agnosia to denote disorders of recognition in contrast to disorders of naming and "visual agnosia" gradually supplanted "mindblindness" as the preferred term for a range of disabilities having to do with the visual apprehension of objects, events, and spatial relations. Various forms of defect were then described. The mindblindness of Munk, Wilbrand, and Lissauer, in which the patient fails to recognize even common objects, was designated as *visual object agnosia,* which will be discussed in Chapter 9. Impairment in the discrimination of forms or complex figures with preserved recognition of common objects came to be known as *visual form agnosia* or *geometric form agnosia.* The inability to recognize familiar persons on the basis of facial characteristics was described as a specific entity, as was symbol agnosia and color agnosia. The inability to grasp the impact of a complex pictorial presentation with preserved recognition of its constituent elements was given the designation of *simultanagnosia.*

Hughling Jackson's concept of "imperception" involved disturbances in visual orientation as well as lack of recognition of familiar persons and places. Visuospatial disability became a topic of much clinical investigation and discussion in the 1880's, particularly among ophthalmologists. An important early contribution was the detailed case report of Badal (1888) describing a patient with preserved central visual acuity who showed spatial disorientation. She could not find her way about the house or the immediate neighborhood and had difficulty in locating objects. She could read letters, numbers, and familiar words, but serial reading was grossly impaired because of directional impairment as she scanned printed material. She recognized objects, but could not estimate their size, distance, or location. Like Jackson's patient, she could not dress herself. Since her disorientation extended to the auditory and somesthetic realms, Badal interpreted her defects as a reflection of a supramodal disability of the "sense of space."

Rather similar cases were described by Foerster (1890), Dunn (1895), and Meyer (1900). The motoric element of "psychic paralysis of gaze" was added to the clinical picture by Balint (1909). On the basis of his observations on younger patients with penetrating brain wounds, Gordon Holmes (1918; Holmes and Horrax, 1919) divided visuospatial disabilities into two major types: disturbances in orientation and size and distance estimation; and disturbances in ocular fixation with consequent inability to "find" objects.

The neurological interest of these early observations came from the demonstration that visuospatial disabilities of the types described were produced by focal posterior brain disease. For example, autopsy examination (Sachs, 1895) of Foerster's case disclosed bilateral softening confined to the occipital and temporal lobes and the brain of Balint's patient showed essentially the same picture. In his cases, Holmes found bilateral lesions involving the angular and supramarginal gyri and extending into adjacent occipital and temporal areas.

Visuoconstructive disabilities were first described under the broader heading of optic apraxia, a term used to designate virtually any disturbance in action referable to defective visual guidance of action. For example, Poppelreuter (1917) described awkwardness in the execution of acts requiring manual dexterity, inability to maintain one's balance in tests of locomotion, and defective imitation of movements, as well as visuoconstructive disabilities, as forms of optic apraxia. Kleist (1923; Strauss, 1924) then singled out constructional apraxia as a separate disorder because of his observation that it could occur independently of other forms of apraxia and his conviction that it possessed a distinctive neuropathological significance. He conceived of it as a particular type of visuoconstructive impairment that reflected an inability to translate an adequate visual perception into appropriate action. It was a perceptuomotor, rather than purely visuoperceptual, disability that occurred as a consequence of a break in the connections between visual and kinesthetic processes. Thus, in Kleist's view, constructional apraxia was essentially a disconnection symptom and he placed the locus of the causative lesion in the posterior area of the dominant hemisphere. Yet, at the same time, he emphasized the spatial nature of the disability, defining it as a disturbance "in formative activities such as assembling, building and drawing, in which the spatial form of the product proves to be unsuccessful, without there being an apraxia of single movements."

After Kleist's description, constructional apraxia was immediately recognized as a form of behavioral disability associated with brain disease. However, his precise formulation that it was neither perceptual nor motor but rather "perceptuomotor" and "executive" in nature was generally ignored and the term was used to designate any visuoconstructive disability, whether or not it appeared within a context of visuoperceptive impairment. Later, Duensing (1953) made a distinction between an "ideational-apractic" type of constructional disability, comparable to Kleist's constructional apraxia, and a "spatio-agnostic" type resulting from visuoperceptive impairment.

DEFECTIVE VISUAL ANALYSIS AND SYNTHESIS

There is a huge literature on this topic describing performance deficits on tasks that make demands on various capacities such as making fine visual discriminations, separating figure from ground in complex configurations, achieving recognition on the basis of incomplete information, and synthesizing disparate elements into a meaningful unity as, for example, when viewing a picture depicting action. Selected aspects of this literature will be reviewed.

Visual discrimination

The question of the frequency with which patients with brain disease show defects in simple visual discrimination, i.e., in altered thresholds for the discrimination of single attributes of a stimulus such as size, brightness, or length has been the subject of two recent studies. Taylor and Warrington (1973) assessed the discrimination of size, length, shading, and curvature in groups of patients with focal lesions confined to the left or right hemisphere and a comparable group of control patients. The mean error score of the controls over all tasks was 1.6. Neither the mean error score (1.8) of the left-hemisphere-damaged patients nor that (2.4) of the right-hemisphere-damaged patients was significantly higher than that of the controls. The poorest performances were made by the subgroup of patients with posterior parietal disease of the right hemisphere; however, even their mean score of 3.7 was not significantly higher than that of the controls. That this failure to find between-groups differences was not due to sampling bias is indicated by the fact that the patients with right-hemisphere lesions were inferior to the controls on two other tasks (dot localization, block designs) that were part of the test battery.

A second study by Bisiach, Nichelli, and Spinnler (1976) approached the problem from the standpoint of signal detection theory and showed that the performances of patients with brain disease were not differentially affected by response biases. Patients with unilateral disease of either hemisphere generally performed at a lower level than controls in the discrimination of length, size, curvature, and brightness. Patients with right-hemisphere disease and with visual-field defects showed the most marked impairment. However, in only one test (discrimination of length) were between-groups differences significant.

Thus the indication from both studies is that impairment in simple visual discrimination is not a particularly frequent occurrence in patients with brain disease. Of all groups of patients, those with posterior parietal disease of the right hemisphere are most likely to show defects of this type. Analogous somesthetic performance presents an interesting contrast in this respect. Raised thresholds for light pressure and passive movement, and impairment in tactile two-point discrimination on the side of the body ipsilateral to the side of lesion have been reported by some investigators to occur with notable frequency in patients with unilateral brain disease (Semmes et al., 1960; Vaughn and Costa, 1962; Carmon, 1971). Similarly, in the field of audition, Milner (1962) found that patient with right temporal-lobe excisions were inferior to both control patients and those with left temporal-lobe excisions in the discrimination of loudness, duration, and pitch.

On the other hand, more impressive between-groups differences are found when patients are required to discriminate between complex visual stimulus-configurations that differ in one or another subtle characteristic, if the task presented is sufficiently difficult that relatively few subjects make perfect performances. A single example will be cited to illustrate the point. Meier and French (1965) studied the visual discrimination of complex figures in patients who had undergone resection of either the right or the left temporal lobe for relief of psychomotor seizures. The two groups were equated for mean age (31–33 yrs.), mean WAIS IQ (96–97), and mean Porteus Maze performance level (13.3–13.5 yrs.). The tasks that were presented assessed the ability to discriminate between fragmented concentric circular patterns on the basis of either a rotational or a structural cue that differentiated one pattern from three other identical patterns. The patients with right-hemisphere lesions were clearly inferior to those with left-hemisphere excisions, their mean error score being 46% higher and the between-groups difference in mean error score being significant at the .01 level. Both brain-diseased groups performed at levels significantly below that of normal subjects.

Figure-ground differentiation

Impairment in the ability to separate figure from ground in the visual perception of complex stimulus-configurations has long been considered to be a cardinal feature of higher-level visuoperceptive defect in patients with brain disease. The ability is typically assessed by tasks requiring the detection of "imbedded" or "mixed" figures. The *Embedded Figure Test* developed by Gottschaldt to investigate the determinants of figure–ground differentiation has been utilized in a number of clinical neuropsychological studies (Teuber and Weinstein, 1956; Weinstein, 1964; Russo and Vignolo, 1967; Orgass et al., 1972). These study findings indicate that: (1) impaired performance is found in a significant proportion of patients with focal brain disease, independently of locus of lesion; (2) among nonaphasic patients with focal brain disease, those with parieto-occipital lesion of the right hemisphere show the most severe impairment; (3) the performance level of aphasic patients with left-hemisphere disease is inferior to that of nonaphasic patients with left-hemisphere disease and comparable to that of nonaphasic patients with posterior right-hemisphere disease; (4) performance level is not significantly associated with the presence or absence of visual field defect.

The reasons for the observed association between aphasic disorder and defective performance on this nonverbal visuoperceptive task have not been clearly identified. One possibility is that the aphasic patients have more extensive lesions than their nonaphasic counterparts with left-hemisphere disease and that their defective imbedded figure-test performances reflect general mental impairment associated with a relatively large loss of neuronal tissue. Although no empirical findings have been marshalled to support this possibility, it cannot be ruled out. An argument against it is that, as will be seen, there are other types of visuoperceptive performance that are not related to the presence of aphasia in patients with left-hemisphere disease. A second possibility is that performance on the Gottschaldt test is language-dependent in the sense that detection of the target figure imbedded in a distracting background is facilitated by implicit verbal mediation processes. If this is so, it would be expected that aphasic patients with disturbances in verbal thinking would perform on a subnormal level. It is perhaps relevant to note that dyslexic children have been found to be deficient on the Gottschaldt test as compared to normal readers with whom they were matched for age and IQ (cf. Goetzinger, Dirks, and Baer, 1960; Lovell, Gray, and Oliver, 1964).

Visual synthesis

Some patients who can identify and name single stimuli are unable to grasp the interrelations among a number of simultaneously presented stimuli and to integrate the separate elements into a meaningful whole. For example, when presented with an action picture, a patient may enumerate the persons and objects in it but not describe what action is taking place or interpret the implications of the action. A task of this type was introduced by Binet in his intelligence scale and found a place in versions of the Binet Scale developed in different countries. Three levels of performance are typically distinguished: enumeration of elements; depiction of action; interpretation of the central meaning of the picture.

Binet considered the task to be an appropriate measure of "intelligence" and defective performance by patients with brain disease was at first interpreted as an expression of general mental impairment. However, Wolpert (1924) advanced the view that failure could reflect a modality-specific deficit in visual "integrated apprehension" (Gesamtauffassung) which prevented the patient from grasping the import of a complex stimulus situation even though each detail in it was recognized. He regarded the deficit as a form of visual agnosia for which he coined the term "simultaneous agnosia" (Simultanagnosie).

The nature and localizing significance of this defect have been the subject of numerous studies (Brain, 1941; Luria, 1959; Ettlinger, 1960; McFie and Zangwill, 1960; Kinsbourne and Warrington, 1962, 1963; Weigl, 1964; Fogel, 1967). Failure on picture description and interpretation tasks in patients with brain disease is certainly not rare. Fogel found that 25% of a heterogeneous group of 100 brain damaged patients performed defectively in the sense that their description of a picture did not go beyond describing elements in it. Fogel also found that failing performance was associated with, but not completely determined by, general mental impairment. When "general mental impairment" was defined as a WAIS IQ score significantly below expectations for the patient's educational background, 32% of the impaired cases showed defective performance as compared to 21% of the unimpaired cases. Some investigators (e.g., Luria; Kinsbourne and Warrington) have related the deficit to either left-sided or bilateral occipital-lobe disease, but the findings of others suggest that failure may be associated with lesions in diverse areas. Fogel, in fact, found in his sample that patients with frontal-lobe disease made the poorest performances. Nor have comparisons of patients with left- and right-hemisphere lesions shown consistent differences. This rather confused assemblage of results is understandable when one considers that the task of interpreting a complex meaningful picture makes demands not only on visual integration but also on ideational-associative capacity, verbal encoding, and verbal fluency. Thus a task such as this may be failed by different patients for different reasons. In the light of these considerations, Weigl (1964) questioned the validity of the concept of "simultaneous agnosia" itself, although he did not deny the potential usefulness of picture description tests in the assessment of brain-diseased patients.

The identification of incomplete and mutilated figures and "closure" tasks such as Mooney's (1957) faces and the figure completion test of Street (1931) furnish rather purer measures of the ability to synthesize visual information. As has already been noted, defective performance on Mooney test is associated with right-hemisphere disease (Lansdell, 1968; Newcombe and Russell, 1969). Impaired perception of incomplete figures has also been related to right-hemisphere lesions. Presenting such a task to patients with unilateral brain disease, Warrington and James (1967) found that patients with right-hemisphere lesions performed significantly worse than either controls or patients with left-hemisphere lesions. Within the right-hemisphere group, those patients with lesions involving the posterior parietal region performed most defectively. In contrast, both aphasic and nonaphasic patients with left-hemisphere disease performed on a level comparable to that of controls. Poor performance on the Street test has also been found in patients with right-hemisphere disease, particularly those with lesions involving the occipital lobe or with visual field defects (Orgass et al., 1972).

IMPAIRMENT IN FACIAL RECOGNITION

The question might well be asked why faces have been singled out for particular study in the field of behavioral neurology as contrasted, for example, to automobiles, buildings, or intricate designs. There are at least two reasons for this special interest. First, as will be seen, there are patients who present as their primary complaint a loss in the ability to identify familiar persons, a defect that has come to be known as *prosopagnosia* or *facial agnosia*. Thus, facial recognition possesses an inherent clinical interest. Secondly, as

Meadows (1974a) has pointed out, facial recognition does occupy a special place in visual experience. Over the course of a lifetime, one learns to discriminate thousands of different faces. There is no other category of nonverbal visual stimulus remotely like it in this respect. It is true that thousands of words can be discriminated but these are verbally analyzable and encodable.

There are two types of impairment of facial recognition that are essentially independent of each other and that have different neurological implications. The first is *facial agnosia* or the inability to identify the faces of familiar persons. The second is defective discrimination or matching of unfamiliar faces which makes no demands on memory or past experience.

Facial agnosia

The primary disability in facial agnosia is a patient's incapacity to recognize persons familiar to him, even the members of his family, on the basis of visual perception of their faces. He may succeed in identifying another person on the basis of stature, a distinctive coiffure, facial mark, type of clothing, voice, or gait. He may be able to give an adequate verbal description of the face of a familiar person and at the same time be unable to identify it on confrontation. Such patients have no difficulty in recognizing objects.

A number of other disabilities are frequently (but not invariably) associated with facial agnosia. The patient may fail to recognize the meaning of such graphic symbols as a red cross or a swastika, even though he perceives them clearly. He may show spatial disorientation, defective perception of colors, loss of topographic memory, or constructional apraxia. Defects in the left visual field are the rule. So-called dyspraxia for dressing has been observed in some patients. Thus, in general, facial agnosia is seen in combination with the constellation of behavioral defects associated with right-hemisphere disease, leading to the conclusion that it also is a "right hemisphere" phenomenon. In support of this conclusion, Hécaen and Angelergues (1963) found in a clinical study of 22 cases of facial agnosia that had 16 right-hemisphere lesions, 4 had bilateral disease, and 2 had left-hemisphere lesions.

However, although there is no doubt that clinical evidence favors an association between facial agnosia and right-hemisphere disease, the analyses by Rondot and Tzavaras (1969), Lhermitte et al. (1972), and Meadows (1974a) of the anatomical findings in these cases strongly suggest that bilateral disease is necessary for the appearance of the deficit. Table 8-2 reproduces the listing of autopsied cases presented by Lhermitte et al. (1972), augmented by the recent case study of Benson, Segarra, and Albert (1974). As will be seen, bilateral lesions have been found in all instances.

Since only a few cases have come to autopsy, these findings do not rule out the possibility that facial agnosia may occur as a consequence of disease confined to a single hemisphere, particularly the right hemisphere. Nevertheless, there is reason to believe that bilateral disease is the context in which prosopagnosia occurs. The fact that it is a quite uncommon symptom suggests that combined lesions

TABLE 8-2   *Autopsy Findings in Facial Agnosia**

AUTHOR	ETIOLOGY	SITES OF LESION
1. Wilbrand (1892)	Encephalomalacia	Right occipital lobe extending to calcarine fissure; left occipital lobe (smaller lesion)
2. Heidenhain (1927)	Encephalomalacia	Right & left occipital lobes extending to lower aspect of calcarine fissures
3. Arseni et al. (1958)	Spongioblastoma	Left temporal lobe; right tapetum corporis callosi
4. Hécaen & Angelergues (1962)	Glioblastoma	Right parieto-occipital tumor infiltrating splenium & extending to left hemisphere
5. Pevzner et al. (1962)	Encephalomalacia	Left angular gyrus extending to parieto-occipital fissure; inferior lip of right striate cortex
6. Bornstein (1965)	Glioblastoma	Left tempoparieto-occipital tumor infiltrating splenium
7. Gloning et al. (1970)	Encephalomalacia	Left frontal lobe, insula & fusiform gyrus; right frontal lobe, insula, supramarginal gyrus & fusiform gyrus
8. Lhermitte et al. (1972)	Encephalomalacia	Left fusiform gyrus; white matter of right fusiform & lingual gyri
9. Benson, Segarra, and Albert (1974)	Encephalomalacia	Left medial occipital area; splenium & right inferior longitudinal fasciculus

* Adapted from Lhermitte et al. (1972).

are required: if posterior right-hemisphere disease involving the lingual and fusiform gyri were a sufficient condition, the deficit would be encountered far more frequently than it is. Moreover, clinical symptomatology in these cases has not proved to be a reliable indication of the unilateral nature of the lesion. As Lhermitte et al. (1972) pointed out, the cases of Hécaen and Angelergues (1962) and Pevzner, Bornstein, and Loewenthal (1962), that are listed in Table 8-2, were judged on clinical grounds to have lesions confined to the right hemisphere but autopsy study showed bilateral involvement. Conversely, Lhermitte et al. (1972) cite a patient with lesions directly compromising the right lingual and fusiform gyri and hippocampus who was not prosopagnostic.

Yet clinical evidence indicates that, within the context of bilateral disease, a lesion in the inferior occipital area of the right hemisphere is a crucial factor. Many years ago, Faust (1955) emphasized the association between left superior quadrantanopia and facial agnosia and this point has been documented by Meadows (1974a) whose tabulation of the field defects found in prosopagnostic patients shows that a left upper quadrantic defect was observed in 33 of 34 patients who presented with either a bilateral or left field defect. As Table 8-2 shows, this indication of right inferior occipital involvement is substantiated by autopsy findings. Meadows points out that the possible functional effect of lesions so situated is to prevent visual information from reaching nonoccipital areas, primarily the temporal lobe.

It might be speculated that this break in connections leads to failure in the associative elaboration of visual percepts with reference to past experience. There remains the problem of why this failure should be more-or-less restricted to facial identification. In any case, prosopagnosia can be viewed as a particular example of Lissauer's "associative agnosia" (see Chapter 9). An alternative conception that the disability is a partial or restricted form of the amnesic syndrome has been advanced by Warrington and James (1967). As Meadows (1974a) points out, arguments can be marshalled for and against the conception.

Defective discrimination of unfamiliar faces
Studies of the capacity of patients to discriminate and identify unfamiliar faces were originally undertaken on the assumption that

the abilities which would be assessed were the same as those under-lying the identification of familiar faces and with the expectation that the results would elucidate the nature of facial agnosia. Subse-quent experience showed that the assumption was unfounded (cf. Benton and Van Allen, 1972). However, as it happens, studies of the discrimination of unfamiliar faces generated findings of clinical interest in their own right and there has been continuing investiga-tion of this type of performance both in patients with brain disease and in normal subjects.

Studies of facial discrimination in patients with unilateral brain disease have consistently shown an association between failing per-formance and the presence of right-hemisphere lesions (DeRenzi and Spinnler, 1966; Warrington and James, 1967; Benton and Van Allen, 1968; DeRenzi, Faglioni, and Spinnler, 1968; Tzavaras, Hé-caen, and LeBras, 1970). The observed frequency of defective per-formance varies from one sample to another, but all studies have found that the relative frequency of defect is more than twice as high in patients with right-hemisphere disease than in those with left-hemisphere lesions. The highest frequency of failure is found in patients with right-hemisphere disease and visual field defect, the latter pointing to the importance of the retrorolandic localization of the lesion. (That visual field defect per se is not an important determinant of performance level is indicated by the finding that left-hemisphere-damaged patients with field defects do not perform less well than those without field defects.) Among patients with left-hemisphere disease, those with posterior lesions and aphasia are most likely to show defective performance.

The inference from clinical investigation that the right hemi-sphere plays a particularly important role in mediating facial dis-crimination is supported by the findings of visual field studies in normal subjects. Presenting tachistoscopically controlled stimuli of brief duration (42-66 msec) to each half-field, Hilliard (1973) found a significant left-field superiority in the accuracy of identification of faces. Similarly, Rizzolati, Umiltà, and Berlucchi (1971) found that reaction time for the recognition of faces was shorter in the left field than in the right.

The clinical inference that impaired discrimination of unfamiliar faces is particularly closely associated with posterior right-hemi-sphere disease is, of course, subject to the same criticisms as is the corresponding inference for a "right hemisphere" localization of prosopagnosia. Since no autopsy studies of patients who showed pronounced defects in facial discrimination during life have been reported, the question cannot be decided on anatomical grounds. In addition, the not infrequent occurrence of failing performance in aphasic patients with posterior left-hemisphere disease indicates that the relationship between performance level and lesional locus is not a simple one.

IMPAIRMENT IN COLOR RECOGNITION

A variety of performance deficits are subsumed under this heading as well as under the terms, "color imperception," "color agnosia," "color anomia," and "amnesia for colors" found in the clinical literature. A patient may be unable to name colors correctly, but not show a correspondingly severe impairment in object naming. He may be unable to point to colors named by the examiner. He may not be able to give the characteristic colors of common objects, e.g., "red" for blood, "white" for snow, etc. Presented with uncolored line drawings of common objects (e.g., a banana or a fork) and a display of different colors, he may make gross errors in matching colors to the drawings, choosing blue for the banana or black for the fork. Presented with a large display of different colors, for example, the Holmgren woolen skeins, he may not achieve an adequate sorting of the colors into categories on the basis of hue. He may perform defectively on tests for color-blindness, such as the Ishihara plates. Finally, he may show a visual field defect for colored targets but not for a white target. These deficits may or may not be the subject of complaint by the patient.

It is obvious that there is no unitary impairment in color recognition. Instead, these diverse performance defects point to the presence of distinctive underlying disabilities of a sensory, perceptual, associative, or linguistic nature, each of which has a different neurological basis. The major forms of deficit are described below.

Impaired perception of colors
It has long been known that defects in the discrimination of colors, roughly analogous to congenital weakness in color discrimination,

may occur as a consequence of brain disease. Central or acquired achromatopsia, dyschromatopsia, color blindness, and color imperception are some of the names that have been employed to designate these defects. Their presence is assessed by the same tests, such as the Ishihara plates and the Farnsworth-Munsell 100 Hue test, utilized to probe for congenital color weakness.

Although acquired color imperception had been the subject of several case reports, the first large-scale study of its occurrence in patients with brain disease was undertaken by DeRenzi and Spinnler (1967). Color perception was assessed by two tests, the Ishihara plates and a color matching task in which the patients had to abstract pairs of identical colors from two sets of colored squares. Failing performance on the color matching test was shown by 17% of the brain-diseased patients, with a decidedly higher frequency in those with right-hemisphere lesions (23%) than in those with left-hemisphere lesions (12%). Essentially the same findings were obtained for the Ishihara test where failing performance was shown by 9% of the total group, 14% of right-hemisphere-damaged patients, and 6% of left-hemisphere-damaged patients. Further analysis showed that failure was particularly frequent among patients with visual field defects. In the patients with left-hemisphere disease, aphasics showed a higher frequency of failure than nonaphasics, but it is not clear whether the aphasic patients also had visual field defects.

A second large-scale study (Scotti and Spinnler, 1970) utilized the Farnsworth-Munsell 100 Hue test to determine whether the observed effects of side-of-lesion and visual field defect could be confirmed and also to investigate performance along the color spectrum in brain-diseased and control patients. The salient findings were that patients with right-hemisphere disease and visual field defect performed most poorly and patients with left-hemisphere disease but without visual field defect performed at a normal level. All groups, including the control patients, showed the same performance profile characterized by a relatively high number of errors in the green-blue section of the spectrum. Essentially similar findings indicating a higher frequency of color imperception in patients with right-hemisphere disease have also been reported by Lhermitte et al. (1969) and Assal, Eisert, and Hécaen (1969). In the latter study, however, the observed between-hemispheres difference was small and nonsignificant.

Two recent studies have addressed the question of the anatomical basis of acquired color imperception in patients with brain disease. Meadows (1974b), on the basis of a review of the clinical literature and a personally observed case, concludes that bilateral lesions in the region of the occipitotemporal junction (i.e., the anterior inferior part of the occipital lobe) represent the crucial pathological basis for the disorder. He points out that all the cases reviewed showed visual field defects, bilateral superior altitudinal defects being particularly frequent. Moreover, the three cases that were studied postmortem showed bilateral inferior occipital lesions. The study of Green and Lessell (1977) of five patients who showed impairment in color perception on the Ishihara plates supports Meadows' conclusion that bilateral occipital disease is the basis for the deficit. The authors of both studies comment on the frequent association of color imperception with facial agnosia. The combination is, of course, understandable since the crucial lesions underlying both symptoms are situated in the same territory.

Impairment in color association
Failure in tasks requiring a patient to indicate the characteristic colors of familiar objects, within the context of intact color perception, is the primary performance deficit covered by this concept. Provided that the patient understands and can produce the names of colors and familiar objects, an appropriate method to probe for the presence of the defect is to ask him what the usual color of an object, such as salt, peas, or a banana, is. Having him match colors to uncolored line drawings of objects either by actually coloring the drawing or pointing to the appropriate color in a display, is a more desirable procedure since it circumvents overt language activity.

The inability of some patients with brain disease to link colors (or their names) to objects with which they are characteristically associated was noted as early as the 1880's by ophthalmologists and neurologists and was the topic of considerable discussion over the course of subsequent decades. Wilbrand and Saenger (1904–1906) postulated a disconnection between the cortical visual center and the speech area in the left hemisphere as the essential basis for the disability. However, Lewandowsky (1908) pointed out that the failure of these patients on nonverbal coloring tasks (sometimes with preserved ability to give the name of the colors associated with objects) indicated a deficit beyond color anomia. Instead, Lewandowsky advanced the idea that the basic deficit consisted of a "splitting" between the concept of form and that of color, leading to a loss of associations between objects and their characteristic colors. All authors acknowledged the close relationship of the disability to aphasic disorder and Sittig (1921) emphasized the crucial role of verbal associative functions in performance.

DeRenzi and Spinnler (1967) included both verbal and nonverbal color association tests in their study of color imperception. The verbal task consisted of asking the patient to name the characteristic color of familiar objects. In the nonverbal task, the patient was given a choice of 10 colored pencils and instructed to color a number of line drawings. Predictably, most of the failures on the verbal color association task were made by aphasic patients. However, a few nonaphasic patients with right-hemisphere disease (about 10%) also failed; most of these showed defects in color perception (Ishihara plates and color matching). No such relationship was evident in the patients with left-hemisphere disease. The results for the nonverbal coloring task were most interesting. About 50% of the aphasics failed the task, i.e., made a score below that of the poorest control. Performance level within the aphasic group showed a modest correlation ($r = .48$) with assessed severity of aphasic disorder. A few nonaphasic patients (11% of those with right-hemisphere disease; 7% of those with left-hemisphere disease) also performed defectively, failure here being closely associated with defective color perception.

A second study by DeRenzi et al. (1972) also demonstrated a close relationship between impaired performance on a nonverbal coloring task and aphasic disorder. When attention was restricted to the 18 poorest performances in a sample of 166 patients with unilateral brain disease (60 of whom were aphasic), it was found that 17 of these were made by aphasic patients. Stated in another way, gross failure on the task was shown by 28% of the aphasic but only 1% of the nonaphasic patients.

A recent study by Guzman (1975) has confirmed these findings. Aphasic patients with significant auditory comprehension defect invariably failed both verbal and nonverbal color association tasks. Impaired performance was shown by 11% of nonaphasic patients with right-hemisphere disease and 10% of those with left-hemisphere disease. Other relevant studies are those of Lhermitte et al. (1969) and Tzavaras, Hécaen, and LeBras (1971).

The remarkable frequency with which aphasic patients fail the nonverbal task of matching colors to line drawings is often interpreted as implying that verbal mediational processes must underlie the matching performance. This is a reasonable conclusion but, as DeRenzi and his co workers have pointed out, it has not been securely established. Another possibility is that defective performance reflects impairment in a cognitive function subserved by left-hemisphere mechanisms and hence likely to be associated with (but not dependent upon) aphasic disorder.

Impairment in the verbal identification of colors

The inability to name colors on visual confrontation or to point to them when their names are supplied by the examiner are the major performance deficits subsumed under this heading. Other tasks that have been used to probe for defective verbal identification of colors are the completion of sentences calling for the name of a color (e.g., "The color of an apple is ———") and controlled word association in which the patient is asked to name as many different colors as he can (cf. Wyke and Holgate, 1973).

It is to be expected that aphasic patients will perform defectively on these tasks, the degree of defect being proportional to the severity of their linguistic disabilities. It is also to be expected that patients with impairment in color perception will perform defectively on visuoverbal tasks. In line with these expectations, DeRenzi and Spinnler (1967) found that 42% of their group of aphasic patients failed a combined test of color naming and identifying colors when the names were supplied, as compared to 10% of nonaphasic patients. Moreover, 5 of the 6 nonaphasic patients with right-hemisphere disease who failed the verbal tests were found to have defective color perception as well. There remained 5 nonaphasic patients with left-hemisphere disease who failed the verbal tests and who did not show impairment in color perception. These patients showed an apparently specific "color anomia" and/or "color name amnesia" not attributable to either linguistic impairment or perceptual deficit.

The most striking examples of specific visuoverbal color disability are seen in alexic patients who fail color naming tasks and at the same time show intact (or only mildly impaired) ability to name objects and pictures. This association of incorrect color verbalization with acquired alexia is highly frequent and is often included in the syndrome of pure alexia (i.e., without agraphia) and right hemianopia (see Chapter 3). Gloning, Gloning, and Hoff (1968) found evidence of "color agnosia" in 19 of 27 patients with pure alexia. Some insight into the neural mechanisms underlying visuoverbal color disabilities has been gained from clinicopathological studies of individual alexic patients. The findings and implications of two detailed case reports, one dealing with an alexic patient with impairment in verbal color identification and the other with an alexic patient without such impairment, will be considered.

Geschwind and Fusillo (1964, 1966) describe a 58-year-old man who, following a vascular accident, manifested pure alexia and right hemianopia as permanent defects after the acute episode. He could not read words aloud or match them to corresponding pictures. He could read a few single letters and some two-digit numbers. He could write to dictation but was not able to read his handwriting. He was able both to spell orally and to identify words spelled to him orally. Speech production, understanding of oral speech, and object naming were intact, as were right–left orientation, finger naming, and oral arithmetic calculation. The single remarkable nonverbal disability was a severe disturbance in topographical orientation, reflected in his inability to give the location of his home or to describe routes in traveling from one place to another.

He was totally unable to name colors (including black, white, and gray) correctly, to identify the colors of pictures of objects where there was no inherent association between the color and the object (e.g., necktie, dress), and even to identify the colors of objects that are associated with specific colors (e.g., white writing paper, red bricks). Nor could he point to colors when their names were supplied by the examiner. In contrast, his performance on nonverbal color tasks was quite adequate. He could match and sort colors and correctly matched colors to uncolored line drawings (e.g., yellow to a banana). His performance on pseudoisochromatic tests of color vision was normal. He was able to state the usual colors of familiar objects such as an apple or the sky.

Postmortem examination disclosed areas of infarction in the left calcarine cortex, the splenium of the corpus callosum, and the left hippocampus, all within the territory of the left posterior cerebral artery.

Geschwind and Fusillo interpret this syndrome of alexia, impaired color cognition, and right hemianopia as the functional outcome of a disconnection between the right occipital cortex and the language area of the left hemisphere. Their interpretation follows the classic explanation that the failure in naming (and identification) of colors as well as the alexia are due to a break in the connections between the visual cortex and the language area. Thus color anomia comes about because visual information cannot reach the language zone of the left hemisphere to be encoded. Faulty identification of colors named by the examiner comes about because verbal information cannot reach the visual cortex to be decoded.

A persisting problem has been how to explain the retained capacity for object naming and object identification by name shown by patients with alexia and color anomia since these sensory-verbal performances also would seem to depend upon the same visual mechanisms that are invoked to explain color naming and identification performances. A number of possible explanations have been advanced, none with great confidence. One possibility is that visually presented objects or pictures arouse tactile associative activity in the brain leading to excitation of anterior areas in the right hemisphere which is then transmitted to the language zone of the left hemisphere through callosal fibers anterior to the splenium. Letters, words, and colors do not arouse such tactile associative activity (cf. Geschwind, 1962). Another possibility is that the naming of familiar objects is such an elementary and automatized performance that (assuming that the splenial fibers have not been completely destroyed) it can be sustained by meager interhemispheric connections (cf. Howes, 1962). This explanation implies that the

patient with alexia and color anomia should have difficulty in naming less familiar objects. The clinical observation that the majority
of alexic patients do in fact exhibit mild word-finding difficulties
can be cited to support the implication. Still another possibility is
that object naming is subserved by neural mechanisms that are
different from those involved in color naming or reading.

As has been noted, color anomia and alexia do not invariably
appear in combination. The case report of Greenblatt (1973) describing an alexic patient without agraphia, hemianopia, or color
anomia is instructive because it points to the possible neural mechanisms underlying each of the two performances. Autopsy study of
this patient disclosed a neoplasm that had invaded the splenium
and inferior part of the left occipital lobe leaving the left calcarine
cortex and optic radiation intact. Thus there was an interruption
in the connection between the left angular gyrus and the right
visual cortex, and a partial interruption between the left angular
gyrus and the left visual cortex, involving the inferior or ventral
connections. Greenblatt suggests that this disconnection was responsible for the patient's isolated alexia and that the remaining
intact dorsal connection from the occipital cortex to the angular
gyrus accounts for the preservation of color naming.

Thus the indications are that specific impairment in verbal operations with colors is explainable in terms of derangement of
specific neural mechanisms and that some progress has been made in
the identification of these mechanisms. Advances in knowledge
depend upon the continued accumulation of detailed clinicopathological correlational data.

VISUOSPATIAL DEFECTS

Patients with brain disease may show any of a variety of performance deficits indicative of faulty appreciation of the spatial aspects of visual experience. Some of the more prominent deficits and
their correlates and interrelations are described below.

Defective localization of points in space

This disability has long been familiar to clinicians who observed
that patients with parieto-occipital injuries exhibited it in particu-

larly severe form (cf. Benton, 1969). In addition, some large-scale studies have assessed its frequency and its association with locus-of-lesion.

Warrington and Rabin (1970) presented two cards containing single dots in a vertical array to patients who were required to state whether or not the position of the dots was the same on the two cards. Both simultaneous and successive presentations were given. The task proved to be rather easy, all groups of patients making relatively low error scores. Nevertheless, it could be shown that the performance of patients with right parietal lesions was significantly poorer than that of patients with left-hemisphere disease or control patients; the latter two groups did not differ from each other.

However, Ratcliff and Davies-Jones (1972), using a different procedure for assessing accuracy of visual localization, obtained rather different results. In their study, patients were required to touch point stimuli on a projection perimeter while maintaining fixation of gaze. Defective localization was defined in terms of an average error greater than that made by any control subject. The essential findings were that patients with posterior parietotemporo-occipital lesions in *either* hemisphere performed defectively while none of the patients with anterior lesions showed defective localization. Visual field defect was not a significant correlate of performance level.

Thus the results of the two studies were in agreement about the importance of parieto-occipital disease in the production of the deficit but differed in their implications about the role of the right hemisphere in the mediation of visual localization performances. However, a more recent investigation by Hannay, Varney, and Benton (1976) has generated strong evidence of a striking difference in the performances of patients with right- and left-hemisphere lesions on a visual localization task. In this study the level of difficulty of the task was deliberately augmented by reducing the exposure time and requiring the patient to identify the locations of simultaneously exposed pairs of dots as well as single dots. Under these experimental conditions, 45% of a group of 22 patients with right-hemisphere lesions performed defectively (i.e., below the level of the poorest control patient). None of the 22 patients with left-hemisphere disease performed defectively and the mean score of this group was practically the same as that of the control patient group. In contrast to the Warrington-Rabin findings, visual field defect was associated with defective performance in this study. And, in contrast to the results of both of the earlier studies, patients with perirolandic lesions of the right hemisphere were found to be impaired as frequently as those with posterior lesions. All three studies were in agreement that patients with unilateral frontal lesions are likely to perform normally.

Possible reasons for the inconsistency of these findings may be considered. Some clinicians have differentiated between the localization of stimuli within "grasping distance" (thus permitting a reaching or pointing response) and those beyond arm's reach, requiring a verbal judgment (cf. Brain, 1941; Birkmayer, 1951). In addition, a distinction is sometimes made between the "absolute" localization of a single stimulus in relation to the observer and "relative" localization involving the spatial relationship between two stimuli as seen by the observer (cf. Kleist, 1923). The pointing responses made by the patients in the study of Ratcliff and Davies-Jones assessed "absolute" localization of stimuli within grasping distance. In contrast, the judgmental and matching responses called for in the Warrington-Rabin and Hannay-Varney-Benton studies assessed "relative" localization of stimuli which could not be touched. Thus it may be that the right hemisphere plays a distinctively important role in the mediation of "relative" but not "absolute" localization performances. A study in which both types of localization tasks are given to the same group of patients could be done to test the cogency of this hypothesis as well as to assess whether the unexpectedly high frequency of defect in the patients with right perirolandic lesions found in the Hannay-Varney-Benton study was a chance finding in a small sample of cases.

Defective judgment of direction and distance

Appreciation of the directional orientation of lines presented as either tactile or visual stimuli has been the subject of a number of investigations designed to determine whether there is a differential hemispheric contribution in the mediation of this spatial performance (Carmon and Benton, 1969; Newcombe and Russell, 1969; Warrington and Rabin, 1970; Fontenot and Benton, 1971, 1972; Benton, Levin, and Varney, 1973; Benton, Hannay, and Varney, 1975). The results of all these studies have been consistent in indicating that perception of directional orientation is mediated primarily by the right hemisphere in right handed subjects. The clearest demonstration of this hemispheric asymmetry, as reflected in the finding of particularly severe defect in patients with right-hemisphere disease, is provided by the study of Benton, Hannay, and Varney (1975).

A task requiring identification of the directional orientation of lines was given to the same patients in whom accuracy of dot localization had been assessed. Both single- and double-line stimuli were presented to central vision for 300 msec and this was followed by the presentation of a response card on which the patient identified the line or lines which he had seen. (Fig. 8-1). Three groups of right handed patients (left-hemisphere lesions, right-hemisphere lesions, controls without history or evidence of brain disease) comparable with respect to age and type-of-lesion were studied. A strikingly high proportion (59%) of the patients with right-hemisphere lesions performed defectively, i.e., at a level below that represented by the lowest score in either the control or the left-hemisphere group (Table 8-3). As in the case of dot-localization performance, patients with right perirolandic lesions performed as defectively as those with right posterior lesions.

The circumstance that both the dot localization and line orientation tasks had been given to the same patients made it possible to assess the relationship between these types of performance. The correlation coefficient between the scores on the two tasks in the group of 22 patients with right-hemisphere lesions was .74, the split-half reliability coefficients of the tasks having been found to be .88 (dots) and .89 (lines). This substantial positive correlation indicates that to a large extent the same factors determine performance level on the two tasks. The higher sensitivity of the lines task to the presence of right-hemisphere disease suggests that it is measuring these factors somewhat more adequately.

As has been noted, analogous tasks assessing the tactile perception of line direction have generated similar results showing hemispheric asymmetry in the mediation of performance. Thus the indications are that the right hemisphere plays a more important role than the

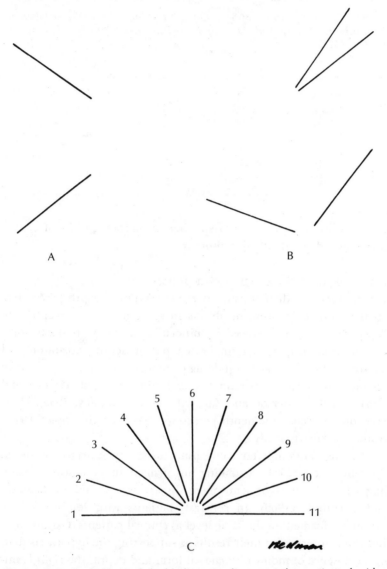

Fig. 8-1 (A-B) Single-line and double-line stimuli presented to patients for identification; (C) multiple-choice card on which patients identified stimuli.

TABLE 8-3 *Distributions of Scores of Control and Brain-Diseased Patients on Tasks Requiring Judgment of Line Direction (Benton, Hannay, and Varney, 1975)*

SCORE	CONTROL	LEFT LESION	RIGHT LESION
31–33	1	1	—
28–30	6	3	1
25–27	12	7	3
22–24	1	8	2
19–21	2	2	3
16–18	—	—	7
<16	—	—	6

left in subserving behavior requiring the apprehension of spatial relations independently of sensory modality.

DEPTH PERCEPTION AND DISTANCE JUDGMENT

It is necessary to distinguish between two types of depth perception, "real" depth perception of objects in space and the perception of "apparent" depth produced by binocular disparity in stereoscopic presentation. Impairment in both types of depth perception and concomitant inaccuracy in judging distances have been described in the clinical literature as sequellae of brain injury (cf. Holmes and Horrax, 1919; Paterson and Zangwill, 1944; Critchley, 1953). However, only stereoscopic depth perception has been the topic of controlled systematic study.

Utilizing random-letter stereograms of the type originally developed by Julesz (1964), a striking impairment in stereoscopic vision in patients with right-hemisphere disease was found by Carmon and Bechtoldt (1969). In contrast, patients with left-hemisphere disease performed on the same level as control patients. Carmon and Bechtoldt interpreted their results as supporting the hypothesis that, in the absence of monocular cues of form and depth, the right hemisphere is "dominant" for stereopsis in right handed subjects. Their results have been confirmed by Benton and Hécaen (1970) and Hamsher (1978). Both of the latter studies found that many patients who failed the random-letter stereoscopic task were able to perform adequately on a conventional test of stereoscopic vision involving defined forms. Thus it seemed evident that the technique devised by Julesz, in which monocular cues are completely excluded, is required to demonstrate the presence of the defect.

As has been indicated, the frequency of impairment in "real" depth perception in patients with brain disease and the relationship of such impairment to locus-of-lesion have not been systematically investigated. A comparative study of both types of depth perception would be informative and in fact is necessary for further understanding of the underlying neural mechanisms.

Defective topographical orientation

The most prominent performance defects in this category are failure to describe the spatial characteristics of familiar surroundings (such as the arrangement of the rooms in one's house), to tell how one would travel from one point to another in one's home town, and to indicate the location of major cities on a map of one's native country. The failure may be on the level of "representation" or "revisualization" rather than of perception, and the patient is apparently unable to call up the detailed schematic framework which he would need to describe routes or make localizations. However, failing performance on some orientational tasks may be due to a specific perceptual defect, namely, failure to attend to one or another part of the stimulus configuration involved in the task.

Hécaen and Angelergues (1963) assessed "topographical memory" by requiring the patients to describe familiar routes, the arrangement of rooms in his house, the street on which the house was located, or the main square of the city. Studying large samples of patients with unilateral or bilateral retrorolandic disease, they found that loss of topographical memory, as reflected in poor performance on these tasks, was shown only by patients with either bilateral or right-hemisphere disease; even in these groups the deficit occurred rather infrequently. The highest incidence of failure (8%) was found in the bilateral cases. The patients with right-hemisphere disease showed a 6% and those with left-hemisphere disease a 1% incidence. Control patients were not studied and it is not made clear how defective performance was defined.

Hécaen and Angelergues also studied geographic orientation (under the heading of "topographical concepts") by having their patients identify the principal cities, regions, and rivers of France on a map. Again, the criteria for judging whether a performance was defective are not explicitly stated. Here the authors found that no less than 21% of the patients with retrorolandic lesions of the right hemisphere performed defectively, as compared to 4% of left-hemisphere cases and 6% of bilateral cases. It is clear from the descriptions in the monograph that failure on this map test was often associated with visual neglect of (i.e., failure to attend to) the left half of the map.

Benton, Levin, and Van Allen (1974) assessed geographic orientation both with a verbal test (requiring the patient to state the direction he would travel in going from one city or state to another) and with a nonverbal test in which he localized cities and states on a large map of the United States. Since educational background is an obvious determinant of performance level on these tasks, normative data were collected on two separate groups of control patients, one with 12 or more years and the other with fewer than 12 years of education. Defective performance was defined as a score 3 or more SD's below the respective group mean on each task. Defective performance on the verbal directions test occurred with equally low frequency (about 5%) in patients with right- or left-hemisphere disease. The frequency of failure on the map localization test was somewhat higher (22%) with only a slight difference between the right- and left-hemisphere groups (25% vs. 20%). However, a "vector" score for the map test, which provided a measure of directional bias in localization, clearly differentiated between the two unilateral groups. The mean "vector" score of the patients with left-hemisphere disease was −3.2, reflecting a systematic shift in localization toward the left or "western" half of the map. The mean "vector" score of the patients with right-hemisphere disease was +4.4, reflecting an even greater systematic shift in localization toward the right or "eastern" half of the map. For the most part, defective performance was shown only by patients with less than a twelfth-grade education.

Our knowledge of the determinants and correlates of defective topographical orientation, in the sense in which the term has been used in this section, is rather scanty. From the anatomical standpoint, it is still not entirely clear that there is an unequal hemispheric contribution to the mediation of these performances, but a predominant role of the right hemisphere is probable. Neglect of the left or right visual field may distort performance and lead to failure on some tasks. Visual neglect is shown more frequently by patients with right-hemisphere disease than those with left-hemisphere lesions (see Chapter 10), thus creating a bias toward a higher incidence of failure in the first group, as Hécaen and Angelergues found. These authors also reported an association between impaired topographical orientation and a number of other defects associated with right-hemisphere disease, such as constructional apraxia, dressing dyspraxia, and a "spatial" type of dyslexia.

Unilateral visual neglect

This term refers to the longstanding clinical observation that some patients do not respond to stimuli in one or the other lateral visual field. "Unilateral spatial agnosia" and "hemianopic weakness of attention" are other terms that have been used to designate the phenomenon. Unilateral neglect is often seen in association with homonymous hemianopia. However, the majority of hemianopic patients, having learned to compensate for their visual defect by postural adjustments, do not show persistent inattention to stimuli in the blind field. Conversely, many patients who are not hemianopic are inattentive to stimuli in the visual field opposite to the side of their lesion. Visual neglect is encountered far more frequently in patients with lesions of the right hemisphere than in those with left-hemisphere disease. Whether this difference implies a special functional property of the right hemisphere or is referable to such factors as extent and type of lesion is a question that is still debated. The one-sided neglect may extend to auditory and tactile, as well as visual, stimuli.

Various features of a patient's behavior make his unilateral neglect apparent to clinical observation. He will brush up against one side of a doorway in going through it. During a bedside visit, he will respond to persons on his right but not to those on his left. In traversing a route, he will go astray, because of a persistent failure to make left turns. During a meal he will "forget" to eat salad or dessert, if the dish has been placed on the left side of the tray.

A number of maneuvers can be employed to elicit evidence of unilateral visual neglect. One is to have the patient mark the midpoint of a horizontal line. Unilateral neglect will be reflected in deviant placement of the mark off the center toward the unaffected side. One supposes that this displacement occurs because the patient does not "see" one end of the line and marks the midpoint of that part of the line which he does perceive. Neglect of this type is likely to occur in hemianopic patients but it is also observed in patients without a demonstrable lateral hemianopia. In addition, some hemianopic patients, who presumably have learned to compensate for their visual deficit by appropriate motor adjustment, place the midpoint off center *toward* the affected side.

Colombo, DeRenzi, and Faglioni (1976) employed bisection of lines to good advantage in a study of visual neglect in patients with unilateral brain disease. Both right- and left-hemisphere-damaged groups showed significant displacement of the center point toward the side of the lesion (refer to Fig. 10-2). Hemianopic patients with right-hemisphere disease showed the most marked displacement but the other subgroups (right nonhemianopic, left hemianopic and nonhemianopic) also showed a significant shift in placement of the center mark toward the side of lesion. Of the four tasks used to elicit lateral neglect, line bisection appeared to be the most sensitive.

Another task that may be used for eliciting evidence of lateral neglect is to present the patient with a display of lines drawn on a sheet of paper and request him to cross each line (cf. Denny-Brown, 1963; Albert, 1973, Fig. 10-3, this volume). As would be expected, normal adults perform at a perfect or near-perfect level, failing to cross only one or two lines at most in an array of 40 or 50 lines. However, some patients with brain disease will fail to cross a larger number of lines as they proceed with the task. The omissions may occur on lines in different localizations on the display, presumably reflecting deficient attention and concentration, or they may be restricted to a particular part of the display, reflecting specific neglect of that part.

Albert (1973) presented a display of 40 randomly placed lines to be crossed to groups of patients with unilateral brain disease. All members of a group of 30 control patients had performed perfectly on the task. Eleven (37%) of 30 patients with right-hemisphere lesion and 11 (30%) of 36 patients with left-hemisphere lesions made one or more omissions. Although the between-hemispheric difference in the frequency of less-than-perfect performances was slight, the patients with right-hemisphere lesions showed a greater severity of defect, their mean omission score being 4.8, as compared to a mean error score of .7 in the left-brain-damaged patients. However, only three patients showed omissions confined to the left or right part of the display; two patients with right-hemisphere lesions showed left neglect and one patient with left-hemisphere disease showed right neglect. Defective performance was associated with visual field defect and a posterior locus of lesion in the right hemisphere group.

Lateral visual neglect may also be disclosed in drawing performances, as in copying figures or drawing an object on verbal command. One side of the drawing, usually the left, will be omitted entirely or drawn poorly (for illustrative examples, see Fig. 10-1 in this volume, Critchley, 1953; Denny-Brown, 1963; Gainotti, Messerli, and Tissot, 1972; Lezak, 1976). Other tasks that may elicit the phenomenon are block construction (see Benton, 1969) and the localization of places on a map (see Benton, Levin, and Van Allen, 1974).

The mechanisms underlying lateral visual neglect have been the subject of much discussion. DeRenzi, Faglioni, and Scotti (1970) have postulated a "mutilated representation of space" as the basic cognitive deficit. The importance of sensory impairment has been emphasized by Gainotti, Messerli, and Tissot (1972). Most recently, Heilman and Valenstein (1972 a,b; Watson et al., 1973; Heilman, Watson, and Schulman, 1974) have proposed that lateral neglect (in any sensory modality) represents the behavioral outcome of a unilateral defect in arousal produced by injury to corticolimbic-reticular activating mechanisms (see pp. 276–298 of Chapter 10). Evidence supporting their hypothesis is derived from the experimental production of the neglect syndrome in animals as well as from study of patients with brain disease. (For a further discussion of neglect see Chapter 10).

VISUOCONSTRUCTIVE DISABILITIES

"Constructional praxis" refers to any type of performance in which parts are put together or articulated to form a single entity or object, for example, assembling blocks to form a design or drawing four lines to form a square or a diamond. Thus it implies organizing activity in which the spatial relations among the component parts must be accurately perceived if these parts are to be synthesized into the desired unity. Following the designation of Kleist (1923), the pathological counterpart of constructional praxis, i.e., a specific defect in spatial-organizational performances, usually has been referred to as "constructional apraxia." However, as the historical sketch presented earlier in this chapter indicates, Kleist had a specific idea of what he meant by "constructional apraxia" and did not think that all forms of constructional failure belonged in that category. For this reason, the neutral and more inclusive term "visuoconstructive disability" is now more often used to refer to failing performances of this type.

Given the very broad definition of the disability as a disturbance in "organizing" or "constructional" activity, it is inevitable that a variety of tasks should have been employed to probe for its presence. The types of tasks that have been used in clinical and investigative work are listed below:

1. Building in the vertical dimension. An illustrative example of some historical interest is shown in Figure 8-2. It appears in Poppelreuter's monograph published in 1917 and is probably the first pictorial representation of defective block construction by a brain-injured patient.

2. Building in the horizontal dimension, as in block design and stick constructions (see Critchley, 1953 for illustrative examples).

3. Three-dimensional block construction, either from a block model or a photograph (see Benton, 1969 and Warrington, 1969, for illustrative examples).

4. Copying line drawings (see Benton, 1962, for illustrative examples).

5. Drawing to verbal command, e.g., a house or a man (see Critchley, 1953 and Warrington, 1969, for illustrative examples).

In practice the level of difficulty of each type of task varies widely. With respect to copying, for example, a patient may be required to reproduce a few single figures, a design comprising several figures in a specific spatial relationship, or an extremely complicated figure containing innumerable details, such as Rey's complex figure (cf.

Fig. 8-2 Defective vertical block building (Poppelreuter, 1917).

Lezak, 1976). The actual block model may be presented to him for block design construction or he may have to proceed on the basis of a reduced schematic representation, as in the WAIS block design subtest. The stimulus for a three-dimensional block construction may be either the actual model or a two-dimensional representation of it. Clearly these diverse tasks are not equivalent in their demands on sustained attention, the capacity for deliberation, perceptual acuity, the apprehension of spatial relationships, judgment of perspective, and motor skill. Yet all are considered to be measures of "constructional praxis."

As has been mentioned, Kleist localized the causative lesion of "constructional apraxia" in the posterior parietal area of the left hemisphere. Subsequent clinical observation supported this localization, in particular, the frequent association of constructional apraxia with other symptoms referable to posterior left-hemisphere disease, such as aphasic disorder, finger agnosia, and right–left disorientation. However, the fact that patients with right-hemisphere disease also showed visuoconstructive disabilities became increasingly evident and, indeed, the indications were that these patients were likely to be more frequently and more severely impaired than those with left-hemisphere lesions.

Systematic studies generally have supported these indications of a hemispheric difference in the direction of more frequent and more severe constructional disability in patients with right-hemisphere disease (e.g., Piercy, Hécaen, and Ajuriaguerra, 1960; Benton, 1962; Benton and Fogel, 1962; Piercy and Smyth, 1962; Arrigoni and De-Renzi, 1964; Benton, 1967; DeRenzi and Faglioni, 1967; Benton, 1968). However, a substantial number of studies have not found important between-hemispheric differences (e.g., Warrington, James, and Kinsbourne, 1966; Benson and Barton, 1970; Benton, 1973; Black and Strub, 1976; Colombo, DeRenzi, and Faglioni, 1976). This inconsistency is only to be expected when one considers the several factors that may determine level of performance on constructional tasks; for the most part these were not controlled in the studies above.

An important factor is the task used to assess constructional ability. Benton (1967) found that impairment in three-dimensional block building and in copying designs was more than twice as frequent in patients with right-hemisphere lesions than in those with left-hemisphere disease; but an approximately equal proportion of patients in the two unilateral groups performed defectively on the WAIS block design subtest. Similarly, Benson and Barton (1970) found differences in the direction of poorer performance by patients with right-hemisphere lesions on a template matching test and the "token-pattern" test of Arrigoni and DeRenzi (1964) but not for three other constructional tasks.

Another factor is intrahemispheric locus of lesion, the general (but not invariable) rule being a trend toward poorer performance on the part of patients with posterior lesions. For example, Black and Strub (1976), investigating performance on three constructional tests in patients with prerolandic and retrorolandic unilateral penetrating brain wounds, found significant between-hemispheres differences in the direction of more defective performance by the patients with right-hemisphere wounds on two of the three tests and a nonsignificant difference in the same direction on the third test. However, more impressive differences were shown in anterior–posterior comparisons, the patients with retrorolandic wounds being consistently poorer than those with prerolandic lesions. Moreover, the findings of some studies suggest an interactive effect of side and intrahemispheric locus of lesion on performance. In the Black-Strub study, the patients with right retrorolandic lesions consistently performed less well than did the patients in the other three "quadrant" groups. Benson and Barton (1970) noted a tendency for patients with either left retrorolandic or right prerolandic lesions to perform most defectively. However, their groups were very small, and this may have been a chance finding.

Still another important correlate of performance level is the presence of sensory aphasic disorder. Benton (1973) compared the performances of nonaphasic patients with right-hemisphere disease on a three-dimensional block construction test with the performances of three discrete groups of patients with left-hemisphere disease: (1) nonaphasics, (2) expressive aphasics with no significant receptive language impairment, and (3) aphasics with significant receptive language impairment. The highest frequency of defect (50%) was shown by the aphasic patients with receptive impairment. The right-hemisphere-damaged patients showed a 36% frequency of defect. The other two groups of patients with left-hemisphere disease (nonaphasics or expressive aphasic only) showed a relatively low frequency of defect (13%).

Still another variable that needs to be considered as a determinant of performance level is the size of the brain lesion. This factor has been invoked to explain between-hemispheric differences in constructional task performance, the argument being that since patients with right-hemisphere disease have more extensive lesions, their performance is generally poorer than that of left-hemisphere-damaged patients. In fact, no empirical evidence has been added to support the contention. In the study of Benson and Barton (1970), the size of lesion was estimated by brain scan in 19 of the 25 cases. The left-frontal group showed the largest mean (and median) size and the right-frontal group the smallest. But the left-frontal patients were superior to the other three "quadrant" groups on all the constructional tasks and, as has been noted, there was a tendency for the right-frontal patients to perform particularly poorly.

The fact that such a wide diversity of tasks has been utilized and the observation that different tasks appear to interact in different ways with other factors to determine performance level have led some researchers to conclude that the visuoconstructive disability concept is too broad to be optimally useful in clinical or investigative work (cf. Benton, 1967; Benson and Barton, 1970). Instead, a classification in terms of types of constructional tasks differing in their demands on visuoperceptive, motor, and linguistic capacities offers greater promise of relating performance to cerebral function.

An initial distinction might be made between assembling performances (such as block building and stick construction) and graphomotor performances (such as drawing from a model or to verbal command). Dissociation in performance level on the two types of tasks, with a patient failing one and not the other, is often encountered in clinical evaluation and large-scale studies also provide justification for the distinction. In a study by Dee (1970), a group of 86 patients with unilateral brain disease were given both a three-dimensional block-construction test and a test of copying designs. Forty-six patients failed one or both tests. Of these 46 patients, 34 (74%) performed defectively on both tests. Thus 26% of the patients performed defectively on one test but not the other.

The differentiation first made by Duensing (1953) between an "ideational-apractic" form of constructional disability and a "spatio-agnostic" form has been utilized by some theorists to explain the fact that defective performance may be shown by patients with lesions of either hemisphere. Following Kleist's original formulation, it is assumed that a perceptuomotor integrative mechanism in the left-hemisphere mediates the motor aspects of constructional activity and that a lesion impairing this mechanism will disrupt performance even in the absence of visuospatial disability. On the other hand, impairment in visuospatial abilities resulting from right-hemisphere disease will also be reflected in defective constructional performance as well as on failure on nonmotor tasks making demands on spatial thinking. If the theory is correct, defective constructional performance should be more closely related to perceptual impairment in patients with right-hemisphere disease than in those with left-hemisphere lesions. But empirical tests of this hypothesis have not confirmed it. Both Piercy and Smyth (1962) and Dee (1970) found that visuoconstructional disability was closely associated with visuo-perceptive impairment in patients with lesions of either hemisphere.

One or another form of constructional disability is shown by a remarkably high proportion of patients with brain disease. One study (Benton, 1967) found that in a sample of 100 patients, the majority of whom had unilateral lesions, 47 showed defective performance on one or more of four constructional tests (copying designs, three-dimensional block construction, stick construction, WAIS block designs). Twenty-two patients performed defectively on at least two tests. Of the 35 patients with right-hemisphere lesions, 54% were defective on at least one test and 29% on two or more tests. Of the 43 patients with left-hemisphere lesions, 35% were defective on at least one test but only 12% on two or more tests. The proportions of patients with bilateral or diffuse disease (bifrontal tumor or degenerative disease) who performed defectively were about the same as in the right-hemisphere group, 55% failing at least one test and 36% failing two or more. Thus these tests may be diagnostically useful in that they often disclose disabilities related to brain disease which are only rarely the subject of complaint on the part of patients.

References

Albert, M. L. (1973). A simple test of visual neglect. *Neurology* 23:658–664.

Arrigoni, G. and DeRenzi, E. (1964). Constructional apraxia and hemispheric locus of lesion. *Cortex 1*:180–197.

Assal, G., Eisert, H. G., and Hécaen, H. (1969). Analyse dés resultats du Farnsworth D15 chez 155 malades atteints de lésions hémisphériques droites ou gauches. *Acta Neurologica et Psychiatrica Belgica 69*:705–717.

Badal, J. (1888). Contribution à l'étude des cécités psychiques: alexie, agraphie, hémianopsie inférieure, trouble du sens de l'espace. *Archives d'Ophtalmologie 8*:97–117.

Balint, R. (1909). Seelenlähmung des "Schauens", optische Ataxie, räumliche Störung der Aufmerksamkeit. *Monatsschr. f. Psychiat. u. Neurol. 25*:51–81.

Benson, D. F. and Barton, M. I. (1970). Disturbances in constructional ability. *Cortex* 6:19–46.

Benson, D. F., Segarra, J., and Albert, M. L. (1974). Visual agnosia-prosopagnosia. *Arch. Neurol.* 30:307–310.

Benton, A. L. (1962). The visual retention test as a constructional praxis task. *Confinia Neurologica* 22:141–155.

Benton, A. L. (1967). Constructional apraxia and the minor hemisphere. *Confinia Neurologica* 29:1–16.

Benton, A. L. (1968). Differential behavioral effects in frontal lobe disease. *Neuropsychologia* 6:53–60.

Benton, A. L. (1969). Disorders of spatial orientation, in *Handbook of Clinical Neurology*, Vol. 3, P. J. Vinken and G. W. Bruyn (eds.). Amsterdam: North-Holland.

Benton, A. L. (1973). Visuoconstructive disability in patients with cerebral disease: its relationship to side of lesion and aphasic disorder. *Documenta Ophthalmologica* 34:67–76.

Benton, A. L., Elithorn, A., Fogel, M. L., and Kerr, M. (1963). A perceptual maze test sensitive to brain damage. *J. Neurol. Neurosurg. Psychiat.* 26:540–543.

Benton, A. L. and Fogel, M. L. (1962). Three-dimensional constructional praxis. *Arch. Neurol.* 7:347–354.

Benton, A. L., Hannay, J., and Varney, N. R. (1975). Visual perception of line direction in patients with unilateral brain disease. *Neurology* 25: 907–910.

Benton, A. L. and Hécaen, H. (1970). Stereoscopic vision in patients with unilateral cerebral disease. *Neurology* 20:1084–1088.

Benton, A. L., Levin, H. S., and Van Allen, M. W. (1974). Geographic orientation in patients with unilateral cerebral disease. *Neuropsychologia* 12:183–191.

Benton, A. L., Levin, H. S., and Varney, N. R. (1973). Tactile perception of direction in normal subjects. *Neurology* 23:1248–1250.

Benton, A. L. and Van Allen, M. W. (1968). Impairment in facial recognition in patients with cerebral disease. *Cortex* 4:344–358.

Benton, A. L. and Van Allen, M. W. (1972). Prosopagnosia and facial discrimination. *J. Neurol. Sci.* 15:167–172.

Birkmayer, W. (1951). *Hirnverletzungen.* Wien: Springer-Verlag.

Bisiach, E., Nichelli, P., and Spinnler, H. (1976). Hemispheric functional asymmetry in visual discrimination between univariate stimuli: an analysis of sensitivity and response criterion. *Neuropsychologia* 14: 335–342.

Black, F. W. and Strub, R. L. (1976). Constructional apraxia in patients with discrete missile wounds of the brain. *Cortex* 12:212–220.

Brain, W. R. (1941). Visual disorientation with special reference to lesions of the right cerebral hemisphere. *Brain* 64:224–272.

Carmon, A. (1971). Disturbances in tactile sensitivity in patients with cerebral lesions. *Cortex* 7:83–97.

Carmon, A. and Bechtoldt, H. P. (1969). Dominance of the right cerebral hemisphere for stereopsis. *Neuropsychologia* 7:29–39.

Carmon, A. and Benton, A. L. (1969). Tactile perception of direction and number in patients with unilateral cerebral disease. *Neurology 19*: 525–532.

Colombo, A., DeRenzi, E., and Faglioni, P. (1976). The occurrence of visual neglect in patients with unilateral cerebral disease. *Cortex 12*:221–231.

Corkin, S. (1965). Tactually-guided maze learning in man: effects of unilateral cortical excisions and bilateral hippocampal lesions. *Neuropsychologia 3*:339–351.

Critchley, M. (1953). *The Parietal Lobes*. London: Edward Arnold.

Dee, H. L. (1970). Visuoconstructive and visuoperceptive deficits in patients with unilateral cerebral lesions. *Neuropsychologia 8*:305–314.

Denny-Brown, D. (1963). The physiological basis of perception and speech, in *Problems of Dynamic Neurology*. L. Halpern (ed). Jerusalem: Hebrew University Medical School.

DeRenzi, E. and Faglioni, P. (1967). The relationship between visuo-spatial impairment and constructional apraxia. *Cortex 3*:327–342.

DeRenzi, E., Faglioni, P., and Scotti, G. (1970). Hemispheric contribution to exploration of space through the visual tactile modality. *Cortex 6*: 191–203.

DeRenzi, E., Faglioni, P., Scotti, G., and Spinnler, H. (1972). Impairment of color sorting behavior after hemispheric damage: an experimental study with the Holmgren skein test. *Cortex 8*:147–163.

DeRenzi, E., Faglioni, P., and Spinnler, H. (1968). The performance of patients with unilateral brain damage on face recognition tasks. *Cortex 4*:17–34.

DeRenzi, E. and Spinnler, H. (1966). Facial recognition in brain-damaged patients. *Neurology 16*:144–152.

DeRenzi, E. and Spinnler, H. (1967). Impaired performance on color tasks in patients with hemispheric damage. *Cortex 3*:194–216.

Duensing, F. (1935). Raumagnostische und ideatorisch-apraktische Störung des gestaltenden Handelns. *Deutsche Z. f. Nervenheilkunde 170*:72–94.

Dunn, T. D. (1895). Double hemiplegia with double hemianopsia and loss of geographic centre. *Transactions of the College of Physicians of Philadelphia 17*:45–56.

Ettlinger, G. (1960). The description and interpretation of pictures in cases of brain lesion. *J. Mental Sci. 106*:1337–1346.

Faust, C. (1955). *Die Zerebralen Herdstörungen bei Hinterhauptverletzungen und ihre Beurteilung*. Stuttgart: Thieme.

Foerster, R. (1890). Ueber Rindenblindheit. *Graefes Archiv für Ophthalmologie 36*:94–108.

Fogel, M. L. (1967). Picture description and interpretation in brain-damaged patients. *Cortex 3*:433–448.

Fontenot, D. J. and Benton, A. L. (1971). Tactile perception of direction in relation to hemispheric locus of lesion. *Neuropsychologia 9*:83–88.

Fontenot, D. J. and Benton, A. L. (1972). Perception of direction in the right and left visual fields. *Neuropsychologia 10*:447–452.

Freud, S. (1891). *Zur Auffassung der Aphasien*. Deuticke: Leipzig und Wien. English Translation by E. Stengel (1953). New York: International Universities Press.

Gainotti, G., Messerli, P., and Tissot, R. (1972). Qualitative analysis of unilateral neglect in relation to laterality of cerebral lesions. *J. Neurol. Neurosurg. Psychiat. 35*:545–550.

Geschwind, N. (1962). The anatomy of acquired disorders in reading, in *Reading Disability*, J. Money (ed). Baltimore: Johns Hopkins Press.

Geschwind, N. and Fusillo, M. (1964). Color-naming defects in association with alexia. *Trans. Am. Neurol. Assoc. 89*:172–176.

Geschwind, N. and Fusillo, M. (1966). Color-naming defects in association with alexia. *Arch. Neurol.* 15:137–146.

Gloning, I., Gloning, K., and Hoff, H. (1968). *Neuropsychological Symptoms and Symptoms and Syndromes in Lesions of the Occipital Lobe and the Adjacent Areas*. Paris: Gauthier-Villars.

Goetzinger, C. P., Dirks, D. D., and Baer, C. J. (1960). Auditory discrimination and visual perception in good and poor readers. *Ann. Otology, Rhinology and Laryngology 69*:121–136.

Green, G. J. and Lessell, S. (1977). Acquired cerebral dyschromatopsia. *Arch. Ophthalmol. 95*:121–128.

Greenblatt, S. H. (1973). Alexia without agraphia or hemianopsia. *Brain 96*:307–316.

Guzman, E. (1975). Color cognition in patients with brain disease. M.A. Thesis, University of Iowa.

Hamsher, K. DeS. (1978). Stereopsis and unilateral brain disease. *Investigative Ophthalmology 4*:336–343.

Hannay, H. J., Varney, N. R., and Benton, A. L. (1976). Visual localization in patients with unilateral brain disease. *J. Neurol. Neurosurg. Psychiat. 39*:307–313.

Hécaen, H. and Angelergues, R. (1962). Agnosia for faces (prosopagnosia). *Arch. Neurol. 7*:92–100.

Hécaen, H. and Angelergues, R. (1963). *La Cécité Psychique*. Paris: Masson.

Heilman, K. M. and Valenstein, E. (1972a). Frontal lobe neglect in man. *Neurology 22*:660–664.

Heilman, K. M. and Valenstein, E. (1972b). Auditory neglect in man. *Arch. Neurol. 26*:32–35.

Heilman, K. M., Watson, R. S., and Schulman, H. M. (1974). A unilateral memory defect. *J. Neurol. Neurosurg. Psychiat. 37*:790–793.

Hilliard, R. D. (1973). Hemispheric laterality effects on a facial recognition task in normal subjects. *Cortex 9*:246–258.

Holmes, G. (1918). Disturbances of visual orientation. *Br. J. Ophthalmol. 2*:449–486, 506–516.

Holmes, G. and Horrax, G. (1919). Disturbances of spatial orientation and visual attention, with loss of stereoscopic vision. *Arch. Neurol. Psychiat.* *1*:385–407.

Howes, D. H. (1962). A quantitative approach to word blindness, in *Reading Disability*, J. Money (ed). Baltimore: Johns Hopkins Press.

Jackson, J. H. (1876). Case of large cerebral tumour without optic neuritis and with left hemiplegia and imperception. *Royal Ophthalmological Hospital Reports. 8*:434–444.

Julesz, B. (1964). Binocular depth perception without familiarity cues. *Science 145*:356.

Kinsbourne, M. and Warrington, E. (1962). A disorder of simultaneous form perception. *Brain 85*:461–486.

Kinsbourne, M. and Warrington, E. (1963). The localizing significance of limited simultaneous form perception. *Brain 86*:699–702.

Kleist, K. (1923). Kriegverletzungen des Gehirns in ihrer Bedeutung für die Hirnlokalisation und Hirnpathologie, im *Handbuch der Arztlichen Erfahrung im Weltkriege, 1914/1918*, Vol. 4, O. von Schjerning (ed). Leipzig: Barth.

Lansdell, H. C. (1968). Effect of extent of temporal lobe ablations on two lateralized deficits. *Physiol. Behav. 3*:271–273.

Lewandowsky, M. (1908). Ueber abspaltung des Farbensinnes. *Montasschr. f. Psychiat. Neurol. 23*:488–510.

Lezak, M. D. (1976). *Neuropsychological Assessment*. New York: Oxford University Press.

Lhermitte, F., Chain, F., Aron, D., Leblanc, M., and Jouty, O. (1969). Les troubles de la vision des couleurs dans les lésions postérieures du cerveau. *Rev. Neurol. 121*:5–29.

Lhermitte, J., Chain, F., Escourolle, R., Ducarne, B., and Pillon, B. (1972). Étude anatomo-clinique d'un cas de prosopagnosie. *Rev. Neurol. 126*: 329–346.

Lissauer, H. (1890). Ein fall von Seelenblindheit nebst einem Beitrag zur Theorie derselben. *Archiv für Psychiatrie und Nervenkrankheiten 21*: 22–270.

Lovell, K., Gray, E. A., and Oliver, D. E. (1964). A further study of some cognitive and other disabilities in backward readers of average nonverbal reasoning scores. *Br. J. Educ. Psychol. 34*:275–279.

Luria, A. R. (1959). Disorders of simultaneous perception in a case of bilateral occipito-parietal brain injury. *Brain 82*:437–449.

McFie, J. and Zangwill, O. L. (1960). Visuo-constructive disabilities associated with lesions of the right cerebral hemisphere. *Brain 82*:243–259.

Meadows, J. C. (1974a). The anatomical basis of prosopagnosia. *J. Neurol. Neurosurg. Psychiat. 37*:489–501.

Meadows, J. C. (1974b). Disturbed perception of colors associated with localized cerebral lesions. *Brain 97*:615–632.

Meier, M. J. and French, L. A. (1965). Lateralized deficits in complex visual discrimination and bilateral transfer of reminiscence following unilateral temporal lobectomy. *Neuropsychologia 3*:261–272.

Meyer, O. (1900). Ein-und doppelseitige homonyme Hemianopsie mit Orientierungsstörungen. *Monatsschr. f. Psychiat. u. Neurol. 8*:440–456.

Milner, B. (1962). Laterality effects in audition, in *Interhemispheric Relations and Cerebral Dominance,* V. B. Mountcastle (ed). Baltimore: Johns Hopkins Press.

Milner, B. (1965). Visually-guided maze learning in man: effects of bilateral hippocampal, bilateral frontal, and unilateral cerebral lesions. *Neuropsychologia 3*:317–338.

Mooney, C. M. (1957). Closure as affected by configural clarity and contextual consistency. *Can. J. Psychol. 11*:80–88.

Munk, H. (1878). Weitere Mittheilungen zur Physiologie der Grosshirnrinde. *Arch. f. Anatomie u. Physiologie 2*:161–178.

Newcombe, F. and Russell, W. R. (1969). Dissociated visual perceptual and spatial deficits in focal lesions of the right hemisphere. *J. Neurol. Neurosurg. Psychiat. 32*:73–81.

Orgass, B., Poeck, K., Kerschensteiner, M., and Hartje, W. (1972). Visuocognitive performances in patients with unilateral hemispheric lesions. *Z. f. Neurol. 202*:177–195.

Paterson, A. and Zangwill, O. L. (1944). Disorders of visual space perception associated with lesions of the right cerebral hemisphere. *Brain 67*: 331–358.

Pavlov, I. P. (1927). *Conditioned Reflexes.* London: Oxford University Press.

Pevzner, S., Bornstein, B., and Loewenthal, M. (1962). Prosopagnosia. *J. Neurol. Neurosurg. Psychiat. 25*:336–338.

Piercy, M., Hécaen, H., and de Ajuriaguerra, J. (1960). Constructional apraxia associated with cerebral lesions: left and right cases compared. *Brain 83*:225–242.

Piercy, M. and Smyth, V. O. G. (1962). Right hemisphere dominance for certain nonverbal intellectual skills. *Brain 85*:775–790.

Poppelreuter, W. (1917). *Die Psychischen Schädigungen durch Kopfschuss im Kriege 1914–1916: die Störungen der niederen und höheren Sehleistungen durch Verletzungen des Okzipitalhirns.* Leipzig: Voss.

Ratcliff, G. and Davies-Jones, G. A. B. (1972). Defective visual localization in focal brain wounds. *Brain 95*:49–60.

Reitan, R. M. and Tarshes, E. L. (1959). Differential effects of lateralized brain lesions on the trail making test. *J. Nervous Mental Dis. 129*:257–262.

Rizzolati, G., Umiltà, C., and Berlucchi, G. (1971). Opposite superiorities of the right and left cerebral hemispheres in discriminative reaction time to physiognomic and alphabetical material. *Brain 94*:431–442.

Rondot, P. and Tzavaras, A. (1969). La prosopagnosie après vingt années d'études cliniques et neuropsychologiques. *J. Psychologie Normale et Pathologique 2*:133–165.

Russo, M. and Vignolo, L. A. (1967). Visual figure-ground discrimination in patients with unilateral cerebral disease. *Cortex 3*:113–127.

Sachs, H. (1895). Das gehirn des Förster'schen Rindenblinden. *Arbeiten der Psychiatrischen Klinik Breslau 2*:55–104.

Scotti, G. and Spinnler, H. (1970). Colour imperception in unilateral hemisphere-damaged patients. *J. Neurol. Neurosurg. Psychiat. 33*:22–28.

Semmes, J., Weinstein, S., Ghent, L., and Teuber, H. L. (1960). *Somatosensory Changes after Penetrating Brain Wounds in Man.* Cambridge: Harvard University Press.

Sittig, O. (1921). Störungen im Verhalten gegenüber Farben bei Aphasischen. *Monatsschr. f. Psychiat. u. Neurol. 49*:63–68, 169–187.

Strauss, H. (1924). Ueber konstruktiv Apraxie. *Monatsschr. f. Psychiat. u. Neurol. 56*:65–124.

Street, R. F. (1931). *A Gestalt Completion Test.* New York: Bureau of Publications, Teachers College.

Taylor, A. M. and Warrington, E. (1973). Visual discrimination in patients with localized brain lesions. *Cortex 9*:82–93.

Teuber, H. L. and Weinstein, S. (1956). Ability to discover hidden figures after cerebral lesions. *Arch. Neurol. Psychiat. 76*:369–379.

Tzavaras, A., Hécaen, H., and LeBras, H. (1970). Le problème de la spécificité du déficit de la reconnaissance du visage humain lors les lésions hémisphériques unilatérales. *Neuropsychologia 8*:403–416.

Tzavaras, A., Hécaen, H., and LeBras, H. (1971). Troubles de la vision des couleurs après lésions corticules unilatérales. *Revue Neurologique 124*: 396–402.

Vaughn, H. G. and Costa, L. D. (1962). Performances of patients with lateralized cerebral lesions. *J. Nervous Mental Dis. 134*:237–243.

Warrington, E. K. (1969). Constructional apraxia, in *Handbook of Clinical Neurology*, Vol. 4, P. J. Vinken and G. W. Bruyn (eds). Amsterdam: North-Holland.

Warrington, E. K. and James, M. (1967). An experimental investigation of facial recognition in patients with unilateral lesions. *Cortex 3*:317–326.

Warrington, E. K., James, M., and Kinsbourne, M. (1966). Drawing disability in relation to laterality of cerebral lesion. *Brain 89*:53–82.

Warrington, E. K. and Rabin, P. (1970). Perceptual matching in patients with cerebral lesions. *Neuropsychologia 8*:475–487.

Watson, R. T., Heilman, K. M., Cauthen, J. C., and King, F. A. (1973). Neglect after cingulectomy. *Neurology 23*:1003–1007.

Weigl, E. (1964). Some critical remarks concerning the problem of so-called simultanagnosia. *Neuropsychologia 2*:189–207.

Weinstein, S. (1964). Deficits concomitant with aphasia or lesions of either cerebral hemisphere. *Cortex 1*:151–169.

Wilbrand, H. (1887). *Die Seelenblindheit als Herderscheinung und ihre*

Beziehungen zur Homonymen Hemianopsie. Wiesbaden: J. F. Bergmann.

Wilbrand, H. and Saenger, A. (1906). *Die Neurologie des Auges,* Vol. 3, Wiesbaden: Bergmann.

Wolpert, I. (1942). Die Simultanagnosie: Störung der Gesamtauffassung. *Z. f. d. gesamte Neurol. u. Psychiatr. 93*:397–415.

Wyke, M. and Holgate, D. (1973). Colour-naming defects in dysphasic patients: a qualitative analysis. *Neuropsychologia 11*:457–461.

9
Agnosia

ALAN B. RUBENS

Agnosia is a relatively rare neuropsychological syndrome defined in the classical literature as a failure of recognition. In its purest form, agnosia should represent, in Teuber's words (1968), ". . . a failure of recognition that is referable neither to subtle changes in the sensory processing of the input nor to disorders of naming. The two limiting sets of conditions: failure of processing and failure of naming, thus bracket, so to speak, the alleged disorder of recognition per se, which would appear in its purest form as a normal percept that has somehow been stripped of its meaning." The notion that there actually exists a separate neuropsychological disturbance of recognition fitting the narrow definition above has come under attack in the modern literature from two separate directions. On the one hand, critics have claimed that agnosic failures can be reduced to the combined affects of a primary sensory processing disturbance and generalized mental deterioration (Bay, 1953; Bender and Feldman, 1972), or to a complex mixture of disturbed perception and faulty sensory-motor exploration (Luria, 1959; Luria et al., 1963). On the other hand, Geschwind has questioned the concept of a unitary psychological process of recognition and has suggested that agnosic errors represent confabulated misnamings elaborated by an intact speech area disconnected from an intact cortical sensory region (Geschwind, 1965). These views will be discussed in greater detail in the section on visual agnosia.

Munk (1881) was the first to demonstrate experimentally in dogs that visual detection could be dissociated from visual recognition. Dogs with partial bilateral occipital lobe excisions neatly avoided obstacles placed in their path and yet failed to recognize and react appropriately to objects that previously had frightened or attracted them. Munk attributed the failure to recognize without actual blindness to a loss of images or memories of previous visual experience and termed the condition "Seelenblindheit" (mind, psychic, or soul blindness). Lissauer (1889) was the first to report in detail a thorough clinical evaluation of a patient with a visual recognition disturbance. The term "agnosia" was introduced by Freud (1891) and eventually came to replace "mind blindness" and other terms such as "asymbolia" (Finkelnburg, 1870) and "imperception" (Jackson, 1876). Liepmann (1900) was the first to provide a clear clinical demonstration of the separation between agnosic and apractic disturbances (see also Chapter 8).

Agnosia is most often modality specific; the patient who fails to recognize material presented through a particular sensory channel such as vision is successful when allowed to handle it or to experience it through some other sensory channel. Visual, auditory, and tactual agnosia have received the most attention and will be reviewed in this chapter. Visual and auditory agnosia have been by far the most thoroughly studied in the recent literature.

VISUAL AGNOSIA

The patient with visual agnosia does not respond appropriately to visually presented material even though visual sensory processing, language, and general intellectual functions are preserved at sufficiently high levels so that their impairment cannot account individually or in combination for the failure to recognize. Poor recognition is usually limited to the visual sphere and appropriate responses occur when the patient is allowed to handle the object or hear it in use. In the clinical setting, one or more of the following correct patient responses are customarily regarded as evidence that visual material has been recognized: (1) supplying the correct name, description, and/or demonstration of use, or otherwise providing an appropriate description (e.g., "the President," "the color of tomatoes," "like the one you are wearing on your wrist that tells time"), or (2) choosing from among a group of items, the one named by the examiner.

When the patient fails to name but can indicate visual recognition by other means (description, gesture, etc.) the failure is considered to be anomic in nature and part of a more general aphasic disturbance.* Unlike the agnosic, the anomic does not improve when the material is presented through another sensory modality (Goodglass et al., 1968; Spreen et al., 1966), and is less apt to improve when he is asked to produce lists of words in specific categories, complete open-ended sentences, or respond to definitions.† In contrast to the spontaneous speech of the nonaphasic agnosic patient, the conversational speech of the anomic may alert the examiner to the possibility of difficulty on visual naming because it contains word-findings pauses, circumlocutions, verbal paraphasias, and a general lack of substantives (see Chapter 2, pp. 46–47).

There is no classification of visual agnosia that has met with universal acceptance. In 1889, Lissauer proposed on theoretical grounds the separation of visual agnosia into two often concurrent types: apperceptive and associative, depending on whether lower or higher levels of sensory processing were disturbed. By apperception, Lissauer meant the final conscious perception of a sensory impression; the piecing together of separate attributes of a visual stimulus into a whole. By association, Lissauer meant the imparting of meaning to the content of perception by matching and linking it to previous experience, a process that requires the participation of association cortex. According to Lissauer, the patient with a defect at the level of apperception will not be able to match or copy

---

* A possible exception is so-called "optic aphasia" regarded by some as a naming disturbance limited to the visual sensory modality.

† In contrast to aphasics with temporoparietal lesions, those with frontal lesions appear to be more successful at generating names on visual confrontation than either in spontaneous speech and/or when asked to produce a list of words in specific categories (Luria, 1966; Goldstein, 1948).

a misidentified object or picture while the patient with an associative deficit will be able to copy because he perceives normally.
Despite arguments against the classification of agnosia into apperceptive and associative forms, Lissauer's dichotomy has been increasingly referred to in the recent literature, and a number of well-
studied cases have been reported that support the usefulness of
this classification, at least as a starting point in the discussion of
visual agnosia.

Visual agnosia has also been classified according to the specific
category of visual material that cannot be recognized. Impairment
in the recognition of faces (prosopagnosia), color (color agnosia),
objects (object agnosia), and inability to read (agnosic alexia) are
found in various combinations and also in isolation (see also Chapter 8). The occurrence of associative visual object agnosia with
alexia, color agnosia, and prosopagnosia is common, but not invariable.

Apperceptive visual agnosia

Well-documented cases of apperceptive visual agnosia are rare. Most
published cases have been criticized as examples of primary sensory
failure and/or faulty visual exploration. Virtually every case has
been associated with pathological processes such as carbon monoxide
poisoning (Von Hagen, 1941; Adler, 1944; Benson and Greenberg,
1969), cardiac arrest (Brown [Case 11], 1972), bilateral strokes
(Stauffenberg, 1914), or an atrophic dementing process that produces
bilateral posterior hemispheric lesions. The behavior of these patients suggests severe visual difficulties. Many are recovering from a
state of cortical blindness. Because of their helplessness in the visual
environment, many are considered still blind until they report that
they can indeed see, but not clearly. Standard testing then reveals
normal or near normal acuity and visual fields, confirming their
subjective report, and distinguishing their deficit from that of
Anton's syndrome (Anton, 1899), denial of cerebral blindness. The
patient of Benson and Greenberg (1969) was thought to be blind
until he was seen coasting down the hospital corridor in his wheelchair avoiding obstacles easily.

Patients with apperceptive visual agnosia fail to recognize because
they do not perceive clearly. They cannot draw misidentified items

or match them to sample. They are unable to point to objects named by the examiner. The impairment involves all elements of the visual environment that require shape and pattern perception (faces, objects, letters). The recognition of even the simplest of line drawings may be impossible. However, bright and highly saturated colors are often recognized. Some patients are able to trace the outlines of letters, objects, or drawings, but often retrace them over and over again because they do not recognize their starting point. The patient of Benson and Greenberg (1969) was able to distinguish small differences in the luminance (0.1 log unit) and wavelength (7–10 μ) of a test aperture subtending a visual angle of approximately 2 degrees. Many patients behave as though they are unaware of and unconcerned about their visual deficit until they are confronted with a visual recognition task. They will then acknowledge that they do not see clearly. They may complain that the visual environment appears to change as they try to scrutinize it and that objects disappear or are not visible until they are moved. They may blame their deficit on the need for new glasses, poor lighting, or the fact that they have not had much prior experience with the particular kind of visual material that they are being asked to identify. Performance may vary considerably from day to day and is very dependent on contextual cues.

It has always been difficult to analyze and describe the visual performance of these patients. Their deficit does not fit the narrow definition of "a percept stripped of its meaning." According to Bay (1953), there is neither a specific gnostic function nor a specific disorder of gnosis, agnosia. Apparent cases of agnosia are actually disorders of primary sensory function due to lesions of the primary sensory fields and their connections. The presence of a generalized dementing process further impairs the interpretation of faulty primary sensory data. Bay reported abnormalities in sensation time (the minimal exposure time sufficient for recognition of portions of the visual field), and local adaptation time (the elapsed time for a visual stimulus to fade from portions of the field) in patients with otherwise normal visual acuity and visual fields. In these patients, visual stimuli tend to drop out of awareness because of abnormal fatigability, particularly at the periphery. This time-dependent lability is referred to as "Funktionswandel," after the Heidelberg school of psychology. Bay applied his tests to a patient with visual agnosia, and, finding an abnormality of Funktionswandel, attributed the recognition deficit to primary visual sensory impairment. Bay's findings, however, cannot be generalized to all agnosics. His argument has since been weakened by the findings of Ettlinger (1956) of similar abnormalities in patients with various combinations of visual sensory impairment and dementia, but who were not agnosic. One patient with prosopagnosia performed at a higher level on these tests than most of the nonagnosic patients. It is evident, therefore, that visual sensory abnormalities as measured by tests of sensation time and local adaptation time are not, even in the presence of dementia, sufficient in themselves to produce an agnosia-like recognition deficit. It is true, however, that many patients with visual agnosia have elements of this type of disturbance and many also have abnormalities in visual attention, search, and exploration which further complicate the analysis of their visual performance.

In a recent paper, Bender and Feldman (1972) strongly re-asserted the claim that visual agnosia represents nothing more than a complex interaction between primary visual sensory abnormalities, various degrees of inattention, ocular fixation, and an organic mental syndrome (dementia). In their opinion, previous reported cases of visual agnosia were insufficiently examined. As evidence they presented data from a retrospective review of patients who had been diagnosed as having visual agnosia. Visual perceptual motor deficits and significant organic mental syndromes were found in all patients. Once again, however, the problem of lack of adequate controls presents itself. The concurrent presence of a visual sensory defect and visual agnosia cannot by itself be used as evidence that in the individual patient the visual defect is sufficient to produce a failure of recognition. It is important when examining such patients to investigate and report not only deficits but also islands of retained ability in order to gain a fuller understanding of the complex dynamics of the problem.

Luria and his associates (Luria, 1959; Luria et al., 1963) have suggested that the phenomenon of simultanagnosia may be the basic underlying disturbance in visual agnosia. The term *simultanagnosia* was introduced by Wolpert (1924) to refer to a condition in which the patient is unable to recognize or abstract the meaning of the whole (pictures or series of pictures) even though the details were correctly appreciated. Luria uses the term in a more literal sense; the patient actually perceives only one thing at a time. Luria equates simultanagnosia with a perceptual deficit often found as part of Balint's syndrome (Balint, 1909) which is composed of the following three defects: (1) psychic paralysis of fixation with inability to voluntarily look into the peripheral field, (2) optic ataxia, manifested by clumsiness or inability to respond manually to visual stimuli, with mislocalization in space when pointing to visual targets, and (3) a disturbance of visual attention affecting mainly the periphery of the visual field and resulting in a dynamic concentric narrowing of the effective field. Balint's syndrome is almost invariably associated with large biparietal lesions (Hécaen and Ajuriaguerra, 1954). Visual fields may be normal by standard perimetric testing but shrink to "shaft vision" when the patient concentrates on his visual environment. Performance may be worse in one hemifield, more often on the left. A striking example of narrowing of visual field is given by Hécaen and Ajuriaguerra (1954). While their patient's attention was focused on the tip of a cigarette held between his lips, he failed to see a match flame offered him and held several inches away. Patients with Balint's syndrome thus do not perceive more than one object or part of an object at a time. It is as though they had bilateral visual neglect with macular sparing. Their problem is compounded by an inability to relate small portions of what they see to the remainder of the stimulus by scanning. Based on the study of several such patients, Luria (Luria, 1959; Luria et al., 1963) concluded that visual agnosia represents a complex perceptuomotor breakdown of the active, serial feature-by-feature analysis necessary for processing elements of a visual scene or pattern.

Kinsbourne and Warrington (1962) described patients with a mild form of this defect which they termed a disorder of simultaneous form perception and which they believed accounted for the reading disturbance which was present. Botez (1975) has identified a group of patients with elements of Balint's syndrome who recognize only moving objects or letters that are slowly drawn in their view. He attributes the deficit, which he calls static visual agnosia, to impairment of the geniculostriate system, and the spared ability to localize and use movement for recognition to the retained function of the more "primitive" tectopulvinar nonstriate system.

It is probable that elements of Balint's syndrome were present in most published cases of apperceptive visual agnosia (e.g., Goldstein and Gelb, 1918; Adler, 1944). For that reason, it may be helpful to compare a recent detailed case report of Balint's syndrome (Tyler, 1968) with that of a patient considered to have apperceptive visual agnosia (Benson and Greenberg, 1969; Efron, 1968). Whether the two are qualitatively different, or simply represent different degrees of severity of the same deficit, is unsettled.

A 66-year-old woman (Tyler, 1968) suddenly developed visual difficulties associated with segmental basilar artery occlusion. Visual acuity was 20/30 with glasses. Visual fields were at first considered normal, but careful re-testing showed that while the left field was normal to movements of large objects, these objects faded from awareness in one to two seconds. With continued testing within that field, awareness of even the movement of large objects was lost. In the right visual field, the central two degrees around fixation were always normal, the surrounding outer 20 degrees fatigued rapidly, and beyond 20 degrees, movement was recognized but objects faded rapidly. The patient could see only one object or part of one object at a time with her central two to four degrees of vision. She scanned normally when looking at predictable objects such as a circle or a square but frequently lost her place when viewing objects and pictures. Slight movement of the page made her lose her place. She reported seeing bits and fragments. For instance, when shown a picture of a flag, she said, "I see a lot of lines, now I see some stars." When shown a dollar bill, she saw a picture of George Washington. Moments later when shown a cup, she said, "A cup with a picture of Washington on it." Eye movement studies revealed a normal number of visual fixations per unit of time and a normal pattern of fixation for small saccades or so-called visual steps. However, there were very few if any so-called long saccades or leaps that relate one part of the picture to another. The patient, therefore, looked for abnormally long periods of time at small portions of the picture.

The verbal reports of Tyler's patient are similar to those of the patient of Adler (1944), who was considered to have a case of apperceptive visual agnosia.

When shown a picture of a boy admiring a sailboat in a toy shop followed by a second picture of the boy bending down and playing with the same boat in a pool, she pointed to each picture and said simply, "A boy." She then pointed to the boat in each picture and identified it but did not recognize that it was the same boat because of its "different color." However, when referring to the color of the boat, she was actually pointing to the blue water.

In contrast to the two patients described above, whose impaired visual recognition is attributable to the combined effects of narrowed effective visual field and failure to adequately compensate for this by visual exploration, the patient reported by Benson and Greenberg (1969) and also by Efron (1968) appears to demonstrate an isolated failure of visual shape discrimination.

The patient was a 25-year-old man who was a victim of accidental carbon monoxide poisoning. He remained in coma for several days and gradually improved. For several months he was thought to be blind and yet was seen one day navigating the corridor successfully in his wheelchair. He was able to name colors and could often follow moving visual stimuli, but yet could not identify by vision alone objects placed before him. He could occasionally identify the letters "X" and "O" if allowed to see them drawn, or if they were moved slowly before his eyes. Visual acuity was at least 20/100 measured by his ability to indicate the orientation of the letter "E", to detect the movement of small objects at standard distances and to reach for fine threads on a piece of paper. Optokinetic nystagmus was elicited bilaterally with fine 1/8" marks on a tape. Visual fields were normal to 3 mm. wide objects with minimal inferior constriction bilaterally to 3 mm. red and green objects. There was an impersistence of gaze with quasi-random searching movements particularly noticeable when he was inspecting an object. His recognition deficit included objects, pictures of objects, body parts, letters, and numbers, but not colors. He could tell which of two objects was the larger and detect very small movements of small targets. He easily identified and named objects tactually and auditorily. He guessed at the names of objects utilizing color, size, and reflectance cues. He was totally unable to match or copy material which he could not identify. However, he was taught to apply a name to each object in a small group of objects which were presented to him one at a time on a piece of white paper. For instance, after he was repeatedly shown the back of a red and white playing card and informed of its identity, he was able on later exposures to identify it. He was thus able to use color and size cues to learn and remember the names of various objects in a closed set. However, when these objects were placed out of context, he was no longer able to name them. His recent memory, spontaneous speech, comprehension of spoken speech and repetition were intact. On psychophysical testing he was able to distinguish small differences in luminance (0.1 log unit), and wave length (7–10 μ), of a test aperture subtending a visual angle of approximately two degrees. However, he was unable to distinguish between two objects of the same luminance, wave length, and area when the only difference between them was one of shape.

The deficit in this patient, therefore, was a low specificity for the attribute of shape while the specificity for the awareness of other attributes of visually discriminated material was retained (Efron, 1968).

It would be impossible with our present level of knowledge of visual perceptual physiology to finely localize the lesions responsible for what has been called apperceptive visual agnosia. As noted above, the presence of bilateral subtotal lesions of striate and peristriate areas have been incriminated. It is interesting to note that monkeys with complete bilateral excisions of striate cortex can learn to discriminate simple patterns (Pasik and Pasik, 1971). There is evidence for (Pasik and Pasik, 1971) and against (Humphrey, 1970) color discrimination ability in these animals. According to Weiskrantz (1972), the destriated animal is like the normal animal with poor acuity (i.e., amblyopic), and it is only when damage extends into prestriate and association cortex that discriminative capacity begins to be limited to total luminous flux. Weiskrantz et al. (1974) recently reported a patient with hemianopia (resulting from the excision of an arteriovenous malformation limited to the striate cortex) who could, in his hemianopic field, discriminate the large letters "X" from "O", reach fairly accurately for stimuli, and differentiate between horizontal, diagonal, and vertical lines. This patient, unlike the patient of Benson and Greenberg, who "saw" but could not recognize, claimed that he did not see targets to which he responded correctly. The term "blind sight" has been applied to this phenomenon. It is clear that the distinction between sensation, perception, and recognition, and the relative participation of striate and extrastriate visual systems in each of these processes is far from settled.††

Associative visual agnosia
The major distinguishing feature of associative visual agnosia is the patient's ability to copy and/or match to sample items that he fails

†† In a recent review of their experience with cortical and subcortical excisions in monkeys, Denny-Brown and his colleagues (Denny-Brown and Chambers, 1976; Denny-Brown and Fischer, 1976) report that with either (1) complete removal of corticomesencephalic fibers and the colliculus or (2) bilateral excisions of area 17 with preservation of large portions of areas 18 and 19, there is a loss of visual recognition of still objects but sparing of visual-spatial orientation, reaching for moving targets, and appreciation of edges, walls, and depth. Selective excision of areas 18 and 19, on the other hand, is associated with no loss of recognition of objects and of individuals.

to recognize visually. In the past decade, a number of detailed case reports of patients in whom adequate visual perception has been documented leave no doubt about the existence of this form of agnosia (Albert et al., 1975; Hécaen et al., 1974; Lhermitte et al., 1973; Lhermitte and Beauvois, 1973; Mack and Boller, 1977; Oxbury et al., 1969; Rubens and Benson, 1971; and Taylor and Warrington, 1971). The patients of Rubens and Benson, Taylor and Warrington, and Newcombe and Ratcliff (1974 [Case 1]) matched to sample and produced strikingly accurate drawings of pictures and objects that they could not identify visually (Fig. 9-1). The patient of Lhermitte and associates performed normally on careful tests of ocular motility and scanning. The patients of Rubens and Benson, and Taylor and Warrington were able to find hidden figures in figure-ground tests. Case 1 of Newcombe and Ratcliff showed no deficits on psychophysical tests of visual function. This disturbance, therefore, cannot be attributed to primary sensory or sensory-motor impairment and fits the narrow definition of agnosia as "perception without meaning."

The core feature of this syndrome is the inability to recognize objects or their pictures. Picture identification is typically more difficult than the identification of real objects and may be the only residual in the recovery period. This dissociation is *not* seen in the naming performance of aphasics (Corlew and Nation, 1975; Hatfield and Howard, 1977), and may serve as a marker for the presence of agnosia in naming tasks. Impairment of recognition of faces (prosopagnosia), color (color agnosia), and of written material (alexia) are usually found in association with object agnosia. Each of these deficits, however, may occur in isolation or in various combinations. For example, the patients of Hécaen and Ajuriaguerra (1956), Lhermitte and Beauvois (1973), and Rubens et al. (1978) had no impairment of facial recognition, and reading was spared in the patients of Davidenkov (1956), Newcombe and Ratcliff (1974), Mack and Boller (1977), and Levine (1978). Levine's patient and Case 1 of Newcombe and Ratcliff had no color agnosia or alexia. Alexia is commonly found alone or with color agnosia; prosopagnosia is frequently an isolated recognition disturbance, but is often associated with acquired achromatopsia. (See Chapter 8.)

Tactile and auditory recognition are typically intact, however, two

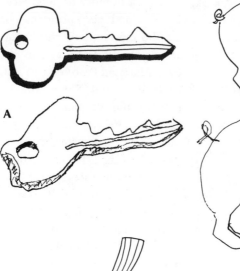

Fig. 9-1 Copies of line drawings by patient with associative visual agnosia. After copies were made, the patient still misidentified drawings as follows:

(A) "I still don't know."
(B) "Could be a dog or any other animal."
(C) "Could be a beach stump."
(D) "A wagon or a car of some kind. The larger vehicle is being pulled by the smaller one."

(From Rubens and Benson, 1971).

patients of Newcombe and Ratcliff and the patient of Taylor and Warrington were not able to identify objects by touch or by vision. Impairment of short-term verbal memory, particularly as measured by paired-word associate learning has been present in every patient in whom memory testing has been reported. Paradoxically, intact short-term nonverbal memory has been documented in many of these same patients. The most common visual defect is a dense, right homonymous hemianopia. Two left-handed patients with left hemianopias have been reported (Newcombe and Ratcliff [Case 2], 1974; Levine, 1978), and, interestingly, reading was spared in both. Normal visual fields have also been reported (Davidenkov, 1956; Newcombe and Ratcliff [Case 1], 1974; Taylor and Warrington, 1971).

The clinical picture is one of a patient who fails to name or to describe verbally or by gesture the nature of visually presented material, but who is able to draw or to match the misidentified material with identical samples. Pointing to objects named by the examiner is typically better than identifying objects verbally or by gesture. In the recovery period, pointing often returns to normal while other signs of "recognition" remain impaired. The disproportional improvement in pointing to named objects is thought to reflect the relative ease of choosing a named item from a closed set compared to choosing the name of a viewed object from an almost infinite list of possible names. However, an equally tenable explanation is that pointing to a named object is an easier task because it does not involve speaking and therefore reduces the chances of an incorrect verbal response adversely affecting subsequent cognitive performance.

Incorrect responses usually are morphological confusions or perseverations. Semantic confusions, however, are not uncommon. Perseverations may represent previously viewed objects or, more commonly, the verbal response to them. It has been claimed that such perseverations are verbal reports of a lingering visual sensory experience of previously viewed material, so-called "palinopsia" (Critchley, 1964). However, the drawings of patients who have perseverated the wrong name in a series of visual presentations are those of the items that they are viewing, not the items whose name they have incorrectly perseverated (Lhermitte and Beauvois, 1973; Rubens and Benson, 1971; Rubens et al., 1978). Successfully copying a misidentified picture does not facilitate identification of that picture. Viewing an object in use or otherwise in context significantly aids in recognition. Partially covering an item or placing it in unusual context hinders identification.

There is much evidence that the initial verbalized response to visual presentation affects otherwise intact abilities, often adversely. The strong perseverative tendency and the disrupting influence of visual naming on tactile identification are examples of this. One might expect that a patient who has already demonstrated adequate blindfolded tactile naming will perform at least as well when he simultaneously inspects and handles the same objects. However, the otherwise superior tactile identification of the patients of Ettlinger and Wyke (1961) and Rubens et al. (1979) fell to the much lower levels of visual identification alone when the patients were allowed to simultaneously view and handle the objects. Requiring the patient to name in writing (Lhermitte and Beauvois, 1973) or to supply a description (Newcombe and Ratcliff, 1974) instead of naming aloud normalized "recognition" in one case and enhanced it in the other. Many patients, however, insist on speaking despite strict instructions to remain silent. Case 1 of Oxbury et al. (1969), who was specifically instructed to demonstrate in silence the use of objects shown her, continued to name them aloud and then to produce an incorrect gesture that corresponded to her verbal misidentification. This same patient, when asked to match a line drawing to one of three real objects, would misname the drawing and then search vainly for an object corresponding to her incorrect name. A recently reported patient of Rubens et al. (1979) consistently misidentified objects and pictures only when naming preceded demonstration of use, but when instructed to first silently (with tongue held between teeth) demonstrate function, he supplied the proper gesture and then followed with the correct name. This patient also was unable to group pictures into categories unless he was strictly instructed to remain silent.

These examples have been described in some detail in order to underline the importance of controlling for the "confabulation factor" when examining various cognitive or gnostic functions. Many authors have commented on the erratic performance of these patients in the test situation and particularly in everyday life. It is not uncommon for patients to function well in their visual environment in everyday life, but then to fail miserably on recognition when formally tested. Much of the variability is, of course, attributable to the facilitatory effects of contextual cues that are congruent with patient expectations in a known environment. It is probable, however, that many of the errors demonstrated in the neuropsychology laboratory represent a test artifact induced by the highly verbal nature of the task.

The failure to sort objects and pictures into categories (articles of clothing, tools, etc.) or to match nonmorphologically identical representations of the same object (a small line drawing of a wrist watch with a real wrist watch) is a common finding. This feature is so prominent that Hécaen et al. (1974) suggested that the basic disorder underlying visual object agnosia is a specific categorization defect for visual inputs. Newcombe and Ratcliff (1974) proposed that the defect lies in an intermediate step between Lissauer's stages of apperception and association. They suggest that an object is first identified on the basis of visual characteristics alone, either by template matching or visual feature extraction. In the absence of such a template, the visual features are extracted individually and a search conducted through some form of lexicon for objects with similar contour, then for objects with similar sheen, etc. The search continues until either a single class of objects has been identified or until more than one class of objects remains and further information must be obtained. A defect in the ability to conduct this kind of search underlies the recognition disturbance of some patients with associative visual agnosia.

The marked variability of performance of patients in the natural setting as opposed to the test setting has been noted by Geschwind (1965) who proposed that agnosia is not a defect of a unitary process of recognition, but is a rather special form of modality-specific naming deficit. He views the misidentifications as confabulated responses elaborated by the intact speech area pathologically disconnected from intact sensory area. Failure to supply the correct gesture results from concomitant disconnection between motor and sensory areas. The common association of visual object agnosia with right homonymous hemianopia, alexia, and color agnosia, a triad known to occur almost invariably with damage to the mesial left occipital lobe and nearby posterior callosal fibers, supports the visual-verbal disconnection hypothesis. Authors arguing against the disconnection hypothesis cite: (1) the occasional finding of normal visual fields; (2) the occasional absence of color agnosia and alexia in the same patient (Newcombe and Ratcliff [Case 1], 1974; Levine, 1978); and finally (3) the question of why a left occipital-splenial lesion produces the syndrome of alexia without agraphia commonly but object agnosia only rarely.

It is probable that there are two or more forms of associative visual agnosia representing impairment at different levels of processing beyond the stage of perception. Patients such as those of Taylor and Warrington (1971) and Newcombe and Ratcliff [Cases 1 and 2] (1974) with diffuse bilateral disease processes, tactile agnosia, and normal visual fields appear to form a separate group from those with right homonymous hemianopsia associated with infarction primarily in the territory of the left posterior cerebral artery. The possibility of disconnection is not ruled out by the presence of normal visual fields and spared reading and color recognition. It is possible that even in these cases, unilateral or bilateral intrahemisphere disconnection and selective destruction of independent pathways mediating various elements of visual recognition play a role. There is evidence, for example, for the specificity of neural pathways for color (Meadows, 1974a). Neuropathological data suggest that sufficient (if not always necessary) pathology for the production of visual object agnosia includes either extensive left mesial occipital lobe destruction with callosal and mesial temporal lobe limbic involvement (Hahn, 1895 [autopsy of Lissauer's patient]), or bilateral cortical-subcortical occipital lobe lesions with disconnection of visual areas from both the left speech area and the limbic system (Benson et al., 1974 [autopsy of the case of Rubens and Benson]). A combined visual-speech and visual-limbic disconnection is suggested by this material.

The nature of pathological processes that affect the posterior part of the brain dictates that many patients with posterior cerebral lesions will have bilateral involvement. For that reason, it is common to see elements of apperception and faulty sensory-motor scanning in patients with associative visual agnosia. The interaction between these levels of impairment makes analysis of visual behavior extremely difficult and often confounds attempts at classification. It is reasonable, however, to attempt to isolate the various elements of perceptual and recognition disturbance, rather than to lump the entire group into a wastepaper basket category of demented patients with poor vision.

Optic aphasia

The term "optic aphasia" was introduced by Freund (1889) to describe the deficit of one of his patients with a right homonymous hemianopia and aphasia due to a left parietal occipital tumor; the patient's naming ability was impaired primarily for objects presented visually. The case report is of little value because of its incompleteness, but Freund's speculations are pertinent. He hypothesized a left speech area–right occipital disconnection as the basis for the visual naming deficit. In current usage, *optic aphasia* refers to the condition in which a patient is unable to name visually presented objects and yet is able to show that he recognizes the object either by indicating its use or by pointing to it when it is named. Tactile and auditory naming are preserved. Certain authors have emphasized the distinction between optic aphasia and visual agnosia, the former representing a naming disorder and the latter a disturbance of recognition. It is probable, however, that the difference is one of severity, not quality. The patient of Lhermitte and Beauvois (1973) whom the authors classified as an optic aphasic (because he could point to objects on command and indicate the use of objects shown him, but could not utter the name of verbally presented objects) could name when he was required to respond in writing. I have personally observed two patients evolve from classical associative visual agnosia in the first several months of their illness to so-called optic aphasia in the chronic period. The fact that certain patients can be made to oscillate between optic aphasia and visual agnosia by varying the instructions given them on a particular task blurs the distinction between a naming disorder and a disturbance of recognition and lends support to Geschwind's contention that visual agnosia is an unusual form of modality-specific naming disorder in which confabulated verbal misnaming interferes with otherwise intact cognitive and gnostic capacities.

Color agnosia

The patient with color agnosia is unable to name colors shown him or to point to a color named by the examiner, yet performs normally on tests of color perception. He is able to read Ishihara plates and to sort colors according to hue, but is unable to operate in the visual-verbal mode. The disorder is usually associated with the syndrome of alexia without agraphia, and is viewed by some as a color anomia. According to Oxbury et al. (1969), there are at least two varieties of the disturbance. One is a visual modality-specific disorder typically associated with alexia without agraphia and thought to result from a disconnection of right visual from left language centers (Geschwind and Fusillo, 1966; Oxbury et al. [Case 1], 1969). The patient is able to respond correctly to verbal-verbal tasks (what is the color of a banana?) and to visual-visual tasks (appropriate color line drawings with crayons). The second variety is considered to be part of a primary dysphasic disorder arising from damage to parietal regions of the left hemisphere. These patients are unable to produce visual-visual and verbal-verbal responses (Oxbury et al. [Case 2], 1969; Kinsbourne and Warrington, 1964). The deficit is similar to that reported in aphasic patients by DeRenzi et al. (1972). Although color agnosia may be found in isolation and can be distinguished from achromatopsia (color blindness) by matching and sorting tasks, it is evident that many patients with a color recognition disturbance have elements of color perception impairment as well. Meadows (1974a) and Green and Lessell (1977) have presented clinical data suggesting that bilateral anterior-inferior occipital-lobe lesions produce persisting impairment of color vision with preservation of primary visual function. The anatomical location and the visual field deficits (altitudinal field defects) are similar to what is found in prosopagnosia, a disturbance commonly associated with acquired achromatopsia. (See also pp. 198–200 in Chapter 8.)

Prosopagnosia

The term *prosopagnosia* was first introduced by Bodamer (1947) to describe the inability to recognize familiar faces. However, patients with this disorder may be able to discriminate and match faces normally (Benton and Van Allen, 1972; Tzavaras et al., 1970). The impairment often extends to other categories requiring special visual experience (i.e., the recognition of cars, types of trees, etc.) and topographical memory (Rondot and Tzaveras, 1969). In some cases, the impairment of facial recognition is so severe that the patient is unable to recognize his own face in the mirror. Patients learn to identify people by utilizing specific cues such as clothing, character-istic footsteps, length of hair, and height. The inability to recognize family members, friends, and hospital staff by face may lead to the mistaken impression that the patient is suffering from a Korsakoff syndrome or a generalized dementia. Meadows (1974b) has shown that patients with prosopagnosia nearly always have a left upper-quadrant visual field defect associated with a right occipitotemporal lesion. A symmetrically placed smaller left-sided lesion is usually associated with this, or, less commonly, a left-sided lesion that does not involve the anterior-inferior temporal lobe. In either case, pro-sopagnosia is a reliable marker of bilateral cerebral pathology. The reader is referred to the excellent recent review of prosopagnosia by Meadows (1974b) for further discussion of this interesting clinical entity. (See also Chapter 8, pp. 198–200.)

AUDITORY AGNOSIA

The term *auditory agnosia* refers to impaired capacity to recognize sounds in the presence of otherwise adequate hearing as measured by standard audiometry. The literature is somewhat confusing be-cause the term has been sometimes used in a broader sense to refer to impaired capacity to recognize both speech and nonspeech audi-tory material, and in a narrower sense to refer to a selective deficit in the recognition of nonverbal sounds only. If one uses the term to refer to the broad spectrum of all auditory recognition problems associated with cerebral auditory dysfunction, the disorder is further subdivided into auditory sound agnosia, auditory verbal agnosia, and a mixed group. Using the more narrow definition, one speaks of auditory agnosia (selective impairment of nonverbal-sound recog-nition) and pure word deafness (selective impairment of speech-sound recognition). The term *cortical deafness* generally has been applied to those patients whose daily activities and auditory be-havior indicate an extreme lack of awareness of auditory stimuli of any kind, and whose audiometric pure tone thresholds are markedly abnormal. The dividing line between cortical deafness and mixed verbal- and nonverbal-sound auditory agnosia is poorly defined. *Receptive* (sensory) *amusia* refers to loss of the ability to appreciate various characteristics of heard music.

Pure word deafness (auditory agnosia for speech, verbal auditory agnosia)

The patient with pure word deafness is unable to comprehend and discriminate spoken language although he can read, write, and speak in a relatively normal manner. This syndrome is "pure" only in the sense that it is relatively free of aphasia symptoms found with other disorders affecting language comprehension such as Wernicke's aphasia and transcortical sensory aphasia. The disorder was first described by Kussmaul (1877) who used the term "reinen Worttaubheit" to refer to patients who were unable to understand spoken words but whose speech and hearing were normal. Lichtheim (1885) later described, using the term "subcortical sensory aphasia," a patient with defective understanding of spoken speech who had no difficulty in speaking, reading, or writing and no impairment of the identification of nonverbal sounds except for music. He postulated a subcortical interruption of fibers from both ascending auditory projections to the left auditory word center. With few exceptions, pure word deafness has been associated with bilateral, rather symmetrical cortical-subcortical lesions involving the anterior part of the superior temporal gyri with some sparing of Heschl's gyrus, particularly on the left side. Several patients were found to have unilateral lesions located subcortically in the temporal lobe, destroying the left auditory radiation as well as the callosal fibers from the opposite auditory region (e.g., Liepmann and Storch, 1902; Schuster and Taterka, 1926). The very low incidence of pure word deafness is attributable to the fact that it takes an unusually placed, very circumscribed lesion of the superior temporal gyrus to involve Heschl's gyrus or its connections and still selectively spare Wernicke's area.

Cerebrovascular disease is the most common cause of pure word deafness. The patient when first seen is often recovering from a full-blown Wernicke's aphasia. As the paraphasias and writing and reading disturbances disappear, the patient still does not comprehend spoken language but can be easily communicated with by writing. Deafness can be ruled out by normal pure-tone thresholds on audiometry. At this stage, the patient may experience auditory hallucinations and exhibit transient paranoid ideation. The inability to repeat speech stimuli that are not comprehended distinguishes pure word deafness, which is a disturbance at the perceptual-discrimination level, from transcortical sensory aphasia in which word sounds are perceived normally, but there is an estrangement of sound from meaning. The absence of florid paraphasia and of reading and writing disturbances distinguishes the disorder from Wernicke's aphasia. The patient with word deafness complains that speech is muffled or sounds like a foreign language. Hemphill and Stengel's patient (1940) stated that "voices come but no words." The patient of Klein and Harper (1956) described speech "as an undifferentiated continuous humming noise without any rhythm" and "like foreigners speaking in the distance." Albert and Bear's patient (1974) said, "Words come too quickly," and they "sound like a foreign language." The speech of these patients may contain occasional word finding pauses and paraphasias and is often slightly louder than normal. Performance in speech perception tasks is very inconsistent and highly dependent on context. Most patients use lip-reading as an aid to auditory comprehension. Patients do much better when they are aware of the category of the subject under discussion. Comprehension often drops suddenly when the topic is changed. Words embedded in sentences are more easily identified than isolated words. Slowing the presentation rate of words in sentences also aids in comprehension. This improvement with slower speech rates may be due to the reduced adverse effects of abnormally slow temporal analysis of auditory stimuli or more plausibly to the fact that the processing of words and their meaning involves an act of constructive synthesis carried on by the listener (Neisser, 1967) and the slower rate of presentation allows the patient more time to make educated guesses.

In a recent case report, Albert and Bear (1974) suggested that the problem in pure word deafness is one of temporal resolution of auditory stimuli rather than specific phonetic impairment. Their patient demonstrated abnormal auditory fusion thresholds for clicks and improvement on auditory comprehension when speech was presented at slower rates. Saffran, Marin, and Yeni-Komshian (1976), on the other hand, in an exceptionally detailed case report, showed that informing their patient of the nature of the topic under discussion—indicating the category of words to be presented or giving the patient a multiple-choice array just before presentation of words

—significantly facilitated comprehension. Words embedded in a sentence were better recognized, particularly when they occurred in the latter part of the sentence. These authors suggest that pure word deafness represents an arrest of speech perception at a prephonetic level. The extreme suppression of right-ear perception on dichotic listening tasks found in the two patients discussed above suggests the inaccessibility of the left-hemisphere phonetic decoding areas (Wernicke's area) to auditory material that has already been acoustically processed by the right hemisphere.

There is evidence that unilateral left-sided hemispheric lesions, particularly those producing Wernicke's aphasia with impaired auditory comprehension, are also associated with impaired ability to match nonverbal sounds with pictures (Vignolo, 1969). These errors, however, are almost exclusively semantic, not acoustic, and thus do not suggest that unilateral left-hemisphere temporal-lobe disease produces a perceptual-discriminative sound recognition disturbance. For that reason, the finding of impaired ability to discriminate nonverbal speech sounds in a patient with pure word deafness suggests bilateral disease, even in the absence of other neurological findings of bilaterality.

Auditory agnosia for nonspeech sounds (auditory sound agnosia)

Auditory agnosia restricted to the recognition of nonspeech sounds is a rarely reported entity. This is probably so because such patients are less likely to seek medical advice than those with a disorder of speech comprehension, and also because nonspecific auditory complaints are often discounted when pure tone audiometric and speech discrimination thresholds are normal.

Vignolo (1969) makes the case for dividing auditory sound agnosia into a perceptual-discriminative form associated mainly with lesions of the right hemisphere and an associative-semantic form associated with lesions of the left hemisphere and closely linked to Wernicke's aphasia. The distinguishing characteristics of these groups are the types of errors made on tasks of sound recognition and discrimination—acoustic confusions as opposed to semantic confusions. This division follows the original classification of Kleist (1928) who distinguished between the inability to perceive isolated sounds or noises (perceptive Geräuschtaubheit) and the inability to understand the meaning of sounds (Geräuschinntaubheit). It resembles also the apperceptive/associative dichotomy of Lissauer (1889). In the verbal sphere, the analogous comparison is between pure word deafness (perceptual-discriminative) and transcortical sensory aphasia (semantic-associative).

Several well-studied cases of auditory sound agnosia have been reported in the recent literature (Albert et al., 1972; Spreen et al., 1965). The patient of Spreen and associates was a 65-year-old right-handed male whose major complaint when seen three years after a left hemiparetic episode was that of "nerves" and headache. Audiometric testing demonstrated moderate bilateral high-frequency loss and speech reception thresholds of 12 db for both ears. There was no aphasia. The outstanding abnormality was the inability to recognize common sounds; understanding of language was fully retained and there were no other agnosic defects. Sound localization was normal. Scores on the pitch test of the Seashore Measures of Musical Talent were at chance level. The patient claimed no experience or talent with music and refused, as many patients do, to cooperate with further testing of musical ability. A failure of recognition at the semantic-associative level was suggested by the fact that the patient was able to match previously heard but misidentified sounds with one of four tape recorded choices. Postmortem examination revealed a sharply demarcated old infarct of the right hemisphere centering around the parietal lobe and involving the superior temporal and angular gyri, as well as a large portion of the inferior parietal, inferior and middle frontal, and long and short gyri of the insula. This case represents the only example of auditory sound agnosia with documented unilateral pathology. In a more recent case report (Albert et al., 1972) there was clinical evidence of bilateral involvement. The authors suggest an associative-level deficit in their patient as well. It is interesting to note that there was complete extinction of the left ear on dichotic presentation of words and musical stimuli.

In the large majority of cases impairment of nonverbal sound recognition is accompanied by impaired recognition of speech sounds. This mixed group frequently evolves from a state of cortical deafness, and it is often difficult to define a clear separation between the two entities.

Cortical deafness

Although it was originally believed that bilateral cortical lesions involving the primary auditory cortex resulted in total hearing loss, recent evidence from animal experiments (Massopoust et al., 1967; Neff et al., 1961) and clinicopathological studies in man (Mahoudeau et al., 1956; Wohlfart et al., 1952) indicates that complete bilateral destruction of primary auditory cortex does not lead to substantial permanent loss of audiometric sensitivity. It is common, however, for an asymptomatic patient with old unilateral temporal-lobe pathology to become suddenly totally deaf with the occurrence of a second lesion in the opposite auditory region. This is most common in cerebrovascular disease where the course is commonly biphasic with a transient deficit (often aphasia and hemiparesis) related to one hemisphere followed in a number of months or years by a second deficit associated with sudden but transient total deafness (Jerger et al., 1969; Jerger et al., 1972). In many patients severe aphasia interferes with further audiometric testing. Occasionally, hearing remains severely affected and the patient appears not to attend to loud noises (Earnest et al., 1977). Even these patients, however, occasionally react to environmental noises such as the ringing of a telephone or an airplane passing overhead. The erratic auditory behavior in these patients often leads to the suspicion of psychogenic hearing loss. It is probable that a large component of the intermittency of auditory detection is due to attentional impairment. Other well-documented causes of cortical deafness include encephalitis and head trauma. Of particular interest is a recently described syndrome found in young children characterized by the occurrence of generalized seizures, progressive hearing loss, and aphasia (Landau and Kleffner, 1957; Gascon et al., 1973). The EEG of these patients reveals bitemporal dysrhythmia thought to result in physiological interference with auditory sensory processing.

Sensory (receptive) amusia

The subject of amusia has been reviewed in detail by Wertheim (1969), Critchley and Henson (1977), and Gates and Bradshaw

(1977). Sensory amusia refers to an inability to appreciate various characteristics of heard music. It occurs to some extent in all cases of sound agnosia and in the majority of cases of aphasia and pure word deafness. As is the case with selective auditory-sound agnosia, the loss of musical perceptual ability is underreported because a specific musical disorder rarely interferes with everyday life. A major obstacle to systematic study of the disorder is the extreme variability of premorbid musical abilities, interests, and skills. It was Wertheim's conclusion (1969) that receptive amusia corresponds more frequently with a lesion of the left hemisphere, while expressive musical disabilities are more apt to be associated with right-hemispheric dysfunction. Recent evidence indicates that cerebral organization of musical ability differs depending on degree of skill and musical sophistication. Musically sophisticated individuals are more likely to perceive music in a more analytical manner and to rely more heavily on the dominant hemisphere. Dichotic listening studies show that the right hemisphere plays a more important role than the left in the processing of musical and nonlinguistic sound patterns (Gordon, 1974). However, the left hemisphere appears to be of major importance in the processing of sequential material of any kind including musical series. According to Gordon (1974), melody recognition becomes less of a right-hemisphere task as the time and rhythm factors become more important for distinguishing the tone patterns. These factors contribute to the lack of definition of the entity of receptive amusia and the difficulty of localizing the deficit to a particular brain region. Further complicating the picture is the fact that pitch, harmony, timbre, intensity, and rhythm may be affected to different degrees and in various combinations in the individual patient. Furthermore, there is recent evidence that aspects of musical denotation (the so-called "real world" events referred to by lyrics), and musical connotation (the formal expressive patterns indicated by pitch, timbre, and intensity) are selectively vulnerable to focal brain lesions (Gardner et al., 1977). For instance, on tests of musical denotation, right hemisphere damaged patients perform well on items where acquaintance with lyrics is required; in contrast, aphasics with anterior lesions are superior to both right-hemisphere patients and to aphasics with posterior lesions on items where knowledge of lyrics is unnecessary. On tests of musical connotation, right-hemisphere patients do better in matching sound patterns to temporally sequenced designs than to simultaneous gestalten. Aphasics with posterior lesions perform relatively well on tests of musical connotation.

TACTILE AGNOSIA

Tactile agnosia is a condition in which objects are not recognized in the tactile modality. As is the case with other forms of agnosia, many authors doubt that impairment of tactile recognition occurs in the absence of a primary sensory deficit. The distinction between the terms "astereognosis" and "tactile agnosia" is not clear and is the source of much confusion in the literature. It is beyond the scope of this chapter to discuss in detail the clinical entity of astereognosis, which has been reviewed in great depth by Critchley (1953). A commonly accepted classification of tactile recognition disorders is that of Delay (1935) who subdivided astereognosis into (1) impaired recognition of the size and shape of objects—*amorphognosis,* (2) impairment in the discrimination of distinctive qualities of objects such as density, weight, texture, and thermal properties—*ahylognosia,* and finally (3) impaired recognition of the identity of objects in the absence of amorphognosis and ahylognosia—*tactile asymboly.* The latter term corresponds to the "tactile agnosia" of other authors.

Semmes (1965) has identified a group of patients without primary sensory tactile impairment who fail in tests of object shape and pattern discrimination. These patients are also found to have significant spatial disability as measured by general tests of spatial orientation. Teuber (1965a,b) interprets the difficulty as a special form of spatial orientation deficit rather than one of agnosia for shape. A recent study (Roland, 1976), has reconfirmed the importance of the anterior part of the middle third of the postcentral gyrus in the production of impairment of size-and-shape discrimination of the hand contralateral to the lesion.

Impairment at the perceptual-discriminative level of tactile identification does not account for instances in which patients are able to tactually match to sample objects that they are not able to identify (Newcombe and Ratcliff, 1974). This type of defect is obviously at the associative level of recognition. The possibility of a tactile–

verbal disconnection resulting in a modality-specific naming deficit analogous to that which is seen in associative visual agnosia is suggested by the remarkable patient of Geschwind and Kaplan (1965) with infarction of and a tumor invading the corpus callosum. The patient was unable to name or supply verbal descriptions of items placed in the left hand but could draw misidentified objects with the left hand and choose a previously manipulated object tactually from a group of other objects. Posterior parietal lesions of the dominant hemisphere may be responsible for the bilateral form of this disturbance. It is therefore important to allow patients who fail on tactile identification to match tactually and to attempt to draw with the hand that failed to identify.

EXAMINATION OF THE PATIENT WITH AGNOSIA

The examination of the agnosic patient has already been discussed in some detail. In distinguishing between agnosic and aphasic errors, it is important to remember that agnosic recognition failures are most often modality-specific. The agnosic without associated aphasia will not manifest word-finding difficulties in spontaneous speech, in generating lists of words in specific categories, in completing open-ended sentences, and in supplying words that correspond with definitions. Except in the rare case of optic aphasia, the agnosic will not be able to identify the misnamed objects by means of circumlocution, and more specifically by indicating function. It is important to determine whether the patient is able to demonstrate the use of objects not in his presence and to follow commands not requiring objects (e.g., salute, wave goodby, and make a fist). Failures of this type in the presence of otherwise intact auditory comprehension indicate apraxia; subsequent failure to demonstrate the use of objects presented on visual confrontation may therefore be apractic, not agnosic.

In pointing and naming tasks, it is important to be certain that the patient is visually fixating on the objects to be identified and that pointing errors are not due to mislocalization in space found with Balint's syndrome. Recognition should be examined both in the context of normal surroundings and in the formal test setting.

In the visual sphere, the recognition of objects, colors, words, geometrical forms, faces, and emblems and signs, should be evaluated. In the event of failure to recognize, the patient should be allowed to match misidentified items to sample and to produce drawings of objects not identified. Correct matching and accurate drawing suggests intact perceptual processing and a failure at the associative level. Cross-modal matching should also be evaluated. It is important to keep in mind that matching a visually presented object to one of four objects presented tactually is different from first presenting an object for palpation and asking that it be chosen from one of four objects presented visually. Line drawings to be copied should contain a certain amount of internal detail so that slavish, slow tracing of an outline can be distinguished from the more detailed drawings of patients with normal perceptuomotor function. Failure to match and to draw accurately does not rule out associative agnosia when perceptuomotor deficits are also present. Hidden figures, visual mazes, and counting tasks (count dots on a white piece of paper, pick up pennies spread over a table top) should also be administered. Visual memory for designs, objects, faces, and colors, should be assessed by delayed drawing and by choosing from a multiple-choice array. The ability to categorize, sort misidentified objects, and pair objects that are not morphologically identical, but represent examples of the same item (lined drawing of a baby and an actual baby doll) should be tested.

The patient should be asked to identify the pictures of well-known people and to identify hospital staff by face. If recognition does not occur, patient should be asked to determine whether the face is of a male or female or whether the face is of a human or animal. Visual agnosics often fail to learn the names of new people and places, but are able to demonstrate recognition by other means such as "He's my doctor." Failure to name a particular face should therefore be further examined by asking for further identification of persons not named. The ability to discriminate faces should also be evaluated by matching tests.

Color perception should be tested with pseudoisochromatic plates and with the Farnsworth Hue test. The patient should be asked to respond to (1) verbal-verbal tasks such as, "What is the color of a banana?" or to list items that are of a certain color, (2) to visual-

visual tasks such as coloring line drawings with crayons and sorting and matching colors according to hue, and finally (3) to carry out visual-verbal tasks such as pointing to named colors and naming colors pointed to by the examiner.

The possibility of confabulation interfering with cognitive and gnostic performance should be considered. Therefore, test performance when the patient is allowed to verbalize should be compared to performance when he is prohibited from verbalizing either by asking him to count backwards, or by having him place his tongue between his teeth. Comparisons between naming and the tactile modality alone and with simultaneous visual and tactile presentation should also be made.

Careful visual fields and visual acuity measures are important. It may be necessary, in testing patients who cannot read, to construct tests of acuity that use nonverbal targets such as the orientation of lines of various lengths and distances from the viewer, or the detection of two points at variable distances from each other and from the patient. If equipment is available, psychophysical tests should be employed. These include detection threshold, local adaptation time, flicker fusion, movement after-effect, and the tachistoscopic presentation of single and multiple items. Depth perception using Julesz figures should be tested. Luminance discrimination should also be tested. The use of an eye-movement monitor is helpful in describing visual scanning behavior.

In the sphere of hearing, standard audiometric testing including speech reception and pure tone audiometry should be determined. The ability to localize in space should also be examined. It should be remembered that patients with acquired auditory-sound agnosia do not ordinarily complain specifically about their problem. Recognition of nonverbal sounds should be tested preferably with the use of a series of tape-recorded sounds. The Seashore Test of Music Abilities may be used to measure musical ability, however, it is important to recognize that in the absence of a history of proven musical talent and interest, the findings on this test are impossible to interpret.

In the tactile sphere, it is important to allow the patient to attempt to draw misidentified objects or to after-select them from a group tactually.

References

Adler, A. (1944). Disintegration and restoration of optic recognition in visual agnosia. *Arch. Neurol. Psychiat. 51*:243–259.

Albert, M., Reches, A., and Silverberg, R. (1975). Associative visual agnosia without alexia. *Neurology 4*:322–326.

Albert, M. L., Sparks, R., Stockert, Th. v., and Sax, D. (1972). A case study of auditory agnosia: linguistic and non-linguistic processing. *Cortex 8*:427.

Albert, M. L. and Bear, D. (1974). Time to understand. A case study of word deafness with reference to the role of time in auditory comprehension. *Brain 97*:373.

Anton, G. (1899). Ueber die Selbstwahrnehmungen der Herderkrankungen des Gehirns durch den Kranken bei Rindenblindheit und Rindentaubheit. *Arch. Psychiat. 32*:86–127.

Balint, R. (1909). Seelenlähmung des "Schauens", optische Ataxie, räumliche Störung der Aufmerksamkeit. *Montasschr. f. Psychiat. u. Neurol. 25*:57–71.

Bay, E. (1953). Disturbances of visual perception and their examination. *Brain 76*:515–550.

Bender, M. B. and Feldman, M. (1972). The so-called "visual agnosias". *Brain 9*:173–186.

Benson, D. and Greenberg, J. (1969). Visual form agnosia. *Arch. Neurol. 20*:82–89.

Benson, D. F., Segarra, J., and Albert, M. L. (1974). Visual agnosia-prosopagnosia. *Arch. Neurol. 30*:307–310.

Benton, A. L. and Van Allen, M. W. (1972). Prosopagnosia and facial discrimination. *J. Neurol. Sci. 5*:167–172.

Bodamer, J. (1941). Die Prosop-Agnosie (die Agnosie des Physiognomieerkennens). *Arch. f. Psychiat. u. Nervenkrankheit 179*:6–53.

Botez, M. I. (1975). Two visual systems in clinical neurology: readaptive role of the primitive system in visual agnosic patients. *Europ. Neurol. 13*:101–122.

Brown, J. W. (1972). *Aphasia, Apraxia, and Agnosia—Clinical and Theoretical Aspects.* Springfield, Ill.: C. C. Thomas.

Corlew, M. M. and Nation, J. E. (1975). Characteristics of visual stimuli and naming performance in aphasic adults. *Cortex 11*:186–191.

Critchley, M. M. (1953). *The Parietal Lobes.* London: Arnold.

Critchley, M. M. (1964). The problem of visual agnosia. *J. Neurol. Sci. 1*:274–290.

Critchley, M. M. and Henson, R. A. (1977). *Music and the Brain: Studies in the Neurology of Music.* Springfield, Ill.: C. C. Thomas.

Davidenkov, S. (1956). Impairments of higher nervous activity: lecture 8, visual agnosias. *Clinical Lectures on Nervous Diseases.* Leningrad: State Publishing House of Medical Literature.

Delay, J. (1935). *Les Astéréognosies. Pathologie du Toucher. Clinique, Physiologie, Topographie.* Paris: Masson.

Denes, G. and Semenza, C. (1975). Auditory modality—specific anomia: evidence from a case of pure word deafness. *Cortex 11*:401.

Denny-Brown, D. and Chambers, R. (1976). Physiological aspects of visual perception. I. Functional aspects of visual cortex. *Arch. Neurol. 33*: 219–227.

Denny-Brown, D. and Fischer, E. G. (1976). Physiological aspects of visual perception. II. The subcortical visual direction of behavior. *Arch. Neurol. 33*:228–242.

DeRenzi, E., Faglioni, P., Scotti, G., and Spinnler, H. (1972). Impairment in associating color to form, concomitant with aphasia. *Brain 95*:293–304.

Earnest, M. P., Monroe, P. A., and Yarnell, P. R. (1977). Cortical deafness: demonstration of the pathologic anatomy by CT scan. *Neurology 27*: 1172–1175.

Efron, R. (1968). What is perception? in *Boston studies in the philosophy of science,* Vol. 4, R. Cohen and M. Wartofsky (eds). New York: Humanities Press and the Netherlands: O. Reidel.

Ettlinger, G. (1956). Sensory defects in visual agnosia. *J. Neurol. Neurosurg. Psychiat. 19*:297–307.

Ettlinger, G. and Wyke, M. (1961). Defects in identifying objects visually in a patient with cerebrovascular disease. *J. Neurol. Neurosurg. Psychiat. 24*:254–259.

Finkelnburg, F. C. (1870). Niederrheinische Gesellschaft in Bonn. Medicinische Section. *Berliner klinische Wochenschrift 7*:449–450, 460–461.

Freud, S. (1891). *Zur Auffasung der Aphasien. Eine Kritische Studie.* Leipzig: Deuticke.

Freund, D. C. (1889). Ueber optische Aphasie und Seelenblindheit. *Arch. f. Psychiat. u. Nervenkr. 20*:276–297, 371–416.

Gardner, H., Silverman, J., Denes, G., Semenza, C., and Rosenstiel, A. K. (1977). Sensitivity to musical denotation and connotation in organic patients. *Cortex 13*:242–256.

Gascon, G., Victor, D., Lombroso, C. T., and Goodglass, H. (1973). Language disorder, convulsive disorder and encephalographic abnormalities. *Arch. Neurol. 28*:156–162.

Gates, A. and Bradshaw, J. L. (1977). The role of the cerebral hemispheres in music. *Brain and Language 4*:403–431.

Geschwind, N. (1965). Disconnexion syndromes in animals and man. *Brain 88*:237–294.

Geschwind, N. and Fusillo, M. (1966). Color-naming defects in association with alexia. *Arch. Neurol. 15*:137–146.

Geschwind, N. and Kaplan, E. (1962). A human deconnection syndrome. *Neurology (Minneapolis) 12*:675–685.

Goldstein, K. (1948). *Language and Language Disturbances.* New York: Grune & Stratton.

Goldstein, K. and Gelb, A. (1918). Psychologische Analyser hirnpathologischer Fälle Grund von Untersuchungen Hirnverletzter. *Z. f. d. gesamte Neurol. u. Psychiat.* 41:1–142.

Goldstein, M. N. (1974). Auditory agnosia for speech ("pure word deafness"): a historical review with current implications. *Brain and Language* 1:195–204.

Goodglass, H., Barton, M. I., and Kaplan, E. F. (1968). Sensory modality and object-naming in aphasia. *J. Speech Hearing Res.* 11:488–496.

Gordon, H. W. (1974). Auditory specialization of the right and left hemispheres, in *Hemispheric Disconnection and Cerebral Function*, M. Kinsbourne and W. L. Smith (eds). Springfield, Ill. C. C. Thomas.

Green, G. L. and Lessell, S. (1977). Acquired cerebral dyschromatopsia. *Arch. Ophthalmol.* 95:121–128.

Hahn, E. (1895). Pathologische-anatomische Untersuchung en de Lissauer'schen Falles von Seelenblindheit. *Arbeiten aus dem Psychiatrischen Klinik in Breslau.*

Hatfield, F. M., Howard, D. et al. (1977). Object naming in aphasia—the lack of effect of context or realism. *Neuropsychologia* 15:717–727.

Hécaen, T. and de Ajuriaguerra, J. (1954). Balint's syndrome (psychic paralysis of visual fixation) and its minor forms. *Brain* 77:373–400.

Hécaen, H. and de Ajuriaguerra, J. (1956). Visual agnosia for inanimate object due to left occipital disease. *Rev. Neurol.* 94:222–233.

Hécaen, H., Goldblum, M. C., Masure, M. C., and Ramier, A. M. (1974). Une nouvelle observation d'agnosie d'objet. Deficit de l'association ou de la categorisation, specifique de la modalité visuelle? *Neuropsychologia* 12:447–464.

Heilman, K. M., Scholes, R., and Watson, R. T. (1975). Auditory affective agnosia. *J. Neurol. Neurosurg. Psychiat.* 38:69–72.

Hemphill, R. C. and Stengel, E. (1940). A study of pure word deafness. *J. Neurol. Psychiat.* 3:251–262.

Humphrey, N. K. (1970). What the frog's eye tells the monkey's brain. *Brain Behav. Evol.* 3:324–337.

Jackson, J. H. (1876). Case of large cerebral tumour without optic neuritis and with left hemiplegia and imperception. *R. Lond. Ophthal. Hosp. Rep.* 8:434. Reprinted (1932). *Selected Writings of John Hughlings Jackson*, Vol. 2, J. Taylor (ed). London: Hodder and Stoughton.

Jerger, J., Weikers, N. J., Sharbrough, F. W., and Jerger, S. (1969). Bilateral lesions of the temporal lobe. A case study. *Acta Oto-Laryngologica Suppl. 258.*

Jerger, J., Lovering, L., and Wertz, M. (1972). Auditory disorder following bilateral temporal lobe insult: report of a case. *J. Speech Hearing Dis.* 37:523.

Kinsbourne, M. and Warrington, E. K. (1962). A disorder of simultaneous form perception. *Brain* 85:461–486.

Kinsbourne, M. and Warrington, E. K. (1964). Observations on colour agnosia. *J. Neurol. Neurosurg. Psychiat.* 27:296–299.

Klein, R. and Harper, J. (1956). The problem of agnosia in the light of a case of pure word deafness. *J. Mental Sci. 102*:112–120.

Kleist, K. (1928). Gehirnpathologische und lokalisatorische Ergebnisse über Hörstörungen, Geräuschtaubheiten und Amusien. *Monatsschr. f. Psychiat. u. Neurol. 68*:853–860.

Kussmaul, A. (1877). Disturbances of speech, in *Cyclopedia of the Practice of Medicine*, Vol. 14, H. von Ziemssen (ed). New York: William Wood.

Landau, W. and Kleffner, F. (1957). Syndrome of acquired aphasia with convulsive disorder in children. *Neurology 7*:523–530.

Levine, D. N. (1978). Prosopagnosia and visual object agnosia: a behavioral study. *Brain and Language.*

Lhermitte, F. and Beauvois, M. F. (1973). A visual-speech disconnexion syndrome. *Brain 96*:695–714.

Lhermitte, F., Chedru, F., and Chain, F. (1973). A propos d'une cas d'agnosie visuelle. *Rev. Neurol. 128*:301–322.

Lichtheim, M. L. (1885). On aphasia. *Brain 7*:433–484.

Liepmann, H. (1900). Das Krankheitsbild der Apraxia ("motorischen asymbolie"). *Monatsschr. f. Psychiat. u. Neurol. 8*:15–44, 102–132, 181–197.

Liepmann, H. and Storch, E. (1902). Der mikroskopische Gehirnbefund bei dem Fall Gorstelle. *Monatsschr. f. Psychiat. u. Neurol. 11*:115–120.

Lissauer, H. (1889). Ein Fall von Seelenblindheit nebst Beitrage zur theorie derselben. *Arch. f. Psychiat. u. Nervenkr. 21*:222–270.

Luria, A. R. (1959). Disorders of "simultaneous perception" in a case of bilateral occipito-parietal brain injury. *Brain 82*:437–449.

Luria, A. R. (1966). *Higher Cortical Functions in Man.* New York: Basic Books.

Luria, A. R., Pravdina-Vinarskaya, E. N., and Yarbus, A. L. (1963). Disorders of ocular movement in a case of simultanagnosia. *Brain 86*:219–228.

Mack, J. L. and Boller, F. (1977). Associative visual agnosia and its related deficits: the role of the minor hemisphere in assigning meaning to visual perceptions. *Neuropsychologia 15*:345–349.

Mahoudeau, D., Lemoyne, J., Dubrisay, J., and Caraes, J. (1956). Sür un cas d'agnosie auditive. *Rev. Neurol. 95*:57.

Massopoust, L. C. and Wolin, L. R. Jr. (1967). Changes in auditory frequency discrimination thresholds after temporal cortex ablation. *Exp. Neurol. 19*:245–251.

Meadows, J. C. (1974a). Disturbed perceptives of colors associated with localized cerebral lesions. *Brain 97*:615–632.

Meadows, J. C. (1974b). The anatomical basis of prosopagnosia. *J. Neurol. Neurosurg. Psychiat. 37*:489–501.

Milner, B. and Teuber, H. (1968). Alteration of perception and memory in man: reflections on methods, in *Analysis of Behavioral Change*, L. Weiskrantz (ed). New York: Harper and Row.

Munk, H. (1881). Ueber die Functionen der Grosshirnrinde. *Gesammelte Mittheilungen aus den Jahren 1877–80.* Berlin: Hirschwald.

Neff, W. D. (1961). Neuronal mechanisms of auditory discrimination, in *Sensory Communication,* Vol. 15, N. A. Rosenblith (ed). Cambridge: The MIT Press.

Neisser, U. (1967). *Cognitive Psychology.* New York: Appleton.

Newcombe, F. and Ratcliff, G. (1974). Agnosia: a disorder of object recognition, in *Les Syndromes de Disconnexion Calleuse chez L'homme,* F. Michel et B. Schott (eds). Colloque International de Lyon.

Oxbury, J. M., Oxbury, S. M., and Humphrey, N. K. (1969). Varieties of color anomia. *Brain 92*:847–860.

Pasik, T. and Pasik, P. (1971). The visual world of monkeys deprived of striate cortex: effective stimulus parameters and the importance of the accessory optic system. *Vision Res. Suppl. 3*:419–435.

Roland, P. E. (1976). Astereognosis. *Arch. Neurol. 33*:543–550.

Rondot, P. and Tzavaras, A. (1969). La prosopagnosie après vingt annes d'études cliniques et neuropsychologiques. *J. Psychol. 66*:133–166.

Rubens, A. and Benson, D. (1971). Associative visual agnosia. *Arch. Neurol. (Chicago) 24*:305–316.

Rubens, A., Johnson, M., and Garwick, D. (1978). Confabulation in visual agnosia. *Brain and Language.*

Saffran, E. M., Marin, O. S. M., and Yeni-Komshian, G. H. (1976). An analysis of speech perceptions in word deafness. *Brain and Language 3*:209–228.

Schuster, P. and Taterka, H. (1926). Beitrag zur Anatomie und Klinik der reinen Worttaubheit. *Z. f. d. gesamte Neurol. u. Psychiat. 105*:494.

Semmes, J. (1965). A non-tactual factor in asterognosis. *Neuropsychologia 3*:295–315.

Spinnler, H. and Vignolo, L. A. (1966). Impaired recognition of meaningful sounds in aphasia. *Cortex 2*:337.

Spreen, O., Benton, A. L., and Allen, M. W. Van. (1966). Dissociation of visual and tactile naming in amnesic aphasia. *Neurology (Minneapolis) 16*:807–814.

Spreen, O., Benton, A., and Fincham, R. (1965). Auditory agnosia without aphasia. *Arch. Neurol. 13*:84.

Stauffenburg, V. (1914). Über Seelenblindheit. *Arbeiten aus dem Hirnanatomischen Institut in Zurich* Heft 8, Wiesbaden: Bergman.

Taylor, A. and Warrington, E. K. (1971). Visual agnosia: a single case report. *Cortex 7*:152–161.

Teuber, H. L. (1965a). Somatosensory disorders due to cortical lesions. *Neuropsychologia 3*:287–294.

Teuber, H. L. (1965b). Postscript: some needed revisions of the classical views of agnosias. *Neuropsychologia 3*:371–378.

Teuber, H. L. (1968). Alteration of perception and memory in man, in *Analysis of Behavioral Change,* L. Weiskrantz (ed.), New York: Harper and Row.

Tyler, H. R. (1968). Abnormalities of perception with defective eye movements (Balint's syndrome). *Cortex 4*:154–171.

Tzavaras, A., Hécaen, H., and Lebras, H. (1970). Le probleme de la specificité du deficit de la reconnaissance du visage humans lors des lesions hémispheriques unilaterales. *Neuropysychologia 8*:403–416.

Vignolo, L. (1969). Auditory agnosia: a review and report of recent evidence, in *Contributions to Clinical Neuropsychology*, A. L. Benton (ed). Chicago: Aldine.

Von Hagen, K. O. (1941). Two clinical cases of mind blindness (visual agnosia), one due to carbon monoxide intoxication, one due to diffuse degeneration process. *Bull. Los Angeles Neurol. Soc. 6*:191–194.

Weiskrantz, L. (1972). Behavioral analysis of the monkey's visual nervous system. *Proc. Roy. Soc. London 182*:427–455.

Weiskrantz, L., Warrington, E. K., Sanders, M. D., and Marshall, J. (1974). Visual capacity in the hemianopic field following a restricted occipital ablation. *Brain 97*:709–728.

Wertheim, N. (1969). The amusias, in *Handbook of Clinical Neurology*, Vol. 4, P. J. Vinken and G. W. Bruyn (eds). Amsterdam: North-Holland.

Wohlfart, G., Lindgren, A., and Jernelius, B. (1952). Clinical picture and morbid anatomy in a case of "pure word deafness." *J. Nervous Mental Disease 116*:818–827.

Wolpert, I. (1924). Die Simultanagnosie: störung der gesamtauffassung. *Z. f. d. gesamte Neurol. u. Psychiat. 93*:397–415.

10
Neglect and Related Disorders
KENNETH M. HEILMAN

DEFINITION

Under a variety of stimulus and performance conditions, patients who do not have elemental sensory or motor defects fail to report, respond, or orient to stimuli presented to the side contralateral to a cerebral lesion. In some patients different behavioral manifestations are seen at different times and in some patients certain behavioral manifestations are never seen. The various behavioral manifestations are explained in the following sections.

Hemi-inattention or hemineglect
The failure to report or respond to unilateral stimuli has been termed *neglect* (hemineglect) or *inattention* (hemi-inattention). In the somesthetic and visual modalities, it is often difficult to separate hemineglect from hemianesthesia or hemianopia; however, a patient with hemineglect may be able to report a stimulus when his attention is drawn to the neglected side. For example, when a patient is touched on his abnormal side, he may not orient to the stimulus or make an appropriate response, but when his attention is drawn to this side he may be able to demonstrate that he does not have an elementary sensory defect.

Patients with profound hemi-inattention may even fail to recognize that their contralesional extremities are their own. We have seen patients who wanted to know why someone else's arm or leg was in bed with them. When confronted with objective evidence, they still denied that their own extremities belonged to them. Patients with milder neglect may be aware that their extremities belong to them (because they are attached), but still refer to their extremities as though they were objects.

Hemiakinesia

Patients with unilateral neglect may not orient their eyes and head to the side opposite their lesion to stimuli presented on that side when following a command or when following a moving object (pursuit). With the use of procedures such as passive head turning ("doll's eyes") or caloric stimulation, one may be able to demonstrate that this gaze preference is not being produced by a disturbance of brainstem mechanisms regulating extraocular movements.

Patients with unilateral neglect may also fail to use the extremities opposite a lesion. For example, when asked to raise both arms, they may raise only one. When attention is focused on the abnormal extremity, they may be able to perform, thus demonstrating that there is no simple motor defect (that is, there is no weakness or paralysis).

Allesthesia

Patients touched on the side opposite their lesion may report that they were touched on the extremity ipsilateral to the lesion (Obersteiner, 1882). This has been called *allesthesia*. A similar defect may be seen in other sensory modalities and in other response modes. For example, a patient addressed from the side opposite a lesion may orient his head and eyes to the other (ipsilesional) side. When a patient is asked to move the extremity touched by the examiner and is then stimulated on the side opposite his lesion, he may respond with the ipsilesional extremity.

Hemispatial neglect

When patients with neglect are asked to draw a picture of a flower, they may draw only half of a flower (Fig. 10-1). When asked to bisect

Fig. 10-1 An example of hemispatial neglect (visuospatial agnosia). Drawing on left performed by examiner. Drawing on right performed by patient.

a line, they may quarter it instead (Fig. 10-2) or may fail to cross out lines distributed over a page (Fig. 10-3). The patients appear to be neglecting one-half of visual space. This has been termed *hemispatial neglect, visuospatial agnosia, hemispatial agnosia, visuospatial neglect,* and *unilateral spatial neglect.*

Although several authors (Gainotti, Messerli, and Tissot, 1972; Battersby et al., 1956) have attributed the original description of this disorder to Holmes (1918), Holmes actually reported six patients with disturbed visual orientation from bilateral lesions. It was Riddoch (1935) who reported two patients without any disturbance of central vision who had visual disorientation limited to homonymous half-fields. Brain (1941) also described three patients who had visual disorientation limited to homonymous half-fields that was

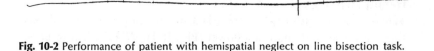

Fig. 10-2 Performance of patient with hemispatial neglect on line bisection task.

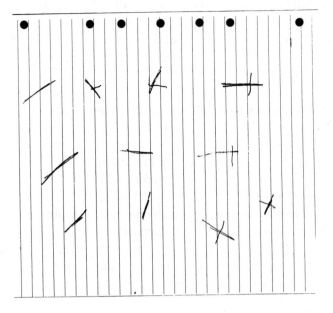

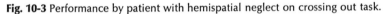

Fig. 10-3 Performance by patient with hemispatial neglect on crossing out task.

not due to defects in visual acuity. Brain attributed this disorder to inattention of the left half of external space and thought it was similar to the "amnesia" for the left half of the body which may follow a lesion of the right parietal lobe. Paterson and Zangwill (1944); McFie, Piercy, and Zangwill (1950); and Denny-Brown and Banker (1954) demonstrated that patients with unilateral inattention (hemispatial neglect) not only had visual disorientation limited to a half-field but also omitted material on one side of drawings and failed to eat from one side of their plates.

Frequently, patients with this disorder also fail to dress or groom the abnormal side. Although this may be considered a form of dressing apraxia, the pathophysiology may be different from that seen with other forms of apraxia (see Chapter 7) or that seen in patients with profound visuospatial disorders (see Chapter 8).

Patients with neglect may also fail to read part of a word or a portion of a sentence (i.e., they may read the word "cowboy" as "boy"). This has been termed *paralexia* (Benson and Geschwind,

1969). Patients may write on only one side of a page (see Chapter 4 on agraphia), or when using a typewriter, they may fail to type letters correctly which are on the side of the keyboard contralateral to their lesion (Fig. 10-4). This has been termed *paragraphia* (Valenstein and Heilman, 1978).

Sensory extinction to simultaneous stimulation

Most patients who initially have hemisensory inattention (hemineglect) from a stable lesion later improve. Whereas initially they ignore stimuli on one side or manifest allesthesia, they become able to correctly detect and lateralize stimuli which are presented on the side opposite their lesion. When given bilateral simultaneous stimulation, however, they often fail to report the stimulus presented to the contralesional side. This phenomenon was first noted by Loeb (1885) and Oppenheim (1885) in the tactile modality and by Anton (1899) and Poppelreuter (1917) in the visual modality; it has been termed *extinction to double simultaneous stimulation*.

A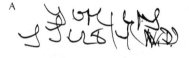

B

C

1   FOUR   SVORQ   ND 40   YER   DGO ..

2   zbrqha   mlincoln

3   AM   IN T THE   HOSPITLW   GWINEV   ILLLLL   E   .   FL

4   I   AM   IN   THE   HOSPITL   AT   GAINSVILLLLE

D   Q W E R T Y U I O P °
    A S D F G H J K L ; "
    Z X C V B N M , . ?

Fig. 10-4

A. Attempting to write, "You are a doctor."
B. Copying.
C. Typing. (1–3) Typewriter directly in front of patient, (4) typewriter moved to patient's right.
D. The typewriter keyboard. Note that the letters missed (A, S, E) are at the left of the keyboard.

Anosognosia

Patients with the neglect syndrome may be unaware of or deny their hemiparesis. They may also deny that their paretic extremity belongs to them. This phenomenon has been termed *anosognosia* (Babinski, 1914). Patients may also deny sensory loss or hemianopia. More frequently, patients may admit that they have a neurological impairment but they appear unconcerned about it. This has been termed *anosodiaphoria* (Critchley, 1969).

Other mental status changes

We have noted (Heilman and Watson, 1977) that patients with neglect are often hypokinetic. They take little interest in their environment and they are generally inattentive, even to stimuli presented to their normal side. They have difficulty in being vigilant (remaining attentive for sustained periods). Because they are inattentive and hypokinetic, they are often said to be "confused." Patients with neglect not only seem unconcerned about their illness or hemiplegia but often appear apathetic about events not related to their illness. These changes in emotional responsiveness are discussed in Chapter 13.

TESTING FOR NEGLECT

Mechanism of stimulation

Various aspects of neglect are detected by observing abnormal responses to sensory stimuli.

Stimuli should be given in at least three modalities: (1) somesthetic, (2) visual, and (3) auditory; however, other stimuli (e.g., gustatory and olfactory) may also be used. Examiners most often request an immediate response; however, delaying the response and using distractor techniques may amplify the symptoms of neglect since patients with neglect have a unilateral memory defect (Heilman, Watson, and Schulman, 1974).

SOMESTHETIC

Although the intensity of a tactile stimulus may be controlled by elaborate equipment, Von Frie hairs, fingers, or cotton applicators are adequate for bedside testing. Other cutaneous stimuli (e.g., pins) can be used.

AUDITORY

Audiometry may be used; however, for bedside testing we either use voice or sounds made by rubbing or snapping the fingers.

VISUAL

For testing visual fields, perimetry and tangent screen should be used when possible; however, for bedside testing we use confrontation techniques. Either a cotton-tipped applicator can be used as the stimulus, or a finger. For simultaneous testing, finger movements are excellent stimuli. A modified Poppelreuter diagram or words and sentences may also be used.

These somesthetic auditory and visual stimuli should be presented to the abnormal (contralesional) side and to the normal side of the body in random order. If the patient responds normally to unilateral stimulation, bilateral simultaneous stimuli may be used. Unilateral stimuli should be interspersed with bilateral simultaneous stimuli. Bender (1952) noted that normal subjects may show extinction to simultaneous stimulation when the stimuli are delivered to two different (asymmetrical) parts of the body (simultaneous bilateral heterologous stimulation). For example, if the right side of the face and the left hand are stimulated simultaneously, normal subjects sometimes report only the stimulus on the face. Normal subjects do not extinguish symmetrical simultaneous stimuli (simultaneous bilateral homologous stimulation). Simultaneous bilateral heterologous stimulation can sometimes be used to test milder defects in patients with neglect (i.e., when the right face and left hand are stimulated, the patient does not report the stimulus on the left hand, but when the left face and right hand are stimulated he reports both stimuli).

Response mode

ORIENTING HEAD AND EYES

Prior to stimulation, any head or eye deviation should be noted. Tests for head and eye orientation may be done without verbal instructions and therefore may be used in aphasics. They may also be used in patients who have a hemiparesis. Two examiners are needed. One examiner stands behind the patient and presents the stimuli (e.g., the examiner may touch the patient on the shoulder, snap his fingers, or move his hand into the patient's field of vision). The other examiner stands in front of the patient and notes any asymmetries of the orienting response (i.e., does the patient turn or orient to stimuli on one side better than he orients to stimuli on the other?). If the patient does not orient to stimuli or if he habituates to stimuli before a definite response bias can be detected, the examiner may then use stronger stimuli (e.g., pin, calling the patient's name) or he may vary the nature of the stimulus.

VERBAL REPORT

The patient is asked where he is being stimulated—right, left, or both (e.g., which side he hears fingers snapping or sees fingers moving).

EXTREMITY MOVEMENTS

The subject is instructed verbally or nonverbally (i.e., by gesture) to move the extremity or extremities the examiner has touched. To ascertain if a patient has unilateral akinesia, the examiner may request that the patient use the extremity on the side opposite to that stimulated. Commands for sustained bilateral action may also help demonstrate a unilateral akinesia. For example, the patient may demonstrate good strength when he is asked to move only one arm, since his attention is focused on that arm, but when asked to raise both arms he may only raise one, or he may raise both and then let one of them drop.

SPATIAL OPERATIONS

Several tests have been designed to determine if a patient has hemispatial neglect: (a) In the crossing out test devised by Horenstein (personal communication), lines are scattered over an 8 × 11 card (see Fig. 10-3). The patient is asked to cross out all the lines. Failure to cross out lines on one side of the card suggests the presence of a hemispatial neglect. (b) In the line bisection task, a 4- to 8-inch line is placed before the patient and the patient is asked to bisect the line ("Cross the line out in the middle."). Patients with hemispatial neg-

lect will usually make their mark to the side of the midline ipsilateral to their lesion (see Fig. 10-2). (c) Having the patient draw a
picture is perhaps one of the best ways to demonstrate hemispatial
neglect because, unlike the crossing out task and the bisecting line
task, the drawing task does not require afferent stimuli. Patients
with unilateral spatial neglect will draw only half of an object (see
Fig. 10-1). Since patients with right-hemisphere lesions commonly
have a visuospatial defect and an associated constructional apraxia,
they may have difficulty with spontaneous drawings. An alternative
test is to have patients place numbers on a clock. Frequently, patients with neglect will write only on one side of the clock; they
may write in only the numbers which belong on that side, or they
may write all 12 numbers on one side.

ANOSOGNOSIA

The examiner should make systematic formal observations as to
whether the patient spontaneously complains about the presence
of weakness, sensory loss, or hemianopia. If the patient does not
spontaneously complain, the examiner should ask whether he does
recognize his disability and if he has an emotional response to this
defect. The patient should be asked if his limbs belong to him and
if they are weak or numb. The manner in which he refers to his
limbs should also be noted (e.g., does he refer to them in the third
person, "It doesn't want to move."). Disturbances of mood should
also be noted (see Chapter 13).

MECHANISMS UNDERLYING NEGLECT
AND RELATED DISORDERS

Hemi-inattention, extinction, and allesthesia

Hemi-inattention, allesthesia, and extinction are best considered
different manifestations of the neglect. Although there must be differences in pathogenesis to explain the behavioral differences among
patients who display these three syndromes, the individual syndromes cannot be properly understood in isolation. As Critchley
(1966) has stated, "the phenomenon of tactile inattention is probably another instance of unilateral neglect made manifest at that
particular moment by the technique of simultaneous stimulation.

. . . This same fundamental disorder, namely unilateral neglect, no doubt enters into the production of such interesting sensory disorders as allochiria or allesthesia. . . ." Our observations are concordant with Critchley. It appears that, in general, as our patients improve, they progress from neglect and allesthesia to extinction.

There have been many explanations of the neglect. Unfortunately, most theories attempt to explain only part of the picture (for example, extinction or hemispatial neglect). Incomplete theories may have arisen because some investigators were unaware that neglect, allesthesia, and extinction represent a clinical spectrum determined by such factors as severity, location, and chronicity of the pathological process. In this chapter, we use the term *neglect* to denote all three manifestations of a defective response to unilateral or bilateral stimuli.

SENSORY AND PERCEPTUAL HYPOTHESIS

Sensory hypothesis. There are several theories of neglect which propose that it is caused by defective sensation. Battersby and associates (1956) thought that neglect in humans resulted from decreased sensory input superimposed on a background of decreased mental function. Sprague and colleagues (1961) made unilateral mesencephalic lesions in cats which produced unilateral neglect involving smell and vision: "The lateral regions of the mesencephalon containing the specific, highly localized long and direct sensory pathways have been thought by many to be restricted to the function of bearing specific information to the formation and forebrain structures." Because one animal with reticular formation damage was asymptomatic and another with more medial damage was hypokinetic but without sensory defects, Sprague and co workers concluded that neglect was caused by loss of patterned sensory input to the forebrain, particularly to the neocortex.

More recently, Eidelberg and Schwartz (1971) proposed a hypothesis similar to Sprague's. They postulated that neglect (extinction) was a passive phenomenon due to quantitatively asymmetrical sensory input into the two hemispheres. The authors based this conclusion on the finding that they could produce neglect from neospinothalamic lesions but not from medial lemniscal lesions. They thought that the neospinothalamic tract carries more tactile information to the hemisphere than does the medial lemniscus. However, since lesions in primary and secondary sensory cortex could also produce neglect, they postulated that the syndrome could also be caused by a reduced functional mass of one cortical area concerned with somatic sensation relative to another.

Body schema. Brain (1941) believed that the parietal lobes contained the body schema and also mediated spatial perception. Parietal lesions therefore caused a patient to fail to recognize not only half of his body but also half of space. Brain thought that allesthesia resulted from severe damage to the schema for one-half of the body causing events occurring on that half, if perceived at all, to be related in consciousness to the surviving schema representing the normal half.

Amorphosynthesis. Denny-Brown and Banker (1954) thought that the parietal lobes were important in cortical sensation and the phenomenon of inattention belonged to the whole class of cortical disorders of sensation (". . . a loss of fine discrimination . . . an inability to synthesize more than a few properties of a sensory stimulus and a disturbance of synthesis of multiple sensory stimuli"). The neglect syndrome was ascribed to a defect in spatial summation (amorphosynthesis).

ATTENTIONAL HYPOTHESIS

Some of the first references in the neglect-syndrome literature referred to defects of attention. Poppelreuter (1917) introduced the word "inattention." Brain (1941) and Critchley (1966) were also strong proponents of this view. Bender and Furlow (1944, 1945), however, challenged the attentional theory; they felt that inattention could not be important in the pathophysiology of the syndrome because having the patient "concentrate" on the neglected side did not alter the deficit.

Recently, Heilman and Valenstein (1972) and Watson and associates (1973, 1974) have again postulated an attention-arousal hypothesis. These authors argued that the sensory and perceptual hypotheses could not explain all cases of neglect, since neglect was often produced by lesions outside of the traditional sensory pathways (see below). Furthermore, neglect is usually multimodal and cannot be explained by a defect in any one sensory modality. Considerable support for the attention-arousal hypothesis of neglect has come from anatomical, physiological, and behavioral experimentation.

Cortical lesions. Lesions in three different cortical areas have been associated with the neglect syndrome: the inferior parietal lobule, the dorsilateral frontal lobe, and the cingulate gyrus.

Patients with unilateral neglect most commonly have lesions in the inferior parietal lobule (Critchley, 1966; Brain, 1941; Heilman and Watson, 1977b). The inferior parietal lobule appears to be a multimodal secondary association area. The primary sensory areas for audition, vision, and somesthesis project to their respective association areas, and each association area in turn projects to the inferior parietal lobule (Pandya and Kuypers, 1969). In monkeys, experimental lesions restricted to this area can produce multimodal neglect (Heilman et al., 1970). By recording cellular electrical activity, Yin and colleagues (1975) demonstrated that there are neurons in the inferior parietal lobule that discharge before the onset of an orienting response to visual stimuli. Stimuli in the contralateral field were most effective in eliciting these responses. Neurons in the same area also responded to auditory stimuli. Auditory stimuli also influenced the cell's usual response to a visual stimulus (Davis and Benevento, 1975).

Pandya and Kuypers (1969) also showed that auditory, visual, and somesthetic association areas project to the dorsilateral frontal lobe, as well as to the inferior parietal lobule. In addition, the inferior parietal lobule projects to the dorsilateral frontal lobe. Lesions in the dorsilateral frontal lobe (a tertiary association area) produces neglect in animals (Kennard and Ectors, 1938; Welch and Stuteville, 1958) and in man (Heilman and Valenstein, 1972).

Heilman and Valenstein (1972) described several patients with unilateral neglect who had discrete lesions in the cingulate gyrus. To confirm these clinical observations, Watson et al. (1973) demonstrated that discrete unilateral lesions in the anterior cingulate gyrus of monkeys produce unilateral neglect. It is of interest that Pandya and Kuypers (1969) showed that the dorsilateral frontal lobe projects to the cingulate gyrus. The three cortical regions which are implicated in the neglect syndrome thus all have prominent corticocortical interconnections. They are all areas which have access directly or indirectly to more than one sensory modality and, as will be seen below, they all have prominent connections with the brainstem reticular formation.

Mesencephalic-reticular formation. Moruzzi and Magoun (1949) showed that the brainstem reticular formation is important in mediating the orienting response. Discrete lesions in the mesencephalic reticular formation have been shown to induce neglect in cats (Reeves and Hagamen, 1971) and monkeys (Watson et al., 1974).

Corticoreticular loop. Heilman and Valenstein (1972) and Watson et al. (1973) postulated that unilateral neglect was a unilateral attention-arousal (alerting) defect induced by a defect in a corticolimbic-reticular loop. The postulated loop is similar to that proposed by Sokolov (1963). The cortex is responsible for stimulus analysis: it distinguishes novel from nonnovel, and biologically significant from nonsignificant stimuli. If a stimulus is novel or significant, corticofugal impulses direct the reticular system to activate the cortex. For this hypothesis to be tenable, there must be both corticofugal projections to the reticular activating system and reticular projections to the cortex.

Corticofugal input may be direct or may travel via the limbic system (cingulate). Nauta (1964) demonstrated that the cingulate gyrus has extensive connections with the mesencephalic reticular formation. Astruc (1971) showed a connection between the dorsilateral frontal lobe (the arcuate gyrus) and the mesencephalic reticular system. French, Hernandez-Peon, and Livingston (1955) studied corticofugal pathways to the reticular system with evoked potentials and physiological neuronographic techniques. They found that corticofugal pathways originated in the arcuate gyrus (dorsilateral frontal lobe), cingulate gyrus, sensorimotor cortex, and posterior parietal-superior temporal gyrus region. Segundo, Naguet, and Buser (1955) induced both diffuse electrocortical and behavioral arousal in the monkey by subconvulsive stimulation of the arcuate gyrus, the posterior parietal-superior temporal gyrus region, and the cingulate gyrus. The same cortical sites which produce reticular firing and behavioral electroencephalographic (EEG) arousal when stimulated, produce neglect when ablated (see above).

The superior colliculus projects to the mesencephalic reticular formation, and may be a portion of a corticoreticular pathway, as well as a sensory integrator in its own right. Astruc (1971) demonstrated that the dorsilateral frontal lobe (arcuate gyrus region) projects to the colliculus. The superior colliculus also receives input from the visual system (optic tracts via the brachia of the superior colliculi), and it receives somesthetic projections from the spinotectal tract. Lesions of the brachia of the superior colliculi produce transient visual neglect but not trimodal neglect (Sprague and Meikle, 1965). Unilateral lesions of the superior colliculus in cats, however, produce trimodal unilateral neglect (Sprague and Meikle, 1965). The lesions produced by Sprague and Meikle injure somesthetic projections to the colliculus, as well as to tectoreticular pathways. Denny-Brown et al. (1952) produced trimodal neglect in monkeys with large superior collicular and tectal lesions. Denny-Brown thought that these areas might be a "primary driver" of the reticular system.

These observations suggest that the superior colliculus is a "sensory integrative center" (Sprague and Meikle, 1965) which has important input into the reticular activating system. Unilateral collicular lesions may reduce collicular "driving" of the reticular formation, and thus produce a unilateral defect in the orienting response.

Two ascending routes have been postulated: a ventral route via basal forebrain areas (lateral hypothalamus and substantia innominata), which is important for desynchronization, and a dorsal route, via the thalamus, which is important in mediating recruitment phenomena (Brodal, 1969).

The lateral hypothalamus and the substantia innominata receive fibers from the mesencephalic reticular formation. Kievit and Kuypers (1975) have demonstrated that these basal forebrain areas project to the cortex. Van Hoesen (1976) has suggested that these areas may be an important relay in the ascending limb of the cortico-limbic-reticular loop proposed by Heilman and Valenstein (1972) and Watson et al. (1973). Marshall, Turner, and Teitelbaum (1971) and Marshall and Teitelbaum (1974) provided evidence to support this notion by producing neglect in rats by ablating the lateral hypothalamus. The ascending reticular hypothalamic pathway and other pathways were included in their lesion. Kievit and Kuypers (1975) noted that the connections from these basal forebrain areas to the cortex were comparable in some respects with the ascending monoaminergic pathways, since these pathways traverse the lateral hypothalamus and substantia innominata on their way to the cortex. Ablating monoaminergic pathways with 6-hydroxydopamine hydrobromide produces the neglect syndrome (Ungerstadt, 1973).

Turner found that lesions of the medial portion of the amygdala produce a similar syndrome to that seen after lateral hypothalamic lesions. However, the relationship of the amygdala to the hypothalamus in the production of the orienting response is still uncertain. Bagshaw and Benzies (1968) found that amygdalectomized monkeys had a defective vegetative orienting response (e.g., galvanic skin response, heart rate, respiratory rate), but their somatic and electrophysiological (EEG) orienting was intact. In a more recent paper, however, Bagshaw et al. (1972) stated that amygdalectomized monkeys have an abnormal visual orienting response. Unfortunately, unilateral neglect could not be assessed because the authors made bilateral lesions. We have examined nine patients following unilateral anterior temporal lobectomy which included the amygdala. None of these patients showed evidence of the unilateral neglect syndrome. Since the stria terminalis is one of the main connections between the hypothalamus and the amygdala, Turner (1973) sectioned the stria terminalis but was not able to produce neglect. There are, however, ventral amygdalofugal pathways which connect these structures, and therefore the relationship between these structures and the orienting response remains unclear.

In a recent article, Marshall and Teitelbaum (1974) proposed that the pathway described by Nauta (1964), ". . . which goes from the frontal cortex to the lateral hypothalamus . . ." and a corticofugal pathway which passes through the subthalamus and terminates in the reticular formation may be involved in the orienting response. Marshall and Teitelbaum's most recent hypothesis appears to be in full agreement with those proposed by Heilman and Valenstein (1972) and Watson et al. (1973): neglect is caused by a disruption in a corticolimbic-reticular loop.

Cortical and subcortical structures known to produce the neglect syndrome when ablated such as the frontal arcuate gyrus (Welch and Stuteville, 1958), the superior colliculus (Sprague and Meikle, 1965), the spinothalamic tract (Eidelberg and Schwartz, 1971), and the mesencephalic reticular formation (Watson et al., 1973) all project to the thalamic intralaminar nucleus. Although stimulation of the intralaminar nuclei at slow frequencies induces a recruitment response, rapid stimulation can induce both behavioral (Jung and Hassler, 1960) and electrophysiological (Weinberger, Velasco, and Lindsley, 1965) arousal. Orem, Schlag-Rey, and Schlag (1973) ablated the intralaminar nucleus and produced visual neglect. Watson and Heilman (1978) ablated the intralaminar nucleus in monkeys and were able to demonstrate multimodal neglect (visual, somesthetic, and auditory), and Watson and Heilman (1978) have described three patients with unilateral neglect associated with thalamic hemorrhage.

Efferent connections of the intralaminar nucleus are less clearly defined primarily because anatomical methods are as yet incapable of following multisynaptic pathways. The most clearly defined efferent connections of the intralaminar nucleus are to the putamen (Mehler, 1966). Although the function of the basal ganglia is only now being elucidated, they have long been known to play a crucial role in motor behavior. Connections from cortical areas 4, 6, and 8 as well as from the parietal lobe and cingulate gyrus enter the putamen (Berke, 1960). Heir et al. (1977) have reported four cases of neglect from putamenal hemorrhage.

Behavioral observations. No critical behavioral experiment has previously been designed to distinguish the sensory from the attentional hypothesis or, perhaps even more important, to differentiate sensory inattention from a loss of intention to make a correct response to a perceived stimulus.

In a recent study, Watson, Miller, and Heilman (1978) trained animals to perform with the extremity contralateral to a stimulus and induced neglect by both frontal intralaminar and mesencephalic lesions. Postoperatively, the monkeys had normal strength. Performance was abnormal with ipsilesional stimulation, but was normal with contralesional stimulation. These findings refute the sensory hypothesis of neglect.

These observations also suggest that the behavioral abnormality seen from lesions in these areas is caused by a loss of intention to perform a motor response to a sensory stimulus (akinesia) rather than by sensory inattention. Valenstein and Heilman (1978) have described a patient with a discrete hemorrhage of the striatum. Unlike many patients with lateral ganglionic hemorrhage who have motor and sensory defects from compression of the internal capsule, this patient had good strength of his contralateral extremities. He did not have a somesthetic defect or a hemianopia and he had normal hearing. When given unilateral or bilateral simultaneous stimulation, his verbal responses were flawless (i.e., "right, left, both"), however, when he was asked to elevate the arm ipsilateral to the side stimulated (e.g., "Raise your right arm when I touch you on the right side, your left arm when I touch you on the left side and both arms when I touch you on both sides."), the patient always had a slower response when touched on the left than on the right. In addition, when touched on both sides, he would usually only raise his right arm; if he raised his left arm at all, it was, after a considerable delay. Because we were concerned that this defect might be induced by mild weakness, we did a reaction time study. The patient depressed one key with each hand; he was required to release the key ipsilateral to a visual stimulus. With unilateral stimulation, reaction times were slower for the left hand than for the right; however, with bilateral stimuli, left-hand reaction times were dramatically slowed. These results suggest that the patient's disorder was caused neither by weakness nor a sensory defect, but rather by a unilateral disorder of initiation of movement (akinesia) which was increased when bilateral movements were required ("motor extinction").

As previously mentioned, Heilman and Valenstein (1972) and Watson, Heilman, and Cauthen et al. (1973) postulated that the behavioral defect seen with the neglect syndrome is a defect in an attention-arousal response (orienting response). Unlike other reaction patterns to sensory stimuli, the orienting response is preparatory rather than consummatory (Lynn, 1966). The orienting response not only reduces threshold to incoming stimuli but also prepares the organism for action. Lesions which induce the unilateral neglect syndrome produce a unilateral reduction of arousal. Because one hemisphere is hypoaroused, it cannot prepare for action and it is therefore akinetic.

It is possible that lesions which induce hypokinesia (e.g., intralaminar, striatum, frontal) affect just the ascending limb of the proposed corticolimbic-reticular loop and that a lesion of the descending limb (e.g., inferior parietal lobe) would also produce sensory inattention and not a defect of intention.

Electrophysiological correlates of neglect: EEG. Since we have proposed that unilateral neglect is a defect of arousal (alerting) produced by a corticolimbic-reticular disconnection, we should be able to demonstrate electrophysiological changes in subjects with neglect. Lindsley (1950) has noted:

Electroencephalography . . . has revealed that alert wakefulness is associated with low voltage, fast discharge of the cerebral cortex, while high voltage slow waves characterize electrocortical activity in drowsiness and sleep. . . . Exciting the reticular core of the brain stem and the basal diencephalon abolished existing electrocortical synchrony and substituted low voltage fast activity in its place, thus reproducing the EEG changes seen in spontaneous awakening or in the arousal reaction to stimuli. . . . Acute brain stem lesions in a position to interrupt the reticular activating system were next found to abolish the EEG pattern of wakefulness and to result in recurring slow waves. . . .

Watson, Andriola, and Heilman (1978) have studied 23 patients with unilateral neglect and compared them with 20 subjects with aphasia without neglect. Twenty-two of the 23 patients with unilateral neglect demonstrated diffuse ipsilateral slowing, but only 7 of 20 aphasic patients showed ipsilateral slowing. The difference between these groups is significant. There were no significant differences between these groups in the frequency of positive brainscans, the size of the scans, or the day between onset of their ictus and the EEG recording. The lesions of most patients were in the parietal lobe (14 of 19 with positive scans).

Electrophysiological correlates of neglect: cortical evoked potential. Although the EEG data appear to support the arousal hypothesis of neglect, they do not rule out the possibility that asymmetrical sensory input is producing these EEG changes. The averaged evoked potential (EP) is obtained by computer averaging segments of EEG time-locked to a repetitive stimulus. The EEG response evoked by the stimulus summates, while the background EEG tends to cancel out. The averaged evoked response has several components. In general, the early components are thought to represent specific sensory conduction, whereas later components reflect arousal, alerting, and attentional neuronal activities. Study of the EP in animals with neglect could therefore separate the sensory responses from the attentional responses. Watson, Miller, and Heilman (1977) studied three unanesthetized monkeys (*Macaca speciosa*) by electrically stimulating the peroneal nerve and recording EPs from the cortical hindlimb area. After preoperative recordings were made, the animals underwent an arcuate gyrus ablation that induced unilateral neglect. Comparing the changes in the EP from the preoperative to the postoperative conditions between the lesioned and nonlesioned sides demonstrated a significant interaction for the late waves but no significant interaction for the early waves. These findings tend to discredit the sensory hypothesis and are compatible with the attention-arousal hypothesis.

INTERHEMISPHERIC HYPOTHESES

Suppression. Interhemispheric hypotheses have been invoked mainly to explain extinction. Bender and Furlow (1944, 1945) noted that the defect in sensation in a patient with neglect was increased by the phenomenon of rivalry. Nathan (1946) noted that although a stimulus was perceived on the abnormal side, it would become imperceptible when a stimulus was applied to the normal side. Nathan therefore postulated that the normal side was suppressing the abnormal side. Reider (1946) also thought that the normal hemisphere suppressed the abnormal hemisphere. The basic mechanism underlying all of these theories is suppression. Although the concept of cortical suppressor action has long been abandoned, interhemispheric inhibition remains a theoretical possibility. For example, Sprague (1966) noted that defects in visually guided behavior in the cat could be produced by either collicular or parietotemporooccipital cortical lesions. When these lesions were made on the same side of the brain, there was a marked potentiation of the defect, however, when cortical and tectal lesions were placed sequentially on opposite sides of the brain, the resultant effects did not summate but instead were opposed (i.e., a contralateral collicular lesion resulted in a return of visually guided behavior in the previously hemianopic field. Sprague's findings included both ectosylvian and calcarine cortex. Cats with lesions confined to the geniculocalcarine system do not have defects of visually guided behavior because they have a second visual system, the collicular system, which is able to mediate certain forms of visually guided behavior. Cats with lesions limited to their ectosylvian area have a defect in visually guided behavior because they have visual neglect (Yamamoto et al., 1975). As previously mentioned, collicular lesions can also induce neglect (Sprague and Meikle, 1965). It is possible that Sprague's (1966) first lesion (which included both the ectosylvian region and the calcarine cortex) interfered with visually guided behavior by inducing neglect. The ipsilesional collicular visual system could not take over the function of visually guided behavior because it was being inhibited by the contralesional colliculus; however, when the contralesional colliculus was also ablated, there was a release from inhibition. To further test the inhibition hypothesis, Sprague again made cortical lesions, inducing a defect of visually guided behavior, and then lesioned the optic brachium, thereby decreasing visual input into the contralesional colliculus. Despite reduced visual input into the colliculus, the defect persisted; however, when the collicular commissure was cut, visually guided behavior returned even though the contralesional colliculus was intact. Recently, we (Heilman et al., 1978) saw a patient with a long standing left-sided somesthetic and auditory neglect (extinction) and a dense left hemianopia or neglect. The patient became transiently blind, then had a right hemianopia and regained vision in his previously hemianopic left visual field. We think that the initial hemianopia was attentional and the second stroke in the geniculocalcarine system released inhibition.

Inertia–interference. Birch, Belmont, and Karp (1967) proposed an interhemispheric mechanism that did not rely on a suppressor. They postulated the inertia–interference model: the damaged hemisphere processes information more slowly than the undamaged hemisphere (inertia) and is therefore subject to interference from the normal side. These authors supported their hypothesis by demonstrating that stimulation of the intact side before stimulation of the abnormal side induced extinction; however, when the abnormal side was stimulated first, extinction was reduced. Defective arousal may be inducing this delayed responsiveness, however, the following alternative hypothesis may help explain extinction.

Release from reciprocal inhibition and bilateral attention-arousal defect. When one side is stimulated, sensory information is transmitted not only to the contralateral hemisphere but also to the ipsilateral hemisphere. Allesthesia may be caused not by a perceptual error of the impaired hemisphere, but by the normal hemisphere responding as if the stimulus were a signal for it to perform. This hypothesis would imply some type of reciprocal interhemispheric inhibition such that under normal circumstances the hemisphere contralateral to a stimulus may inhibit the ipsilateral hemisphere from performing and under abnormal circumstances this inhibition is released.

As previously mentioned, during recovery the organism goes from the stage of allesthesia to extinction. At this stage, the normal ("released") hemisphere can direct an appropriate response to either a contralateral or ipsilateral stimulus. When simultaneous stimuli are presented, however, the contralateral stimulus preoccupies the normal hemisphere and the ipsilateral stimulus is neglected.

The reciprocal inhibition model has been elaborated by Kinsbourne (1970) who proposed that each hemisphere inhibits the other by callosal mechanisms, the neglect syndrome being produced by a decrease in transcallosal inhibitory influence on the normal hemisphere. We also feel that the head and eye deviation seen in neglect is evoked by an imbalance of orientation tendencies (Heilman and Watson, 1977), however, whereas Kinsbourne believes the imbalance to be due to relatively increased activity of the nonlesioned side, we think it is due to decreased activity of the lesioned hemisphere. Patients with neglect do not appear to be hyperattentive to stimuli ipsilateral to their lesions. On the contrary, most of them appear hypokinetic. We think these patients are hypokinetic because they have bilateral arousal defects, the lesioned side being more hypoaroused than the nonlesioned side.

There is physiological evidence which supports our hypothesis. Moruzzi and Magoun (1949) produced bilateral cortical activation by unilaterally stimulating the brainstem reticular formation: the ipsilateral cortex showed a stronger arousal response than the contralateral cortex. Segundo, Naguet, and Buser (1955) showed that cortical stimulation could effect behavioral and EEG arousal. They also found that unilateral stimulation induced bilateral arousal. The anatomy of reticulocortical projections has not been completely elucidated; however, Rossi and Brodal (1956) demonstrated that each hemisphere projects bilaterally to the reticular formation.

There is also behavioral evidence which supports our hypothesis. Gainotti and Tiacci (1971) noted that although patients with unilateral neglect make more errors on the side contralateral to their lesions than on the ipsilesional side, they also make more errors on the ipsilesional side than do controls. Reaction times are one measure of arousal and correlate with EEG evidence of arousal (Lansing, Schwartz, and Lindsley, 1959). We have measured visual reaction time of patients with unilateral neglect. Their reaction times were very slow, even though the stimulus was delivered to both fields and the ipsilesional hand performed the movements. A warning stimulus normally reduces reaction time by increasing arousal (Lansing, Schwartz, and Lindsley, 1959). Warning stimuli failed to reduce reaction time in patients with neglect (Heilman, 1978), even when warning and reaction time stimuli were given to the side ipsilateral to the lesion. As another measure of arousal, we used a galvanic skin response (Heilman, Schwartz, and Watson, 1978). We stimulated and recorded from the hand ipsilateral to the lesion. With the galvanic skin response set at maximal sensitivity and with electrical stimuli that were judged by the patient as uncomfortable, there was minimal or no galvanic skin response in patient with neglect. In contrast, aphasic controls showed an excellent response.

Hemispatial neglect

The mechanism underlying the defective behavior seen in hemispatial neglect has not been elucidated. Several hypotheses can be advanced.

SENSORY HYPOTHESIS (HEMIANOPIA)

Patients with hemispatial neglect are frequently hemianopic and therefore do not see one half of space. When asked to bisect a line, they quarter it because they only see one half of the line. McFie et al. (1950), however, noted that some of their patients with hemispatial neglect were not hemianopic. Rosenberger (1974) tested patients' visual discrimination of bisected lines and found that hemianopic patients did not perform any differently than nonhemianopic patients. DeRenzi, Faglioni, and Scotti (1970) found that hemispatial neglect was not limited to the visual modality.

ATTENTIONAL HYPOTHESIS

Brain (1941) proposed that the mechanism underlying hemispatial neglect is attentional. The patient can see the entire line to be bi-

sected but he attends to only a portion of the line and bisects only
that portion.

UNILATERAL AKINESIA HYPOTHESIS

As previously mentioned, Watson, Miller, and Heilman (1977)
trained animals to move the extremity contralateral to a stimulus
and then induced unilateral neglect with a unilateral hemispheric
lesion. The experimental animals showed unilateral akinesia: when
stimulated on the neglected side (contralateral to the lesion), they
performed normally with their ipsilesional arm; however, when
stimulated on the nonneglected side (ipsilateral to their lesion), they
failed to use the extremity opposite the lesion, despite normal
strength. Based on this observation, we proposed (Heilman and
Watson, 1977b) that patients with hemispatial neglect fail at line
bisection and similar tasks (drawing, crossing out lines) because
akinesia associated with neglect is not limited to the contralateral
extremity but is an akinesia for any act which must be performed
in the neglected (contralesional) hemispatial field.

To determine which of the hypotheses described above was correct, we used a modified line bisection task (Heilman and Valenstein, 1979). Prior to bisecting a line, the patient had to read a letter on the right or left end of the line ("starting point"). If either
the hemianopic or attentional hypothesis were correct, identifying
the letter contralateral to the lesion should improve performance,
since looking at that letter will displace the line toward the normal field and will insure that the patient has attended to the
end of the line which is usually neglected. We tested six patients
with unilateral left-sided neglect on this task and found that the
"starting point" did not significantly affect performance. We next
administered the same test, but placed the line either to the left or
to the right of the patient. It is important to realize that the patient's hemispatial field is not the same as his visual field. The
hemispatial field refers to the space to one side of the midline of
the patient's body. If the patient has a hemispatial akinesia, then
his performance should improve when the line is in the hemispatial
field ipsilateral to the lesion and should get worse when the line is
placed in the contralateral hemispatial field, and not vary with
"starting point."

Performance was significantly better when the lines were placed on the right side (ipsilesional) than when they were placed on the left side (contralesional). These observations tend to discredit the sensory and sensory inattention hypotheses and support the hypothesis that patients with hemispatial neglect have a contralesional hemispatial akinesia.

In addition to the results of our study, observations of normal subjects suggest that each hemisphere is responsible not only for mediating distal movements of the contralateral extremity and processing contralateral sensory input, but also for mediating behavior in the contralateral spatial field independent of which extremity is used. In normal subjects, the time taken to react to a lateralized visual stimulus is determined by the anatomical connections between the receiving hemiretina and the responding hand. Ipsilateral responses (i.e., stimulus presented to the right field and the right hand responds) which are mediated by intrahemispheric neuronal circuits are faster than contralateral responses (i.e., stimulus presented to the right field and the left hand responds) which require interhemispheric transfer (Berlucchi et al., 1971). Reaction times to a lateralized stimulus can be affected by changing the spatial position of the responding hand (Simon, Hinrichs, and Craft, 1970). If the hands are crossed so that the right hand is on the left side of the body and the left hand is on the right side of the body, stimuli on one side (e.g., left side) are responded to faster by the contralateral extremity (e.g., right hand) than by the ipsilateral extremity (e.g., left hand). This phenomenon has been termed *stimulus response compatibility* (Anzola et al., 1977) and has been thought to reflect a natural tendency to respond with the hand which is already in the appropriate hemispatial field. An alternative explanation is that each hemisphere is responsible not only for moving the contralateral extremity and processing contralateral sensory stimuli but also for mediating behavior in the contralateral hemispatial field. When an arm is crossed, it enters the other hemisphere's field (crossed operations) and interhemispheric communication is required. Although both crossed and uncrossed operations have ipsilateral responses (e.g., stimulus is presented to the right field and response is made with the right hand) because the crossed operation (e.g., where the right hand is to the left side of the body) requires bilateral hemispheric processing (e.g., the left hemisphere processes visual stimuli and controls the right hand and the right hemisphere controls operations in the left field) it is slower than uncrossed operations which require only intrahemispheric processing.

HEMISPATIAL MEMORY HYPOTHESIS

Heilman et al. (1974) have demonstrated that patients with neglect have a unilateral auditory memory defect. Although Samuels et al. (1971) did not test their subjects for neglect, they tested patients with right parietal lesions and demonstrated a similar phenomenon in the visual modality. William James (1890) noted that "an object once attended will remain in the memory whilst one inattentively allowed to pass will leave no trace behind." Although patients with neglect may be able to see the full extent of a line, it is possible that the side of the line in the left hemispatial field does not form a stable trace. As the subject explores the remainder of the line he "forgets" the left side of the line and performs as if he has not seen it (Heilman and Valenstein, 1979).

Anosognosia

PSYCHODYNAMIC

Von Monakow (1885) and Anton (1899) noted that patients with visual disturbances from cortical lesions lacked awareness of their defect. Anton (1899) noted that many of these patients appeared hysterical. Although anosognosia is most frequently associated with right parietal disease, it can also be seen with lesions in many different regions of the nervous system. Goldstein (1939) therefore thought that the defect was a "quite normal biological reaction to a very grave defect." In a similar fashion, Schilder (1935) proposed that there was an instinctive urge to maintain the body's integrity and that anosognosia was a form of repression motivated by that urge. Weinstein and Kahn (1955) studied patients who denied their illness and found that they had certain personality characteristics (i.e., they were compulsive and perfectionistic) and that in their premorbid behavior they tended to deny problems.

DISORDERS OF BODY SCHEMA

Head and Holmes (1911) studied the individual's perception of his own body (postural schema or body schema) and subsequently many authors discussed the nature and genesis of this schema. Fredericks (1969), who reviews the ontogenesis of the body schema concept, defines it as ". . . the peripheral schematically conscious, structured, plastically bordered spatial perception of one's own body, constructed from previous and current (especially somesthetic) sensory information." It has been postulated that this schema resides in the parietal lobes (Schilder, 1935; Neilsen, 1948) and, with damage to this schema, one not only neglects one-half of the body but also denies the existence of defects on the neglected side.

Although neglect of one side of the body caused by either a disturbance in the body schema (Neilsen, 1948) or by attentional-arousal defects (Heilman and Watson, 1977a, 1977b) might explain an implicit neglect of a paralyzed half of body, neither of these theories can explain the explicit denial of illness (which Fredericks [1969] terms *verbal anosognosia*). The psychodynamic, body schema, attention-arousal theories also fail to explain what Babinski (1918) first noted: that anosognosia is seen more commonly with right- than with left-hemisphere lesions. There are several possible explanations for this asymmetry: The neglect syndrome is more severe with right-hemisphere lesions than it is with left-hemisphere lesions (see page 296). Dominant-hemisphere lesions are frequently associated with language disturbances and it is difficult for patients with aphasia to be verbally explicit.

EMOTIONAL DISORDERS

It has been demonstrated that patients with neglect have emotional flattening. It has been postulated that the right hemisphere is important in mediating emotion (see Chapter 13). Another hypothetical explanation of anosognosia is that right-hemisphere lesions induce emotional defects that are responsible for the denial of illness. Although the emotional flattening seen with right-hemisphere disease may be responsible for the flattened emotional responses to one's illness (anosodiaphoria), flattening of emotions cannot explain verbal anosognosia (explicit denial of illness).

DISCONNECTION

An explicit denial of illness may be considered a confabulatory response. Geschwind (1965) has postulated that the confabulatory response may be an attempt to fill gaps in the information available to the speech area. Perhaps right-hemisphere lesions disconnect the right hemisphere which processes left-sided afferent stimuli from the left hemisphere which contains the language area (Green, 1976). A simple test of this disconnection hypothesis is to see if explicit denial is eliminated by bringing the left paretic arm into the right field of vision (which has access to the speech areas) and asking the patient to move the arm. Patients with explicit denial of illness seldom improve with this maneuver.

In summary, although there are many explanations of denial of illness, most of them can only explain anosodiaphoria and not the explicit denial of illness, which often accompanies the neglect syndrome.

Mental status changes

Many patients with the unilateral neglect syndrome have an altered mental status (Battersby, Bender, and Pollack, 1956). Although they have a lesion restricted to one hemisphere, they look like the akinetic mute with bilateral frontal or cingulate disease. We (Heilman and Watson, 1977b) think these patients are hypokinetic because they have bilateral arousal (alerting) defects, the lesioned side being more hypoaroused than the nonlesioned side, and we have already summarized the evidence supporting this hypothesis.

Most of the hypokinetic patients we see with the unilateral neglect syndrome have right-hemisphere lesions. Our clinical observations suggest that neglect from right-hemisphere lesions produces a greater ipsilateral arousal (alerting) defect than do lesions of the left hemisphere. Evidence to support this observation comes from DeRenzi and Faglioni (1965) who studied patients with unilateral lesions with a reaction time paradigm. When the hand ipsilateral to the lesion was used, one would have expected normal reaction times, but these investigators found that reaction times were slowed from lesions in either hemisphere. They also found that lesions of the right hemisphere caused greater slowing than did lesions of the left hemisphere. DeRenzi and Faglioni suggested that reaction time is proportional to the extent and severity of a cerebral lesion irrespective of its focus. They thought that, since right-hemisphere lesions tend to be less symptomatic than left hemisphere lesions, their patients with right-hemisphere disease had bigger lesions. Subsequently, Howes and Boller (1975) studied reaction times in brain-damaged subjects. Although the lesions of the left hemisphere that they observed tended to be larger than those of the right, patients with lesions on the right had greater slowing of reaction time than patients with left-hemisphere lesions. In patients with cortical lesions, the greatest slowing appeared with posterior parietal lesions, the nondominant lesions producing the greatest defect. As mentioned, reaction time correlates with EEG evidence of activation (Lansing, Schwartz, and Lindsley, 1959) and neglect is most often associated with nondominant parietal lesions. Although Howes and Boller (1975) alluded to a loss of topographical sense as possibly being responsible for their subjects' prolonged reaction times, they were careful not to draw any conclusions about why nondominant parietal-lobe lesions produced slowed reaction times. We would propose that their data support our hypothesis and suggest that a unilateral nondominant parietal lesion with neglect produces a bilateral defect in arousal, the lesioned hemisphere being even less aroused than the nonlesioned hemisphere. Unfortunately, Howes and Boller did not report testing their patients for neglect. However, it is of interest that, of the neglect patients we previously mentioned with abnormal galvanic skin reaction and reaction times (to stimuli delivered to their normal side), all but one had right-hemisphere lesions.

There are, however, additional data on normal subjects that also provide some evidence for a specific role of the right parietal region in attention-arousal. Beck, Dustman, and Sakai (1969) noted that when the evoked potential was used as a measure of attention, the greatest amplitude change with increased attention was always seen in those responses recorded from the right parietal leads. Bowers and Heilman (1976) gave 16 normal subjects either a verbal or nonverbal warning stimulus followed by a neutral reaction-time stimulus. Reaction times by the right hand were significantly faster with verbal warning stimuli than with nonverbal warning stimuli. There were, however, no significant differences for the left hand between verbal and nonverbal warning stimuli. Wood and Goff (1971) reported that auditory evoked potentials were different over the left hemisphere, although identical over the right, during linguistic and nonlinguistic analyses of the same signal. Perhaps both

Bowers and Heilman (1976) and Wood and Goff (1971) have demonstrated that the left hemisphere is alerted by a specific stimulus—language—whereas, the right hemisphere is alerted by all stimuli.

Moreover, if right-side lesions do induce a more severe hypokinesia than left-side lesions and if the mechanism underlying the hypokinesia is hypoarousal, it would appear that the right hemisphere has more of an influence on left hemisphere arousal than vice versa. To test this hypothesis, Van Den Abell and Heilman (1978) studied reaction times in normal subjects and demonstrated that warning stimuli delivered to the right hemisphere (left visual field) reduce reaction times of the right hand (increased left hemisphere arousal) more than do warning stimuli delivered directly to the left hemisphere (right visual field).

Hemispheric asymmetries

Several early investigators reported that neglect in man was induced primarily by right-sided lesions (Brain, 1941; Critchley, 1966; Mc-Fie, Piercy, and Zangwill, 1950), however, Denny-Brown and Banker (1954) reported amorphosynthesis (neglect) from left parietal lesions. Battersby, Bender, and Pollack (1956) studied 122 patients with unilateral hemisphere lesions. Of the 65 patients with neglect, 41 had right-hemisphere lesions and 24 had left-sided lesions. Although Battersby, Bender, and Pollack's finding would suggest that neglect was more frequent after right-hemisphere lesions, 10 of the left-hemisphere impaired patients could not be tested. If these 10 subjects had been added to the 24 patients with right-sided neglect, the incidence of neglect following right-hemisphere lesions would not have been significantly greater than the incidence of neglect following left-hemisphere lesions. Albert (1973) used Horenstein's crossing out task as a test for neglect. He tested 65 patients, 36 with left-hemisphere lesions and 30 with right-hemisphere lesions. He did not exclude aphasics. Thirty-seven percent of patients with right-hemisphere lesions and 30% of patients with left-hemisphere lesions failed to cross out lines. Although this asymmetry of incidence was small, when severity was determined, it was shown that right-sided lesions produced a more pronounced defect than did left-sided lesions. Gainotti, Messerli, and Tissot (1972), Faglioni, Scotti, and Spinnler (1971), Costa et al. (1969), Colombo, DeRenzi, and Faglioni (1976), and others have demonstrated similar findings.

VISUOSPATIAL HYPOTHESIS

It has been demonstrated that the right hemisphere is dominant for visuospatial processing (Joynt and Goldstein, 1975; Benton, Hannay, and Varney (1975) (see also Chapter 8), and it has been postulated that neglect may be more severe with right-sided lesions for that reason (Albert, 1973; McFie, Piercy, and Zangwill, 1950). The major problem with this explanation is that dominance implies field independence rather than dependence. For example, patients with a language disturbance such as Wernicke's aphasia cannot read words in either the left or the right visual field. While right-hemisphere visuospatial dominance may explain why patients with neglect have constructional apraxia, it does not explain why they have a higher incidence and greater severity of visuospatial neglect.

AROUSAL HYPOTHESIS

Several behavioral and physiological studies have demonstrated that language induces left-hemisphere activation (Kinsbourne, 1974; Bowers and Heilman, 1976). If the symptoms of neglect are induced by asymmetries of hemispheric activation (see above), then left-hemisphere activation would decrease the imbalance caused by left-hemisphere lesions and enhance the imbalance caused by right hemisphere lesions. Kinsbourne (1970b) has postulated that, since patients think and communicate verbally (especially when being tested), the left hemisphere is usually preferentially activated and therefore neglect is more evident with right-sided lesions.

We (Heilman and Watson, 1978) tested this hypothesis using six patients with unilateral neglect from right-side lesions. The subjects were given six trials of crossing out tasks. In these, they were presented with sheets containing three six-letter words (i.e., school, center, doctor) randomly distributed across a card. The subjects were instructed to cross out one of the words (e.g., doctor) whenever they saw it on the card. In the other three crossing out tasks, the patients were presented with a card that had lines oriented vertically. horizontally, and diagonally. Again, the subjects were instructed to cross out only a specific type of line (e.g., vertical) wherever they saw it on the card. All six subjects with left-sided neglect demonstrated less neglect—crossed out more lines and went further to their left on the page—in the visuospatial condition than they did in the language condition. These results give partial support to Kinsbourne's hypothesis, but we are not certain that the mild effect seen in our study can account for the gross asymmetries seen with the neglect syndrome.

As previously mentioned, Sokolov (1963) proposed a two-stage attentional-arousal model in which the cortex analyzes stimuli and the reticular formation mediates arousal. The attentional-arousal response is preparatory rather than consummatory (Lynn, 1966). To determine whether there is a hemispheric dominance for mediating this attentional-arousal response, we measured EEG desynchronization to visual warning stimuli (Van Den Abell and Heilman, 1978). The right parietal lobe appears to be focally activated by stimuli projected into either field. The left hemisphere, however, is only activated by stimuli projected into the right field. Unlike the left hemisphere, stimuli projected to the right hemisphere can prepare either hemisphere for action. Since the right hemisphere appears to be dominant for mediating the attentional-arousal response (i.e., processing stimuli presented on both sides and preparing both hemispheres for a response), when the left parietal lobe is injured, the right parietal lobe continues to process ipsilateral stimuli and prepares both hemispheres for action. However, since the left hemisphere cannot process ipsilateral stimuli, lesions of the right hemisphere induce a profound deficit in the attentional-arousal response.

NEUROPATHOLOGY OF NEGLECT

As mentioned previously, neglect in man can be seen to accompany lesions in the following areas: (1) inferior parietal lobule (Critchley, 1966; Watson and Heilman, 1978); (2) dorsolateral frontal lobe (Heilman and Valenstein, 1972); (3) cingulate gyrus (Heilman and Valenstein, 1972); (4) neostriatum (Heir et al., 1977); (5) thalamus (Watson and Heilman, 1978).

The most common cause of neglect from cortical lesions is cerebral infarction (from either a thrombosis or embolus) and the most common cause of subcortical neglect is intracerebral hemorrhage. Neglect can also be seen with tumors. Rapidly growing malignant tumors (e.g., metastatic or glioblastoma) are more likely to produce neglect than slowly growing tumors. It is unusual to see neglect as the result of degenerative disease, because the degeneration is most often bilateral and insidious. However, the akinesia often seen with this disease may be bilateral neglect (Heilman and Valenstein, 1972; Watson et al., 1973) which we believe is the cause of akinetic mutism. We have also seen a transient neglect syndrome as a post-ictal phenomenon in a patient with idiopathic right temporal-lobe seizures, and the transient bilateral akinesia seen with other types of seizures may also be induced by similar mechanisms (Watson et al., 1974).

RECOVERY OF FUNCTION AND TREATMENT

Natural history

Unfortunately, in man no one has systematically observed the natural course of recovery from neglect. From our observations, however, it appears that some patients demonstrate a characteristic syndrome of acute symptoms after an ictus: neglect of their extremities or an allesthetic response, hemispatial neglect, head-and-eye deviation, and an explicit (verbal) denial of illness. In a period of weeks to months, profound hemineglect and allesthesia abate and the neglect syndrome can be demonstrated with simultaneous stimulation. Hemispatial neglect also diminishes and, although an explicit denial of illness abates, patients continue to show a flattening of affect and anosodiaphoria. Extinction, emotional flattening, and anosodiaphoria may persist for years.

Unlike man, who recovers from the neglect syndrome slowly or not at all, monkeys rarely ever show any evidence of neglect after one month. The neural mechanisms underlying this recovery are poorly understood. There are multiple theoretical mechanisms which may underlie recovery, and some of these are discussed in Chapter 17.

One theoretical possibility, however, is that with unilateral stimuli, the nonlesioned hemisphere in part processes the ipsilateral stimulus and has learned not to produce an allesthetic response. With bilateral simultaneous stimuli, however, it is "busy" processing the contralateral stimuli and therefore the abnormal hemisphere must process the stimulus and fails. If with unilateral stimulation the contralesional stimulus reaches the ipsilateral (normal) hemisphere via the corpus callosum or anterior commissure, then destruction of these commissures should retard recovery; if there is recovery to unilateral stimuli, bilateral stimuli should not then produce extinction.

Hughlings Jackson (cited by Taylor, 1932) postulated that certain functions could be mediated at several levels of the nervous system (hierarchical representation). Lesions of higher areas (e.g., cortex) would release phylogenetically more primitive areas which may take over the function of the lesioned cortical areas. Perhaps after disruption of the corticolimbic-reticular loop, a subcortical area, rather than the opposite hemisphere, takes over function and is responsible for mediating response. Ideally, the area which substitutes for the lesioned area must have some similar characteristics to the areas which, when lesioned, produce neglect. It must have multimodal afferent input, and must not only have reticular connections but also be capable of inducing activation with stimulation. Lastly, ablation of this area should induce the neglect syndrome, even if transient. The superior colliculi not only receives optic fibers but also receives somesthetic projections from the spinotectal tract (Sprague and Meikle, 1965) and fibers from the medial and lateral lemnisci and from the inferior colliculus (Truex and Carpenter, 1964). Sprague and Meikle believe that the colliculus is more than a reflex center controlling eye movements. They think it is a sensory integrative center. Tectoreticular fibers project to the mesencephalic reticular formation and ipsilateral fibers are more abundant than contralateral fibers (Truex and Carpenter, 1964). Stimulation of the colliculus (like stimulation of the arcuate gyrus or the inferior parietal lobe) produces an arousal response (Jefferson, 1958). Unilateral lesions of the superior colliculus produce a multimodal unilateral neglect syndrome, and combined cortical collicular lesions produce a more profound disturbance regardless of the order of removal (Sprague and Meikle, 1965). Therefore, another possibility is that in the absence of the corticoreticular loop a collicular-reticular or similar subcortical system takes over function.

Treatment

It must be remembered that the neglect syndrome is a behavioral manifestation of underlying cerebral pathology and the evaluation and treatment of the underlying disease is of primary importance.

In regard to treating the symptoms of the neglect syndrome, there are several things that can be done. The patient with neglect should have his bed placed so that his "good" side faces the area where interpersonal actions are most likely to take place. When he must interact with people or things, these interactions should take place on his good side. When discharged home, his environment should be adjusted in a similar manner. So long as a patient has the neglect syndrome, he should not be allowed to drive or work with anything that, if neglected, will induce injury to himself or others.

During the acute stages when patients have anosoagnosia, rehabilitation is difficult; however, in most patients, this symptom is transient. In addition, because patients with neglect remain inattentive to their left side and in general are poorly motivated, training is laborious and in many cases nonrewarding; however, Diller and Weinberg (1977) were able to train patients with neglect to look to their neglected side.

It is hoped that in the future neuropharmacological or electrophysiological means may be used in treating these behavioral disorders, however, at present operant conditioning and similar behavioral modification paradigms are the best hope of giving patients relief from this behaviorally devastating syndrome.

References

Albert, M. C. (1973). A simple test of visual neglect. *Neurology* 23:658–664.

Anton, G. (1899). Ueber die selbstawahmenhmungen der herderkankungen des Gehirns durch den Kranken bei Rindenblindheit und Rindentaubheit. *Arch. Psychiat. Nervenkr.* 32:86–127.

Anzola, G. P., Bertoloni, A., Buchtel, H. A., and Rizzolatti, G. (1977). Spatial compatibility and anatomical factors in simple and choice reaction time. *Neuropsychologie* 15:295–302.

Astruc, J. (1971). Corticofugal connections of area 8 (frontal eye field) in Macaca mulatta. *Brain Res.* 33:241–256.

Babinski, J. (1914). Contribution à l'etude des troubles mentaux dans l'hémiplégie organique cerebrale (agnosognosie). *Rev. Neurol.* 27:845–847.

Bagshaw, M. H. and Benzies, S. (1968). Multiple measures of the orienting reaction and their dissociation after amygdalectomy. *Exp. Neurol.* 26:175–187.

Bagshaw, M. H., Mackworth, N. H., and Probram, K. H. (1972). The effects of resections of the inferotemporal cortex and the amygdala on visual orienting and habituation. *Neuropsychologia* 10:153–162.

Battersby, W. S., Bender, M. B., and Pollack, M. (1956). Unilateral spatial agnosia (inattention) in patients with cerebral lesions. *Brain 79*:68–93.

Beck, E. C., Dustman, R. E., and Sakai, M. (1969). Electrophysiological correlates of selective attention, in *Attention in Neurophysiology*, C. R. Evans and R. B. Mulholland (eds). New York: Appleton.

Bender, M. B. (1952). *Disorders in Perception*. Springfield, Ill.: C. C. Thomas.

Bender, M. B. and Furlow, C. T. (1944). Phenomenon of visual extinction and binocular rivalry mechanism. *Trans. Am. Neurol. Assoc. 70*:87–93.

Bender, M. B. and Furlow, C. T. (1945). Phenomenon of visual extinction on homonymous fields and psychological principles involved. *Arch. Neurol. Psychiat. 53*:29–33.

Benson, F. and Geschwind, N. (1969). The alexias, in *Handbook of Neurology*, Vol. 4, P. J. Vinken and G. W. Bruyn (eds). Amsterdam: North-Holland.

Benton, A., Hannay, H. J., and Varney, N. R. (1975). Visual perception of line direction in patients with unilateral brain disease. *Neurology 25*: 907–910.

Berke, J. J. (1960). The claustrum, the external capsule, and the extreme capsule of Macaca mulatta. *Comp. Neurol. 115*:297–331.

Berlucchi, G., Heron, W. Hyman, R., Rizzolatti, G., and Umiltà, C. (1971). Simple reaction times of ipsilateral and contralateral hand to lateralized visual stimuli. *Brain 94*:419–430.

Birch, H. G., Belmont, I., and Karp, E. (1967). Delayed information processing and extinction following cerebral damage. *Brain 90*:113–130.

Bowers, D. and Heilman, K. M. (1976). Material specific hemispheric arousal. *Neuropsychologia 14*:123–127.

Brain, W. R. (1941). Visual disorientation with special reference to lesions of the right cerebral hemisphere. *Brain 64*:224–272.

Brodal, A. (1969). *Neurological Anatomy*. London: Oxford University Press.

Colombo, A., DeRenzi, E., and Faglioni, P. (1976). The occurrence of visual neglect in patients with unilateral cerebral disease. *Cortex 12*:221–231.

Costa, L. D., Vaughan, H. G., Horwitz, M., and Ritter, W. (1969). Patterns of behavior deficit associated with visual spatial neglect. *Cortex 5*: 242–263.

Critchley, M. (1966). *The Parietal Lobes*. New York: Hafner.

Davis, B. and Benevento, L. A. (1975). Single cell responses to auditory and visual stimuli in the preoccipital gyrus and superior temporal gyrus in the macaque monkey. Presented at the Society of Neuroscience. New York.

Denny-Brown, D. and Banker, B. Q. (1954). Amorphosynthesis from left parietal lesions. *Arch. Neurol. Psychiat. 71*:302–313.

Denny-Brown, D., Meyer, J. S., and Horenstein, S. (1952). The significance of perceptual rivalry resulting from parietal lesion. *Brain 75*:434–471.

DeRenzi, E., and Faglioni, P. (1965). The comparative efficiency of intelligence and vigilance tests detecting hemispheric damage. *Cortex 1*:410–433.

DeRenzi, E., Faglioni, P., and Scotti, G. (1970). Hemispheric contribution to the exploration of space through the visual and tactile modality. *Cortex 6*:191–203.

Diller, L. and Weinberg, J. (1977). Hemi-inattention in rehabilitation: the evolution of a rational remediation program, in *Advances in Neurology*, Vol. 18, E. A. Weinstein and R. P. Friedland (eds). New York: Raven Press.

Eidelberg, E. and Schwartz, A. J. (1971). Experimental analysis of the extinction phenomenon in monkeys. *Brain 94*:91–108.

Faglioni, P., Scotti, G., and Spinnler, H. (1971). The performance of brain-damaged patients in spatial localization of visual and tactile stimuli. *Brain 94*:443–454.

Fredericks, J. A. M. (1969). Disorders of body schema, in *Handbook of Clinical Neurology*, Vol. 4, P. J. Vinken and G. W. Bruyn (eds). New York: Wiley.

French, J. D., Hernandez-Peon, R., and Livingston, R. (1955). Projections from the cortex to cephalic brainstem (reticular formation) in monkeys. *J. Neurophysiol. 18*:74–95.

Gainotti, G., Messerli, P., and Tissot, R. (1972). Qualitative analysis of unilateral spatial neglect in relation to laterality of cerebral lesions. *J. Neurol. Neurosurg. Psychiat. 35*:545–550.

Gainotti, G. and Tiacci, C. (1971). The relationships between disorders of visual perception and unilateral spatial neglect. *Neuropsychologia 9*:451–458.

Geschwind, N. (1965). Disconnexion syndromes in animals and man. *Brain 88*:237–294, 585–644.

Glick, S. D., Jerussi, T. P., and Zimmerberg, B. (1977). Behavioral and neuropharmacological correlates of nigrostriatal asymmetry in rats, in *Lateralization in the Nervous System*, S. Harnad, R. W. Doty, L. Goldstein, J. Jaynes, and G. Krauthamer (eds). New York: Academic Press.

Goldstein, K. (1939). *The Organism, a Holistic Approach to Biology Derived from Pathological Data in Man*. New York: American Book Company.

Green, J. B. and Hamilton, D. O. (1976). Anosognosia for hemiplegia: somatosensory evoked potential studies. *Neurology 26*:1141–1144.

Head, H. and Holmes, G. (1911). Sensory disturbances from cerebral lesions. *Brain 34*:102–254.

Heilman, K. M., Miller, B. D., and Valenstein, E. (1978). Return of vision in a hemianopic field (in preparation).

Heilman, K. M., Pandya, D. N., and Geschwind, N. (1970). Trimodal inattention following parietal lobe ablations. *Trans. Am. Neurol. Assoc. 95*:259–261.

Heilman, K. M., Schwartz, H. D., and Watson, R. T. (1978). Hypoarousal in patients with the neglect syndrome and emotional indifference. *Neurology 28*:229–232.

Heilman, K. M. and Schwartz, H. (1978). Reaction times in neglect (in preparation).

Heilman, K. M. and Valenstein, E. (1972). Frontal lobe neglect in man. *Neurology 22*:660–664.

Heilman, K. M. and Valenstein, E. (1979). Mechanisms underlying hemispatial neglect. *Ann. Neurol. 5*:166–170.

Heilman, K. M. and Watson, R. T. (1977a). Mechanisms underlying the unilateral neglect syndrome, in *Advances in Neurology*, Vol. 18, E. A. Weinstein and R. P. Friedland (eds). New York: Raven Press.

Heilman, K. M. and Watson, R. T. (1977b). The neglect syndrome—a unilateral defect in the orienting response, in *Lateralization in the Nervous System*, S. Harnad, R. W. Doty, L. Goldstein, J. Jaynes, and G. Krauthamer (eds). New York: Academic Press.

Heilman, K. M. and Watson, R. T. (1978). Changes in the symptoms of neglect induced by changes in task strategy. *Arch. Neurol. 35*:47–49.

Heilman, K. M., Watson, R. T., and Schulman, H. (1974). A unilateral memory defect. *J. Neurol. Neurosurg. Psychiat. 37*:790–793.

Heir, D. B., Davis, K. R., Richardson, E. T., et al. (1977). Hypertensive putaminal hemorrhage. *Ann. Neurol. 1*:152–159.

Holmes, G. (1918). Disturbances of vision of cerebral lesions. *Br. J. Ophthalmol. 2*:353–384.

Howes, D. and Boller, F. (1975). Evidence for focal impairment from lesions of the right hemisphere. *Brain 98*:317–332.

Jackson, J. Hughlings. (1932). *Selected Writings of John Hughlings Jackson*, J. Taylor (ed). London: Hodder and Stoughton.

James, W. (1890). *The Principles of Psychology*. Vol. 2 New York: Holt.

Jefferson, G. (1958). Substrates for integrative patterns in the reticular core, in *Reticular Formation*, M. E. Scheibel and A. B. Scheibel (eds). Boston: Little, Brown.

Joynt, R. J. and Goldstein, M. N. (1975). Minor cerebral hemisphere, in *Advances in Neurology*, Vol. 7, W. J. Friedlander (ed). New York: Raven Press.

Jung, R. and Hassler, R. (1960). The extrapyramidal motor system, in *Handbook of Physiology and Neurophysiology*, Vol. II, J. Field (ed). Washington, D.C.: American Physiological Society.

Kennard, M. A. and Ectors, L. (1938). Forced circling movements in monkeys following lesions of the frontal lobes. *J. Neurophysiol. 1*:45–54.

Kievit, J. and Kuypers, H. G. J. M. (1975). Basal forebrain and hypothalamic connections to frontal and parietal cortex in rhesus monkeys. *Science 187*:660–662.

Kinsbourne, M. (1970). A model for the mechanism of unilateral neglect-of space. *Trans. Am. Neurol. Assoc. 95*:143.

Kinsbourne, M. (1974). Direction of gaze and distribution of cerebral thought processes. *Neuropsychologia 12*:270–281.

Kinsbourne, M. (1977). Hemi-neglect and hemisphere rivalry, in *Advances in Neurology*, Vol. 18, E. A. Weinstein and R. P. Friedland (eds). New York: Raven Press.

Kirvel, R. D., Greenfield, R. A., and Meyer, D. R. (1974). Multimodal sensory neglect in rats with radical unilateral posterior isocortical and superior collicular ablations. *J. Comp. Physiol. Psychol.* 87:156–162.

Lansing, R. W., Schwartz, E., and Lindsley, D. B. (1959). Reaction time and EEG activation under alerted and nonalerted conditions. *J. Exp. Psychol.* 58:1–7.

Lindsley, D. B., Schreiner, L. H., Knowles, W. B., and Magoun, H. W. (1950). Behavioral and EEG changes following chronic brainstem lesions in a cat. *Electroencephalography and Clinical Neurophysiology* 2:483–498.

Loeb, J. (1885). Die elementaren storunger eirfacher functionennach oberflachlicher umschriebener Verletzung des Grosshirns Pfluger's. *Arch. f. Physiologie* 37:51–56.

Lynn, R. (1966). *Attention, Arousal and the Orientation Reaction*. Oxford: Pergammon Press.

McFie, J., Piercy, M. F., and Zangwill, O. L. (1950). Visual spatial agnosia associated with lesions of the right hemisphere. *Brain* 73:167–190.

Marshall, J. F. and Teitelbaum, P. (1974). Further analysis of sensory inattention following lateral hypothalamic damage in rats. *J. Comp. Physiol. Psychol.* 86:375–395.

Marshall, J. F., Turner, B. H., and Teitelbaum, P. (1971). Sensory neglect produced by lateral hypothalamic damage. *Science* 174:523–525.

Mehler, W. R. (1966). Further notes on the center median nucleus of Luys, in *The Thalamus*, D. P. Purpura and M. D. Yahr (eds). New York: Columbia Press.

Moruzzi, G. and Magoun, H. W. (1949). Brainstem reticular formation and activation of the EEG. *Electroencephalography and Clinical Neurophysiology* 1:455–473.

Nathan, P. W. (1946). On simultaneous bilateral stimulation of the body in a lesion of the parietal lobe. *Brain* 69:325–334.

Nauta, W. J. H. (1964). Some efferent connections of the prefrontal cortex in the monkey, in *The Frontal Granular Cortex and Behavior*, J. M. Watten and K. Akert (eds). New York: McGraw-Hill.

Nielsen, J. M. (1948). *Agnosia, Apraxia, Aphasia*. New York: Hafner.

Obersteiner, H. (1882). On allochiria—a peculiar sensory disorder. *Brain* 4:153–163.

Oppenheim, H. (1885). Ueber eine durch eine klinisch bisher nicht verwertete Untersuchungs-methode ermittelte Form der Sensibilitatsstorung bei einseitigen Erkrankungen des Grosshirns. *Neurol. Centrabl.* 4:529–533. Cited by Benton, A. L. (1956). Jacques Loeb and the method of double stimulation. *J. Hist. Med. Allied Sci.* 11:47–53.

Orem, J., Schlag-Rey, M., and Schlag, J. (1973). Unilateral visual neglect and thalamic intralaminar lesions in the cat. *Exp. Neurol.* 40:784–797.

Pandya, D. M. and Kuypers, H. G. J. M. (1969). Cortico-cortical connections in the rhesus monkey. *Brain Res. 13*:13–36.

Paterson, A. and Zangwill, O. L. (1944). Disorders of visual space perception associated with lesions of the right cerebral hemisphere. *Brain 67*: 331–358.

Poppelreuter, W. L. (1917). Die psychischen Schadigungen durch Kopfschuss Krieg im 1914–1916: Die Storungen der niederen und hoheren Leistungen durch Verletzungen des Oksipitalhirns. Vol. 1, Leipzig: Leopold Voss. Referred to by Critchley, M. (1949). *Brain 72*:540.

Reider, N. (1946). Phenomena of sensory suppression. *Arch. Neurol. and Psychiatry 55*:583–590.

Reeves, A. G. and Hagamen, W. D. (1971). Behavioral and EEG asymmetry following unilateral lesions of the forebrain and midbrain of cats. *Electroencephalography and Clinical Neurophysiology 30*:83–86.

Riddoch, G. (1935). Visual disorientation in homonymous half-fields. *Brain 58*:376–382.

Rosenberger, P. (1974). Discriminative aspects of visual hemi-inattention. *Neurology 24*:17–23.

Rossi, G. F. and Brodal, A. (1956). Corticofugal fibers to the brainstem reticular formation. An experimental study in the cat. *J. Anat. 90*: 42–63.

Samuels, I., Butters, N., and Goodglass, H. (1971). Visual memory defects following cortical-limbic lesions: effect of field of presentation. *Physiol. Behav. 6*:447–452.

Schilder, P. (1935). *The Image and Appearance of the Human Body.* London: Kegan Paul, Trench, Trubner.

Segundo, J. P., Naguet, R., and Buser, P. (1955). Effects of cortical stimulation on electrocortical activity in monkeys. *J. Neurophysiol. 18*:236–245.

Simon, J. R., Hinrichs, J. V., and Craft, J. L. (1970). Auditory S-R compatibility: reaction time as a function of ear-hand correspondence and ear-response-location correspondence. *J. Exp. Psychol. 86*:97–102.

Sokolov, Y. N. (1963). *Perception and the Conditioned Reflex.* Oxford: Pergamon Press.

Sprague, J. M. (1966). Interaction of cortex and superior colliculus in mediation of visually guided behavior in the cat. *Science 153*:1544–1547.

Sprague, J. M., Chambers, W. W., and Stellar, E. (1961). Attentive, affective and adaptive behavior in the cat. *Science. 133*:165–173.

Sprague, J. M. and Meikle, T. H. (1965). The role of the superior colliculus in visually guided behavior. *Exp. Neurol. 11*:115–146.

Truex, R. C. and Carpenter, M. B. (1964). *Human Neuroanatomy.* Baltimore: Williams and Wilkins.

Turner, B. H. (1973). Sensorimotor syndrome produced by lesions of the amygdala and lateral hypothalamus. *J. Comp. Physiol. Psychol. 82*: 37–47.

Ungerstedt, U. (1973). Selective lesions of central catecholamine pathways: application in function studies, in *Neuroscience Research*, Vol. 5, S. Ehrenpreis and I. Kopin (eds). New York: Academic Press.

Valenstein, E. and Heilman, K. M. (1978). Apraxic agraphia with neglect induced paragraphia. *Arch. Neurol.* (in press).

Valenstein, E. and Heilman, K. M. (1978). Motor extinction (in preparation).

Van Den Abell, T. and Heilman, K. M. (1978). Lateralized warning stimuli, phasic hemisphere arousal and reaction time. Presented before the International Neuropsychologic Association. Minneapolis.

Van Hoesen, G. (1976). Personal communication.

Von Monakow, C. (1885). Experimentelle und pathologisch-anatomische Untersuchungen uber die Beziehungen der sogenannten Sehsphare zu den infrakortikalen Opticuscentren und zum N. opticus. *Arch. Psychiat.* 16:151–371.

Watson, R. T., Andriola, M., and Heilman, K. M. (1977). The EEG in neglect. *J. Neurol. Sci.* 34:343–348.

Watson, R. T. and Heilman, K. M. (1978). Thalamic neglect (in preparation).

Watson, R. T., Heilman, K. M., Cauthen, J. C., and King, F. A. (1973). Neglect after cingulectomy. *Neurology* 23:1003–1007.

Watson, R. T., Heilman, K. M., Miller, B. D., and King, F. A. (1974). Neglect after mesencephalic reticular formation lesions. *Neurology* 24: 294–298.

Watson, R. T., Miller, B., and Heilman, K. M. (1977). Evoked potential in neglect. *Arch. Neurol.* 34:224–227.

Watson, R. T., Miller, B. D., and Heilman, K. M. (1978). Nonsensory neglect. *Ann. Neurol.* 3:505–508.

Weinburger, N. M., Velasco, M., and Lindsley, D. B. (1965). Effect of lesions upon thalamically induced electrocortical desynchronization and recruiting. *Electroencephalography and Clinical Neurophysiology 18*: 369–377.

Weinstein, E. A. and Kahn, R. L. (1955). *Denial of Illness*. Springfield, Ill.: C. C. Thomas.

Welch, K. and Stuteville, P. (1958). Experimental production of neglect in monkeys. *Brain 81*:341–347.

Wood, C. and Goff, W. (1971). Auditory evoked potentials during speech perception. *Science 173*:1248–1251.

Yin, T. C. T., Lynch, J. C., Talbot, W. H., and Mountcastle, V. G. (1975). Neuronal mechanisms of the parietal lobe for directed visual attentions. Presented at the Society of Neuroscience, New York.

Yamamoto, T., Horenstein, S., and Young, P. (1975). Visual inattention resulting from lesions of the nonvisual temporal cortex in cat. *Neurology* 24:348.

11

The Callosal Syndrome

JOSEPH E. BOGEN

In spite of evidence affirming it, the callosal syndrome, whose principal elements were magnificently described before 1908, has been discussed, forgotten, rediscovered, denied, proven, put in doubt; it continues a subject for argument in 1975.

Brion and Jedynak

The corpus callosum is by far the largest of those nerve fiber collections which directly connect one cerebral hemisphere with the other, and which are called "the cerebral commissures." These include the anterior commissure, the hippocampal commissure and, for some purposes, the massa intermedia. Not included are the posterior and habenular commissures (parts of the midbrain) as well as other commissures of the spinal cord and brainstem (Cumming, 1970; Selnes, 1974; Pandya, 1975).

When the cerebral commissures have been surgically divided (the "split-brain" operation) and the patient has recovered from the acute effects of the operation, a variety of deficits in interhemispheric communication can be demonstrated. These make up "the syndrome of the cerebral commissures," also known as "the syndrome of brain bisection" or "the syndrome of hemisphere disconnection" (Sperry, Gazzaniga, and Bogen, 1969). It is an interesting fact of clinical neurology that many of these same deficits can occur with only a *partial* interruption of the commissures (for example, a portion of the corpus callosum) when this partial disconnection occurs in a setting of acute, naturally occurring disease such as a thrombosis (Geschwind, 1965). Earlier cases were often described as examples of "the anterior cerebral artery syndrome" (Foix and Hillemand, 1925a; Critchley, 1930; Ethelberg, 1951).

Callosal lesions may be accompanied by damage to neighboring structures. As a result, the callosal syndrome consists of two distinct types of signs (and symptoms). These are: (1) signs of hemisphere disconnection and (2) neighborhood signs. The situation may also be complicated by nonlocalizing signs, such as meningismus when the callosal lesion is associated with hemorrhage from an anterior communicating aneurysm, or signs of increased intracranial pressure when the callosal lesion is a tumor. In this chapter, attention will be given only to signs of the first two types, mainly the first. A brief history of studies of the corpus callosum will help us to understand how the disconnection signs have come to be emphasized, and why we often take the trouble to speak of "the cerebral commissures," including the anterior commissure, rather than just the corpus callosum. After this historical account, the callosal syndrome will be described. Because I have been associated with human split-brain patients since 1961, and have followed many (as their physician) over the years, emphasis will be given to the effects of complete cerebral commissurotomy. The next section will focus on the clinical approach to naturally occurring lesions, and the concluding section will touch on two problems as examples of the ongoing controversy in this area.

HISTORICAL BACKGROUND

The history of studies of the corpus callosum can be considered to have five periods, each characterized by the views of leading contributors:

1. The humoral anatomists.
2. The traffic anatomists.
3. The classical neurologists.
4. The critics.
5. The two-brain theorists.

Contributors not mentioned here are cited in the extensive reviews included in the bibliography (Lévy-Valensi, 1910; Mingazzini,

1922; Bremer, Brihaye, and André-Balisaux, 1956; Geschwind, 1965; Unterharnscheidt, Jalnik, and Gott, 1968; Bogen and Bogen, 1969; Elliot, 1969; Doty and Negrão, 1972; Berlucchi, 1972; Joynt, 1974; Brion and Jedynak, 1975; Rudel, 1978).

The humoral anatomists

By "humoral anatomists" I mean those writers of antiquity whose concepts of brain function emphasized the contents of the brain cavities and the flow of various fluids such as air, phlegm, CSF, blood, etc. For them, the corpus callosum seemed largely a support-ing structure. Even that original genius, Vesalius, believed the cor-pus callosum to serve mainly as a mechanical support, maintaining the integrity of the various cavities. In 1543 he wrote:

There is a part [whose] external surface is gleaming white and harder than the substance on the remaining surface of the brain. It was for this reason that the ancient Greeks called this part *tyloeides* [*callosus* in Latin] and, following their example, in my discourse I have always referred to this part as the corpus callosum. If you look at the right and left brain . . . and also if you compare the front and rear, the corpus callosum is observed to be in the middle of the brain; . . . Indeed, it relates the right side of the cere-brum to the left; then it produces and supports the septum of the right and left ventricles; finally, through that septum it supports and props the [fornix] so that it may not collapse and, to the great detriment of all the functions of the cerebrum, crush the cavity common to the two [lateral] ventricles of the cerebrum. [Clarke and O'Malley, 1968, p. 597]

The traffic anatomists

With the "traffic anatomists," there was a major step forward. As in-dicated by Joynt (1974), it was at about the time of Willis (1664) that anatomists began thinking more in terms of a traffic or com-munication between the more solid parts of the brain. This view became quite explicit in the statement of Viq d'Azyr who wrote in 1784:

It seems to me that the commissures are intended to establish sympathetic communications between different parts of the brain, just as the nerves do between different organs and the brain itself. . . . [Clarke and O'Malley, 1968, p. 592]

For over two centuries, beliefs about callosal function consisted almost solely of inferences from its central location, widespread connections, its large size (larger than all those descending and ascending tracts, taken together, which connect the cerebrum with the outside world). Willis, Lapeyronie, and Lancisi among others thought the corpus callosum a likely candidate for "the seat of the soul"; or they used some other expression intended to cover that highest or ultimate liaison which brings coherent, vital unity to a complex assemblage.

The observations of the early anatomists have been supported by subsequent anatomical observations, including the large number of callosal fibers, some 200 million of them, and the important fact that the callosal fibers myelinate quite late, indicating that they probably serve later-developing functions. It certainly seems reasonable to suppose that the cerebral commissures have to do with the "highest," most educable and characteristically human functions of the cerebrum.

Inference of function from observable structure is time-honored and productive. On the other hand, such inference has its limitations. The physiological evidence has only partially sustained anatomical inference. We now know from various data (notably the split-brain) that the corpus callosum does indeed serve as an important integrative structure; we also know it is neither sufficient nor crucial, providing only one of a number of integrative mechanisms. That it is not the exclusive "seat of the soul" is evident from the apparent overall normality of patients who have had complete cerebral commissurotomies. That it is an important intergrating mechanism is clear from the peculiarities of such patients. These include, among other things, a unilateral tactile *anomia,* a left *hemialexia,* and a unilateral *apraxia.* That is, for the right-hander with complete cerebral commissurotomy, there is an inability to name aloud objects felt with the left hand, an inability to read aloud written material presented solely to the left half-field of vision, and an inability to execute with the left hand actions verbally named or described by the examiner. The apraxia usually recedes in a few months whereas the hemialexia and unilateral anomia persist for years.

Such deficits are now easily and clearly demonstrable in individuals who have had surgical section of the cerebral commissures. But such deficits were first recognized, by a number of exceptionally astute clinicians, in patients with vascular disease causing very complex and continually evolving syndromes.

The classical neurologists

In the closing decades of the nineteenth century (or more broadly construed, in the period between the American Civil War and the First World War) there emerged that group of neurologists whose discoveries and formulations are still the core of current clinical knowledge; even the issues which they debated among themselves remain live issues today. Among them were several, including Wernicke, Liepmann, Dejerine, and Goldstein, who interpreted various neurological symptoms as resulting from disconnection, and more specifically, interruption of information flow through the corpus callosum.

The concept of apraxia was developed by Liepmann expressly to describe a patient who could carry out commands with one of his hands but not with the other. Liepmann and Maas (1908) described a right-hander whose callosal lesion caused a left apraxia as well as a left-hand *agraphia*—an inability to write—in the absence of aphasia. These disabilities have subsequently been observed many times. Unilateral apraxia and the unilateral agraphia are not always present, and they may subside when a stroke victim progressively recovers, but they remain among the cardinal signs of hemisphere disconnection.

Among Liepmann's ideas were two which he considered to be necessarily connected, but whose acceptance, in fact, has waxed and waned independently. We can call them: (1) the concept of callosal motor mediation or "the callosal concept" and (2) the concept of left-hemisphere motor dominance or "motor dominance."

According to the first concept, interruption of transcallosal interhemispheric communication resulted in apraxia. Liepmann considered the corpus callosum instrumental in left-hand responses to verbal command: the verbal instruction was comprehended only by the left hemisphere and the left hand followed instructions which were delivered not by a directly descending pathway (what we would now call "ipsilateral control") but by a route involving callosal interhemispheric transfer from left to right and then by way of what we now call "contralateral control," that is, by right hemisphere control of the left hand. Necessarily then, callosal interruption would result in an inability to follow verbal commands with the left hand although there would be no loss of comprehension (as expected from a left-hemisphere lesion). And there would be no weakness or inco-ordination of the left hand (as would usually result from a right-hemisphere lesion). This view was largely ignored or rejected (particularly in the English-speaking countries) for nearly half a century, although it is now thought to be essentially correct. Correspondingly, we now recognize the notion of spatial or pictorial instructions understood by the right hemisphere and requiring callosally mediated interhemispheric communication for correct right-hand execution. This right-to-left aspect of callosal function was not part of Liepmann's original callosal concept although, in retrospect, it seems a natural corollary.

Second, there was Liepmann's concept of the left hemisphere as the organizer of complex (particularly learned) motor behavior. Indeed, according to Goldstein (1953) it was Liepmann who made ". . . the important discovery of the dominance of the left hemisphere." Unlike the callosal concept, this idea of motor dominance was readily accepted, along with the already established concept of language dominance by the left hemisphere. Almost everyone came to think of the left hemisphere as *generally* "the dominant hemisphere" (Benton, 1977). The reemergence in the 1960's of interest in the corpus callosum (as described below) was coincidentally accompanied by a recognition of right-hemisphere dominance for certain nonverbal processes, including their motor expression. Hence, while Liepmann's callosal concept was regaining popularity, his motor dominance concept was losing much of its appeal. This seems to be an example of how ideas thought by their inventor to be necessarily linked can be separated by the judgments of others. Whether, and in what way, the left hemisphere is dominant for skilled movements generally (and not just those linguistically initiated) is currently a matter of active controversy (Kimura and Archibald, 1974; Denckla, 1974; Geschwind, 1975; Albert et al., 1976; Kimura et al., 1976; Mateer and Kimura, 1977; Haaland et al., 1977; Denckla and Rudel, 1978). For a further discussion of apraxia (including callosal apraxia) see Chapter 7.

Meanwhile, Liepmann's callosal concept is now hardly doubted. But this was not always so.

The critics

Even during the time of Liepmann, there were critics and doubters; they became progressively more influential in the ensuing decades. In addition to the criticism of hemisphere disconnection as a cause of symptoms, the situation was clouded by certain distractions which we can consider briefly before returning to the central theme of disconnection.

MENTAL SYMPTOMS WERE DISPUTED

Distractions arose as the result of attempts to correlate lesions, especially tumors of the corpus callosum, with mental symptoms. For example, a mental callosal syndrome was formulated by Raymond, Lajonne, and Lhermitte (1906) and their views were widely accepted for many years. They observed a certain loss of connectedness of ideas but no delirium, a difficulty with recent memory, a "bizarreness" of manner, and a lability of mood. One is impressed with the extent to which this resembles symptoms which are now commonly attributed to frontal-lobe damage (Botez, 1974; Barbizet et al., 1977).

Alpers (1936) redescribed the callosal syndrome emphasizing "imperviousness": a certain indifference to stimuli as if the threshold were elevated, difficulties in concentration, and a lack of elaboration of thought.

After reviewing the relevant literature, and on the basis of personal cases, Brihaye agreed with the observation of Le Beau (1943) that, "There is a certain apathy, that is to say, a clouding without somnolence which is possibly very specific. . . ." (Bremer et al., 1956). When we actually read Le Beau, we find that the rest of his sentence is, ". . . but this, in any case, is insufficient to permit more than a clinical suspicion of localization in the corpus callosum. Most of the time, there is nothing of the sort." [page 1370] And on the very first page of his extensive article, Le Beau says, "The clinical diagnosis of these tumors is hardly possible, because there is no callosal syndrome." [page 1365] And in his summary, ". . . in particular there is no characteristic mental deficit and no apraxia." [page 1381]

In my experience, patients with anterior callosal lesions often *do* have "a certain apathy." This "imperviousness" occurs in patients with acute or progressive callosal lesions—especially the malignancy which is sometimes called a "butterfly glioma" because it spreads its wings into both frontal lobes. The patient who is impervious to instructions will eventually respond, and often appropriately, but only after repeated requests and considerable delay, and sometimes incompletely. We are now inclined to attribute this symptom not to involvement of the genu of the corpus callosum (which is, to be sure, involved) but rather to involvement of the medial aspects of the frontal lobes including the anterior cingulate gyri. And we suppose the imperviousness to be a milder form of the akinesia, often approaching a mute immobility, of a patient who has what is sometimes called "the subfrontal syndrome" consequent to bleeding from an anterior cerebral artery aneurysm, or with an anterior third ventricle tumor. (Also see Chapters 10 and 12, on the neglect syndrome and the frontal lobes, respectively).

In any event, imperviousness can be a useful sign of anterior callosal lesions, although it is probably not a result of callosal interruption. This seems, in retrospect, a good example of anatomical relationships being important clinically, although misleading from the point of view of physiological theory.

Neighborhood signs have also been noted with posterior callosal lesions, with involvement of the hippocampi. Translating Escourolle et al. (1975):

A certain number of our tumors of the splenium [twice as common as genu gliomas] were accompanied by memory dysfunction, whereas the anterior tumors were more often manifested by akinetic states with mutism, probably because of bilateral anterior cingulate involvement. [page 48]

DISCONNECTION SIGNS WERE OFTEN NOT SEEN
The demise of Liepmann's understanding of the corpus callosum was only partly attributable to clouding of the issue with neighborhood signs; mainly it was from an unwillingness to accept as meaningful such disconnection signs as unilateral apraxia, unilateral agraphia, and hemialexia. The objections which were raised included the following six points:

1. Callosal lesions are rarely if ever isolated, so that deficits attributed to such lesions may well result, at least in part, from associated damage.

This problem is real enough; the only solution is to obtain a sufficient variety of cases so that one can reasonably attribute to their common anatomical aspects those clinical features which they also have in common. This is reminiscent of the generally accepted attitude among scientists that a belief becomes more secure through the convergence of widely differing lines of evidence.

A good example of such scientific convergence can be seen in the now general acceptance of dominance by the right cerebral hemisphere for facial recognition. This idea originally arose from the usual association of prosopagnosia (an inability to recognize faces) with posterior right-hemisphere lesions (Hécaen and Angelergues, 1962; Bornstein et al., 1969; Rondot and Tzavaras, 1969; Whiteley and Warrington, 1977). But prosopagnosics usually have other lesions, known or reasonably suspected; on lesion evidence alone, therefore, the dominance of the right hemisphere for facial recognition was uncertain (Pevzner et al., 1962; Gloning et al., 1970; Lhermitte et al., 1972; Meadows, 1974; Benson et al., 1974; Cohn et al., 1977).

Various tests of facial recognition were then devised. Although these tests sometimes give normal results in patients with overt prosopagnosia, they did show that deficits in facial recognition could be elicited even in patients who did not complain of trouble recognizing faces. Again, the right hemisphere was implicated (Warrington and James, 1967; DeRenzi et al., 1968; Lansdell, 1968; Milner, 1968; Newcombe and Russell, 1969; Benton and Van Allen, 1972; Vilkki and Laitinen, 1974; Levin et al., 1975).

Then, supporting evidence came from testing of intact ("normal") subjects. Presentation of faces to the right hemisphere (via the left visual half-field) usually (but not always) resulted in better scores than presentation to the left hemisphere (Rizzolati, Umiltà, and Berlucchi, 1971; Geffen, Bradshaw, and Wallace, 1971; Hilliard, 1973; Berlucchi et al., 1974; Pirozzolo and Rayner, 1977; Broman, 1979).

Furthermore, chimeric (split-stimulus) tests of split-brain subjects showed a greater reliability of the right hemisphere identification of faces, as well as suggesting that the association of names with faces was quite difficult when both hemispheres were present but disconnected (Levy, Trevarthen, and Sperry, 1972). Similar results were obtained using chimeric stimuli in a naturally occurring case of hemisphere disconnection (Lhermitte et al., 1974–76).

And there is EEG evidence, as yet meager, that the right hemisphere is dominant for faces (Dumas and Morgan, 1975; Glass, Butler, and Heffner, 1975).

2. Signs attributable to callosal lesions often subside or disappear altogether.

This criticism is correct, especially for younger patients with unimanual dyspraxia and unimanual dysgraphia. But it does not apply to all callosal signs, notably the unilateral anomia and the hemialexia following commissurotomy. Even if it did, subsidence does not mean that a sign was without significance, any more than the frequent subsidence of aphasia means that it is not a reliable sign (in right-handers) of a left-hemisphere lesion. Progressive compensation following focal damage is one of the most characteristic features of the brain.

3. In numerous cases of callosal disease the expected disconnection signs were not elicited; this included cases of toxic degeneration of the corpus callosum (such as Marchiafava-Bignami disease) as well as the far more common cases of callosal tumor or callosal infarction.

In retrospect, these negative findings can often be attributed to a lack of looking; it is not everyone's routine to look for dysgraphia in the left hand or even for an anomia; and hemialexia in the left half-field can be even more elusive, particularly if no precautions are taken to prevent shift of gaze (such as using a tachistoscope so that stimuli appear, in one visual half-field or the other, for only a fraction of a second). In addition, disconnection signs may not be demonstrable because patients with callosal tumors or toxic degeneration are often too obtunded to be appropriately tested. When patients with toxic malfunction of the corpus callosum are testable, and appropriately tested, such signs as unilateral anomia and dyspraxia have been found (Lechevalier et al., 1975; Lhermitte et al., 1977).

4. Patients with agenesis of the corpus callosum (and/or callosal lipoma) do not manifest most of the so-called callosal signs.

Lévy-Valensi (1910) was an ardent admirer of Liepmann, gave him the credit for the concept of apraxia, and said, ". . . apraxia is part of the callosal syndrome." But he, like so many others, was particularly troubled by callosal agenesis and admitted, "The physiologist is no less embarrassed than the anatomist by these disconcerting cases." A sizable number of callosal agenesis patients have been seen in the past few years; and a few deficits in interhemispheric transfer have seemed to be present (Jeeves, 1965a, 1965b; Lehmann and Lampe, 1970; Dixon and Jeeves, 1970; Kinsbourne and Fisher, 1971; Sadowsky and Reeves, 1975).

But there has been no disconnection syndrome typical of the split-brain in such patients. This observation cannot be explained away on methodological grounds since it is true even with the most extensive, systematic testing (Saul and Sperry, 1968; Ettlinger et al., 1974; Ferriss and Dorsen, 1975; Reynolds and Jeeves, 1977; Gott and Saul, 1978).

The presence of interhemispheric transfer in spite of callosal agenesis has been attributed to various causes, most notably the use of other commissural systems such as the anterior commissure. There may also be a duplication of function (such as speech in each hemisphere) or the compensatory appearance, during brain development, of unusually effective ipsilateral fiber tracts.

The anterior commissure explanation is appealing because the available postmortem evidence indicates that individuals with callosal agenesis (if they reach an age sufficient for psychological testing) all have anterior commissures, sometimes larger than normal (Bruce, 1890; Segal, 1935; Kirschbaum, 1947; Slager et al., 1957; Loeser and Alvord, 1968; Bossy, 1970; Iro et al., 1972; Sheremata et al., 1973; Shoumura et al., 1975; Carleton et al., 1976).

The anterior commissure has been shown in animal experiments to serve visual transfer nearly as well as the splenium (Downer, 1962; Black and Myers, 1964; Gazzaniga, 1966; Doty and Overman, 1977; Sullivan and Hamilton, 1973). And it is now known that in the chronic, stabilized state, splenial remnants can effect sufficient interhemispheric exchange to avoid the usual signs of disconnection (Gorden, Bogen, and Sperry, 1971; Gazzaniga et al., 1975; Ozgur et al., 1977). This conclusion is based on cases having very extensive but not quite complete commissurotomy, that is, section of the anterior commissure and all of the corpus callosum except for a part (about one half) of the splenium. In the second half of this chapter you will find an extensive list of deficits reliably found after a complete cerebral commissurotomy; they are not found after surgery if the splenium is spared. Two points are important:

a. An apparent lack of callosal symptoms in cases of long-standing partial lesion (or of callosal agenesis) is largely due to the remarkable compensatory capabilities of the remaining commissural fibers.

b. Partial lesions are not usually compensated immediately. Hence, disconnection symptoms are more likely to occur after a sudden partial lesion (such as a stroke), or in the presence of progressive lesions (such as tumors) where the deficit is increasing faster than it can be compensated.

The paucity of disconnection deficits in patients with callosal agenesis is not wholly explained by the presence of the anterior commissure. It should be kept in mind that compensation for loss of the splenium, by the anterior commissure, was not 100% in animal experiments. Nor does the anterior commissure compensate completely for splenial loss in the human, as is shown by the hemialexia usually persisting after splenial section (Trescher and Ford, 1937; Maspes, 1948; Gazzaniga and Freedman, 1973; Iwata et al., 1974).

Interhemispheric transfer via the anterior commissure seems to be, in surgical cases, incomplete (Goldstein and Joynt, 1969; Goldstein et al., 1975). When present, it is largely restricted to visual information (Risse et al., 1978). Even if the anterior commissure is responsible for visual transfer in cases of callosal agenesis, how are we to explain the somesthetic transfer in such cases? One consideration is that agenesis cases typically have a large longitudinal bundle of fibers along the medial aspect of each hemisphere (the bundle of Probst). As pointed out by R. Saul (personal communication) this bundle might make available to the anterior commissure some types of information which it does not ordinarily transfer. In any event, the presence of Probst's bundle fits the view that brains with callosal agenesis differ from normal brains in ways other than disconnection.

Also implying that such a brain is peculiar in its principles of operation is the notion of increased function of ipsilaterally descending or ascending fiber tracts. In this regard, Dennis (1976) confirmed that callosal agenesis is accompanied by deficits *within* each hemisphere, appearing as a loss of finely differentiated tactile localization and individual finger movements. This was attributed to a lack of inhibitory action by the corpus callosum during early development of the brain. The corpus callosum, she suggests, ordinarily suppresses information contained in uncrossed pathways. Somewhat related are the suggestions: (a) that unilateralization of language (and other engrams) depends on callosal inhibition active at the time of engram acquisition (Doty, Negrão, and Yamaga, 1973); (b) that the development of hemispheric specialization depends on competitive interaction between the hemispheres during early childhood (Galin, 1977).

Some reservation is necessary with respect to the interpretation of intrahemispheric deficits in callosal agenesis, since the condition is so often associated with other anomalies. Hence, any deficit in intrahemispheric function might easily be coincidental, not a direct result of the absence of commissures. Further evidence may be forthcoming from animal experiments in which the cerebral commissures are severed shortly after birth (Jeeves and Wilson, 1969; Sechzer et al., 1976).

5. *Callosal section in animal experiments did not produce any significant deficits;* this includes the experiments of Zinn (1748), Magendie, Muratow, Roussy, Franck and Pitres, Koranyi, Dotto and Pusateri, Lo Monaco, and Baldi, all reviewed by Lévy-Valensi (1910) whose own monkey experiments were (to his dismay) also negative. Also negative were the experiments of Lafora and Prados (1923), Hartmann and Trendelenburg (1927), and Seletzky and Gilula (1928).

In retrospect, all of these negative results were attributable to a lack of relevant testing (as will be discussed in the following section). Besides, the more striking signs and symptoms seen in human patients are attributable to hemispheric specialization which is poorly developed or absent in cats, dogs, or even monkeys (Warren and Nonneman, 1976; Doty and Overman, 1977; Hamilton, 1977; Stamm et al., 1977; Dewson, 1977).

6 *Surgical section of the corpus callosum is often asymptomatic.* Walter Dandy went so far as to say in 1936:

The corpus callosum is sectioned longitudinally . . . no symptoms follow its division. This simple experiment puts an end to all of the extravagant hypotheses on the functions of the corpus callosum.

Even more persuasive was the negative testing by Akelaitis of patients who had callosal section. These results were admitted by Tomasch (1954,1957) whose interest in the corpus callosum and anterior commissure led him to make the now widely accepted estimates of their fiber content. Of the Akelaitis results he wrote:

They showed very clearly and in accordance with some earlier authors like Dandy, Foerster, Meagher and Barre, whose material however was not so extensive, that the corpus callosum is hardly connected with psychological functions at all.

Ethelberg (1951), after extensive review, concluded:

It may be premature to consider the recent clinical, surgical and experimental observations an obituary of Leipmann's concepts as to the role played by the corpus callosum in the development of "true" apraxia. But they certainly suggest the need of some hesitance in accepting them. [page 117]

About the same time, Fessard (1954) summarized the view which was then generally accepted:

. . . there is a great deal of data showing [that] section of important associative white tracts such as corpus callosum does not seem to affect mental performances. Other similar observations in man or animals are now accumulated in great number and variety. These results are so disturbing that one may be tempted to admit the irrational statement that a heterogeneous system of activities in the nervous system could form a whole in the absence of any identified liaison.

Such sentiments are similar to others, even better known, although less well documented. Warren McCullough is reputed to have said (possibly at a 1948 Cal Tech conference) that the corpus callosum seems to serve only the purpose of transmitting seizure activity from one hemisphere to the other. Karl Lashley is supposed to have commented that the corpus callosum also serves to keep the two cerebral hemispheres from collapsing into each other (reminiscent of the opinion of Vesalius). Apparently taking his cue from these knowledgeable acquaintances of his, Norbert Wiener wrote:

There is some evidence that the long-distance paths in the brain have a tendency to run outside of the cerebrum altogether, and to traverse the lower centers. This is indicated by the remarkably small damage done by cutting some of the long-distance cerebral loops of white matter . . . the direct connectors between the hemispheres—the cerebral commissures—in a brain as large as that of man, are so few in number that they are of very little use; and the interhemispheric traffic must go by roundabout routes through the brain-stem. As a consequence, the processes associated with speech and writing are very likely to be involved in a traffic jam, and stuttering is the most natural thing in the world. [Wiener, 1948, pp. 177–179]

Some facts relevant to this wild assertion are that the cerebral commissures are proportionately *more extensive* in human brains than in other creatures, that the cerebral commissures *are* of considerable use, and that hemisphere disconnection does *not* cause stuttering.

We now realize that most of the negative findings resulted from two sources:

a. As already mentioned, when surgical section of the commissures is incomplete, a remarkable capacity for maintaining cross-communication between the hemispheres may be retained by even quite small commissural remnants, particularly when the part remaining is at the posterior end of the corpus callosum (in other words, in the splenium).

b. Negative findings often result from the use of inappropriate or insensitive testing techniques. What one finds depends on what one looks for: whereas Dandy (1936) said that callosal section produces no observable deficits, among his own patients was the one reported by Trescher and Ford (1937) to have hemialexia.

The two-brain theorists

A dramatic reversal of opinion occurred during the 1960's, following publication of the "split-brain" experiments on cats and monkeys.

Current views on callosal function are attributable in large part to studies, under the aegis of R. W. Sperry, of our patients with surgical section of the cerebral commissures. These patients are indeed without, in Dandy's words, "any deficits" in the ordinary social situation, or even as determined by a routine neurological examination, for the most part (Bogen and Vogel, 1975; Botez and Bogen, 1977). In specially devised testing situations, however, they can be shown to have a wide variety of deficits in interhemispheric communication (Gazzaniga, 1970; Gazzaniga, Bogen, and Sperry, 1962, 1963,

1965, 1967; Gazzaniga and Sperry, 1967; Sperry, 1970, 1974; Sperry and Gazzaniga, 1967; Sperry, Gazzaniga, and Bogen, 1969).

The split-brain patients confirmed in a particularly dramatic way the importance of the commissural fibers for interhemispheric communication. But the essential facts had already been described in animal experiments during the 1950's, initiated by Myers and Sperry (1953; Myers, 1956). It was found that each hemisphere of a cat or monkey could learn solutions to a problem different from (even conflicting with) the solutions learned by the other hemisphere. This made it clear that effective functioning could occur independently in the two hemispheres. As Sperry (1961) put it:

Callosum-sectioned cats and monkeys are virtually indistinguishable from their normal cagemates under most tests and training conditions. [But] if one studies such a "split-brain" monkey more carefully, under special training and testing conditions where the inflow of sensory information to the divided hemispheres can be separately restricted and controlled, one finds that each of the divided hemispheres now has its own independent mental sphere or cognitive system—that is, its own independent perceptual, learning, memory, and other mental processes . . . it is as if the animals had two separate brains. [page 1749]

It is important to understand that the duality of minds seen after hemisphere disconnection is not an inference solely from certain striking clinical cases, and a handful of surgical patients, as is sometimes said. Split-brain experiments have been carried out with many different species by hundreds of investigators around the world. They are virtually unanimous in concluding that each of the disconnected hemispheres can act independently of the other (Bogen, 1977). Let us consider two examples of variation on the basic idea of what has been called the "double brain" (Dimond, 1972).

1. One of the most reliable signs of a bilateral prefrontal lobectomy in monkeys is their inability to do delayed-alternation tasks. It was long supposed that this inability might be explained as the result of the hyperactivity and/or distractability which is also characteristic of such monkeys. This supposition can be tested in a split-brain monkey, where each hemisphere can function separately. If one hemisphere has had a prefrontal lobectomy, it performs poorly on the delayed-alternation task. This poor performance by the lobectomized hemisphere is not accompanied by hyperactivity or

distractability. Apparently, the remaining frontal lobe keeps the monkey quiet and attentive even though the intact hemisphere is not participating in the recognition of various stimuli or the evaluation of their significance (Glickstein, Arora, and Sperry, 1963).

2. A truly dramatic example occurs when only one hemisphere of a split-brain monkey has had a temporal lobectomy. A bitemporal monkey manifests the Klüver-Bucy syndrome, which includes difficulties in the visual identification of objects, orality (often mouthing inappropriate objects), hypersexuality, hypomotility, and tameness in the presence of humans. When the intact hemisphere can see, the split-brain rhesus monkey behaves in the usual rhesus manner, manifesting a fierce fear of humans. But if only the temporal lobectomized hemisphere receives the visual information, the split-brain animal acts like a Klüver-Bucy monkey, particularly as regards its relative tameness. When this was reported (Downer, 1961, 1962) it was so amazing that many of us doubted it, although we were already convinced of the duality of mind in the split-brain monkey. Little room for doubt remains because this finding has, in its essentials, been reported by a number of other investigators (Bossom, Sperry, and Arora, 1961; Horel and Keating, 1969, 1972; Doty, Negrão, and Yamaga, 1971, 1973; Doty and Overman, 1977).

It was knowledge of the split-brain experiments in laboratory animals that alerted Geschwind and Kaplan (1962) to the possibility of a hemisphere-disconnection syndrome in the human. This led them, when a likely patient appeared, to search in a deliberate way for the disconnection effects. From a complex, evolving picture, they expertly teased out the relevant phenomena.

One of the first things Geschwind and Kaplan found was that although the patient wrote clearly with his right hand, he wrote "aphasically" with his left (and was astonished when he looked at what he had written). Among other things they found that an object placed in his left hand was handled correctly and was correctly retrieved by feel, but it could not be named; nor could it be retrieved by feel with his right hand. In their words,

. . . he behaved as if his two cerebral hemispheres were functioning nearly autonomously. Thus, we found that so long as we confined stimulation and response within the same hemisphere, the patient showed correct performance.

In contrast, the patient performed incorrectly when the stimulus was provided to one hemisphere and the response was required from the other. They concluded that the best explanation was to suppose that his hemispheres were disconnected by a lesion of the corpus callosum. Their anatomical prediction was eventually confirmed by autopsy. Their conclusions were soon amply confirmed by the surgical cases whose description we come to next.

Liepmann's callosal concept has been resurrected. There is now widespread acceptance of an idea long ignored. It is an interesting example of what Kuhn (1962) called scientific "revolutions." Geschwind (1974) wrote,

What was astonishing was the fact that this work had been so grossly neglected . . . that important confirmed scientific observations could almost be expunged from the knowledge of contemporary scientists.

Geschwind has suggested in correspondence that there was a widespread revulsion against attempts to link brain to behavior, associated with the rise of psychoanalysis; and he had another sociological explanation:

Henry Head had been shrewd enough to point out that much of the great German growth of neurology had been related to their victory in the Franco-Prussian war. He was not shrewd enough to apply this valuable historical lesson to his own time and to realize that perhaps the decline of the vigor and influence of German neurology was strongly related to the defeat of Germany in World War I and the shift of the center of gravity of intellectual life to the English-speaking world, rather than necessarily to any defects in the ideas of the German scholars. [Geschwind, 1964]

But there were other factors. One thing that was missing was a widespread conviction that the essential facts could be observed repeatedly in humans under controlled, prospective circumstances. Such observations are possible with persons who have had a complete cerebral commissurotomy.

A SYNOPSIS OF THE SYNDROME FOLLOWING COMPLETE CEREBRAL COMMISSUROTOMY

Clarification and extensive confirmation of the callosal syndrome came from observations on patients whose forebrain commissures were sectioned to control severe intractable epilepsy. Results were favorable in our early patients (Bogen and Vogel, 1962; Bogen, Fisher, and Vogel, 1965). These results led to continued application of the operation which included section of the entire corpus callosum and anterior and hippocampal commissures plus in some cases the massa intermedia—all in a single operation. The increased number of patients exhibit a wide spectrum of disconnection deficits. At one extreme, our first patient, who had grossly apparent right-frontal atrophy, was oldest at the time of brain injury (age 30), the oldest at time of operation (age 45), and subsequently showed the most severe apraxic and related symptoms. Least affected was a 13-year-old boy who had the smoothest postoperative course, relatively little brain damage before surgery, early date of brain injury (birth), was youngest at time of operation, and whose left-hand apraxia was minimal. Following a similar operation by others (Wilson et al., 1975, 1977) further variation has been encountered, but the crucial observations have been the same. The following briefly outlines some of the typical findings. (Left-handers are excluded.)

Overall effects

Within a few months after operation, the symptoms of hemisphere disconnection tend to be compensated to a remarkable degree. In personality, and in social situations the patient appears much as before. However, with appropriate tests the disconnected hemispheres can be shown to operate independently to a large extent. Each of the hemispheres appears to have its own learning processes and its own separate memories, all of which are largely inaccessible to the other hemisphere.

Visual effects

Visual material can be presented selectively to a single hemisphere by having the patient fix his gaze on a projection screen onto which pictures of objects or symbols are backprojected to either right, left, or both visual half-fields, using exposure times of 1/10 sec or less. The patients can read and describe material of various kinds in the right half-field at a level substantially the same as before surgery. When stimuli are presented to the left half-field, however, the patients usually report that they see "nothing" or at most "a flash of light."

The difficulty in the left half-field is not visual but one of verbal communication since the same visual stimuli which the subject denies having seen are correctly identified through nonverbal means, for example, by correctly retrieving with the left hand (but not the right) an object pictured briefly in the left half-field. If a pair of objects or images are presented simultaneously, one left and one right, the left hand (but not the right) can be used to pick out by touch, from an unseen group of objects, the specific item pictured in the left half-field. If then asked (before he sees it) what he has chosen with the left hand, the patient replies incorrectly, often naming what was seen in the right half-field.

An object identified in the left visual half-field cannot be recognized as the same when it reappears in the right half-field. Words or other material presented to left and right of the vertical midline are responded to quite separately. Each separated hemisphere seems to have its own visual images and memories, as if two separate brains were viewing left and right halves of the visual field. Only one, the left hemisphere, is able to communicate what it sees through speech or writing.

Auditory suppression

Following cerebral commissurotomy, the patient readily identifies single words (and other sounds) if they are presented to one ear at a time. But if different words are presented to both ears simultaneously (so-called "dichotic listening") only the words presented to the right ear will be reliably reported (Milner et al., 1968; Sparks and Geschwind, 1968; Springer and Gazzaniga, 1975; Gordon, 1975; Cullen, 1975; Zaidel, 1976; Efron et al., 1977).

This phenomenon is usually considered to be the result of two concurrent circumstances: (1) the ipsilateral pathway from the left ear (to the left, speaking, hemisphere) is suppressed by the presence of simultaneous but differing inputs, as it is in intact individuals during dichotic listening (Kimura, 1967). (2) The contralateral pathway from the left ear (to the right hemisphere) conveys information which cannot reach the left (speaking) hemisphere by the callosal pathway which has been severed. Although left-ear words are not reported, their perception by the right hemisphere is occasionally evidenced by appropriate actions of the left hand (Gordon, 1973).

Motor function

The degree of left-hand dyspraxia is subject to large individual differences. Immediately after surgery all the patients showed some left-sided apraxia to verbal commands such as "Wiggle your left toes." or "Make a fist with the left hand." This left-limb dyspraxia is attributable to the simultaneous presence of two deficits: poor comprehension by the right hemisphere (which has good control of the left hand), and poor ipsilateral control by the left hemisphere (which understands very well). Subsidence of the dyspraxia could therefore result from two compensatory mechanisms: increased right-hemisphere comprehension of words, and increased left-hemisphere control of the left hand. The extent of ipsilateral motor control can be tested by flashing to right or left visual half-field sketches of thumb and fingers in different postures, for the subject to mimic with one or the other hand. Responses are poor with the hand on the side opposite the visual input, simple postures such as closed fist or open hand being attainable after further recovery. As recovery proceeds, good ipsilateral control is first attained for responses carried out by the more proximal musculature. After several months, most of the patients can form a variety of hand and finger postures with either hand to verbal instructions, for example, "Make a circle with your thumb and little finger.", etc.

Subsidence of the apraxia continues so that eventually it is hardly in evidence. But even many years later, it can be demonstrated to some degree, especially if the patient is fatigued or naive to the task (Zaidel and Sperry, 1977).

The capacity of either hemisphere, and particularly the left hemisphere, to control the ipsilateral hand varies from one patient to another both in the immediate postoperative period and many years later. This, together with variations in right-hemisphere language, probably accounts for many of the discrepancies in descriptions of the callosal syndrome as presented by various authors.

Somesthetic symptoms

The lack of interhemispheric transfer following brain bisection can be demonstrated with respect to somesthesis (including touch, pressure, and proprioception) in a variety of ways.

CROSS-RETRIEVAL OF SMALL TEST OBJECTS

Unseen objects in the right hand are handled, named, and described in normal fashion. In contrast, attempts to name or describe the same objects held out of sight in the left hand consistently fail. In spite of the patient's inability to name an unseen object in his left hand, identification of the object by the right hemisphere is evident from appropriate manipulation of the item showing how it is used, or by retrieval of the same object with the left hand (but not the right) from among a collection of other objects screened from sight.

CROSS-REPLICATION OF HAND POSTURES

Specific postures impressed on one (unseen) hand by the examiner cannot be mimicked in the opposite hand. Also, if a hand posture in outline form is flashed by tachistoscope to one visual half-field, it can be copied easily by the hand on that side but usually not by the other hand.

A convenient way to test for lack of interhemispheric transfer of proprioceptive information is as follows: the patient extends both hands beneath the opaque screen (or vision is otherwise excluded) and the examiner impresses a particular posture on one hand. For example, one can put the tip of the thumb against the tip of the little finger and have the other three fingers fully extended and separated (or the other three fingers can be kept close together, as the examiner wishes). One then says, "Now make a fist—good—now put it back the way it was." Then one says, "Keep your hand just the way it is and do exactly the same with your other hand." The patient with complete cerebral commissurotomy cannot mimic with the other hand a posture being held by the first hand. When assuring oneself of the presence of hemisphere disconnection, this procedure should be repeated with various postures and in both directions. In this way, one can establish quite clearly (in the absence of malingering) that there is a hemisphere disconnection.

CROSS-LOCALIZATION OF FINGER TIPS

After complete cerebral commissurotomy there is a partial loss of the ability to name exact points stimulated on the left side of the body.

This defect is least apparent, if at all, on the face and it is most apparent on the distal parts, especially the finger tips. This is not a deficit dependent upon language since it can be done in a nonverbal fashion and in both directions (right-to-left and vice versa). An easy way to demonstrate the defect is to have the subject's hands extended, palms up (again with vision excluded). One touches the tip of one of the four fingers with the point of a pencil, asking the patient to then touch the same point with the tip of the thumb of the same hand. Repeating this maneuver many times produces a numerical score, about 100% in normals for either hand. In the absence of a parietal lesion, identification of any of the four finger tips by putting the thumb tip upon the particular finger can be done with great reliability. It can be done at nearly 100% level by the split-brain patient.

One then changes the task so that the finger tip is to be indicated, not by touching it with the thumb of the same hand but by touching the *corresponding* finger tip of the other hand with the thumb of that (other) hand. Sometimes the procedure should be demonstrated with the patient's hand in full vision until the patient understands what is required. This cross-localization cannot be done by the split-brain patient at a level much better than chance (25%). Normal adults almost always do better than 90%.

It is of interest that an inability to cross-localize has been found in young children, possibly because their commissures are not yet fully functioning (Galin et al., 1977).

Verbal comprehension by the right hemisphere

Auditory comprehension of words by the disconnected right hemisphere is suggested by the subjects' ability to retrieve with the left hand various objects if they are named aloud by the examiner. Visual comprehension of printed words by the right hemisphere is often present; after a printed word is flashed to the left visual halffield, the subjects are often able to retrieve with the left hand the designated item from among an array of hidden objects. Control by the left hemisphere in these tests is excluded because incorrect verbal descriptions given immediately after a correct response by the left hand show that only the right hemisphere knew the answer.

The language capabilities of the right hemisphere, including certain right-hemisphere influences on linguistic processing by the left hemisphere, have recently been of considerable theoretical interest (Smith, 1966; Gazzaniga and Sperry, 1967; Gazzaniga and Hillyard, 1971; Levy, Nebes, and Sperry, 1971; Kinsbourne, 1971; Zurif and Ramier, 1972; Caplan et al., 1974; Kinsbourne, 1975; Brown and Jaffe, 1975; Moscovitch, 1976; Selnes, 1976; Burklund and Smith, 1977; Bradshaw et al., 1977; Sasanuma et al., 1977; Rogers et al., 1977; Winner and Gardner, 1977; Bradshaw and Gates, 1978; Marcel and Patterson, 1978).

Right-hemisphere language capabilities are distinctly more in evidence when the left hemisphere has been removed. Indeed, if the left hemisphere is removed (or was severely incapacitated) in infancy, these capabilities may seem normal (Smith, 1974; Kohn and Dennis, 1974; Smith and Sugar, 1975; Dennis and Whitaker, 1976). But when the left hemisphere is present and relatively intact, they are largely absent, or suppressed. The disconnected right hemisphere's receptive vocabulary can grow considerably over the years, reaching levels comparable with the vocabulary of a 10 or even a 16 year old. But this impressive single-word comprehension is not accompanied by speech. This is true even of the patient, who, in a broad spectrum of patients, is the most extreme case to date of right-hemisphere language ability in a right-handed (and left-hemisphere speaking) split-brain subject (Gazzaniga et al., 1977; LeDoux et al., 1977).

In addition to the absence of speech, right-hemisphere language in the split-brain subject has other limitations, syntactic ability being rudimentary at best (E. Zaidel, 1973, 1977, 1978a, 1978b). Studying a few cases in great depth for over seven years, Zaidel concluded:

Whereas phonetic and syntactic analysis seem to specialize heavily in the left hemisphere, there is a rich lexical structure in the right hemisphere. The structure of the right hemisphere lexicon appears to be unique in that it has access to a severely limited short term verbal memory, and it has neither phonetic encoding nor grapheme-to-phoneme correspondence rules . . . [this] represents the limited linguistic competence that can be acquired by a nonlinguistic, more general purpose (or other purpose) cognitive apparatus. . . . [Zaidel, 1978]

Right-hemisphere dominance
Following commissurotomy, we can test each hemisphere separately. It is thus possible to demonstrate in a positive way those things

which each hemisphere can do better than the other, rather than inferring what a hemisphere does from the loss of function when it is injured. Right-hemisphere dominance for faces has already been discussed, and other aspects will be mentioned in the following section. For those particularly interested in right-hemisphere dominance in the commissurotomized human, representative reviews are included in the bibliography (Bogen and Bogen, 1969; Milner and Taylor, 1972; Levy, 1974; Nebes, 1974; Sperry, 1974).

CLINICAL TESTING FOR CALLOSAL
SIGNS AND SYMPTOMS

Following are some abbreviated descriptions of what one can look for using simple maneuvers in the clinic, when hemisphere disconnection is suspected. The descriptions apply to right-handers. In left-handers the situation is rarely a simple reversal; usually it is quite complex, as the reader can see in referring to the case histories cited in the bibliography (Liepmann, 1900; Hécaen and Ajuriaguerra, 1964; Gloning et al., 1966; Botez and Crighel, 1971; Tzavaras et al., 1971; Heilman et al., 1973; Schott et al., 1974; Aptman et al., 1977; Hirose et al., 1977).

History
Discussions with the patient, relatives, or nursing personnel often disclose sensations or occurrences suggesting hemisphere disconnection. As usual, if one is aware of what can sometimes happen, one is more apt to elicit the relevant report.

DISSOCIATIVE PHENOMENA
If the extra-callosal damage is small enough that each hemisphere can retain a capacity for integrative behavior (as distinguished from cases with dense hemiplegia for example), conflicting actions may occur more or less simultaneously. The commonest of these (which is not very helpful because it often occurs in "normal" people) is a disparity between facial expression and verbalization. More meaningful is a dissociation between what the left hand is doing and what the patient is saying. Or there may be a dissociation between general bodily actions (rising, walking, etc.) and what is being done by either hand or what is being said.

One suspects a conversion hysteria when dissociative phenomena occur. But such dissociations have occurred sufficiently often following callosal section in animals (Trevarthen, 1965) and in humans with cerebral commissurotomy as well as in naturally occurring cases, that they should arouse suspicion of a hemisphere disconnection. Indeed, there may be some substance to the view that such conative or volitional ambivalence, when it occurs in intact people, might be attributable, on some occasions at least, to a lack of information transfer by anatomically intact commissures (Galin, 1974; Hoppe, 1977).

In contrast with volitional ambivalence, emotional ambivalence (such as the report by the patient of possessing two conflicting internal feelings simultaneously) has not been a symptom of commissurotomy nor of most reported natural cases. Indeed, individuals with cerebral commissurotomy are *less* apt than normal individuals to discuss their feelings, conflicting or otherwise (Hoppe and Bogen, 1977).

INTERMANUAL CONFLICT

The dissociative phenomenon most clearly identifiable with hemisphere disconnection is intermanual conflict, in which one hand is acting at cross purposes to the other. Almost all of our complete commissurotomy patients manifested some degree of intermanual conflict in the early postoperative period. For example, a few weeks after a certain patient underwent surgery, his physiotherapist said, "You should have seen Rocky yesterday—one hand was buttoning up his shirt and the other hand was coming along right behind it undoing the buttons!" Similar phenomena were observed after commissurotomy by Wilson et al. (1977) and by Akelaitis (1944–45) who called it "diagonistic dyspraxia." And the phenomenon has been described in many individual case reports of callosal infarcts or tumors. Such behavior soon subsides, probably because of other integrative mechanisms supplementing or replacing commissural function. But when it occurs, the phenomenon is quite striking, and probably pathognomonic.

THE ALIEN HAND

Possibly a lesser form of intermanual conflict is what Brion and Jedynak (1972) called, "la main étrangère." This is a circumstance in which one of the patient's hands, the left hand in the right-handed patient, behaves in a way which the patient finds "foreign," "alien," or at least uncooperative. Among our patients it has been most flagrant in a patient with a rather flamboyant personality which we believe contributed materially to her frequent complaints about "my little sister" in referring to whomever or whatever it was that made her left hand behave peculiarly. And it may be that when the "strange hand" accompanies callosal tumors or infarcts, some predisposing peculiar personality features play a part, particularly since so many patients with definite callosal lesions do not emphasize this problem. However, even Rocky, a rather stolid fellow, complained for several years of an inability to get his left foot to go in the same direction as the rest of him.

AUTOCRITICISM

There is a related phenomenon, emphasized by Brion and Jedynak (1975), which they called "L'autocritique interhémisphérique." They refer to the fairly frequent expressions of astonishment by the patient with respect to the capacity of the left hand to behave independently of their conscious volition. The patient may say, when the left hand makes some choice among objects, that "my hand did that," rather than taking the responsibility themselves. A patient was described by Sweet (1945) as saying, "Now you want me to put my left index finger on my nose." She then put that finger into her mouth and said, "That's funny; why won't it go up to my nose?" [page 88].

Split-brain patients soon accept the idea that they have capacities of which they are not conscious, such as left-hand retrieval of objects not namable. But even many years after operation the patients will occasionally be quite surprised when some well-coordinated or obviously well-informed act has just been carried out by the left hand. This is particularly common under conditions of continuously lateralized input (Zaidel, 1977, 1978b).

Examination

Most naturally occurring cases of hemisphere disconnection are in a process of recovery (as with a stroke) or are worsening (as with a tumor) or may be fluctuating (as with remitting vascular disease or fluctuating edema). Findings which are quite clear on one occasion may be doubtful later (or earlier). Hence, repeated examinations at different times are most informative.

Various neighborhood signs can prevent the demonstration of disconnection signs. The imperviousness from certain bifrontal lesions may render the patient insufficiently cooperative. Forced deviation of gaze, not uncommon with unilateral hemispheric involvement, can interfere. The anterior cerebral artery syndrome classically includes a unilateral crural (leg) weakness of the "pyramidal" type and/or a strong grasp reflex, uni- or bilateral. Such an abnormality (especially forced grasping) makes testing for disconnection quite difficult. Most neighborhood signs will eventually subside after a stroke, with the emergence of a period during which disconnection signs can be demonstrated for awhile, before compensation supervenes.

UNILATERAL "VERBAL ANOSMIA"

Following complete cerebral commissurotomy, the patient is unable to name odors presented to the right nostril, even though they can be named quite readily when presented to the left nostril. This is not a defect of smell with the right nostril, since the patient can select, by feeling with the left hand, an object which corresponds to the odor, such as selecting a plastic banana or a plastic fish after having smelled the related odor (Gordon and Sperry, 1969). This has been confirmed in a case (including section of the anterior commissure) from a different surgical series (Gazzaniga et al., 1975). Callosotomy without section of the anterior commissure does not affect smell (Risse et al., 1978). Naturally occurring cases await investigation.

DOUBLE HEMIANOPIA

Most clinicians do not have routinely available a tachistoscope or other means for lateralizing visual information. But the disconnection (if it includes the splenium) can sometimes be demonstrated with simple confrontation testing of the visual field. The patient is allowed to have both eyes open but does not speak, and is allowed to use only one hand (sitting on the other hand, for example). Using the free hand, the subject indicates the onset of a stimulus, such as the wiggling of the examiner's fingers. With such testing there may appear to be an homonymous hemianopia contralateral to the indicating hand (the patient reliably points to the right half-field stimulus with the right hand but not to a left half-field stimulus). When the patient is tested with the *other* hand, there seems to be an homonymous hemianopia in the *other* half-field. Occasionally a stimulus in the apparently blind half-field (on the left when the right hand is being used) will produce turning of the head and eyes toward the stimulus and *then* the hand will point.

When the stimuli appear in both fields simultaneously, the patient, if free to do so, will often use both hands simultaneously. But if one hand is restrained, only one half-field will be indicated. This peculiar situation must be distinguished from the much more commonly occurring extinction or hemi-inattention deficits from a hemispheric lesion (commonly right parietal) such that the patient tends to indicate only one stimulus when the stimuli are in fact bilaterally present. An observable difference is that the double hemianopia is a symmetrical phenomenon (the deficit occurs on each side) whereas extinction or hemi-inattention is typically one-sided, more commonly for the left side. Another difference is that the double hemianopia is the result of a sharply defined projection system combined with the commissural disconnection, that is, it is thought to be a relatively primitive sensory loss. In contrast, the phenomenon of hemi-inattention is usually considered to be a higher-order derangement (Heilman and Watson, 1977; Weinstein and Friedland, 1977). For a further discussion of hemi-inattention, see Chapter 10 which covers the neglect syndrome.

Each hemisphere can exert a modicum of ipsilateral control, especially for gross arm movements. As a result, stimuli in the right half-field (seen only by the left hemisphere) may be pointed to when the patient is using only the left hand, and similarly for the left half-field stimuli when only the right hand is available. But such pointing is unreliable and inaccurate, as compared with the dependable response and precise localization possible when the patient is using the hand contralateral to the stimulated hemisphere.

When a patient has a left hemiplegia, one cannot prove that an apparent left hemianopia (when the patient is responding verbally or with right hand) is the result of a commissural lesion; but if threats in the left half-field produce wincing or flinching, failure to point to left half-field stimuli with the right hand is suggestive of a disconnection.

HEMIALEXIA

When the splenium is affected, it may sometimes be possible to demonstrate a hemialexia by the brief presentations of cards, on which are printed letters or short words, in the left half-field. The patient is often unable to read a card presented this way, although he can readily read it when it is presented in the right half-field. Eye movements are usually too active for such simple testing methods; but hemialexia was, in fact, observed by such methods long before its demonstration by tachistoscopic presentation (Trescher and Ford, 1937). It is necessary to show that the hemialexia is not merely a matter of a left hemianopia, for example by having the patient retrieve correctly objects which are briefly shown in the left half-field. Less reliable but suggestive is to see the patient point quickly (with the left hand) to stimuli (which cannot be read) when they appear in the left half-field. Sometimes a patient can name objects in the left half-field although hemialexic in that half-field and reading normally in the right.

Quite often the patient will manifest normal visual fields by perimetry and tangent screen examination (particularly if permitted to use both hands to indicate the appearance of the stimulus). There may be a partial homonymous defect in the left half-field caused by extension into the right hemisphere of the callosal lesion; but the defect would be insufficient to account for the hemialexia if it were not accompanied by a callosal lesion (Wechsler, 1972).

UNILATERAL (LEFT) IDEOMOTOR APRAXIA

Historically the first described callosal symptom was unilateral ideomotor apraxia, by which we mean that in response to verbal command the subject is unable to carry out with the left hand some behavior which is readily executed with the right hand. This ready execution demonstrates that the failure is not ascribable to a lack of understanding. It is also necessary to demonstrate that the inability is not accounted for by either weakness (paresis) or incoordination (ataxia) in the left hand (Wilson, 1908; Nielsen, 1936; Denny-Brown, 1958; Bogen, 1969; Geschwind, 1975).

Strength and coordination in the left hand can be demonstrated in various ways. The main problem is not to confuse an ideomotor (also called "ideokinetic") apraxia with the much more commonly occurring loss of dexterity which is called "kinetic dyspraxia" or "limb-kinetic dyspraxia" or "innervatory apraxia" or "melokinetic dyspraxia." This occurs in the left hand as the result of various right-hemisphere lesions, which can cause a mild weakness, or a release of excessive grasping or groping tendencies which interfere with function. In the words of K. Poeck (personal communication), "This is no apraxia at all!" What many of us, including Poeck, consider the hallmark of apraxia is the appearance of well-executed but incorrect movements. These so-called *parapraxias* are analogous to the paraphasias (incorrect sounds or entire words) which are so characteristic of most aphasic speech. (For another view, see Chapter 7, *Apraxia*.)

Nor should ideokinetic apraxia be confused with "ideational apraxia" in which a sequence of movements is ineffective to some overall purpose in spite of adequate performance of individual movements. Ideational apraxia can be seen in either or both hands, often in association with linguistic deficit. It can result from a left-hemisphere lesion, but usually is caused by diffuse brain disease. (For further discussion, see Chapter 7.)

The best way to demonstrate an absence of weakness or incoordination in the left hand is to see the patient carry out exactly the same behavior (which could not be carried out to verbal instruction) on some other occasion. This may either occur spontaneously or it may result from some different (nonverbal) instruction. The right-handed patient with callosal disconnection often cannot follow a verbal command such as "pretend you are turning a door knob" or "pretend you are combing your hair" while using the left hand. In contrast, the very same behavior will be readily executed when the patient is actually confronted with a real door knob to turn, or given (into the left hand) some article whose use is to be demonstrated.

Left-handed apraxia can sometimes be easily demonstrated simply by requesting a number of individual finger motions such as "stick out your little finger." When the patient is attempting to cooperate with the left hand, such a request may result in a parapraxis, or only in bewilderment on the patient's part, whereas the left little finger is adroitly extended when one silently demonstrates the desired action. In the most pronounced cases, the disability may include such relatively crude acts as opening or closing the fist, or even whole arm movements such as saluting, waving goodby, etc., when they are verbally requested.

When a patient has a pronounced inability to perform certain movements in the left hand under the circumstances just described, there is a strong presumption for a callosal lesion. One problem is that the dyspraxia commonly is accompanied by some weakness, because the naturally occurring callosal lesion is usually accompanied by some extension toward one or the other hemisphere. When the dyspraxia is accompanied by paresis or forced grasping, it can nonetheless be quite suggestive, especially if it is out of proportion to any weakness or incoordination simultaneously present.

UNILATERAL (LEFT) AGRAPHIA

Right-handers can write legibly, if not fluently, with the left hand. This ability is commonly lost with callosal lesions, especially those which cause a unilateral apraxia. An inability to write to dictation is common with left-hemisphere lesions, but these almost always affect the right hand at least as much as they affect the left. The left hand may be dysgraphic because it is affected by a right hemispheric lesion, such as a frontal lesion causing forced grasping. That the left dysgraphia is not simply attributable to an incoordination or paresis resulting from a right-hemisphere lesion can be established if one can demonstrate some *other* ability in the left hand requiring as much control as would be required for writing. One cannot expect to see spontaneous left-handed writing, since the right hemispheres of most individuals rarely possess sufficient language capacity for this (Gazzaniga and Sperry, 1967; Sperry and Gazzaniga, 1967; Gazzaniga and Hillyard, 1971; Levy, Nebes, and Sperry, 1971; Zaidel, 1973; Gazzaniga, LeDoux, and Wilson, 1977). But one can sometimes see the left hand spontaneously doodling, or one can ask the patient to use the left hand to copy various designs or diagrams. Here, as elsewhere, it is not so much the presence of a deficit but rather the *con-*

trast between certain deficits and certain retained abilities which is most informative.

Simple or even complex geometric figures can often be copied by a left hand which cannot write, or which cannot even copy writing previously made with the patient's own right hand (Bogen and Gazzaniga, 1965; Bogen, 1969; Kumar, 1977; Zaidel and Sperry, 1977). Copying of block letters may be present when the copying of cursive writing is not; this may not be an example of printing with the left hand but rather a copying of geometric figures which happen also to have linguistic content.

UNILATERAL (LEFT) TACTILE ANOMIA

One of the most convincing ways to demonstrate hemisphere disconnection is to ask the patient to feel with one hand and then to name various small, common objects such as a button, coins, safety pin, paper clip, pencil stub, rubber band, key, fingernail file, comb, etc. When these are placed into the patient's hand, it is essential that vision be occluded. A blindfold is notoriously unreliable. It is better to have an assistant hold the patient's eyelids closed, or to put a pillowcase over the patient's head for the brief testing session. (For longer testing sessions, one should use an opaque screen.)

The patient with a hemisphere disconnection will generally be unable to name or describe an object in the left hand although he readily names such objects in the right hand. Sometimes the patient will be able to give a vague description of the object although he is unable to name it; in this case there can still be a contrast with the ability to readily name the object when it is placed into the right hand.

To establish hemisphere disconnection, it is necessary to exclude other causes of unilateral anomia, particularly astereognosis (or even a gross sensory deficit) as may occur with a right-parietal lesion. The best way to exclude astereognosis is to show that the object has in fact been recognized, although it cannot be verbally identified or described. The most certain proof that the object has been identified is for the subject to retrieve it correctly from a collection of similar objects. Such a collection is most conveniently placed in a shallow box about 12–15 cm in diameter, around which the subject can shuffle the objects with one hand while exploring for the test object. Even without the evidence of correct retrieval, one can often reasonably exclude astereognosis by observing the rapid, facile, and appropriate manipulation of an object in spite of its unavailability to naming or verbal description.

In testing for anomia, one must be aware, in certain clever patients, of strategies for circumventing the defect. For example, the patient may drop an object, or may manipulate it in some other way (such as running a fingernail down the teeth of the comb) and in one of these ways produce a characteristic noise by which the object can be identified. In the same vein, a subject may identify a pipe or some other object by a characteristic smell and thus circumvent the inability of the left hemisphere to identify, by palpation alone, an object in the left hand.

UNILATERAL (RIGHT) CONSTRUCTIONAL APRAXIA

By "constructional praxis" we mean the ability to put together a meaningful configuration. This can be an object (in three dimensions) or a complex drawing (in two dimensions). Constructional dyspraxia is the inability to get several parts into a configuration, in spite of a normal ability to handle or draw the individual parts (Benton, 1962; Benton and Fogel, 1962). Constructional dyspraxia can occur from lesions in either hemisphere; left lesions usually result in an absence of some of the parts and in simplified versions of a model, whereas right-hemisphere lesions result in inappropriate relationships among the parts, including a loss of perspective in drawings intended to represent three dimensions (Paterson and Zangwill, 1944; Warrington, James, and Kinsbourne, 1966; Benton, 1967; Hécaen, 1969; Gainotti et al., 1977). (See Chapter 8.)

Constructional apraxia can be quite prominent in the right hand of right-handers with callosal lesions. The simplest way to test for this is to ask the patient to copy with one hand (and subsequently with the other) various geometric figures which can either be drawn by the examiner or which have been prepared beforehand. It is usually better to proceed from simple squares and triangles to more complex figures, eventually including drawings which represent three dimensional objects such as a cube, stairway or a house. Drawing with a felt pen is often easier than with a pencil.

Hemisphere disconnection (in a right-hander) is strongly suggested if the patient can copy designs better with the left hand. Of course, if a callosal lesion is accompanied by right-hemisphere involvement, the left hand may be paretic or ataxic so that the patient does no better with the left hand than with the right.

SPATIAL ACALCULIA

Because hemisphere disconnection (or a right-hemisphere lesion) can cause a right-hand disability for spatial forms, such a patient may have difficulties using pencil and paper to solve problems. This deficit may be mild and not noticeable, unless the patient has an occupation in which sketching is regularly employed. Sometimes the deficit is so severe that it interferes with the use of pencil and paper in doing arithmetic problems. In our patients with complete cerebral commissurotomy we usually observed some difficulty in doing written arithmetic following the operation, a deficit which progressively receded (Bogen, 1969, page 92). On a few occasions we were surprised to note that a patient would have difficulty in doing arithmetic on paper whereas comparable problems could be done "in the head," that is, by mental calculation. This was a rather elusive phenomenon and was never pursued; that it was, in fact, a sign of hemisphere disconnection is suggested by the report of a similar situation in the case of a 41-year-old woman with a callosal hematoma associated with an (operated) anterior cerebral artery aneurysm (Brion and Jedynak, 1975).

It must surely be rare to find a patient who can do arithmetic to verbal instruction but who cannot do similar problems presented on paper, in spite of normal reading and writing skills. But the phenomenon is sufficiently dramatic and is of sufficient scientific interest that looking for it, in appropriate circumstances, is probably worthwhile.

THE LACK OF SOMESTHETIC TRANSFER

The foregoing signs of disconnection are all dependent on hemispheric dominance—either left or right depending upon the particular task. Even more convincing are disconnection signs appearing with tests for which there is little if any dominance. These include the transfer of somesthetic information whether tactile, proprioceptive, or stereognostic. How to test for these was described in the preceding section.

TWO EXAMPLES OF REMAINING PROBLEMS

Postcommissurotomy mutism

Following complete section of the cerebral commissures, there is a mutism, sometimes lasting many days; the patient does not talk although he is quite cooperative and often writing readily. I first thought this was simply a neighborhood sign, a partial form of akinetic mutism (without the akinesia) which resulted from retraction around the anterior end of the third ventricle during section of the anterior commissure. But it may be a disconnection sign, since I have now seen a number of patients with similar retraction but whose commissural section spared the splenium, and who did *not* have mutism. So I now favor the speculation that the mutism results either from some hemispheric conflict (possibly at a brainstem level) or from a bilateral diaschisis which affects speech much more than it affects writing (Bogen, 1976). Whatever the speculative explanation for these postsurgical observations, clinical experience indicates that when mutism occurs with naturally occurring callosal lesions, the disease process probably involves the anterior cingulate regions bilaterally (above the callosum) or the septal area (below the callosum).

Alexia without agraphia

Stroke patients who can write but are unable to read, even what they have just written correctly to dictation, are not extremely rare. This remarkable dissociation of reading from writing has been known for nearly a century (Dejerine, 1892). How can it be explained? A popular explanation is as follows: since such a patient usually has a right homonymous hemianopia resulting from a left occipital-lobe lesion, nothing can be seen, much less read, in the right half-field. Hence, visual information can reach the left hemisphere language zone only from the left half-field via the right occipital cortex and then crossing via the splenium. In addition, another (or confluent) splenial lesion (usually present in such cases) has disconnected the right occipital cortex from the left hemisphere. On this explanation, the left hemisphere still retains a competence to write to dictation but no longer has access to information arriving in the right occipital lobe from the left visual half-field (Foix and Hillemand, 1925b; Geschwind and Fusillo, 1966; Benson and Geschwind, 1969; Geschwind, 1970; Cumming et al., 1970; Ajax et al., 1977; Benson, 1977; Damasio, 1977).

As its proponents have recognized, there are some difficulties with this explanation. For example, after surgical section of the splenium leaving the anterior commissure intact, patients can often name objects, or pictures of objects, in the left half-field, showing that information *can* reach the language zone from the left half-field (Iwata et al., 1974). In at least some cases of complete callosotomy with retained anterior commissure, there may be no alexia for the left half-field (Risse et al., 1978). Moreover, alexia without agraphia can sometimes occur without an accompanying loss of the right visual half-field (Ajax, 1967; Heilman et al., 1971; Goldstein et al., 1971; Greenblatt, 1973; Vincent et al., 1977). And there occur cases of alexia without agraphia in which the splenium is thought to be largely intact (Wechsler, 1972; Hécaen and Gruner, 1975; Greenblatt, 1976; a personal (Bogen) post-traumatic case with CAT scan lesion in the left temporoparietal region).

Some of the problems in explaining alexia without agraphia can be seen in the very first, famous case of Dejerine (1892). This 68-year-old man, "of above average intelligence and culture" suffered a left occipital infarct. He was followed for four years during which he continued to manage his business affairs. On a number of different testing sessions it was found that he could write without error entire pages, none of which he could read. An accomplished musician and sight-reader, he readily learned difficult passages by ear following his stroke, but he could no longer read "a single musical note." Nor could he name a single written letter. But he readily named written numbers as well as real objects, and he could do arithmetic problems which were written on paper. Moreover, his hemianopia was not terribly dense, objects being obscure and colorless (gray) in his right visual half-field. His callosal (splenial) lesion was quite small and was dismissed by Dejerine as irrelevant to the behavioral deficit. (Also see Chap. 3, pp. 70–73.)

Alexia without agraphia has been argued for nearly a century; it is still a puzzle. Part of the answer may be, among other things, that reading is a multistage process which can be disturbed in a variety of ways (Hécaen and Kremin, 1976; Greenblatt, 1977). There is a good deal more to be learned about this striking condition in which the ability to read is disturbed far out of proportion to disturbance in other abilities.

In the past 20 years, our understanding of commissural function has been greatly enriched and clarified. But there remain many unresolved issues. The foregoing (postcommissurotomy mutism, and alexia without agraphia) are but two of these.

References

Ajax, E. T. (1967). Dyslexia without agraphia. *Arch. Neurol. 17*:645–652.

Ajax, E. T., Schenkenberg, T., and Kosteljanetz, M. (1977). Alexia without agraphia and the inferior splenium. *Neurology 27*:685–688.

Akelaitis, A. J. (1944–45). Studies on the corpus callosum IV. Diagnostic dyspraxia in epileptics following partial and complete section of the corpus callosum. *Am. J. Psychiat. 101*:594–599.

Akelaitis, A. J. (1944). A study of gnosis, praxis and language following section of the corpus callosum and anterior commissure. *J. Neurosurg. 1*:94–102.

Albert, M. L., Silverberg, R., Reches, A., and Berman, M. (1976). Cerebral dominance for consciousness. *Arch. Neurol. 33*:453–454.

Alpers, B. J. (1936). The mental syndrome of tumors of the corpus callosum. *Arch. Neurol. Psychiat. 35*:911–912.

Aptman, M., Levin, H., and Senelick, R. C. (1977). Alexia without agraphia in a left-handed patient with prosopagnosia. *Neurology 27*:533–536.

Bale, P. M. and Reye, R. D. K. (1976). Epignathus, double pituitary and agenesis of corpus callosum. *J. Pathol. 120*:161–164.

Barbizet, J., Degos, J. D., Duizabo, Ph., and Chartier, B. (1974). Syndrome de déconnexion interhémisphérique d'origine ischémique. *Rev. Neurol. 130*:127–142.

Barbizet, J., Duizabo, Ph., Bouchareine, A., Degos, J. D., and Poirier, J. (1977). *Abrégé de Neuropsychologie.* Paris: Masson.

Benson, D. F. (1977). The third alexia. *Arch. Neurol. 34*:327–331.

Benson, D. F. and Geschwind, N. (1969). The alexias. *Handbook Clin. Neurol. 4*:112–140.

Benson, D. F., Segarra, J., and Albert, M. L. (1974). Visual agnosia—prosopagnosia. *Arch. Neurol. 30*:307–310.

Benton, A. L. (1962). The visual retention test as a constructional praxis task. *Confin. Neurol. 22*:141–155.

Benton, A. L. (1967). Constructional apraxia and the minor hemisphere. *Confin. Neurol. 29*:1–16.

Benton, A. L. (1977). Historical notes on hemispheric dominance. *Arch. Neurol. 34*:127–129.

Benton, A. L. and Fogel, M. L. (1962). Three-dimensional constructional praxis. *Arch. Neurol. 7*:347–354.

Benton, A. L. and Van Allen, M. W. (1972). Prosopagnosia and facial discrimination. *J. Neurol. Sci. 15*:167–172.

Berlucchi, G. (1972). Anatomical and physiological aspects of visual functions of corpus callosum. *Brain Res. 37*:371–392.

Berlucchi, G., Brizzolara, D., Marzi, C. A., Rizzolatti, G., and Umiltà, C. (1974). Can lateral asymmetries in attention explain interfield differences in visual perception? *Cortex 10*:177–185.

Black, P. and Myers, R. E. (1964). Visual function of the forebrain commissures in the chimpanzee. *Science 146*:799–800.

Bogen, J. E. (1969). The other side of the brain I. Dysgraphia and dyscopia following cerebral commissurotomy. *Bull. Los Angeles Neurol. Soc. 34*:73–105.

Bogen, J. E. (1969). The other side of the brain II. An appositional mind. *Bull. Los Angeles Neurol. Soc. 34*:135–162.

Bogen, J. E. (1976). Language function in the short term following cerebral commissurotomy, in *Current Trends in Neurolinguistics*, H. Avakian-Whitaker and H. A. Whitaker (eds). New York: Academic Press.

Bogen, J. E. (1977). Further discussion on split-brains and hemispheric capabilities. *Br. J. Phil. Sci. 28*:281–286.

Bogen, J. E. and Bogen, G. M. (1969). The other side of the brain III: The corpus callosum and creativity. *Bull. Los Angeles Neurol. Soc. 34*: 191–220.

Bogen, J. E., Fisher, E. D., and Vogel, P. J. (1965). Cerebral commissurotomy: a second case report. *J. Am. Med. Assoc. 194*:1328–1329.

Bogen, J. E. and Gazzaniga, M. S. (1965). Cerebral commissurotomy in man: minor hemisphere dominance for certain visuospatial functions. *J. Neurosurg. 23*:394–399.

Bogen, J. E., Sperry, R. W., and Vogel, P. J. (1969). Commissural section and the propagation of seizures, in *Basic Mechanisms of the Epilepsies*, H. H. Jasper, A. A. Ward, and A. Pope (eds). Boston: Little, Brown.

Bogen, J. E. and Vogel, P. J. (1962). Cerebral commissurotomy in man. *Bull. Los Angeles Neurol. Soc. 27*:169–172.

Bogen, J. E. and Vogel, P. J. (1975). Neurologic status in the long term following cerebral commissurotomy, in *Les Syndromes de Disconnexion Calleuse chez l'Homme*. F. Michel and B. Schott (eds). Lyon: Hopital Neurologique.

Bornstein, B., Sroka, H., and Munitz, H. (1969). Prosopagnosia with animal face agnosia. *Cortex 5*:164–169.

Bossom, J., Sperry, R. W., and Arora, H. (1961). Division of emotional behavior patterns in split-brain monkeys. *Caltech. Biol. Ann. Rep.* p. 127.

Bossy, J. G. (1970). Morphological study of a case of complete, isolated and asymptomatic agenesis of the corpus callosum. *Arch. Anat. Histol. and Embryol. 53*:289–340.

Botez, M. (1974). Frontal lobe tumours. *Handbook Clin. Neurol. 17*:234–280.

Botez, M. I. and Bogen, J. E. (1976). The grasp reflex of the foot and related phenomena in the absence of other reflex abnormalities following cerebral commissurotomy. *Acta Neurol. Scandinav. 54*:453–463.

Botez, M. I. and Crighel, E. (1971). Partial disconnexion syndrome in an ambidextrous patient. *Brain 94*:487–494.

Bradshaw, J. L., Gates, A., and Nettleton, N. C. (1977). Bihemispheric involvement in lexical decisions: handedness and a possible sex difference. *Neuropsychologia 15*:277–286.

Bremer, F., Brihaye, J., and André-Balisaux, G. (1956). Physiologie et pathologie du corps calleux. *Arch. Suisses Neurol. Psychiat. 78*:31–87.

Brion, S. and Jedynak, C. P. (1972). Troubles du transfert interhémisphérique (callosal disconnection) a propos de 3 observations de tumeurs du corps calleux. Le signe de la main étrangère. *Rev. Neurol. 126*:257–266.

Brion, S. and Jedynak, C. P. (1975). *Les Troubles du Transfert Interhémisphérique*. Paris: Masson.

Broman, M. (1979). Reaction time differences in right and left hemispheres for face and letter discrimination in children and adults. *Cortex* (in press).

Brown, J. W. and Jaffe, J. (1975). Hypothesis on cerebral dominance. *Neuropsychologia 13*:107–110.

Bruce, A. (1890). On the absence of corpus callosum in the human brain, with the description of a new case. *Brain 12*:171–190.

Burklund, C. W. and Smith, A. (1977). Language and the cerebral hemispheres. *Neurology 27*:627–633.

Caplan, D., Holmes, J. M., and Marshall, J. C. (1974). Word classes and hemispheric specialization. *Neuropsychologia 12*:33–337.

Carleton, C. C., Collins, G. H. and Schimpff, R. D. (1976). Subacute necrotizing encephalopathy (Leigh's disease): two unusual cases. *South Med. J. 69*:1301–1305.

Clarke, E. and O'Malley, C. D. (1968). *The Human Brain and Spinal Cord*. Berkeley: Univ. Calif. Press.

Cohn, R., Neumann, M. A., and Wood, D. H. (1977). Prosopagnosia: A clinicopathological study. *Ann. Neurol. 1*:177–182.

Critchley, M. (1930). The anterior cerebral artery, and its syndromes. *Brain 53*:120–165.

Cullen, J. K. (1975). *Tests of a Model for speech information flow*. Ph.D. Thesis, Louisiana State Univ., 1975.

Cumming, W. J. K. (1970). An anatomical review of the corpus callosum. *Cortex 6*:1–18.

Cumming, W. J. K., Hurwitz, L. J., and Perl, N. T. (1970). A study of a patient who had alexia without agraphia. *J. Neurol. Neurosurg. Psychiat. 33*:34–39.

Damasio, A. R. (1977). Varieties and significance of the alexias. *Arch. Neurol. 34*:325–326.

Dandy, W. E. (1936). Operative experience in cases of pineal tumor. *Arch. Surg. 33*:19–46.

Dejerine, J. (1892). Contribution a l'étude anatomo-pathologique et clinique des différentes variétés de cécité verbale. *Comptes rendus des séances et mémoires de la Soc. de Biol.* Vol. *44* (vol. 4 of Series 9) (Second section-Mémoires):*61*–90.

Denckla, M. B. (1974). Development of motor coordination in normal children. *Dev. Med. Child Neurol. 16*:729–741.

Denckla, M. B. and Rudel, R. G. (1978). Anomalies of motor development in hyperactive boys. *Ann. Neurol. 3*:231–233.

Dennis, M. (1976). Impaired sensory and motor differentiation with corpus callosum agenesis: A lack of callosal inhibition during ontogeny? *Neuropsychologia 14*:455–469.

Dennis, M. and Whitaker, H. A. (1976). Language acquisition following hemidecortication: linguistic superiority of the left over the right hemisphere. *Brain and Language 3*:404–433.

Denny-Brown, D. (1958). The nature of apraxia. *J. Nervous Mental Dis. 126*:9–32.

DeRenzi, E., Faglioni, P., and Spinnler, H. (1968). The performance of patients with unilateral brain damage on face recognition tasks. *Cortex 4*:17–34.

Dewson, J. H. III (1977). Preliminary evidence of hemispheric asymmetry of auditory function in monkeys, in *Lateralization in the Nervous System*, S. Harnad et al. New York: Academic Press.

Dimond, S. J. (1972). *The Double Brain*. London: Churchill-Livingstone.

Dixon, N. F., and Jeeves, M. A. (1970). The interhemispheric transfer of movement aftereffects: a comparison between acallosal and normal subjects. *Psychon. Sci. 20(4)*:201–203.

Doty, R. W. and Negrão, N. (1972). Forebrain commissures and vision, in *Handbook of Sensory Physiology VII/3*, R. Jung (ed). Berlin: Springer-Verlag.

Doty, R. W., Negrão, N., and Yamaga, K. (1973). The unilateral engram. *Acta Neurobiol. Exp. 33*:711–728.

Doty, R. W. and Overman, W. H. (1977). Mnemonic role of forebrain commissures in macaques, in *Lateralization in the Nervous System*, S. Harnad et al. New York: Academic Press.

Doty, R. W., Yamaga, K., and Negrão, N. (1971). Mediation of visual fear via the corpus callosum. *Proc. Soc. Neurosco., 1*:104.

Downer, J. L. de C. (1961). Changes in visual gnostic functions and emotional behavior following unilateral temporal pole damage in the "split-brain" monkey. *Nature 191*:50–51.

Downer, J. L. de C. (1962). Interhemispheric integration in the visual system, in *Interhemispheric Relations and Cerebral Dominance*, V. B. Mountcastle (ed). Baltimore: Johns Hopkins Press.

Dumas, R. and Morgan, A. (1975). EEG asymmetry as a function of occupation, task, and task difficulty. *Neuropsychologia 13*:219–228.

Efron, R., Bogen, J. E., and Yund, E. W. (1977). Perception of dichotic chords by normal and commissurotomized human subjects. *Cortex 13*: 137–149.

Escourolle, R., Hauw, J. J., Gray, F., and Henin, D. (1975). Aspects neuropathologiques des lésions du corps calleux, in *Les Syndromes de Disconnexion Colleuse Chez l'Homme*, F. Michel and B. Schott (eds). Lyon: Hospital Neurologique.

Elliot, F. A. (1969). The corpus callosum, cingulate gyrus, septum pellucidum, septal area and fornix. *Handbook Clin. Neurol.* 2:758–775.

Ethelberg, S. (1951). Changes in circulation through the anterior cerebral artery. *Acta Psychiat. Neurol. Suppl. 75*:3–211.

Ettlinger, G., Blakemore, C. B., Milner, A. D., and Wilson, J. (1972). Agenesis of the corpus callosum: a behavioral investigation. *Brain 95*: 327–346.

Ettlinger, G., Blakemore, C. B., Milner, A. D., and Wilson, J. (1974). Agenesis of the corpus callosum: a further behavioural investigation. *Brain 97*:225–234.

Ferriss, G. D. and Dorsen, M. M. (1975). Agenesis of the corpus callosum: neuropsychological studies. *Cortex 11*:95–122.

Fessard, A. E. (1954). Mechanisms of nervous integration and conscious experience, in *Brain Mechanisms and Consciousness*, J. F. Delafresnaye (ed). Springfield, Ill.: C. C. Thomas.

Foix, Ch. and Hillemand, P. (1925a). Les syndromes de l'artère cérébrale antérieure. *Encéphale 20*:209–232.

Foix, Ch. and Hillemand, P. (1925b). Role vraisemblable du splénium dans la pathogénie de l'alexie pure par lésion de la cérébrale postérieure. *Bull. Mém. Soc. Méd. Hôp. 49*:393–395.

Gainotti, G., Miceli, G., and Caltagirone, C. (1977). Constructional apraxia in left brain-damaged patients: a planning disorder? *Cortex 13*:109–118.

Galin, D. (1974). Implications for psychiatry of left and right cerebral specialization. *Arch. Gen. Psychiat. 31*:572–583.

Galin, D. (1977). Lateral specialization and psychiatric issues: speculations on development and the evolution of consciousness. *Ann. New York Acad. Sci. 299*:397–411.

Galin, D., Diamond, R., and Herron, J. (1977). Development of Crossed and Uncrossed Tactile Localization on the fingers. *Brain and Language 4*:588–590.

Gardner, H. and Zurif, E. (1975). Bee but not be: oral reading of single words in aphasia and alexia. *Neuropsychologia 13*:181–190.

Gazzaniga, M. S. (1966). Interhemispheric communication of visual learning. *Neuropsychologia 4*:183–189.

Gazzaniga, M. S. (1970). *Hhe Bisected Brain*. New York: Appleton.

Gazzaniga, M. S., Bogen, J. E., and Sperry, R. W. (1962). Some functional effects of sectioning the cerebral commissures in man. *Proc. Nat. Acad. Sci. 48*:1765–9.

Gazzaniga, M. S., Bogen, J. E., and Sperry, R. W. (1963). Laterality effects in somesthesis following cerebral commissurotomy in man. *Neuropsychologia 1*:209–215.

Gazzaniga, M. S., Bogen, J. E., and Sperry, R. W. (1965). Observations on visual perception after disconnexion of the cerebral hemispheres in man. *Brain 88*:221–236.

Gazzaniga, M. S., Bogen, J. E., and Sperry, R. W. (1967). Dyspraxia following division of the cerebral commissures. *Arch. Neurol. 16*:606–612.

Gazzaniga, M. S. and Freedman, H. (1973). Observations on visual processes after posterior callosal section. *Neurology 23*:1126–1130.

Gazzaniga, M. S. and Hillyard, S. A. (1971). Language and speech capacity of the right hemisphere. *Neuropsychologia 9*:273–280.

Gazzaniga, M. S., LeDoux, J. E., and Wilson, D. H. (1977). Language, praxis, and the right hemisphere: clues to some mechanisms of consciousness. *Neurology 27*:1144–1147.

Gazzaniga, M. S., Risse, G. L., Springer, S. P., Clark, E., and Wilson, D. H. (1975). Psychologic and neurologic consequences of partial and complete cerebral commissurotomy. *Neurology 25*:10–15.

Gazzaniga, M. S. and Sperry, R. W. (1967). Language after section of the cerebral commissures. *Brain 90*:131–148.

Geffen, G., Bradshaw, J., and Wallace, G. (1971). Interhemispheric effects on reaction time to verbal and non-verbal visual stimuli. *J. Exp. Psychol. 87*:415–422.

Geschwind, N. (1964). The development of the brain and the evolution of language, in *Monograph Series on Language and Linguistics*, Vol. 17, C. I. J. M. Stuart (ed). Washington: Georgetown Univ. Press.

Geschwind, N. (1965). Disconnexion syndromes in animals and man. *Brain 88*:237–294, 585–644.

Geschwind, N. (1970). The organization of language and the brain. *Science 170*:940–944.

Geschwind, N. (1974). *Selected Papers on Language and the Brain*. Boston: Reidel.

Geschwind, N. (1975). The apraxias: neural mechanisms of disorders of learned movement. *Am. Sci. 63*:188–195.

Geschwind, N. and Fusillo, M. (1966). Colour-naming defects in association with alexia. *Arch. Neurol. 15*:137–146.

Geschwind, N. and Kaplan, E. (1962). A human cerebral deconnection syndrome: a preliminary report. *Neurology 12*:675–685.

Glass, A., Butler, S. R., and Heffner, R. (1975). Asymmetries in the CNV elicited by verbal and non-verbal stimuli. *10th Int. Cong. Anat., Tokyo.*

Glickstein, M., Arora, H. A., and Sperry, R. W. (1963). Delayed-response performance following optic tract section, unilateral frontal lesion, and commissurotomy. *J. Comp. Physiol. Psychol. 56*:11–18.

Gloning, I., Gloning, K., Jellinger, K., and Quatember, R. (1970). A case of "prosopagnosia" with necropsy findings. *Neuropsychologia* 8:199–204.

Gloning, I., Gloning, K., Jellinger, K., and Tschabitscher, H. (1966). Zur dominanzfrage beim Syndrom: Reine wortblindheit-farbagnosie. *Neuropsychologia* 4:27–40.

Goldstein, K. (1953). Hugo Karl Liepmann, in *The Founders of Neurology*, W. Haymaker (ed). Springfield, Ill.: C. C. Thomas.

Goldstein, M., and Joynt, R. (1969). Long-term follow-up of a callosal-sectioned patient. *Arch. Neurol.* 20:96–102.

Goldstein, M. N., Joynt, R. J., and Goldblatt, D. (1971). Word blindness with intact central visual fields. *Neurology* 21:873–876.

Goldstein, M., Joynt, R., and Hartley, R. (1975). The long-term effects of callosal sectioning. *Arch. Neurol.* 32:52–53.

Gordon, H. W. (1973). *Verbal and Non-verbal Cerebral Processing in Man for Audition.* Thesis, California Institute of Technology.

Gordon, H. W. (1975). Comparison of ipsilateral and contralateral auditory pathways in callosum-sectioned patients by use of a response-time technique. *Neuropsychologia* 13:9–18.

Gordon, H. W., Bogen, J. E., and Sperry, R. W. (1971). Absence of deconnexion syndrome in two patients with partial section of the neocommissures. *Brain* 94:327–336.

Gordon, H. W. and Sperry, R. W. (1969). Lateralization of olfactory perception in the surgically separated hemispheres of man. *Neuropsychologia* 7:111–120.

Gott, P. S. and Saul, R. E. (1978). Agenesis of the corpus callosum: limits of functional compensation. *Neurology* 28:1272–1279.

Greenblatt, S. (1973). Alexia without agraphia or hemianopsia. *Brain* 96:307–316.

Greenblatt, S. H. (1976). Subangular alexia without agraphia or hemianopsia. *Brain and Language* 3:229–245.

Greenblatt, S. H. (1977). Neurosurgery and the anatomy of reading: a practical review. *Neurosurg.* 1:6–15.

Greenwood, P., Wilson, D. H., and Gazzaniga, M. S. (1977). Dream report following commissurotomy. *Cortex* 13:311–316.

Haaland, K. Y., Cleeland, C. S., and Carr, D. (1977). Motor performance after unilateral hemisphere damage in patients with tumors. *Arch. Neurol.* 34:556–559.

Hamilton, C. R. (1977). Investigations of perceptual and mnemonic lateralization in monkeys, in *Lateralization in the Nervous System*, S. Harnad et al. New York: Academic Press.

Harnad, S., Doty, R. W., Goldstein, L., Jaynes, J., and Krauthamer, G. (1977). *Lateralization in the Nervous System.* New York: Academic Press.

Hécaen, H. (1969). Aphasic, apraxic and agnosic syndromes in right and left hemisphere lesions. *Handbook Clin. Neurol.* 4:291–311.

Hécaen, H. and Ajuriaguerra, J. (1964). *Left Handedness.* New York: Grune & Stratton.

Hécaen, H. and Angelergues, R. (1962). Agnosia for faces (prosopagnosia). *Arch. Neurol.* 7:92–100.

Hécaen, H. and Gimeno Alava, A. (1960). L'apraxie idéo-motrice unilatérale gauche. *Rev. Neurol.* 102:648–653.

Hécaen, H. and Gruner, J. (1975). Alexie "pure" avec intégrité du corps calleux, in *Les Syndromes de Disconnexion Calleuse Chez l'Homme,* F. Michel and B. Schott (eds). Lyon: Hospital Neurologique.

Hécaen, H. and Kremin, H. (1976). Neurolinguistic research on reading disorders resulting from left hemisphere lesions: aphasic and "pure" alexias, in *Studies in Neurolinguistics* H. Whitaker and H. A. Whitaker (eds). New York: Academic Press.

Heilman, K. M., Coyle, J. M., Gonyea, E. F., and Geschwind, N. (1973). Apraxia and agraphia in a left-hander. *Brain* 96:21–28.

Heilman, K. M., Safran, A., and Geschwind, N. (1971). Closed head trauma and aphasia. *J. Neurol. Neurosurg. Psychiat.* 34:265–269.

Heilman, K. M. and Watson, R. T. (1977). The neglect syndrome—a unilateral defect of the orienting response, in *Lateralization in the Nervous System,* S. Harnad et al. New York: Academic Press.

Hilliard, R. D. (1973). Hemispheric laterality effects on a facial recognition task in normal subjects. *Cortex* 9:246–259.

Hirose, G., Kin, T., and Murakami, E. (1977). Alexia without agraphia associated with right occipital lesion. *J. Neurol. Neurosurg. Psychiat.* 40: 225–227.

Hoppe, K. D. (1977). Split brains and psychoanalysis. *Psychoanalytic Quart.* 46:220–244.

Hoppe, K. and Bogen, J. E. (1977). Alexithymia in twelve commissurotomized patients. *Psychother. Psychosom.* 28:148–155.

Horel, J. A. and Keating, E. G. (1969). Partial Kluver-Bucy syndrome produced by cortical disconnection. *Brain Res.* 16:281–284.

Horel, J. A. and Keating, E. G. (1972). Recovery from a partial Kluver-Bucy syndrome in the monkey produced by disconnection. *J. Comp. Physiol. Psychol.* 79:105–114.

Iro, M., Yashiki, K., and Hirata, T. (1972). Agenesis of the corpus callosum in man. *Acta Anat. Nippon* 47:391–402.

Iwata, M., Sugishita, M., Toyokura, Y., Yamada, R., and Yoshioka, M. (1974). Étude sur le syndrome de disconnexion visuo-linguale apres la transection du splenium du corps calleux. *J. Neurol. Sci.* 23:421–432.

Jeeves, M. A. (1965). Agenesis of the corpus callosum—physiopathological and clinical aspects. *Proc. Austr. Assoc. Neurol.* 3:41–48.

Jeeves, M. A. (1965). Psychological studies of three cases of congenital agenesis of the corpus callosum, in *Functions of the Corpus Callosum,* E. G. Ettlinger (ed). London: Churchill.

Jeeves, M. A. and Wilson, A. F. (1969). Tactile transfer and neonatal callosal section in the cat. *Psychon. Sci.* 16 (5):235–237.

Joynt, R. J. (1974). The corpus callosum: history of thought regarding its function, in *Hemispheric Disconnection and Cerebral Function,* M. Kinsbourne and W. L. Smith (eds). Springfield, Ill.: C. C. Thomas.

Kimura, D. (1967). Functional asymmetry of the brain in dichotic listening. *Cortex 3*:163–178.

Kimura, D. and Archibald, Y. (1974). Motor functions of the left hemisphere. *Brain 97*:337–350.

Kimura, D., Battison, R., and Lubert, B. (1976). Impairment of nonlinguistic hand movements in a deaf aphasic. *Brain and Language 3*:566–571.

Kinsbourne, M. (1971). The minor cerebral hemisphere as a source of aphasic speech. *Arch. Neurol. 25*:302–306.

Kinsbourne, M. (1975). Minor hemisphere language and cerebral maturation, in *Foundations of Language Dev.,* H. Lenneberg and E. Lenneberg (eds). New York: Academic Press.

Kinsbourne, M. and Fisher, M. (1971). Latency of uncrossed and of crossed reaction in callosal agenesis. *Neuropsychologia 9*:471–473.

Kinsbourne, M. and Smith, W. L. (1974). *Hemispheric Disconnection and Cerebral Function.* Springfield, Ill.: C. C. Thomas.

Kirschbaum, W. R. (1947). Agenesis of the corpus callosum and associated malformations. *J. Neuropath. Exp. Neurol. 6*:78–94.

Klein, R. and Ingram, I. M. (1958). Functional disorganization of the left limbs in a tumour of the corpus callosum infiltrating the hemispheres. *J. Mental Sci. 104*:732–742.

Krashen, S. D. (1976). Cerebral asymmetry, in *Studies in Neurolinguistics,* H. Whitaker and H. A. Whitaker (eds). New York: Academic Press.

Kohn, B. and Dennis, M. (1974). Patterns of hemispheric specialization after hemidecortication for infantile hemiplegia, in *Hemispheric Disconnection and Cerebral Function,* M. Kinsbourne and W. L. Smith (eds). Springfield, Ill.: C. C. Thomas.

Kuhn, T. S. (1962). *The Structure of Scientific Revolutions.* Chicago: Univ. Chicago Press.

Kumar, S. (1977). Short-term memory for a non-verbal tactual task after cerebral commissurotomy. *Cortex 13*:55–61.

Lansdell, H. (1968). Effect of extent of temporal lobe ablations on two lateralized deficits. *Physiol. Behav. 3*:271–273.

Le Beau, J. (1943). Sur la chirurgie des tumeurs du corps calleux. *Union Méd. Canada 72*:1365–1381.

Lechevalier, B., Andersson, J. C., Morin, P., and Poilpre, E. (1975). Syndrome de disconnexion calleuse avec trouble de la coordination visuomotrice croisée (phénomène d'évitement croisé) au cours d'une maladie de Marchiafava-Bignami (cas anatomoclinique), in *Les Syndromes de Disconnexion Calleuse Chez l'Homme,* F. Michel and B. Schott (eds). Lyon: Hospital Neurologique.

LeDoux, J. E., Wilson, D. H., and Gazzaniga, M. S. (1977). A divided mind:

observations on the conscious properties of the separated hemispheres. *Ann. Neurol.* 2:417–421.

Lehmann, H. J. and Lampe, H. (1970). Observations on the interhemispheric transmission of information in 9 patients with corpus callosum defect. *Europ. Neurol.* 4:129–147.

Levin, H. S., Hamsher, K. S., and Benton, A. L. (1975). A short form of the test of facial recognition for clinical use. *J. Psychol.* 91:223–228.

Levy, J. (1974). Cerebral asymmetries as manifested in split-brain man, in *Hemispheric Disconnection and Cerebral Function*, M. Kinsbourne and W. L. Smith (eds). Springfield, Ill.: C. C. Thomas.

Levy, J., Nebes, R. D., and Sperry, R. W. (1971). Expressive language in the surgically separated minor hemisphere. *Cortex* 7:49–58.

Levy, J., Trevarthen, C., and Sperry, R. W. (1972). Perception of bilateral chimeric figures following hemispheric deconnexion. *Brain* 95:61–78.

Lévy-Valensi, J. (1910). *Le Corps Calleux* (Paris Theses 448). Paris: G. Steinheil.

Lhermitte, F. and Beauvois, M. F. (1973). A visual-speech disconnexion syndrome. *Brain* 96:695–714.

Lhermitte, F., Chain, F., and Chedru, F. (1975). Syndrome de déconnexion interhémisphérique: étude des performances visuelles, in *Les Syndromes de Disconnexion Calleuse Chez l'Homme*, F. Michel and B. Schott (eds). Lyon: Colloque International.

Lhermitte, F., Chain, F., Chedru, F., and Penet, C. (1974). Syndrome de déconnexion interhémisphérique. Étude des performances visuelles. *Rev. Neurol.* 130:247–250.

Lhermitte, F., Chain, F., Chedru, F., and Penet, C. (1976). A study of visual processes in a case of interhemispheric disconnexion. *J. Neurol. Sci.* 28:317–330.

Lhermitte, F., Chain, F., Escourolle, R., Ducarne, B., and Pillon, B. (1972). Étude anatomoclinique d'un cas de prosopagnosie. *Rev. Neurol.* 126: 329–346.

Lhermitte, F., Marteau, R., Serdaru, M., and Chedru, F. (1977). Signs of interhemispheric disconnection in Marchiafava-Bignami disease. *Arch. Neurol.* 34:254.

Liepmann, H. (1900). Das Krankheitsbild der Apraxie ("motorische Asymbolie") auf Grund eines Falles von einseitiger Apraxie. *Monatsschr. f. Psychiat. u. Neurol.* 8:182–197.

Leipmann, H. (1905, 1906). Der Weitêre Krankheitsverlauf bei dem einseitig Apraktischen und der Gehirnbefund auf Grund von Serienschnitten. *Monatsschr. f. Psychiat. u. Neurol.* 17:289–311; 19:217–243.

Liepmann, H. and Maas, O. (1908). Fall von linksseitiger Agraphie und Apraxie bei rechtsseitiger Lähmung. *J. f. Psychol. u. Neurol.* 10:214–227.

Loeser, J. E. and Alvord, E. C. (1968). Agenesis of the corpus callosum. *Brain* 91:553–570.

Maspes, P. E. (1948). Le syndrome expérimental chez l'homme de la section du splénium du corps calleux. Alexie visuelle pure hémianopsique. *Rev. Neurol.* 80:100–113.

Mateer, C. and Kimura, D. (1977). Impairment of nonverbal oral movements in aphasia. *Brain and Language* 4:262–276.

Meadows, J. C. (1974). The anatomical basis of prosopagnosia. *J. Neurol. Neurosurg. Psychiat.* 37:489–501.

Michel, F. and Schott, B. (eds) (1975). *Les Syndromes de Disconnexion Calleuse Chez l'Homme.* Lyon: Hospital Neurologique.

Milner, B. (ed) (1975). *Hemispheric Specialization and Interaction.* Cambridge: MIT Press.

Milner, B. (1968). Visual recognition and recall after right temporal-lobe excision in man. *Neuropsychologia* 6:199–209.

Milner, B. and Taylor, L. (1972). Right-hemisphere superiority in tactile pattern-recognition after cerebral commissurotomy: evidence for nonverbal memory. *Neuropsychologia* 10:1–15.

Milner, B., Taylor, L., and Sperry, R. W. (1968). Lateralized suppression of dichotically presented digits after commissural section in man. *Science* 161:184–186.

Mingazzini, G. (1922). *Der Balken.* Berlin: Springer.

Moscovitch, M. (1976). On the representation of language in the right hemisphere of right-handed people. *Brain and Language* 3:47–71 and 3:590–599.

Myers, R. E. (1956). Function of corpus callosum in interocular transfer. *Brain* 79:358–363.

Myers, R. E. and Sperry, R. W. (1953). Interocular transfer of a visual form discrimination habit in cats after section of the optic chiasma and corpus callosum. *Anat. Record* 115:351–352.

Myers, R. E. and Sperry, R. W. (1958). Interhemispheric communication through the corpus callosum. Mnemonic carry-over between the hemispheres. *Arch. Neurol. Psychiat.* 80:298–303.

Nebes, R. D. (1974). Hemispheric specialization in commissurotomized man. *Psychol. Bull.* 81:1–14.

Newcombe, F. and Russell, W. R. (1969). Dissociated visual perceptual and spatial deficits in focal lesions of the right hemisphere. *J. Neurol. Neurosurg. Psychiat.* 32:73–81.

Nielsen, J. M. (1936). *Agnosia, apraxia, aphasia. Their value in cerebral localization.* New York: Hoeber.

Ozgur, M. H., Johnson, T., Smith, A., and Bogen, J. E. (1977). Transcallosal approach to third ventricle tumor: case report. *Bull. Los Angeles Neurol. Soc.* 42:57–62.

Pandya, D. N. (1975). Interhemispheric connections in primates, in *Les Syndromes de Disconnexion Calleuse Chez l'Homme,* F. Michel and B. Schott (eds). Lyon: Hospital Neurologique.

Paterson, A. and Zangwill, O. L. (1944). Disorders of visual space perception associated with lesions of the right cerebral hemisphere. *Brain 67*: 331–358.

Pevzner, S., Bornstein, B., and Loewenthal, M. (1962). Prosopagnosia. *J. Neurol. Neurosurg. Psychiat. 25*:336–338.

Pirozzolo, F. J. & Rayner, K. (1977). Hemispheric specialization in reading and word recognition. *Brain and Language 4*:248–261.

Preilowski, B. F. B. (1972). Possible contribution of the anterior forebrain commissures to bilateral motor coordination. *Neuropsychologia 10*: 267–277.

Raymond, F., Lejonne, P., and Lhermitte, J. (1906). Tumeurs du corps calleux. *Encéphale. 1*:533–565.

Reeves, D. L. and Courville, C. B. (1938). Complete agenesis of the corpus callosum. *Bull. Los Angeles Neurol. Soc. 3*:169–181.

Reynolds, D. McQ. and Jeeves, M. A. (1977). Further studies of tactile perception and motor coordination in agenesis of the corpus callosum. *Cortex 13*:257–272.

Risse, G. L., LeDoux, J., Springer, S. P., Wilson, D. H., and Gazzaniga, M. S. (1978). The anterior commissure in man: functional variation in a multisensory system. *Neuropsychologia 16*:23–31.

Rizzolatti, G. and Buchtel, H. A. (1977). Hemispheric superiority in reaction time to faces: a sex difference. *Cortex 13*:300–305.

Rizzolatti, G., Umiltà, C., and Berlucchi, G. (1971). Opposite superiorities of the right and left cerebral hemispheres in discriminative reaction time to physiognomical and alphabetical material. *Brain 94*:431–442.

Rogers, L., TenHouten, W., Kaplan, C. D., and Gardiner, M. (1977). Hemispheric specialization of language: an EEG study of bilingual Hopi Indian Children. *Internat. J. Neurosci. 8*:1–6.

Rondot, P. and Tzavaras, A. (1969). La prosopagnosie, après vingt années d'études cliniques et neuropsychologiques. *J. Psychologie 2*:133–165.

Rudel, R. G. (1978). Neuroplasticity: implications for development and education, in *Education and the Brain*, J. Chall and A. Mersky (eds). New York: 77th NSSE Yearbook.

Sadowsky, C. and Reeves, A. G. (1975). Agenesis of the corpus callosum with hypothermia. *Arch. Neurol. 32*:744–776.

Sasanuma, S., Itoh, M., Mori, K., and Kobayashi, Y. (1977). Tachistoscopic recognition of kana and kanji words. *Neuropsychologia 15*:547–553.

Saul, R. E. (1969). Relearning following cerebral deconnection. A case report. *Excerpta Medica 193*:779.

Saul, R. and Sperry, R. W. (1968). Absence of commissurotomy symptoms with agenesis of the corpus callosum. *Neurology 18*:307.

Schott, B., Michel, F., Michel, D., and Dumas, R. (1969). Apraxie idéomotrice unilatérale gauche avec main gauche anomique: syndrome de déconnexion calleuse? *Rev. Neurol. 12*:359–365.

Schott, B., Trillet, M., Michel, F., and Tommasi, M. (1974). Le syndrome de disconnexion calleuse chez l'ambidextre et le gaucher, in *Les Syn-*

dromes de Disconnexion Calleuse Chez l'Homme, F. Michel and B. Schott (eds). Lyon: Colloque International.

Sechzer, J. A., Folstein, S. E., Geiger, E. H., and Mervis, R. F. (1976). The split-brain neonate: a surgical method for corpus callosum section in newborn kittens. *Dev. Psychobiol. 9*:377–388.

Selnes, O. A. (1974). The corpus callosum: some anatomical and functional considerations with special reference to language. *Brain and Language 1*:111–139.

Selnes, O. A. (1976). A note "On the representation of language in the right hemisphere of right-handed people." *Brain and Language 3*:583–589.

Segal, M. (1935). Agenesis of the corpus callosum in man. *S. Afr. J. Med. Sci. 1*:65–74.

Sheremata, W. A., Deonna, T. W., and Romanul, F. C. A. (1973). Agenesis of the corpus callosum and interhemispheric transfer of information. *Neurology 23*:390.

Shoumura, K., Ando, T., and Kato, K. (1975). Structural organization of "callosal" OBg in human corpus callosum agenesis. *Brain Res. 93*:241–252.

Slager, U. T., Kelly, A. B., and Wagner, J. A. (1957). Congenital absence of the corpus callosum. *New Engl. J. Med. 256*:1171–1176.

Smith, A. (1966). Speech and other functions after left (dominant) hemispherectomy. *J. Neurol. Neurosurg. Psychiat. 29*:467–471.

Smith, A. (1974). Dominant and nondominant hemispherectomy, in *Hemispheric Disconnection and Cerebral Function,* M. Kinsbourne and W. L. Smith (eds). Springfield, Ill.: C. C. Thomas.

Smith, A. and Sugar, O. (1975). Development of above-normal language and intelligence 21 years after left hemispherectomy. *Neurology 25*:813–818.

Sparks, R. and Geschwind, N. (1968). Dichotic listening in man after section of neocortical commissures. *Cortex 4*:3–16.

Sperry, R. W. (1961). Cerebral organization and behavior. *Science 133*:1749–1757.

Sperry, R. W. (1970). Perception in the absence of the neocortical commissures. *Assoc. Res. Nervous Mental Dis. 48*:123–138.

Sperry, R. W. (1974). Lateral specialization in the surgically separated hemispheres, in F. O. Schmitt and F. G. Worden (eds), *Neuroscience 3rd Study Prog.,* Cambridge: MIT Press.

Sperry, R. W. and Gazzaniga, M. S. (1967). Language following surgical disconnection of the hemispheres. *Brain Mechanisms Underlying Speech and Language.* New York: Grune & Stratton.

Sperry, R. W., Gazzaniga, M. S., and Bogen, J. E. (1969). Interhemispheric relationships: The neocortical commissures; syndromes of hemisphere disconnection. *Handbook Clin. Neurol. 4*:273–290.

Springer, S. P. and Gazzaniga, M. S. (1975). Dichotic testing of partial and complete split-brain subjects. *Neuropsychologia 13*:341–346.

Stamm, J. S., Rosen, S. C., and Gadotti, A. (1977). Lateralization of functions in the monkey's frontal cortex, in *Lateralization in the Nervous System,* S. Harnad, R. W. Doty, L. Goldstein, J. Jaynes, and G. Krauthamer (eds). New York: Academic Press.

Sullivan, M. C. and Hamilton, C. R. (1973). Interocular transfer of reversed and non-reversed discriminations via the anterior commissure in monkeys. *Physiol. Behav. 10*:355–359.

Sullivan, M. C. and Hamilton, C. R. (1973). Memory establishment via the anterior commissure in monkeys. *Physiol. Behav. 11*:873–879.

Sweet, W. H. (1945). Seeping intracranial aneurysm simulating neoplasm. Syndrome of the corpus callosum. *Arch. Neurol. Psychiat. 45*:86–104.

Tomasch, J. (1954). Size, distribution, and number of fibres in the human corpus callosum. *Anat. Record 119*:7–19.

Tomasch, J. (1957). A quantitative analysis of the human anterior commissure. *Acta Anat. 30*:902–906.

Towns, L. C., Giolli, R. A., and Haste, D. A. (1977). Corticocortical fiber connections of the rabbit visual cortex: a fiber degeneration study. *J. Comp. Neurol. 173*:537–560.

Trescher, H. H. and Ford, F. R. (1937). Colloid cyst of the third ventricle. Report of a case; operative removal with section of posterior half of corpus callosum. *Arch. Neurol. Psychiat. 37*:959–973.

Trevarthen, C. (1974). Functional relations of disconnected hemispheres with the brain stem, and with each other: monkey and man, in *Hemispheric Disconnection and Cerebral Function,* M. Kinsbourne and W. L. Smith (eds). Springfield, Ill.: C. C. Thomas.

Trevarthen, C. (1965). Motor responses in split-brain animals, in *Functions of the Corpus Callosum,* E. G. Ettlinger (ed). London: Churchill.

Trevarthen, C. and Sperry, R. W. (1973). Perceptual unity of the ambient visual field in human commissurotomy patients. *Brain 96*:547–570.

Tzavaras, A., Hécaen, H., and Le Bras, H. (1971). Troubles de la réconnaissance du visage humain et latéralisation hémisphérique lésionnelle chez les sujets gauchers. *Neuropsychologia, 9*:475–477.

Unterharnscheidt, F., Jalnik, D., and Gott, H. (1968). Der balkenmangel. *Monographien a. d. gesamtgebiete Neurol. Psychiat. 128*:1–232. New York: Springer.

Vilkki, J. and Laitinen, L. V. (1974). Differential effects of left and right ventrolateral thalamotomy on receptive and expressive verbal performances and face-matching. *Neuropsychologia 12*:11–19.

Vincent, F. M., Sadowsky, C. H., Saunders, R. L., and Reeves, A. G. (1977). Alexia without agraphia, hemianopia, or color-naming defect: a disconnection syndrome. *Neurology 27*:689–691.

Warren, J. M. and Nonneman, A. J. (1976). The search for cerebral dominance in monkeys. *Ann. N.Y. Acad. Sci. 280*:732–744.

Warrington, E. K. and James, M. (1967). An experimental investigation of facial recognition in patients with unilateral cerebral lesions. *Cortex* 3:317–326.

Warrington, E. K., James, M., and Kinsbourne, M. (1966). Drawing disability in relation to laterality of cerebral lesion. *Brain* 89:53–82.

Wechsler, A. F. (1972). Transient left hemialexia. *Neurology* 22:628–633.

Wechsler, A. F., Weinstein, E. A., and Antin, S. P. (1972). Alexia without agraphia. *Bull. Los Angeles Neurol. Soc.* 37:1–11.

Weinstein, E. A. and Friedland, R. P. (1977). *Hemi-Inattention and Hemisphere Specialization*. New York: Raven Press.

Whiteley, A. M. and Warrington, E. K. (1977). Prosopagnosia: a clinical, psychological, and anatomical study of three patients. *J. Neurol. Neurosurg. Psychiat.* 40:395–403.

Wiener, N. (1948). *Cybernetics*. New York: Technology Press.

Wilson, D. H., Culver, C., Waddington, M., and Gazzaniga, M. (1975). Disconnection of the cerebral hemispheres. *Neurology* 25:1149–1153.

Wilson, D. H., Reeves, A., Gazzaniga, M., and Culver, C. (1977). Cerebral commissurotomy for control of intractable seizures. *Neurology* 27:708–715.

Wilson, S. A. K. (1908). A contribution to the study of apraxia. *Brain* 31:164–216.

Winner, E. and Gardner, H. (1977). The comprehension of metaphor in brain-damaged patients. *Brain* 100:717–729.

Zaidel, E. (1973). Linguistic competence and related functions in the right hemisphere of man following cerebral commissurotomy and hemispherectomy. Ph.D. thesis, California Institute of Technology. *Dissertation Abstracts International* 34:2350B (University Microfilms #73-26, 481).

Zaidel, E. (1976). Language, dichotic listening, and the disconnected hemispheres, in *BIS Conference Report #42*, D. O. Walter, L. Rogers, and J. M. Finzi-Fried (eds). Los Angeles: University of California.

Zaidel, E. (1977). Unilateral auditory language comprehension on the Token Test following cerebral commissurotomy and hemispherectomy. *Neuropsychologia* 15:1–18.

Zaidel, E. (1978a). Lexical organization in the right hemisphere, in *Cerebral Correlates of Conscious Experience*, P. Buser and A. Rougeul-Buser (eds). Amsterdam: Elsevier.

Zaidel, E. 1978b). Concepts of cerebral dominance in the split-brain, in *Cerebral Correlates of Conscious Experience*, P. Buser and A. Rougeul-Buser (eds). Amsterdam: Elsevier.

Zaidel, D. and Sperry, R. W. (1977). Some long-term motor effects of cerebral commissurotomy in man. *Neuropsychologia* 15:193–204.

Zurif, E. B. and Ramier, A. M. (1972). Some effects of unilateral brain damage on the perception of dichotically presented phoneme sequences and digits. *Neuropsychologia* 10:103–110.

12

The Frontal Lobes

ANTONIO DAMASIO

METHODOLOGICAL CONSIDERATIONS

Dysfunction of the frontal lobes is reflected in a number of relatively specific behavioral manifestations, in the sense that dysfunction elsewhere in the brain generally does not produce them. However, the notion that frontal-lobe lesions are associated with a single characteristic picture (the "frontal-lobe syndrome") is not supported either by clinical experience or by animal experiments. All the manifestations need not be present at the same time or to the same degree and, in fact, they tend to appear in various combinations. Yet a survey of the literature on the subject shows that authors have traditionally insisted on the concept of a "frontal-lobe syndrome" and have regarded the frontal lobes as a morphological unit.

The frontal lobes make up roughly half of the cerebral cortex of man and have diverse connections with other areas of the cortex, with the subcortical limbic system, and with the basal ganglia. But this has not deterred researchers who study the overall behavioral effects of large lesions of the frontal lobes from treating such a vast morphological arrangement as a whole. This disregard for anatomical subunits, even when the concept of frontal lobe is restricted to the prefrontal areas, has not helped to unravel the so-called "riddle

360

of the frontal lobe." As a consequence, attempts to shape significant syndromes out of the diverse manifestations of frontal-lobe dysfunction have been somewhat unsatisfactory. Although we have gone beyond the frontal lobe as a whole and established some useful clinicoanatomical correlations, it is clear that they are still imprecise.

Critical review of clinical data shows that the location of lesions are crucial for the determination of frontal-lobe syndromes. Side of lesion, for instance, is quite important, as there is evidence that some lesions of the dominant frontal lobe interfere with verbal behavior more so than do corresponding nondominant lesions. Lack of fluency, loss of quality of syntactic structuring, and of the drive to communicate verbally may be indexes of lateralized dominant involvement. Certain emotional changes may also be related to the left–right dichotomy, with nondominant frontal lesions presenting more significant alterations. On the other hand, there is evidence that bilateral lesions present a different clinical picture both quantitatively and qualitatively. The site of damage within a frontal lobe is also relevant to the production of a given syndrome. This regional effect may determine distinctive clinical configurations and allow the prediction of whether the involvement is predominantly mesial or dorsolateral. It is possible that at least one broad locus of lesion, inferior orbital, may be associated with a separate clinical picture.

Analysis of the behavioral effects of different loci of damage must also take account of the nature of the lesion. The effects of infarction of the mesial portion of a frontal lobe may differ from gliomatous involvement of the connections of the same area, and hence the behavioral effects of one cannot be equated with those of the other. The discrepancies arising from such comparisons need not be treated as another riddle in the frontal-lobe mystery. As in the case of any lesion of the CNS, the rate of development of damage is a vital factor.

Depth of lesion is also an important variable, probably as much so as surface extent of damage. Many signs of frontal-lobe dysfunction seem to be a consequence of severed subcortical connections, and a deep lesion has a better chance of destroying linking pathways.

The time elapsed after a lesion has fully developed is still another factor which influences the clinical picture. Recovery is more likely with frontal lesions than with lesions in the posterior sensory cortex, but the degree of recovery will be different according to the time at which the patient is evaluated. Often a patient with severe symptomatology will experience a remarkable remission within a period of weeks.

Another temporal factor is the age at which the dysfunction begins. There is evidence that lesions starting in childhood or adolescence produce different effects from those starting in adulthood, particularly if they are extensive and bilateral. Level of education and acculturation are probably closely related to the age factor. Characteristics of the premorbid personality are almost certainly of importance.

If these factors are not taken into account, it will not be possible to make an adequate clinical evaluation of patients, and clinical research may produce paradoxical results. But even if all the rules are observed, there are other problems associated with the evaluation and investigation of the frontal-lobe patient. These are the consequence of the particular mode of expression of frontal-lobe dysfunction, be it related to mesial, dorsolateral, or infraorbital lesions, in the right or the left hemispheres. Signs and symptoms of frontal-lobe dysfunction do not lend themselves easily to quantitative measurement. Unlike the impairment of the elementary instrumental abilities, which is the hallmark of lesions in the rolandic cortex or in the postrolandic sensory cortex, frontal-lobe dysfunction is more readily described as changes in quality. In this, it shares the shortcomings of measuring dysfunction of the anterior and mesial temporal cortex and of the elusive structures of the subcortical limbic brain and the basal ganglia. The contradiction between the claim that the frontal lobes control the highest forms of behavior in man and the claim that intelligence test performance is not affected after extensive frontal damage is a manifestation of the problem of what to measure and how. Both claims are correct since they stem from types of analysis addressing different forms of frontal defect. Patients with frontal-lobe dysfunction are unlikely to show quantifiable impairments when language and allied abilities are objectively assessed. But that hardly guarantees that the patient's personality has not been damaged. Even objective manifestations of frontal-lobe dysfunction such as bradykinesia or release of primitive reflexes challenge quantification. As to the most telling signs, they correspond to often subtle changes in alertness, affect, emotional response, and appropriate control of regulatory behaviors. These disturbances have so far eluded direct measurement. The same can be said about impairment of high-level problem solving, the result of which is the inability to plan one's actions appropriately. This defect, which is characteristic of rather extensive and bilateral frontal-lobe dysfunction, places these syndromes close to some psychiatric entities, although the distinctions remain clear.

This reviewer knows of no study which has met the challenge of measurement or has successfully avoided the methodological pitfalls indicated above. As a consequence, it is probably wise to consider the diagnosis and classification of frontal-lobe syndromes to be limited, for the time being, by lack of precise knowledge.

ANATOMY

One of the most promising lines of research in the problem is the study of neuroanatomy both by itself and within the framework of neurophysiological investigation. Knowledge of anatomy may well prove to be the vital step in the understanding of the roles of the frontal lobe. Since nomenclature used to describe the morphology of the frontal lobe is generally confusing, a brief review is probably useful at this point.

Frontal cortex

Inspection of the external surface of the lobe reveals three important natural borders, the rolandic sulcus, the sylvian fissure, and the corpus callosum; and three large expansions of cortex, in the lateral convexity, in the mesial flat aspect which faces the opposite lobe, and in the inferior concave aspect which corresponds to the roof of the orbit. Traditional anatomy has divided this cortex in the following principal regions: the precentral cortex, the premotor cortex, the prefrontal cortex, and the limbic cortex.

The designation of precentral cortex corresponds to the long gyrus immediately anterior to the rolandic fissure and which also forms its anterior bank and depth. This area continues into the mesial portion of the lobe, ending in the cingulate sulcus. Histologically it is a region of agranular cortex and its function as the principal motor area is well known. The presence of *Betz* cells is a distinguishing feature. In Brodmann's map it corresponds to field 4 (for Brodmann's map, see Fig. 1-1, p. 6). Anterior and parallel to this region lies the premotor cortex which in man corresponds to the posterior portion of the three horizontally placed frontal gyri. Histologically this is transitional cortex, the function of which is closely related to motor activity. For the most part, this is field 6 in Brodmann's map, but the lower region, which comprises a portion of the third (inferior) frontal gyrus, is referenced as field 44 and presumably corresponds to Broca's area. Field 45 is closely connected to 44, both anatomically and, in all probability, functionally. In the mesial prolongation of this zone, which also terminates in the cingulate sulcus, lies the supplementary motor area. Anterior to both the precentral and premotor regions lies the prefrontal cortex which makes up most of the frontal cortex and encompasses the pole of the lobe. Macroscopically, three major aspects may be distinguished: Mesial, dorsolateral, and orbital. Histologically this is granular cortex which corresponds in Brodmann's map to fields 8, 9, 10, 11, 12, 13, 47, 46, 32, and part of 24. This is the enigmatic area that most authors have in mind when they speak of the frontal lobe in relation to behavior. Little is known about the contribution of each of these separate areas, with the exception of field 8, the so-called eye-field, which presumably serves a monitoring function in relation to eye and head involvements. Finally, the cingulate gyrus, limited by the cingulate sulcus above and the corpus callosum below, forms the frontal surface of the limbic system. It corresponds to most of field 24 of Brodmann.

Frontal-lobe connections

Understanding the prefrontal lobe depends upon knowledge of the company it keeps; that is, its afferent and efferent connections. Some of these connections are with other neocortical structures, mainly from and to association areas in the temporal, parietal, and occipital lobes, including special areas of multimodal convergence. The same may be said of the premotor region by means of which a motor cortical link may be achieved. There are significant connections with the limbic cortex of the cingulate gyrus and with limbic

and motor subcortical structures. Some projections seem to be uni-
directional, such as those to the caudate and putamen. Some seem
to be bidirectional such as those with the nucleus medialis dorsalis
of the thalamus. The latter is a particularly important connection,
so much so that some authors have defined the prefrontal cortex as
that region which is coextensive with projections from the nucleus
medialis dorsalis. The arrangement of projections is quite specific:
the orbital aspect is linked with the pars magnocellularis, the dorsolateral cortex with the pars parvocellularis. Other major subcortical
connections are with the hippocampus by way of the cingulate and
hippocampal gyri, with the amygdala by way of the uncinate fasciculus, and with the hypothalamus, the septum, and the mesencephalon by direct pathways.

The prefrontal cortex thus receives input (by more than one
channel) from the sensory regions of the cortex, it is closely woven
with the limbic system, and it can affect the motor system in more
than one way. The functionally central position of the frontal lobe
can be made more clear by a brief review of its efferent and afferent
connections in nonhuman primates. The frontal lobe of the monkey
is roughly comparable to that of man in shape, limits, connections,
and cytoarchitecture. Important differences, other than size, are apparent in the dorsolateral aspect where the three horizontally oriented gyri are substituted by two fields placed in a dorsal and ventral position in relation to a single sulcus, the principalis (see
Figure 1-2, p. 17). One other major sulcus, the arcuate, arch-shaped
and more-or-less vertically oriented, represents the seam between
prefrontal and premotor cortex. It is in this transition zone, particularly in the rostral bank of the sulcus, that Brodmann's field 8
is located. Sources used in the following description of subcortical
and cortical projections include: Ward and McCulloch, 1947; Bailey
and Von Bonin, 1951; Pribram and MacLean, 1953; Pribram, Chow
and Semmes, 1953; Whitlock and Nauta, 1956; Nauta, 1962; Crosby,
Humphrey, and Lauer, 1962; Nauta, 1964; Akert, 1964; De Vito
and Smith, 1964; Kuypers, Szwarcbart, and Mishkin, 1965; Powell,
Cowan, and Raisman, 1965; Valverde, 1965; Johnson, Rosvold, and
Mishkin, 1968; Nauta and Haymaker, 1969; Pandya and Vignolo,
1971; Pandya, Dye, and Butters, 1971; Kievit and Kuypers, 1974;
Chavis and Pandya, 1976; and Rosene, Mesulam, and Van Hoesen,
1976; Yeterian and Van Hoesen, 1977; Goldman and Nauta, 1977.

SUBCORTICAL CONNECTIONS

Projections from the hypothalamus. Direct projections from the hypothalamus have not been as easy to identify as the ones in the opposite direction, which may possibly reflect a different functional significance. At any rate, there is some evidence that there are such projections to several regions above and below the arcuate sulcus and to the rostral part of the principal sulcus. These projections may be parallel to the monoaminergic projections arising in the mesencephalic tegmentum, and may indeed be interwoven with them, since the latter are known to travel in the lateral hypothalamic region and possibly articulate there.

Projections from the amygdala and the hippocampus. There are projections from the amygdala to the orbital cortex, particularly in its most posterior and medial region. But the amygdala also projects to the mesial aspect of the frontal lobe, particularly into area FL, which includes the gyrus rectus and the subcallosal portion of Brodmann's area 24. The amygdala (like the hippocampus) projects to areas of the diencephalon and mesencephalon to which the prefrontal lobe itself strongly projects.

Projections from the thalamus. The afferent projections from the thalamus mostly originate in the regions where the efferent projections from the prefrontal cortex terminate, that is, in both the medial and lateral aspects of the mediodorsal nucleus. But there are also important projections from intralaminar nuclei. The medial thalamus thus appears as a transforming station for inputs from the prefrontal regions. In addition, direct and indirect relationships with the activating system are achieved by means of projections to and from the intralaminar nuclei which are also known to be distributed to the specific thalamic nuclei. Projections of the medial pulvinar to area 8 have also been described.

Projections to amygdala and hippocampus. These arise mostly from the orbital aspect and partly from the inferior ventral dorsolateral aspect and travel in the uncinate fasciculus. Some fibers may go directly to the amygdala, although most go to rostral temporal cortex which in turn projects to the amygdala. Projection to the hippocampus is indirect via the limbic cortex of the cingulate and hippocampal gyri.

Projections to hypothalamus. Direct connections to various hypothalamic nuclei have been known for a long time. The most striking projections are to the preoptic region of the hypothalamus and to the more lateral hypothalamic regions although fibres also terminate in the dorsal hypothalamic area and the posterior hypothalamic nucleus. Almost in continuum with the latter, there are projections to the mesencephalic tegmentum, namely to the anterior half of the periaqueductal grey matter. These are areas to which both the hippocampus and the amygdala send strong projections.

Projections to the septum. These probably arise from the upper bank of the sulcus principalis. A reciprocal connection is probably involved.

Projections to the thalamus. Other than the well-known projections to the nucleus dorsalis medialis, fibers also terminate in the intralaminar thalamic complex.

Projections to the striatum. Projections to the caudate and the putamen but not the pallidum have been identified. It was once thought that the frontocaudate projection was limited to the head, but it has recently been shown that the prefrontal cortex projects to the whole caudate, even if all the fibers enter the caudate at the level of the head. Of particular interest is the fact that regions of the cortex with which the frontal lobe is reciprocally innervated, e.g., in the parietal lobe, seem to project to the caudate in approximately the same area.

Projections to claustrum, subthalamic region, and mesencephalon. Projections to the claustrum travel in the uncinate fasciculus and originate in the orbital and inferior dorsolateral aspects. Projections to the regions of the subthalamic nucleus and the red nucleus also seem to come primarily from the orbital aspects. Projections to the central grey seem to come from the convexity only.

Projections to cerebellum. These are projections which travel to the pons where they relay before joining the cerebellar cortex. They originate from roughly the same area that produces the striatal projections.

CORTICAL CONNECTIONS

Projections from visual, auditory, and somatosensory cortex. Practically all areas of the cortex project to the frontal lobe. In the rhesus monkey these projections have been studied in relation to two distinct regions, the periarcuate cortex, which surrounds the arcuate sulcus, and the prearcuate cortex, which includes all of the frontal pole lying anterior to the former region and which encompasses the region of the sulcus principalis.

Projections terminating in the periarcuate cortex arise from the caudal portion of the superior temporal gyrus, the lateral peristriate belt, the superior parietal lobule, and the anterior portion of the inferior parietal lobule. Projections terminating in the prearcuate cortex arise from the middle region of the superior temporal gyrus, the caudal and inferior temporal cortex, and the middle portion of the inferior bank of the intraparietal sulcus.

Direct projections to the orbital cortex come mainly from the anterior region of the superior temporal gyrus. But there are indirect projections which also reach this area by way of the mediodorsal thalamus; they originate in the middle and inferior temporal gyri and share the same route of projections from the olfactory cortex.

Considerable overlap takes place in relation to these connections, for instance, between the first-order visual and auditory projections in the periarcuate region, or between second-order visual, auditory, and somatosensory projections in prearcuate cortex.

Projections from olfactory cortex. The pyriform cortex projects to the frontal lobe by way of the mediodorsal nucleus of the thalamus. In this way, olfactory information joins that of the other modalities creating a convergence absent in the posterior sensory cortex.

Projections to temporal cortex. The temporal cortex receives projections from the region of the sulcus principalis in a well-organized fashion. The anterior third projects mainly to the anterior third of the superior temporal sulcus and of the superior temporal gyrus. The middle third connects with both the anterior and middle portions of the superior temporal sulcus. The posterior third mainly projects to the more caudal region of the superior temporal sulcus. The orbital aspect of the frontal lobe also projects to the rostral areas of the temporal lobe.

Projections to posterior sensory cortex. These are mainly directed to the inferior parietal lobule and originate in the posterior third of the sulcus principalis and in the arcuate sulcus.

Projections to limbic cortex. Both the anterior and middle thirds of the sulcus principalis project to the cingulate gyrus, the latter in a more intense fashion, as do areas in the concavity of the arcuate sulcus. This is an interesting projection that courses all along the cingulate distributing fibers to the overlying cortex but then continues as a bundle to reach the hippocampal gyrus.

Projections within the frontal lobe. The lower bank of the sulcus principalis is connected to the orbital aspect of the frontal cortex. The region of the arcuate sulcus connects anteriorly to portions of the frontal pole.

RELATIONSHIP BETWEEN ANATOMY AND FUNCTION

We think it is possible to propose a workable model of frontal-lobe function by reflecting upon the anatomical connections in the light of modern physiology and clinical neurology. Although it is outside the scope of this chapter to present the development of a theoretical model, we will outline some of the principles which, in our view, govern the activity of the frontal lobes.

Analysis of the pattern of anatomical connections underscores the diversity of frontal-lobe structures. Some fundamental organizational trends clearly emerge, such as: (1) The strong cortical and subcortical bidirectional linkage with the limbic and reticular activating systems, (2) The intimate bidirectional linkage with the association areas of the posterior sensory cortex, and (3) The intimate associations with the motor system, at cortical (premotor and precentral) and subcortical (striatal and cerebellar) levels.

The overall distinctive pattern consists in the insertion of the limbic and arousal systems between the sensory and motor systems. Interestingly, the limbic system processes the same sensory information which is projected frontally from the posterior neocortex. On the basis of the morphology, one is probably justified in saying that the frontal lobe is suited to act as a comparator. With it the nervous system has achieved the maximal structural separation between stimulus and response, and has gone further away from reflex activity. What lies between S and R is a complex chain of decisions, such as how to process S to the best advantage and how to respond to S in the way more suitable to the set of immediate and long-term goals of the individual. In morphological terms, this probably corresponds to a complicated voyage through the several hierarchies of the limbic and arousal systems. The frontal lobe judges and regulates ongoing external perception, and calculates appropriate responses to what is being perceived, according to the principle of preservation of the individual's equilibrium.

Such a principle applies to the most diverse levels of stimulus, simple and complex, and to the most varied forms of response. Planning on the best course to take to avert the falling of an object, or to achieve a given social position, would be governed by the same process of computation of S, and organization of R according to a set of stabilizing goals. The core of the nervous system is probably continuously engaged in operations which contribute to maintaining the organization "in purpose" (the preservation of its own life, the maintenance of lineage). The correct choice and execution of suitable actions is co-extensive with (or accompanied by) reward, or maybe even *maintained* by reward obtained by the perception of relevant stimuli. An example of such a form of regulatory activity is the function of the hypothalamic nuclei (Olds, 1958; Valenstein, 1966, 1969, 1970). It appears that the role of the hypothalamic reinforcement system is to evaluate the motivational relevance and hedonic value of stimuli that promote a certain behavior. Such an action is under the control of "gate" mechanisms in which motivational state and past experience play a role. Some gate mechanisms are in all probability "located" in hypothalamic structures, but others, particularly those that have to do with complex acquired contingencies, most certainly depend on the frontal lobe. In the hypothalamus, the control of the internal milieu is obtained by means of a response (such as the secretion of a hormone or a hormone-stimulating factor, the triggering of a drive for a given action, or the triggering of a pattern of emotional display) to a given unbalancing variable (such as pain or a change in serum osmolality, level of blood sugar, temperature, or amount of light in the environment). The response, or set of responses, will produce directly or indirectly, the annulation or minimization of the unbalancing variable and therefore contribute to rewarded (rewarding) equilibrium. But achieving homeostasis is a function of environmental contingencies too, and, as a consequence, in the case of man, on contingencies of an environment regulated by complex rules of interpersonal and objectal relationship. In terms of this environment the mere evaluation of S and managing of R are not satisfactory and the need to override such quasi-automatic nonacquired responses has probably been answered by the development of complex decision chains ("gate" systems again) able to judge at progressively more elaborate levels, according to external as well as internal rules, and according to medium, long-term, and immediate goals.

We propose that the structures capable of performing the environmentally related "gating" of diencephalic innate behaviors are in the frontal lobe. Hence we see the frontal lobe engaged in the same type of regulatory activity as the hypothalamus. The difference lies in the complexity of the stimulus configuration about which decisions are made and in the complexity of the response. It is the ability to handle hypercomplex environmental contingencies in the framework of the individual's own history, and in the perspective of his desired future course, that distinguishes frontal-lobe operation. On the other hand, the similarity lies in the fact that ultimately even the most complex calculations and decisions include a "hypothalamic" component which, regardless of how indirectly, rewards or punishes an action.

According to this view, we consider the frontal lobe to be primarily concerned with high-level cognition. The fact that affective and emotional disorders are the most dramatic signs of disease in the frontal lobe is in keeping with that hypothesis: frontal-lobe structures mediate the cognition necessary to harmonize internal and external pressures by modulating primitive forms of response. In simple terms, frontal-lobe disease would downgrade the quality of "gate" mechanisms and allow less elaborate responses to complex environmental situations to take place.

This broad main principle describing frontal-lobe function is compatible with the idea that differently located foci of damage may produce different clinical manifestations. Indeed, the diversity of morphological machinery necessary to carry out the various levels of processing encompassed by such a principle underscores the absurdity of the notion of a single frontal-lobe syndrome.

Another important principle of frontal-lobe function pertains to learning. We conceive of the frontal lobe as an outpost of the hypothalamus informed by learning rather than by inheritance. We presume that the matrices which interweave internal and external representations of the world come about as a result of learning, and that programs to *S-R* action are tried, selected, and learned on the basis of those matrices. The role of specific chemical mediation systems, such as those of acetylcholine, noradrenaline, dopamine, and serotonin, in that acquisition process is almost certainly of high relevance. Knowledge of their widespread distribution in frontal-lobe areas and of their organized anatomical course in limbic-system structures makes it possible that some regional pathochemical conditions may be produced by certain neuropathological conditions. It is obviously too early to speculate further on this matter. We also hypothesize that in the process of consolidation of learning, more and more programs of action are "taught" to nonfrontal-lobe structures, such as those in the posterior sensory cortex, so that a different level of semiautomatic response ability is created and frontal-lobe structures are freed for further learning and programming. In this fashion, the "gating" networks are progressively reproduced in the posterior regions of the brain, possibly by means of a "kindling" process. The substrate for this process may be the efferent corticocortical connections to the posterior association areas. Some "gating" networks, however, would never be "kindled" back, particularly those relating to the more refined aspects of judgment and creativity. Such an explanation could possibly reconcile the disparate results of frontal-lobe ablations in children and adults, as well as the relative preservation of intelligence, as measured by standard intelligence tests, in the face of major changes in personality and appropriate social behavior.

In the following pages, some evidence supporting this model will be discussed, including that coming from human research, clinical observation, and animal experimentation.

HUMAN STUDIES

Case studies

During the first half of this century single case studies and the results of prefrontal leucotomy and lobotomy were the principal sources of information concerning the function of the frontal lobes. As would be expected, the cases and the circumstances in which the studies were carried out had little in common and they were used as the basis for markedly divergent conclusions. At its most radical, these encompassed the opinion that the frontal lobe was indispensable for superior forms of human behavior as compared to the claim that intellectual competence is not impaired by the absence of frontal-lobe structures. Some of the more interesting single case studies involved in the controversy, such as those of Brickner (1934, 1936), Hebb and Penfield (1940), and Ackerly and Benton (1948), will be reviewed.

Brickner's patient, known as *A*, was a 39-year-old New York stockbroker, who, until one year before surgery, led a normal life. Slowly progressive headaches, which became more and more severe, and finally the sudden onset of mental obtundation, brought him to medical attention. A diagnosis of a frontal mass was made which, at surgery, proved to be a voluminous meningioma of the falx compressing both frontal lobes. The neurosurgeon, Walter Dandy, had to undertake an extensive, bilateral resection of frontal tissue performed in two stages. On the left side all the frontal tissue rostral to Broca's area was removed. On the right, the excision was even larger and included all the brain anterior to the motor area. The patient's condition gradually stabilized and no motor or sensory defect could be detected. For months there were frequent periods of restlessness, but akinesia or changes in tone were never noted, nor were there any signs of motor perseveration. Orientation to person, place, and time seemed intact as well as remote and recent memory. *A* was able to understand the circumstances of his illness, the surgical intervention he had been subject to, and he was aware of the efforts of his family and physician to make him recover as much as possible. The range of his intellectual ability could be inferred from his capacity to play checkers, sometimes at a quick and expert pace, to explain the meaning of proverbs, and, occasionally, to discuss with lucidity the meaning of his predicament for himself, for his relatives, and for his friends. On the negative side, his behavior had undergone a marked deterioration in terms of ability to focus attention, and to adjust his emotional reaction to almost any daily event. Furthermore, his affect was shallow. *A* became boastful, constantly insisting on his professional, physical, and sexual prowess and he showed little restraint not only in describing his mythical adventures but in verbalizing uninhibited judgments of people and circumstances surrounding him. His train of thought was often hypomanic-like, with facetious remarks to match, but he could suddenly become difficult and aggressive, if frustrated. Frequently he tried to be witty, generally at the expense of others. He was particularly nasty towards his wife; prior to surgery he had always been kind to her although not unusually considerate. His sex life, which the wife described as normal before the operation, changed radically. He became impotent and, after a few frustrated attempts at intercourse, never again sought his wife or indeed any other partner, although much of his conversation would revolve around his sexual exploits. Ability to plan daily meaningful activity had been clearly lost and so had his initiative and creativity. Although he constantly spoke of returning to work, he never made any effort to do so and continued living in close dependence on his relatives. Certain levels of learning ability however, both verbal and nonverbal, seemed intact and in the face of his constant distractability and lack of interest, he was taught how to operate proficiently a complex printing machine, on which he produced visiting cards. Moreover, when faced with strangers in a reasonably non-demanding situation, he would be charming, display impeccable manners and be considerably restrained. Independent examiners, including clinical neurologists, would then be unable to detect any abnormality even after fairly long conversations.

Brickner's painstaking description produced different impressions on the readers of the time. The overall view was that the intervention had had a crippling effect on A's mental ability. But for Egas Moniz, the enterprising pioneer of frontal leucotomy (1936), the case of Brickner's patient was remarkable in that it proved bilateral frontal damage to be compatible with maintenance of major operational abilities and especially because it demonstrated a change in affect and emotional response with pronounced reduction of anxiety. This view is likely to have played a role in the theorization behind the leucotomy project.

The question of whether the changes reported in this case were due primarily to the frontal-lobe resection is not entirely resolved. For the most part they probably were. However, it is not possible to exclude preoperative damage produced by silent growth of the tumor and a period of sustained intracranial pressure. In view of the location and size of the neoplasia, damage to the septal and hypothalamic regions was a possibility and although the autopsy report on this case (Brickner, 1952) mentioned no such evidence, there may have been basal forebrain changes. The report is clear in noting that the cortical territory of the anterior cerebral arteries was intact (which might have been predicted from the patient's lack of crural paresis). Nevertheless, the autopsy did becloud the issue by revealing several meningiomas, one of which was of significant size and located in the right occipital area. In retrospect it seems clear that the latter tumor was not large at the time of operation since the patient developed a new set of symptoms six to seven years after surgery. Such findings should not be used to minimize the significance of this case, as it is unlikely that they played any role in the patient's behavior.

Hebb and Penfield (1940) described an example of relatively successful bilateral removal of frontal tissue with a more straightforward possibility of a clinico-anatomical correlation:

This patient had been normal until age 16 and had then sustained a compound frontal fracture which damaged both frontal lobes, produced the formation of scar tissue, and resulted in a severe convulsive disorder. At age 28, the patient was operated and the frontal lobes were extensively resected bilaterally, exposing both orbital plates back to the lesser wing of the sphenoid and transecting the frontal horns of the ventricles. The anterior cerebral arteries were spared. At least a third of the frontal lobes was removed. In terms of the anatomical result the intervention is not very different from that of Brickner's patient. But unlike A this patient's brain had not been distorted and edematous prior to resection and the ablation took place under optimal surgical circumstances. In the postoperative period seizures practically stopped and the behavioral disturbances associated with interictal periods disappeared. The authors suggest that the patient's personality actually improved and that his intellectual ability was probably better than before the surgical intervention. We take this to mean that comparison with the period of convulsive disorder was favorable and bore out the lack of interictal behavior deviation. Comparison with the period prior to the initial damage would certainly not be as favorable, as we believe this patient's intellectual and affective maturation had been considerably affected by his frontal-lobe lesion. Even if he is described as relatively independent, socially adequate, and intellectually intact, some observers have felt that his personality development seemed arrested at the age of the accident and a certain resemblance with the patient of Ackerly and Benton has been indicated. In a later study, Hebb conceded (1945) that in spite of the patient's apparently good adjustment, his long-term planning and initiative ability may have been impaired.

The patient of Ackerly and Benton (1948), on the other hand, sustained bilateral frontal-lobe damage either at birth, or during the perinatal period. A neurosurgical exploration was performed at age 19 and revealed cystic degeneration of the left frontal lobe and absence of the right one, probably as a result of atrophy. This patient's history was marked throughout childhood and adolescence by severe behavioral problems, in school and at home. He could not hold a job, generally because after some days of being an obedient and even charming employee, he would suddenly show bursts of bad temper, lose interest in his activity, and often end up by stealing or being disorderly. He reacted badly to frustration and departure from routine would easily frustrate him. Except for periods of frustration and catastrophic reaction, his docility, quietness, and polite manners were quite impressive. His general health seems to have been good. His sexual interests were apparently dim and he never had an emotional involvement with any partner although, for a time, he did have occasional sex with prostitutes. As a whole, his behavior was described as stereotyped, unimaginative, and lacking in initiative. He never developed any particular professional skill or hobby and this deficit never seemed to bother him. He also failed to plan for the future, either immediate or long range, and previous reward and punishment did not seem to influence the course of his behavior. In keeping with this, his memory was described as capricious, showing at times a remarkable capacity (such as his ability to remember the makes of automobiles) and at other times an inaccurate representation of events. There was no evidence of the common varieties of neurotic disorder, no signs of somatization or of deliberate antisocial behavior, or of addiction. Apparently he could not be described in terms of being joyful or happy and it looked like both pleasure and pain were short lived and directly related to the presence or absence of frustration.

When reevaluated 15 years later, there had been no remarkable personality changes except for a higher frustration threshold. But intellectually, recent memory deficits were now noticeable and an inability to perform the Wisconsin Card Sorting Test was recorded.

Reflection on these cases is most rewarding. There seems to be some superficial similarity among them, particularly between the two latter patients. Both shared a rigid, perseverative attitude in their approach to life and both had the courteous manner described as "English valet politeness," though in the judgment of several examiners Hebb and Penfield's patient led a clearly more productive, but not fully independent, existence. The evolution of the personality in Hebb's patient seems to have been somewhat arrested at the time of his accident, when he was 16, while in Ackerly's patient the defect came early in development. Ackerly's case could thus be viewed as an example of learning and personality development without the frontal lobes, whereas Hebb's would represent an arrest of development in adolescence at an age where some positive adaptation would still be possible. Brickner's patient, on the other hand, had a normal development and sustained frontal-lobe damage in adult life. If an overall assessment can be made he was, in some aspects, the more impaired of the three, but also the one who had sustained more severe and acute damage. Premorbid personality and the fact that lesion was sustained at an age when plasticity of the nervous system was limited may have been important factors. But in spite of the differences, the patient shared many features with the other two: lack of originality and creativity; inability to organize future activity, hold gainful employment, and be fully independent; inability to focus attention (distractability); recent memory vulnerable to interference; tendency to present a favorable view of himself often to the point of boastfulness; stereotyped but pleasant manners in nonthreatening situations; tendency to display inappropriate emotional reactions; diminished ability to experience pleasure and probably also to react to pain; diminished sexual and exploratory drives; lack of motor, sensory, or communication defects; overall intelligence scale within average for age and education.

It seems probable that bilateral damage to the frontal lobe in infancy or childhood produces a more devastating effect on personality and cognitive ability than the same amount of damage sustained elsewhere in the brain at any time in the course of development. This point is illustrated by cases of early hemispherectomy on either side and by cases of extensive unilateral or bilateral lesions of the parietal, occipital, and posterior temporal lobes which demonstrate almost normal maturation of personality. Few cases comparable to Ackerly and Benton's have been published, an exception being that reported by Russell (1959) whose findings are in accord with this view. We would surmise that early lesions of the frontal lobe, just like lesions of the anterior temporal lobe, the limbic system, and the anterior and dorsomedial thalami, are not compatible with normal development of intellectual abilities and affect and consequently are not compatible with normal maturation of personality.

The results of prefrontal leucotomy and prefrontal lobotomy have been a constant source of controversy. Although Moniz (1936, 1949) had been impressed by the lack of pronounced defects of motor, sensory, and communicative function in cases of frontal-lobe lesion, it is clear that he attributed several important functions to the frontal lobe. One was related to learning. He reasoned that in cases of schizophrenic thought disorder or of obsessive compulsive disease, "wrongly learned" thinking processes were dependent on frontal-lobe function and based on reverberating circuitry connecting the frontal lobe to midline subcortical structures and to the posterior cortical areas. Such "repetitive linkages" called for surgical interruption. He also hypothesized a relation between the aberrant thought process and the accompanying emotional status of the patient and assumed that a lesion that altered one would also alter the other. He recalled the frequent observation of affective indifference in frontal-lobe patients, as well as the remarkable affective changes shown in Jacobsen's chimpanzees (Fulton and Jacobsen, 1935) after frontal-lobe surgery. As Jacobsen (Fulton, 1951) put it "the animals had joined the happiness cult of the Elder Micheaux and had placed their burdens on the Lord." It is clear that Moniz conceived of the frontal lobes as important for cognitive maturation and for the regulation of emotion and that, far from designing an innocuous intervention, he was planning the active introduction of defects in patients whose previous abnormality might benefit from such diminution.

Objective assessment of the results of prefrontal surgery is extremely difficult. Several surgical methods have been devised involving various amounts of damage to different structures and these have been performed with more or less precision according to the technique. All cases suffered from preexisting psychiatric disease or intractable pain, generally of considerable severity and duration. Finally, the methods of behavioral assessment have been different in scope and quality, and have often been unconsciously biased.

Nevertheless, several general conclusions may be drawn from a survey of the literature in this area. The first is that bilateral surgically controlled frontal-lobe damage, particularly when it involves the mesial and inferior orbital aspects, produces modifications in the affective and emotional sphere. These changes may also appear as a result of dorsolateral lesions but seem less pronounced. On the other hand, measurable intellectual impairment more often follows dorsolateral involvement. Recent accounts supporting this view can be found in Hamlin (1970) and in Scoville and Bettis (1977) and are in keeping with the predictions that might have been formulated on the basis of studies such as those of Faust (1966). Changes related to higher levels of regulatory behavior are difficult to disentangle from the results of previous and ongoing psychiatric processes. These will probably be approachable as a result of the introduction of fractionated forms of psychosurgery. But possibly the most scientifically revealing trend in psychosurgery has been the attempt to produce behavior modification not by frontal-lobe lesions but by direct approach to the hypothalamic centers, with which the frontal lobe has an intimate and possibly regulatory relationship (Dieckmann and Hassler, 1977; Nádvornik, Šramka, and Patoprstá, 1977; Schneider, 1977).

Neuropsychological studies

After World War II, new knowledge of neuroanatomy and neurophysiology was gained, stimulating studies of a more experimental nature. In one of the more significant, Brenda Milner (1963) was able to demonstrate a measurable deficit as a result of frontal-lobe lesions. Her subjects were epileptic patients undergoing frontal resections for treatment of convulsive disorder. There were no patients with tumors in the group. All patients had atrophic lesions and most of them were studied before and after the operation. Measure-

ment of IQ after the operation showed a mean loss of 7.2 points in
the frontal-lobe group, which was less than the loss shown by the
left temporal and left parietal-lobe groups, and by the general control group which showed a mean loss of 8.4 points. Against this
background, Milner then demonstrated the remarkable impairment
which her frontal patients showed in the Wisconsin Card Sorting
Test.

The Wisconsin Card Sorting Test had been first used by Berg
(1948) and by Grant and Berg (1948). The subject is shown four
cards whose figures are different in color, form, and number of
elements, (a red triangle, two green stars, three yellow crosses, and
four blue circles). The subject is handed a pack of 128 cards which
vary according to color, form, and number, and is requested to sort
each consecutive card from the pack (response cards) and place it in
front of one of the four cards (stimulus cards) where he thinks it
belongs. After he has made a choice, he is told whether his approach
is right or wrong and asked to use that information in an attempt
to make as many correct choices as possible. The first sorting criterion is color and any other choice is called wrong. After the subject
achieves ten consecutive correct color choices, the sorting criterion
changes without the subject being told so, and color choices are
called wrong. A shift to form will then be called right and after ten
correct form choices, the criterion will again change without warning, this time to number. The procedure is repeated until six
changes have been completed using the order: color, form, number,
color, form, number.

Milner found that all her frontal patients performed more poorly
after the operation, in clear contrast to patients in her control group
which included several cases of resection of the left temporal lobe,
left parietal lobe, right temporoparietal-occipital and of combined
orbitotemporal resections. Postoperatively, the frontal patients
tended to stick to one choice and to perseverate throughout the test
without shifting into further sorting categories. Milner described an
additional group of patients tested only after the operation and the
results were so similar that she felt justified in combining the data
into a final, larger group.

The findings were interpreted as proof that the ability to shift
from one strategy to another in a sorting task is more compromised

by frontal-lobe damage than by rolandic or posterior sensory-cortex damage. The manifest perseveration which made patients rigidly adhere to one criterion and ignore the examiner's guiding information was interpreted as an inability to overcome an established response set.

A complex question raised by this study relates to the difficulty of the Wisconsin Card Sorting Test. It is known that many normal subjects perform poorly in it, and one tends to expect a brain-damaged patient to do even worse. However, Milner's control group answers that comment fairly well by showing a clear difference between frontal and nonfrontal cases. Since the intelligence quotients were comparable and since the background conditions of all patients in terms of disease and production of lesion were similar, it is probable that the defect of performance was a consequence of frontal-lobe damage. Further support for this view comes from the patient of Scoville and Milner (1957) who, in spite of bilateral hippocampal lesions and severe memory loss, performed the Card Sorting Test remarkably well, achieving at least four categories.

Another question bears upon the correlation between the changes and the area of frontal-lobe involvement. Apparently there were no differences between right- and left-frontal lesions in terms of the card sorting procedure, and lesions on either side produced the same defect. This result is difficult to accept, except for the period immediately after the operation, but since no other study of the magnitude of Milner's has addressed this problem, the question is unsettled. Another problem regarding anatomical correlation comes when Milner describes the pertinent lesions as dorsolateral. At least 15 of the 18 patients had as much mesial involvement as they had dorsolateral. Furthermore, the dorsolateral involvement varied considerably and, judging from the diagrams, it was in some cases restricted to prefrontal cortex while in some others there seems to have been invasion of transitional and premotor cortex. Also the extent of orbital involvement is not known except for one case. Under the circumstances, it is possible to say that the abnormal behavior of these patients was correlated with extensive and bilateral frontal-lobe damage, predominantly prefrontal, but not necessarily allocated to the dorsolateral, mesial, or orbital aspects.

Milner's results are at variance in several respects with those of

Teuber (1964) who pointed out that although many of his frontal patients failed the Wisconsin Sorting Test, some did very well and individual variation was striking. This seems not to have been the case in Milner's study. On the other hand, Teuber's controls did not do as well as Milner's and thus the overall differences were minimized. The nature of the pathological process (gunshot wounds in Teuber's study) and the locus of lesion may be crucial factors, the probability being that Teuber's cases had a lesser mesial involvement. One final point is that the procedure in the administration of the test was changed for Teuber's patients, in that they were informed that there would be changes in the sorting criteria, thus making the task easier.

Rosvold (1964) reported observing impairment in the Wisconsin Card Sorting Test in lobotomized patients. The defects were very pronounced one month after operation, but the patients subsequently improved and some recovered completely. His observation calls attention to the element of time after lesion as a factor in the disturbances related to frontal-lobe damage. However, it is not possible to equate the results of the predominantly white-matter damage produced by lobotomy procedures with those from radical lobectomies.

Another important finding related to frontal-lobe damage reported by Milner (1964) pertains to verbal behavior. Using Thurstone's Word Fluency Test, she showed that patients with left frontal lobectomies which spared Broca's area, scored very poorly in this test although there was no evidence of aphasia. The result was in keeping with traditional clinical observations of marked paucity of speech after frontal-lobe damage, but Milner went one step further and demonstrated that right frontal-lobe resections did not produce the defect. Controls with temporal lobectomies performed as well as patients with right-frontal lobectomies. Interestingly, both left and right frontals performed at the same level in a task of verbal memory, suggesting the relative independence of the mechanism underlying fluency. The temporal-lobe controls did poorly on the verbal memory task.

Benton (1968) arrived at the same conclusions using a group of patients with left, right, and bilateral frontal damage. The task used to test fluency was an oral version of the Thurstone test, in which the patient is requested to say as many words as come to mind, beginning with a given letter of the alphabet. Not only did the left-hemisphere patients do remarkably worse than the right-hemisphere ones, but bilaterally damaged patients also performed more poorly than those with right-hemisphere damage only. The observations of Ramier and Hecaen (1970) were in essential accord with these results.

The findings of Milner and Benton provide empirical confirmation of the classic views of Feuchtwanger (1923) and Kleist (1936), according to which "dominant" frontal lesions but not "minor" frontal ones, interfere with verbal processes, particularly in respect to spontaneity and the ability to maintain a flow of verbal evocation, without actually producing one of the typical aphasias. They are in opposition to the views of Jefferson (1937) and Rylander (1940), who denied any lateralization of defect after frontal lobectomies.

As suggested by Milner's results in the task of verbal memory, the impairment in fluency seems to have an independent mechanism, and is not necessarily associated with verbal learning defects. Benton noted that left-hemisphere patients were not worse than right-hemisphere ones in tasks of verbal paired-associate learning.

Benton's study also demonstrated that right-hemisphere-damaged subjects perform significantly worse than left-hemisphere-damaged subjects on visuoconstructive tasks. The findings confirm earlier results of Corkin (1964) and support the notion of lateralized differences in function. Along the same lines, Milner (1971) showed right frontal-lobe patients to be defective in spatial learning, and noted that those defects seemed dissociated from nonspatial learning.

Teuber's contribution to the problem of frontal-lobe function (1964, 1966) is of special interest. At a time when researchers were primarily looking at the sensory aspect of the problem, he emphasized the motor end and introduced the concept of corollary discharge. In brief, this is defined as the preparatory action which the motor system exerts on the sensory system to announce the intention of incoming movement, correct for displacement of perception, and assure smooth perceptual continuity once movement is carried out. Teuber viewed this mechanism as being dependent on frontal-lobe structures and considered it to be a basic physiological function of the frontal lobe. In keeping with this idea, he hypothesized that most signs of frontal-lobe dysfunction in animals and man were derived from impairment of the corollary discharge mechanism. Indications of dysfunction as disparate as delayed response deficits in monkeys, perseveration, and the inability to handle sorting principles were seen to result from the absence of a motor sensory alerting signal.

There is no doubt that some mechanism of corollary discharge exists and is essential for the continuity of perception. But it is not clear that frontal-lobe structures are indispensable to corollary information processes. Nor does it seem probable that a single impaired mechanism can explain the variety of clinical and experimental signs of frontal-lobe damage.

The observations that led Teuber to his concept of corollary discharge were made in patients with penetrating gunshot wounds involving the frontal lobes. In agreement with other authors, Teuber found no major deficit in intelligence or in performance on memory tests (Teuber and Weinstein, 1954, 1956; Weinstein and Teuber, 1957; Ghent, Mishkin, and Teuber, 1962), but he and his co-workers were unable to replicate Milner's findings on the Wisconsin Card Sorting Test. As noted, the discrepancy may have been due to the difference in type of lesions as well as to different procedures and experimental design (Teuber, 1964).

Objective evidence of dysfunction in Teuber's patients was reflected in impairment in a series of perceptuomotor tasks which included tests of visuopostural orientation, visual-searching, body-orientation, and reversal-of-perspective ability. The visuopostural task (Teuber and Mishkin, 1954) called for the mechanical setting of a brightly luminous rod in the vertical position. The test was conducted in a dark room with the patient under different conditions of body tilt. Frontal-lobe subjects did poorly in this task. But if the task was strictly visual and no intermodal (visuoproprioceptive) conflict was established, the subjects performed normally. The visual search and body orientation tasks involved active head-and-eye-movement in the search for certain patterns, or else rapidly shifting left-to-right pointing responses on the patient's body. The reversal-of-perspective task was performed with two Necker cubes with the patient being requested to signify his perception of left or right perspective reversal by pressing levers placed to his left and to his right. Since all of these tasks are difficult for a normal human being to perform and probably more so for a brain-damaged individual, the strength of the results lies in the verification that patients with nonfrontal brain damage perform consistently better than those with frontal disease. The preliminary results of Teuber and co-workers suggested that this was so.

Luria's contribution to the study of frontal-lobe function encompasses many years of extensive investigation of patients and normals (Luria, 1964, 1966, 1969). As in so many other studies on the frontal lobe, the importance of the results is somewhat limited by the choice of the subjects for experimentation. Most of the patients studied by Luria and his co-workers had large frontal tumors, some intrinsic and some extrinsic. Some involved subcortical limbic-system structures such as the septum. Some had associated hydrocephalus and some not. Most patients had associated nonfrontal dysfunction, due to mass effect or compromise of vascular supply elsewhere in the brain. The location within the frontal lobe was also variable. The limits of studies performed under such unsatisfactory methodology are obvious. Nevertheless, Luria's concept of frontal-lobe function and dysfunction is quite stimulating.

His interpretation emphasizes the verbally mediated activating and regulatory role of the frontal lobes, and the role of the frontal lobes in problem solving. He suggests that the orienting reaction, as measured by galvanic skin response or suppression of the alpha rhythm in the EEG, cannot be stabilized by verbal stimuli in patients with frontal-lobe lesions. In normal subjects, the presentation of verbally meaningful instructions is expected to prevent habituation to stimuli, and therefore prevent the orienting response from disappearing (Homskaya, 1966). Apparently nonaphasic patients with tumors, gunshot wounds, or strokes involving the posterior sensory cortex, behave like normals in terms of verbal stabilization of the verbal orienting responses even in the presence of praxic and gnosic defects. In patients with frontal-lobe lesions, however, the verbal signal does not prevent habituation. Moreover, subjects with damage to the frontal poles and to the mesial and basal aspects of the frontal structures tend to be more affected than those with dorsolateral involvement.

Additional evidence for altered orienting responses in frontal-lobe patients comes from studies of visual potentials evoked by verbally tagged stimuli. Stimuli which would have increased the amplitude of visual evoked potentials in normals, failed to do so in patients with frontal-lobe damage (Simernitskaya and Homskaya, 1966, and Simernitskaya, 1970).

Another aspect of frontal-lobe function impaired by disease concerns the possibility of directing the execution of complex actions by verbal mediation. Several authors have pointed out that frontal-lobe patients may be able to repeat correctly the instructions for a given task while making no use whatever of the information in performing a task. Thus, while performing a sorting task, subjects may make perseverative sorting errors even while they are verbalizing the correct strategy. The same has been said regarding the utilization of perceived error: patients will verbally admit the mistake but fail to correct it. Luria has repeatedly called attention to this type of defect and considers it one of the hallmarks of frontal-lobe dysfunction. He attempted to objectify the defect in a series of experiments in which patients were requested to follow progressively more complex verbal instructions. He noted that patients were able to perform only the more direct and simple commands and would fail to carry out more complex instructions, particularly if they involved some change in principle or some conflict with additional cues provided by the examiner. Since the patient would still be able to repeat the initial verbal instruction, Luria concluded that the primary difficulty was one of verbal guidance of actions (Luria and Homskaya, 1964). Again, the weakness of these studies resides in the subjects used for the observations, i.e., patients with massive bilateral tumors of the frontal lobes. Attempts at replication have met with difficulties (Drewe, 1975). Some defects of the kind reported by Luria were found, but the dissociation between verbal and motor ability was not verified and the author considered it unlikely that a loss of verbal regulatory action was the mechanism underlying impaired performance.

A similar objection may be raised about Luria's description of the changes in problem solving behavior that attend massive lesions of the frontal lobes. A state of confusion seems to underlie many of the disturbances of planning and calculation exhibited by his patients. Naturally, one can respond to this argument by stating that a more-or-less marked confusional state is part of the frontal-lobe syndrome to begin with. But this is not always the case. Confusion may be produced by CNS changes that have little to do with frontal-lobe dysfunction although they may coincide with it and derive from a common cause. Also, confusion is not a necessary accompaniment of frontal-lobe damage; it is associated more with acute and massive damage of frontal tissue and is clearly changeable with time, as adaptation to the pathological process occurs.

Nevertheless, Luria's observations are very suggestive, and his proposals have heuristic value. The idea that patients have trouble in the choice of programs of action, that their strategy for gathering information necessary for the solution of the problem is impoverished, and that they seldom verify whether their actions meet the original intent, are interesting interpretations of some of the defects that can be found, together or in isolation, in instances of frontal-lobe damage. In addition, it is our impression that even when these defects cannot be demonstrated by an experimental task in the immediate and consistent manner claimed by Luria, one can still encounter them at more complex levels of behavior, for instance, in goal-oriented decision processes in long-term planning operations.

ANIMAL STUDIES

A detailed review of animal experiments on frontal-lobe function is outside the scope of this chapter. Nevertheless, consideration of some of the major results of animal research is in order because of their bearing on clinical issues.

The original findings of Jacobsen regarding the impairment in delayed responses in chimpanzees (Jacobsen, 1935; Jacobsen and Nissen, 1937) still dominates this area of study. During the past three decades an impressive number of researchers have replicated Jacobsen's results for both the delayed response and the delayed alternation tasks and extended the verification of the defects to rhesus monkeys, cats, dogs, and rats. Furthermore, within the prefrontal cortex, damage to the region of the sulcus principalis has been identified as the crucial region for the production of the defect (Blum, 1952). However, nobody has been able to reproduce the same delayed response defect in man no matter how intense the attempt (Chorover and Cole, 1966).

The delayed response procedure consists of the presentation of two or more empty food wells, one of which is baited in front of the animal. The wells are then covered and hidden from view, during a delay of at least 5 seconds, after which the animal is again allowed to view the covered wells and requested to retrieve the bait. The number of errors the animal makes reaching for the food is the basis for the score. Jacobsen noted that animals with bilateral removals of the prefrontal lobes did very poorly in this task, unlike animals with bilateral lesions elsewhere in the brain. The initial interpretation was that of an immediate memory defect. But this hypothesis was abandoned since the same animals that failed the delayed response task would pass a visual discrimination procedure which necessitates immediate memory. If, for instance, one of the food wells was made different by the addition of a specific visual feature, the animal would make a correct choice after the delay. The fact that similar animals would perform normally if left in the dark during the delay, suggested that retroactive erasing of traces was at stake. Also if animals were allowed a rewarded response before the first trial, they would perform normally or with few errors, a finding which pointed to the obvious role of limbic reinforcement in the type of response (Malmo, 1942; Finan, 1942).

The delayed alternation tasks operate in the same setup but the procedure is made more complicated by consecutive switching of the bait from one well to the other. Since delayed alternation naturally requires memory in a way that delayed response does not, performance in the two tasks may be dissociated by bilateral lesions of the hippocampus, which compromise delayed alternation but not delayed response (Orbach, Milner, and Rasmussen, 1960; Pribram, Wilson, and Connors, 1962). But destruction of the head of the caudate impairs both, in a manner similar to that produced by lesions in the region of the sulcus principalis, and electrical stimulation of the caudate during the trials also impairs the response (Rosvold and Delgado, 1956; Dean and Davis, 1959; Battig, Rosvold, and Mishkin, 1960). Bilateral stimulation of the region of the sulcus principalis impairs both tasks too (Mishkin and Pribram, 1955, 1956; Pribram, 1961; Stamm, 1961). Furthermore, it has been shown that ablation or stimulation of the middle sector of the sulcus principalis disrupts delayed response or delayed alternation response, whereas ablation or stimulation of the anterior sector does not produce any impairment (Stamm, 1969; Butters and Pandya, 1969). Results of involvement of the posterior sector have been controversial. Finally, only lesions of both the upper and lower banks of the middle third (but not lesions of either upper or lower, in isolation), seem capable of producing the defects (Butters et al., 1971). The suggestion that lesions in the nucleus medialis dorsalis of the thalamus might impair delayed response (Schulman, 1969) has not been unquestionably verified.

The reason for the failure of nonhuman primates and other animals in the delayed response and delayed alternation tasks has not been unequivocally established. Lack of a so-called second signaling system does not explain the question entirely. Other factors that have been proposed are impairment of processing of spatial and temporal cues, and the effect of interference. Several studies tend to support the importance of these factors. For instance, Grueninger and Pribram (1969) showed that the performance of monkeys with dorsolateral lesions is impaired by distraction from the processing of spatial cues which raises the possibility that changes in spatial information act as distractors in the delayed alternation task. This, in turn, suggests that the role of dorsolateral frontal-lobe structures is that of an inhibitor of interference. That this inhibitory action might be more marked for spatial than nonspatial information is suggested by the better performance of monkeys with dorsolateral frontal-lobe damage in nonspatial and "go/no go" problems (Mishkin, 1964).

Yet another cause for the delayed response defect may be the lack of limbic "tagging" of the stimuli, a circumstance that could arise from the destruction of a frontal region vital for the relay of sensory information into the limbic system. The fact that (a) the crucial area for delayed response impairment, the sulcus principalis, projects to the limbic system via the cingulate and from there to the hippocampus, (b) that other areas of the anterior frontal cortex project to the caudate (from which similar defects may be obtained by stimulation), and, in addition, (c) the fact that delayed alternation defects can be obtained from almost anywhere in the limbic structures, support the view that blocking the entry of input into this system is of importance in the determination of such defects. Both distractability and weakness of limbic marking are compatible with Konorski and Lawicka's (1964) interpretation of the defect on the basis of an abnormally rapid decay of the conditioning signal during the delay. In summary, it seems that delayed response defects result from the interaction of several factors, among which the limbic connection may be singled out as particularly important.

The idea that frontal-lobe damage produces changes in the processing of information by altering the orienting response has also been approached in the animal. Although it is not possible to draw a parallel with the human results in which the changes seem to derive, at least in part, from lack of verbal control, animal studies have demonstrated the presence of abnormal orienting responses which fail to appear, or appear in an inconsistent manner (Kimble, Bagshaw, and Pribram, 1965; Grueninger et al., 1965).

If damage to the region of the sulcus principalis has been found to be the crucial one for the type of intellectual defects shown by Jacobsen's monkeys, "Becky" and "Lucy," damage to the orbital cortex seems to have been essential for their so-called "bluntness of affect."

Following their own observations that monkeys with orbital-ablations showed marked and long-lasting changes in emotional behavior (Butter, Mishkin, and Rosvold, 1963) which seemed to be related to an increase in aversive reactions and a concomitant decrease in aggressive reactions (Butter, Mishkin, and Mirsky, 1968), Butter, Snyder, and McDonald (1970) made a careful study of aversive and aggressive behaviors in two groups of monkeys, one with orbital lesions, the other with temporal lesions. The orbital (but not temporal) lesions produced a clear reduction in aggressive behaviors, a change which was consistent and could still be seen after ten months. This reduction seemed to be situational, as there were noticeable differences in the way the animals reacted to different potentially threatening stimuli, and the animals could still demonstrate aggression when brought back to the colony where they had been dominant figures. This suggests that a regulatory mechanism of aggression had been impaired and that the capacity to display aggression had not been eliminated. The authors point out that the dependence on environmental configuration and the variety of possible emotional responses are not consistent with a permanent state of "bluntness of affect" used to describe similar changes in animals or in lobotomized patients, even if superficially the animals do look "blunted" and are indeed more "tame" in many situations.

Anatomical study of the lesions indicated that the posteromedial region of the orbital aspect of the frontal lobe was closely associated with the reported changes. This in turn suggests involvement of that particular region in the regulation of aggressive behaviors. This area of the cortex is intimately connected to the amygdala and furthermore, along with the dorsomedial nucleus of the thalamus, the amygdala and posteromedial orbital cortex projects to roughly the same regions of the hypothalamus. The combination of behavioral and anatomical data supports the conjecture that these three structures form an integrated system capable of controlling certain types of emotional reaction.

It is clear that animal studies have made important contributions to the understanding of frontal-lobe function. The most relevant results have been the unraveling of the anatomical connections, referred to at the beginning of the chapter and the demonstration that monkeys with bilateral frontal damage are not able to utilize reinforcement properly and thus are prevented from guiding their behavior in terms of reward or punishment.

CLINICAL ASSESSMENT

Patients with frontal-lobe damage share some clinical characteristics. If it is possible to speak in general terms at all, these are patients who tend to think that nothing serious is the matter with them although they will not actively deny a disease state. They seldom complain of pain, and their emotional response is inadequate. Often their history has to be obtained from relatives since information given by the patient is unreliable. Not infrequently patients are listless, distractable, and lacking in spontaneity. Their ability to communicate and move appropriately may be impoverished by phenomena such as perseveration, that is, a tendency to persist in the execution of an act long after it has ceased to be valuable. In many instances there will be unpredictable and generally inappropriate changes in emotional stance. Such signs point to abnormalities in various aspects of nervous activity, namely, in arousal mechanisms, in mechanisms of control of emotion and affect, and in overall regulation of motor activity, including that involved in communication. Not all of these manifestations need be present in one patient at the same time. As noted before, variations are the rule rather than the exception. The identification of clear-cut syndromes is hazardous and anatomical inferences from them should be made cautiously. Nevertheless, some presentations can be utilized to advantage in clinical practice.

The vascular syndromes are the most distinctive, particularly those related to the anterior cerebral artery. Bilateral involvement is a common cause of mutism with akinesia. Unilateral left-sided involvement gives rise to transcortical motor aphasia (see Chapter 2). Damage is predominantly to the mesial aspect of the frontal lobe. In many cases the artery is involved distal to the anterior communicating artery. Embolus and thrombosis have been recorded, but the most common cause of abnormalities in flow is rupture of an anterior communicating artery aneurysm. Instances of proximal involvement, before or immediately after the origin of Heubner's artery, give rise to unilateral syndromes with predominant motor manifestations. Critchley's description of such distinctive cases is still unsurpassed, and the interested reader is referred to his publication (1930). The frontal branches of the middle cerebral artery may also be involved, the more frequent causes being thrombosis and embolism. In cases in which such a process is present, compromise is almost always unilateral and predominantly affects the dorsolateral aspect of the lobe.

Tumor syndromes naturally vary with location and histological nature. Intrinsic and extrinsic tumors may be present. Extrinsic tumors, such as meningiomas, may be located subfrontally or in the falx, where they involve the mesial aspect of the lobes and produce bilateral changes. They may also have a more lateral origin and compress the dorsolateral aspect of one frontal lobe only. Intrinsic tumors may also show up unilaterally or bilaterally. The distinction often depends on time, as an originally unilateral glioma may invade the corpus callosum and cross to the opposite side.

Not uncommonly, frontal-lobe tumors present with widespread intellectual and affective impairment which justifies the use of the term dementia, so "diffuse" is the disorganization of normal behavior. For this reason, the diagnosis of frontal-lobe tumor (e.g., neoplasia, subdural hematoma) should always be considered in the study of a dementia syndrome. Confusional states are also frequently associated with tumors in the frontal lobe, perhaps more so than with tumors anywhere else in the central nervous system (Hécaen, 1964). Disturbances of mood and character, although less frequent than confusion or dementia, were noted almost as frequently in Hécaen's study (1964).

Other pathological processes may produce lesions in the frontal lobes. Wounds related to head injury—whose clinical pictures were vividly described by Kleist (1936) and Goldstein (1948), infections such as syphilis, or degenerative processes such as Pick's disease, may have a preponderant frontal involvement and present with a combination of frontal-lobe signs. However, more often than not, manifestations suggestive of disease elsewhere in the brain will also be evident.

The importance of the rate of development of the lesion, of time elapsed since peak development was attained, and of the age and education of the patient when struck by disease have been stressed and are indispensable to the evaluation of the frontal-lobe case. The possibility of worsening, stabilization, or recovery depends on the nature of the underlying pathological process. Most stroke patients tend to stabilize and then improve slowly, while the course of patients with tumors is a function of the degree of cytological and mechanical malignancy of the tumor and of the type of surgical or medical treatment adopted.

Detailed neurological examination often discloses few so-called hard signs. Nevertheless, a comprehensive neurological evaluation will reveal a variety of manifestations, most of which unmistakably suggest pathological involvement of the anterior areas of the brain. Some of the more significant ones are listed below under clinically convenient headings, which do not necessarily reflect the pathophysiological mechanism which may underlie them.

Neurological signs

ABNORMAL REFLEXES

The more significant are the grasp reflex, the groping reflex, and the snout and sucking reflexes. Traditionally these abnormal responses have been termed "psychomotor signs," calling attention to the fact that they almost invariably appear in the setting of an abnormal mental status.

The most useful of the group is the grasp reflex (the "prehension reflex" of Kleist, the "forced grasping" of Adie and Critchley) which may appear unilaterally or bilaterally, in the hands or in the feet. It consists of a more-or-less forceful prehension of an object that has come into contact with the palm of the hand or the sole of the foot. It can be elicited by touching or by stroking the skin, particularly in the region between the thumb and the index finger. Most maneuvers used to elicit the plantar reflex may produce a grasp reaction of the foot and may even mask an abnormal extensor response which, in that case, may be obtained from stimulation of the lateral side of the foot. The degree of the grasp reflex varies from patient to patient and it is generally more intense in cases with impaired mentation. In more alert states, it is characteristic that the patient cannot release the prehension even if told to do so and even if he wishes to do so. The reflex may extinguish after repeated stimulation and reappear after a period of rest. Classic descriptions used to refer to changes in lateralization induced by positioning of the head and body but such changes are not reliable and probably should not be used for clinical localization.

The groping reflex is less frequent than the grasp and generally appears in conjunction with the latter. The hand of the patient, as well as the eyes, tend to follow an object or the fingers of the examiner in a magnetic fashion. For a brief period, the patient behaves as if stimulus bound.

The sucking reflex is elicited by touching the lips of the patient with a cotton swab, while the snout reflex may be obtained by tapping the skin of the upper perioral region with finger or hammer. These responses are often present in patients with disease confined to the frontal lobe but, more so than the grasp reflex, they appear in a wide variety of dementia syndromes associated with more wideranging damage. Furthermore, the snout reflex, just like the palmomental reflex, may appear in patients with basal ganglia disorders and even in normal older individuals.

Traditionally, these signs have been interpreted as an indication of release of primitive forms of reflex response, kept in abeyance by normal inhibitory function of frontal-lobe structures. This view seems entirely valid.

ABNORMAL TONE

Patients with lesions in the prefrontal areas often show changes in muscle tone. These may be more closely associated with lesions in the dorsolateral aspect of the frontal lobes, particularly near the premotor regions. The most characteristic sign is Kleist's *Gegenhalten,* also referred to as counterpull, paratonia, opposition, or the Mayer-Reisch phenomenon. This is another of the so-called "psychomotor signs" and it may be wrongly interpreted as a deliberate negative attitude on the part of the patient. When the examiner tries to assess tone by passively moving the arm, he may find a sudden resistance to the extension maneuver and note that the counteracting flexion movement actually increases in intensity in an attempt to neutralize the action. The patient may or may not be aware of this development and, as with the grasp reflex, he will be unable to suppress the reflex even if he so wishes. Rigidity may also be present, but since it is not associated with tremor, it will not have "cogwheel" characteristics. The degree of rigidity may show little consistency and vary between observations. It is best described as "plastic" in type. Periodic hypotonia resembling cataplexy is quite rare (Ethelberg, 1949).

BRADYKINESIA

Many patients with lesions in the frontal lobe will show bradykinesia i.e., they will perform movements slowly, have difficulty in initiating or stopping actions, and will be unable to carry out more than one motor program simultaneously. It will usually be noted, however, that their facial expression is vacuous rather than merely hypomimic, or that their blinking is normal rather than reduced. Both hypomimia and impaired blinking are evident in most cases of parkinsonism, a condition dominated by bradykinesia but in which patients generally behave in an alert and intelligent fashion. Nevertheless, in frontal-lobe patients it may prove difficult to disentangle bradykinesia from lowered arousal, loss of orienting responses, and lack of drive. In most clinical circumstances it should be clear that the patient with frontal-lobe lesions suffers from a more-or-less profound disinclination to act, a loss of *Antrieb* (drive) in Kleist's description, which lessens his inclination to dress or wash or initiate any purposeful activity. The comparison with parkinsonism may again be helpful, as the motor impairment present in that condition generally coexists with a normal drive for useful activity. Naturally, the further we move away from the core of the parkinsonian syndrome, i.e., idiopathic Parkinson's disease, and into the several fringe syndromes, the more blurred the distinctions become. In our view the distinction also becomes blurred when we consider parkinsonian patients after one or more decades of disease, even in the post-dopamine era.

ABNORMAL GAIT AND POSTURE

Patients with severe frontal-lobe damage often show abnormalities of gait. A wide range of characteristic changes may be present, including walking with short steps but without festination, loss of balance with retropulsion or, inability to walk as in cases of so-called gait apraxia. The latter may be seen in a variety of conditions, most frequently in the intriguing syndrome of normal-pressure hydrocephalus, which may well be a frontal-lobe syndrome consequent to periodically raised intraventricular pressure. In diagnosing gait apraxia, an effort should be made to demonstrate that the patient can execute in bed, while recumbent, all the movements he is unable to perform while standing when his feet become "glued" to the floor.

The designation "frontal ataxia" probably does not cover a manifestation typical of frontal-lobe lesions—as even Bruns admitted when he coined the term. A tendency to fall backward rather than to the side and a predominance of deficits in the trunk rather than in the extremities is evident in some cases.

Abnormalities of posture are possible, though not pathognomonic or frequent. In some cases, the examiner will be able to place the arms of the patient in various bizarre positions and note the waxy flexibility with which the patient will remain in those unlikely positions. True catalepsy and sudden freezing of posture have also been described but seem rare.

CHANGES IN CONTROL OF EYE MOVEMENTS

The control of eye and head movements is part of a highly developed system tuned to orient the organism toward possibly important stimuli and therefore aid perception of the environment. The role of the frontal eye-fields, located bilaterally in area 8 of Brodmann, in the control of these movements is still a matter of controversy. The paucity of spontaneous head and eye movement toward new stimuli, which is commonly described in connection with the impairment of orienting responses of frontal-lobe patients, is possibly related to eye-field function. But, on the whole, the value of eye-movement defects in the assessment of higher levels of behavior disturbance is limited.

Frontal seizures, originating in lesions in or near one eye field, may be characterized by turning of the eye and head away from the side of the lesion. On the other hand, structural damage of one eye field, particularly if acute, will produce turning of eyes and head toward the side of lesion.

Clear anomalies of conjugate gaze mechanism have their greatest value in the assessment of the comatose patient, where their relation to a concomitant paresis may decide whether the damage is in the frontal lobe or in the brainstem.

CHANGES IN SPHINCTER CONTROL

It is often noted that patients with frontal-lobe damage have disturbances of sphincter control. The setting in which the disturbances occur is characteristic in that the patient shows little concern about urinating or even defecating in socially unacceptable circumstances. Bilateral involvement of the mesial aspect of the frontal lobe is the rule in these cases. Resection of an underlying tumor will often improve this manifestation which tends to recover in cases of stroke. Extensive lesions of the white matter may also produce incontinence, as the early techniques of frontal lobotomy used to demonstrate. This defect is probably the result of the loss of inhibitory action which the frontal lobe presumably exerts over the spinal detrusor reflex.

CHANGES IN AROUSAL AND ORIENTING RESPONSE

As has been noted, it may prove difficult to distinguish bradykinesia from changes in the mechanisms of arousal. Patients who move little, or not at all, often pay little or no attention to new stimuli and show few signs of spontaneous activity. Changes in arousal mechanisms may also produce periods of sleepiness and confusion which further complicate the clinical picture. The type of abnormality described by Fisher (1968) as "intermittent interruption of behavior" in cases of anterior cerebral artery infarction probably results from a transient change in arousal. Occasionally, in a paradoxic fashion, patients with poor orienting responses are hyperactive and distractable and actually present with hyperactivity.

Concerning the orienting response, it has been recently demonstrated that it is impaired in dorsolateral or cingulate-gyrus damage. The changes generally appear in the setting of a neglect to stimuli arriving in the space contralateral to the lesion, with the associated hypomobility of the neglected side (Heilman and Valenstein, 1972). Lesions in the arcuate region in primates may produce unilateral neglect (Kennard and Ectors, 1938; Welch and Stuteville, 1958), not unlike that determined by lesions of multimodal parietal association areas (Heilman et al., 1971). Lesions in the cingulate gyrus itself may also produce neglect, as Watson et al., (1973) demonstrated, again in monkeys, in a study that clearly separated the effect produced by cingulate damage from that resulting from lesions in the supplementary motor area. Furthermore, unilateral neglect may be produced by lateral hypothalamic lesions, that is, by damage in yet another region with which prefrontal areas are closely connected (Marshall, Turner, and Teitelbaum, 1971; Marshall and Teitelbaum, 1974). These defects are clinically similar to the neglect described in parietal damage in man, particularly in the right hemisphere. In cases of bilateral lesion, the neglect may be bilateral and produce the picture of the inattentive, aspontaneous "frontal lobe" patient. The implication of the limbic and arousal systems in the genesis of neglect and impairment of the orienting response is inescapable. Naturally, lesions of key areas of the frontal lobe, where these systems interweave with the sensory and motor ones, are associated with these defects. (For a further discussion of neglect, see Chapter 10.)

MUTISM

Mutism, generally associated with some degree of bradykinesia, is a very frequent sign of frontal-lobe dysfunction. It probably denotes bilateral mesial involvement of the frontal lobe. The most frequent cause for its appearance is impairment in the blood supply of the anterior cerebral artery territories. Rupture of aneurysms of the anterior communicating artery is the usual antecedent event. The patient is silent and nearly motionless although tracking movements of the eyes, blinking, and some movement of the lips are always preserved. The ability to ambulate is maintained, provided that a paraparesis is not associated. The facial expression is empty and the patient makes no effort to communicate, verbally or otherwise although rare utterances may be produced. He also gives no sign of comprehending questions and no emotional reaction is ever manifested. Repetition of single words can occasionally be performed.

The diagnosis of mutism should only be made after careful judgment of accompanying signs and of the whole context of the clinical presentation. Patients with mutism often suggest psychiatric disease and if it were not for a clarifying previous history, a primarily neurological nature could go unnoticed for some time.

Mutism must be distinguished from anarthria, a condition in which the inability to speak is accompanied by an obvious frustrated intent to communicate verbally. Mutism must also be distinguished from disorders specifically related to verbal communication, such as the transcortical motor aphasias, in which speech is sparse and nonfluent but possible nevertheless, and in which word and sentence repetition is always preserved. A general diminution of verbal communication, reflected in slow, but well-articulated speech, is evident in many cases of bilateral or left frontal-lobe damage and should be differentiated from mutism or the transcortical aphasias (see Chapter 2). In addition, speech may be halted by seizure phenomena related to foci in both frontal lobes if the supplementary motor area is involved (Penfield and Roberts, 1959; Fedio, 1976).

The possibility that mutism associated with frontal-lobe lesions corresponds to a very intense degree of bilateral neglect is an interesting one and some evidence has been marshalled to its support (see Chapter 10). Mutism may also derive from lesions in the diencephalon and mesencephalon (Segarra, 1970) and this must be considered in the evaluation. The differential diagnosis with "locked-in states" and with acute psychotic states or bizarre conversion reactions, must be considered in cases with unclear history.

CHANGES IN AFFECT AND REGULATION
OF EMOTIONAL RESPONSE

The standard descriptions of affective and emotional changes in frontal-lobe patients include the mention of *Witzelsucht,* a term coined by Oppenheim (1889) to describe the facetiousness of these patients, and *moria,* a term coined by Jastrowitz (1888), to denote a sort of caustic euphoric state that is almost inseparable from *Witzelsucht.* Phenomena which resemble such descriptions are occasionally found but it should be understood that in no patients are such changes a permanent feature. Indeed a patient who appears facetious and boastful will look apathetic and indifferent at some later time, or else may show a sudden burst of short-lived anger. The instability of humor also applies to the traditional and somewhat misleading descriptions of "tameness" and "bluntness" of emotion which may be quite changeable and actually give way to unbridled aggressive behavior against a background of poor affect. External circumstances, particularly if they are stressful, as during an examining session, may "set" the patient's emotional tone. Frequently, reaction will be found inappropriate to the circumstances, but not necessarily in a consistent or predictable manner.

When present, facetiousness often has a sexual content, but this is kept within verbal limits and rarely, if ever, does a patient attempt to act according to the wishes or judgments expressed in his profane remarks. The lack of appreciation of social rules is usually quite evident but even so there is no intentional viciousness associated with this type of behavior. Nor is there any indication that it produces pleasure: indeed, affect tends to be shallow. Inability to enjoy pleasurable stimulation particularly if it involves rewards of social, intellectual, and aesthetic nature, is probably characteristic of such patients and is in keeping with restricted response to pain. Both underscore the elementary disorder of affect.

Depressive or hypomanic states, are not encountered. Frontal-lobe patients rarely show the concern and preoccupation which depressed patients do. They may look psychopathic and show expansive, puerile behavior but they lack the organization of the psychopathic personality. The same applies to the so-called hypomania of frontal-lobe disease, which more often consists of an unstable state of exuberance occasionally interrupted by a flareup of irritation. An interesting discussion of these distinctions is provided by Blumer and Benson (1975).

Primary regulatory behaviors associated with positive reward are markedly disturbed and it is common to note the impairment of sexual drive and exploratory drive. Eating habits are commonly disturbed.

The association of changes in affect and in emotional control with predominant involvement of a specific region of the frontal lobe is still unsettled. Many patients with significant disturbances suffer from such extensive lesions that it is necessary to take account of effects elsewhere in the brain, particularly in the nearby limbic-system. However, there is little doubt that the orbital aspect of the frontal lobe is particularly involved in many patients presenting with emotional changes, particularly if the patient's conflicts are with society rather than being only intrapersonal. It is too early to say whether lateralization of lesions may also be important as has been suggested for interictal behavioral disorders (Bear and Fedio, 1977), or for the differences in discriminating affect (Heilman, Scholes, and Watson, 1975). Nevertheless, clinical experience suggests that bilateral or right-frontal damage is probably more conducive to the disturbances than is left-frontal damage. (For a further discussion of emotional changes see Chapter 13.)

CHANGES IN COGNITION AND COMMUNICATION

Impairments of cognitive ability, as measured by standard intelligence tests, are not striking in most patients with frontal-lobe lesions, even when bilateral. With the exception of patients who present with confusion or dementia (as may be the case with large tumors), studies have shown that patients with frontal-lobe lesions may still perform at average levels of intelligence although their overall performance may be lower than expected for age and education. One need only recall Hebb's patient whose IQ was 98, or the very disturbed patient of Brickner who scored 80 one year after operation, but 12 months later actually reached 99. But as Zangwill (1966) clearly pointed out, intelligence tests are unlikely to address the type of cognitive ability lost by frontal-lobe patients. In reality, most forms of objective neuropsychological assessment could be covered by Zangwill's criticism and, accordingly, few such tests disclose any abnormality unless patients have associated confusion or nonfocal brain damage. A partial exception to this rule is impairment in constructive ability, which requires visuomotor coordination to carry out a relatively complex building plan. Such impairment may be seen with some, but by no means all, cases of bilateral or right frontal-lobe damage. It may also be seen in cases of left-hemisphere damage (see Chapter 8).

Verbal fluency, as measured by verbal association tests, can also be objectively impaired. This may be noted in the absence of any detectable change in speech output. A curious instance is Brickner's patient *A*. He spoke fluent and well-articulated speech, often at high rates, manifesting a free flow of verbal association of almost manic nature. However, when given a certain word, his ability to produce morphologically similar words, by changing a letter or letter positions, was impaired. This ability is also impaired in the clinically apparent cases of transcortical motor aphasia.

Broca's aphasia, ideomotor apraxia, and "sympathetic" apraxia, are outside the scope of this chapter, although they are often present in the setting of changes in affect and higher cognition suggestive of damage to more anterior areas of the brain. (See Chapters 2 and 7 on aphasia and apraxia, respectively.) This is probably explained by the characteristics of some lesions producing Broca's aphasia which, by their location and depth, may damage association pathways between the orbital aspect of the frontal lobe and the anterior temporal lobe and limbic system, e.g., the uncinate fasciculus.

The problem of so-called frontal-lobe memory deficit deserves comment. It is doubtful that the presence of marked impairment of recent memory is ever associated with lesions confined to the frontal lobes. Patients with a "Korsakoff-like" deficit probably suffer from pathological involvement elsewhere in the brain, e.g., hippocampus, the fornices, the mamillary bodies, or the dorsomedial thalami. In our experience, some frontal-lobe patients are unusually forgetful, in an absent-minded sort of way. We have noted this to be generally associated with, and probably even produced by, distractability and diminished arousal. In those circumstances, retention or recall may seem to be poor but performance on a different occasion may show no deficit whatever, again underscoring the inconsistency of behavior which marks so many of these cases.

CHANGES IN GOAL-ORIENTED BEHAVIOR

These are the most characteristic changes resulting from frontal-lobe damage and the most difficult to evaluate. The assessment of changes of this level of behavior implies a notion of the limits of normal variation of several aspects of human personality. Naturally, only a relative judgment is possible, taking into account the patient's age, educational level, social and cultural group, and previous achievements. Knowledge of the clinical pictures of the more frequent dementias as well as an acquaintance with the principal psychiatric entities is necessary for this aspect of diagnosis.

In spite of these difficulties, several relatively objective abnormalities can be detected. Lack of insight and lack of foresight are usually quite prominent. Even if able to act on their own, few patients will see the significance of their decisions for themselves and for those around them. Often patients will be unable to organize their daily activity, and planning of near and long-term future will not be possible. As a consequence, during the acute phase of frontal-lobe damage, patients are invariably dependent on relatives or guardians, even if perception and communication abilities are intact. In the more fortunate cases, moderate degrees of independence will be achieved after recovery from major lesions. No patient who has sustained major frontal-lobe lesions will ever engage in creative endeavors or in the pursuit of meaningful interpersonal relationships. Taste, in the social sense, and aesthetic sense, are traits which the frontal-lobe-damaged patient will find difficult or impossible to cultivate.

Such impairments may result from an inability to assess the value of each new action, or lack of action, in terms of goals which are not overtly specified in the immediate environment. We presume that the disturbance of "abstract reasoning," of which so much has been made in analyses of the frontal lobe, really corresponds to this inability to reason according to a program not clearly expounded. One is tempted to hypothesize that either (a) the "master plan" is not available for adequate assessment, or (b) the configuration of stimuli producing action or nonaction is not fully appreciated, or (c) whatever decisions are made are not carried out as planned. Specific derangements which may impair affective coloring of stimuli or which may curtail drive for action may be important, but it seems more likely that the impairment in goal-oriented behavior is ultimately the consequence of a high-level cognitive defect.

CONCLUDING REMARKS

It should be clear from this review that the frontal lobes are not a homogeneous anatomical structures and that damage to them is not manifested by a single syndrome. Certain organizational trends and functional principles can be discerned by reflecting upon the connections of frontal-lobe structures with the rest of the brain, and by considering the behavioral changes produced by different types of lesions at different ages. Although the diversity of clinical presentations and the variety of discrete functions are the keynote, and no single pathognomonic sign can be isolated, the various combinations of syndrome associated with frontal-lobe damage are distinct from those produced by lesions elsewhere in the brain, and therefore contribute to a large pool of manifestations of frontal-lobe dysfunction.

The mere fact that we still resort to the term "frontal lobes" for want of a better heading underscores our modest knowledge of the form and function of this large portion of brain. As noted at the beginning of the chapter, this state of affairs results as much from methodological limitations as from the complexity of the problem under investigation. But recent advances and current developments in neuroanatomy and neurophysiology, make it likely that the enigma of the frontal lobes will be solved in the near future.

References

Ackerly, S. S. and Benton, A. L. (1948). Report of a case of bilateral frontal lobe defect. Research Publication of the Association for Research in Nervous and Mental Disease 27:479–504.

Akert, K. Comparative anatomy of frontal cortex and thalamofrontal connections, in *The Frontal Granular Cortex and Behavior,* J. M. Warren and K. Akert (eds). New York: McGraw-Hill, 1964.

Bailey, P. and Von Bonin, G. *The Isocortex of Man.* Urbana: University of Illinois Press, 1951.

Battig, K., Rosvold, H. E., and Mishkin, M. (1960). Comparison of the effects of frontal and caudate lesions on delayed response and alternation in monkeys. *J. Comp. Physiol. Psychol.* 53:400–404.

Bear, D. M. and Fedio, P. (1977). Quantitative analysis of interictal behavior in temporal lobe epilepsy. *Arch. Neurol. 34*:454–467.

Benton, A. L. (1968). Differential behavioral effects in frontal lobe disease. *Neuropsychologia 6*:53–60.

Berg, E. A. (1948). A simple objective technique for measuring flexibility in thinking. *J. Genet. Psychol. 39*:15–22.

Blum, R. A. (1952). Effects of subtotal lesions of frontal granular cortex on delayed reaction in monkeys. *Arch. Neurol. Psychiat. 67*:375–386.

Blumer, D. and Benson, D. F. (1975). Personality changes with frontal and temporal lobe lesions, in *Psychiatric Aspects of Neurologic Disease,* D. F. Benson and D. Blumer (eds). New York: Grune & Stratton, 1975.

Brickner, R. M. (1934). An interpretation of frontal lobe function based upon the study of a case of partial bilateral frontal lobectomy. Research Publication of the Association for Research in Nervous and Mental Disease *13*:259–351.

Brickner, R. M. (1952). Brain of patient "A" after bilateral frontal lobectomy; status of frontal lobe problem. *Arch. Neurol. Psychiat. 68*:293–313.

Brickner, R. M. (1936). *The Intellectual Functions of the Frontal Lobes: Study Based Upon Observation of a Man After Partial Bilateral Frontal Lobectomy.* New York: Macmillan.

Butter, C. M., Mishkin, M., Mirsky, A. F. (1968). Emotional responses toward humans in monkeys with selective frontal lesions. *Physiol. Behav. 3*:213–215.

Butter, C. M., Mishkin, M., and Rosvold, H. E. (1963). Conditioning and extinction of a food rewarded response after selective ablations of frontal cortex in rhesus monkeys. *Exp. Neurol. 7*:65–75.

Butter, C. M., Snyder, D. R., and McDonald, J. A. (1970). Effects of orbital frontal lesions on aversive and aggressive behaviors in rhesus monkeys. *J. Comp. Physiol. Psychol. 72*:132–144.

Butters, N. and Pandya, D. (1969). Retention of delayed-alternation: effect of selective lesions of sulcus principalis. *Science 165*:1271–1273.

Butters, N., Pandya, D., Sanders, K., and Dye, P. (1971). Behavioral deficits in monkeys after selective lesions within the middle third of sulcus principalis. *J. Comp. Physiol. Psychol. 76*:8–14.

Chavis, D. A. and Pandya, D. N. (1976). Further observations on corticofrontal connections in the rhesus monkey. *Brain Res. 117*:369–386.

Chorover, S. L. and Cole, M. (1966). Delayed alternation performance in patients with cerebral lesions. *Neuropsychologia 4*:1–7.

Corkin, S. H. Somesthetic function after focal cerebral damage in man. Unpublished doctoral thesis, McGill University, 1964.

Critchley, M. (1972). Inter-hemispheric partnership and interhemispheric rivalry, in *Scientific Foundations of Neurology,* M. Critchley, J. L. O'Leary, and B. Jennett (eds). London: Heineman.

Critchley, M. (1930). The anterior cerebral artery and its syndromes. *Brain* 53:120–165.

Crosby, E. C., Humphrey, T., and Lauer, E. W. (1962). *Correlative Anatomy of the Nervous System.* New York: Macmillan.

Dean, W. H. and Davis, G. D. (1959). Behavior following caudate lesions in rhesus monkey. *J. Neurophysiol. 22*:524–537.

DeVito, J. L. and Smith, O. E. (1964). Subcortical projections of the prefrontal lobe of the monkey. *J. Comp. Neurol. 123*:413.

Dieckmann, G. and Hassler, R. Treatment of sexual violence by stereotactive hypothalamatomy. in *Neurosurgical Treatment in Psychiatry, Pain, and Epilepsy,* W. H. Sweet, S. Obrador, and J. G. Martín-Rodríquez (eds). Baltimore: University Park Press, 1977.

Drewe, E. A. (1975). An experimental investigation of Luria's theory on the effects of frontal lobe lesions in man. *Neuropsychologia 13*:421–429.

Ethelberg, S. (1949). On "Cataplexy" in a case of frontal lobe tumour. *Acta Psychiat. Neurol. 24*:421–427.

Faust, C. I. (1966). Different psychological consequences due to superior frontal and orbito-basal lesions. *Intern. J. Neurol. 5*:3–4.

Fedio, P. and VanBuren, J. M. (1976). Functional representation on the medial aspects of the frontal lobes in man. *J. Neurosurg. 44*:275–289.

Feuchtwanger, E. (1923). Die funktionen des stirnhirns, in *Monographien aus dem Gesamtgebiete der Neurologie und Psychiatrie,* O. Förster and K. Willmanns (eds). Berlin: Springer.

Finan, J. L. (1942). Delayed response with predelay reinforcement in monkeys after removal of the frontal lobes. *Am. J. Psychol. 55*:202–214.

Fisher, C. M. (1968). Intermittent interruption of behavior. *Trans. Am. Neurol. Assoc. 93*:209–210.

Freeman, W. and Watts, J. W. (1947). Retrograde degeneration of the thalamus following prefrontal lobotomy. *J. Comp. Neurol. 86*:65.

Fulton, J. F. (1951). *Frontal Lobotomy and Affective Behavior.* New York: Norton.

Fulton, J. F. and Jacobsen, C. F. (1935). The functions of the frontal lobes, a comparative study in monkeys, chimpanzees and man. *Advan. Mod. Biol. (Moscow) 4*:113–123.

Ghent, L., Mishkin, M., and Teuber, H.-L. (1962). Short-term memory after frontal-lobe injury in man. *J. Comp. Physiol. Psychol. 55*:705–709.

Goldman, P. S. and Nauta, W. J. H. (1977). An intricately patterned prefrontocaudate projection in the rhesus monkey. *J. Comp. Neurol. 171*: 369–386.

Goldstein, K. (1948). *Aftereffects of Brain Injuries in War.* New York: Grune & Stratton.

Grant, D. A. and Berg, E. A. (1948). A behavioral analysis of degree of reinforcement and ease of shifting to new responses in a Weigl-type card-sorting problem. *J. Exp. Psychol. 38*:404–411.

Grueninger, W. E., Kimble, D. P., Grueninger, J., and Levine, S. E. (1965).

GSR and corticosteroid response in monkeys with frontal ablations. *Neuropsychologia 3*:205–216.

Grueninger, W. E. and Pribram, K. H. (1969). The effects of spatial and non-spatial distractors on performance latency of monkeys with frontal lesions. *J. Comp. Physiol. Psychol. 68*:203–209.

Hamlin, R. M. (1970). Intellectual function 14 years after frontal lobe surgery. *Cortex 6*:299–307.

Hebb, D. O. (1945). Man's frontal lobes: a critical review. *Arch. Neurol. Psychiat. 54*:421–438.

Hebb, D. O. and Penfield, W. (1940). Human behavior after extensive bilateral removals from the frontal lobes. *Arch. Neurol. Psychiat. 44*: 421–438.

Hécaen, H. (1964). Mental symptoms associated with tumors of the frontal lobe, in *The Frontal Granular Cortex and Behavior*, J. M. Warren and K. Akert (eds). New York: McGraw-Hill.

Heilman, K. M., Pandya, D. N., Karol, E. A., and Geschwind, N. (1971). Auditory inattention. *Arch. Neurol. 24*:323–325.

Heilman, K. M., Scholes, R., and Watson, R. T. (1975). Auditory affective agnosia: disturbed comprehension of affective speech. *J. Neurol. Neurosurg. Psychiat. 38*:69–72.

Heilman, K. M. and Valenstein, E. (1972). Frontal lobe neglect in man. *Neurology 22*:660–664.

Homskaya, E. D. (1966). Vegetative components of the orienting reflex to indifferent and significant stimuli in patients with lesions of the frontal lobes, in *Frontal Lobes and Regulation of Psychological Processes*, A. R. Luria and E. D. Homskaya (eds). Moscow: Moscow University Press.

Jacobsen, C. F. (1935). Functions of the frontal association area in primates. *Arch. Neurol. Psychiat. 33*:558–569.

Jacobsen, C. F. and Nissen, H. W. (1937). Studies of cerebral function in primates. IV. The effects of frontal lobe lesion on the delayed alternation habit in monkeys. *J. Comp. Physiol. Psychol. 23*:101–112.

Jastrowitz, M. (1888). Beiträge zur Localisation im Grosshirn and über deren praktische Verwerthung. *Deutsche Medizinische Wochenschrift 14*:81.

Jefferson, G. (1937). Removal of right or left frontal lobes in man. *Br. Med. J. 2*:199.

Johnson, T. N., Rosvold, H. E., and Mishkin, M. (1968). Projections from behaviorally defined sectors of the prefrontal cortex to the basal ganglia, septum, and diencephalon of the monkey. *Exp. Neurol. 21*: 20.

Kennard, M. A. and Ectors, L. (1938). Forced circling movements in monkeys following lesions of the frontal lobes. *J. Neurophysiol. 1*:45–54.

Kievit, J. and Kuypers, H. G. J. M. (1974). Basal forebrain and hypothalamic connections to frontal and parietal cortex in the rhesus monkey. *Science 187*:660–662.

Kimble, D. P., Bagshaw, M. H., and Pribram, K. H. (1965). The GSR of monkeys during orienting and habituation after selective partial ablations of the cingulate and frontal cortex. *Neuropsychologia, 3*:121–128.

Kleist, K. (1936). *Gehirnpatholgie*. Leipzig: Barth.

Konorski, J. and Lawicka, W. (1964). Analysis of errors by prefrontal animals on the delayed-response test, in *The Frontal Granular Cortex and Behavior*, J. M. Warren and K. Akert (eds). New York: McGraw-Hill.

Kuypers, H. G. J. M., Szwarcbart, M. K., and Mishkin, M. (1965). Occipito-temporal cortico-cortical connections in the rhesus monkey. *Exp. Neurol. 11*:245.

Luria, A. R. (1969). Frontal lobe syndrome, in *Handbook of Clinical Neurology*, Vol. 2, P. J. Vinken and G. W. Bruyn (eds). Amsterdam: North-Holland.

Luria, A. R. (1966). *Human Brain and Psychological Processes*. New York: Harper & Row.

Luria, A. R. and Homskaya, E. D. (1964). Disturbances in the regulative role of speech with frontal lobe lesions, in *The Frontal Granular Cortex and Behavior*, J. M. Warren and K. Akert (eds). New York: McGraw-Hill.

Malmo, R. B. (1942). Interference factors in delayed response in monkeys after removal of frontal lobes. *J. Neurophysiol. 5*:295–308.

Marshall, J. F. and Teitelbaum, P. (1974). Further analysis of sensory inattention following lateral hypothalamic damage in rats. *J. Comp. Physiol. Psychol. 86*:375–395.

Marshall, J. F., Turner, B. H., and Teitelbaum, P. (1971). Sensory neglect produced by lateral hypothalamic damage. *Science 174*:523–525.

Milner, B. (1963). Effects of different brain lesions on card sorting. *Arch. Neurol. 9*:90–100.

Milner, B. (1971). Interhemispheric differences in the localisation of psychological processes in man. *Br. Med. Bull. 27*:272–277.

Milner, B. (1964). Some effects of frontal lobectomy in man, in *The Frontal Granular Cortex and Behavior*, J. M. Warren and K. Akert (eds). New York: McGraw-Hill.

Mishkin, M. (1964). Perseveration of central sets after frontal lesions in monkeys, in *The Frontal Granular Cortex and Behavior*, J. M. Warren and K. Akert (eds). New York: McGraw-Hill.

Mishkin, M. and Pribram, K. H. (1955). Analysis of the effects of frontal lesions in monkeys: I. Variations of delayed alterations. *J. Comp. Physiol. Psychol. 48*:492–495.

Mishkin, M. and Pribram, K. H. (1956). Analysis of the effects of frontal lesions in the monkey: II. Variations of delayed response. *J. Comp. Physiol. Psychol. 49*:36–40.

Moniz, E. (1949). Confidências de um investigador científico. Lisboa: Livraria Atica.

Moniz, E. (1936). *Tentatives Operatoires dans le Traitement de Certaines Psychoses*. Paris: Masson and Cie.

Nádvornik, P., Šramka, M., and Patoprstá, G. (1977). Transventricular anterior hypothalamatomy in stereotactic treatment of hedonia, in *Neurosurgical Treatment in Psychiatry, Pain, and Epilepsy*, W. H. Sweet, S. Obrador, and J. G. Martín-Rodríquez (eds). Baltimore: University Park Press.

Nauta, W. J. H. (1962). Neural associations of the amygdaloid complex in the monkey. *Brain 85*:505–520.

Nauta, W. J. H. (1964). Some efferent connections of the prefrontal cortex in the monkey, in *The Frontal Granular Cortex and Behavior*, J. M. Warren and K. Akert (eds). New York: McGraw-Hill.

Nauta, W. J. H. and Haymaker, W. (1969). *The Hypothalamus*. Springfield, Ill.: C. C. Thomas.

Olds, J. (1958). Effects of hunger and male sex hormone on self-stimulation of the brain. *J. Comp. Physiol. Psychol. 51*:320–324.

Oppenheim, H. (1889). Zur pathologie der grosshirngeschwülste. *Arch. Psychiat. 21*:560.

Orbach, J., Milner, B., and Rasmussen, T. (1960). Learning and retention in monkeys after amygdala-hippocampal resection. *Arch. Neurol. 3*: 230–251.

Pandya, D. N., Dye, P., and Butters, N. (1971). Efferent cortico-cortical projections of the prefrontal cortex in the rhesus monkey. *Brain Res. 31*:35–46.

Pandya, D. N., Hallett, M., and Mukherjee, S. K. (1969). Intra- and inter-hemispheric connections of the neocortical auditory system in the rhesus monkey. *Brain Res. 13*:49.

Pandya, D. N. and Kuypers, H. G. J. M. (1969). Cortico-cortical connections in the rhesus monkey. *Brain Res. 13*:13.

Pandya, D. N. and Vignolo, L. A. (1971). Intra- and interhemispheric projections of the precentral, premotor and arcuate areas in the rhesus monkey. *Brain Res. 26*:217–233.

Penfield, W. and Evans, J. (1935). The frontal lobe in man: a clinical study of maximum removals. *Brain, 58*:115–139.

Penfield, W. and Roberts, L. (1959). *Speech and Brain-Mechanisms*. Princeton: Princeton University Press.

Powell, T. P. S., Cowan, W. M., and Raisman, G. (1965). The central olfactory connexions. *J. Anat. (London) 99*:791.

Pribram, K. H. (1961). A further experimental analysis of the behavioral deficit that follows injury to the primate frontal cortex. *Exp. Neurol. 3*:432–466.

Pribram, K. H., Chow, K. L., and Semmes, J. (1953). Limit and organization of the cortical projection from the medial thalamic nucleus in monkey. *J. Comp. Neurol. 98*:433–448.

Pribram, K. H. and Luria, A. R. (eds). (1973). *Psychophysiology of the Frontal Lobes.* New York: Academic Press.

Pribram, K. H. and MacLean, P. D. (1953). Neuronographic analysis of medial and basal cerebral cortex: II. Monkey. *J. Neurophysiol. 16*: 324–340.

Pribram, K. H., Wilson, W. A., and Connors, J. (1962). Effects of lesions of the medial forebrain on alternation behavior of rhesus monkeys. *Exp. Neurol. 6*:36–47.

Ramier, A.-M. and Hécaen, H. (1970). Rôle respectif des atteintes frontales et de la latéralisation lésionnelle dans les déficits de la "fluence verbale." *Rev. Neurol. 123*:17–22.

Rosene, D. L., Mesulam, M-M., and Van Hoesen, G. W. (1976). Afferents to area FL of the medial frontal cortex from the amygdala and hippocampus of the rhesus monkey. *Neuroscience Abstracts,* Vol. 2, Part 1. Bethesda, Md.: Society for Neuroscience.

Rosvold, H. E. and Delgado, J. M. R. (1956). The effect on delayed-alternation test performance of stimulating or destroying electrically structures within the frontal lobes of the monkey's brain. *J. Comp. Physiol. Psychol. 49*:365–372.

Rosvold, H. E. (1964). In discussion on B. Milner's presentation in *The Frontal Granular Cortex and Behavior,* J. M. Warren and K. Akert (eds). New York: McGraw-Hill.

Rubens, A. B. (1975). Aphasia with infarction in the territory of the anterior cerebral artery. *Cortex 11*:239–250.

Russell, W. R. (1959). *Brain, Memory and Learning.* New York: Oxford University Press.

Rylander, G. (1940). *Personality Changes After Operations on the Frontal Lobes.* Copenhagen: Munksgaard.

Schneider, H. (1977). Psychic changes in sexual delinquency after hypothalamotomy, in *Neurosurgical Treatment in Psychiatry, Pain, and Epilepsy,* W. H. Sweet, S. Obrador, and J. G. Martín-Rodríquez (eds). Baltimore: University Park Press.

Schulman, J. S. (1969). Electrical stimulation of monkey's prefrontal cortex during delayed response performance. *J. Comp. Physiol. Psychol. 67*: 535–546.

Scoville, W. B., and Bettis, D. B. (1977). Results of orbital undercutting today: a personal series, in *Neurosurgical Treatment in Psychiatry, Pain, and Epilepsy,* W. H. Sweet, S. Obrador, and J. G. Martín-Rodríquez (eds). Baltimore: University Park Press.

Scoville, W. B. and Milner, B. (1957). Loss of recent memory after bilateral hippocampal lesions. *J. Neurol. Neurosurg. Psychiat. 20*:11–21.

Segarra, J. and Angelo, J. (1970). Anatomical determinants of behavioral change, in *Behavioral Change in Cerebrovascular Disease*, A. L. Benton (ed). New York: Harper & Row.

Simernitskaya, E. G. (1970). *Evoked Potentials as an Indicator of the Active Process*. Moscow: Moscow University Press.

Simernitskaya, E. G. and Homskaya, E. D. (1966). Changes in evoked potentials to significant stimuli in normal subjects and in lesions of the frontal lobes, in *Frontal Lobes and Regulation of Psychological Processes*, A. R. Luria and E. D. Homskaya (eds). Moscow: Moscow University Press.

Stamm, J. S. (1961). Electrical stimulation of frontal cortex in monkeys during learning of an alternation task. *J. Neurophysiol. 24*:414–426.

Stamm, J. S. (1969). Electrical stimulation of monkeys' prefrontal cortex during delayed-response performance. *J. Comp. Physiol. Psychol. 67*: 535–546.

Teuber, H.-L. (1966). The frontal lobes and their function: further observations on rodents, carnivores, subhuman primates, and man. *Intern. J. Neurol. 5*:282–300.

Teuber, H.-L. (1964). The riddle of frontal lobe function in man, in *The Frontal Granular Cortex and Behavior*, J. M. Warren and K. Akert (eds). New York: McGraw-Hill.

Teuber, H.-L. and Mishkin, M. (1954). Judgment of visual and postural vertical after brain injury. *J. Psychol. 38*:161–175.

Teuber, H.-L. and Weinstein, S. (1956). Ability to discover hidden figures after cerebral lesions. *Arch. Neurol. Psychiat. 76*:369-379.

Teuber, H.-L. and Weinstein, S. (1954). Performance on a formboard-task after penetrating brain injury. *J. Psychol. 38*:177–190.

Valenstein, E. S. (1969). Behavior elicited by hypothalamic stimulation: a prepotency hypothesis. *Brain Behav. Evol. 2*:295–316.

Valenstein, E. S. (1966). The anatomical locus of reinforcement, in *Progress in Physiological Psychology*, Vol. 1, E. Stellar and J. Sprague (eds). New York: Academic Press.

Valenstein, E. S. (1970). Stability and plasticity of motivational systems, in *The Neurosciences: Second Study Program*, F. O. Schmit (ed). New York: Rockefeller University Press.

Valverde, F. (1965). *Studies on the Piriform Lobe*. Cambridge, Mass.: Harvard University Press.

Van Buren, J. M. and Fedio, P. (1976). Functional representation on the medial aspect of the frontal lobes in man. *J. Neurosurg. 44*:275–289.

Ward, A. A. and McCulloch, W. S. (1947). The projection of the frontal lobe on the hypothalamus. *J. Neurophysiol. 10*:309–314.

Watson, R. T., Heilman, K. M., Cauthen, J. C., and King, F. A. (1973). Neglect after cingulectomy. *Neurology 23*:1003–1007.

Watson, R. T., Heilman, K. M., Miller, B. D., and King, F. A. (1974). Neglect after mesencephalic reticular formation lesions. *Neurology 24*: 294–298.

Weinstein, S. and Teuber, H.-L. (1957). Effects of penetrating brain injury on intelligence test scores. *Science 125*:1036–1037.

Welch, K. and Stuteville, P. (1958). Experimental production of neglect in monkeys. *Brain 81*:341–347.

Whitlock, D. C. and Nauta, W. J. H. (1956). Subcortical projections from the temporal neocortex in *Macaca mulatta*. *J. Comp. Neurol. 106*:183–212.

Yeterian, E. H. and Van Hoesen, G. W. (1977). Cortico-striate projections in the Rhesus monkey: the organization of certain cortico-caudate connections. *Brain Res. 139*:43–63.

Zangwill, O. L. (1966). Psychological deficits associated with frontal lobe lesions. *Intern. J. Neurol. 5*:395–402.

ACKNOWLEDGMENTS

The author thanks Drs. Arthur Benton and Gary Van Hoesen for their critique of the manuscript and Dr. Hanna Damasio for help in researching and preparing the text.

13

Emotional Disorders Resulting From Lesions of the Central Nervous System

EDWARD VALENSTEIN AND
KENNETH M. HEILMAN

INTRODUCTION

Patients with neurological diseases may react to illness with emotions such as depression, anxiety, denial, or anger. Emotional states may also cause, intensify, or simulate neurological disease. For example, tension headaches may result from anxiety, emotional states may intensify seizure disorders, and the hysterical patient may simulate weakness or sensory loss. In this respect, neurological diseases are not different from diseases of other organ systems. Diseases affecting the CNS (central nervous system), however, have the additional opportunity to affect directly the structures that mediate emotional behavior and thus to produce emotional change as a symptom. In this chapter we will discuss neither emotional reactions to illness nor emotionally induced diseases. We will only deal with changes in emotional state that are directly caused by diseases which affect the CNS.

A knowledge of normal physiology would be helpful in understanding how CNS diseases affect emotions; however, as is so often the case in the CNS (especially when dealing with complex behavior), little is known about the normal physiology of emotion. In fact, the investigation of pathological states has so far been the most helpful means of understanding normal physiology. Nevertheless, speculation about the psychophysiology of emotion may provide a framework for discussing the pathophysiology of emotions.

THE PSYCHOPHYSIOLOGICAL BASIS OF EMOTION

William James (1890) proposed that emotions were actually the experience of bodily changes which result from perceiving a set of stimuli. ". . . the bodily changes follow directly the perception of the exciting fact, and . . . our feeling of the same changes as they occur is the emotion." I cry, therefore I must be sad. Subsequent work tended to refute James' theory. Dana (1921) found that patients who had high cervical spinal cord transections (and thus had no feeling of bodily changes below the neck) still had emotions. Cannon (1927) cited this finding as well as similar evidence from animals to refute James' theory. In addition, he pointed out that similar bodily changes occur with different emotions.

Cannon regarded the thalamus as an important central structure for the mediation of emotions. It could be stimulated either by peripheral sensory input or by cortical impulses. He proposed that thalamic activity would excite both the cortex and the viscera: cortical activation produced the conscious emotional state, while visceral changes occurred simultaneously and served adaptive purposes. Bard (1934) demonstrated that the hypothalamus was, in fact, the major effector of emotional expression. It regulates both the endocrine system and the autonomic nervous system. Papez (1937) proposed that the limbic system, which has important connections with the hypothalamus, is important in the regulation of emotion.

The concept of cortical activation by emotion was central to Cannon's theory. Subsequent physiological work led to a better understanding of the physiology of arousal. Berger (1933) noted that during behavioral arousal the electroencephalographic (EEG) pattern decreased in amplitude and increased in frequency. This was termed EEG "desynchronization." EEG desynchronization also occurs during emotional states (Lindsley, 1970). Animals stimulated in the non-specific thalamic nuclei or in the mesencephalic reticular formation also show behavioral arousal and EEG desynchronization (Moruzzi and Magoun, 1949). In addition, stimulation of certain cortical areas activates the mesencephalic reticular formation

(French et al., 1955) and elicits an arousal response (Segundo et al., 1955). The limbic system, which has strong input into the reticular activating system, is one pathway by which cortical stimulation can produce arousal (Heilman and Valenstein, 1972; Watson et al., 1973).

These studies provided some understanding of the anatomy and physiology underlying arousal. The relationship of arousal to the experience of emotion was, in part, defined in studies on normal human subjects. Maranon (1924) induced physiological arousal by injecting sympathomimetic drugs and found that most of his subjects felt no emotions, but many experienced "as if" feelings. When Maranon provided his subjects with an affective memory which was not strong enough to produce an emotion in the normal state, emotional reactions occurred if there was concomitant pharmacological arousal. Schacter (1970) aroused normal subjects pharmacologically, placed them in a stressful situation, and found subjective and objective evidence of emotion. Pharmacological arousal alone did not produce emotion, and the stressful situation produced less emotion when the subjects were not pharmacologically aroused.

These studies support the hypothesis that in order to feel an emotion one must have the appropriate cognitive state plus a certain degree of arousal. Arousal depends on the brainstem reticular formation, nonspecific thalamic nuclei, and certain regions of the neocortex. Emotions are accompanied by visceral changes that are mediated by the hypothalamus. The hypothalamus is strongly influenced by the limbic system which, in turn, has considerable input from the neocortex (especially the frontal lobes). An emotion thus depends on varied anatomic structures: (1) cortical systems to produce the appropriate cognitive set; (2) limbic structures to activate the brainstem and thalamic activating centers and to control hypothalamic output; (3) the hypothalamus to regulate endocrine and autonomic responses; (4) the brainstem and thalamic activating systems to produce cortical arousal.

THE LIMBIC SYSTEM AND HYPOTHALAMUS

In 1878, Broca designated a group of anatomically related structures on the medial wall of the cerebral hemisphere "le grand lobe limbique." Because those structures were in proximity to structures of

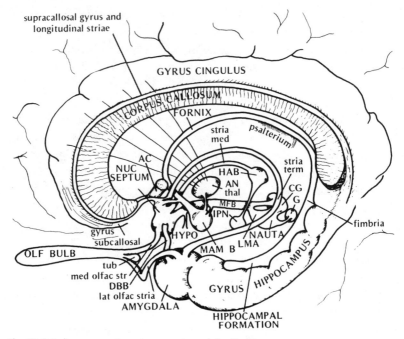

Fig. 13-1 A diagrammatic representation of the limbic system.

AC—Anterior commissure,
ANthal—Anterior Nucleus of the thalamus,
CG—Central gray matter of the midbrain,
DBB—Diagonal Band of Broca,
G—Gudden's deep tegmental nucleus,
HAB—Habenula,
HYPO—hypothalamus,
IPN—Interpeduncular nucleus,
LMA NAUTA—Lateral midbrain area of Nauta,
lat olf str—lateral olfactory stria,
med olf str—medial olfactory stria,
MFB—median forebrain bundle,
MAM B—mamillary bodies,
stria med—stria medullaris,
stria term—stria terminalis.

the olfactory system, it was assumed that they all had olfactory or related functions. In 1901, Ramon y Cajal concluded on the basis of histological studies that portions of the limbic lobe (the hippocampal-fornix system) had no more than a neighborly relationship with the olfactory apparatus. Papez (1937) postulated that a "circuit" in the limbic lobe (cingulate-hippocampus-fornix-mamillary bodies-anterior thalamus-cingulate) was an important component of the central mechanism subserving emotional feeling and expression. Bard (1934) had demonstrated that the hypothalamus was important in mediating a rage response and Papez postulated that the hypothalamus was the effector of emotion. In 1948, Yakovlev added the basolateral components (orbitofrontal, insular and anterior temporal lobe cortical region, amygdala and dorsomedial nucleus of the thalamus) to the medial system and together these were designated as the limbic system (MacLean, 1952).

Experimental observations in animals

There has been a myriad of stimulation and ablation experiments in animals which have attempted to define the role of the limbic system in regulating emotion (Valenstein, 1973). Many of these studies have provided confusing and contradictory results. Some of the difficulty undoubtedly results from the complex organization within each component of the limbic system (Isaacson, 1974). There is probably significant functional differentiation within each component. Adding to this is the difficulty of measuring affect in animals; most experiments use techniques such as active or passive avoidance and infer the emotional state from the animal's behavior. Finally, species differences may be significant, even in this phylogenetically older portion of the cerebral hemispheres, and it is not clear that the results of animal experiments are directly relevant to the study of human emotions.

One of the earliest and most important animal observations was that bilateral ablation of the anterior temporal lobe changes the aggressive rhesus monkey into a tame animal (Klüver and Bucy, 1937). Such animals also demonstrated hypersexuality and visual agnosia. Akert et al. (1961) demonstrated that removal of the temporal lobe neocortex did not produce this tameness. Ursin (1960) stimulated the amygdaloid nucleus and produced a rage-like response and an increase in emotional behavior. Amygdala ablation (Woods, 1956) produced placid animals.

Septal lesions in animals, on the other hand, produce a rage-like state (Brady and Nauta, 1955) and septal stimulation produces an apparently pleasant state in which animals will stimulate themselves without additional reward (Olds, 1958). Decortication in animals produces a state of pathological rage ("sham rage"). In a series of experiments, Bard (1934) demonstrated that the caudal hypothalamus was mediating this response. Both the amygdala (a component of the basolateral circuit and the septal region (a portion of both limbic circuits) have great input into the hypothalamus (Yakolev, 1948). MacLean (1952) has proposed that the septal pathway is important for species preservation (that is, social-sexual behavior), while the amygdala circuit is more important for self preservation (fight and flight).

Limbic dysfunction in man
DISCRETE LESIONS AND STIMULATION

Some of the findings in man have been analogous to the results reported in animals. In man, for example, tumors in the septal region have been reported to produce rage-like attacks and increased irritability (Zeman and King, 1958; Poeck and Pilleri, 1961), while stimulation is reported to be pleasant and sexually arousing (Heath, 1964). Bilateral temporal lobe lesions in man entailing the destruction of the amygdala, uncus, and hippocampal gyrus have been reported to produce placidity (Poeck, 1969). In aggressive patients, stereotactic amygdaloidectomy has been reported to reduce rage (Mark, Sweet, and Erwin, 1972). Anterior temporal lobectomy for seizure disorders has been reported to increase sexuality (Blumer and Walker, 1975). An unexpected finding in man was that bilateral hippocampal removal produces a profound and permanent deficit in recent memory, an effect which cannot be demonstrated with certainty in animals (see Chapter 14).

NATURAL DISEASE AFFECTING THE LIMBIC SYSTEM

Inflammatory conditions. Several inflammatory and viral diseases have been known to affect the limbic system. Herpes simplex encephalitis has a predilection for destroying the orbitofrontal and anterior temporal regions and thus selectively destroys much of the limbic system. Impulsivity, memory loss, and abnormalities of emotional behavior such as depression are frequent early manifestations of this infection. Limbic encephalitis may also be associated with carcinoma. There is degeneration and inflammation of amygdaloid nuclei, hippocampi, cingular gyri, as well as other structures. Clinically, the picture is similar to herpes infection with memory loss and abnormalities of emotional behavior including depression, agitation, and anxiety (Corsellis et al., 1968). Rabies, which also has a predilection for limbic structures such as the hippocampus (as well as hypothalamic and brainstem regions), also has prominent emotional symptomatology including profound anxiety and agitation.

Temporal-lobe epilepsy. Partial (focal) seizures with complex symptomatology (temporal-lobe epilepsy, psychomotor epilepsy) have long been known to produce emotional symptomatology. This symptomatology may be considered under three headings: ictal phenomena (phenomena directly related to the seizure discharge), post-ictal phenomena (occurring directly after a seizure), and inter-ictal behavior (occurring between overt seizures).

1. Ictal phenomena. One of the strongest arguments supporting the notion that the limbic system is of importance in emotional behavior is the observation that emotional change as a manifestation of a seizure discharge is highly correlated with foci in or near the limbic system, particularly with foci in the anteromedial temporal lobes. Phenomena include visceral sensations (such as a "rising" feeling in the abdomen and thorax or, rarely, sexual stimulation), emotions (most often fear, but sometimes rage or elation), and complex states (deja vu, depersonalization). True rage attacks are rare, but well documented, ictal manifestations of temporal-lobe epilepsy.

2. Post-ictal phenomena. Many patients are confused, restless, and combative after a seizure and apparently particularly after a temporal-lobe seizure. Instances of aggression in this state are common but usually consist only of the patient struggling with persons trying to restrain him.

3. Inter-ictal phenomena. This has proven to be the most difficult of issues, and has yet to be resolved. Patients with temporal-lobe epilepsy are said to have a dramatic, and possibly specific, disorder of personality (Blumer and Benson, 1975). Slater and Beard (1963) described "schizophreniform" psychosis in patients with temporal-lobe epilepsy, but they described selected cases and could not comment

on the incidence of this disorder in temporal-lobe epileptics. Other studies (Currie et al., 1971) have failed to show a higher than expected incidence of psychosis in temporal-lobe epileptics, but it can still be maintained that less severe psychiatric abnomalities could have eluded these investigators. Other studies which claim to show no difference in emotional makeup between temporal-lobe and other epileptics (Stevens, 1966; Guerrant et al., 1962) have been reinterpreted (Blumer, 1975) to indicate that there is, in fact, a difference: temporal-lobe epileptics are likely to have more serious forms of emotional disturbance.

The "typical personality" of the temporal-lobe epileptic has been described in roughly similar terms over many years (Blumer and Benson, 1975; Geschwind, 1975, 1977). These patients are said to have a deepening of emotions; they ascribe great significance to commonplace events. This can be manifested as a tendency to take a "cosmic" view; hyper-religiosity (or intensely professed atheism) is said to be common. Concern with minor details results in slowness of thought and circumstantiality and can also be manifested by hypergraphia, a tendency of such patients to record in writing minute details of their lives (Waxman and Geschwind, 1974). In the extreme, psychosis, often with prominent paranoid qualities, can be seen (the "schizophreniform" psychosis noted above) but, unlike schizophrenics, these patients do not have a "flat" affect and they tend to maintain interpersonal relations better. Inter-ictal aggressiveness is common. Hyposexuality is often described.

Bear and Fedio (1977) have recently designed a questionnaire specifically to detect personality features. They found that these personality changes are significantly more common among temporal-lobe epileptics than among normal subjects. Furthermore, in accordance with other studies (Flor-Henry, 1969; McIntyre, Pritchard, and Lombroso, 1976), they found that patients with right-hemisphere foci are more likely to show emotional tendencies (elation, sadness, etc.) and denial, while patients with left-temporal-lobe foci show ideational abberations (paranoia, sense of personal destiny) and dissocial behavior. This study is the first to show in a systematic way that temporal-lobe seizures are associated with inter-ictal disturbances in personality. Since a control population with seizure foci in other sites was not used, however, the specificity of these changes to limbic regions can still be questioned.

THE CORTEX

Although a well-developed limbic system appears to be the common denominator of mammalian brains (MacLean, 1952), with the development of a large neocortex, certain functions relative to self-preservation were usurped by the neocortex. In man, the neocortex is important in sensory and perceptual analysis, cognitive activity, and motor programs. Externally directed activity aimed at preservation of the self or the species is mediated for the most part by the neocortex. The limbic system and hypothalamus monitor the internal milieu and induce drive states. They are responsible for internally directed self-preservation activity.

The frontal lobes

Although the posterior neocortex has some projections to the limbic system, its major projections are to the frontal lobes. The anterior frontal lobes receive projections not only from the posterior neocortical regions but also from limbic areas. The frontal lobes also project to the limbic system, motor areas, and posterior neocortex. In this manner, the limbic system influences the frontal lobes and modulates externally directed higher forms of drives, and the neocortex influences the limbic system, altering internally directed drive states. Lesions of the frontal lobes therefore produce a dissociation between these systems: there is less neocortical influence on the limbic system and less limbic influence on neocortical function.

The emotional symptomatology of frontal-lobe lesions appears to vary depending on the site of the lesion. The orbital (basal) aspect of the frontal lobes have extensive connections to the septal area and the amygdala. Lesions in the orbitofrontal cortex produce disinhibition of these areas. Patients with orbitofrontal lesions not uncommonly demonstrate inappropriate irritability and anger, as well as inappropriate sexual activity. The dorsolateral aspect of the frontal lobe has input into the cingulate gyrus and the reticular activating system. Patients with lesions of the dorsolateral frontal lobe often have a defect in phasic arousal: although they can develop the correct cognitive state in response to external stimuli, they fail to be aroused. When they note something which should produce an emotional reaction, they appear unemotional (emotional blunting). Lesions in portions of the limbic system which modulate this arousal also can produce emotional blunting (for example, lesions of the amygdala, cingulate, and lateral hypothalamus) (see Chapter 12).

Perceptual and cognitive function

The development of an emotional cognitive state is dependent on the perception of a set of stimuli. Lesions which interfere with sensory end-organs or with the conduction of impulses from these end-organs to the CNS will obviously prevent a cognitive state from being formed on the basis of stimuli of that sensory modality. In addition, however, it appears that for certain types of input, there are significant asymmetries in hemispheric processing which have a bearing on the perception of stimuli which normally produce emotional responses.

LANGUAGE

Language may be said to carry two different sorts of information simultaneously: the linguistic content and the affective content. The linguistic content is conveyed by a complex code familiar to all of us which requires phonemic and semantic decoding. The affective content is conveyed by the pitch, tempo, and tonal contours of speech (Paul, 1909), and consequently requires a different sort of processing. In most people (particularly in right-handers), the left hemisphere is clearly superior to the right in the decoding of linguistic content. Patients with left-hemisphere lesions, especially in the posterior temporal and parietal region, may not be able to comprehend propositional language. When the development of an emotional state is dependent on the comprehension of propositional language, patients with aphasia may not be able to form the appropriate cognitive state.

Aphasic patients with poor comprehension of language may nevertheless be able to comprehend affective intonation (how something is said, rather than what is said). We recently tested a global aphasic who had a large left-hemisphere perisylvian infarction. This patient could not follow simple pointing commands, nor could he respond correctly to yes/no questions. We placed before him pictures of four faces (happy, sad, angry, and indifferent) and read neutral sentences with different affective tones. This patient flawlessly pointed to the appropriate face. Observations of this man and other patients with similar language comprehension disturbances thus suggest that these patients can develop an appropriate cognitive state from the affective intonation of language.

In contrast, patients with right-hemisphere lesions have difficulty with the same task. Heilman et al. (1975) compared the performance of patients with right temporoparietal infarctions with that of aphasic patients with left temporoparietal infarctions on this task. The performance of patients with right-hemisphere lesions was much poorer than that of the aphasic controls.

Studies in normals using the dichotic listening technique (Kimura, 1967) lend support to the notion that the left and right hemispheres process different aspects of language. In the dichotic task, two different auditory stimuli are presented simultaneously to the two ears and the subject is asked to recall what he has heard. The ear with superior performance is contralateral to the hemisphere dominant for processing the auditory stimulus. Using this technique, Haggard and Parkinson (1971) and Carmon and Nachshon (1973) presented words spoken with emotional tones. When the subjects were asked to recall which words they heard, they recalled more of the words presented to the right ear; however, when asked to recall the emotional mood of the speaker, the subjects recalled more moods presented to the left ear.

The failure of right-hemisphere-damaged patients to distinguish affective tones in speech may be purely perceptual or it may reflect a cognitive deficit. To distinguish between these alternatives, Tucker et al. (1977) required patients with right-hemisphere lesions to discriminate between pairs of sentences that had the same words but were spoken with either the same or different tonal contours. The patient did not have to identify the emotion but merely to tell if the sentences sounded the same or different. These patients performed more poorly in this task than aphasic controls. This result indicated a perceptual difficulty. A similar group of patients was asked to identify the emotion conveyed by different stories which were read without affective intonation. The stories clearly conveyed an emotion, but they did not name the emotion (that is, the words sad, happy, or angry were not used). On this task, patients with right-hemisphere disease performed as well as controls. These patients thus have not lost the concept of what different emotions mean.

VISUOSPATIAL

Gardner et al. (1975) found that the ability to choose the most humorous of a group of cartoons was impaired equally in right- and left-hemisphere-damaged patients. Right-hemisphere-damaged patients, however, performed better on items with captions, while left-hemisphere-damaged patients performed better on captionless items.

Lesions of the right hemisphere may interfere with the ability to recognize faces (prosopagnosia, see Benton and Van Allen, 1968). In normal subjects, emotional faces are recognized better when projected to the left half of the visual field than when they are projected to the right half, suggesting that the perception of emotional faces is mediated by the right hemisphere (Suberi and McKeever, 1977). These observations on normal subjects would suggest that right-hemisphere lesions should interfere with the recognition of emotional faces. We have tested nine patients with right temporo-parietal lesions and compared them to eight aphasic controls with left-hemisphere lesions and nine patients without hemispheric lesions (DeKosky et al., 1979). We tested the subjects' ability (1) to match faces (same/different), (2) to recognize the emotion expressed by a face, (3) to match emotions expressed on the same face (same/different), and (4) to recognize the emotion brought to mind by scenes which depict situations similar to those described in the stories mentioned before. Right-hemisphere-impaired patients demonstrated an inability to match faces, as previously reported (Benton and Van Allen, 1968). Both right- and left-hemisphere-impaired patients had difficulty recognizing emotional faces and there was a trend for the right-hemisphere-impaired patients to perform more poorly than those impaired on the left. Similarly, the right-hemisphere group did not match emotional faces as well as those impaired on the left. When we covaried for prosopagnosia, the right- and left-hemisphere groups were no longer different, suggesting that the same defect underlying these patients' prosopagnosia may be underlying their inability to recognize and match emotional faces. More specifically, it appears that these patients have difficulty discriminating faces, rather than a specific defect for recognizing emotional faces.

Arousal

Goldstein (1948) noted that patients with left-hemisphere lesions and aphasia demonstrated a profound depression which he termed the catastrophic reaction. Hécaen et al. (1951) and Denny-Brown et al. (1952) noted that patients with right-hemisphere disease appear inappropriately indifferent.

Gainotti (1972) studied the emotional reactions of 160 patients with lateralized brain damage, and his findings supported earlier clinical observations that patients with left-hemisphere disease suffer catastrophic reactions and those with right-hemisphere disease show indifference. To explain these asymmetries, Gainotti postulated that the catastrophic reaction in patients with left-hemisphere disease was basically a normal response to a serious deficit in physical and cognitive functions. He felt the indifference reaction was an abnormal mood associated with denial of illness. We (Gasparrini et al., 1977) gave the Minnesota Multiphasic Personality Inventory (MMPI) to a group of right- and left-hemisphere-impaired patients. Both right- and left-hemisphere groups were examined with a battery of cognitive tests (e.g., Wechsler Adult Intelligence scale) and manual skill tests (e.g., finger tapping). Although there were no differences between the right- and left-hemisphere groups' performance on the cognitive tests, there was a difference on scale 2 (depression) of the MMPI, the left-hemisphere impaired group being more depressed than the group impaired on the right. These results confirm the previous clinical observations and demonstrate that the differences between the emotional states seen with right- and left-hemisphere disease cannot be explained by differences in the severity of cognitive deficits.

To ascertain if patients with the indifference reaction had normal arousal, Heilman et al. (1977) tested them by stimulating their normal side with an electrical stimulus and recording galvanic skin responses (GSR), also from the normal side. The GSR is a measure of peripheral sympathetic activity which correlates well with other central measures of arousal such as EEG. Patients with the indifference reaction showed less arousal response than non-brain-damaged

controls. Aphasic patients showed not only a greater arousal response than patients with the indifferent response but also showed
a greater arousal response than did the non-brain-damaged controls.

Patients with indifference reaction from right-hemisphere disease
have unilateral neglect (Denny-Brown et al., 1952; Gainotti, 1972;
Heilman and Valenstein, 1972); also, see this volume, Chapter 10).
We have proposed that unilateral neglect is an attention-arousal defect caused by dysfunction in a corticolimbic-reticular loop (Heilman and Valenstein, 1972; Watson et al., 1973). The corticoreticular
loop is similar to that proposed by Sokolov (1963), the cortex being
responsible for stimulus analysis (novel versus nonnovel; significant
versus nonsignificant), and the reticular formation mediating arousal.
Unilateral stimulation of the reticular formation produces bilateral
arousal, the ipsilateral hemisphere demonstrating more arousal than
the controlateral hemisphere (Moruzzi and Magoun, 1949). Unilateral cortical stimulation also produces bilateral arousal. The areas
of the cortex which produce bilateral arousal when stimulated, produce neglect when ablated (Segundo et al., 1955).

In addition to the GSR data mentioned above, there is other evidence that right temporoparietal lesions are associated with bilateral arousal disturbances. Reaction times, which are a measure of
activation, are slower after right-hemisphere lesions than after left-
hemisphere lesions (DeRenzi and Faglioni, 1965), DeRenzi and
Faglioni postulated that this interhemispheric difference resulted
from a tendency for right-hemisphere lesions to be larger than left-
hemisphere lesions, but Howes and Boller (1975) demonstrated that
it was not lesion size which produces this asymmetry. Howes and
Boller also found that of all cortical lesions, those in the right parietal lobe produce the greatest slowing of the reaction time. We
have seen fluent and global aphasics with an indifference reaction
and neglect associated with left-posterior-hemisphere lesions. We
had the opportunity to test one of these patient's GSR to stimuli
and noted that he had a bilateral defect in arousal similar to that
seen in our patients with right-sided neglect.

Although an indifference reaction and neglect can be seen in patients with posterior aphasia, the two disorders are more common
and are more severe with right- than with left-hemisphere disease.
Utilizing this data, we have proposed that it is the right hemisphere

that is dominant for mediating an attention-arousal-activation response (Heilman et al., 1977).

In addition to parietal-lobe lesions (Critchley, 1966), unilateral lesions in the following areas in man can also produce contralateral neglect: dorsolateral frontal lobes (Heilman and Valenstein, 1972), cingulate gyrus (Watson et al., 1973), mesencephalic reticular formation (Watson et al., 1974), and thalamic reticular formation (Watson and Heilman, 1968). We believe lesions in these areas produce neglect because they interrupt the corticolimbic-reticular loop postulated to be important in mediating an arousal-activation response. These lesions have been predominantly right-sided. Lesions in all of these areas have also been associated with the indifference reaction. Bilateral lesions in the same areas (i.e., frontal, cingulate, and reticular) produce an even more pronounced arousal-activation disorder: whereas patients with unilateral lesions are hypokinetic and indifferent, patients with bilateral lesions become akinetic and emotionally unresponsive (Nielson and Jacobs, 1951; Segarra and Angelo, 1970; Heilman and Valenstein, 1972; Watson et al., 1973, 1974). (For further discussion see Chapter 10.)

Cortical control of emotional expression

Hemispheric asymmetries also appear to be present when expressive speech is examined. Patients with aphasia from left-hemisphere lesions frequently have difficulty expressing their emotions using propositional speech; however, as Hughlings Jackson first noted, there are aphasic patients who can, by varying tempo, pitch, and timbre, convey a rich variety of emotional feeling, despite their incapability of producing propositional speech. These same nonfluent aphasic patients may also be able to curse quite fluently.

Patients with right-hemisphere lesions, on the other hand, are able to use propositional speech to express emotions, but may be incapable of using affective intonation (Tucker et al., 1977). When asked to repeat a neutral sentence (for example, "The boy went to the store.") with emotional feeling, these patients repeat the sentence in a monotone, often denoting the emotion by using propositional speech (for example, "The boy went to the store. He was sad.").

We have compared the ability of six right- and six left-hemisphere-impaired patients to make emotional faces and found no difference, however a recent study suggests the right hemisphere may be dominant (Sackeim et al., 1978).

SUBCORTICAL STRUCTURES

Arousal

Since an arousal response is dependent on a corticolimbic-reticular loop, diseases which affect the subcortical white matter (e.g., hydrocephalus, lacunar state), the reticular activating system, and related structures may also produce hypokinesia and an indifference reaction.

Endogenous and exogenous drugs and toxins may also affect the reticular activating system, producing sedation and indifference. Many drugs alter catecholamine metabolism. Catecholamines may be transmitters in the ascending system important in mediating arousal. A review of psychopharmacology is beyond the scope of this chapter.

The basal ganglia

The basal ganglia, consisting of the caudate, putamen, globus pallidus, subthalamus, and related brainstem structures, are a group of subcortical nuclei with extensive cortical and subcortical connections. Because disorders of movement are prominent with certain types of pathology in these regions, the basal ganglia have been investigated extensively in connection with the motor system. There are diseases which are associated with lesions in the basal ganglia, however, which also have prominent behavioral and emotional symptomatology. Although the mechanisms by which these diseases produce emotional and behavioral changes are still obscure, it has been found that some of the diseases are associated with abnormalities of neurotransmitter function.

PARKINSON'S DISEASE

Parkinson's disease is associated with depigmentation and neuronal loss in the substantia nigra. The prominent neurological findings consist of tremor, rigidity, bradykinesia, and loss of postural reflexes. Patients often appear emotionally unresponsive or depressed; however, emotional responsiveness and expression are difficult to study since parkinsonian patients typically are hypokinetic and have "masked" facies.

The nigrostriatal pathway which specifically degenerates in patients with parkinsonism is a dopamine-containing pathway. The
dramatic improvement in many features of the disease following
treatment with L-dopa (a precursor of dopamine) is thought to substantiate the importance of the lack of dopamine in this syndrome.
Some patients who are treated with L-dopa, however, develop a depression. More rarely, they may become manic.

HUNTINGTON'S CHOREA

Huntington's chorea is a dominantly inherited condition which is
characterized pathologically by severe cell loss and consequent shrink-
age of the caudate and putamen with concomitant cell loss in the
frontal neocortex. Clinically, the patients exhibit chorea (a movement disorder characterized by unpredictable movements of the face
and extremities) and dementia. In addition, patients often present
with emotional and behavioral disturbances. Sometimes these disturbances are clearly related to dementia (for example, inappropriate
jocularity, impulsiveness, and the like). Some patients, however, may
present with disturbances in affect which mimic manic-depressive
psychosis, a "functional" psychiatric illness (McHugh and Folstein,
1975). Suicide is the most common cause of death early in the course
of this disease (Reed and Chandler, 1958). The depressions seen
may be accompanied by delusions and psychomotor retardation, and
they may be responsive to antidepressant medication and to electroconvulsive therapy (ECT). Manic episodes are less frequently seen.
In addition, hallucinations and delusions may occur and lead to an
incorrect diagnosis of schizophrenia.

As noted above, the caudate receives a large dopaminergic input
from the substantia nigra. It is of interest to note that L-dopa,
which may induce depression and mania in parkinsonians, may also
induce choreiform movements. The dopaminergic systems have been
among those implicated in the arousal response and patients with
Huntington's chorea are often apathetic; however, the large variety
of emotional problems noted above cannot be explained so simply.
Furthermore, evidence suggests that the dopaminergic pathway mediating arousal is different from the nigrostriatal pathway. Patients
with Huntington's chorea have been shown to have a decreased concentration of GABA in their caudate nuclei (Bird and Iverson,
1974). The role of GABA in emotional responses is, as yet, un-

known. Finally, it should be noted that the caudate and putamen are particularly rich in opiate receptors. These receptors have not yet been studied in Huntington's chorea and their importance in emotional responsiveness is as yet unclear.

Subcortical control of emotional expression

Wilson (1924) postulated a pontobulbar area responsible for emotional facial expression. Lesions which interrupt the corticobulbar motor pathways bilaterally will release reflex mechanisms for facial expression from cortical control.

The syndrome consists of involuntary laughing or crying (or both). As with many forms of release phenomena, this excess of emotional expression is stereotypic and does not show either a wide spectrum of emotions or different degrees of intensity of expression. It can be triggered by a wide variety of stimuli, but it cannot be initiated or stopped voluntarily. Examination usually shows weakness of voluntary facial movements and increase in the facial and jaw stretch reflexes.

The location of the centers for the control of facial expression is not known and, although Wilson postulated it to be in the lower brainstem, Poeck (1969) has postulated centers in the thalamus and hypothalamus. Although bilateral lesions are usually responsible, the syndrome has been described with unilateral lesions on either side (Bruyn and Gathier, 1969).

Patients with this syndrome report feeling normal emotions, despite the abnormality of expression. Commonly, their family and physicians speak of them as being "emotionally labile," implying that they no longer have appropriate internal emotional feeling. It is important to make the distinction between true emotional lability (as may be seen with bilateral frontal-lobe disturbance) and pseudobulbar lability of emotional expression (with normal inner emotions).

PSYCHIATRIC DISTURBANCES

Evidence has been accumulating that several diseases previously thought to be "functional" in fact have an "organic" substrate. *Infantile autism* has much in common with less severe language disturbances in children, and is associated with structural abnormalities of the brain (see Chapter 17). *Gilles de la Tourette syndrome,* which is characterized by unusual tics progressing to involuntary outbursts of foul language (coprolalia), has a familial incidence (Eldridge et al., 1977; Pollack et al., 1977) and a dramatic response to medication (haloperidol) (Pollack et al., 1977), indicating a probable organic basis.

Similar arguments have been advanced to support the notion that schizophrenia and some of the other functional psychoses have an organic basis (Pincus and Tucker, 1978). Since there have been no reliable neuropathological abnormalities found in these disorders, one cannot make clinicopathological correlations. Recent advances in psychopharmacology (Iversen and Iversen, 1975) have provided an important avenue for research. Further discussion of these disorders, however, is beyond the scope of this chapter.

Psychiatric disturbances are also commonly associated with endocrine dysfunction. Postpartum depression, premenstrual tension, and steroid psychosis are examples. The mechanisms by which endocrine hormones produce behavioral changes are not known, although there is now evidence of receptors for certain hormones in the brain. Martin, Reichlin, and Brown (1977) review these disorders.

TREATMENT

The treatment of any behavioral neurological disorder should first be aimed at treating the underlying disease (e.g., tumor, vascular disease, infection, etc.) and preventing further insults. If the emotional disorder is being caused by seizures, then appropriate anticonvulsants should be used.

Neurosurgery
If a seizure focus is confined to one anterior temporal lobe and the seizures cannot be controlled by conservative methods (e.g., anticonvulsant therapy), anterior temporal lobectomy may be indicated. Although surgical treatment for seizures is a well-accepted procedure, psychosurgery (surgical treatment for behavioral disorders) remains controversial. Today psychosurgery is used mainly to treat

patients with physical and psychic pain (i.e., patients with intractable hyperemotional functional neurosis). Psychosurgery has also been used to treat aggressive patients, but the use of surgery for social reasons is very controversial. Psychosurgery has not been demonstrated to be useful in patients with known structural disease who have an emotional disorder as a result of their disease. Until further research is done, we would not recommend surgical intervention in these patients (unless it is aimed at treating the underlying disease, such as a tumor).

Education of Patients and Family

Most people have been brought up with psychoanalytic concepts. Although they will readily attribute motor or sensory deficits to neurological dysfunction, they tend to ascribe emotional disorders to interpersonal, intrapersonal, and environmental conflicts, even when the emotional disorder coexists with motor and sensory defects. For example, the spouses of several of our aphasic and right-hemiparetic patients thought that the irritability and agitated depression demonstrated by the patients were being produced by a breakdown of interpersonal relations. When the nature of their spouse's disorder was explained, there was a release from personal guilt, which allowed more effort to be expended on constructive modes of therapy, as discussed below.

Alternate strategies

Finding alternative strategies would work most successfully in patients who have difficulty developing the appropriate cognitive state. If the defect is modality specific (i.e., deafferentation or agnosia), alternative modalities should be used. Within a modality, if a perceptual defect prevents the patient from understanding affective intonation ("how it is said"), the affective content should be stated. If a patient cannot understand "what is said," one should attempt to communicate either by "how it is said" or by the use of another modality.

Similarly, alternative strategies may be used when there is a disorder of expression. Aphasic patients may communicate by "how it is said" or by gestures or faces. Patients whose expression lacks affective intonation may communicate by "what is said" or by gestures or facial expression. Patients who cannot control facial muscles may communicate verbally. It is important that family members and others who have frequent contact with the patient also learn these alternative strategies so that they can communicate with the patient and understand the patient's emotional expressions.

Psychopharmacological treatment

Many psychopharmacological agents have a profound affect on arousal. Many sedatives and hypnotics work directly on the reticular activating system. Phenothiazine-like drugs block ascending catecholamine systems and mood-elevating drugs increase catecholamines. Although there are indications for the use of drugs to treat functional emotional disorders, benefits from the pharmacological treatment of emotional disorders induced by neurological disease have not been established. It is possible that drugs which stimulate the cortex (via the reticular activating system) would benefit patients whose emotional disorder results from a defect in arousal, but no controlled clinical trial has been done. Although L-dopa and the phenothiazines appear effective in the treatment of rigidity in parkinsonism and in the treatment of chorea (respectively), their affect on emotional disorders in these syndromes is not established.

References

Akert, K., Gruesen, R. A., Woolsey, C. N., and Meyer, D. R. (1961). Kluver-Bucy syndrome in monkeys with neocortical ablations of temporal lobe. *Brain 84*:480–498.

Bard, P. (1934). Emotion. I. The neuro-humoral basis of emotional reactions, in *Handbook of General Experimental Psychology*, C. Murchison (ed). Worcester, Mass.: Clark University Press.

Bear, D. M. and Fedio, P. (1977). Quantitative analysis of interictal behavior in temporal lobe epilepsy. *Arch. Neurol. 34*:454–467.

Benson, D. F. and Geschwind, N. (1976). The aphasias and related disturbances, in *Clinical Neurology*, Vol. 1, Chap 8, A. B. Baker and L. H. Baker (eds). Hagerstown, Md.: Harper & Row.

Benton, A. L. and Van Allen, M. W. (1968). Impairment in facial recognition in patients with cerebral disease. *Cortex 4*:344–358.

Berger, H. (1933). Uber das electrenkephalogramm des menschen. *Arch. f. Psychiat. u. Nervenk. 99*:555–574.

Bird, E. D. and Iverson, L. L. (1974). Huntington's chorea: post-mortem measurements of glutamic acid decarboxylase, choline acetyltransferase and dopamine in basal ganglia. *Brain 97*:457–472.

Blumer, D. (1975). Temporal lobe epilepsy and its psychiatric significance, in *Psychiatric Aspects of Neurological Disease,* D. F. Benson and D. Blumer (eds). New York: Grune & Stratton.

Blumer, D. and Benson, D. F. (1975). Personality changes with frontal and temporal lobe lesions, in *Psychiatric Aspects of Neurological Disease,* D. F. Benson and D. Blumer (eds). New York: Grune & Stratton.

Blumer, D. and Walker, A. E. (1975). The neural basis of sexual behavior, in *Psychiatric Aspects of Neurological Disease,* D. F. Benson and D. Blumer (eds). New York: Grune & Stratton.

Brady, J. V. and Nauta, W. J. (1955). Subcortical mechanisms in control of behavior. *J. Comp. Physiol. Psychol. 48*:412–420.

Broca, P. (1878). Anatomie comparee des enconvolutions cerebrales: le grand lobe limbique et al scissure limbique dans la serie des mammiferes. *Rev. Anthrop. 1*:385–498.

Bruyn, G. W. and Gathier, J. C. (1969). The opercular syndrome, in *Handbook of Clinical Neurology,* Vol. 2, Chap. 5, P. J. Vinken and G. W. Bruyn (eds). Amsterdam: North Holland.

Cannon, W. B. (1927). The James-Lange theory of emotion: a critical examination and an alternative theory. *Am. J. Psychol. 39*:106–124.

Carmon, A. and Nachshon, I. (1973). Ear asymmetry in perception of emotional and non-verbal stimuli. *Acta Psychol. 37*:351–357.

Corsellis, J. A. N., Goldberg, G. J., and Norton, A. R. (1968). Limbic encephalitis and its association with carcinoma. *Brain 91*:481–496.

Critchley, M. (1966). *The Parietal Lobes.* New York: Hafner.

Currie, S., Heathfield, K. W. G., Henson, R. A., and Scott, D. F. (1971). Clinical course and prognosis of temporal lobe epilepsy. A survey of 666 patients. *Brain 94*:173–190.

Dana, C. S. (1921). The autonomic seat of the emotions: a discussion of the James-Lange theory. *Arch. Neurol. Psychiat. 6*:634–639.

DeKosky, S., Heilman, K. M., Bowers, D., and Valenstein, E. (1979). Recognition and discrimination of emotional faces and pictures. *Brain and Language* (in press).

Denny-Brown, D., Meyer, J. S., and Horenstein, S. (1952). The significance of perceptual rivalry resulting from parietal lesions. *Brain 75*:434–471.

DeRenzi, E. and Faglioni, P. (1965). The comparative efficiency of intelligence and vigilance detecting hemisphere damage. *Cortex 1*:410–433.

DeRenzi, E. and Spinnler, H. (1966). Facial recognition in brain damaged patients: an experimental approach. *Neurology 16*:145–152.

Eldridge, R., Sweet, R., Lake, C. R., Ziegler, M., and Shapiro, A. K. (1977). Gilles de la Tourette's syndrome: clinical, genetic, psychologic and biochemical aspects in 21 selected families. *Neurology 27*:115–124.

Flor-Henry, P. (1969). Schizophrenic-like reactions and affective psychoses associated with temporal lobe epilepsy: etiologic factors. *Am. J. Psychiat. 216*:400–403.

French, J. D., Hernandex-Peon, R., and Livingston, R. (1955). Projections from the cortex to cephalic brainstem (reticular formation) in monkeys. *Brain 18*:74–95.

Gainotti, G. (1972). Emotional behavior and hemispheric side of lesion. *Cortex 8*:41–55.

Gardner, H., Ling, P. K., Flam, L., and Silverman, J. (1975). Comprehension and appreciation of humorous material following brain damage. *Brain 98*:399–412.

Gasparrini, W., Satz, P., Heilman, K. M., and Coolidge, F. (1977). Hemispheric asymmetries of affective processing as determined by the Minnesota Multiphasic Personality Inventory. Presented before the International Neuropsychological Society, Santa Fe, New Mexico. February.

Geschwind, N. (1975). The clinical setting of aggression in temporal lobe epilepsy, in *The Neurobiology of Violence,* W. S. Fields and W. H. Sweet (eds). St. Louis: Warren H. Green.

Geschwind, N. (1977). Behavioral changes in temporal lobe epilepsy. *Arch. Neurol. 34*:453.

Goldstein, K. (1948). *Language and Language Disturbances.* New York: Grune and Stratton.

Guerrant, J., Anderson, W. W., Fischer, A., Weinstein, M. R., Janos, R. M., and Deskins, A. (1962). *Personality in Epilepsy.* Springfield, Ill.: Charles C. Thomas.

Haggard, M. P. and Parkinson, A. M. (1971). Stimulus and task factors as determinants of ear advantages. *Quart. J. Exp. Psychol. 23*:168–177.

Heath, R. G. (1964). Pleasure response of human subjects to direct stimulation of the brain: physiologic and psychodynamic considerations, in *The Role of Pleasure in Behavior,* R. G. Heath (ed). New York: Harper & Row.

Hécaen, H., Ajuriaguerra, J. de, and Massonet, J. (1951). Les troubles visuoconstructifs par lesion parieto-occipitale droit. *Encephale 40*:122–179.

Heilman, K. M., Scholes, R., and Watson, R. T. (1975). Auditory affective agnosia: disturbed comprehension of affective speech. *J. Neurol. Neurosurg. Psychiat. 38*:69–72.

Heilman, K. M., Schwartz, H., and Watson, R. T. (1977). Hypoarousal in patients with the neglect syndrome and emotional indifference. *Neurology 28*:229–232.

Heilman, K. M. and Valenstein, E. (1972). Frontal lobe neglect. *Neurology 22*:660–664.

Howes, D. and Boller, F. (1975). Simple reaction times: evidence for focal impairment from lesions of the right hemisphere. *Brain 98*:317–332.

Isaacson, R. L. (1974). *The Limbic System.* New York: Plenum Press.

Iversen, S. D. and Iversen, L. L. (1975). *Behavioral Pharmacology.* New York and Oxford: Oxford University Press.

James, W. (1890). *The Principles of Psychology.* New York: Holt.

Kluver, H. and Bucy, P. C. (1937). "Psychic blindness" and other symptoms following bilateral temporal lobectomy in Rhesus monkeys. *Am. J. Physiol.* 119:352–353.

Kimura, D. (1967). Functional asymmetry of the brain in dichotic listening. *Cortex 3*:163–178.

Lindsley, D. (1970). The role of nonspecific reticulo-thalamo-cortical systems in emotion, in *Physiological Correlates of Emotion,* P. Black (ed). New York: Academic Press.

MacLean, P. D. (1952). Some psychiatric implications of physiological studies on the frontotemporal portion of the limbic system (visceral brain). *EEG Clin. Neurophysiol.* 4:407–418.

Maranon, G. (1924). Contribution aletude de l'action emotive de l'adrenoline. *Revue Franc d' Endocrin.* 21:301–325. As quoted in Fehr, F. S. and Stern, J. A. (1970): Peripheral physiological variables and emotion: the James-Lange theory revisited. *Psychol. Bull.* 74:411–424.

Mark, V. H., Sweet, W. H., and Ervin, F. R. (1972). The effect of amygdalectomy on violent behavior in patients with temporal lobe epilepsy, in *Psychosurgery,* E. Hitchcock, L. Laitinen, and K. Vernet (eds). Springfield, Ill.: C. C. Thomas.

Martin, J. B., Reichlin, S., and Brown, G. M. (1977). *Clinical Neuroendocrinology.* Philadelphia: F. A. Davis Co.

McHugh, P. R. and Forstein, M. F. (1975). Psychiatric syndromes of Huntington's chorea: a clinical and pharmacologic study, in D. F. Benson and D. Blumer (eds). *Psychiatric Aspects of Neurologic Disease.* New York: Grune & Stratton.

McIntyre, M., Pritchard, P. B., and Lombroso, C. T. (1976). Left and right temporal lobe epileptics: a controlled investigation of some psychological differences. *Epilepsia 17*:377–386.

Moruzzi, G. and Magoun, H. W. (1949). Brain stem reticular formation and activation of the EEG. *EEG Clin. Neurophysiol.* 1:455–475.

Nielsen, J. M. and Jacobs, L. L. (1951). Bilateral lesions of the anterior cingulate gyri: report of a case. *Bull. Los Angeles Neurol. Soc. 16*:321–334.

Olds, J. (1958). Self-stimulation of the brain. *Science 127*:315–324.

Papez, J. W. (1937). A proposed mechanism of emotion. *Arch. Neurol. Psychiat. 38*:725–743.

Paul, H. (1909). *Principien der Sprachgeschichte,* 4th ed. Hall a.S: Niemeyer.

Pincus, J. H. and Tucker, G. J. (1978). *Behavioral Neurology,* 2nd ed. New York: Oxford University Press.

Poeck, K. (1969). Pathophysiology of emotional disorders associated with brain damage, in *Handbook of Neurology,* Vol. 3, P. J. Vinken and G. W. Bruyn (eds). New York: American Elsevier.

Poeck, K. and Pilleri, G. (1961). Wutverhalten und pathologischer Schlaf bei Tumor der vorderen Mittellinie. *Arch. f. Psychiat. u. Nervenkr.* *201*:593–604.

Pollack, M. A., Cohen, N. L., and Friedhoff, A. J. (1977). Gilles de la Tourette's syndrome familial occurrence and precipitation by methlyphenidate therapy. *Arch. Neurol. 34*:630–632.

Ramon y Cajal, S. (1955). *Studies on the Cerebral Cortex (Limbic Structures),* L. M. Kraft (Translator). London: Lloyd-Luke, Ltd.

Reed, T. E. and Chandler, J. R. (1958). Huntington's chorea in Michigan. I. Demography and genetics. *Am. J. Hum. Genet. 10*:201–225.

Sackeim, H. A., Gur, R. C., Saucy, M. C. (1978). Emotions are expressed more intensely on the left side of the face. *Science 202*:434–436.

Segarra, J. M. and Angelo, J. N. (1970). Presentation I in *Behavioral Change in Cerebrovascular Disease,* A. L. Benton (ed). New York: Harper & Row.

Segundo, J. P., Naguet, R., and Buser, P. (1955). Effects of cortical stimulation on electrocortical activity in monkeys. *J. Neurophysiol. 18*:236–245.

Schacter, S. (1970). The interaction of cognitive and physiological determinants of emotional state, in *Advances in Experimental Social Psychology,* Vol. 1, L. Berkowitz (ed). New York: Academic Press.

Slater, E. and Beard, A. W. (1963). The schizophrenia-like psychoses of epilepsy. *Br. J. Psychiat. 109*:95–150.

Sokolov, Y. N. (1963). *Perception and the Conditioned Reflex.* Oxford: Pergamon Press.

Stevens, J. R. (1966). Psychiatric implications of psychomotor epilepsy. *Arch. Gen. Psychiat. 14*:461–471.

Suberi, M. and McKeever, W. F. (1977). Differential right hemisphere memory storage of emotional and nonemotional faces. *Neuropsychologia 15*:757–768.

Tucker, D. M., Watson, R. T., and Heilman, K. M. (1977). Affective discrimination and evocation in patients with right parietal disease. *Neurology 27*:947–950.

Ursin, H. (1960). The temporal lobe substrate of fear and anger. *Acta Psychiat. Scandinav. 35*:378–396.

Valenstein, E. S. (1973). *Brain Control. A Critical Examination of Brain Stimulation and Psychosurgery.* New York: Wiley-Interscience.

Watson, R. T., Heilman, K. M., Cauthen, J. C., and King, F. A. (1973). Neglect after cingulectomy. *Neurology 23*:1003–1007.

Watson, R. T., Heilman, K. M., Miller, B. D., and King, F. A. (1974). Neglect after mesencephalic reticular formation lesions. *Neurology 24*:294–298.

Watson, R. T. and Heilman, K. M. (1978). Thalamic neglect. *Neurology 28*:396.

Waxman, S. G. and Geschwind, N. (1974). Hypergraphia in temporal lobe epilepsy. *Neurology 24*:629–636.

Wilson, S. A. K. (1924). Some problems in neurology. II. Pathological laughing and crying. *J. Neurol. Psychopathol. 16*:299–333.

Woods, J. W. (1956). Taming of the wild Norway rat by rhinocephalic lesions. *Nature 170*:869.

Yakolev, P. I. (1948). Motility, behavior, and the brain: stereodynamic organization and neural coordinates of behavior. *J. Nervous Mental Dis. 107*:313–335.

Zeman, W. and King, F. A. (1958). Tumors of the septum pellucidum and adjacent structures with abnormal affective behavior: an aterior midline structure syndrome. *J. Nervous Mental Dis. 127*:490–502.

14

Amnesic Disorders

NELSON BUTTERS

GENERAL SYMPTOMS OF PERMANENT AMNESIA

Severe memory deficits are common symptoms following damage to a number of limbic system structures. Difficulty in learning new materials and recalling remote events arises after hippocampal lesions (e.g., anoxia, herpes encephalitis, cerebrovascular accidents involving the posterior cerebral artery and surgical removal) (Milner, 1970), atrophy of medial diencephalic structures including n. medialis dorsalis and the mammillary bodies (e.g., alcoholic Korsakoff's Disease) (Victor, Adams and Collins, 1971) and lesions of the fornix (e.g., tumors) (Heilman and Sypert, 1977). Despite the locus of the lesion or the etiology of the disease, the patients share four outstanding clinical characteristics. First, all amnesics have *anterograde amnesia*. This means that the patient is unable to learn new verbal and nonverbal information from the time of onset of his illness. He will not remember the names of his physician and nurses, and will even

Some of the research reported in this paper was supported by funds from the Veterans Administrations' Medical Research Service and by NIAAA Grant AA-00187 to Boston University. The author wishes to thank Ms. Kathleen Montgomery for her assistance in preparing this manuscript.

439

have difficulty learning the name of the hospital in which he is being treated. Events that occurred hours or even minutes before will be lost to the amnesic individual. Not only does he fail to learn the names of important people and places but often he will not remember previous encounters with these individuals. Experimentally, this severe learning deficit can be demonstrated by the great difficulty the patient has in learning even short lists of paired associates. That is, when the patient is presented with a list of word pairs (e.g., handle–sun) in which he must learn to associate the second word (e.g., sun) with the first (e.g., handle), the acquisition of these associations may require 70 or 80 trials instead of the three or four presentations needed by intact individuals.

The second major symptom of amnesia is *retrograde amnesia.* The patient has difficulty retrieving from long-term memory events that occurred before the onset of his illness. When asked who was President of the United States before Mr. Carter, the patient might answer "Eisenhower" or perhaps "Kennedy." If asked whether any other Presidents held office between Mr. Carter and "Kennedy," the patient often will say no. In general, this difficulty in retrieval of old memories is more pronounced for events just before the onset of the illness while remote events from the patient's childhood are often well remembered. This temporal "gradient" has been demonstrated in numerous studies. Seltzer and Benson (1974), using a multiple-choice questionnaire, found that alcoholic Korsakoff patients could remember famous events from the 1930's and 1940's better than events from the 1960's and early 1970's. Marslen-Wilson and Teuber (1975) presented Korsakoff patients with photographs of famous people and found that the patients had much more difficulty identifying famous faces from the 1960's than from the 1930's and 1940's. Further evidence for this temporal gradient is found in studies of electroconvulsive therapy with depressed patients. Squire, Slater, and Chace (1975) reported that ECT resulted in a loss of memory for television shows aired during the year before therapy while the patients' memory for shows aired several years before ECT remained intact.

Warrington and her associates have challenged the existence of this gradient and have presented evidence that amnesic patients have as much difficulty retrieving remote (e.g., childhood) as recent events. Sanders and Warrington (1971) administered a famous events questionnaire and a test of famous faces to five amnesics (mixed etiology). Their patients were impaired relative to the control group on all tests and for all periods of time. Unlike the other studies reviewed, the patients' impairment was of equal severity at all time periods. The authors believe that the gradient often attributed to the patients' retrograde problems is due to a lack of control of the difficulty of the test items representing the various decades. That is, questions and famous faces from the 1930's and 1940's may be easier than those from the 1960's and 1970's. Warrington believes that if one insures that all questions are of equal difficulty then the "gradient" of retrograde amnesia disappears, and the patient shows equal difficulty in recalling remote and recent past events.

Albert, Butters, and Levin (1979) have recently reexamined retrograde amnesia in light of Warrington's criticisms of other studies. Three tests were developed: a famous faces test, a recall questionnaire, and a multiple-choice recognition questionnaire. Each test consisted of items from the 1920's to the 1970's that had been assessed on a large population of normal controls before their inclusion in the final test battery. Half of the items were "easy" as judged by the performance of the standardization group; the other half were difficult or "hard" judged by the same criterion. In addition, the famous faces test included photographs of some individuals early and late in their careers. For example, photographs of Marlon Brando from the 1950's and from the 1970's were both in the test battery.

When this retrograde battery was administered to a group of 11 amnesics (alcoholic Korsakoff patients) and a group of 15 normal controls matched to the amnesics for age and educational background, little evidence supporting Sanders and Warrington's (1971) contentions was found. As shown in Figures 14-1 and 14-2, the classical gradient was evident regardless of the difficulty of the items. For both easy and hard items (Fig. 14-1), the Korsakoff patients identified more photographs from the 1930's and 1940's than from the 1960's. Furthermore, while the normal controls were more accurate at identifying famous people later than earlier in their careers, the Korsakoff patients performed in the opposite manner. On the recall test of famous events (Figure 14-2), the same pattern

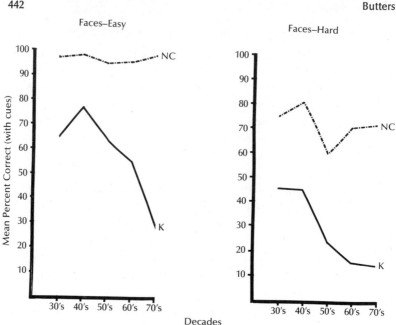

Fig. 14-1 Identification of famous faces from 1930's–70's by alcoholic Korsakoff patients (K) and normal controls (NC).

emerges. For both easy and hard items, the Korsakoff patients recalled more information from the 1930's and 1940's than from the 1960's. On the basis of this evidence, and the other studies reviewed, it seems fair to conclude that temporal gradients do exist in the retrograde memory deficits of at least some amnesic patients. Whether the gradients reported for alcoholic Korsakoff patients (Seltzer and Benson, 1974; Marslen-Wilson and Teuber, 1975; Albert et al., 1979) are also characteristic of other groups of amnesic patients (e.g., postencephalitic patients) remains to be determined.

The third characteristic of amnesic patients is their tendency to *confabulate* when faced with questions they cannot answer. When asked to relate his activities from the previous day an amnesic patient may "fill in" this gap in his memory with a story concerning a trip to his home or to a sporting event that may have actually occurred many years ago. This confabulatory tendency is not a constant or necessarily permanent feature of amnesic patients, and there are marked individual differences among amnesic populations.

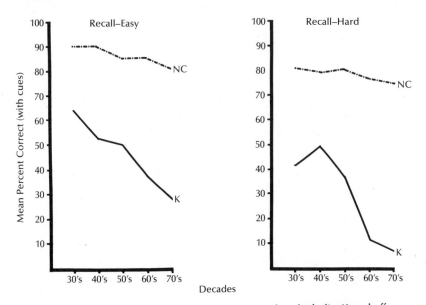

Fig. 14-2 Recall of famous events from 1930's–70's by alcoholic Korsakoff patients (K) and normal controls (NC).

In general, confabulation is most marked during the acute stages of the illness and becomes progressively less noticeable as the patient adjusts to his disorder. It is relatively easy to elicit confabulation from a patient in a Wernicke-Korsakoff confusional state, but such responses are rare in chronic alcoholic Korsakoff patients who have had this disease for five or more years.

The fourth characteristic of amnesic patients is their relatively *intact intellectual functions* as measured by standardized intelligence tests such as the Wechsler Adult Intelligence Scale (WAIS). Table 14-1 shows the WAIS performances of nine amnesic alcoholic Korsakoff patients and nine intact normal controls matched on the basis of age (mean = 53 years), socioeconomic class (working class), and educational background (mean = 11 years of formal education). Except for the digit-symbol subtest, there are no significant differences between the Korsakoff patients and the normal controls. Special notice should be made of the Korsakoff patients' normal performance on the digit-span subtest, a task that is often considered a measure of immediate memory. Drachman and Arbit (1966) have demon-

Table 14-1 *Mean Performance (Scaled Scores) of Alcoholic Korsakoff Patients (N = 9) and Nonalcoholic Controls (N = 9) on the WAIS*

	KORSAKOFFS	NONALCOHOLIC CONTROLS
Age	53.4	53.2
Years of education	10.77	10.88
Full scale WAIS IQ	102.55	99.22
Verbal IQ	105.33	99.77
Performance IQ	98.55	97.22
Information	10.66	10.55
Comprehension	11.55	9.00
Arithmetic	9.66	9.55
Similarities	10.55	9.44
Digit span	9.44	8.77
Vocabulary	10.77	9.77
Digit symbol	3.44	6.88
Picture completion	9.55	9.77
Block design	8.22	7.77
Picture arrangement	7.77	7.77
Object assembly	8.66	6.55

strated that postencephalitics, like normals, can repeat seven or eight numbers immediately after presentation but are severely impaired in attempting to learn supraspan lists of 12 numbers. Presumably, once the list has been lengthened to include 12 numbers, the first three or four numbers are no longer in immediate memory but rather in the patients' impaired short-term storage.

Figure 14-3 shows the verbal IQ, performance IQ, full-scale IQ, and memory quotient (MQ based upon the Wechsler Memory Scale) of nine amnesic alcoholic Korsakoff patients, 47 long-term alcoholics (non-amnesic), and 28 normal controls. Again there are no differences between the amnesics and the other two groups on the IQ scores, although the MQ's of the amnesics are clearly impaired. This 20–30 point scatter between IQ and MQ is the hallmark of the amnesic syndrome.

Despite the amnesic patient's normal IQ, his cognitive performance is not completely intact. A full neuropsychological evaluation usually reveals a number of secondary defects that may or may not contribute to the patient's severe memory problems. Among alcoholic Korsakoff patients, the most common deficits involve visuo-

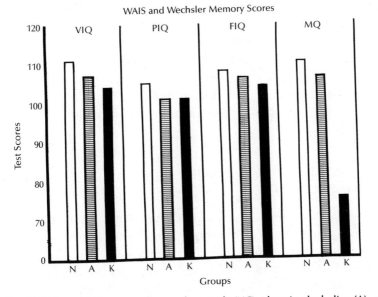

Fig. 14-3 IQ and MQ scores of normal controls (NC), chronic alcoholics (A), and alcoholic Korsakoff patients (K). VIQ = verbal IQ; PIQ = performance IQ; FIQ = full-scale IQ; MQ = memory quotient.

perceptive and visuospatial capacities. Korsakoff patients are impaired on digit-symbol and symbol-digit substitution tasks (Glosser, Butters, and Kaplan, 1977; Kapur and Butters, 1977), hidden or embedded figure tests (same authors), and on various tests that require the sorting of complex visual stimuli (Oscar-Berman, 1973; Oscar-Berman and Samuels, 1977). Such visuoperceptive deficits should not be surprising since chronic alcoholics who are not clinically amnesic have been reported to have the same perceptual problems (e.g., Kleinknecht and Goldstein, 1972; Goodwin and Hill, 1975; Parsons, Tarter, and Jones, 1971; Goldstein and Shelly, 1971; Parsons, 1975). Although there are some indications that these visuoperceptive deficits, like the memory disorder, may be due to atrophy of limbic structures surrounding the third ventricle (Jarho, 1973), most investigators have attributed such disorders to atrophy of cortical association areas (e.g., Parsons et al., 1971; Parsons, 1975).

While the secondary cognitive deficits of other types of amnesics have not been formally studied, their existence is obvious, as shown by clinical and neuropsychological evaluation. Patients who have survived herpes encephalitis are often left with some aphasic symptoms (e.g., anomia, paraphasia) as well as varying degrees of constructional apraxia as noted by low performance IQ's and difficulty with drawing and copying complex geometric figures. A similar combination of aphasic and constructional problems is usually associated with patients whose permanent amnesia is due to anoxia or trauma.

NEUROPSYCHOLOGICAL STUDIES OF AMNESIC STATES

Unfortunately for neuropsychologists, brain damage in human populations is rarely limited to a single brain structure. In most cases the patient's disorder involves a combination of lesions that may or may not be confined to a single region (e.g., the thalamus) of the brain. For example, Korsakoff patients whose amnesia is related to alcohol intoxication and malnutrition have lesions involving n. medialis dorsalis, the mammillary bodies, the vermis of the cerebellum, the oculomotor nucleus, and in some cases association cortex (for review, see Talland, 1965; Victor, Adams, and Collins, 1971). Similarly, patients with Alzheimer's disease whose amnesic symptoms are part of a general intellectual decline have progressive lesions of the hippocampus and of posterior and anterior association cortex (Tomlinson, 1977). Even postencephalitic patients whose amnesic symptoms are due to a herpes virus that directly attacks the hippocampus usually have considerable involvement of temporal and frontal neocortical areas (Haymaker et al., 1958; Drachman and Adams, 1962; Johnson, Olson, and Buescher, 1968). When the multiplicity and variability of the patients' lesions are combined with a lack of postmortem verification of lesion sites, an assessment of what individual structures are contributing to a patient's amnesic symptomatology becomes nearly impossible.

In addition to the problems with localization of lesions, the scientific inquiry into the memory of brain-damaged patients is handicapped by the lack of specificity and definition of the terms psychologists use to study memory. Constructs like "storage," "retrieval," and "encoding" are widely employed but poorly defined in the human memory literature. The havoc such lack of specificity produces for students of amnesia can be easily exemplified. Some amnesic patients perform better with cued than with free recall. They may be unable to recall the name of their doctor on direct inquiry but quickly supply the name when reminded that the physician's name begins with a "B" or is "something associated with bread." Such demonstrations of cueing have led investigators to propose that amnesia represents a problem with retrieval not storage (Warrington and Weiskrantz, 1970, 1973). That is, the patient can and does store information normally but is impaired in his ability to retrieve the name. While this explanation seems plausible, it makes the implicit assumption that storage is all-or-none and not partial, an assumption that has little support in the literature on normal human memory. If in fact humans can partially store new information or store it in an inadequate form (e.g., poorly encoded) then the cueing phenomenon becomes equally consistent with a storage hypothesis. Retrieval processes may be quite normal although some form of phonemic or semantic cue may be required to retrieve a partially or inadequately stored (i.e., degraded) engram. Of course the point of this example is that since "storage" is not fully understood in normal memory, attempts to separate storage and retrieval difficulties in amnesic patients have not been completely successful.

Despite the lack of preciseness with regard to lesions and memory concepts, there has been an increasing interest in the study of amnesic patients during the past 15 years. Some of the neuropsychological studies have dealt with the localization and lateralization of memory functions, others with a description of the capacities and deficits of amnesic patients, and still others with the application of theories of information processing to the amnesic syndromes. The major findings of these neuropsychological studies will be reviewed in the following sections.

Amnesia following bilateral lesions of the mesial temporal region

The neuropsychological studies of Brenda Milner at the Montreal Neurological Institute (McGill University) have left little doubt that the mesial temporal region is directly associated with memory processes in man (Scoville and Milner, 1957; Penfield and Milner,

1958; Milner, 1966, 1970). Scoville and Milner (1957) described the severe memory disorder of a young man (H.M.) who had undergone bilateral mesial temporal lobe ablations to treat an uncontrolled form of epilepsy. This radical surgery was performed only after other more conservative therapies had failed to control H.M.'s severe epileptic seizures. Upon recovering from surgery H.M. manifested a severe inability to learn new information (i.e., anterograde amnesia) and was even unable to recall many events that had occurred prior to surgery (i.e., retrograde amnesia). In addition to H.M., Scoville and Milner described the memory disturbances of eight psychotic patients who had received bilateral mesial temporal removals; it was hoped that such treatment would improve their psychotic thought disorders. Severe anterograde amnesia was noted in those cases in which the lesions included the anterior sector of the hippocampus but was not evident when the lesion was limited to the uncus and the amygdala, sparing the hippocampus. On the basis of these nine patients (H.M. and the eight psychotic patients), the investigators concluded that an intact hippocampus was necessary for the acquisition of new memories and the maintenance or retrieval of old traces.

H.M.'s surgery was successful in treating his seizures, but he has been left with a permanent memory defect that has been extensively studied by Brenda Milner, her colleagues, and students. H.M. continues to show a severe anterograde amnesia as evidenced by his inability to learn the names of friends or his new address. He has difficulty recalling events occurring just prior to the time of his operation but is able to remember events from his early childhood. His postoperative IQ is in the high-normal range and somewhat improved over his preoperative score. He is reported to have been a placid individual before surgery and there has been no change in this personality evaluation in the years since surgery.

In addition to this general clinical evaluation, a wide range of formal learning and cognitive tasks has been administered to H.M. Two investigations (Prisko, 1963; Sidman, Stoddard, and Mohr, 1968) have shown that H.M. is impaired on short-term memory tasks. In Prisko's study, H.M. was presented with two stimuli from the same modality separated by intervals ranging from zero to 60 seconds; he was then asked to indicate whether the second stimulus was identical or different from the first. The stimuli were either nonverbal visual stimuli such as light flashes and shades of red or nonverbal auditory material such as clicks and tones. The results were striking: while H.M. performed normally with very short delays between the two stimuli, his performance deteriorated as the delays increased. After a 60-second delay his performance approached chance guessing. This short-term memory deficit stands in marked contrast to H.M.'s normal immediate memory span. If seven single-digit numbers are presented in succession, H.M. can recall all numbers in order if recall is attempted immediately following presentation. When, however, more than seven digits are presented or when a delay intervenes between presentation and recall, H.M. is severely impaired on this task. H.M.'s performance on the digit span task is, as noted previously, typical of all amnesics and represents one of the distinguishing features between amnesia (i.e., a severe memory defect with no general intellectual decline) and dementia (a severe memory defect as part of a general intellectual decline). While the amnesic patient usually has a normal immediate memory span (about seven digits), the dementing patient's span is often limited to four or five items.

H.M.'s ability to learn and retain motor and maze tasks has been evaluated (Milner, 1962; Milner, Corkin, and Teuber, 1968). Although H.M. could learn and retain for several days mirror-drawing and pursuit rotor skills, his performance on visual and tactile mazes was grossly impaired. When Milner (1962) attempted to train H.M. on a visual stylus-maze (with 28 choice points), H.M. failed to show any progress in 215 trials. A subsequent study (Milner, 1968) indicated that H.M.'s failure on this test was because the 28 rights and lefts were well beyond his immediate memory span. When H.M. was tested on a shorter seven-choice point maze that was within his immediate span, he was able to attain criterion after 155 trials and 256 errors. What is most remarkable is that when H.M. was tested on this shortened version of the visual maze two years later he showed 75% savings despite the fact that he did not remember the previous testing session. Gardner (1975) has noted a similar phenomenon in a patient with a traumatic amnesia (i.e., severe amnesic symptoms following a closed head injury in an automobile accident). This patient had been taught to play a melody on the piano and retained this skill despite a total inability to remember the original learning sessions. It appears then that H.M., and other amnesics as well, have great difficulty in acquiring new information, but once this material achieves long-term storage it can be retained fairly well.

Except for his severe and persistent memory defect, H.M. was found to have few other cognitive deficits. He performed normally on the Wisconsin Card Sorting Task and on a number of visuoperceptual tasks such as the Mooney face perception task. Since these tasks have been shown to be sensitive to frontal (Milner, 1963, 1964) or to temporal-parietal (Lansdell, 1968; Newcombe and Russell, 1969) cortical lesions, respectively, it was concluded that H.M.'s severe memory problems must be related to the mesial temporal ablations (probably the hippocampus) and not to any accessory cortical lesions.

Verbal and nonverbal memory deficits after
unilateral temporal lobectomies

While the case of H.M. and of other patients receiving bilateral mesial temporal lesions clearly established the importance of the mesial temporal region in memory, it has been the investigations of patients with unilateral temporal lobectomies that have pointed to the lateralized contributions of the two temporal regions to memory. Like H.M., the patients with unilateral temporal lobectomies have had surgical intervention to treat uncontrollable epileptic seizures. In most cases the surgery has been successful with regard to seizure activity, and the patients have returned to productive lives without any obvious amnesic symptoms. However, close examination of these patients has uncovered subtle memory defects that are dependent on whether the left or right temporal lobe has been removed, and the severity of the memory problem seems to depend upon the amount of hippocampus ablated.

Removal of the left temporal lobe is followed by verbal memory deficits. Patients with left temporal lobectomies have more difficulty learning and retaining verbal materials (both visually and auditorally presented) than do patients with right temporal lobectomies. For example, patients with left temporal lobectomies are impaired in the recall of prose passages, in verbal paired-associate learning, and on Hebb's digit sequence task which assesses the patient's ability to learn a recurring sequence of numbers exceeding the patient's digit span (Milner, 1971; Gerner, Ommaya, and Fedio, 1972). On a short-term memory task employing a distractor technique left temporals show faster decay of consonant trigrams than do patients with right temporal lobectomies (Corsi, 1969).

The results of these ablation studies have recently been supported and expanded by a study concerning the effects of electrical stimulation on language and memory processes (Fedio and Van Buren, 1974). The patients for this study were seven temporal-lobe epileptics who were candidates for unilateral temporal lobectomies. Before such a patient undergoes neurosurgery it is necessary to map via electrical stimulation the speech areas of the patient's brain. The results of this procedure allow the surgeon to avoid ablating tissue that is crucial for the patient's language capacities. In the Fedio and Van Buren study the patients were administered a naming and memory task as part of this mapping procedure. The task involved the presentation of a series of pictures of common objects (e.g., hand, tree, clock) with short delays between successive pictures. The patient was instructed to first name the object in the picture before him and then to recall the name of the object presented on the immediately preceding trial. As expected, electrical stimulation of the left (but not the right) temporal lobe led to a variety of anomic (dysphasic) naming errors, but the new and important findings concerned the patients' memory (recall) performance during stimulation of the temporal lobes. Two distinct areas were found within the left temporal lobe: stimulation of the anterior sector of the left temporal lobe resulted in anterograde amnesia, while stimulation of the posterior (temperoparietal) region produced retrograde problems. If points in the anterior temporal region were stimulated while the patient was correctly naming a presented picture, he often would be unable to recall this picture on a later trial when no stimulation was present. Somehow stimulation of this anterior point had prevented the consolidation or acquisition of the picture's name. In contrast, electrical stimulation of points in the posterior left temporal region resulted in a failure to recall the picture exposed on the preceding trial despite the fact that at the time of original exposure and naming no stimulation was being applied to the brain. That is, electrical stimulation of the posterior region made it difficult for patients to recall events that had occurred prior to the stimulation (i.e., retrograde amnesia). The investigators suggest that structures in the anterior portion of the left temporal lobe (e.g., the hippocampus) may play a role in the consolidation or storage of verbal materials, while sectors of the left posterior temporal region may be important in the retrieval of previously stored verbal stimuli.

While patients with right temporal lobectomies are unimpaired on verbal memory tasks, they have been found to be impaired in comparison to the lefts on tasks that require the processing of nonverbal patterned materials. Right-temporal patients have difficulty remembering whether they have previously seen an unfamiliar geometric pattern (Kimura, 1963) and are impaired in the learning of visual and tactile mazes (Milner, 1965; Corkin, 1965). They have difficulty in the recognition of tonal patterns (Milner, 1967) and faces (Milner, 1968) after a short delay. Patients with left temporal ablations are not impaired on any of these tasks.

The temporal lobectomies performed on the McGill patients have involved a number of neuroanatomical structures such as the amygdala, uncus, hippocampus, anterior temporal neocortex, and parahippocampal gyrus, but there is now substantial evidence from Milner's laboratory that the ablation of the hippocampus is the critical factor in the patients' memory deficits. These studies were facilitated by the surgeons' care in recording the locus and the extent of their temporal-lobe lesions. When the left- and right-temporal groups were divided according to the amount of hippocampal involvement, it was found that the degree of behavioral deficit correlated with the amount of hippocampus removed. Corsi (1969) found that patients with left temporal ablations with extensive hippocampal damage were more impaired on short-term memory tasks and in the learning of supraspan digit sequences (Hebb's digit sequence task) than were patients with little or no involvement of the hippocampus. On the other hand, maze learning (Milner, 1965; Corkin, 1965) and recognition of faces from photographs (Milner, 1968) were impaired only with extensive lesions of the right hippocampus. It should be stressed that temporal-lobe lesions that involved the amygdala, uncus, and cortex, but left the hippocampus relatively intact, produced no noticeable defects on the verbal and nonverbal memory tasks. On the basis of these studies it seems fair to conclude that H.M.'s severe amnesic syndrome, that involves both verbal and nonverbal materials, is due to the bilateral and extensive ablation of the hippocampus.

Neuropsychological studies of the anterograde amnesia of alcoholic Korsakoff patients

While the importance of an intact hippocampus for normal memory is now well established, it is evident from neuropathological and neuopsychological studies of alcoholic Korsakoff patients that other mesial brain structures also play some role in memory. The essential clinical symptoms of this alcoholic disorder have been known for approximately 100 years (for review see Talland, 1965). The patient has combined chronic alcoholism and a specific nutritional deficiency (i.e., thiamine) into a neurological syndrome characterized by changes in motor, sensory, cognitive, and personality processes. In the acute stage the patient presents with ataxia, nystagmus, confusion with regard to time and place, and various peripheral neuropathologies (e.g., pain or loss of sensation in the extremities). If the patient is treated with large doses of thiamine, the motor and sensory abnormalities slowly improve over a four- to eight-week period, but the patient is left in most cases with a severe amnesia and striking personality alterations. Regardless of the patient's premorbid personality he is extremely passive, malleable, and emotionally flat in the chronic Korsakoff state. His memory disorder is equally severe and permanent and closely resembles that of H.M.

Until recently, hippocampal lesions were believed to be responsible for the Korsakoff patients' memory problems (for reviews, see Talland, 1965; Victor, Adams, and Collins, 1971), but the neuropathological analysis of an extensive series of alcoholic Korsakoff brains (Victor et al., 1971) has shown the critical lesions to involve mesial thalamic structures. Every Korsakoff patient who had an amnesic syndrome also showed atrophy of the dorsal medial nucleus of the thalamus, but lesions of the hippocampus were not found consistently. Case studies demonstrating that tumors (Kahn and Crosby, 1972) and shrapnel wounds (Jahro, 1973) of the midline diencephalic region result in amnesic problems also point to thalamic or

hypothalamic (mammillary bodies) involvement in memory. Teuber, Milner, and Vaughn (1968) have reported a single case (Case
N.A.) of amnesia resulting from a stab wound that damaged sectors
of the rostral midbrain.

Coinciding with the recent neuropathological findings, there have
been a number of extensive neuropsychological studies of Korsakoff
patients (for reviews, see Cermak and Butters, 1973; Butters and
Cermak, 1974, 1975, 1976). These studies have focused upon the patients' short-term memory capacities and the role of interference
and encoding in retention problems. Although Baddeley and Warrington (1970) reported no differences between their amnesics and
their normal controls on short-term memory tasks, a number of
other investigators have consistently found that alcoholic Korsakoff
patients are impaired in their retention of information after delays
of only a few seconds (for review, see Butters and Cermak, 1975;
Kinsbourne and Wood, 1975; Piercy, 1978). If the Korsakoff patients
are presented (visually or orally) with three words (e.g., apple, pen,
roof) and then required to count backward from 100 by two's to prevent rehearsal (i.e., a distractor task), they will be impaired in the
recall of the three words after only 9 or 18 seconds of such counting
activity (Fig. 14-4). While there is some evidence that the Korsakoff
patient's nonverbal STM is superior to their verbal retentive capacities (Butters et al., 1973), it now appears that this superiority is
related to the verbal nature of the distractor activity. Counting
backward is a verbal task, and it interferes more with verbal than
with nonverbal materials. The introduction of a nonverbal distractor activity can lead to better performance with verbal than nonverbal materials (DeLuca, Cermak, and Butters, 1975).

In a recent report, Squire and Slater (1978) have administered
short-term memory tasks to a patient with a lesion (from a stab
wound) localized in the area of n. medialis dorsalis and found severe impairments in this patient's ability to retain verbal information beyond a few seconds.

The importance of the distractor task for the Korsakoff patient's
performance exemplifies one of the most prominent features of his
anterograde amnesia, i.e., increased sensitivity to proactive interference. The patients are unable to acquire new information because
of interference from previously learned materials. The evidence for

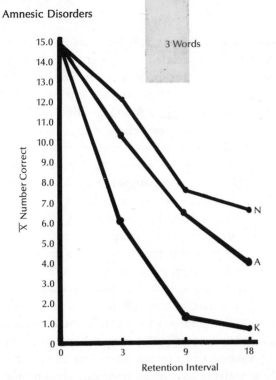

Fig. 14-4 Performance of alcoholic Korsakoff patients (K), chronic alcoholics (A), and normal controls (N) on short-term memory test with three words (word triad) as the to-be-remembered materials.

this interference phenomenon stems from three sources: (1) the nature of the Korsakoff patient's errors on learning tasks, (2) demonstrations of normal performance when partial information is provided at the time of retrieval (Warrington and Weiskrantz, 1970, 1973), and (3) demonstrations of improved retention when the learning conditions are structured to reduce proactive interference (Butters and Cermak, 1975). As noted previously, Korsakoff patients are severely impaired on short-term memory (distractor) tasks, but this impairment is not manifested in an equivalent manner throughout the test session. On early trials of the session the patients will often perform normally, but their recall will deteriorate very rapidly on subsequent trials. It has been shown that Korsakoff patients may recall as much as 90% of the presented materials on trials 1 and 2 but may recall less than 50% of the information shown on the fifth trial of the session (Cermak, Butters, and Moreines, 1974). This rapid drop in performance seems related to a rapid increment in proactive interference. On trial 5 the patient is still recalling the material presented on trials 1 and 2. These intralist intrusions suggest that the learning of material on trials 1 and 2 is hindering the patients' attempt to recall the stimuli from trial 5. Figure 14-5 shows the types of errors made by Korsakoff patients, normal controls, and dementing patients with Huntington's disease. It is evident that both the Korsakoff and the dementing patients make many errors on this short-term memory task but that the type of errors they produce differs significantly. The Korsakoff patients' errors are primarily intrusions from prior list items while the patients with Huntington's disease make many omission errors (that is, a failure to make any response). Interference then does not appear to be a crucial factor in the memory disorders of all brain-damaged patients.

With methods of retrieval that reduce interference, the performance of amnesic patients may not differ from that of intact normal controls. Warrington and Weiskrantz (1970) have shown that while amnesics are severely impaired when unaided recall or recognition tests are employed, these patients do retrieve normally when partial

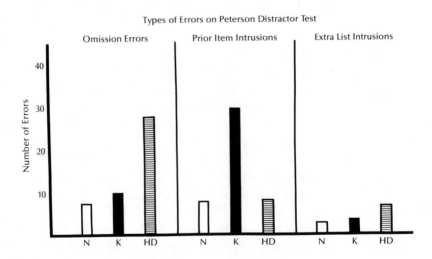

Fig. 14-5 Types of errors on short-term memory test. N = normal controls; K = alcoholic Korsakoff patients; HD = patients with Huntington's disease.

information such as the first two letters of the to-be-remembered words is provided. Warrington and Weiskrantz (1973) believe that the superiority of the partial information method stems from the limitations it places on interference from previously learned information. If the first two letters of the to-be-recalled word are "ST," the number of words that can possibly interfere with the recall of the target word "STAMP" are greatly limited. Apparently free recall and recognition procedures do not limit proactive interference to the same degree.

It is well known from the literature on normal human memory that proactive interference may be reduced by specific manipulations of the conditions under which learning is attempted. For example, distributed practice results in less interference than does massed practice. Also, a consonant trigram (e.g., J R N) will interfere less with the retention of a word triad (e.g., rose, ship, camel) than will another word triad (e.g., tulip, car, horse). When the distractor task was administered with distributed (one minute rest between successive trials) rather than massed (6 seconds between trials) presentation to Korsakoff patients, patients with Huntington's disease, and alcoholic controls, the Korsakoff patients and the controls showed significant improvements in their performance (Butters et al., 1976). In fact, the Korsakoff patients recalled as many items with distributed practice as the controls did with massed practice. However, this reduction in interference (via distribution of trials) had no effect upon the memory deficits of the dementing Huntington's patients; they performed as poorly with distributed as with massed practice. Almost identical results have been found when a word triad was preceded by a consonant trigram rather than another word triad (Butters et al., 1976). Again, low interference conditions led to improvement in the short-term memory of alcoholic Korsakoff patients and normal controls but to no changes in the poor performances of Huntington patients.

While Warrington and Weiskrantz (1973) have been content to accept interference as an explantion of amnesia, other investigators have viewed "interference theory" as primarily descriptive rather than explanatory (Piercy, 1978) and have offered hypotheses to account for both the patients' retention and interference problems. Butters and Cermak (1974, 1975) have suggested that the Korsakoff

patient's verbal memory impairment is related to a failure to encode, at the time of storage, all of the attributes of the stimulus. The
Korsakoff patients may fully categorize verbal information according to its phonemic and associative attributes, but they seem inadequate in their analysis of the semantic features of the materials. Information that is not fully analyzed (encoded) may be stored in a
degraded fashion and thus be more sensitive to interference. The
evidence supporting this conclusion stems from cueing studies in
which phonemic (e.g., rhymes) and semantic (e.g., superordinate)
cues were compared in terms of their ability to facilitate recall.
In general, phonemic cues worked as well for Korsakoff patients as
for controls, but semantic cues only aided the recall of the control
subjects. While the results of some studies have been consistent with
the semantic encoding hypothesis (Cermak et al., 1974), the findings
of other investigations have not confirmed this theory (Winocur and
Weiskrantz, 1976).

To determine whether the Korsakoff patients' deficits in semantic
encoding might represent a specific example of a more general limitation in the patients' ability to extract the features of complex
stimuli, Glosser, Butters, and Samuels (1976) employed a modified
version of the dichotic listening technique with alcoholic Korsakoff
patients, chronic alcoholics, and normal controls. Their dichotic
technique involved a simultaneous presentation of two single digits
to the patient, one to his right and one to his left ear. The patient
was instructed to press a response key whenever the digit pairs had
certain preselected spatial and/or identity features.

Under the first preselection condition, the patients were instructed
to press the response key if the number "10" was presented to their
right (or left) ear. In the second condition, the patients were to respond if the critical number "10" appeared in either ear. The third
condition required that the patients respond only when the digit
pair "9–10" appeared simultaneously in his two ears. If one of the
two critical digits was paired with a noncritical digit (e.g., "7"), the
patients were instructed not to respond. The fourth condition required that the patients respond only when the digit "9" occurred
in the right (left) ear and "10" in the left (right) ear. For all these
conditions the interval between successive pairs of digits was 1.2
seconds. For a fifth and sixth condition (virtually repeats of the

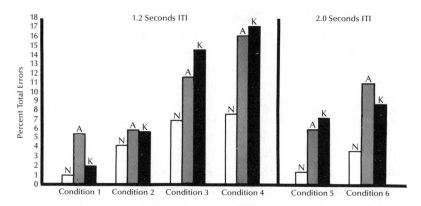

Fig. 14-6 Performance of alcoholic Korsakoff patients (K), chronic alcoholics (A), and normal controls (N) on the six conditions of the dichotic listening task of Glosser et al.

third and fourth conditions) the interpair interval was increased from 1.2 seconds to 2.0 seconds.

Results for all conditions are shown in Figure 14-6. As can be seen, the alcoholic Korsakoff patients did not differ significantly from the normal controls on Conditions 1 and 2, but on Conditions 3 and 4 the differences between these two groups were significant. It might also be noted that except for their unexplainable difficulty with Condition 1, the alcoholics showed the same pattern of deficits as the Korsakoff patients. As more and more features of the dichotic stimuli had to be processed, the Korsakoffs and the chronic alcoholics became increasingly impaired. On Conditions 5 and 6, both alcoholics and Korsakoff patients improved their performance, but they continued to make more errors than did the normal controls.

The pattern of commission errors made by the Korsakoff patients in Condition 4 suggests the nature of their difficulty on these dichotic tasks. They made no more errors than the normal controls when both dichotically presented digits were noncritical (e.g., "3" in the right ear, "8" in the left ear). However, when only one of the critical digits was present, or when the ear placement of the two critical digits was inverted, the Korsakoff patients made many more errors than did the normal controls. It appeared that when the decision processes become complicated, the Korsakoff patients did not fully analyze all the incoming information. They failed to process both channels of inputs and/or they failed to process both stimulus dimensions (phonemic, spatial).

The alcoholic Korsakoff patients' impairments on the third and fourth conditions of this experiment further confirm the hypothesis that they have a general deficit in analyzing or processing all the dimensions of new information. Whether the stimuli be visual patterns (Oscar-Berman and Samuels, 1977), names of common items (Cermak, Butters, and Gerrein, 1973), or digits presented dichotically (Glosser et al., 1976), the alcoholic Korsakoff patient has difficulty processing all of the features of the stimuli. The present experiment also suggests that what processing a Korsakoff patient can perform takes more than the normal amount of time. Given additional time to process information (Conditions 5 and 6), the alcoholic Korsakoff patient's performance does improve. This fact had also been observed previously (Cermak et al., 1974) on a task in which patients were required to determine whether or not an "A" and an "a" had the same name. Under these conditions Korsakoff patients took longer to respond than did controls.

Most recently, the limited encoding hypothesis has been applied to some of the Korsakoff patients' nonverbal cognitive deficits. In addition to their problems with verbal memory, alcoholic Korsakoff patients are significantly impaired on a number of visuoperceptive tasks such as retention of random geometric forms (DeLuca et al., 1975), digit-symbol substitution tasks (Talland, 1965; Glosser et al., 1977; Kapur and Butters, 1977), hidden figure tests (Talland, 1965; Glosser et al., 1977; Kapur and Butters, 1977), and on visual card sorting tasks (Oscar-Berman, 1973; Oscar-Berman and Samuels, 1977). Oscar-Berman and Samuels (1977) provided some evidence that the Korsakoff patient's perceptual problems may reflect an incomplete analysis of all attributes of visual stimuli. Such patients were trained to discriminate between complex visual stimuli differing on a number of relevant dimensions (e.g., color, form, size, position) and then were administered transfer tasks to determine which of the relevant stimulus dimensions had been noted. While the intact controls showed transfer to all of the relevant stimulus dimensions, the Korsakoff patients' discriminations were based upon only one or two relevant features of the stimuli.

To assess the possibility that the alcoholic Korsakoff patients' visuo-perceptual problems are attributable to a limit or deficiency in their analyses of nonverbal stimuli, Dricker et al. (1978) employed a series of facial recognition and matching tasks. On the first test, subjects were presented with two sets of photographs of college students. Set 1 was a 4 × 3 array of 12 photographs. The subject was allowed to inspect the array for 45 seconds, after which the photographs were removed. Ninety seconds later the subjects were given a 5 × 5 matrix of 25 photographs and asked to select the 12 faces that had appeared in the original inspection set. Not only did the Korsakoff patients perform at chance level on this delayed matching task, but they also made numerous errors on an immediate matching task when a single target photograph and the 25 comparison faces were both present at the same time.

The second test involved a facial matching task (developed by Diamond and Carey, 1977) that compares the subjects' tendency to use superficial piecemeal cues (such as paraphernalia and expression) and more advanced configurational cues in their analyses of faces. Configurational relationships refer to the spatial relationships between the nose, mouth, and eyes. As shown in Figure 14-7 this matching test involves five basic problems. On each trial of a given problem the subject is shown a card with three photographs of unfamiliar faces, one at the top (the target face) and two at the bottom (the comparison faces). The subject is asked to indicate which of the two comparison faces is the same as the one at the top of the card. In Type I and II problems, paraphernalia (hat) is used to fool the subjects; if the subject bases identity on similar paraphernalia (hat), he has made an incorrect choice. In Type III and IV problems, expression is used to fool the subject; judgments based upon similar expressions (smiling or frowning) would be incorrect. To perform consistently well on these four problem types, the subject must rely on the configurational aspects of the faces. In addition to the four experimental problems, there was a control problem in which neither paraphernalia nor expression were manipulated to fool the subjects. To qualify for inclusion in this study, a patient had to demonstrate accurate performance on the control problems.

The results with the Diamond-Carey face recognition task are shown in Figure 14-8. It is clear that the Korsakoff patients were

Control

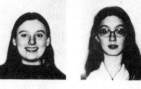

Type I

Type II

Type III

Type IV

Fig. 14-7 The Diamond-Carey Face Matching Task.

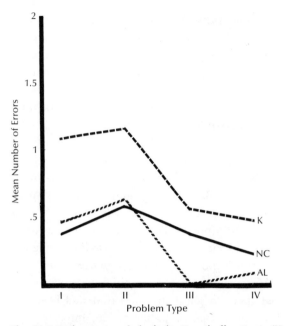

Fig. 14-8 Performance of alcoholic Korsakoff patients (K), normal controls (NC), and chronic alcoholics (AL) on the four problem types of the Diamond-Carey task.

often fooled by both paraphernalia and by expression in their match-ing of faces, although paraphernalia seems to be the more distract-ing of the two cues. These findings suggest that Korsakoff patients do not analyze all of the relevant features of unfamiliar faces. While normal subjects utilize configurational features of faces, the Korsa-koff patients rely upon more piecemeal or superficial features such as paraphernalia and expression and seem to ignore the configura-tional features of faces. If such limited perceptual analysis is charac-teristic of the Korsakoff patient, it may at least partially explain the patients' difficulties in learning, remembering, and even perceiving nonverbal patterned materials. Just as the amnesic may fail to re-trieve verbal material because of faulty or incomplete encoding, so a similar impairment in perceptual processing may be responsible for the patient's nonverbal visual memory and perceptual deficits.

While this author and his collaborators have stressed a general limitation in encoding as the source of the Korsakoff patient's amnesic problems, other investigators (Kinsbourne and Wood, 1975; Huppert and Piercy, 1976; Winocur and Kinsbourne, 1978) have suggested that such memory deficits reflect a specific failure to encode the contextual attributes of new information. That is, they may be able to encode many of the specific physical or semantic attributes of a stimulus but fail to note the temporal and spatial contexts in which the stimulus was encountered. As a consequence of this deficit, these patients may later recognize the stimulus as familiar but be unable to "recall" when or where they experienced the stimulus. This hypothesis is consistent with the often noted clinical observation that Korsakoff patients can accurately select from a room full of people those individuals they have seen before but are unable to recall under what circumstances the interaction occurred. Huppert and Piercy (1976) have provided some experimental evidence for this hypothesis. They presented Korsakoff patients and control subjects with a series of familiar and unfamiliar pictures and later asked them to select the ones that had been exposed previously. While the Korsakoff patients were impaired for both familiar and unfamiliar pictures, their performance was much better with the unfamiliar pictures. The investigators believe that this disparity in performance was due to the fact that familiar, but not unfamiliar, pictures require the patients to make a contextual judgment. For the correct identification of an unfamiliar stimulus the Korsakoff patient only has to determine whether he has, or has not, seen the picture before. However, for correct identification of a familiar picture the patient must not only determine that he has seen the picture previously (i.e., that it is familiar) but also whether the familiar picture had been included in the series administered by the investigator. The patients' failures with the familiar pictures is supposedly due to their inability to associate the pictures with the testing context.

Winocur and Kinsbourne (1978) have supplied additional evidence for this contextual encoding theory. Amnesic patients were required to learn lists of verbal paired associates under conditions which maximized the interference between successive lists (e.g., both lists contained the same stimulus but different response elements). While this proactive interference made learning almost impossible for the Korsakoff patients, their performance could be greatly improved by increasing the saliency (e.g., use of different colored inks, background music) of the contextual cues in the learning environment.

It should be noted by the reader that the application of information processing concepts to neuropsychological studies of amnesia is a relatively new venture and that a solid empirical base upon which to develop theories is still lacking. Few should be surprised then that all of the currently popular theories of amnesia are deficient in their explanation of the myriad of symptoms (e.g., the gradient associated with the patients' retrograde amnesia) associated with the amnesics' symptoms. More complete and valid theories must await a more thorough empirical knowledge of the amnesic patients' performance on various processing tasks.

Similarities and differences among amnesics
Since amnesia has been associated with a number of etiologies (e.g., vascular, alcohol, viral, trauma) and brain sites (e.g., hippocampus, mammillary bodies, mesial thalamus), it is of some importance to determine whether or not all amnesias reflect the same underlying impairments. Warrington and her collaborators have championed the position that amnesia is a unitary disorder regardless of the etiology or locus of the disease (e.g., Baddeley and Warrington, 1970; Warrington and Weiskrantz, 1973). Their investigations of amnesia have included patients with alcoholic, viral, anoxic, and surgical etiologies, and they report that all patients have performed similarly on their various learning and cognitive tasks. All of their amnesic patients are reported to perform normally on short-term memory tasks with distractors, to be highly sensitive to proactive interference, and to exhibit the same encoding strategies. Two other sets of investigators have addressed this problem by comparing populations of alcoholic Korsakoff patients and postencephalitic (herpes simplex encephalitis) patients. Lhermitte and Signoret (1972) compared these groups on four tasks that involved the learning and memory of a spatial array, of a verbal sequence, of a logical arrangement, and a code. On the first task the Korsakoff patients showed better retention than did the postencephalitic patients, but on the other three tasks the postencephalitics not only were superior to the Korsakoff patients, they also did not differ from normal controls. This author

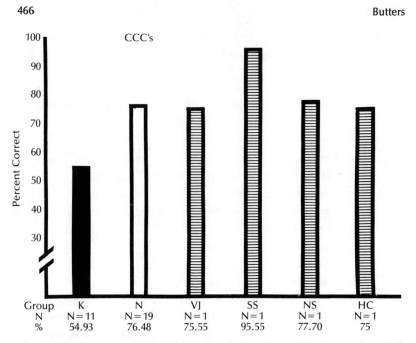

Fig. 14-9 Performance of 11 alcoholic Korsakoff patients (K), 19 normal controls (N), and four individual postencephalitics (VJ, SS, NS, and HC) on a short-term memory test with three consonants (CCC's) as the to-be-remembered materials.

has compared 11 alcoholic Korsakoff patients and four postencephalitics on short-term memory tasks. As shown in Figure 14-9 all four postencephalitic patients performed within the normal range and as a group they recalled significantly more items than did the Korsakoff patients. The findings of these two experimental studies substantiate Zangwill's (1966) clinical observations of Korsakoff and postencephalitic patients. Zangwill suggested that the alcoholic Korsakoff patients, but not the postencephalitics, manifest cognitive changes that include an increased tendency to confabulate and a lack of insight into the nature of their illness.

Despite the postencephalitics' superiority on tests of short-term memory, their performance on tests of retrograde amnesia is often worse and does not demonstrate the same temporal gradient discussed in the first section of this chapter. Figure 14-10 shows the performance of 11 alcoholic Korsakoffs, 15 normal controls, and three postencephalitics on the famous faces test of Albert, Butters, and Neff

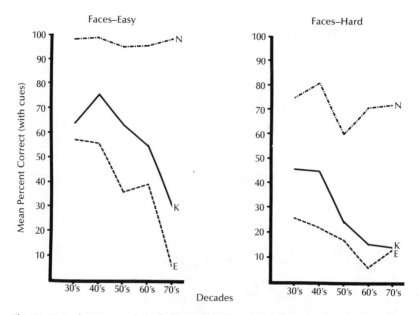

Fig. 14-10 Performance of alcoholic Korsakoff patients (K), postencephalitics (E), and normal controls (N) on famous faces test of Albert et al.

(1978). For easy items, the encephalitics perform more poorly than do the Korsakoff patients but show the same temporal gradient as do the Korsakoff patients. For hard items, the postencephalitics not only perform more poorly but also demonstrate little temporal gradient in their retrograde problems. It may be of some import that postencephalitics, but not alcoholic Korsakoff patients, provide data consistent with Sanders and Warrington's (1971) conceptions of retrograde amnesia.

This double dissociation between Korsakoff patients and postencephalitics on tests of short-term memory and retrograde amnesia not only emphasizes possible differences among amnesic populations but also suggests that anterograde-retrograde amnesic symptoms may not necessarily be correlated (Benson and Geschwind, 1967). The ability to learn new information and the capacity to recall past events may depend upon different cognitive processes and ultimately upon different neuroanatomical structures. Certainly, Fedio and Van Buren's (1974) demonstration that anterograde and retrograde deficits may be separated by stimulation along the anterior-posterior axis of the left temporal lobe is consistent with the noted behavioral dissociations.

Butters and Cermak (1976) have reported that the memory disturbances of alcoholic Korsakoff patients and of dementing patients with Huntington's disease can be empirically differentiated on short-term memory tasks. Huntington's disease is a genetically transmitted disorder in which the patient (usually about 40 years of age) undergoes progressive motor and intellectual deterioration. During the early and middle stages of the disease the patient complains of memory problems, but his amnesic symptoms are only one aspect of a general intellectual dementia as witnessed by his loss of arithmetic, linguistic, and conceptual capacities. The lesions responsible for this severe disorder include the caudate nucleus and the frontal and temporal lobes. Like the Korsakoff patients, the patients with Huntington's disease are severely impaired on short-term memory tasks (Butters and Cermak, 1976; Caine, Ebert, and Weingartner, 1977) but their disturbances seem relatively unrelated to proactive interference (see Fig. 14-5). As noted previously, the Korsakoff patients' recall improves when low-interference (e.g., distributed rather than massed presentation of trials) conditions are used, but such manipulations of interference have little or no effect upon the performance of the dementing Huntington patient. Comparisons of free versus cued recall have shown that the memory disorder of Huntington patients cannot be attributed to a specific encoding problem.

Amnesic Korsakoff patients and Huntington patients also differ in the degree to which they benefit from rehearsal. Butters and Grady (1977) employed a modified short-term memory task (distractor technique) in which a 0, 2, or 4-second delay intervened between presentation of the to-be-recalled verbal stimulus and the beginning of the counting (i.e., distractor) procedure. The 2 and 4-second predistractor delays were used to allow the patients additional time to rehearse (and thus encode) the verbal stimuli. The results (Fig. 14-11) showed that while the predistractor delays led to improved recall in the Korsakoff patients, they had virtually no effect on the Huntington patients. Apparently the Korsakoff patients, but not the dementing patients, could utilize the 2 and 4-second predistractor delays to analyze additional stimulus features to improve their recall.

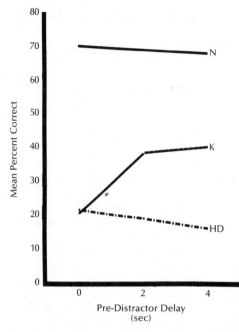

Fig. 14-11 Performance of alcoholic Korsakoff patients (K), patients with Huntington's disease (HD), and normal controls (N) on short-term memory test with 0, 2, and 4-second predistractor delays.

While the exact processing deficits involved in the amnesic symptoms of various brain-damaged groups remain largely unknown, the evidence does suggest that the amnesic disorders manifested by patients with differing disease etiologies may not be identical on neuropsychological tests. Damage to the hippocampus, lesions of the mammillary bodies and the mesial thalamus, and perhaps even damage of other subcortical and cortical structures may all produce memory disturbances, but the specific processes underlying these memory deficits may vary depending on the lesion site. Intact memory may depend on an intact limbic-diencephalic-cortical circuit, but damage at different points in the circuit does not necessarily result in the same pattern of neuropsychological deficits.

References

Albert, M., Butters, N., and Neff, J. (1978). Retrograde amnesia of alcohol and nonalcohol related amnesias. Paper presented at the annual convention of the International Neuropsychological Association, Minneapolis, Minn.

Albert, M. S., Butters, N., and Levin (1979). Temporal gradients in the retrograde amnesia of patients with alcoholic Korsakoff's disease. *Archiv. Neurol.* (in press).

Baddeley, A. D. and Warrington, E. K. (1970). Amnesia and the distinction between long- and short-term memory. *J. Verbal Learning and Verbal Behav.* 9:176–189.

Benson, D. and Geschwind, N. (1967). Shrinking retrograde amnesia. *J. Neurol. Neurosurg. Psychiat.* 30:539–544.

Butters, N., Lewis, R., Cermak, L. S., and Goodglass, H. (1973). Material-specific memory deficits in alcoholic Korsakoff patients. *Neuropsychologia, 11*:291–299.

Butters, N. and Cermak, L. S. (1974). The role of cognitive factors in the memory disorder of alcoholic patients with the Korsakoff syndrome. *Ann. New York Acad. Sci. 233*:61–75.

Butters, N. and Cermak, L. S. (1975). Some analyses of amnesic syndrome in brain damaged patients, in *The Hippocampus*, K. Pribram and R. Isaacson (eds). New York: Plenum Press.

Butters, N. and Cermak, L. S. (1976). Neuropsychological studies of alcoholic Korsakoff patients, in *Empirical Studies of Alcoholism*, G. Goldstein and C. Neuringer (eds). Cambridge, Mass.: Ballinger Press.

Butters, N., Tarlow, S., Cermak, L. S., and Sax, D. (1976). A comparison of the information processing deficits of patients with Huntington's chorea and Korsakoff's syndrome. *Cortex 12*:134–144.

Butters, N. and Grady, M. (1977). The role of temporal processing factors in the short-term memory performance of patients with Korsakoff's and Huntington's disease. *Neuropsychologia 15*:701–706.

Caine, E. D., Ebert, M. H., and Weingartner, H. (1977). An outline for the analysis of dementia: the memory disorder of Huntington's disease. *Neurology 27*:1087–1092.

Cermak, L. and Butters, N. (1973). Information processing deficits of alcoholic Korsakoff patients. *Quart. J. Studies Alcohol 34*:1110–1132.

Cermak, L., Butters, N., and Gerrein, J. (1973). The extent of the verbal encoding ability of Korsakoff patients. *Neuropsychologia 11*:85–94.

Cermak, L., Butters, N., and Moreines, J. (1974). Some analyses of the verbal encoding deficit of alcoholic Korsakoff patients. *Brain and Language 1*:141–150.

Corkin, S. (1965). Tactually-guided maze-learning in man: effects of unilateral cortical excisions and bilateral hippocampal lesions. *Neuropsychologia 3*:339–351.

Corsi, P. M. Verbal memory impairment after unilateral hippocampal excisions. Paper presented at the 40th Annual Meeting of the Eastern Psychological Association, Philadelphia, April 1969.

DeLuca, D., Cermak, L., and Butters, N. (1975). An analysis of Korsakoff patients' recall following varying types of distractor activity. *Neuro-psychologia 13*:271–279.

Diamond, R. and Carey, S. (1977). Developmental changes in the representation of faces. *J. Exp. Child Psychol. 23*:1–22.

Drachman, D. A. and Adams, R. D. (1962). Herpes simplex and acute inclusion body encephalitis. *Arch. Neurol. 7*:45–63.

Drachman, D. A. and Arbit, J. (1966). Memory and the hippocampal complex. *Arch. Neurol. 15*:62–61.

Dricker, J., Butters, N., Berman, G., Samuels, I., and Carey, S. (1978). Face perception in alcoholic Korsakoff patients. *Neuropsychologia,* in press.

Fedio, P. and Van Buren, J. (1974). Memory deficits during electrical stimulation of the speech cortex in conscious man. *Brain and Language 1*: 29–42.

Gardner, H. (1975). *The Shattered Mind.* New York: Alfred Knopf.

Gerner, P., Ommaya, A., and Fedio, P. (1972). A study of visual memory: verbal and nonverbal mechanisms in patients with unilateral lobectomy. *Intern. J. Neurosci. 4*:231–238.

Glosser, G., Butters, N., and Samuels, I. (1976). Failures in information processing in patients with Korsakoff's syndrome. *Neuropsychologia 14*:327–334.

Glosser, G., Butters, N., and Kaplan, E. (1977). Visuoperceptual processes in brain damaged patients on the digit symbol substitution test. *Intern. J. Neurosci. 7*:59–66.

Goldstein, G. and Shelly, C. H. (1971). Field dependence and cognitive, perceptual and motor skills in alcoholics. *Quart. J. Studies Alcohol 32*: 39–40.

Goodwin, D. W. and Hill, S. Y. (1976). Chronic effects of alcohol and other psychoactive drugs on intellect, learning, and memory, in *Alcohol, Drugs and Brain Damage,* J. Rankin (ed). Ontario: Addiction Research Foundation.

Haymaker, W., Smith, M. G., Bogaert, L. U., and de Chenar, D. (1958). Pathology of viral disease in man characterized by nuclear inclusions, in *Viral Encephalitis,* W. S. Fields and R. J. Blatiner (eds). Springfield, Ill.: C. C. Thomas.

Heilman, K. and Sypert, G. W. (1977). Korsakoff's syndrome resulting from bilateral fornix lesions. *Neurology 27*:490–493.

Huppert, F. A. and Piercy, M. (1976). Recognition memory in amnesic patients: effect of temporal context and familiarity of material. *Cortex 12*:3–20.

Jarho, L. (1973). *Korsakoff-Like Amnesic Syndrome in Penetrating Brain Injury.* Rehabilitation Institute for Brain Injured Veterans in Finland, Helsinki.

Johnson, R. T., Olson, L. C., and Buescher, E. L. (1968). Herpes simplex virus infections of the nervous system. *Arch. Neurol. 18*:260–264.

Kahn, E. and Crosby, E. (1972). Korsakoff's syndrome associated with surgical lesions involving the mammillary bodies. *Neurology 22*:317–325.

Kapur, N. and Butters, N. (1977). Visuoperceptive deficits in long-term alcoholics with Korsakoff's psychosis. *J. Studies Alcohol 38*:2025–2035.

Kimura, D. (1963). Right temporal-lobe damage. *Arch. Neurol. 8*:264–271.

Kinsbourne, M. and Wood, F. (1975). Short-term memory processes and the amnesic syndrome, in *Short-Term Memory*, D. Deutsch and J. A. Deutsch (eds). New York: Academic Press.

Kleinknecht, R. A. and Goldstein, S. G. (1972). Neuropsychological deficits associated with alcoholism. *Quart. J. Studies Alcohol 33*:999–1019.

Lansdell, H. (1968). Effects of extent of temporal lobe ablations on two lateralized deficits. *Physiol. Behav. 3*:271–273.

Lhermitte, F. and Signoret, J. L. (1972). Analyse neuropsychologicue et differenciation des syndromes amnesiques. *Rev. Neurol. 126*:161–178.

Marslen-Wilson, W. D. and Teuber, H. L. (1975). Memory for remote events in anterograde amnesia: recognition of public figures from newsphotographs. *Neuropsychologia 13*:347–352.

Milner, B. (1962). Les troubles de la memoire accompagnant des lesions hippocampiques bilaterales, in *Physiologie de l'Hippocampe*. Paris: C.N.R.S. (English translation in P. M. Milner and S. Glickman (eds) (1965). *Cognitive Processes and the Brain*. Princeton: Van Nostrand.)

Milner, B. (1963). Effects of different brain lesions on card sorting. *Arch. Neurol. 9*:90–100.

Milner, B. (1964). Some effects of frontal lobectomy in man, in *The Frontal Granular Cortex and Behavior*, J. M. Warren and K. Akert (eds). New York: McGraw Hill.

Milner, B. (1965). Visually-guided maze learning in man: effects of bilateral hippocampal, bilateral frontal, and unilateral cerebral lesions. *Neuropsychologia 3*:317–338.

Milner, B. (1966). Amnesia following operation on the temporal lobes, in *Amnesia*, C. W. M. Whitty and O. L. Zangwill (eds). London: Butterworths.

Milner, B. (1967). Brain mechanisms suggested by studies of the temporal lobes, in *Brain Mechanisms Underlying Speech and Language*, F. L. Darley (ed). New York: Grune & Stratton.

Milner, B. (1968). Visual recognition and recall after right temporal-lobe excisions in man. *Neuropsychologia 6*:191–210.

Milner, B., Corkin, S., and Teuber, H. L. (1968). Further analysis of the hippocampal amnesic syndrome. *Neuropsychologia 6*:267–282.

Milner, B. (1970). Memory and the medial temporal regions of the brain, in *Biology of Memory*, K. H. Pribram and D. E. Broadbent (eds). New York: Academic Press.

Milner, B. (1971). Interhemispheric differences in the localization of psychological processes in man. *Br. Med. Bull. 27*:272–275.

Newcombe, F. and Russell, R. (1969). Dissociated visual perceptual and spatial deficits in focal lesions of the right hemisphere. *J. Neurol. Neursurg. Psychiat. 32*:73–81.

Oscar-Berman, M. (1973). Hypothesis testing and focusing behavior during concept formation by amnesic Korsakoff patients. *Neuropsychologia 11*:191–198.

Oscar-Berman, M. and Samuels, I. (1977). Stimulus-preference and memory factors in Korsakoff's syndrome. *Neuropsychologia 15*:99–106.

Parsons, O. A., Tarter, R. E., and Jones, B. (1971). Cognitive deficits in chronic alcoholics. *Il Lavoro Neuro Psichiatrico 49*:5–14.

Parsons, O. (1975). Brain damage in alcoholics: altered states of unconsciousness, in *Alcohol Intoxication and Withdrawal*, Vol. II, M. Gross (ed). New York: Plenum Press.

Penfield, W. and Milner, B. (1958). Memory deficit produced by bilateral lesions in the hippocampal zone. *A.M.A. Arch. Neurol. Psychiat. 79*: 475–497.

Piercy, M. (1978). Experimental studies of the organic amnesic syndrome, in *Amnesia*, 2nd ed., C. W. M. Whitty and O. L. Zangwill (eds). London: Butterworths.

Prisko, L. (1963). Short-term memory in focal cerebral damage. Unpublished Ph.D. thesis, McGill University.

Sanders, H. I. and Warrington, E. K. (1971). Memory for remote events in amnesic patients. *Brain 94*:661–668.

Scoville, W. B. and Milner, B. (1957). Loss of recent memory after bilateral hippocampal lesions. *J. Neurol. Neurosurg. Psychiat. 20*:11–21.

Seltzer, B. and Benson, D. F. (1974). The temporal pattern of retrograde amnesia in Korsakoff's disease. *Neurology 24*:527–530.

Sidman, M., Stoddard, L. T., and Mohr, J. P. (1968). Some additional quantitative observations of immediate memory in patient with bilateral hippocampal lesions. *Neuropsychologia 6*:245–254.

Squire, L., Slater, P. C., and Chace, P. M. (1975). Retrograde amnesia: temporal gradient in very long-term memory following electroconvulsive therapy. *Science 187*:77–79.

Squire, L. R. and Slater, P. C. (1978). Anterograde and retrograde memory impairment in chronic amnesia. *Neuropsychologia 16*:313–322.

Talland, G. (1965). *Deranged Memory*, New York: Academic Press.

Teuber, H.-L., Milner, B., and Vaughan, H. (1968). Persistent anterograde amnesia after stab sound of the basal brain. *Neuropsychologia 6*:267–282.

Tomlinson, E. (1977). Pathology of dementia, in *Dementia*, 2nd ed., C. Wells (ed). Philadelphia: F. A. Davis.

Victor, M., Adams, R. D., and Collins, G. H. (1971). *The Wernicke-Korsakoff Syndrome*, Philadelphia: F. A. Davis.

Warrington, E. K. and Weiskrantz, L. (1970). Amnesic syndrome: consolidation or retrieval? *Nature 228*:628–630.

Warrington, E. K. and Weiskrantz, L. (1973). An analysis of short-term and long-term memory defects in man, in *The Physiological Basis of Memory,* J. A. Deutsch (ed). New York: Academic Press.

Winocur, G. and Weiskrantz, L. (1976). An investigation of paired-associate learning in amnesic patients. *Neuropsychologia 14*:97–110.

Winocur, G. and Kinsbourne, M. (1978). Contextual cueing as an aid to Korsakoff amnesics. *Neuropsychologia.* In press.

Zangwill, O. L. (1966). The amnesic syndrome, in *Amnesia,* C. W. M. Whitty and O. L. Zangwill (eds). London: Butterworths.

15

Dementia

ROBERT J. JOYNT AND IRA SHOULSON

Dementia is a loss of intellectual function. The term is loosely used so that qualification is necessary. It means an unusual loss of intellectual function as there is an inexorable, noticeable decline in certain mental powers. It is also usually interpreted as an acquired loss as opposed to mental retardation in which the intellect was never normal. It does not necessarily mean a gradual loss of these functions, for it may be of sudden onset, e.g., following an episode of anoxia or a cerebrovascular accident.

Intellectual function covers a variety of mental operations but the phrase generally means orientation, cognition, and memory. Other operations are affected in dementia, such as language, praxis or skilled movement, and perceptions. However, isolated neurological defects like aphasia are not usually classified as dementia. This latter statement is controversial and some investigators believe that aphasic patients do have defects in intelligence and suffer the loss of an internal speech. Regardless of that argument, in clinical practice, language disorders such as aphasia, alexia, and agraphia are usually excluded from the general classification of dementia. Likewise, sensory defects such as denial of illness, hemiplegia of body parts, or a restricted sensory abnormality like Gerstmann's syndrome, would not be included. Some would even exclude circumscribed memory disorders such as Wernicke-Korsakoff syndrome since in these cases mental operations seem to function well on what memories the patient can use. Generally, however, memory disorders are regarded as dementias.

INTRODUCTION

In this chapter we will center our discussion upon the most common and typical forms of dementia. We will emphasize Alzheimer's disease as it is by far the most common dementia encountered. It is not our purpose to discuss the multifarious causes and treatments but to assist in the recognition and differentiation so that more definitive studies and treatment plans can be initiated. We will emphasize practical aids in diagnosis but will not discuss the many neuropsychological tests that are useful and should be applied for more exact measurement of the intellectual defects. After this introductory section, the chapter will present a classification followed by a discussion of subtypes, diagnostic evaluation, and some general statements about care. In the discussion of the various types of dementia, we will include some of the modes of presentation and differential diagnosis.

Two important admonitions about the problem of dementia must be stated. The first is that dementia is a symptom of many disorders and not a diagnostic entity. The second point follows from the first: since dementia has different etiologies, some cases are remediable.

The important principle that dementia is a symptom emphasizes a basic observation about the reaction of the brain to disease. Irrespective of the cause of the disorder, the symptoms will be a function of the locus and not the type of disease. Therefore, atrophy affecting the frontal lobes or tumor invading the same region may present in similar fashion. Not recognizing this principle may lead to egregious errors in diagnosis. However, it must be recognized that all brain lesions are not confined to discrete anatomical regions; some spread through certain systems or cell groups. In the latter case certain types of diseases preferentially attack certain systems or groups of cells. An example of this is the propensity of Alzheimer's disease to selectively affect association areas early in the disease. Another factor that must be considered in the production of signs and symptoms is the speed of onset of the disease. Hughlings Jackson referred to this as the "momentum" of the lesion. An illustration of this is the observation that denial of illness, anosognosia, is much more frequent after strokes than with tumors. This happens even when both may occupy approximately the same amount of brain in an identical location. This acute effect or disaschisis, to use von Monakow's term, also applies to dementia. Usually the more prominent disturbance seen after an acute episode clears, and residual signs and symptoms then depend on the location and extent of the lesion. The initial acute effect does not abrogate our fundamental observation about the response of the brain. With acute lesions such as strokes there is widespread physiological disruption which goes beyond the bounds of brain destruction and renders large undamaged areas inactive temporarily.

The second point—that some dementias are treatable and may be remedied or at least halted—places a great responsibility on the clinician. It is becoming more obvious in this day of more effective cardiopulmonary resuscitation that the chief aim of all of medicine is to keep the nervous system functioning. The specter of dementia, a failing mind in a healthy body, is so dreadful that a missed chance for treatment has immense implications for the patient and his family. A more optimistic outlook is noted in the section on diagnostic evaluation.

CLASSIFICATION

Dementias may be classified in a number of ways, e.g., by age of onset, etiology, accompanying neurological signs, or by whether or not they are treatable. From a diagnostic standpoint it is most useful to classify them on the basis of their localization because the signs and symptoms are dependent on this and not, for example, on their etiology. This type of classification has drawbacks for many of the dementias which progressively involve more and more of the brain so that strict categorization becomes meaningless. However, at that point it takes no skill in diagnosis to detect global brain involvement. The worth of such a classification is to help in early recognition and categorization so that further efforts at diagnosis, management, and prognosis have a rational basis.

The classification system we will use, recognizing its obvious faults, is:

   I. Localized dementia
     A. Cortical
     B. Subcortical
     C. Axial
  II. Global dementia

For each of the above we will take one example to typify that category: Alzheimer's disease for cortical, Huntington's disease for subcortical, and Wernicke-Korsakoff syndrome for axial. Global dementia is best typified by advanced Alzheimer's disease. The defects of the classification are immediately obvious for we know that Alzheimer's disease involves subcortical areas and Huntington's disease produces cortical changes. Another defect in classification is that anyone involved in the care of these patients is aware of the variegated behavioral pattern of demented patients. Geschwind (1975) has emphasized the variable nature of brain disease, pointing out that any one feature, such as memory disorder, may be prominent in one and lacking in another.

The outward manifestations of brain disease are, as we have emphasized, based on the location and extent of the disease. This view must be reconciled with the clinical and pathological observations that some functions appear to be dependent not on the location and extent of brain damage but on the total amount of brain damage irrespective of location. This propels us into the age-old controversy of the localizationists versus the holists (also see Chapter 1). There is no question that certain areas do have very circumscribed functions. But when one is considering such functions as cognition, orientation, memory, abstraction, adaptation, and reaction to stress, localizing and assigning these functions to discrete brain areas is difficult. The best study of the behavioral effect of measured brain removal was that of Chapman and Wolff (1959). They found that if less than 120 grams of cortical tissue were removed, memory and orientation were intact but certain adaptive responses were impaired. It is not to be denied on the basis of present data that holistic views of cerebral function are valid. However, to measure accurately or even to define such abstruse concepts as adaptation or drive is almost insurmountable. When the behavioral task, no matter how complex, is broken down into its basic components it is possible to make more accurate anatomic and clinical correlations. Thus, the view that certain mental functions are not assignable to specific brain areas is quite likely a condemnation of our inadequate observation and testing.

Cortical dementias are characterized by defects in abstraction, orientation, judgment, and memory. In addition, these patients have deficits in those association areas serving expressive and comprehensive language, skilled movements, and sensory interpretation. Defects in these areas result in aphasias, apraxias, and agnosias which are usually of limited intensity. Because such symptoms are limited, they may not be detected. Our concept of aphasia, for example, is founded mainly by observing patients with vascular and neoplastic disease where there is often complete, but circumscribed, brain parenchymal loss. In dementias, this is not the pathogenetic mechanism since the cell loss is diffuse and not total and therefore complete syndromes are not present early.

The concept of a subcortical dementia is new. The prominent feature is a gradual decline in cognitive powers but without signs of loss of associative cortical areas. Therefore, aphasia, agnosias, and perceptual disturbances like cortical blindness are absent. McHugh and Folstein (1975) emphasize that these features along with a profound apathy constitute the "subcortical dementia syndrome."

Axial dementias are so designated because they involve the axial structures of the brain such as the medial portion of the temporal lobes, hippocampus, fornix, mammillary bodies, and hypothalamus. It is those areas which are concerned with the registration of memory, as documented by Victor and his co-workers (1971). The prominent feature of this dementia is marked disturbance in recent memory which makes learning a new task is almost impossible. Equally striking is the absence of other intellectual disturbances, a prominent feature in the other dementias. (See Chapter 14.)

While we have emphasized intellectual function such as cogni-

tion, memory, orientation, and language in the differentiation of
these dementias, a very important feature is the general changes in
emotions and behavior. Indeed, it is often the behavioral features
which are paramount in alerting the family and acquaintances to
the existence of the dementia. Often the more subtle cognitive
changes are not noted until detected in the examination. Accompanying some of the dementias are nonspecific and specific neurological signs. In many of the cortical and subcortical dementias there
are signs such as the grasp reflex, the palmomental reflex, and
brisk muscle stretch reflexes. In dementias like Huntington's disease, the choreic movements are characteristic and form part of the
basis for diagnosis. Specific laboratory procedures are also useful
such as studies for spinal fluid absorption in normal pressure hydrocephalus and computerized tomographic (CT) scan for cortical
atrophy and ventricular enlargement.

Specific diagnosis for dementia is therefore primarily dependent
on (1) case history usually supplied by the relatives regarding behavior and mental functioning; (2) physical examination, not neglecting the general examination; (3) mental status assessment; and
(4) appropriate laboratory tests.

CORTICAL DEMENTIAS

Alzheimer's disease and senile dementia are a single process. The
basis for this conclusion rests on excellent neuropathological studies.
The artificial differentiation of a presenile and senile dementia, depending on the age of onset, has clouded this diagnosis for years.
The foolishness of this thinking is exemplified in the artificial shift
of the age of onset for the diagnosis from 60 to 65, reflected in the
literature on the disorder. In this discussion, Alzheimer's disease and
senile dementia will be used interchangeably.

There is no doubt that Alzheimer's disease is one of the most
prominent public health problems today. It is estimated that about
5% of the population over 65 has a severe dementia and about 10%
has a mild to moderate dementia. In pointing out this prevalence,
Katzman (1976) estimated that senile dementias are likely the
fourth or fifth most common cause of death in this country, as the
presence of dementia in elderly patients considerably shortens their
expected life spans. There is evidence that this is likely an under-

estimation, e.g., one report quoted by Arie (1973) estimates that over 80% of moderate to severely demented patients were not known to be so by their family physician.

Presentation
The mode of presentation of these patients is often useful in the diagnosis. It is extremely rare that a person with Alzheimer's disease will be self-referred. Occasionally, a person who is concerned about a failing memory will seek consultation. A few, but not many, of these patients will turn out to have a progressive dementia. Most are usually active people in their 40's or 50's who normally perform at a high intellectual level and become concerned when they feel that they cannot maintain this performance. Many turn out to be patients with a depression. The reason for the lack of self-referral is the concomitant loss of insight which blunts the person's sensitivity to his own shortcomings. Characteristic patterns of referral were noted by Arie (1973). Many of these are crisis referrals in which the patient is brought by the family for an initial evaluation and already found to be grossly demented. He noted the "Monday morning syndrome" in which family members who infrequently visit their aging parents or parent find on one weekend that the patient is not doing as well. Because of the infrequent contact, this appears to be a worsening, and the doctor is called "first thing" after the weekend. Another type is the "Friday afternoon crisis" when the family that was taking care of the demented parent and has need of a respite and arrives at the hospital prior to a short vacation.

Many of these referrals are caused by some change in the patient's health or living situation. Elderly patients with moderate dementia may do quite well living alone in familiar surroundings and with a regular routine. However, some mild illness or the initiation or change in medication of almost any type may increase their confusion. Changes in routine such as a move to a nursing home or the closing of a neighborhood grocery store may make their underlying dementia more obvious.

Behavioral changes
Behavioral changes are often prominent much earlier than problems with orientation, cognition, and memory. Three prominent behavioral features are commonly encountered. They are (1) accen-

tuation of prior behavioral traits to the point of eccentricity, (2) an apathetic attitude which precludes taking on novel ventures, and (3) the inability to handle multiple mental operations with a marked distractability when required to do so. The latter characteristic is very subject to fatigue.

Accentuation of previous behavior traits is very common. While it can generally be said that many of the social graces and neatness of dress eventually disappear in senile dementias, it is not unusual for a housewife noted for her cleanliness to become obsessive about household tasks. The patients who are secretive and suspicious become frankly paranoid and make severe recriminations about the behavior of close friends, family, and spouses. Individuals who have been sexually active may pursue this activity indiscriminately, and eventually have to suffer embarrassing and even legal consequences.

Novel undertakings of any type are very difficult for patients with dementia. The urging of concerned family or a concerned spouse that a change of scenery is necessary may often end up with a disastrous worsening. As the dementia progresses, this reluctance to take on new things evolves into a marked apathy. With this the patient's appearance degenerates. The man no longer shaves or washes. The woman leaves her hair uncombed and is generally unkempt.

Many of the patients with dementia can carry on with their work or with their hobbies if they are not called upon to handle more than a few operations at a time. The shopkeeper may handle one customer without difficulty, but the appearance of a few more people waiting to be served is very disquieting and many precipitate an outburst of temper.

Another less frequent but often prominent feature is the loss of a sense of humor. This has been stressed as an early sign of intellectual loss. Unfortunately, many people, including some of the examining physicians, may not have a particularly well-developed sense of humor. Thus, to quantitate the loss when both the patient and the physician have varying standards may not be useful. There have been efforts at standardizing these responses by presenting captioned cartoons. But the authors of this article disagreed on which cartoons, if any, were humorous. Laughter at macabre situations is obviously inappropriate, but this is rarely an early sign of dementia.

The vacillation of emotional response with wide mood swings is not, in our experience, as common as stated. It does occur but usually represents an exaggeration of a previously unstable temperament.

The behavioral abnormalities discussed above as well as the patients' intellectual capabilities are subject to fatigue. After a night of rest many patients are quite lucid, but as their day goes on their ability to cope with intellectual material lessens and, along with this, behavior disintegrates. Therefore, mental status testing and behavioral observations are necessary throughout the day to accurately assess the degree of impairment.

Intellectual changes

The earliest signs of intellectual deficit in most patients is the impairment of memory. The immediate or "scratch-pad" memory is characteristically preserved but holding material for several minutes may be impossible. Patients often use *aide-memoires* like writing notes to themselves, but even these may be misplaced. Frequently a spouse will report that there are literally hundreds of notes in various places in the home. Items of apparel may be forgotten or put on improperly, pots may boil dry on the stove, and familiar friends may be misnamed.

Defects in abstract thinking are more difficult to detect. Sometimes examples may be garnered from the history. Unfortunately, it is the defect in abstract thinking and comprehension which blunts the insight of the patient. With this poor appreciation of their defect they may continue on in positions of authority and responsibility. It is frightening to find patients with major intellectual deficits who are responsible for decisions affecting the lives and fortunes of others.

As cortical dementias progress, those mental operations which are localizable such as language and perception become affected. As noted earlier, these are usually partial defects by nature of the progress of the disease: loss of brain cells is gradual and diffuse. Eventually, well developed aphasic, apractic, and agnostic syndromes may emerge. Early language problems are usually manifested by word-finding difficulties and gradual attrition of complex language capabilities, both in expression and comprehension. Items are misnamed and phonemic substitutions are made. Subtleties of language such as subjunctive and complex sentence forms disappear.

More and more jargon is uttered when the patient is stimulated to speak. Other forms of communication such as reading and writing suffer along with the deterioration in speech.

Practic disorders are usually present in well-developed cases. General clumsiness may increase to marked confusion about the sequence of motor acts. Taking a match from a book and striking it may tax the patients' abilities so they sit dumbfounded when asked to do this. On the other hand, overlearned motor behavior, eating, for example, may persist undisturbed even when other functions have severely deteriorated.

Perceptual disorders are usually manifested by problems with spatial perception and route finding. Patients may get lost even in every-day familiar surroundings. This is particularly true if they also suffer with defective vision or hearing. Confusion at night is common because sensory input is lessened. Most perceptual defects are negative symptoms but positive symptoms of visual and auditory hallucinations may occur. Any medications which sedate and depress awareness may precipitate hallucinations.

Cranial Nerve, Motor, and Sensory Abnormalities

These are adjuncts for diagnosis since the early signs of dementia are reflected in decline of intellectual function. However, with gradual decrease in the population of nerve cells, gross neurological signs appear. They are largely due to loss of inhibition of rudimentary reflexes with the appearance of the so-called frontal release signs: the snout reflex, grasp reflex, and palmomental reflex along with a general increase in muscle stretch reflexes. In advanced stages, Babinski responses may appear. Rarely, there are positive signs of cerebral involvement with myoclonic, focal, and generalized seizures.

Laboratory studies also contribute to the diagnosis. The evidence of cortical atrophy can now be determined by the CT scan. In most instances, this has eliminated the need for pneumoencephalography, a procedure which is uncomfortable for the patient and, in certain cases, precipitates rapid worsening.

SUBCORTICAL DEMENTIAS

The concept of subcortical dementia is recent, although the dementia accompanying subcortical disease states has been well observed and described. The term is used to designate the dementia seen with disease of subcortical regions and the most prominent examples are Huntington's disease, Parkinson's disease, progressive supranuclear palsy and thalamic surgery. That these are not identical in location and extent of lesion is evidenced by different patterns of neurological deficit present in each. Also, in many of these disorders the lesion is more widespread than the subcortex. This group also illustrates another complexity: our views of brain structure amalgamate structure and function. The demonstration that some diseases are lesions of certain transmitter systems must revise our concept of neuroanatomy. We have really not begun to make good sense out of the behavioral defects related to biochemical lesions. In spite of this hiatus in our knowledge, there are certain features which bind together the diseases which present with subcortical dementias. Albert and his co-workers (1974) pointed out that there are defects in timing and activation with slowing of memory, thought, and motor performance. The hallmark of these dementias is the prominent appearance of signs relating to deficits in frontal-lobe function *without* signs of language involvement. The most characteristic is the clinical picture of a patient with Huntington's disease. We will emphasize the mental status and behavior dysfunction and not the movement disorder.

Behavioral changes

There are certain behavioral changes unique to Huntington's disease which are not seen in the other subcortical dementias. This is due to the hereditary nature of the disease. In at-risk relatives or in patients with early disease the specter of the progressive dilapidation of mental function along with the distressing movement disorder colors their lives. Thus, a marked anxiety and preoccupation with their health is common. This occasionally culminates in major depressive symptoms with suicide as one of the outcomes.

The behavioral features common to all the subcortical dementias are the marked apathy and the slowing of thinking and memory. This leads to gradual withdrawal of these patients from former activities and severing of old friendships. Attention to their work, to their interpersonal relationships, and to their own appearance wanes. As with most patients with frontal-lobe disease, there is disinhibition of emotional responses so that outbursts of temper and violent behavior may occur.

Prominent psychotic changes may be seen in patients with Huntington's disease. McHugh and Folstein (1975) describe two types: mood disorders resembling manic-depressive psychosis, and delusionary-hallucinatory states resembling schizophrenia.

Intellectual changes

The cognitive changes seen in subcortical dementias resemble those seen in the cortical dementias with the prominent exception of preserved language function. Most authors have noted that almost all aspects of language function are undisturbed including reading, writing, speaking, and comprehension. There may be nonspecific word-finding difficulties, but the prominent jargon seen in patients with Alzheimer's disease, for example, is not seen in the subcortical dementias. Speech may suffer because of motor involvement with problems in coordination, resulting in dysarthria. Other cortical defects also escape so that major apraxias and agnosias are not prominent. Occasionally, we detect some problems with spatial perception in patients with Huntington's disease.

Memory function is usually affected after the cognitive defects appear. In memory testing, these patients are easily distracted. The deficit in memory is usually not present early in the disease and never approaches the severity seen in axial dementia. However, it is difficult for them to learn extensive new material. We noted in testing those patients who were cognizant of their memory problem and susceptibility to distraction that they would personally take great pains to shut out competing stimuli; they would turn off radios and television sets and shut doors prior to memory testing (also, see Chapter 14 on memory).

The intellectual defects progress much slower in patients with Huntington's disease than with Alzheimer's disease. The end result in both is similar except for the preservation of language in Huntington's disease.

Cranial Nerve, Motor, and Sensory Abnormalities

The subcortical dementias are accompanied by various types of neurological abnormalities depending on the underlying disease. In Huntington's disease there is a generalized chorea accompanied by dystonic posturing of the extremities and the trunk. The neurological abnormalities may precede or follow the onset of intellectual dysfunction.

AXIAL DEMENTIA

The axial structures of the brain are essential for the proper registration and retention of new material. (Memory disorders are discussed in Chapter 14.) Some argue that these disorders are not dementias because the patients often function quite adequately with the information they have retained. However, they often seem to be unaware of their disturbance, a characteristic which is out of keeping with the statement that all functions except memory are intact. The most flagrant example of this disorder is the Wernicke-Korsakoff syndrome. The disorder is caused by nutritional deficiency and is probably selective for those patients who have enzyme systems which are particularly dependent on thiamine. Other conditions which may cause similar memory disturbances are the aftermath of head injuries, normal-pressure hydrocephalus, and the sequelae of encephalitis (particularly those varieties with a propensity to medial temporal-lobe involvement like herpes simplex encephalitis).

Behavioral changes
The behavior of a patient with Wernicke-Korsakoff syndrome secondary to alcoholism may be clouded by other mental changes seen in chronic alcoholics. In most instances, there are few overt behavioral abnormalities. The patients do lack initiative and are generally unaware or are not disturbed about their profound memory loss. The swings in mood seen with other types of dementia are not a feature of the axial dementias. In fact, most of the patients appear placid and cooperative. The social amenities are ordinarily preserved, and most patients are mindful of their personal appearance.

Intellectual changes
The most striking change is in memory. The patient does have some degree of retrograde memory loss which may extend back for weeks or years. This is usually a discontinuous loss with some islands of preserved memories.

It is almost impossible for the patient to retain new material. Commonly, series of figures may be parroted back, but anything delayed for more than several seconds is lost. Tests of abstraction may be performed if the patient is working on old retained information or if he is capable of quickly thinking through the problem prior to the loss of new information being used. Language problems are not encountered.

Confabulation is not a sine qua non for the diagnosis of this disorder but is frequently present.

Cranial Nerve, Motor, and Sensory Abnormalities

These depend on the underlying condition. In the Wernicke-Korsakoff syndrome seen with thiamine deficiency, there may be signs of Wernicke's encephalopathy with eye-movement disorders and ataxia. There are no specific abnormalities seen with all axial dementias.

SUMMARY

As noted above, dementias may be classified into cortical, subcortical, and axial. If the disturbance is progressive or is accompanied by other brain disease, the classification loses its worth and the loose term, global dementia, is used. However, early in the disease this classification is useful as it gives a basis for diagnosis, further investigation, and management. While faulty, the following categorization of dementias is proposed:

Cortical dementias	Subcortical dementias	Axial dementias
Alzheimer's disease	Huntington's disease	Wernicke-Korsakoff syndrome
Multi-infarct dementia	Parkinson's disease	Normal-pressure hydrocephalus
Creutzfeldt-Jakob disease	Progressive supranuclear palsy	Herpes encephalitis
Head injury (extent)	Head injury (extent)	Head injury (extent)
Neoplastic (extent)	Neoplastic (extent)	
Metabolic		
Infections such as meningitis and encephalitis		
Anoxia		

The common forms of dementia and their clinical features are listed in the sections that follow.

Multi-infarct dementia (MID)

Multi-infarct dementia is recognized clinically by the accumulation of abrupt vascular episodes (strokes), generally associated with focal neurological deficits. The hypertensive patient is most susceptible to repeated lacunar infarcts; features of the lacunar state may develop eventually. Multiple, embolic, cerebral infarcts from extracranial atheromatous disease (carotid artery disease) or from cardiac origins (atrial fibrillation) may also contribute to the development of multi-infarct dementia. "Cerebral arteriosclerosis" is a vague entity, commonly mistaken as a cause of dementia. The clinical distinction of multi-infarct dementia is important because the disability may be favorably altered by therapy (control of hypertension, and, more controversially, the use of anticoagulants, or vascular surgery).

Post-traumatic dementia

Post-traumatic dementia, like the more global form of alcoholic dementia, is an acknowledged but ill-defined entity. Many clinicians believe that intellectual failure is an unusual sequelae of closed head injury; however, the results of psychological testing do not support this viewpoint. Meticulous assessment of memory and learning skills following head concussions has demonstrated fixed, cognitive deficits in a substantial proportion of patients. In general, the intellectual impairment is global and shows some improvement with the passage of time. Instances of progressive post-traumatic dementia, particularly following repeated head injury, are well recorded. The "post-concussion syndrome" of irritability, poor concentration, fatigue, and headache may occasionally be a prodrome of post-traumatic dementia. Longitudinal studies of intellectual functioning are needed in these patients.

Infectious dementias

Increasing investigative interest has been accorded to the viral pathogenesis of CNS diseases associated with dementia. A relatively acute onset, prominent disturbances in attention, focal and evanescent neurological deficits, and rapid progression are the hallmarks of the infectious (viral) dementias. Brain biopsy may be warranted in patients with presumed herpes encephalitis and should be considered in patients with suspected multifocal leukoencephalopathy or subacute sclerosing panencephalitis. Creutzfelt-Jakob disease is often accompanied by EEG changes and myoclonic jerking; however, the EEG alterations are not pathognomonic, and myoclonus has been observed in other categories of dementia. Antiviral chemotherapy appears established in the treatment of herpes encephalitis, and represents a promising strategy in other viral dementias.

Nutritional-endocrine-metabolic dementias

The dementing disorders resulting from nutritional deficiencies (vitamin and protein depletion) and endocrine-metabolic disturbances (thyroid/adrenal/parathyroid disease, carbohydrate intolerance, and lipoproteinemic disturbances) deserve their accorded emphasis. Although these disorders are frequently remediable, their occurrence is relatively rare. Screening batteries have heightened attention to unsuspected endocrine-metabolic disorders, particularly calcium, magnesium, and phosphorus disturbances. The protein deficiency states and hypovitaminoses deserve reemphasis because of the advent of intravenous hyperalimentation and of renal dialysis.

Toxic dementias

Iatrogenic or surreptitious drug exposure appears to be a more common cause of dementia than that contributed by the combined nutritional-endocrine-metabolic disorders. The published data are probably a conservative estimate of the numbers of patients whose intellectual performance improves after discontinuation or dose reduction of existing medications. The anticholinergics, antipsychotics, and sedative-hypnotics account for a substantial proportion of drug-related dementias. These observations suggest that "drug holidays" be considered in the evaluation of dementia. Recent evidence suggests that manganese and aluminum may play a substantive role in the pathogenesis of Parkinsonian and Alzheimer's dementias; screening batteries for heavy metals may help clarify the role of these presumed CNS toxins. The contribution of environmental toxins to the prevalence of dementia has gained some popular attention, and prospective investigative approaches are clearly needed.

DIAGNOSTIC EVALUATION

"Dementia" is a useful term as applied to the symptom complex of intellectual failure that results from a variety of diseases affecting the brain. For diagnostic purposes, the terms "dementia" or "unclassified dementia" describe those patients with intellectual failure whose underlying diseases have not yet been identified. In fact, the number of patients with unclassified organic brain syndrome is quite small. A specific clinical diagnosis can be formulated in the overwhelming number of patients with unclassified dementia, through the process of a systematic and comprehensive clinical evaluation. This contention is supported by the studies of Seltzer and Sherwin (1978) who were able to arrive at a specific diagnosis in 96% of patients with previously unclassified dementia. Furthermore, the specific diagnosis can be established on the basis of clinical evaluation alone, and only rarely requires pathological confirmation. Of course, the evaluation is not often accomplished with great ease. Historical information is usually incomplete, the patients may be less than cooperative during the examination and laboratory investigation, and repeated assessment is frequently needed. However, these obstacles should not prevent the skilled and experienced clinician from establishing a specific diagnosis. Of greatest importance, Seltzer and Sherwin found that identification of the underlying disease has direct therapeutic importance in the treatment of approximately 50% of patients with unclassified dementia. In all patients, the evaluation process may help focus on the needs and concerns of patients and family.

The skill and experience required in the assessment of the patient with dementia precludes the use of a simple algorithmic approach in the evaluation process. The basic precept offered is that all patients with presumed intellectual impairment undergo a complete clinical appraisal, based on a systematic and comprehensive history, examination, and laboratory investigation.

History
The approach in obtaining the history is somewhat unconventional since the most helpful and reliable historical information is not ob-

tained directly from the patient but rather from a relative or friend. Of course, the manner in which the patient relates the history, if he does so at all, is a critical part of the examination process. In our experience, it is unusual for the patient with dementia to initiate the clinical contact. If the patient initiates the clinical evaluation process, especially when expressing concerns of a memory disturbance, the examiner should be alerted to the possibility of a pseudodementia, particularly depression.

Several salient features in the history are worthy of emphasis. Rapidity of onset is an important indicator. A sudden, definable onset implies more precipitous causes of dementia such as multi-infarcts, head traumas, or infections. On the other hand, the more insidious development of symptoms suggests a steadily progressive disorder such as Alzheimer's dementia. The course of the illness in rate and pattern of progression also has bearing in defining the underlying disorder. Some types of dementia are typically rapid or steadily progressive such as Creutzfeldt-Jakob disease or space taking dementias. A slow course characterizes Alzheimer's or Huntington's disease. Some dementias may be slow but show episodic step-wise deterioration such as multi-infarct dementias.

The history may also provide a focus for the types of mental operations which appear to be most affected. Particular inquiry should be made into possible drug, toxic, or infectious exposure. Specific information should be obtained regarding the patient's education and vocational background. A review of the patient's nutritional status may provide clues to readily remediable causes of dementia. Likewise, the presence of a previous psychiatric illness may provide a precise diagnostic focus. Finally, a complete family history should be obtained for the propositus and family in as many generations as possible. The recognition of a hereditary dementia is critical not only for the patient but for his family members as well.

Examination
The examination of the patient should include a full mental status, cranial nerve, motor, sensory, and general physical examination. Although much cognitive and behavioral information is obtained through the interview, a systematic examination of mental status should be made. The examiner should evaluate and record the patient's performance in all cognitive functions including: level of re-

sponsiveness, attention, language, memory, constructional abilities (perception), and reasoning (judgment and interpretation). The procedure varies depending on the clinical situation. In some, memory testing may need the most thorough scrutiny, and in others abstraction may be most critical. The practical importance of systematically evaluating all mental operations derives from the fact that specific patterns of cognitive impairment are encountered in the underlying diseases of dementia. For example, in Korsakoff syndrome, the memory disturbance is prominent and perception may be somewhat impaired, but other mental operations are typically intact. In Alzheimer's or other cortical dementias, more global intellectual failure is observed in language, memory, perception, attention, and reasoning. The subcortical dementias show little, if any, language impairment.

NEUROLOGICAL EXAMINATION

Comments regarding observations of behavior and emotions have already been made. The patient should also be observed for attention and responsiveness. Vague terms such as obtunded, semicomatose, and drowsy are useless. The response to stimuli should be noted. This is a quantitative measure which will be useful in grading progression over time and will have some meaning to other examiners.

Mental status. The examination of mental status is a skill acquired by contact with many patients. Attempts to quantitate these tests are worthy but do not take into account many of the variables which objective scoring misses. For example, the patient's education and background, proficiency in the language used in the examination, sensory problem such as deafness and blindness, and reactions to answers by the examiner all affect his performance, as does the environment in which the test is conducted and the medication being used by the patient. Many of the standard batteries use tests of current events such as the incumbent governor, past presidents, and other such questions—it is sad, but true, that many people have little interest in these matters so their failures mean disinterest but not memory loss.

To give a quick appraisal of mental status, orientation, memory, abstraction, judgment, perception, and language should be tested.

Orientation is assessed by questions about persons, places, and time. It is rare that a person does not know who he is, but this does occur in advanced global dementias. Place disorientation is common, but here consideration must be given to the state of the patient's alertness when he was brought to the hospital. Time information includes day, date, month, year, hour, and season. The date is often off a few days when a patient has been in the hospital several days. Missed questions about dates are often noted in the chart by physicians who have to ask the date or consult a calendar to put the proper dated entry in the chart.

Memory is broken down into immediate, recent, and remote. Immediate is best tested by remembering digit sequences. Most patients can parrot back five or more digits. Reversing the digits is more difficult because the patient has to hold and manipulate these. An excellent test to pick up more subtle loss is to have the patient learn and repeat back a ten-digit sequence. Most people succeed after four to seven trials if the numbers are slowly repeated to them after each trial. Ten trials are given and the results noted. Most normal people will pass this test which measures intact recent memory, concentration, and attention. Normal subjects can usually retain three items for five minutes, a useful guide for testing recent memory. Remote memory is tested by referring back to past current events, keeping in mind the admonition already mentioned, and events relating to early life which can be confirmed from a spouse or relative. For additional discussion of memory, see Chapter 14.

Abstraction is usually tested by proverb interpretation. Again, one must be careful as certain cultures do not employ proverbs, and young patients not exposed to the McGuffey's reader or to the early teaching of proverbs conveying moral concepts do not use or understand proverbs. Another way to approach this is to pick a terse newspaper headline or heading and ask what it means and what are the implications of the information.

Judgment can best be assessed by information from the relatives who in most instances of dementia can cite examples of poor judgment. A good assessment of judgment is the patient's attitude in the testing. The unimpaired patient will recognize the significance and object of the examination. Those with impaired judgment will question, resent, ignore, or answer with absurdities or in poor taste.

Perception is most easily tested in the visual area. Copying figures or constructing simple geometric designs test both perception and constructional ability. If there are defects, more extensive testing can be done. Also, see discussion of visuospatial disorders in Chapter 8.

Language testing is treated elsewhere (see Chapter 2) but a quick survey can be done in the course of the conversation. Observations should be made regarding spontaneous production of speech, complexity of speech, use of correct names, and comprehension. Simple tests of object recognition should be done, as a patient who seems to have normal speech may fail on this test. A test for subtle aphasic problems is the ability to produce several words in one category like the names of ten flowers, all the words one can think of beginning with a certain letter, or all the synonyms of a common word.

More extensive testing can be done during the hospitalization period. Also, testing should be performed at different times of the day. Many patients who are depressed and anxious do much better when they become more familiar with the examiner or after a few days of rest.

A formal review of psychiatric or behavioral features during the mental status examination is frequently overlooked. The need to examine mood, emotional status, reality-testing, and thought content of the patient is as compelling as the evaluation of cognitive functions. In some underlying diseases that produce a picture of dementia, failure to recognize psychiatric as well as cognitive impairment may deprive the patient of appropriate therapeutic measures. Moreover, the cognitive impairment may appear more prominent because of existing but unrecognized psychiatric disturbances. The finding of Seltzer and Sherwin that 11% of their patients with unclassified dementia actually had psychiatric disorders is testimony to the admonition.

Cranial nerve, motor, and sensory examination. The formal neurological examination of the patient with dementia has undergone considerable refinement in recent years. The critical appraisal of the neurological examination in the elderly patient has provided some needed reference standards, as pointed out by Klawans et al. (1971) and Critchley (1956). The motor examination deserves attention because appraisal of motor functions lends itself to quantitative measures. Evaluation of gait, station, and posture may have important therapeutic as well as diagnostic implications. The presence of a hesitant, reluctant, or festinating gait may suggest Parkinsonism or normal-pressure hydrocephalus, both of which may be amenable to appropriate therapy. Evaluation of altered tone suggesting plastic or paratonic rigidity or dystonia may help in defining basal ganglia or cortical dysfunction. The presence of focal weakness or prominent asymmetry of the muscle stretch reflexes may suggest a more focal disease, such as a stroke or a mass lesion. A group of complex, polysynaptic reflexes has been accorded increased attention in the evaluation of the patient with dementia. Those reflexes which may indicate diffuse or focal cortical involvement include nucocephalic reflex, motor impersistence, perseveration, tonic foot responses, glabellar blink, and a variety of oral responses as noted by Jenkyn et al. (1977), Paulson (1977), and Joynt et al. (1962). A comprehensive eye examination should not be overlooked. The uniquely responsive pupillary patterns of Argyll-Robinson may provide the only physical clue to neurosyphilis. Impairment in gaze, visual tracking, and eye-head coordination may be important indicators of cortical disease as emphasized by Herman and Atkin (1976) and Hurwitz (1968).

GENERAL PHYSICAL EXAMINATION

The general physical examination is an essential part of the patient's evaluation. An accurate assessment and recording of vital signs, cardiovascular condition, and pulmonary status is needed in all patients. Many of the readily remediable disease producing dementia may surface as a result of the general physical examination. These include the metabolic encephalopathies, endocrine disturbances, hyperlipidemic disorders (Mathew et al., 1976), and cardiogenic dementia (*Lancet,* 1977).

LABORATORY EXAMINATION

The laboratory evaluation of the patient with dementia has been refined by the introduction and application of computerized tomography. The accuracy of tomography in the identification of brain atrophy associated with dementia has been demonstrated to be comparable to pneumoencephalography or gross pathological examination of the brain as shown by Huckman et al. (1977) and Menzer et al. (1975). At present we consider the CT scan to be an integral part of the laboratory evaluation of the patient with dementia. Of course, it should not be implied that the CT scan is a screen for dementia; rather, it serves as an aid in assessing the particular types of diseases that produce recognized dementia. Other tests considered essential in the laboratory investigation of the patient with dementia include: serological tests for syphilis; metabolic screens for electrolytes, calcium, magnesium, and hepatic and renal function; urinalysis; and chest x-ray. Screening tests for endocrine dysfunction, drug or heavy metal exposure, and vitamin deficiences are appropriate in certain individuals. A drug holiday may be indicated for those patients receiving drugs at the time of evaluation. In patients where surgical procedures are contemplated, cisternography, pneumoencephalography, or angiography may be warranted. With the advent of newer technologies, the value of the electroencephalogram has been underemphasized. The EEG may assist in the recognition of metabolic disorders or in the identification of a focal versus a global nature of some dementing diseases (Wilson, 1977).

NEUROPSYCHOLOGICAL TESTING

The role of formal psychological testing in the evaluation of the patient with dementia is somewhat controversial. In most instances, the systematic process of a comprehensive mental status examination should suffice for the formulation of a specific diagnosis. At times, however, psychological testing is a useful adjunctive procedure in evaluation. Psychological testing may also be important in establishing a baseline for follow-up evaluation of patients with dementia. Several brief rating scales of intellectual performance have been formulated in recent years and may prove useful to the clinician in follow-up evaluations (Jacobs et al. 1977; Coblentz et al., 1973; Wells, 1977; Straub and Black, 1977). Formal psychological testing, including the objective quantification of cognitive performance, is essential in clinical investigations of patients with dementia, particularly in evaluating efficacy of therapy.

RELATIVE IMPORTANCE OF METHODS OF EVALUATION

At this time, it is difficult to gauge the relative importance of the history, examination, and laboratory investigation in the evaluation process. In some patients, history-taking may be of greater assistance than the examination; in others, the diagnosis may come as a surprise on the basis of the screening laboratory evaluation. It would appear worthwhile to assess the relative contribution of history-taking, examination, and laboratory evaluation in an unselected group of patients with unclassified dementia as has been done for other disorders by Hampton et al. (1975). From such a study, certain dementias might be identified for which particular parts of the evaluation process are more or less critical. Also, the contribution of each constituent of the evaluation process could be evaluated in terms of its effect on patient care.

Few patients should emerge from the comprehensive process of diagnostic evaluation with the label of "unclassified dementia" or "organic brain syndrome." In the Seltzer and Sherwin (1978) series, only 4% of patients were placed in this category. Of course, the reliability of clinical evaluation techniques needs to be scrutinized further and subjected to pathological examination whenever indicated or postmortem examination whenever possible.

TREATMENT

The recently empirically derived data of several clinical investigations do not support the widespread therapeutic nihilism regarding treatment of patients with dementia. Conservative estimates from the Seltzer and Sherwin study showed that 10% of their patients with unclassified dementia had readily remediable conditions. An additional 35% had diseases that existing therapy could ameliorate considerably or retard. The data of Seltzer and Sherwin are strikingly similar to three other studies where various selected groups of individuals with unclassified dementia were evaluated: those of Marsden and Harrison (1972), Katzman (1976), and Freemon (1976). All of these studies support the critical need for a systematic and comprehensive evaluation of patients, not for nosological purposes, but because of the therapeutic implications.

Some dementing disorders, if appropriately recognized, may be readily remediable. Common examples include the endocrine disorders, nutritional deprivation states, and drug-induced dementias. The progress of some disorders may be potentially reversed or aborted if the disease is properly recognized. Examples include multi-infarct dementia, normal-pressure hydrocephalus, and pseudodementia, the latter affecting a large group of patients. Some dementias may require specific care needs such as family and genetic counseling as in Huntington's disease (Shoulson and Fahn, 1978). Some diseases, such as the dementias produced by transmissible viruses described by Gajdusek et al. (1977), may require special precautions in the handling of materials from patients. Finally, the recognition of certain types of dementing disease that at present continue to be characterized by inexorable progress is important for patients and families. It is our contention that the proper management of all patients is critically dependent on comprehensive and systematic clinical evaluation. Even domiciliary care can be improved on the basis of proper recognition of the underlying disease state.

Pharmacological studies in the field of dementia have been prompted largely by serendipitous observations of drug efficacy. In general, various drugs have been employed to treat the impairment in cognitive functioning or the psychiatric and behavioral disturbances. However, there is a striking lack of systematically conducted studies comparing the efficacy of drugs widely employed in the treatment of patients with dementia (Prien, 1973). The role of pharmacotherapy of dementia is entering a new era. With the advent and application of neurochemical techniques, more well-ordered pharmacotherapeutic approaches have been developed. Studies of postmortem brains from patients with Alzheimer's disease have demonstrated a prominent reduction in choline acetyl transferase, the synthetic enzyme for acetylcholine (Davies and Maloney, 1976). Attempts to treat these patients with choline, the precursor of acetylcholine are underway and preliminary results have, however, shown only modest success (Etienne et al., 1978). This rational approach to pharmacotherapy holds promise in the treatment of patients with dementia and already represents a conceptual achievement in combating the widespread therapeutic nihilism.

Several modest efforts are underway to evaluate the efficacy of current care procedures in patients with inexorably progressive forms of dementia. The simple recognition of impaired functional capacities and the emphasis on preserved functions may help in the care of the patient with Alzheimer's disease.

There are certain guidelines for treating all patients with dementia. Obviously, if an etiology is found, then specific therapy is directed that way. In many instances this is not the case. Any general medical condition should be corrected if possible. The correction of cardiac failure, for example, may help in clearing confusion. Inasfar as possible, the fewest and simplest drugs should be used. Relatives of patients with dementia, in their frustration, seek help from many sources so that the patients may end up on multiple drugs. In most instances a greater service is done for the patient by withdrawal, and not addition, of drugs. Simple analgesics for pain are best. Judicious use of alcohol may prove to be the best and least troublesome sedative. Patients should be kept in familiar surroundings if that is possible. Many elderly patients with mild dementia can carry on very well in their own home or apartment. Often the family with all good intentions wishes to move them to a more comfortable retirement or nursing facility. They are fearful that the patient may fall or become ill without their notice. In general, taking that chance is better than displacing such patients from their surroundings.

Hazlitt said in the nineteenth century, "The worst old age is that of the mind." The challenge is there, but the efforts to meet it are as yet woefully inadequate.

References

Albert, M. L., Feldman, R. G., and Willis, A. L. (1974). The subcortical dementia of progressive supranuclear palsy. *J. Neurol. Neurosurg. Psychiat.* 37:121.

Arie, T. (1973). Dementia in the elderly: diagnosis and assessment. *Br. Med. J.* 4:540.

Chapman, L. F. and Wolff, H. G. (1959). The cerebral hemispheres and the highest integrative functions of man. *Arch. Neurol.* 1:357.

Coblentz, J. M., Mattis, S., Zingesser, L. H., Kasoff, S. S., Wisniewski, H. M., and Katzman, R. (1973). Presenile dementia. *Arch. Neurol.* 29:299.

Critchley, M. (1956). Neurologic changes in the aged. *J. Chron. Dis.* 3:459.

Davies, P. and Maloney, A. J. F. (1976). Selective loss of central cholinergic neurons in Alzheimer's disease. *Lancet* ii:1403.

Editorial (1977). Cardiogenic dementia. *Lancet* i:27.

Etienne, P., Gauthier, S., Johnson, G., Collier, B., Mendis, T., Dastoor, D., Cole, M. and Muller, H. F. (1978). Clinical effects of choline in Alzheimer's disease. *Lancet* i:508.

Freemon, F. R. (1976). Evaluation of patients with progressive intellectual deterioration. *Arch. Neurol 33*:658.

Gajdusek, D. C., Gibbs, C. J., Asher, D. M., Brown, P., Diwan, A., Hoffman, P. Nemo, G., Rohwer, R. and White, L. (1977). Precautions in medical care of, and in handling materials from, patients with transmissible virus dementia (Creutzfeldt-Jakob Disease). *N. Engl. J. Med. 297*:1253.

Geschwind, N. (1975). The borderland of neurology and psychiatry: some common misconceptions, in *Psychiatric Aspects of Neurological Disease,* F. Benson and D. Blumer (eds). New York: Grune & Stratton.

Hampton, J. R., Harrison, M. J. G., Mitchell, J. R. A., Prichard, J. S., and Seymour, C. (1975). Relative contributions of history-taking, physical examination, and laboratory investigation to diagnosis and management of medical outpatients. *Br. Med. J. 2*:486.

Herman, P. and Atkin, A. (1976). A modification of eye-head coordination by CNS disease. *J. Neurol. Sci. 28*:301.

Huckman, M. S., Fox, J. H., and Ramsey, R. G. (1977). Computed tomography in the diagnosis of degenerative diseases of the brain. *Seminars in Roentgenology 12*:63.

Hurwitz, L. J. (1968). Neurological aspects of old age and capacity. *Gerontol. Clinica 10*:146.

Jacobs, J. W., Bernhard, M. R., Delgado, A., and Strain, J. J. (1977). Screening for organic mental syndromes in the medically ill. *Ann. Intern. Med. 86*:40.

Jenkyn, L. R., Walsh, D. B., Culver, C. M., and Reeves, A. G. (1977). Clinical signs in diffuse cerebral dysfunction. *J. Neurol. Neurosurg. and Psychiat. 40*:956.

Joynt, R. J., Benton, A. L., and Fogel, M. L. (1962). Behavioral and pathological correlates of motor impersistence. *Neurology 12*:876.

Katzman, R. (1976). The prevalence and malignancy of Alzheimer disease: a major killer. *Arch. Neurol. 33*:217.

Klawans, H. L., Tufo, H. M., Ostfeld, A. M., Shekelle, R. B. and Kilbridge, J. A. (1971). Neurological examination in an elderly population. *Dis. Nerv. Sys. 32*:274.

Marsden, C. D. and Harrison, M. J. G. (1972). Outcome of investigation of patients with presenile dementia. *Br. Med. J. 2*:249.

Mathew, N. T., Meyer, J. S., Achari, A. N., and Dodson, R. F. (1976). Hyperlipidemic neuropathy and dementia. *Europ. Neurol. 14*:370.

Menzer, L. Sabin, T., and Mark, V. H. (1975). Computerized axial tomography, use in the diagnosis of dementia. *J.A.M.A. 234*:754.

McHugh, P. R. and Folstein, M. F. (1975). Psychiatric syndromes of Huntington's chorea: a clinical and phenomenologic study, in *Psychiatric Aspects of Neurological Disease,* F. Benson and D. Blumer (eds). New York: Grune & Stratton.

Paulson, G. W. (1977). The neurological examination in dementia, in *Dementia,* C. Wells (ed). Philadelphia: F. A. Davis.

Prien, R. F. (1973). Chemotherapy in chronic organic brain syndrome—a review of the literature. *Psychopharm. Bull.* *9*:5.

Seltzer, B. and Sherwin, I. (1978). "Organic brain syndromes": an empirical study and critical review. *Am. J. Psychiat.* *135*:13.

Shoulson, I. and Fahn, S. (1979). Huntington's disease: clinical evaluation and care, *Neurology, 29*:1–3.

Straub, R. L. and Black, F. W. (1977). Composite mental status examination, in *The Mental Status Examination in Neurology,* Appendix 2, p. 163. Philadelphia: F. A. Davis.

Victor, M., Adams, R. D., and Collins, G. H. (1971). *The Wernicke-Korsakoff Syndrome.* Philadelphia: F. A. Davis.

Wells, C. E. (1977). Diagnostic evaluation and treatment in dementia, in *Dementia,* C. Wells (ed). Philadelphia: F. A. Davis.

Wilson, W. P., Musella, L., and Short, M. J. (1977). The electroencephalogram in dementia, in *Dementia,* C. Wells (ed). Philadelphia: F. A. Davis.

16
Recovery and Treatment

ANDREW KERTESZ

The study of recovery from CNS lesions has been difficult since it requires that patients be followed for months or years. Clinicians observing patients in the acute state often do not have the opportunity to follow them this long, while rehabilitation specialists rarely see them during the early stages of their illness. Compounding this difficulty is the tendency for rehabilitation therapists to attribute recovery to treatment, thus underestimating the extent of spontaneous recovery. Those interested primarily in clinical and pathological diagnosis, on the other hand, tend to disregard changes in performance or in the clinical pattern of deficits and thus view the neuropsychological deficit as stable. Despite these difficulties, a considerable body of information is accumulating on recovery of function and there are several recent reviews of its various aspects (Stein, Rosen, and Butters, 1974; CIBA Foundation Symposium, 1975; Lebrun and Hoops, 1976; Sullivan and Kommers, 1977; Fingers, 1978).

The mechanisms underlying recovery of function are incompletely understood. Before discussing the patterns of recovery in specific clinical situations, I will review the major theories proposed to explain recovery of function, as well as some of the experimental evidence supporting these theories.

THEORETICAL AND EXPERIMENTAL
CORRELATES OF RECOVERY

Acute changes

Some of the recovery occurring in the first one to three weeks after an acute lesion can be ascribed to the reversal of early physiological abnormalities. Blood flow may increase to areas not irreversibly damaged (Kohlmeyer, 1976); edema may subside; cellular infiltrates may resolve; and pressure associated with hemorrhage or dynamic changes in the flow of cerebrospinal fluid may return to normal.

Long-term improvement

The resolution of edema, ischemia, cellular infiltration, and other acute physiological changes may account for recovery occurring in the first one to three weeks after an acute lesion; however, recovery often continues after this time. The rate of recovery is maximal for two to three months after an acute lesion and then slows. Beyond one year, recovery is less likely to occur. Many mechanisms have been proposed to explain the second phase of recovery.

THEORY OF EQUIPOTENTIALITY

It can be argued that since destruction of a particular area of brain does not result in permanent loss of function, a particular function cannot be "localized" to the destroyed portion of the brain. In other words, according to this view, rigid localization of function in the nervous system cannot be reconciled with the repeated observation that recovery does occur. One of the earliest opponents of phrenological localization was Flourens (1824), who demonstrated recovery after ablative experiments in pigeons. Lashley (1938) based his well-known theory of equipotentiality on similar extensive ablations. He also found 18 cases in the clinical literature in which he could correlate the degree of recovery from motor aphasia with the estimated magnitude of lesions in the frontal lobe. The correlation was negative (-0.9). He considered this analogous to the finding that learning in brain-lesioned animals was positively correlated with the amount of remaining intact cortical tissue.

SUBSTITUTIONIST THEORIES

Fritsch and Hitzig (1870) observed dogs with motor system dysfunction from unilateral cortical lesions, and proposed that the opposite hemisphere was taking over motor function for the injured hemisphere. In adult animals, however, destruction of an analogous area in the opposite hemisphere did not interrupt recovery. In man, observations of patients with hemispherectomies (Smith, 1966) and callosal sections (Gazzaniga, 1970) provided evidence that the right hemisphere is capable of assuming some speech functions such as comprehension (nouns better than verbs) and automatic nonpropositional speech. Kinsbourne (1971) argued that the right hemisphere may be the source of some aphasic speech. In the adult, however, the extent to which this recovery occurs is finite, both in cases of hemispherectomy and in global aphasics. In fact, the behavior of hemispherectomized patients is very similar to the behavior of global aphasics with extensive perisylvian infarction. This indicates that the remaining language function of global aphasics is probably subserved entirely by the right hemisphere. That the restitution of speech is often due to the activity of the opposite hemisphere is known as Henschen's axiom. Henschen (1922) gave credit to Wernicke and other contemporaries for this principle. Nielsen (1946) further advocated the idea that recovery occurs to a large extent by the variable capacity of the right hemisphere to develop speech. Geschwind (1969) also believes there is a considerable amount of individual variation in hemispheric substitution. Some people can make use of certain commissural connections and can activate some cortical mechanisms in the right hemisphere more than others. Munk (1881) thought that regions of the brain previously "not occupied" could assume certain functions (vicarious functioning). Lashley (1938), on the other hand, thought that preservation of part of a system concerned with the same function is necessary. Bucy (1934), however, performed "reverse ablations," which indicated that areas which are needed for recovery do not necessarily contribute to normal function. Clinically, it is evident that right-hemisphere lesions will not cause aphasia in most people, even though the right hemisphere subserves some language functions.

HIERARCHICAL RE-REPRESENTATION

Jackson (1973) proposed that the nervous system is organized hier-archically, with higher centers controlling lower ones. Damage at a higher level releases lower ones from inhibition and leads to "com-pensation." Geschwind (1974) cited examples of neuronal systems that could take over function when released by destruction of higher centers: the spinal cord innervation of the diaphragm is one such system.

DIASCHISIS

Von Monakow (1914) postulated that damage to one part of the nervous system deprives other areas of normal stimulation, and thereby creates a state of shock. He coined the term *diaschisis* for this phenomenon, which occurs during recovery from the initial deficit. Eventually, the undamaged portions of the brain resume normal functioning. Physiological changes have been found which may be related to diaschisis. Following unilateral cerebral infarc-tion, there is bilateral reduction of cerebral blood flow (Meyer, 1970) which can persist for up to two months. Release of catechol-amines has also been demonstrated during this period (Meyer et al., 1974). It is not known, however, whether these changes cause dias-chisis or whether they are merely associated phenomena. Diaschisis is more marked after acute lesions such as infarcts or trauma than it is with lesions which progress slowly, e.g., slowly growing tumors. This may be one reason why animals tolerate two-stage removal of a particular brain area better than removal of the same area in one stage (Ades and Raab, 1946), a phenomenon called the "serial lesion effect." Clinically, it is not unusual to see patients who have no lan-guage deficits despite large, slowly growing tumors in the speech areas.

Factors influencing recovery

Several factors help to explain the variability of behavioral effects among patients who suffer similar lesions and the variability in rate and completeness of recovery.

PLASTICITY

Transfer of function occurs more easily in the immature nervous system. Kennard and McCulloch (1943) demonstrated that unilateral precentral lesions in immature animals have minimal effects when compared to similar lesions in adults. In children, recovery from aphasia acquired before the age of ten to twelve is excellent Basser, 1962; Hécaen, 1976). Maturation of the left hemisphere appears to inhibit the language abilities of the right hemisphere. Lesions in the left speech area early in life release this inhibition and enable recovery to occur (Milner, 1974). It has been proposed that the functional plasticity of the young may depend on the adaptability of Golgi Type II cells (Hirsch and Jacobson, 1974). These cells remain adaptive while cells with long axons responsible for the major transmission of information in and out of the CNS are under early and exacting genetic specification and control. In man, the flexibility of these neurons may be terminated in the teens by hormonal changes. This may explain the age limit on the relocalization of language. It is of interest that acquisition of a foreign language without an accent also appears to be limited by puberty (personal observations). Although comparisons between species are risky, there appears to be an analogous effect of hormone levels on bird song acquisition (Nottebohm, 1970).

ANATOMICAL AND FUNCTIONAL VARIATIONS

The anatomy of the speech areas is variable, so that lesions of similar size may affect language differently in different patients. In addition, there is some variability in the degree to which language is lateralized: in particular, left-handers are more likely to have language function in both hemispheres. Consequently, aphasias in left-handers are more common, less severe, and more likely to improve than aphasias in right-handers (Gloning, et al., 1969; Geschwind, 1974).

THE NATURE OF THE LESION

The nature of the injury may provide another variable. Rubens (1977) explained the dramatic recovery from thalamic hemorrhage in one patient by the fact that dysfunction was caused by the distortion of neural structures by the hemorrhage rather than by their destruction.

Physiological changes underlying recovery of function

The physiological mechanisms underlying recovery of function from CNS lesions are not well understood. The physiological changes which may accompany diaschisis and the possible importance of Golgi Type II neurons in explaining plasticity were mentioned. In addition, other physiological mechanisms have been proposed as being important in recovery of function.

REGENERATION

Although for quite some time it was thought that regeneration occurred only in the peripheral nervous system, it is now known to occur in the CNS. Axonal regrowth has been demonstrated in ascending catecholaminergic fibers; growing zones tend to invade vacant terminal spaces (Schneider, 1973). In addition, neighboring neurons may sprout and send fibers to synapse on vacant terminals (collateral sprouting) (Liu and Chambers, 1958). Both regenerative and collateral sprouting have been demonstrated by Moore (1974). Collateral sprouting appears to be more important, whether from intact axons or from collaterals of the damaged axons.

CENTRAL DENERVATION HYPERSENSITIVITY

Denervation hypersensitivity (Stavraky, 1961) may explain why some central structures become more responsive to stimulation after damage. The remaining fibers from the damaged area may produce a greater effect on the denervated region, thereby promoting recovery. The opposite effect, however, has also been argued. The initial hypersensitivity could induce inhibition of function (diaschisis) and the appearance of collateral sprouting might reduce the denervation and the accompanying inhibition (Goldberger, 1974).

PHARMACOLOGICAL ASPECTS

Pharmacological aspects of recovery are most complex. Cholinergic agents (Ward and Kennard, 1942), anticholinesterases (Luria et al., 1969), and amphetamines (Braun et al., 1966) accelerate recovery,

while barbiturates slow recovery (Watson and Kennard, 1945). Catecholamines may inhibit recovery (Meyer et al., 1974) and bicuculline
may facilitate recovery (Duffy, 1976).

Functional compensation

Functional compensation explains recovery by employing a behavioral rather than a neural model. Instead of rerouting connections,
the brain-damaged organism develops new solutions to problems
using residual structures. Substituted maneuvers or tricks have been
described and documented by Sperry (1947). Luria (1969) formulated the theory of retraining, which claims that the dynamic reor-
ganization of the nervous system is promoted by specific therapy.

Motivational factors

Motivational factors, which have been shown to affect postlesion behavior in animals, have been demonstrated to be important in humans. Karl Lashley illustrates this in a poignant anecdote. He bet a
patient of Dr. Franz who could not learn the alphabet after nine
hundred repetitions, one hundred cigarettes that he could not learn
it in a week. "After ten trials, he was letter perfect, and remembered
it until the debt was paid." Many patients develop functional disorders superimposed on their organic deficit. A passive attitude and
depression are particularly likely to impede recovery. Increasing motivation enhances recovery. The experiments of Franz and Odin
(1917) where subjects were forced to use paralyzed limbs, provided
evidence that intense motivation is effective. Stoicheff (1960) demonstrated the effect of positive and negative verbal comments on the
performance of aphasics. Improvement was promoted by positive reinforcement, and actual worsening was observed with negative reinforcement.

RECOVERY FROM APHASIA

Factors affecting the natural history of recovery

Until recently, most long-term studies of aphasic patients concerned
speech therapy. Vignolo (1964) was the first to include the objective
assessment of untreated patients at various intervals. Subsequent
studies of spontaneous recovery have been performed by Culton

(1969); Sarno, Silverman, and Sands (1970); Sarno and Levita (1971); Hagen (1973), Basso, Faglioni, and Vignolo (1975), and Kertesz and McCabe (1977). These studies are difficult to compare. The methods of evaluation differed. The patient populations were not comparable, since some authors restricted their study to severe aphasics (Sarno et al., 1970; Sarno and Levita, 1971) while others did not (Kertesz and McCabe, 1977). Finally, different classification systems were used: Hagen (1973), for example, used Schuell's system (Schuell, Jenkins, and Jimenez-Pabon, 1964), while Basso et al. (1975) divided their patients into only two categories—Broca's and Wernicke's aphasics (see Chapter 2 for definitions of aphasic syndromes.)

In spite of these diversities, several important factors in the recovery of treated and untreated patients emerge.

ETIOLOGY

Recovery and prognosis depend to some extent on etiology. Patients with post-traumatic aphasia recover better than patients with aphasia following stroke (Butfield and Zangwill, 1946; Wepman, 1951; Luria, 1970; Marks, Taylor, and Rusk, 1957; Godfrey and Douglass, 1959). Complete recovery was seen in more than half of our post-traumatic cases (Kertesz and McCabe, 1977). Dramatic spontaneous recovery, such as a global aphasia improving to a mild anomic state, occurred after closed head injury, but not in patients with vascular lesions with a similar degree of initial impairment (Fig. 16-1). Age and extent of lesion were confounding variables: many of the patients with traumatic aphasia were younger (although the age scatter was considerable), and the extent and severity of lesions in our motor vehicle accident population was variable (most had closed head injuries, but a few had contusion or subdural hemorrhage).

Aphasias resulting from subarachnoid hemorrhage showed a wide variation in rate of recovery. This variability was presumably related to the extent of hemorrhage and to the variable presence of infarction or tissue destruction (Fig. 16-2). To some extent, the prognosis was predictable from the initial severity of the aphasia. It is of interest that some of the worst jargon and global aphasias were seen following ruptured middle-cerebral-artery aneurysms.

APHASIA TYPE

Head (1926) recognized that some types of aphasia improve more rapidly than others. Weisenburg and McBride (1935), Butfield and

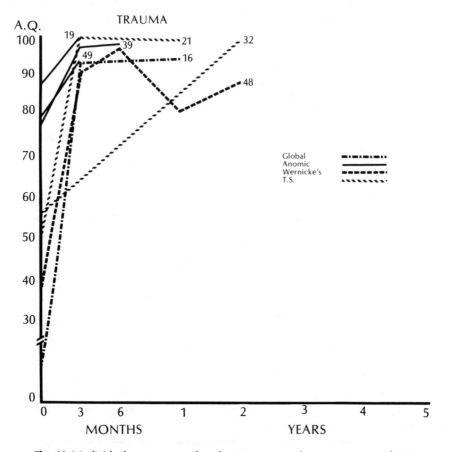

Fig. 16-1 Individual recovery graphs of various types of post-traumatic aphasics. A.Q. = overall score out of 100. Ages of patients are at the ends of the graph lines.

Zangwill (1946), Messerli et al. (1976), and Kertesz and McCabe (1977) considered Broca's or "expressive" aphasics to improve most, while Vignolo (1964) considered expressive disorders to have a poor prognosis, and Basso et al. (1975) did not find any difference between the recovery of fluent and nonfluent aphasic patients. The variability of conclusions in part reflects problems in classification. For example, an "expressive" disorder is found in many different kinds of aphasias.

We assessed the prognosis of 47 patients with aphasia following stroke who had both an initial examination in the acute stages of

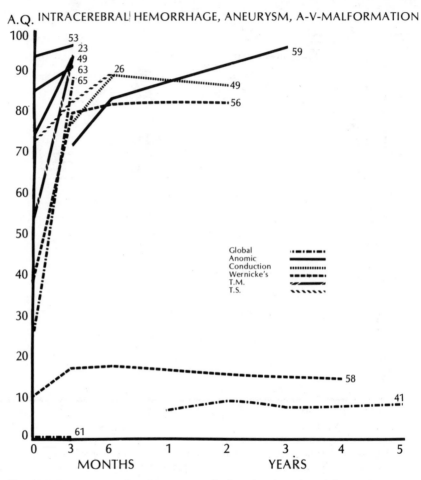

Fig. 16-2 Recovery graphs after intracerebral and subarachnoid hemorrhage. A.Q. = overall score (aphasia quotient).

illness and a follow-up test performed at least one year later (Kertesz and McCabe, 1977). The outcome after this long-term follow-up (average 28.6 months) was categorized on the basis of the Aphasia Quotient (AQ), a summary of the Western Aphasia Battery (Kertesz and Poole, 1974) (Table 16-1). Almost all of the global aphasics remained impaired. Broca's and Wernicke's aphasics showed a wider range of outcome (Figs. 16-3 and 16-4). Some patients with Wer-

TABLE 16-1   *Final Outcome of Aphasia*

PERCENTILE GROUP	N	0–25 (poor)	25–50 (fair)	50–75 (good)	75–100 (very good)
Global	16	13	2	0	1
Broca's	12	0	6	6	1
Conduction	6	0	1	1	4
Wernicke's	13	4	6	3	0
Isolation	1	0	1	0	0
Transcortical motor	2	0	0	2	0
Transcortical sensory	3	0	0	1	2
Anomic	13	0	0	3	10
Total	67	17 (25.4%)	16 (23.9%)	16 (23.9%)	18 (26.9%)

nicke's aphasia retain fluent jargon for many months. After a while, however, they lose their phonemic paraphasias and their language deficit consists of verbal substitutions and anomia. Broca's aphasics have an intermediate outlook, just about evenly divided between fair and good recovery. Anomic, conduction, and transcortical aphasics have a uniformly good prognosis, the majority of cases showing excellent spontaneous recovery. Some of the completely recovered patients were not even included in this analysis because they were not tested again after their three months' repeat scores were normal (as were almost half of the anomic aphasia patients' scores). The overall prognosis, regardless of aphasia type, for these 47 patients was as follows: poor for 28%, fair for 19%, good for 13%, and excellent for 40%.

The determination of complete recovery from aphasia depends on the definition of normal language function. We used an arbitrary cutoff AQ of 93.8. This was the actual mean score of a standardization group of brain-damaged patients who were judged clinically not to be aphasic (Kertesz and Poole, 1974). Final AQs indicated that twelve anomic, five conduction, two transcortical sensory, and one transcortical motor aphasic reached this criterion of recovery. Although this represents only 21% of the 93 patients having aphasias with various etiologies that we studied (Kertesz and McCabe,

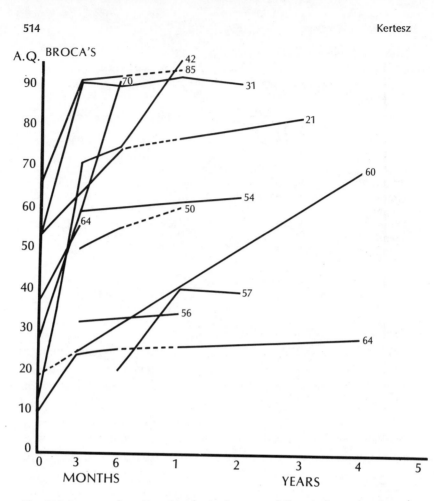

Fig. 16-3 Recovery from Broca's aphasia. Interrupted lines indicate duration of speech therapy. A.Q. = overall score.

1977), it represents 62.5% of the conduction, 50% of the transcortical, and 48% of the anomic patients (Table 16-2).

SEVERITY

The initial severity of the aphasia is closely tied in with the type of aphasia, and it is considered to be highly predictive of outcome (Godfrey and Douglass, 1959; Schuell et al., 1964; Sands et al., 1969; Sarno et al., 1970; Gloning et al., 1976; Kertesz and McCabe, 1977). Unfortunately, it is not always considered in studies of recovery.

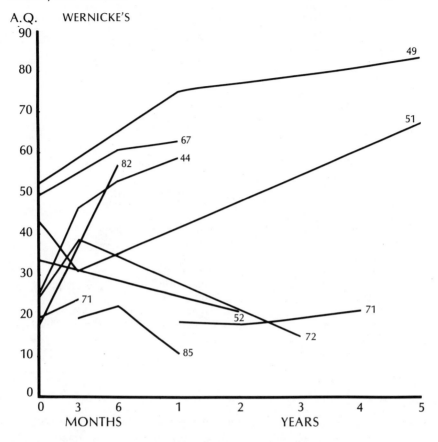

A.Q.   WERNICKE'S

Fig. 16-4 Recovery from Wernicke's aphasia. None of these patients received speech therapy. A.Q. = overall score.

The most severely affected patients show little gain, whether treated or not (Sarno et al., 1970), even though they have the most room for improvement. Mildly affected patients, on the other hand, more often recover completely (Kertesz and McCabe, 1977).

AGE

The influence of age is controversial. There is a clinical impression that younger patients recover better (Wepman, 1951; Eisenson, 1949; Vignolo, 1964). We demonstrated an inverse correlation between age and initial recovery rates (from 0 to 3 months), but when

TABLE 16-2   *Evolution of Aphasia from Initial to Endstage Classification and Percentages of Complete Recovery*

| CLASSIFICATION | | % RECOVERED |
INITIAL	ENDSTAGE	COMPLETELY
Globals (22)	2 Broca	
	1 Transcortical motor	
	1 Conduction	
	1 Anomic	
Broca's (17)	1 Transcortical motor	
	3 Anomic	
Conduction (8)	2 Anomic	
	5 Nonaphasic ————————	(62.5%)
Wernicke's (13)	1 Global	
	1 Transcortical sensory	
	4 Anomic	
Isolation (2)	1 Anomic	
Transcortical 3 motor ⎫	2 Anomic	
⎬ (6)	1 Nonaphasic ⎫ ———————	(50%)
Transcortical 3 sensory ⎭	2 Nonaphasic ⎭	
	1 Anomic	
Anomic (25)	12 Nonaphasic —————	(48%)
Total 93		21%

we excluded the post-traumatic group whose mean age was well below that of the patients with infarction, the trend just missed being significant (Kertesz and McCabe, 1977). Others have failed to show any correlation between age and recovery (Sarno and Levita, 1971; Culton, 1971; Smith et al., 1972). Clinicians also observe remarkable improvement in some elderly patients, and lack of recovery in some young patients.

SEX

Recent studies (McGlone and Kertesz, 1973) suggest that language and visuospatial functions are differently organized in men and women. The more bilateral representation in women would predict better recovery from aphasia in women; however, this is not substantiated by our data (Kertesz and McCabe, 1977), which demonstrate no significant sex differences in rates of recovery from aphasia.

HANDEDNESS

The data from Subirana (1969) and Gloning et al. (1969) indicate that left-handers recover better from aphasias than right-handers. Gloning (1969) also suggested that left-handers are likely to become aphasic regardless of which hemisphere is damaged. Interestingly, right-handers with a history of left-handedness among parents, siblings, or children, recover, on the average, better than right-handers without such a family history (Geschwind (1974)).

OTHER FACTORS

Darley (1972) considered premorbid intelligence, health, and social milieu to have significant influence on recovery. Although intellectual and educational level influence what the patient and his relatives consider recovery to be, Kennan and Brassel's study (1974) indicated that health, employment, and age had little if any prognostic value when compared to factors such as "listening" and "motor speech" (comprehension and fluency). Sarno et al. (1970b) similarly showed that recovery in severe aphasia was not influenced by age, sex, education, occupational status, pre-illness language proficiency, or current living environment.

Time-course of recovery

There is a surprising amount of agreement about the time course of the recovery process. A large number of stroke patients recover a great deal in the first two weeks (Kohlmeyer, 1976). The greatest amount of improvement occurs in the first two or three months after onset (Vignolo, 1964; Culton, 1969; Sarno and Levita, 1971; Basso et al., 1975; Kertesz and McCabe, 1977). After six months, the rate of recovery significantly drops (Butfield and Zangwill, 1946; Sand et al., 1969; Vignolo, 1964; Kertesz and McCabe, 1977). In the majority of cases, spontaneous recovery does not seem to occur after a year (Culton, 1969; Kertesz and McCabe, 1977); however, there are reports of improvement in cases under therapy many years after the stroke (Schuell et al., 1964; Marks et al., 1957; Smith et al., 1972; Broida, 1977).

Linguistic features of recovery

Not only do the various types of aphasia recover differently, but the various components of language do also. Of course, types of aphasia and language components are interdependent, a fact that is sometimes ignored. Kreindler and Fradis (1968) found that naming, oral imitation, and comprehension of nouns showed the most improvement. In the study of Broca's aphasics by Kenin and Swisher (1972), gains were greater in comprehension than in expressive language; but no such difference was found by Sarno and Levita (1971). Hagen (1973) found improvement in language formulation, auditory retention, visual comprehension, and visual motor abilities in a three- to six-month period after the onset of symptoms. Ludlow (1977) found the greatest improvement in Digit Repetition Reverse, Identification by Sentence, and Word Fluency in fluent aphasics; while Digit Repetition Forward, Sentence Comprehension, and Tactile Naming improved most in Broca's aphasics. We studied various language components in four groups of 31 untreated aphasics (Lomas and Kertesz, 1978). Comprehension (as examined by Yes-No questions), sequential commands, and repetition were the most improved components, while word fluency improved least. In fact, word fluency remained impaired while all other language factors improved, indicating that word fluency measures a nonlanguage factor in addition to language-related factors. This is corroborated by the observation that word fluency is often impaired in nonaphasic brain-damaged subjects. The highest overall recovery scores were attained by the low-fluency high-comprehension group. The groups with low initial comprehension showed recovery in Yes-No comprehension and repetition tasks, while patients with high comprehension recovered in all tasks except word fluency.

Other linguistic features have also been studied. Ludlow (1977) studied mean sentence length, grammaticability index, and sentence production index as measures of recovery in Broca's and fluent aphasics. Both groups showed the greatest gains in the second month after onset of symptoms. Alajouanine (1956) distinguished four stages of recovery in severe expressive aphasia: (1) differentiation by intonation, (2) decreased automatic utterances, (3) less-rigid stereotypic utterances, and (4) volitional, slow, agrammatical speech. Ker-

tesz and Benson (1970) pointed out the predictable pattern of linguistic recovery in jargon aphasia. Copious neologistic or phonemic
jargon is replaced by verbal paraphasias or semantic jargon, and
eventually anomia, or more rarely a "pure" word deafness, develops. The fact that overproduction of jargon is replaced by anomic
gaps or circumlocutions indicates that there is recovery of regulatory
or inhibitory systems.

   We have also studied the evolution of aphasic syndromes, docu-
menting the patterns of transformation from one clinically distinct
aphasic type into another, as defined by subscores on subsequent examinations using the Western Aphasia Battery (Kertesz and Mc-
Cabe, 1977). We found that anomic aphasia is a common end-stage
of evolution, in addition to being a common aphasic syndrome
de novo (Table 16-2). Four of 13 Wernicke's, 4 of 8 transcortical, 4
of 17 Broca's, 2 of 8 conduction, and 1 of 22 global aphasias evolved
into anomic aphasia. Reversal of the usual direction of evolution
of aphasic patterns (Table 16-2) should make the clinician suspect
that a new lesion has appeared, as from an extension of a stroke or
a tumor. Thus, for example, an anomic aphasic should not in the
course of recovery become nonfluent, nor should he develop fluent
paraphasic or neologistic jargon. Leischner (1976) has also studied
the transformation of aphasic syndromes three months after stroke,
specifying the degree of improvement, as well. A significant number of patients with total aphasia and "mixed aphasia" evolved toward motor-amnestic aphasia.

Recovery from alexia

Recovery from alexia is scantily documented. Newcombe et al.
(1976) drew recovery curves for the performance of two patients
who were followed for six months and four years, respectively, after
removal of occipital lesions (abscess and meningioma). Without language therapy, the rate of recovery of the ability to read word reading lists was maximal initially and decelerated until eight to ten
weeks after surgery, at which time a slower rate was achieved. Object naming curves showed that the patient with an abscess recovered more slowly and retained more residual errors, in contrast to a
post-traumatic patient, who exhibited better recovery of naming.
Newcombe et al., classified linguistic errors as (1) visual confusions

(BEG → leg), (2) failure of grapheme-phoneme translation (OF → off), (3) semantic substitutions (BERRY → grape), and (4) combinations of these. "Pure dyslexics" tended to make visual errors and patients with dysphasic symptoms showed more grapheme-phoneme mistranslations; semantic errors were rare. Mixed errors were numerous initially, with many neologistic errors. In the residual phase the visual errors seemed independent of the syntactic class of words, but in cases of persistent aphasia, syntax had a marked effect; nouns were easier to read than verbs or adjectives.

RECOVERY OF NONVERBAL FUNCTION

In contrast to the increasingly large literature on recovery and treatment of aphasias, there is very little information available concerning recovery of nonverbal function.

Recovery of nonverbal function in aphasics

Previous studies of aphasic patients showed that performance on Raven's Colored Progressive Matrices (RCPM), a nonverbal intelligence test, was impaired, with some exceptions. Culton (1969) used Raven's Standard Progressive Matrices in testing aphasics, and found that considerable recovery of nonverbal performance had occurred after two months, while no further recovery occurred after 11 months. Our own analysis of RCPM performance in aphasic patients suggested that of all the subtests in the aphasia battery, language comprehension correlated best with performance on the RCPM (Kertesz and McCabe, 1975). If the neuropsychological functions underlying language comprehension and nonverbal performance on the RCPM are related, recovery of language comprehension should parallel recovery of performance on the RCPM. At present, we are studying recovery in aphasic and nonaphasic (right-hemisphere-damaged) patients using the RCPM and various language tests. The initial portion of the study included 44 aphasic patients studied with the RCPM and the Western Aphasia Battery within a month of their stroke and three months later. Twenty aphasics were studied for three to six months and 19 were studied for six to twelve months. Correlations were made between the recovery rates of RCPM performance and the Aphasia Quotient (AQ), as well as other verbal and nonverbal performance subtests. Recovery of language function significantly correlated with performance on the RCPM during the first six months. Significant correlations were also obtained between recovery of RCPM scores and subtests such as auditory word discrimination (comprehension), object naming, sentence completion, responsive speech, and repetition. Correlation was poor with recovery of sentence comprehension, fluency, information content, calculation and praxis, and surprisingly with other nonverbal performance tasks such as drawing and block design. Recovery curves for the RCPM in various aphasic groups indicated that performance on the RCPM recovers in excess of language function in global aphasics but there is less than expected recovery of RCPM and more scatter of initial RCPM performance among Broca's, Wernicke's, conduction, and anomic aphasics.

In conclusion, although recovery of nonverbal function as measured by the RCPM seems to correlate in a general way with recovery of language function, more severely affected global aphasics seem to recover more from this nonverbal impairment than others. Recovery of some language functions, such as comprehension of words, naming, and repetition, seems to correlate better than recovery of other language functions with nonverbal recovery. The results suggest that recovery of language and nonlanguage function are not always parallel.

Recovery of function in nonaphasic brain-damaged patients

NEGLECT

Lawson (1962) emphasized that unawareness of left unilateral neglect retards recovery, and that active treatment is needed to overcome it. Campbell and Oxbury (1976) examined the performance of right-hemisphere-damaged patients three to four weeks (and then six months) after a stroke, on verbal and nonverbal tasks, including block design and matrices. Those who demonstrated neglect on the initial drawing tests remained impaired on visuospatial tests six months later, in spite of the resolution of neglect. Other reports describe unilateral neglect remaining up to 12 years after onset. (For further discussion of recovery from neglect, see Chapter 10.)

BILATERAL INJURY FROM TRAUMA

Performance skills on the Wechsler Adult Intelligence Scale took longer to recover than verbal intelligence in patients with traumatic brain injuries (Bond, 1975). The most rapid recovery occurs during the first six months; recovery then slowly reaches a maximum at 24 months. Psychosocial outcome, which was affected by intellectual and personality changes, correlated negatively with the duration of post-traumatic amnesia.

CORTICAL BLINDNESS AND VISUAL AGNOSIA

Recovery from cortical blindness and related syndromes of the parietal and occipital lobes has been described by Gloning et al. (1968). There appear to be regular stages of progression from cortical blindness through visual agnosia and partially impaired perceptual function to recovery. (For further discussion of visual agnosia, see Chapter 9.)

RECOVERY OF MEMORY

The etiology of the most frequently studied memory loss is trauma. The prognosis of post-traumatic memory impairment has been correlated with the duration of post-traumatic amnesia by Russel (1971): 82% of his patients returned to full duty, 92% of these in less than three weeks. Learning capacity may continue to be impaired after the acute amnesia has subsided (the postconcussional syndrome). The phenomenon of shrinking retrograde amnesia, seen with head trauma (Russel and Nathan, 1946; Benson and Geschwind, 1967), suggests that during the amnestic period memories are not lost but rather cannot be activated (retrieved).

Memory loss secondary to alcoholic, postinfectious, and toxic causes, when severe, tend to persist (Talland, 1965), while ECT-induced memory loss is rarely permanent (Williams, 1966). The acute amnestic confabulatory syndrome (Wernicke's encephalopathy) often subsides within weeks, becoming a more chronic state of Korsakoff psychosis. Korsakoff, himself, was optimistic about the prognosis but did not have reliable reports beyond the acute stage. Later clinicians denied seeing complete remissions. Victor and Adams

(1953) arrived at a more hopeful conclusion but noted that "complete restoration of memory is . . . unusual when the defect is severe." Amnestic symptoms from unilateral infarctions subside in a few months, but more lasting deficit occurs with bilateral posterior cerebral artery involvement (Benson et al., 1974). (For a further discussion of memory disorders, see Chapter 10.)

RECOVERY FROM HEMIPLEGIA

Even though hemiplegia is not a subject covered by this book, the parallels between recovery of neuropsychological function and motor function cannot be ignored. There is an extensive body of information on this subject. The testing of hemiplegia is a more uniform procedure than the testing of neuropsychological disorders, and in spite of the variability of recovery, there is general agreement about many aspects. For example, the recovery of the upper extremity is not as good as that of the lower extremity. Motion begins proximally and then occurs in the more distal portions of the arm. The initial motion occurs from one to six weeks following the stroke. A study by Van Buskirk (1954) concluded that restitution of function occurs chiefly in the first two months and it appears to be a spontaneous process. When full recovery occurs, initial motion begins within two weeks, and full motion occurs within three months. About 45% recover full motion, 40% partial motion, and 15% do not recover the function of the upper extremity (when followed for more than seven months). The role of cerebral dominance was examined in the recovery of ambulation. Right hemiplegics recovered independent ambulation more often and faster than left hemiplegics. The spatial-perceptual deficiencies of left hemiplegics were considered to be more resistant to recovery, and hampered recovery of ambulation (Cassvan et al., 1976). The influence of impaired sensory feedback was investigated by Van Buskirk et al. (1955). Newman (1972) suggested that much of the early recovery (especially in the upper limb) could be due to return of circulation to ischemic areas. Transfer of function to undamaged neurons is suggested as the mechanism underlying late recovery (especially in the lower limbs). (For a discussion of the recovery from apraxia, see Chapter 7.)

LANGUAGE THERAPY

The treatment of aphasics is an established practice, even though only a few studies have considered spontaneous recovery in assessing the efficacy of therapy. The first systematic study of treatment (Butfield and Zangwill, 1946) did not utilize untreated controls, but an attempt was made to describe the method of therapy—mainly the use of oral drills and transmodal cues. Gains after six months were attributed to therapy, assuming that further spontaneous recovery was not significant at that time. Vignolo (1964) studied treated and untreated patients and did not find a significant difference between these groups; nevertheless, he suggested that therapy between the second and sixth months may be beneficial. Sarno et al. (1970a) compared global aphasics who underwent stimulation therapy and programmed instruction with untreated controls and found no significant difference.

There are two studies utilizing untreated controls in the literature which present evidence that therapy is effective. Hagen (1973) compared ten treated aphasics matched for severity and type (sensorimotor type III of Schuell) to ten untreated aphasics and found significantly better recovery in language formulation, speech production, reading comprehension, spelling, and arithmetic in the treated group. Most improvement occurred during the first six months of treatment. Auditory comprehension, auditory retention, visual comprehension, and visuomotor abilities improved equally in the treated and control group. All patients were included in the study at three months and treatment began at six months after the stroke. The second study by Basso, Faglioni, and Vignolo (1975) included 91 treated aphasics and 94 controls who could not come for therapy for personal or logistic reasons. The control group was significantly older than the treated group. The etiologies were said to be the same for the two groups, but no data were published to support this statement, although etiology is a crucial factor to control in a study of recovery. A minimum of six months of therapy was shown to significantly affect the oral expression of aphasics; the longer the duration of aphasia before therapy was begun, the less effective the therapy. Unfortunately, the experimental design lumped all aphasics into two categories, possibly allowing more global or severe-jargon aphasics to be included in the untreated sample. This is bound to occur in every-day therapy situations, as therapists are much less likely to persist with global or severe-jargon patients who do not improve. Another important problem of this retrospective study is that instead of controlling the time of inclusion after the onset, it examined the "effect of this variable" in improvement. This, in fact, allowed patients seen soon after their stroke who would be expected to have more spontaneous recovery to be over-represented in the treated group, and patients seen longer after their stroke when recovery is less likely to occur to be overrepresented in the untreated group. To design a study of treatment of aphasia, it is essential to match patients for initial severity, type, etiology, and time from onset. Hagen's study is the only one which complies with this requirement.

Therapy itself is most complex and difficult to standardize. It is said that there are as many varieties of aphasia treatment as there are aphasics. Therapists, pointing out the need to tailor therapy to the needs of the individual, are reluctant to follow rigidly prescribed treatment programs. The content of therapy, as well as the methods, differs considerably, creating overlapping categories. Lately, the contribution of psycholinguistic principles to the content of therapy has been increasing.

A cooperative study of aphasia therapy, by Wertz et al. (1978), followed stroke patients undergoing stimulus-response speech therapy and compared them to the results of "social interaction" group therapy. The results showed significant gains, as measured by the PICA, in both groups, individually treated patients doing slightly better. Other measures, such as RCPM, showed less overall improvement. Maximum improvement occurred in the first three months. Significant improvement occurred in the language performance between 26 and 48 weeks in both groups, and it was assumed that spontaneous recovery was not operational at that time. This allowed the authors only to speculate about the efficacy of therapy, since no true control group was studied. If, however, one assumes that the social interaction group was, in effect, a control group, one might interpret their data as indicating that more structured speech therapy did not contribute much to recovery.

The following methods of therapy are in use at present. The first two are used by most therapists (Darley, 1975).

1. Stimulation approach. Wepman (1951) recognized that aphasics are, in fact, stimulated rather than educated during treatment. Familiar materials relevant to the patient are used. The patient is not pressured; every response is accepted and reinforced. Schuell's (1964) approach is similar; (1) use intensive *auditory stimulation,* i.e., meaningful patterns and high-frequency words, adjusting the rate, loudness, and length of presentation to the needs of each patient, (2) utilize highly repetitive stimulation, (3) elicit, rather than force, some response to every stimulus, (4) stimulate more responses rather than correct errors, and (5) use different language modalities for facilitation: spelling aloud to help writing, writing to help auditory retention, etc. Various forms of the specific stimulation approach were defined by Taylor (1964): (1) association approach: attempting to elicit associated words by structuring sessions around families of words—such semantic units as body parts, furniture, etc.—using the maximum possible word environments for each target word; (2) situational approach: every-day situations are acted out, facilitating learning functionally useful vocabulary or statements; and (3) minimal differences approach: similarly sounding words and similar-looking written material are used as stimuli for teaching.

Other varieties of stimulation are less structured. These are variously called: (1) environmental stimulation: everybody around the patient talks to him as much as possible; (2) rapport approach: a warm relationship is established between the clinician and the patient without regard to the content and method of contact; (3) socialization approach: individual or group sessions include informal "fun" activities; (4) interest approach: subjects related to the patient's previous group or individual work activities and interests are discussed; and (5) psychotherapeutic approach: problems of anxiety and loss of self-esteem are focused upon.

2. Programmed instruction. The desired language behavior is defined and programs to reach it are constructed. Martha Taylor Sarno and associates defined and developed this approach (Taylor, 1964). Many individual steps from preverbal programs to practicing syntax are used to achieve the desired language behavior (Sarno et al., 1970a). Although repeatable and quantifiable, it is very difficult to design and persist in such a program. This is also called the *psycho-linguistic approach* when careful attention is directed to the rules of language and the language deficit itself. Goda (1962) advocated using the patient's own spontaneous speech to design programs and drill material. *Language Oriented Therapy,* as described by Shewan (personal communication), also uses an operant paradigm while the content is based on knowledge about language impairment in aphasics. It considers the language modalities of training and the level at which the patient should be trained. Criteria for moving from one level to another are predetermined. The purpose is to teach strategies rather than responses.

Various other more-or-less distinct therapeutic approaches can be identified from the literature. This is far from a complete catalog:

3. Deblocking method. Weigl (1968) described a special kind of stimulation which uses an intact channel to eliminate a block in understanding or expression via other channels. A response is evoked in an intact channel (e.g., recognition of a printed word) just before presenting the same stimulus to a blocked channel (auditory comprehension). This is similar to Schuell's intermodality facilitation, see above.

4. Preventive method. This is a specific application of a linguistic theory by Beyn and Shokhor-Trotskaya (1966). Instead of object naming, patients work on expressions as a whole, preventing the occurrence of telegraphic speech.

5. Compensatory approach. This encourages the patients to use their own compensatory strategies (e.g., the patient who needs repetition to understand is encouraged to ask for it). Patients with word-finding difficulty are encouraged to circumlocute (Holland, 1977).

6. Operant conditioning with automatic teaching machines. These have been described by Keith and Darley (1967). Patients universally and understandably prefer human contact!

7. Melodic Intonation Therapy (MIT). This has been tried for global aphasics (Sparks et al., 1974) based on evidence that many severely affected aphasics can sing words better than they speak and that muscal, tonal abilities are subserved by the right hemisphere. The patient intones a melody for simple statements (like opera).

8. Visual Communication (VIC). Nonverbal symbols are used to train global aphasics to express themselves, since there has been a successful demonstration that the chimpanzee can be taught a non-verbal communication system (Glass et al., 1973). Gardner et al. (1976) taught patients to recognize and manipulate symbols in order to respond to commands, answer questions, describe their actions, and express desires and feelings. A similar approach is the use of hand signals to teach global aphasics basic communication (Eagleson et al., 1970).

9. Drug treatment. Drugs used to treat aphasia include dexamethasone, sodium amytal, priscol, meprobamate, and hyperbaric oxygen —with unimpressive results (Darley, 1975).

10. Direct psychotherapy and hypnosis. These have at times been considered useful to reduce the emotional problems of aphasics and to facilitate recovery.

11. Special therapies for various modalities have been suggested. For example, therapies for correcting "verbal apraxia" (Rosenbeck et al., 1973) or for retraining of writing (Hatfield and Weddell, 1976).

Brookshire (1977) attempted to analyze the relationship between clinician behavior and patient behavior. He is developing a system for recording and coding events during therapy. He has aptly stated that "a definite study of the effects of treatment on recovery from aphasia will be impossible without some means of describing objectively and unambiguously the exact nature of the treatment program or programs employed in the study."

References

Ades, H. W. and Raab, D. H. (1946). Recovery of motor function after two-stage extirpation of area 4 in monkeys. *J. Neurophysiol. 9*:55–60.

Alajouanine, T. (1956). Verbal realization in aphasia. *Brain 79*:1–28.

Basser, L. S. (1962). Hemiplegia of early onset and the faculty of speech with special reference to the effects of hemispherectomy. *Brain 85*:427–460.

Basso, A., Faglioni, P., and Vignolo, L. A. (1975). Etude controlee de la reeducation du langage dans l'aphasie: comparaison entre aphasiques traites et non-traitee. *Rev. Neurol. 131*:607–614.

Benson, D. F. and Geschwind, N. (1967). Shrinking retrograde amnesia. *J. Neurol. Neurosurg. Psychiat. 30*:539–544.

Benson, D. F., Marsden, C. D., and Meadows, J. C. (1975). The amnesic syndrome of posterior cerebral artery occlusion. *Acta Neurol. Scandinav. 50*:133–145.

Beyn, E. S. and Shokhor-Trotskaya (1966). The preventive method of speech rehabilitation in aphasia. *Cortex 2*:96–108.

Bond, M. R. (1975). Assessment of psychosocial outcome after severe head injury, in *Outcome of Severe Damage to the Central Nervous System*. Amsterdam: Elsevier.

Brookshire, R. H. 1977). A system for recording events in patient-clinician interactions during aphasia treatment sessions, in *Rationale for Adult Aphasia Therapy*, Univ. of Nebraska Medical Centre.

Braun, J. J., Meyer, P. M., and Meyer, D. R. (1966). Sparing of a brightness habit in rats following visual decortication. *J. Comp. Physiol. Psychol. 61*:79–82.

Broida, H. (1977). Language therapy effects in long term aphasia. *Arch. Phys. Med. Rehabil. 58*:248–253.

Bucy, P. C. (1934). The relation of the premotor cortex to motor activity. *J. Nervous Mental Dis. 79*:621–630.

Butfield, E., and Zangwill, O. L. (1946). Re-education in aphasia: a review of 70 cases. *J. Neurol. Neurosurg. Psychiat. 9*:75–79.

Campbell, D. C., and Oxbury, J. M. (1976). Recovery from unilateral visuospatial neglect. *Cortex 12*:303–312.

Cassvan, A., Ross, P. L., Dyer, P. R., and Zane, L. (1976). Lateralization in stroke syndromes as a factor in ambulation. *Arch. Phys. Med. Rehab. 57*:583–587.

CIBA Foundation Symposium (1975). *Outcome of Severe Damage to the Nervous System*. Amsterdam: Elsevier.

Culton, G. L. (1969). Spontaneous recovery from aphasia. *J. Speech Hearing Res. 12*:825–832.

Culton, G. L. (1971). Reaction to age as a factor in chronic aphasia in stroke patients. *J. Speech Hearing Disorders 36*:563–564.

Darley, F. L. (1972). The efficacy of language rehabilitation in aphasia. *J. Speech Hearing Disorders 30*:3–22.

Darley, F. L. (1975). Treatment of acquired aphasia, in *Advances in Neurology*, Vol. 7, Current reviews of higher nervous system dysfunction, W. S. Friedlander (ed). New York: Raven.

Duffy, F. et al. (1976). Pharmacological reversal of deprivation amblyopia in the cat. Paper read at the 28th annual meeting of the American Academy of Neurology, Toronto.

Eagleson, H. M., Vaughn, G. R., and Knudson, A. B. C. (1970). Hand signals for dysphasia. *Arch. Phys. Med. 51*:111–113.

Eisenson, J. (1949). Prognostic factors related to language rehabilitation in aphasic patients. *J. of Speech Hearing Disorders, 14*:262–264.

Fingers, S. (ed) (1978). *Recovery from Brain Damage*. New York: Plenum.

Flourens, P. (1824). *Recherches Experimentales sur les Proprietes et les Fonctions du Systeme Nerveux dans les Animaux Vertebres*. Paris: Crevot.

Franz, S. I., and Oden, R. (1917). On cerebral motor control: the recovery from experimentally produced hemiplegia. *Psychobiol. 1*:3–18.

Fritsch, G. and Hitzig, E. (1870). Über die elektrische Erregbarkeit des Grosshirns. *Arch. Anat. Physiol., Leipzig 37*:300-332.

Gardner, H., Zurif, E. B., Berry, T., and Baker, E. (1976). Visual communication in aphasia. *Neuropsychologia 14*:275–292.

Gazzaniga, M. S. (1970). *The Bisected Brain*. New York: Appleton.

Geschwind, N. (1969). Problems in the anatomical understanding of the aphasias, in *Contributions to Clinical Neuropsychology*, A. Benton (ed). Chicago: Aldine.

Geschwind, N. (1974). Late changes in the nervous system: An overview, in *Plasticity and Recovery of Function in the Central Nervous System.* D. Stein, J. Rosen, and N. Butters (eds). New York: Academic Press.

Glass, A. V., Gazzaniga, M. S., and Premack, D. (1973). Artificial language training in global aphasics. *Neuropsychologia 11*:95–103.

Gloning, I., Gloning, K., and Haff, H. (1968). *Neuropsychological symptoms and syndromes in lesions of the occipital lobes and adjacent areas.* Paris: Gauthier-Villars.

Gloning, I., Gloning, K., Haub, G., and Quatember, R. (1969). Comparison of verbal behavior in right-handed and non-right handed patients with anatomically verified lesion of one hemisphere. *Cortex 5*:43–52.

Gloning, K., Trappl, R., Heiss, W. D., and Quatember, R. (1976). *Prognosis and Speech Therapy in Aphasia in Neurolinguistics. 4. Recovery in Aphasics.* Amsterdam: Swets & Zeitlinger, B.V.

Goda, S. (1962). Spontaneous speech, a primary source of therapy material. *J. Speech Hearing Disorders 27*:190–192.

Godfrey, C. M., and Douglass, E. (1959). The recovery process in aphasia. *Can. Med. Assoc. J. 80*:618–624.

Goldberger, M. E. (1974). Recovery of movement after CNS lesions in monkeys, in *Plasticity and Recovery of Function in the Central Nervous System*, D. Stein, J. Rosen, and N. Butters (eds). New York: Academic Press.

Hagen, C. (1973). Communication abilities in hemiplegia: effect of speech therapy. *Arch. Phys. Med. Rehab. 54*:454–463.

Hatfield, F. and Weddell, R. (1976). *Re-Training in Writing in Severe Aphasia, in Neurolinguistics. 4. Recovery in Aphasics.* Amsterdam: Swets & Zeitlinger, B.V.

Head, H. (1926). *Aphasia and Kindred Disorders of Speech.* Cambridge: University Press.

Hécaen, H. (1976). Acquired aphasia in children and the ontogenesis of hemispheric functional specialization. *Brain and Language 3*:114–134.

Henschen, S. E. (1922). *Klinische und anatomishe Beitrage zur Pathologie des Gehirns.* Stockholm: Nordiska Bokhandelin, Vol. 5, 6, 7.

Hirsch, H. V. B. and Jacobson, M. (1974). The perfect brain, in *Fundamentals of Psychobiology*, M. S. Gazzaniga and C. B. Blakemore (eds). New York: Academic Press.

Holland, A. L. (1977). Some practical considerations in aphasia rehabilitation, in *Rationale for adult aphasia therapy,* M. Sullivan and M. S. Kommers (eds)., University of Nebraska Medical Center.

Jackson, J. H. (1873). On the anatomical and physiological localization of movements in the brain. *Lancet 1*:84–85, 162–164, 232–234.

Keenan, S. S. and Brassel, E. G. (1974). A study of factors related to prognosis for individual aphasic patients. *J. Speech Hearing Disorders. 39*: 257–269.

Keith, R. L. and Darley, F. L. (1967). The use of a specific electric board in rehabilitation of the aphasic patient. *J. Speech Hearing Disorders 32*: 148–153.

Kenin, M. and Swisher, L. (1972). A study of pattern of recovery in aphasia. *Cortex 8*:56–68.

Kennard, M. A. and McCulloch, W. S. (1943). Motor response to stimulation of cerebral cortex in absence of areas 4 and 6 *(Macaca mulatta). J. Neurophysiol. 6*:181–190.

Kertesz, A. and Benson, D. F. (1970). Neologistic jargon: a clinicopathological study. *Cortex 6*:362–387.

Kertesz, A. and Poole, E. (1974). The aphasia quotient: the taxonomic approach to measurement of aphasic disability. *Can. J. Neurol. Sci. 1*: 7–16.

Kertesz, A. and McCabe, P. (1975). Intelligence and aphasia: performance of aphasics on Raven's Coloured Progressive Matrices (RCPM). *Brain and Language 2*:387–395.

Kertesz, A. and McCabe, P. (1977). Recovery patterns and prognosis in aphasia. *Brain 100*:1–18.

Kinsbourne, M. (1971). The minor cerebral hemisphere as a source of aphasic speech. *Arch. Neurol. 25*:302–306.

Kohlmeyer, K. (1976). *Aphasia due to Focal Disorders of Cerebral Circulation: Some Aspects of Localization and of Spontaneous Recovery, Neurolinguistics. 4. Recovery in Aphasics.* Amsterdam: Swets & Zeitlinger B.V.

Kreindler, A. and Fradis, A. (1968). *Performances in Aphasia. A Neurodynamical, Diagnostic and Psychological Study.* Paris: Gauthier-Villars.

Lashley, K. S. (1938). Factors limiting recovery after central nervous lesions. *J. Nerv. Mental Diseases 88*:733–755.

Lawson, I. R. (1962). Visual-spatial neglect in lesions of the right cerebral hemisphere: a study in recovery. *Neurology 12*:23–33.

Lebrun, Y. and Hoops, R. (1976). *Neurolinguistics. 4. Recovery in Aphasics.* Amsterdam: Swets & Zeitlinger, B. V.

Leischner, A. (1976). *Aptitude of Aphasics for Language Treatment in Neurolinguistics. 4. Recovery in Aphasics.* Amsterdam: Swets & Zeitlinger B.V.

Liu, C. N. and Chambers, W. W. (1958). Intraspinal sprouting of dorsal root axons. *Arch. Neurol. (Chicago) 79*:46–61.

Lomas, J., and Kertesz, A. (1978). Patterns of spontaneous recovery in aphasic groups: a study of adult stroke patients. *Brain and Language* 5:388–401.

Ludlow, C. (1977). Recovery from aphasia: a foundation for treatment, in *Rationale for Adult Aphasia Therapy*, M. A. Sullivan and M. S. Kommers (eds). University of Nebraska Medical Center.

Luria, A. R., Naydin, V. L., Tsvetkova, L. S., and Vinarskaya, E. N. (1969). Restoration of higher cortical function following local brain damage, in *Handbook of Clinical Neurology*, Vol. 3, R. J. Vinken and G. W. Bruyn (eds). Amsterdam: North Holland.

Luria, A. R. (1970). *Traumatic Aphasia*. Hague: Mouton.

Marks, M. M., Taylor, M. L., and Rusk, L. A. (1957). Rehabilitation of the aphasic patient: a survey of three years' experience in a rehabilitation setting. *Neurology* 7:837–843.

Messerli, P., Tissot, A., and Rodriguez, J. (1976). *Recovery from Aphasia: Some Factors of Prognosis in Neurolinguistics. 4. Recovery in Aphasics.* Amsterdam: Swets & Zeitlinger, B.V.

Meyer, J. S. et al. (1974). Disordered neurotransmitter function. *Brain 97*: 655–64.

Meyer, J. S., et al. (1970). Diaschisis result from acute unilateral cerebral infarction. *Arch. Neurol. 23*:241–247.

Milner, B. (1974). Hemispheric specialization: scope and limits, in *The Neurosciences: Third Study Program*, F. O. Schmitt and F. G. Worden (eds). Cambridge: M.I.T. Press.

Moore, R. Y. (1974). *Central Regeneration and Recovery of Function: The Problem of Collateral Reinnervation in Plasticity and Recovery of Function in the Central Nervous System*. New York: Academic Press.

Munk, H. (1881). *Ueber die funktionen der Grosshirnrinde, Gesammelte Mitteilungen aus den Jahren 1877–1880*. Berlin: August Hirshwald.

McGlone, J. and Kertesz, A. (1973). Sex differences in cerebral processing of visuospatial tasks. *Cortex 9*:313–320.

Newman, M. (1972). The process of recovery after hemiplegia. *Stroke 3*: 702–710.

Newcombe, F., Hiorns, R. W., and Marshall, J. C. (1976). *Acquired Dyslexia: Recovery and Retraining. Neurolinguistics. 4. Recovery in Aphasics*. Amsterdam: Swet & Zeitlinger B.V.

Nielsen, J. M. (1946). *Agnosia, Apraxia, Aphasia*. New York: Hoeber.

Nottebohm, F. (1970). Ontogeny of bird song. *Science 167*:950–956.

Rosenbeck, J. C., Lemme, M. L., Ahern, M. B., Harris, E. H., and Wertz, R. T. (1973). A treatment for apraxia of speech in adults. *J. Speech Hearing Disorders 38*:462–472.

Rubens, A. (1977). The role of changes within the central nervous system during recovery from aphasia, in *Rationale for Adult Aphasia Therapy*, M. A. Sullivan and M. S. Kommers (eds). University of Nebraska Medical Center.

Russel, W. R., and Nathan, P. W. (1946). Traumatic amnesia. *Brain 69*: 280–300.

Russel, W. R. (1971). *The Traumatic Amnesias*. London: Oxford University Press.

Sands, E., Sarno, M. T. and Sankweiler, D. (1969). Long-term assessment of language function in aphasia due to stroke. *Arch. Phys. Med. Rehab. 50*:202–222.

Sarno, M. T., Silverman, M., and Sands, E. (1970a). Speech therapy and language recovery in severe aphasia. *J. Speech Hearing Res. 13*:607–623.

Sarno, M. T., Silverman, M., and Levita, E. (1970b). Psychosocial factors and recovery in geriatric patients with severe aphasia. *J. Am. Geriatr. Soc. 18*:405–409.

Sarno, M. T., and Levita, E. (1971). Natural course of recovery in severe aphasia. *Arch. Phys. Med. Rehab. 52*:175–179.

Schneider, G. E. (1973). Early lesions of superior colliculus: factors affecting the formation of abnormal retinal projections. *Brain Behav. Evol. 8*: 73–109.

Schuell, A., Jenkins, J. J., and Jimenez-Pabon (1964). *Aphasia in Adults*. New York: Harper & Row.

Smith, A. (1966). Speech and other functions after left (dominant) hemispherectomy. *J. Neurol. Neurosurg. Psychiat. 29*:467–471.

Smith, A., Chamoux, R., Leri, J., London, R., and Muraski, A. (1972). *Diagnosis, Intelligence and Rehabilitation of Chronic Aphasics*. Ann Arbor: University of Michigan Department of Physical Medicine and Rehabilitation.

Sparks, R., Helm, N., and Albert, M. (1974). Aphasia rehabilitation resulting from melodic intonation therapy. *Cortex 10*:303–316.

Sperry, R. W. (1947). Effect of crossing nerves to antagonistic limb muscles in the monkey. *Arch. Neurol. Psychiat. 58*:452–473.

Stavraky, G. W. (1961). Supersensitivity following lesions of the nervous system. Toronto, Canada: University of Toronto Press.

Stein, D. G., Rosen, J. J., and Butters, N. (1974). *Plasticity and Recovery of Function in the Central Nervous System*. New York: Academic Press.

Stoicheff, M. L. (1960). Motivating instructions and language performance of dysphasic subjects. *J. Speech Hearing Res. 3*:75–85.

Subirana, A. (1969). Handedness and cerebral dominance, in *Handbook of Clinical Neurology*, P. J. Vinken and G. W. Bruyn (eds). Amsterdam: North Holland.

Sullivan, M., and Kommers, M. S. (1977). *Rationale for Adult Aphasia Therapy*. University of Nebraska Medical Center.

Talland, G. A. (1965). *Deranged Memory*. New York: Academic Press.

Taylor, M. L. (1964). Language therapy, in *The Aphasic Adult: Evaluation and Rehabilitation*, H. G. Burr (ed). Charlottesville: Wayside Press.

Van Buskirk, C. (1954). Return of motor function in hemiplegia. *Neurology 4*:919–928.

Van Buskirk, C. (1955). Prognostic value of sensory defect in rehabilitation of hemiplegics. *Neurology (Minneap.) 6*:407–411.

Von Monakow, C. (1914). *Die Lokalisation im Grosshirnrinde und der Abbau der Funktion durch korticale Herde.* Wiesbaden: J. F. Berg-mann.

Victor, M., and Adams, R. D. (1953). The effect of alcohol on the nervous system. *Proc. Assoc. Res. Nervous Mental Disorders 32*:526–573.

Vignolo, L. A. (1964). *Evolution of aphasia and language rehabilitation: a retrospective exploratory study. Cortex 1*:344–367.

Ward, A. A., Jr. and Kennard, M. A. (1942). Effect of cholinergic drugs on recovery of function following lesions of the central nervous system. *Yale J. Biol. Med. 15*:189–229.

Watson, C. W. and Kennard, M. A. (1945). The effect of anticonvulsant drugs on recovery of function following cerebral cortical lesions. *J. Neurophysiol. 8*:221–231.

Weigl, E. (1968). On the problem of cortical syndromes, in *The Reach of Mind,* M. L. Simmel (ed). New York: Springer.

Weisenburg, T., and McBride, K. E. (1935). *Aphasia: A Clinical and Psychological Study.* New York: Commonwealth Fund.

Wepman, J. M. (1951). *Recovery from Aphasia.* New York: Ronald Press.

Wertz, R. T., Collins, M. J., Brookshire, R. H., Friden, T., Kurtzke, J., Pierce, J., and Weiss, D. (1978). The Veterans Administration Co-operative Study on Aphasia: A Comparison of Individual and Group Treatment. Presentation to the Academy of Aphasia Meeting, Chicago, October 16.

Williams, M. (1966). Memory disorders associated with electroconvulsive therapy, in *Amnesia,* C. W. M. Whitby and O. L. Zangwill (eds). London: Butterworths.

17
Childhood Learning Disabilities

MARTHA BRIDGE DENCKLA

INTRODUCTION

This chapter is perforce more strictly clinical than the rest of this volume, reflecting the youthful status of both the subspecialty and the patients it represents. Nosology itself is controversial in this field; some leading figures in the analysis of symptoms urge us to foreswear "syndromes" in favor of less medically based constructs. Our patients outlive us; deprived of anatomy, we reason by analogy. The "mechanisms" of which we are able to speak are inferred from clusters or correlations of functions or dysfunctions, at best longitudinally sequential in time; they have not yet been demonstrably proven chains of causality. Furthermore, intensely aware of the interplay between nature and nurture in the developmental period, we offer up our bits of "neurologizing by analogy" as might an archaeologist hold aloft a potsherd from beneath the rubble, crying "Look! Brain factors here!" Yet I submit that our cheerful (though cautious) plagiarism of assumptions and tests from classic adult-referenced neuropsychology has heuristic value; colleagues from other disciplines are often surprised that they arrive at conclusions similar to those derived from the neurological model. And I am glad to have been compulsively preoccupied with nosology in the decade

535

preceding computer-assisted tomography (the CAT-scan), which may soon provide us with in vivo anatomy for "syndromes," and increasingly sophisticated electroencephalography (EEG), which may help us understand physiology.

In this chapter, I will follow in the historic path of classical neuropsychology and describe the *most extreme* and *most pure* examples of what is seen clinically, rather than the most common. To put the choice in a frame of reference familiar to readers who are trained to diagnose adults (a frame of reference to which I shall return repeatedly in this chapter): the disorders described here are closer to circumscribed aphasias than to dementias, although dementias (often with aphasias embedded therein) are far more commonly encountered. "Specific learning disability" is to "mental retardation" roughly as "aphasia" is to "dementia." The issue of where either "specific learning disability" or "minimal brain dysfunction" stand with respect to "mental retardation," whether the differences are of degree only or of a qualitative nature, is important but too large in scope for this chapter. Broadly speaking, "mental retardation" is both more severe and less selective than either of the other categories. Just as one often says of an adult patient, "He's not demented, he's just aphasic" and yet knows that in a sense any aphasia is a restricted subset of dementia, the same subtle relationship, bal-

TABLE 17-1 *Clinical Syndromes Presenting to a Clinic Specializing in Learning Disabilities, Over a Two-Year Period in which 484 New School-Age (6–16) Patients Were Seen and Diagnosed**

---

1. *Dyslexia-plus,* i.e., combined dyslexia/hyperactivity: 60% of total (any combination 4,5,7,8/2,3,6 below)
2. *Hyperactivity,* syndrome (motor slow-for-age and behavior immature for age): 10%
3. Other *hyperactivity* syndromes, with EEG deviations/anomalies (epileptiform or other): 8%
4. *Dyslexia,* mixed-global language disorder: 7%
5. *Dyslexia,* anomic-repetition disorder: 5%
6. *Prechtl's Choreiform Syndrome:* 3%
7. *Dyslexia,* articulatory-graphomotor syndrome: 2% (Mattis et al., 1975)
8. *Dyslexia,* dysphonemic-sequencing disorder: 2%
9. *Developmental Gerstmann Syndrome:* 1%
10. *Miscellaneous,* other, unclassified, etc.

---

* Calendar years 1974 and 1975. Percentages rounded off.

ancing "specific" and "general" factors, pervades the field of developmental disorders.

The ten most common (prevalent) developmental clinical syndromes are listed in Table 17-1. It is apparent that in order to understand these, the reader must overlap (like a double-exposure photograph) the contents of this chapter and the next chapter on hyperactivity (Chapter 18), as most learning-disabled children suffer from attentional and self-control deficiencies (Peters et al., 1975; Denckla, 1977). In this chapter I will describe not the attentional but the processing disorders (Kinsbourne, 1977).

A section on acquired aphasia is included because, despite its rarity and the paucity of correlative pathological anatomical data, the little we do know is of importance as a transition between adult and developmental neuropsychology.

ACQUIRED DISORDERS OF LANGUAGE IN CHILDHOOD

Within the last decade, little has been added to the literature on acquired aphasia in preadolescence. As the sole "cortical function" consultant in a large neurological institute, between 1969 and 1976 I saw only seven cases of acquired aphasia in children under ten years of age. The salient characteristic of all such cases is their shared nonfluency, ranging from marked reduction in speech to absolute mutism.

Alajouanine and Lhermitte, in their extensive and oft-quoted 1965 report on 32 childhood aphasics, actually cited only nine cases whose left-hemisphere lesions occurred between ages five and ten. No breakdown into localization (anterior/posterior) within the left hemisphere is given for these cases. Eight of the nine who were less than ten years old had severely impaired writing and impaired comprehension of spoken as well as written language, and all nine had articulatory "phonetic disintegration" and severe reduction in verbal expression. Interestingly, recovery of reading was slower in children who sustained acquired aphasic syndromes before age ten years than in those over ten; only three of the 23 in the 11 to 15 age group had severe and seven more had mild impairment of reading comprehension. Impaired writing and "phonetic disintegration" were seen in less than half (ten) of the 11 to 15-year-olds. Intercorrelations among impairments were not given. Recovery was *slower* in *onset* in the under-ten-years-old group, and the picture emerges of quite severe acute language loss in the first decade (second pentad) of life, albeit with good spoken language recovery within a year. On IQ testing, block design was the best score of most of these 32 childhood (ages 5 to 15) aphasics; they scored poorly on arithmetic, coding, picture arrangement, and "retention of figures and narratives." None of the 32 reported could make normal academic progress. It is also important (when transferring inferences from acute acquired to developmental cases) to note the marked reluctance to speak and the withdrawal from communicative attempts of most children with acquired aphasia. It is presumed that children, unlike adults, have not sufficiently practiced and overlearned the articulatory rules and social habits of speech; therefore, even in the presence of preserved "anterior" cortex anatomical substrate for speech, lack of "posterior" inputs is not enough to sustain speech. What is increasingly intriguing is the issue of inputs of a social-emotional nature (perhaps limbic, independent of lateralization, or perhaps from right hemisphere) being just as critical as those from more conventionally language-related left-hemisphere systems.

Left-sided lesions accompanying right infantile hemiplegia disturb articulation of speech more than other aspects of language. There are more right than left infantile hemiplegics (of equal intellect) who are dysarthric or dysarticulate, suggesting that some individuals—especially those without familial sinistrality—cannot fully compensate for loss of left-hemisphere systems subserving the motor production of speech (Annett, 1973). Developmental delay in speech is equally common among right and left infantile hemiplegics (Basser, 1962; Annett, 1973). Frank aphasia does not follow hemispherectomy, either left or right, when the hemisphere removed has sustained an infantile lesion, usually large and epileptogenic, which was the indication for the drastic surgery (Basser, 1962). Yet syntactic understanding is less proficient after left (than after right) hemidecortication in such infantile hemiplegics (Dennis and Kohn, 1975). Intracarotid amytal tests have revealed persistence of left-hemisphere-dependent speech and language in persons with early onset of left-sided lesions to be less dramatic in extent than in those treated by hemidecortication or hemispherectomy (Branch et al., 1964; Wada, 1969).

Annett (1973) has evidence that sex and familial handedness interact with infantile hemiplegia as correlates of outcome for speech, language, and intellectual handicap. Anatomical organization of brains as well as timing of insult with respect to puberty interact to cause variable affects from early acquired lesions as well. Dennis (1977) has evidence for this with respect to sex/age interaction in spatial ability among congenital hydrocephalics. Thus, if anyone can collect a sufficiently large group of childhood cases with acquired aphasia, attention should be directed not only to chronological age, handedness, anatomical localization, and nature of pathology, but also to the sex, familial lateral preference pattern, and physiological (bone, pubertal) age of the patient ("to what brain did this happen?") What seems clear, however, is that speech production and syntactic comprehension are selectively most vulnerable to left-sided infantile insults.

Besides general agreement about acute nonfluency in acquired aphasia of childhood, there is also virtually universal agreement that children recover useful conversational language more completely and rapidly than do adults: weeks or few months for children as opposed to many months or years for adults (Alajouanine and Lhermitte, 1965; Lenneberg, 1967). This happy prognosis for spoken language is to be tempered by the findings that higher-order verbal abilities (concepts, humor, nonliteral usage, metaphor) as well as academic skills (reading, spelling, writing) are almost never acquired normally in children who have "recovered" from aphasia. The inability of children with subclinical or "recovered" aphasia to make progress in regular school subjects is an important link in the chain of reasoning to which I will return in the section on dyslexia of the developmental type.

Progressive subacute acquired aphasia associated with convulsive disorder and bilateral EEG abnormalities has been reported and discussed in two recent papers (Gascon et al., 1973; Rapin et al., 1977), both of which refer back to earlier recognition of these associations. Both papers postulate bilateral temporal-lobe pathology (type unknown) and emphasize the coexistence, *without causal* interpretation, of the seizure-EEG abnormalities with the progressive, then prolonged plateau, aphasia; successful treatment of the seizures or spontaneous normalization of EEG's did not affect the aphasia. Similarity of the aphasia to the syndrome of pure word-deafness

(with the notable exception of fluency) is common to both interpretations (Gascon et al., 1973; Rapin et al., 1977). Rapin et al. make
the additional point that one of their cases had a brother with the
same "verbal auditory agnosia" but without known onset or EEG
abnormality; they suggest that some congenital or developmental
cases may be identical to the progressive acquired type now recognized and "suggest that the distinction between acquired and developmental receptive difficulty for speech may not be as sharp as previously supposed."

The only autopsied case in the literature of a child with congeni-
tal/developmental language disability was that of a ten-year-old boy
with a severe comprehension (and expression) deficit—early on
thought to be deafness—who had old cystic infarcts involving superior temporal gyri bilaterally, with retrograde degeneration of both
medial geniculate nuclei (Landau et al., 1960). On this note of comparison with the adult pathology underlying "pure word deafness,"
I shall move on to a discussion of those far more prevalent clinical
entities, the developmental language disorders (failures of language
acquisition).

DEVELOPMENTAL OR CONGENITAL
LANGUAGE DISORDERS

Receptive disorders (also called verbal auditory agnosia, congenital word deafness, central auditory imperception)

I am using the conventional, albeit inaccurate, name only to avoid
creating further confusion; in fact, it is implicit (but must be made
explicit) that expressive output difficulties are universal in "receptive," indeed in all, language disorders of childhood and that it is
only to emphasize the distinctive feature of impaired comprehension that the term "receptive" is used. All patients with comprehension difficulties show severe retardation in development of spoken
language. Ingram (1969) classifies developmental speech disorders
in a hierarchical-quantitative manner, with "very severe" and "severe" being those in which comprehension is impaired; when comprehension is normal Ingram (1969) labels the syndrome "moderate"
or "mild." This quantitative-hierarchical description *may* reflect underlying anatomical degree of involvement (*bilateral* brain abnor-

mality quite possibly being a necessary condition for failure to comprehend, as in the one autopsied case), although we don't know whether, at the opposite extreme, congenital "pure severe articulatory failure" also requires bilateral lesions. From a functional-developmental point of view, also, lack of comprehension may well have severe consequences comparable to those of profound hearing loss, a point to which I will return later in the section on the problem of thought and language in children. From a clinical point of view, however, I disagree with Ingram's (1969) "more-or-less of speech-and-language," (quantitative-hierarchical) model in that my experience has included qualitatively different language syndromes of similar degree of severity. Furthermore, there is a confounding effect of each end of the spectrum (from comprehension to speech production); longitudinally and developmentally, these are not independent variables. Thus the age of the patient must be taken into account when his syndrome is described. The *same* child who at three was virtually inarticulate but had age-appropriate (three-year-old) comprehension may at six have the speech pattern of a three-year-old and the comprehension of a four-year-old. Lack of ability to engage in the give-and-take of conversation may impair the growth of comprehension or at least retard the rate of that growth. The relative preservation of comprehension still differentiates the profile from that of other syndromes. Depending upon when the clinician first sees the child (or gets a reliable history), "chickens and eggs" may be difficult to sort out.

Table 17-2 lists the characteristics of receptive language disorders. Children with comprehension difficulties who have not acquired a few single words by the age of three years may, like the hearing-impaired, never develop sufficient spoken language to be useful in daily life. Sign language may be the most realistic means of communication for such children. Often diagnosis is achieved only after the differential responses to therapy have become apparent, including a "therapeutic trial" of sign language of the deaf (Ingram, 1969; Denckla, 1974). Differential diagnosis of congenital receptive language disorder necessitates "ruling out" mental retardation and peripheral hearing loss; neither is easy to discard. Reliable assessment of intellect in a young child who does not understand instructions (and may be motorically and attentionally deficient as well)

TABLE 17-2 *Characteristics of Children with Receptive Language Disorder, Developmental Onset*

1. May appear deaf or hard-of-hearing
2. Show inconsistent responses to sounds in general and speech sounds in particular
3. Attention to speech sounds not maintained as well as attention to play-room toys
4. May react dysphorically to sound (dysacusis) or be easily distracted by very soft sounds (hyperacusis)
5. Nonverbal assessments of intellectual development are at least age-appropriate when child is less than seven years old (may fall thereafter)
6. Speech milestones are delayed, but a subgroup shows precocious reading aloud ("hyperlexia") and/or echolalia (not necessarily both)
7. Articulation is nonspecifically indistinct but is best when naming pictures or reading aloud
8. Social adjustment is at best shy, mostly limited (overdependent-symbiotic), and overlaps with autistic withdrawal
9. Motor clumsiness and impulsivity-attentional deficits commonly coexist with language delay

may be virtually out of the question; rather the clinician has to take the approach of looking for and accepting "islands" of age-appropriate function, rather like rays of light shining through a predominantly cloudy sky. I have observed a remarkable increase in concentration and good performance with puzzles, formboards, and imaginative play in children who, approached with formal testing, looked globally mentally retarded (Denckla, 1974).

The issue of hearing loss is a complex one, also not easily settled with a single test, since there are rare cases of "word-deaf" children who are also "sound-deaf" centrally (*total* auditory agnosia, not limited to verbal speech sounds); more seriously—because this element is potentially remediable—there are cases in which peripheral auditory pathways are impaired as well as central ones. Congenital rubella cases in particular may show this mixture of peripheral and central impairment of response to sounds (Chess, 1971; Ames et al., 1970). Increased sophistication in the audiological evaluation of retrocochlear lesions and the use of EEG (auditory evoked potentials) have helped clarify the peripheral/central issues (Goldstein, 1967; Rapin and Graziani, 1967). It has been my experience that the centrally impaired children who behave substantially like the deaf have been best served in schools for the deaf; but the same controversies, revolving about teaching use of sign language versus spoken language, apply to the centrally impaired. It appears that trial therapy, with a flexible willingness to change course if spoken language progress is negligible, is the best we have to offer at present. A promising approach, involving prolongation of the rapidly changing initial portion of the acoustic spectrum of stop consonants, has been described by Tallal (1976).

The most dramatic recent change in clinical concepts of receptive language disorders has been the shift from "rule out" (differential diagnosis) to "recognize overlap of" the syndrome of infantile autism. As reviewed by Rutter (1974) it has been found that only three symptoms are both universal for and specific to the autistic group: (1) profound and general failure to develop social relationships; (2) language disorder, not a simple delay, but with profoundly impaired comprehension, echolalia, and prenominal reversal; and (3) ritualistic and/or compulsive behaviors. It has been noted that children with severe developmental receptive disorders (as in Table 17-2) may slowly develop some of the characteristics of autism; and prognosis for autism has been known for 30 years to be intimately linked to the acquisition of speech by six years of age. Many psychiatrists had thought that the language failure of autistic children was motivational in nature, i.e., entirely secondary to the social withdrawal, a situation better described as "wouldn't" rather than "couldn't" speak. It was often observed, however, that social improvement was not followed by language improvement; that language improvement is not usually carried over into appropriate social usage; and that very early (infantile) inability to respond to the spoken language of adults (perhaps including auditory affective components) might play a causal role in asocial deviation of development. Studies of the language deficits of autistic children, compared with children showing receptive developmental language disorder (where both groups were restricted to boys of normal nonverbal intelligence) revealed many similarities between the two groups. Language comprehension was more seriously impaired in the autistic group, both at semantic and syntactic levels; relatively spared in the autistic group is response to phonological level, rote "meaningless" memory for speech sounds, and the "meaningless" echolalia (which Rutter considers the cause of the prenominal reversal) so characteristic of the autistic syndrome (Rutter, 1974). To a neurologist familiar with the syndrome of "isolation of the speech areas," this description of the profile of language disorder with preserved meaningless speech production and memorization capability certainly "rings a bell" of reminiscence. Of related interest is the syndrome of the "hyperlexic" child (overlap again; some nearly autistic and some more nearly normal socially) who calls out words on cereal packages at age three, reads aloud, and spells to dictation, but cannot understand or converse in spoken language. Unfortunately, such children do not understand what they read aloud any better than they understand what is said to them (Huttenlocher and Huttenlocher, 1973; Elliott and Needleman, 1976).

I have observed that the best-preserved language skill of "hyperlexic" receptively impaired children is the naming of colors and pictured objects on visual confrontation (Denckla, 1974). This is another reason why I disagree with Ingram's "more-or-less" rather than qualitatively descriptive model. Thus there appear to be children who can repeat and memorize speech sounds but not connect speech sounds with meaning; and a closely related group of children who are able to connect visual configurations with speech sounds (name and read aloud) but have far greater difficulty going in the other direction (with the curious circumscribed exception of spelling to dictation) or comprehending intralinguistic speech sound relationships, and in syntax. These examples of selectivity of language impairment possibly reflect some very localized failures of brain development. The clinical picture of the "hyperlexic" is strikingly like that described by Heilman et al. (1976), as a case of mixed transcortical aphasia with intact naming.

With respect to the place of infantile autism among the brain-based developmental disorders, Hauser et al. (1975) have made a landmark contribution in their report of pathological pneumoencephalographic findings—most prominently, but not exclusively, enlargement of left temporal horn (15 out of 18 cases). Overlap exists again in this report, in that one case with mild dilatation of left temporal horn did not have abnormal social interactions. The authors stated that they were unable to correlate degree of left-temporal enlargement with severity of clinical picture. I would expect bilateral lesions, possibly with a left preponderance, in these cases and would hope for computer tomography clarification of more subtle deviations of anatomy. It is possible that disconnection which is not readily visualized anatomically underlies the "isolation"-like character of the infantile autism syndrome. The report of Hauser et al. (1975) does bring up the issue of the temporal lobe being an anatomical "neighborhood" in which both social/emotional and language-development substrates are in proximity. Whether to view the autistic child's language and social/emotional status as causally linked (Rutter's discussion, 1974) or as coexisting is an argument reminiscent of that surrounding the issue of the hostile-paranoid behavior of many (not all) patients with Wernicke's aphasia. Both are classic neuropsychological dilemmas; illustrating the dangers of reasoning that, *cum hoc, ergo propter hoc* (a variation on *post hoc, . . .*).

As for causes of developmental disorders involving impaired comprehension, no coherent pattern of matching syndrome to etiology has as yet emerged. The gamut of causes, from familial (only hypothetically genetic) through every sort of perinatal insult, can be involved, and often the clinician is confronted with "feast" (several possible causes) or "famine" (a dearth of suspect events or relatives). The same can be said for all of the remaining disorders to be discussed in this chapter; rare exceptions will be noted.

Articulatory disorders

Grouped under this heading are the children with late as well as poor speech, not the mild dyslalia (Ingram, 1969) of those who start to speak at a normal age, have plenty of words, and make errors similar to those of healthy younger children. We are concerned here with children who are unintelligible at age five years; Morley (1965) in a British study, found 4% of all Newcastle kindergarteners to be this seriously handicapped. By definition, comprehension is said to be normal in this group, and indeed it is for all intents and purposes functional for daily life; but, analogous to the carefully studied adults with Broca's aphasia, children with speech-production disorders severe enough to render them unintelligible at school entrance usually show deficits in comprehension of morphological and syntactical distinctions; and they are definitely handicapped in the appreciation of the phonemic detail (the phonological level) of language (discussed further below under "dyslexia" heading). Not only does speech-sound production begin late; it also progresses at a slower rate than in normal children, although speech sounds still tend to be acquired in the same order (e.g., labials before linguals) (Ingram, 1969). In the majority of cases, as speech becomes intelligible it becomes apparent that language is not normal but telegramlike; words of syntactical and/or unstressed character are omitted and, again, the pattern of Broca's aphasia comes to mind. In a pathetic minority, speech remains so limited, sparse, and unintelligible (unless one knows the stimulus, e.g., a picture being named), that linguistic involvement, if any, is hidden; my experience is that inarticulate status past the age of eight years carries a dismal prognosis.

Many speech pathologists, exemplified by Morley (1965), refer to the speech-sound production disorder as "dyspraxia of speech," a dyspraxia selectively involving lips, tongue, and palate. Arguments adduced in favor of these concepts are that such children articulated better when they pronounce single words and when they are given visual or somesthetic information by which to guide their articulatory musculature than when they attempt running, spontaneous speech. I would agree to the label "dyspraxia" if it can be demonstrated that an articulatory movement can, in fact, be produced at normal speed in response to visual or haptic stimuli. However, merely demonstrating slowness and clumsiness (which would mean lack of smoothly flowing, connected speech) production within the context of normal nonarticulatory movements does not fit the definition of "dyspraxia." It is difficult, of course, to characterize *any* developmental dyspraxia according to the classic adult terminology concerning loss of skilled movement, but it does not seem useful to employ the term "dyspraxia" unless there are indications that a movement pattern can be acquired under one set of circumstances and not under another. We really do not know whether circumscribed lesions of classic cerebellar or corticobulbar systems, if congenital, might cause slowness and clumsiness. There is a tendency to think that pseudobulbar palsy must include all of the known features of a complete orobuccofacial spastic-paretic picture, yet such is not the case universally even in adults with diseases affecting bilateral corticobulbar tracts. We also lack clinical expertise in ruling out intraoral sensory or perceptual loss, although such cases, with consequent motor control impairment, have been described (Chase, 1967). Speech, being the most demanding of the maneuvers of the mouth, may be dramatically selectively involved in some instances. In children, the articulatory disorder is so central a concern that concomitant mild drooling, choking, or inefficient mastication may go relatively unnoted until the neurologist makes the point that there is a wider and more elementary motor handicap, really "cerebral palsy above the neck." This is not just a theoretical point; years of frustratingly ineffectual speech therapy may be based upon incorrect diagnosis of "dyspraxia."

Tallal (1976) takes another approach to severe articulatory disturbance, emphasizing inadequate ability to perceive, and hence produce and monitor, critical acoustic information presented at the usual rate. This emphasis upon speech perception bears further examination, despite the initial objection that if such children comprehend speech they must perceive it adequately; but adequate for comprehension may not be adequate for production. Studies of dyslexia have made it clear, moreover, that perception adequate for semantic-level contact is not necessarily adequate for phonological-level contact with language symbols (and vice versa); and our experiences with "hyperlexic" children show that their articulation when reading aloud or naming pictures is far clearer than their spontaneously or conversationally produced speech. Longer duration, as well as difference of sensory modality of stimulation, may be a critical feature in such cases.

Moderate developmental disorders of language
This group of disorders usually does not come to clinical attention before the school years. Therefore, they will actually be discussed in greater detail under the heading "dyslexia," because in clinical reality that is the chief complaint or index symptom which brings children to attention. Occasionally, a sophisticated parent or teacher will refer a child with one of these disorders, but because their language skills for daily-life preschool survival are adequate (if marginal) and their speech and language acquisition milestones are not delayed in time of beginning, these "middling" cases muddle along

until classroom instruction and books enter their lives. These children are analogous to the classic adult "fluent aphasics" and may even be described as "very verbal" if of the anomic type.

AUDIOPHONETIC DISORDERS

Consonant with Tallal's (1976) observations of rate-related disorders of language, but not necessarily at the same basic acoustic level, these disorders manifest in children who need to receive short messages slowly. The tendency of such children to say "What" is often dismissed by parents as inattentiveness; their ability to "understand" a message in a familiar context (e.g., a three-stage command at bedtime is carried out) does not prepare parents for the child's inability to follow directions in a classroom. They appear dazed, glazed-of-eye, and inattentive as longer, faster strings of language come at them. Their articulation is normal. Repetition and naming errors are predominantly phonemic substitutions and errors of serial order. Morphology and syntax often lag years behind (i.e., are learned more slowly than) meaningful vocabulary. These children deserve more fine-grained study in terms of issues at the phonological and syntactic level: discrimination, span, sequencing (at the sentence structure as well as polysyllabic word level). At present we know enough to say that single-word semantic vocabulary growth is good in these children but they show "a tin ear for language." A paradoxical situation, changing over time, exists as these children learn to read; although slow to learn, particularly in initial mastery of the phonics-and-blending (analytic-synthetic) method, such children are greatly benefited by reading once they reach a certain critical level of mastery. Written language, by staying before them and with them longer than spoken language and being susceptible to slower rates of processing at their own comfort level, helps them to comprehend complex language (Unger, 1976). Such a child may have trouble *both* understanding and following directions in the classroom *and* learning to read in grades one through three; by fourth grade he may be relatively good at reading, master spelling lists by visuomotor learning (usually his spelling in composition work is poor), and be at most disadvantage when the teacher is lecturing or the coach is explaining a football "play"! He may grow

up to be a well-read adult who avoids parties and jobs which require
long conversational meetings.

ANOMIC-REPETITION OF "EXPRESSIVE"
LANGUAGE DISORDERS
(I preserve the latter term out of deference to its familiarity, not
its precision.) The two terms refer to a large group of children who
may talk a great deal, understand quite well, but have trouble with
word-retrieval. I have never seen a child in this group whose sentence and digit repetition was completely normal at the age of ten
or under; just what happens at ten or above to permit normal repetition (and I have seen this "breakthrough" in cases followed longitudinally) is a matter for speculation, although one is tempted to
relate it to the well-known "normalization" of visual-graphomotor
(design-copying) skills over the age of ten and then relate both
developmental phenomena to myelination of posterior-to-anterior
cortical–cortical connections (to be discussed below, under "developmental lag"). At any rate, the word-finding and naming difficulty
is the more persistent and distinctive part of the clinical picture. A
parent may describe it as "poor memory" yet note with perplexity
that the same youngster has "a photographic memory aside from
words." These children may or may not be late talkers or poor ar-
ticulators; unless *per annum* rate of new words (especially nouns) is
charted, their dysnomia is not of consequence until school starts.
Upon arriving at kindergarten and being asked for his birthday,
such a child may circumlocute, "between the summer and when the
snow falls." The habit of circumlocution and of talking by slow associative approximations may be remarkably well-established by
kindergarten; the child may arouse teacher or peer-group irritation
or derision which, in turn, may elicit or promote stuttering. Dysnomia is, in fact, one of the best-established antecedents of that
common but otherwise mystifying affliction, stuttering or stammer-
ing (Rutherford, 1977). Aside from its impact on the acquisition
of reading (see section below), dysnomia has a profound effect upon
the social-emotional life (as in fact do all of the "middling"-severe
developmental language disorders—a fertile area for psychiatric research). The higher the child's general verbal intelligence, including measures of vocabulary other than those calling for direct single-

word retrieval, the more likely he is to be disturbed by the effect of his dysnomia, since he cannot produce up to the expectations generated, by teachers, parents, and himself, on the basis of his other gifts.

The dysnomic child should be differentiated from the child with a verbal memory problem, who may also have slow vocabulary acquisition and be a "good thinker." Differences between the "amnesioid" and the "aphaseoid" both of whom exhibit poor word retrieval are under active investigation at this time and are not of theoretical interest only; suitable types of academic careers, high school and beyond, may be quite different for these two subgroups. The dysnomic has inconsistent "here today and gone tomorrow" retrieval but may make better use of associative maneuvers, whereas the poor memorizer behaves like a slow learner for whom repetition of multiple trials has to take place before he registers new information. Again, as I follow children I am confronted with the paradox that the poor memorizer is a relatively more skillful reader but a poorer classroom participant than is the dysnomic at junior high school levels. Furthermore, the dysnomic is often able to read for comprehension far better than he reads or spells aloud, but this happens only after a threshold value of fourth-grade reading has been consolidated (Lieben, 1976). The reading behavior of the dysnomic dyslexic in the second decade of life is likely to evoke memories of adult patients with anomic aphasia or conduction aphasia.

DYSLEXIA

In this section, I will discuss children who fail to acquire the skill of reading at the expected rate, despite evidence of adequate intelligence and motivation in other developmental achievements.

From the preceding section it is obvious that I take a strong position, which I will restate. Within the past five years there has been a remarkable confluence of evidence to support the view that dyslexia is usually the index symptom of a developmental language disorder too subtle to lead to a referral of the child in preschool life. (I have already indicated that these subtle language disorders do, in fact, appear to trouble the life of the school-age child and adolescent, even beyond their trouble with books.) In this context, it is important to note that a patient in adult life who speaks as well as a five-year-old kindergarten child would not be called significantly "aphasic."

I am not stating that language disorder is either always necessary or always sufficient to explain dyslexia but rather that the symptoms most universally found among and most specifically related to dyslexia are those of verbal learning and verbal behavior. Many, but not all are familiar from an "aphaseological context" (Critchley, 1970). Verbal memory deficit is more akin to a mild version of what is seen in an adult with left-temporal lobectomy or Korsakoff's syndrome than to an aphasia; it has not yet been adequately studied. I have already discussed the "hyperlexic" state, i.e., precocious decoding level reading aloud, seen in some severely language-disabled preschoolers. My point is that most adequately speaking, intelligent poor readers have some weakness in a component of spoken language with which the written language makes contact (Shankweiler and Liberman, 1976). Further research may even clarify that the set of subtle, intimately related weaknesses manifest in both spoken and written language of this majority of dyslexic children are the consequences of some more basic underlying deficiency in "left-hemisphere-mediated" skills; such has been suggested in terms of temporal-order perception, sequencing, and acoustic analysis. The clinical terminology in which phenomena are described does not preclude delving further into such mechanisms.

I will not attempt to define "dyslexia," but will refer the reader to Critchley (1970), Benton (1975), and Rutter (1976). Social-cultural relativism pervades the issue of definition, so that a single "cutting-point" for defining disability eludes us, unless we know expectancy for both child (intrinsic) and community (extrinsic). However, the *task* to which I am referring is the decoding of written language; the term "dyslexia" as a symptom-description is not being used to refer to failures to comprehend what has been successfully read aloud. Even when we restrict ourselves to children of middle-range intelligence and middle-class communities, with all the usual exclusionary clauses about hearing, vision, and physical and emotional health, we are still left with a complex of brain factors. Even with a neurological model in mind (which, presumably, I need not defend in the context of the present volume) there is no *one* entity, dyslexia but a group of dyslexias, as in adult neurology these are the alexias. Specific dyslexia, meaning (Rutter, 1977) that reading does not match community and intellectual expectation, may still be "dyslexia-plus" coexisting with components of hyperactive syndrome (attention and impulse control deficient), graphomotor deficits, and other "minimal brain dysfunctions." In fact, the term "minimal brain dysfunctions" was originally concocted to cover the frequent overlap of dyslexia with hyperactivity (Peters et al., 1975), a situation reflected in Table 17-1. Even so, within the heterogeneous group of children with "minimal brain dysfunctions," those who *can* read up to expectation have considerably less expressive language impairment than do those who lag in reading (Denckla and Rudel, 1976a, b). This approach—comparing "dyslexic-MBD" to "nondyslexic MBD" groups—is analogous to comparing left- and right-hemisphere-damaged groups on a behavioral task: neither group performs as well as normals but the degree and style of failure may be different. In the search for neuropsychological correlates of dyslexia, the comparison of groups with heterogeneous brain impairments has helped us to set aside certain factors which, although intuitively reasonable to relate to dyslexia, do not in fact turn out to be specifically relevant. For a review of these recently discredited candidates for correlates, including visual perception and intersensory integration, see Vellutino (1978). Briefly Vellutino's analysis of the psychological test findings suggests that apparent perceptual and intersensory integration problems are secondary manifestations of verbal encoding deficiencies.

Another approach is to try to look at "pure" dyslexia (free of all life-history and examination deviations unrelated to school skills) and ask what correlates are found. Table 17-3 lists what I have found and previously reported (Denckla, 1977b). Disorders of verbal learning and language dominate this picture; this has been true even when a small percentage of "visually perceptually impaired specific dyslexics" has been found (Mattis et al., 1975). The "visual-perceptual" factors appear to account for some early but relatively transient reading difficulties (Satz, 1978; Jansky, 1978). The "purest" but most severe, persistent cases I have followed are those who are dysnomic, i.e., naming and word-finding are the particular low points within their globally reduced language functions. Those with

TABLE 17-3   *"Pure" Dyslexia: Clinical Characteristics*

1. Global-mixed language disorder
   a. All tests of language fall below age expectations (comprehension, repetition, and naming tests)
   b. Verbal IQ is below 90 and performance IQ is at least 95
2. Articulatory-graphomotor disorder (Mattis et al., 1975)
   a. Fine motor coordination and pencil use deficient
   b. Language tests normal; articulation deficient
3. Anomic-repetition disorder
   a. Circumlocutory and paraphasic errors account for most excessive errors on confrontation naming
   b. Sentence and digit span shorter than, as well as qualitatively worse than, expected for age group (not true after ten years)
   c. Articulation and comprehension normal
   d. "Scatter" among subtests on verbal IQ
4. Dysphonemic-sequencing disorder
   a. Sentence and digit span "failed" by virtue of omissions, substitutions, errors of sequence
   b. Naming errors (not excessive in number) also characteristically phonemic and/or sequential details
   c. Complex syntactical constructions misunderstood
   d. Articulation and verbal IQ at least average
5. Verbal learning (memorization) deficiency
6. Correlational (sequential-simultaneous?) deficiency

Note: numbers 1, 2, 3, and 4 also recognized by Mattis, 1977.

solid verbal intelligence and dysnomia constitute the most dramatic cases, of course, because the gap between expectancy and achievement is greatest. Two of the boys whom I first met as kindergarten children whose dysnomia included color names (a rather severe and relatively rare problem) are now teenagers "stuck" at the second-grade level, despite superb special schooling and above-average full-scale (average verbal, superior performance) intelligence quotients. My clinical experience has confirmed that a serious dysnomia is *sufficient* to predict long-lasting, "hard-to-learn" dyslexia.

However, the most numerous are *not* the "pure" but the "specific," and in most cases the dyslexia is the outcome of multiple subtle risk factors—additive but susceptible to remediation. Some language factor from the list in Table 17-3 is usually present. On the other hand, I have seen children who present to a clinic with other learning disabilities, but adequate reading, who also turn out to have some language-risk factor (Table 17-3). Why these children "compensate" and others do not may take years of research to unravel, since the initial method and quality of teaching, the nature of emotional support from home, and effects of community standards and peer group competition are all variables difficult to document. Looking at neuropsychological factors in compensation, however, may be more accessible and feasible. My clinical sense is that quantification or strengths is one way to approach understanding of "compensation," i.e., how much *above* average does one have to be in one relevant skill in order to compensate for another relevant weakness? For example, I have followed three boys who have mild right hemiparesis, low verbal IQ, and poor reading/spelling skills (Denckla, 1977b); of these three, only one achieves average grades in mathematics, and he is the one who is above the ninety-fifth (95) percentile on Raven's Coloured Progressive Matrices, Block Design, and Object Assembly. The others are solidly average on these "spatial" tasks, but that doesn't seem to permit average achievement in mathematics.

Why is the dysnomic so particularly, so "purely" a difficult case? The relationship between the word-finding and reading process is an intimate, subtle, yet complex one (Wolf-Ward, 1977). I find it easiest to understand it in the context of Shankweiler and Liberman's (1976) discussion of the several levels at which written language can make contact with the spoken language of the reader; the dysnomic has trouble at all such interfaces, whether it be retrieving phoneme for grapheme (not a one-to-one task in English!) or retrieving a whole spoken word for ideogram.

The "hyperlexic" severely uncomprehending child represents an opposite dissociation, with *only* the "narrow channel capacity" to make associations between configurations (letters, words, pictures) and spoken sound-sequences (Elliot and Needleman, 1976). When the dysnomic child is under ten he usually has span and/or sequencing problems, so that his resynthesis (blending) of sounds usually suffers from omissions and reversals even when he has been able to learn some (and there are lots) of the basic phoneme-grapheme correspondences. Phonics-and-blending, never meant to be a persistent way of reading (only of entering the reading process) can also become a handicap if the child gets "stuck" at that level.

Word–picture associations in a storybook or workbook are often spontaneously discovered by the bright dysnomic child, so that his comprehension of large, substantive pictureable words may far out-run his ability to read aloud "little words." Some special educators (Johnson, 1977) explicitly use this approach (visual-visual) while others argue against it as noncontributory to spelling and writing progress. The neurologist seeing a child who understands (and shows it by correct multiple-choice or picture-matching responses in workbook) "stegosaurus" but is unable to read "the" may occasionally indulge a rescue fantasy by authoritatively snatching such a child from the jaws of a psychodynamic interpretation and a referral for insight psychotherapy. The neurological model makes it comprehensible that "big words" with pictureable (and/or actually pictured) referents could be handled differently from "little words" devoid of such associations.

The important position of dysnomia as a correlate of dyslexia is emphasized by the findings of Mattis et al. (1975) that over 50% of dyslexics suffered from a language disorder in which anomia was the necessary defining feature (with articulatory, comprehension, and repetition deficits variables additionally present).

Articulation and dyslexia

Mattis (1975–1977) having described the "articulatory-graphomotor syndrome" has addressed the therapeutic implications and life history thereof. He has found that initial avoidance of phonics-and-blending, in favor of building upon word families (varying only the first letter) plus whole sight words, works best in these children who have difficulty pronouncing and blending the sounds. He reports that as articulation becomes normal, these children can be returned to explicit analysis of words into phonemic segments. This appears to be both a nice illustration of the motor theory of speech perception and a demonstration of the close relationship between speech status and reading instructional method, both of which must be monitored, as they change year by year. My own experience with children severely unintelligible at eight years or older is that their reading is, much like that of the persistently dysnomic group, limited to silent direct-association comprehension of pictureable words. Again, this is consistent with the concept of early normal reading, i.e., the usual "decoding stage," as speaking or "re-encoding for speech output." The "output" skills of spelling and composition remain overtly correlated with elegance and precision of speech.

Dysphonemic-Sequencing (Dysphonetic, Audiophonetic) Factors

Boder (1971) has independently described a classification, based on reading/spelling error analysis, in which one group is clearly dysphonetic, i.e., unable to decipher or spell words on the basis of word-analysis (phonetic) skills. They read globally, responding to the configurations (and memory-of-configuration for spelling). Boder felt that this was by far the largest group of dyslexic children—a point to which I will return later in my discussion.

Pirozzolo et al. (1977) have studied in detail a twenty-one-year-old "dysphonetic dyslexic" (developmental, not acquired) whose word recognition was fifth grade but whose oral reading was two grades lower, mainly due to errors on grammatical words. On tachistoscopic (left or right) word presentation, this patient showed lack of right-field superiority and, in contradistinction to normal subjects, made most of his errors on acoustically confusable words. This man was at his best reading major lexical items and correctly responding to visual distinctions (configurations) among flashed words.

I have reported (1977b) in a retrospective study of 52 "pure dyslexic" children (found among 297 patients seen in one year) seven with *dysphonemic-sequencing* difficulty, characterized by the phonemic substitutions and mis-sequencing of phonemes within words (as well as words within sentences) elicited on tasks of repetition and naming. Their naming scores are normal (their error types rather than error numbers being salient) and articulation of speech sounds is normal. The dysphonemic-sequencing group (Denckla, 1977b) had the highest percentage of familial-only, as opposed to "risk factor" history, of any of my "pure" dyslexic children (although still not statistically significant). Since the time of the study (although I did not systematically address this issue then) I have been increasingly impressed by the subtle comprehension limitations of this group, bringing them closer to the audiophonetic language disorder group (see above and in Denckla, 1974) in that rapid, lengthy, syntactically complex spoken language also places a strain on them. In colloquial terms, the dysphonemic-sequencing or dysphonetic group are people with "a tin ear for language" (Boder, 1971). Yet single-word vocabulary and general semantic competence in nearly every manner of measurement may be superior: the "message" of meaning is theirs, even if the "medium" is insecure. Mattis (1978) has confirmed the existence of the group, stating that he has documented in 16 dyslexic children the absence of anomia or articulatory defect, poor scores on WISC digit span subtest, Spreen-Benton sentence repetition, and WISC picture arrangement. Furthermore, confirming my ongoing clinical observations about syntactic comprehension, Mattis reports that the latter sections of the Token Test (see Chapter 2) are indeed difficult for this group of children (Mattis, 1978).

To "flesh out" the picture, here are some examples from a closely followed case (IQ 140): he reports that a statue represents "the Merchant (Virgin) Mary," admonishes his mother not to stop the car to pick up "hijackers" (hitch-hikers); offers to get his brother's new eyeglasses from the "optimist" (optometrist); and is uncertain as to whether he is thinking of ordering a "muffin" or "waffle" for breakfast. On the Oldfield-Wingfield naming test (Denckla and Rudel, 1976a) he produces "mindwill" for "windmill" and "shoe-horse," yet obtains an average total score.

As for the *sequencing* issue, this has received ample study in recent years, most specifically by Senf (1969) who found greater disabilities in the temporal ordering of intermingled auditory/visual stimuli than with visual alone (critically analyzed by Vellutino, 1978a); and Bakker (1972) who proposes a complex model of the relationship between reading and "temporal-order perception (TOP)," his term for sequencing. Bakker proposes a critical period of development in which TOP interacts with learning to read, with an upper phase (6 to 8 years for boys, 4 to 6 years for girls) determined by a critical TOP threshold. Bakker is aware of the interaction between verbal codes and TOP and relates TOP for verbally coded material (not TOP for all material equally) to left-hemisphere specialization. He, like Tallal (1976) and Doehring (1976), is caught in the difficulty of getting at the "pure" sequencing task, for we can always ask, "sequencing *what?*" The problem is again that of cause/effect versus "two outward manifestations of a yet-more-profound neuropsychological level of left-hemisphere specialization." The phenomenology (certain tasks, as quoted above from Mattis, 1978) of what we call sequencing failures in our test data stands up well; the mechanism or understanding thereof eludes us. A further complication is that large-scale, impeccably conducted studies of reading failure (Owen et al., 1971; Symmes and Rappaport, 1972) come up with the WISC profile (Digit Span, Arithmetic, and Coding) which by factor analysis indicates the common denominator not only of sequencing but also of attention. Here again comes overlap with Kinsbourne (1970, 1974) in the sense that certain aspects of selective attention have been thought of as left-hemisphere-dependent.

It is in the context of this confusing yet challenging convergence of neuropsychological variables upon left-hemisphere mediation that the dysphonemic-sequencing syndrome of dyslexia becomes most interesting. Neither (1) most severe in prognosis nor (2) most numerous in a *clinical* referral setting (probably (2) is related to (1) as a dependent variable) this syndrome leads us inexorably toward issues of genetic "advantage" (as in Symmes and Rappaport's 1972 nondeficit model), role and meaning of cerebral dominance, male preponderance, and maturational lag in dyslexia. These children speak and understand their native language well enough to rise above Critchley's (1964) criteria for dyslexia (except for some amusing "mord-wixing"), do not have significant verbal IQ lowering, and do not have trouble responding to whole-word configurations. Their disabilities also tend to change with age from reading/spelling retardation to spelling retardation alone, a clinical observation uncorrelated with either errors of order or errors of a phonetic nature (Nelson and Warrington, 1976). Yet they go on to have difficulty with phonetic aspects of learning foreign languages.

It is interesting to combine the data of Symmes and Rappaport (1972) who postulate genetically determined spatial excellence as the other side of the coin of sequencing deficit with that of Witelson (1976) who suggests both right- and left-hemisphere commitment to spatial-holistic strategies in dyslexic boys. Taken together, these studies suggest that a variation in cognitive style may be correlated with a variation in the substrate of neurological organization, such that bilateral cerebral representation of spatial processing (restated, lack of usual cerebral dominance/laterality effects) precludes left-hemisphere proficiency in its (the left's) mediation of linguistic, analytic, and sequential processing. In fact, Witelson's bilateral tactual shape-discrimination task could also be interpreted in the "attention"-subserving frame of reference of Kinsbourne, 1970 (since hand-order effects cannot be ruled out). Reconciling Bakker's 1972 TOP data with these concepts, we encounter age and sex as maturational variables in the life history of an individual who is specialized for spatial-holistic gifts and confront the issue of thresholds or "good-enough" plateaus in development.

Rourke (1976) has reviewed his own work in comparison to that of Satz et al. (1974, 1978) as both relate to paradigms of "developmental lag" versus "deficit" explanations of reading retardation. I propose to mediate the issue by pointing out that, depending on syndrome, both are sometimes true descriptions. I note that neither Rourke nor Satz makes subgroupings or syndromes of dyslexic readers but rather compares good (adequate) and poor readers. Satz and his group postulate a specific lag in the development (maturation) of the left hemisphere which delays, in turn, (1) sensorimotor-perceptual, and later (2) verbal-conceptual skills. Satz has added that the "developmental lag" model implies that performance patterns of older disabled readers should qualitatively resemble those of younger normal readers. The longitudinal studies of Satz et al. have been consistent with this putative lag in a qualitatively normal ontogenetic sequence, and Rourke's group has confirmed that "catch-up" is observed in certain fairly simple, early-emerging abilities but not on tests of higher-order skills. Rourke and Satz appear to differ in their views on (1) which tests have low "ceilings" within development; (2) at which ages such ceilings are critical for the catch-up model; and (3) which tests involve left-hemisphere mediation (a construct validity issue). It is of particular interest to me that Rourke finds Sentence Memory to be in the catch-up paradigm group (see my remarks above with respect to repetition in the second decade of the anomic-repetition syndrome).

Also, if Bakker's observations are correct with respect to sequencing (his TOP) having a critical period with an upper phase ("upper phase" meaning "ceiling" developmentally), then the sequencing component of the dysphonemic-sequencing disorder might be expected to be worse in the early grades; and this has been my observation, nicely backed by the Pirozzolo study of the developmentally dyslexic adult who did not show "sequencing" but only dysphonetic output errors. It is of interest that tests of repetition (digit span, sentence memory) do have steep curves and a ceiling at about 12–13 years; Wechsler (1941) commented that digit span was not a very "intellectual" or G-factor-loaded subtest but that it appeared to be compromising to intellect to have less than a basal (floor or threshold) capability in digit span. Span and sequencing appear to be critical early elements (and with respect to phonological and linguistic elements I doubt that relationships to left hemisphere is open to question) which in fact need only reach a "good-enough floor" or threshold value, not even the "ceiling" for "normal controls," necessary for reading skill to be subserved. Access to names and verbal encoding strategies for memory may on the other hand have not only higher "ceilings" (if any) but higher "good-enough" thresholds. Recall that this is not a hierarchical model, because higher-order skills like broad semantic or categorical competence are not as well related to skill levels in reading/spelling as are naming and memorizing. Semantic and categorical competence may serve as compensatory strategies in the context of a "deficit" paradigm, however. Thus we may be able to observe in the dysphonemic-sequencing group of dyslexics *both* "catch-up" of a developmental lag in sequencing (it just needs to be "good-enough") and compensation (semantic and categorical) for a persistent deficit in phonological precision.

Rudel and I (1979) have studied the word-finding competencies of dyslexic, other-learning-disabled, and normal boys and girls; we have found that the normal boys *share* with dyslexic boys a tendency to make dysphonemic-sequencing errors far more frequently than do girls. The normal boys are rescued, however, by their overall excellence in word-finding; normal boys are *better* than normal girls in terms of total active recall of vocabulary, whereas girls (when correct) are faster. Dyslexic children rank lowest on both score and latency measures. The dysphonemic-sequencing error tendency of normal boys detracted from the drama of their totally larger vocabularies; had we not penalized the normal boys for lack of phonetic detail/sequence precision, their vocabulary advantage would have outraged the Women's Liberation Movement!

Thus we have come to the point of convergence of evidence suggesting that all males, consistent with a slower-maturing neurological substrate (brain as a whole, left side in particular) process and
produce phonological sequences less well at early school ages; an
exaggerated degree of this "male lag" may be the other side of the
coin of special gifts in spatial-holistic strategies. If, either through
premature or excessively phonics-dependent instruction, such a male
fails in reading, or if there is additional deficit imposed by fluctuating conductive hearing loss or attentional problems, "dyslexia" will
result. Dysnomia, on the other hand cannot be thought of as "exaggerated male lag" and represents a departure in the quality, not
just the quantity of development. (Caution: that tells us nothing
about etiology, i.e., genetic versus brain insult. But males cannot
be said simply to have global left-brain "lag" unless (as implicit in
Tallal's and Rourke's 1976 reviews, already cited) we narrow the
focus of left-hemisphere-mediated processes to fine acoustical and/or
phonological distinctions, those precision-and-speed-requiring aspects of language.) We know that the right hemisphere semantically
"knows" a large vocabulary of words (Dennis and Whitaker, 1976)
and we can infer that in childhood this is even more likely to be so;
a right-hemisphere style is not incompatible with the picture we see
in dysphonemic-sequencing dyslexia or in normal boys. I think there
is a powerful analogy between this right–left analysis of language in
childhood and findings on the so-called "visual perception" form-
copying tests—which are really visuomotor tests. It is well known
that the same dyslexic child who is inadequate at copying forms at
age eight will, quite spontaneously, copy them perfectly at age
twelve; furthermore, Owen et al. (1971) have demonstrated that the
eight-year-old in question is an excellent judge of whether others'
copies, in fact, match the standard designs. With Rudel and Bro-
man-Petrovics (1979) I have reported a similar "lag and then leap"
phenomenon in the map-walking (route-finding) skills of a dyslexic
group. Pushing a pencil or one's whole body through a sequence
of moves may again be a left-hemisphere-mediated component (sequencing, again) of each of these "visual-spatial" tasks, so that even
an excellent right hemisphere lacks motor expressive outlet until
some critical "good-enough floor" threshold is reached—thought of
as a skill at the psychological level, the substrate maturing at the
neurological level. It is tempting to speculate from what we know

of myelogenetic schedules (Yakovlev and Lecours, 1967) as to what substrates may reach threshold in the second decade, even if no curve is ever jumped (from lower to higher percentile) and no ceiling is ever reached. From a practical point of view, prognosis may be best when examination reveals that weakness (whether "lag" or "deficit") is in a function for which "ceiling" is relatively early and universal (e.g., digit span, copying forms; twelve-year-old level is good for *life!*).

Correlational dyslexia

This rarest (I see one per year) and "purest" of the "pure" is illustrative of the discussions above (dominance and development, lateralization and lag) but of limited practical import. These children are usually reading at grade level (hence they would never make their way into the literature of dyslexia) and are of superior intelligence, without the least verbal–performance spread. They may be relatively low, i.e., just average, on the familiar trial of digit span, arithmetic, and coding. Their troubles, however, are hard to find unless, as a neuropsychologist, you detect imbalance of strategies. For example, in copying (direct and recall) a complex figure, such children may vacillate between and never integrate an "outer configuration" approach with a "bits-and-details" approach. In two extreme cases, the children spontaneously wrote with right hand, drew pictures with the left, and alternated hands when copying complex figures. Block design may show, and be slowed down by, similar indecisiveness. Digits backwards is low for age, whereas digits forwards may be above age expectations. Matching (within modality) from temporally ordered sequences to spatial-simultaneous "equivalences" is selectively difficult. On timed coordination tasks (e.g., foot-and-finger tapping) the right-preferring child may be faster than average on the right and slower than average on the left, resulting in a huge right–left asymmetry. All of the findings disappear, without remediation, in the second decade (after puberty). I leave it to the reader to review developmental neuroanatomy, particularly myelogenesis (Yakovlev and Lecours, 1967) and hazard his own speculations as to the mechanism underlying this clinical syndrome, as well as formulate his own "treatment" advice for parents and teachers.

Hand, foot, and eye preference patterns

Although I have eschewed repetition of some of the older proposed correlates of dyslexia, there is one from which I have tried in vain to escape. I have been haunted by the issue of left-handedness (pathological or familial), left-eyedness, and degrees of right-handedness. I continue to see a majority of "not strictly right-preferring" children in a clinical setting, with 65% accounted for by the description "right-handed, right-footed, and left-eyed." As one might suspect, centrally determined left-eyedness has to do with an oculomotor function, scanning (Money, 1972), and may account for right-to-left scan direction preference as a risk factor in early reading. As a "marker" of variation in organization of cerebral asymmetry (dominance) left-eyedness turns out to be an interesting correlate of familial left-handedness (correlation coefficient of 0.8, centrally determined left-eyed have at least one left-handed first-degree relative; five years' retrospective chart review, my own unpublished data). Annett (1964, 1972) has demonstrated that the range of degrees of cerebral ambilaterality is represented in a far-from-bimodal distribution of manual asymmetry. Putting together the left-eyed, the incompletely right-handed, and the overtly left-handed, we confront a set of motor markers for what may be partial or risk factor correlates of dyslexia. The issue is allied to the larger controversy about distribution of abilities in left-handers, as Witelson (1976) makes explicit in her discussion of the putative bilateral spatial representation in her right-handed dyslexic group. Verbal IQ and language development in young children (4 and 6.5 years) has been reported to conform to a rank order highest for fully (RRR) congruous right-preferring children (McBurney and Dunn, 1976). With such young children the confounding variable is maturation rate as a whole underlying both clearly expressed lateral preference and any other skill measured. Among infantile hemiplegics, familial sinistrality is associated with more severe intellectual and language handicap in right hemiplegics and left hemiplegic males (Annett, 1973). In my clinical retrospective chart reviews, a confounding but intriguing variable is the occupational bias, toward engineers, artists, architects, mechanics, musicians and other "right-hemisphere dominant" types of skills, among the adult relatives of the noncongruous (mostly RRL) and nondextral patients. (We rarely have access to data about eyedness or the full spectrum of handedness.) Within one family, there may *not* be tight intercorrelations of non-right-handedness, occupation bias, and history of reading disability. Analysis of the variables is exceedingly complex and makes me wary of interpretation of results in normative sample studies of skewed ability in nondextrals, even when the issue of "pathological" determination of motor preference is set aside. Anatomical evidence for ambicerebrality in nondextrals (LeMay, 1976) tempts me to relate the problem of skewed abilities in nondextrals to the reportedly unpredictable "either spatial or linguistic" imbalance found with callosal agenesis (Dennis, 1977). There is a possibility that ambicerebrality, or lack of cerebral lateral asymmetry of function, may predispose an individual to imbalanced intellect or overspecialization of the sort postulated by Symmes and Rappaport (1972) and Witelson (1976). One can only conclude that noncongruous dextrals and nondextrals experience developmental "risks" for which we have not discovered clear biological reasons or compensatory advantages (unless one proposes later better recovery from aphasia as the long-term *raison d'être*).

Summary statement

In summary, most school-age children with at least average intelligence, no major emotional maladjustment, and no neurodevelopmental signs who present with dyslexia really have dyslexia-plus syndrome. (Refer to Table 17-1.) "Dyslexia-plus" and "pure dyslexia" (see Table 17-3) children share deficits falling within the general categories of speech, language, and verbal memory, when contrasted with nondyslexic children in their age group. The dyslexia-plus group (Denckla, 1977b) has milder oral language problems which are compounded by patchy dyscontrol-attentional (most common), fine and graphomotor (very common), and visuospatial (least common) deficits. The purely dyslexic children may also have profiles of patchy impairment but are more likely to have restricted and more severe spoken language deficits, although most in this group are not considered to have significant speech or language problems before they enter school. Tentative conclusions are that a high degree of proficiency in certain aspects of spoken language, including speed and accuracy, is *necessary* for successful early reading (decoding); and that *average* development with respect to perceptual, motor, spatial, or other cognitive abilities is not sufficient to spontaneously compensate for these specific deficits. There is no such thing as "dyslexia," if by "thing" we mean a single entity. Even when "pure," dyslexia is a life complaint which means that outside of the particular constraints of the world of books, the person's subtle deficits do not obviously handicap him (her). In the sense that there are such subtle brain problems or deficits (of several etiologies and even several types, with no established one-to-one correspondence between etiology and clinical type), then there *is* such a thing as dyslexia.

There appear to be various forms of dyslexia, with clinical presentations and life histories distinctive to each. Not surprisingly, all forms seem to reflect deficiencies in traditionally left-hemisphere-dependent neuropsychological functions. "Developmental lag" and "permanent deficit" may characterize different forms and components within forms, as exemplified by dysphonemic-sequencing disorder. A spectrum of risk factors has been presented, dysnomia being the most serious and specific to dyslexia and noncongruous motor preference pattern (RRL) residing at the other extreme. Pieces of the puzzle include sex differences and cognitive style variations in neuropsychological task profile. Omitted from, but overlapping with, the factors discussed here is the huge problem of attention; in fact, if asked what is necessary and sufficient for normal acquisition of reading, I might paraphrase Freud and answer, "To speak and to work."

LANGUAGE AND THOUGHT:
RELATIONSHIP AND PROGNOSIS

In the opening paragraphs of this chapter I proposed the analogy, "Aphasia is to dementia as specific developmental disability is to MBD and/or mental retardation." For the child whose index symptom is dyslexia, a subtle disorder of language may have social and emotional consequences far beyond those of reaction to failure in reading and academic work. Sometimes there is the paradox that the once-dyslexic person prefers to get information from reading rather than from lectures or discussions. Those of us who follow these youngsters into adolescence are impressed with the problems posed for them by independent social or job functioning. We realize then the usefulness of rapid comprehension and full fluency (Rutherford, 1977). For those whose language is impaired enough to come to clinical attention in the preschool years, the situation is even more serious. Here the clinician becomes involved in the controversy about thought existing independent of and prior to language (Vigotsky, 1962) as well as the role of speech in self-control (Luria, 1961).

The developmentally language-impaired present us with an "experiment of nature" in this ontogenetic sequence of language and intelligence. My own clinical experience has confirmed my neurologist's bias toward "splitting" rather than "lumping," for language is not one monolithic "thing" (and neither is "thought," although of the latter, of course, we know even less). The word-deaf develop like the deaf; their nonverbal scores on conventional psychometric tests drop after age seven years, even if there has been excellent remedial work with slow, steady improvement in spoken language. If one designs special tests for the word-deaf, that is, carefully chooses what sort of "thought" or problem-solving is to be utilized, then, as with the deaf, some normal ability may be demonstrated (Furth, 1966). Age-appropriate changes in motor function and EEG rhythms usually reassure us that falling IQ scores do not signify progressive deterioration of brain tissue, and "good-enough" basal conversational skills as well as vocational skills can be achieved in the developmentally word-deaf. Those who are "hyperlexic" at age three years tend to arouse false hopes in parents and professionals alike; but, unlike the reported cases of acquired verbal auditory agnosia (Rapin et al., 1977) these developmental cases do not comprehend what they read aloud any better than they comprehend what they hear (Huttenlocher and Huttenlocher, 1973; Elliot and Needleman, 1976).

For children with less severe syndromes (and presumably a substrate of less extensive bilateral lesions), time may bring higher scores on tests like performance IQ and Raven's Coloured Progressive Matrices, and special aptitudes, usually "right-hemisphere-dependent" emerge; these are the late-bloomers; often their genetic substrate is suggestive of "right-hemisphere style" reflected in familial occupations. Yet certain kinds of "thought" or problem-solving which depend upon verbal or analytic strategies remain impaired, even when the total context is one of solid life progress. The cost in terms of slowness may lead to abandonment of verbal activities in favor of a less social as well as less academic life. Yet it appears that a basal level of some verbal competence has made possible the development of the average nonverbal abilities on standard tests; and that ability to comprehend spoken language, semantically if not syntactically, is critical at this basal or permissive level. Word-finding appears to be more critical than phonemic-phonetic precision, again at the basal level. Remarkable talents and accomplishments notwithstanding, the moderately language-impaired do demonstrate that the elusive "G" of general intelligence is not fully accessible when the "S" (specific) contribution of precise language is inadequate. The next challenge is to chart the contributions to intelligence of those *other* nonlanguage, nonanalytic brain systems so recently emerging into focus from historic dominance of language (Denckla, 1978a, b).

Tests Available for the Assessment of the Speech and Language Status of Children.

I. Sources which list multiple tests of a variety of functions
    1. Dennis, Maureen and Whitaker, Harry A. (1976). Language acquisition following hemidecortication: linguistic superiority of the left over the right hemisphere. *Brain and Language 3,* 404–433.
    2. Gaddes, William H. and Crockett, David J. (1975). The Spreen-Benton Aphasia Tests, normative data as a measure of normal language development. *Brain and Language 2* 257–280.
    3. Mattis, S., French, J. H., and Rapin, I. (1975). Dyslexia in children and young adults: three independent neuropsychological syndromes. *Devel. Med. Child. Neurol. 17,* 150–163.

II. Sources which describe tests of a single function; tests available by writing to first author, unless (*) indicates test materials available from publisher's catalog.

A. Tests of Comprehension (Receptive Language)
   1. The Token Test*
      Spreen, O. and Gaddes, W. H. (1969). Developmental norms
      for 15 neuropsychological tests, ages 6 to 15. *Cortex 5,*
      171–191.
      Noll, J. D. (1970). "The use of the token test with children."
      Paper presented at the annual convention of the American
      Speech and Hearing Association, New York, 1970.
   2. Single-word vocabulary comprehension
      Dunn, L. M. (1965). Peabody Picture Vocabulary Test. Circle
      Pines, Minnesota, American Guidance Service* (available
      through Western Psychological).
   3. Syntax
      Dennis, Maureen and Kohn, Bruno (1975). Comprehension
      of syntax in infantile hemiplegics after cerebral hemidecor-
      tication: left hemisphere superiority. *Brain and Language 2,*
      472–482.
      Menyuk, Paula (1963). A preliminary evaluation of gram-
      matical capacity in children. *Journal of Verbal Learning and
      Verbal Behavior 2,* 429–439.
      Menyuk, Paula (1963). Syntactic structures in the language
      of children. *Child Development 34,* 407–422.
B. Tests of Repetition*
   1. Digit Span subtest from Wechsler Intelligence Test for Chil-
      dren. Revised, 1975, New York: The Psychological Cor-
      poration.
   2. Sentence Memory (at each age level), from Stanford-Binet In-
      telligence Test, 1960, New York: Houghton-Mifflin Company.
C. Tests of Naming
   1. Picture-naming (pictured objects)
      Jansky, J. J. and DeHirsch, K. *Preventing Reading Failure*
      (1973). New York: Harper and Row.
      Denckla, M. B. and Rudel, R. G. (1976). Naming of object-
      drawings by dyslexic and other learning-disabled children.
      Brain and Language 3, 1–15.
   2. Repeated naming (different classes of stimuli)
      Denckla, M. B. and Rudel, R. G. (1974). Rapid "automa-
      tized" naming of pictured objects, colors, letters and num-
      bers by normal children. *Cortex 10,* 186–202.

Denckla, M. B. and Rudel, R. G. (1976). Rapid "automatized" naming (R.A.N.): dyslexia differentiated from other learning disabilities. *Neuropsychologia 14*, 471–479.

References

Alajouanine, T. and Lhermitte, F. (1965). Acquired aphasia in children. *Brain 88*:653–662.

Ames, M. D., Plotkin, S. A., Winchester, R. A., and Atkins, T. E. (1970). Central auditory imperception: a significant factor in congenital rubella deafness. *J.A.M.A. 213*:419–421.

Annett, M. (1964). A model of the inheritance of handedness and cerebral dominance. *Nature (London) 204*:59–60.

Annett, M. (1972). The distribution of manual asymmetry. *Br. J. Psychol. 63*:343–358.

Annett, M. (1973). Laterality of childhood hemiplegia and the growth of speech and intelligence. *Cortex 9*:4–33.

Bakker, D. J. (1972). *Temporal Order in Disturbed Reading.* Rotterdam: Rotterdam University Press.

Basser, L. S. (1962). Hemiplegia of early onset and the faculty of speech with special reference to the effects of hemispherectomy. *Brain 85*: 427-460.

Benton, A. L. (1975). Developmental dyslexia: neurological aspects, in *Advances in Neurology,* Vol. 7, W. J. Friedlander (ed). New York: Raven Press.

Branch, C., Milner, B., and Rasmussen, T. (1964). Intracarotid sodium amytal for the lateralization of cerebral dominance. *J. Neurosurg. 21*: 399-405.

Boder, E. (1971). Developmental dyslexia: prevailing diagnostic concepts and a new diagnostic approach, in *Progress in Learning Disabilities,* Vol. II, H. R. Myklebust (ed). New York: Grune & Stratton.

Chase, R. A. (1967). Abnormalities in motor control secondary to congenital sensory deficits: a case study, in *Symposium on Oral Sensation and Perception,* J. S. Bosma (ed). Springfield, Ill.: Charles C. Thomas.

Chess, S. (1971). Autism in children with congenital rubella. *J. Autism Child Schizophrenia 1*:33–47.

Critchley, MacDonald (1970). *The Dyslexic Child.* Springfield, Ill.: Charles C. Thomas.

Denckla, M. B. (1974). Language Disorders, in *The Child with Disabling Illness,* J. Downey and N. Low (eds). Philadelphia: W. B. Saunders.

Denckla, M. B. (1977a). The neurological basis of reading disability, in *Reading Disability: a Human Approach to Learning,* 3rd ed., F. G. Roswell and G. Natchez (eds). New York: Basic Books.

Denckla, M. B. (1977b). Minimal brain dysfunction and dyslexia: beyond diagnosis by exclusion, in *Child Neurology,* M. E. Blaw, I. Rapin, and M. Kinsbourne (eds). New York: Spectrum Publications.

Denckla, M. B. (1978a). Critical review of "electroencephalographic and neurophysiological studies in dyslexia," in A. L. Benton and D. Pearl (eds). *Dyslexia,* New York: Oxford University Press.

Denckla, M. B. (1978b). Minimal brain dysfunction: current understanding of MBD and related disorders (e.g. hyperactivity and learning disability) in relation to educational policy and practice, in *Education and the Brain,* J. Chall and A. Mirsky (eds). National Society for the Study of Education, Chicago: University of Chicago Press.

Denckla, M. B. and Rudel, R. G. (1976a) Naming of pictured objects by dyslexic and other learning-disabled children. *Brain and Language 3*: 1–15.

Denckla, M. B. and Rudel, R. G. (1976b). Rapid "automatized" naming; dyslexia differentiated from other learning disabilities. *Neuropsychologia 14*:471–479.

Denckla, M. B., Rudel, R. G., and Broman, M. (1979). Spatial orientation in normal, learning-disabled, and neurologically-impaired children, in *Maturational and Biological Factors in Language and Cognition,* D. Caplan (ed). Cambridge, Mass.: M.I.T. Press (in press).

Dennis, Maureen (1977). Cerebral dominance in three forms of early brain disorder, in *Child Neurology,* M. E. Blaw, I. Rapin and M. Kinsbourne (eds). New York: Spectrum Publications.

Dennis, Maureen and Kohn, Bruno (1975). Comprehension of syntax in infantile hemiplegics after cerebral hemidecortication: left-hemisphere superiority. *Brain and Language 2*:472–482.

Dennis, Maureen and Whitaker, Harry A. (1976). Language acquisition following hemidecortication: linguistic superiority of the left over the right hemisphere. *Brain and Language 3*:404–433.

Doehring, Donald G. (1976). Evaluation of two models of reading disability, in *The Neuropsychology of Learning Disorders: Theoretical Approaches,* R. M. Knights and D. J. Bakker (eds). Baltimore: University Park Press.

Elliott, Dale E., and Needleman, Rosa M. (1976). The syndrome of hyperlexia. *Brain and Language 3*:339–349.

Furth, H. G. (1966). *Thinking without Language: the Psychological Implications of Deafness.* New York: Free Press.

Gascon, G., Victor, D., Lombroso, C. T., and Goodglass, H. (1973). Language disorder, convulsive disorder, and electroencephalographic abnormalities. *Arch. Neurol. 28*:156–162.

Goldstein, R. (1967). Electrophysiologic evaluation of hearing, in *Deafness in Childhood,* F. McConnell and P. H. Ward (eds). Nashville, Tenn.: Vanderbilt University Press.

Hauser, S. L., DeLong, G. R., and Rosman, N. P. (1975). Pneumographic findings in the infantile autism syndrome—a correlation with temporal lobe disease. *Brain 98*:667–688.

Heilman, K. M., Tucker, D. M., and Valenstein, E. (1976). A case of mixed transcortical aphasia with intact naming. *Brain 99*:415–426.

Huttenlocher, P. R. and Huttenlocher, J. (1973). A study of children with hyperlexia. *Neurology (Minneap.) 23*:1107–1115.

Ingram, T. T. S. (1969). Developmental disorders of speech, in *Handbook of Clinical Neurology*, Vol. 4, *Disorders of Speech, Perception and Symbolic Behavior*, P. J. Vinken and G. W. Bruyn (eds). Amsterdam: North Holland.

Jansky, J. (1978). A critical review of "some developmental and predictive precursors of reading disabilities, in *Dyslexia: An Appraisal of Current Knowledge*, A. L. Benton (ed). New York: Oxford University Press.

Johnson, Doris J. (1977). Psychoeducational evaluation of children with learning disabilities: study of auditory processes, in *Learning Disabilities and Related Disorders: Facts and Current Issues*, J. G. Millichap (ed). Chicago: Yearbook Medical Publishers.

Kinsbourne, M. (1970). The cerebral basis of lateral asymmetries in attention. *Acta Psychologica 33*:193–201.

Kinsbourne, M. (1974). Direction of gaze and distribution of cerebral thought processes. *Neuropsychologia 12*:279–281.

Kinsbourne, M. (1977). Selective difficulties in learning to read, write, and calculate, in *Learning Disabilities and Related Disorders: Facts and Current Issues*, J. G. Millichap (ed). Chicago: Yearbook Medical Publishers.

Landau, W. M., Goldstein, R., and Kleffner, F. R. (1960). Congenital aphasia: a clinicopathologic study. *Neurology 10*:915–921.

LeMay, Marjorie (1976). Morphological cerebral asymmetries of modern man, fossil man, and non-human primate. *Ann. N.Y. Acad. Sci. 280*: 349–366.

Lenneberg, E. H. (1964). Language disorders in childhood. *Harvard Educ. Rev. 34*:152–177.

Lenneberg, E. H. (1967). *Biological Foundations of Language*. New York: Wiley.

Lieben, Beatrice (1976). Personal communication.

Luria, A. R. (1961). *The Role of Speech in the Regulation of Normal and Abnormal Behavior*. London: Pergamon Press.

Mattis, Steven (1978). Dyslexia syndromes: a working hypothesis that works, in A. L. Benton (ed). New York: Oxford University Press.

Mattis, S., French, J. H., and Rapin, I. (1975). Dyslexia in children and young adults: three independent neuropsychological syndromes. *Dev. Med. Child Neurol. 17*:150–163.

McBurney, A. K. and Dunn, H. G. (1976). Handedness, footedness, eyedness: a prospective study with special reference to the development of speech and language skills, in *The Neuropsychology of Learning Dis-*

orders: Theoretical Approaches, R. M. Knights and D. J. Bakker (eds). Baltimore: University Park Press.

Money, Jean (1972). Studies on the function of sighting dominance. *Quart. J. Exp. Psychol. 24*:454–464.

Morley, M. E. (1965). *The Development and Disorders of Speech in Child-hood,* 2nd ed. Edinburgh: E. and S. Livingstone, Ltd.

Nelson, Hazel E. and Warrington, Elizabeth K. (1976). Developmental spelling retardation, in *The Neuropsychology of Learning Disorders: Theoretical Approaches,* R. M. Knights and D. J. Bakker (eds). Baltimore: University Park Press.

Owen, F. W., Adams, P. A., Forrest, T., Stolz, L. M., and Fisher, S. (1971). Learning disorders in children: sibling studies. *Monograph of the Society for Research in Child Development,* Vol. 36, no. 4. Chicago: University of Chicago Press.

Peters, J. E., Romine, J. S., and Dyckman, R. A. (1975). A special neurological examination of children with learning disabilities. *Dev. Med. Child, Neurol. 17*:63–78.

Pirozzolo, F. J., Rayner, K., and Whitaker, H. A. (1977). Left hemisphere mechanisms in dyslexia: a neuropsychological case study. (Presented at the Fifth Annual Meeting of International Neuropsychology Society, February 5, 1977.)

Rapin, I. and Graziani, L. J. (1967). Auditory evoked responses in normal, brain-damaged, and deaf infants. *Neurology (Minneap.) 17*:881–894.

Rapin, I., Mattis, S., Rowan, A. J., and Golden, G. G. (1977). Verbal auditory agnosia in children. *Dev. Med. Child Neurol. 19*:192–207.

Rourke, Byron P. (1976). Reading retardation in children: developmental lag or deficit, in *The Neuropsychology of Learning Disorders: Theoretical Approaches,* R. M. Knights and D. J. Bakker (eds). Baltimore: University Park Press.

Rudel, R. G. and Denckla, M. B. (1979). The effect of varying stimulus context on word-finding ability in normal, dyslexic, and other learning-disabled children. Submitted for publication.

Rutherford, David (1977). Speech and Language Disorders and MBD, in *Learning Disabilities and Related Disorders: Facts and Current Issues,* J. G. Millichap (ed). Chicago: Year Book Medical Publishers.

Rutter, Michael (1974). The development of infantile autism. *Psychol. Med. 4*:147–163.

Rutter, Michael (1978). Prevalence and types of dyslexia, in *Dyslexia—An Appraisal of Current Knowledge,* A. L. Benton (ed). New York: Oxford University Press.

Rutter, M. and Yule, W. (1975). The concept of reading retardation. *J. Child Psychol. Psychiat. 16*:181–197.

Satz, P., Friel, J., and Rudegeair, F. (1974). Differential changes in the acquisition of developmental skills in children who later became dyslexic: a three-year follow-up, in *Plasticity and Recovery of Function in the Central Nervous System,* D. Stein, J. Rosen, and N. Butters (eds). New York: Academic Press.

Satz, P., Taylor, H. G., Friel, J., and Fletcher, J. (1978). Some developmental and predictive precursors of reading disabilities: a six-year follow-up, in *Dyslexia: An Appraisal of Current Knowledge,* A. L. Benton (ed). New York: Oxford University Press.

Senf, G. M. (1969). Development of immediate memory for bisensory stimuli in normal children and children with learning disorders. *Dev. Psychol. 6:* pt 2, 28.

Shankweiler, Donald and Liberman, Isabelle, Y. (1976). Exploring the relations between reading and speech, in *The Neuropsychology of Learning Disorders: Theoretical Approaches,* R. M. Knights and D. J. Bakker (eds). Baltimore: University Park Press.

Symmes, J. S. and Rappaport, J. L. (1972). Unexpected reading failure, *Am. J. Orthopsychiat. 42:*82–91.

Tallal, Paula (1976). Auditory perceptual factors in language and learning disabilities, in *The Neuropsychology of Learning Disorders: Theoretical Approaches,* R. M. Knights and D. J. Bakker (eds). Baltimore: University Park Press.

Unger, Dorothy (1976). Personal communication.

Vellutino, Frank R. (1978a). Toward an understanding of dyslexia: psychological factors in specific reading disability, in *Dyslexia—an Appraisal of Current Knowledge,* A. L. Benton (ed). New York: Oxford University Press.

Vellutino, Frank R. (1978b). *Theory and Research in Dyslexia.* Cambridge, Mass.: M.I.T. Press.

Vigotsky, L. S. (1962). *Thought and Language.* Cambridge, Mass.: M.I.T. Press.

Wada, J. A. (1969). Interhemispheric sharing and shift of cerebral speech function. *Excerpta Medica Int. Congr. Series 193:*296–297.

Witelson, Sandra F. (1976). Abnormal right hemisphere specialization in developmental dyslexia, in *The Neuropsychology of Learning Disorders: Theoretical Approaches,* R. M. Knights and D. J. Bakker (eds). Baltimore: University Park Press.

Wolf-Ward, Maryanne (1978). The word-finding process and specific reading disability. Qualifying paper submitted for the Ph.D. requirement, Harvard University Graduate School of Education.

Yakolev, P. I. and Lecours, A. (1967). The myelogenetic cycles of regional maturation of the brain, in *Regional Development of the Brain in Early Life,* A. Minkowski, (ed). Oxford: Blackwell.

18
The Syndrome of Hyperactivity

MARTHA BRIDGE DENCKLA AND
KENNETH M. HEILMAN

TERMINOLOGY

Hyperactivity is an index sign (or symptom) of excessive restlessness or inappropriate, non-goal-directed movement.

*Hyperactive synd*rome is a term which designates a set of behaviors in which hyperactivity is often the index sign (symptom); the younger the child, the more likely the occurrence of hyperactivity.

The hyperactive child is an ambiguous term which may be used to designate either the child who manifests hyperactivity, *or* the child who exhibits the hyperactive syndrome. (In this chapter, the term will indicate the presence of the hyperactive syndrome.)

MBD (minimal brain dysfunction) means that an observed disorder of behavioral or mental status is inferred to be based on brain abnormality (i.e., a significant part of the etiology is physical). This vague, overly inclusive term does not suffice for more sophisticated clinical neuropsychological diagnosis and teatment.

HISTORY

Still (1902) described children (mainly boys) who were hyperactive as a result of gross brain lesions. He also described children of normal intelligence who did not have brain damage but were nevertheless hyperactive. He linked this hyperactivity to a variety of etiological factors, both genetic and behavioral. Tredgold (1908), however, postulated that hyperactive behavior followed minimal brain injury, e.g., that caused by anoxia. Similarly, most early workers assumed that brain damage was causing this disorder even if it could not be grossly demonstrated—hence, the term *minimal brain damage*. Childers (1935), however, noted that hyperactivity could be related to brain damage in only a small number of children and he attempted to find criteria which would help differentiate brain-damaged from non-brain-damaged hyperactive children. Since one cannot infer brain damage from behavior, Bax and McKeith (1963) recommended that the term *minimal brain dysfunction* (MBD) replace minimal brain damage. Although there are many other terms (e.g., the World Health Organization has selected the term *hyperkinetic syndrome* and the American Psychiatric Association calls it *hyperkinetic reaction of childhood,* and has recently introduced *attentional deficit syndrome*), many investigators have legitimately asked if there really is a *syndrome* (a set of symptoms which occur together: the sum of signs of any morbid state—*Dorland's Medical Dictionary,* 24th edition).

CLINICAL DESCRIPTION

Clinical symptoms are in part dependent on both age and environmental factors. In addition, there are both behavioral manifestations and neurological findings. "Hyperactivity" is not a syndrome; it is the index sign shared by a group of syndromes involving behavioral difficulties in children.

Motility disorders are important correlates of the behavioral disorder that we are interested in, but they are not the core of the problem. It is important to note, as Kinsbourne (1973) does, that in child development bodily activity reflects different things about mental activity at different stages. Only when a child is very young does the physical activity level go along with the thought processes. Kinsbourne states (1973) that in the course of *all* children's development, thought increasingly dissociates itself from overt movement. The implications for longitudinal follow-up of the "hyperactive syndrome" are two-fold. First, there is no question that, if one focuses on consequences of physical restlessness (the child who runs away from you in a supermarket, who takes everything off the shelves, who breaks your grandmother's china), these problems will go away. Entering their second decade of life, overtly restless, hyperactive children will outgrow overt, physical restlessness. But, as one mother said, "his body doesn't wander anymore, but his mind sure does." That expresses the core of the problem. Second, when diagnosis is at issue in the adolescent, the problem of the wandering mind comes more and more center-stage. One adolescent told his physician, "My mind is like a television set on which someone is always switching the channels." There is a great deal to be learned from children who, although academically adequate and motorically no longer restless, have persistently high Conners ratings of behavioral deficiency. Again, to quote Kinsbourne, if you happen to be bright and gifted enough at the particular kinds of things that the school teachers want you to learn, to the great consternation of the school teacher, you will learn "with half an eye and half an ear." So, there are children who are not academically disabled but who underachieve relative to measured intellectual potential because they do not work hard and hand in assigned work. They are often viewed as "lazy" or "unmotivated" even if not disruptive or aggressive.

A child with the hyperactive syndrome may present with one of five different clinical pictures. These are discussed in order of frequency and presumed prevalence in clinical settings.

The immaturity syndrome
The most common picture is the immaturity syndrome, clinically best described as "developmental lag" (whether or not the mechanism is really "simple delay"). These children act too young for their age and are distractable and impulsive. Although one would suspect from the name that the major behavioral sign would be hyperactivity, several studies have demonstrated that hyperactive children

do not have more daily activity than normal children (Pope, 1970). Rather than having overall increased activity, the main problem is that these children are active at inappropriate times. Rather than hyperactivity, the three major features of the behavioral syndrome appear to be: (1) inattentiveness and short attention span (decreased vigilance); (2) a learning disability; and (3) misconduct which is often refractory to punishment.

Often the first signs of the hyperactive syndrome can be seen in infancy. These children often show an irregularity in both their physiological and psychological functioning. They tend to have sharp mood swings, appear to have an increased activity pattern, and cry readily. Frequently, these infants sleep poorly (Ross and Ross, 1976).

At the preschool level, hyperactive children may show, in addition to inattentiveness, profound conduct problems with low frustration tolerance, fits of violence, inappropriate behavior, destructive behavior, lack of concern for others, disobedience, or accident-proneness. Others are quiet but impersistent and passively noncompliant with demands.

At the elementary school level, the behavior problems associated with the hyperactive syndrome become more manifest to the community. Now, not only does the child disrupt the home but also the school and the neighborhood. Often the children now appear to have superimposed psychiatric difficulties because of their poor self-concept (Ament, 1974) and rejection by parents, sibs, peers, and teachers. These children frequently have a co-existent learning disability and appear not to acquire social skills (Ross and Ross, 1976). In the school, the main problems are not only misconduct and poor social skills but also poor attention and work habits. Some children are not able to stay in their seats; others sit but do not follow oral directions. They do not correct or learn from their mistakes as well as others do. Their performance is erratic and, although they may be intelligent, they fail to learn as rapidly as their peers; if of superior endowment, they learn well but do not produce work upon demand.

Douglas (1976) has coined the term "stop, look and listen" for this group of children. Often they behave well during the structured, fast-moving portions of the examination, particularly on the first visit. Only when the familiarity of the setting and the unstructured portions of the time in the office promote relaxation will behavior become uncontrolled. The examination is remarkable for "slow-for-age" motor coordination and excessive overflow movements for age (Denckla and Rudel, 1978).

Several authors have reported that hyperactivity diminishes with adolescence and adulthood (Werry, 1968). However, others have noted that, although the hyperactivity diminishes, there remain the problems of poor educational achievement and psychopathology (Weiss et al., 1971; Wender, 1976), including attentional and social-emotional immaturity, with pervasively poor self-esteem. Sometimes, the main residual problem is difficulty with the law. More frequently, scholastic and vocational underachievement—the not-doing-as-one-should—is more devastating than the wrong-doing. It may be that if followed into their thirties, if they were not emotionally disturbed by what happened to them during their formative years, "hyperactive" children of the common "immature-for-age" type would show spontaneous improvement or would learn compensatory strategies.

What we have called the "immaturity syndromes" conforms to the usual description of the hyperactive syndrome but we think it is worth distinguishing four other syndromes which are probably often lumped together with the immaturity syndrome, but whose distinguishing features may indicate a different pathogenesis and response to treatment.

Prechtl's choreiform syndrome

Prechtl's choreiform syndrome was originally described 16 years ago, but has been revised in subsequent descriptions to deemphasize reading disability (Touwen and Prechtl, 1970). It is a subtle, involuntary movement disorder. These children are often very bright, and quick. As a matter of fact, their motor coordination may be very good but it is repeatedly interrupted by irregular jerky movements. Such children are also prone to tic behavior (Denckla et al., 1976), sometimes observed to have evolved into the Gilles de la Tourette syndrome.

An epidemiological study by Wolff and Hurwitz (1973) involved the detection of a single sign, choreiform movements, which oc-

curred in 11% of a previously unreferred and unselected public
school population. Wolff and Hurwitz have shown that if one looks
at the boys and girls with choreiform movements, comparing them
with age-matched and IQ-matched controls within the same school
system, then teachers' behavioral rating sheets show a definite and
significant correlation of certain behavioral characteristics such as
poor cooperation, impulsivity, general behavioral immaturity, clumsiness, and short attention span. Curiously, the girls with choreiform
movements had significantly higher IQ scores than their matched
controls, but this was not true of the boys. Nonetheless, the behavioral ratings on girls with choreiform movements revealed that
this motor sign of CNS dysfunction correlated significantly with a
cluster of behavioral "differentness" on the negative side of the
teacher evaluation spectrum.

Hypokinetic underactivated syndrome
Children in this group are distinctively hypokinetic and appear
under-aroused. They are often very sluggish and seem to need
more sleep. Their intellect may be normal, but they are poorly motivated and hence they under-achieve. They often have associated
signs implicating subcortical systems such as abnormalities of cerebellar function, eye movements, or postural reflexes, but these traditional neurological signs are subtle and do not indicate a progressive disease. They are therefore called "soft" signs. EEGs often show
slow activity, reported as "borderline because of excessive slow activity for age." Occasionally, unusual sleep activity or bursts suggestive of absence-like attacks may be reported.

Anhedonic drive syndrome
These children, described by Wender (1971), do not present themselves to neurologists as much as to psychiatrists. Often they are
categorized as schizophrenic. Older literature refers to brain-
damaged children as acting driven (showing stimulus hunger), and
this quality may be present in this syndrome. The subjects roam
around the environment as if trying to feed themselves in some way,
to find some elusive satisfaction. Often they have unmeasurable intelligence (due to lack of test-compliant behavior) or islands of
astonishing intelligence. Clumsiness is often the reason for neuro-

logical consultation. Poor interpersonal relations often overshadow other deficiencies, but restlessness, impulsivity, and lack of sustained attention make them a subset of "hyperactive" syndrome. Paul Wender's idea that anhedonia was fundamental through almost all of the MBD behavioral disorders, or "hyperactive syndrome" in all its forms, seems best suited to the driven, sullen, unhappy, remote children of this subset.

Episodic dyscontrol syndrome

The last group is difficult to name and surrounded by controversy. "Episodic dyscontrol," a term some reject on grounds of social implication, herein refers to children who have EEGs which look epileptiform. There is not enough follow-up data to say whether children in this rare "hyperactive" group ever do develop overt seizures, but anticonvulsants may improve their behavior disorder. They are clinically distinctive because, in addition to daily attentional-organizational problems, episodically they will explode, often with extremely violent behavior: one such child literally destroyed a principal's office. Every neurologist will recognize the relationship of the picture in childhood to the controversial "rage attacks" discussed in literature about adults, as well as the issues of interictal behavior and personality in persons with "temporal lobe epilepsy."

EVALUATION OF THE HYPERACTIVE CHILD

A complete evaluation of a child suspected of having the hyperactive syndrome is essential in order to: (1) confirm diagnosis of a brain-based disorder, (2) decide on the type of management, and (3) provide an objective assessment so that the effectiveness of treatment may be measured. Assessment of a hyperactive child usually requires a multidisciplinary approach—medical, educational, and psychological.

Medical evaluation

HISTORY

In obtaining history from parents, it is imperative to learn as much as possible about the mother's pregnancy (e.g., maternal age, parity, illness, drugs, alcohol, smoking, injuries, etc.); and the child's delivery, neonatal period (prematurity, respiratory distress, low Apgar, etc.), and infancy (feeding difficulty, sleeping difficulties, diseases, drugs, etc.). A detailed history of developmental milestones is also essential. Because there is frequently a family history, one must probe for familial hyperactivity and also determine whether other learning disabilities or psychiatric disorders (especially alcoholism, repeated surgery, and trouble with the law) are present in the family. The clinician must spend extra time to obtain from the parents the age of onset of the major behavioral characteristics and the factors which influence signs and symptoms. The parents' own style of child-rearing must be explicitly described. The school setting must be similarly investigated.

PHYSICAL AND NEUROLOGICAL EXAMINATION

Because hyperactive children have a high incidence of physical abnormalities, a thorough physical examination is imperative. Dysgenetic features and head circumference should be noted.

Neurological findings have been divided into "hard" and "soft" signs (Hertzig, Bortner, and Birch, 1969). Hard signs are reliable, reproducible, and are the type unequivocally associated with brain disease. Soft signs are of two types (Denckla, 1978). There are soft signs which are similar in kind to hard signs, but are of a lesser degree and significance. There are other soft signs in which the child acts or performs like a younger child. Hard signs are associated with brain damage. Although soft signs are frequently associated with MBD, their exact diagnostic or prognostic meaning is as yet unclear.

Hyperactivity is not usually apparent in the office, and the clinician must depend in part on other observations. The younger the child, the more likely is overt restlessness or noncompliance; the older the child, the more the clinician must look for the motor correlates of the syndrome, such as overflow movements or choreiform movements.

LABORATORY EVALUATIONS

The laboratory studies one selects should be based on history and physical findings. A strongly episodic or "phasic" history dictates an EEG. The EEG and psychophysiological tests or arousal may be worthwhile if the evaluator is familiar with norms for children.

Unless a patient has hard neurological findings, computer tomography brain scanning may be unnecessary, and in the absence of hard neurological signs, studies such as arteriography and pneumoencephalography are contraindicated. Blood tests or special chromosomal studies are indicated where the history or physical examination suggest an etiology, but at present, cannot be justified in the absence of such data.

Educational and intellectual assessment

INTELLIGENCE TESTS

The main reason for intelligence tests is to make certain that the hyperactive child is not retarded. Attentional deficits must be taken into account in the interpretation of scores. "Paradoxical" slowness of response on timed tests is also seen in "hyperactive" children. Specific profiles can suggest the diagnosis to the experienced clinician. The most common profile is that of low Digit Span, Coding, and Arithmetic. The most widely accepted and useful test is the *Wechsler Intelligence Scale for Children,* individually administered and not only scored but qualitatively assessed for error types.

ACHIEVEMENT TESTS

Readiness or achievement tests are designed to ascertain whether a child is ready for school or what he has achieved in school. In children with the hyperactive syndrome, periodic achievement tests may give objective evidence as to the success or failure of a treatment mode. Although many are available, the most frequently used are the *Metropolitan Achievement Test* and the *Peabody Individual Achievement Test.* Teacher rating scales and unstructured anecdotal descriptions of classroom adjustment are just as important as "standard" tests, because many older children do not produce on a daily basis what they can achieve on a test.

Behavioral assessment

Although a child's behavioral abnormalities may be seen in the clinic, they often are at least in part environmentally dependent. Even normal children, when fatigued before bedtime or when overstimulated, appear hyperactive, and hyperactive children, when slightly anxious or in the structured environment of the clinic, may appear normal. Therefore, the clinician must rely on parents' and teachers' observations. Narrative descriptions of a child's behavior are important; however, questionnaires are useful. Although abnormal behavior may affect the child's daily academic achievement as well as his performance on achievement and intelligence tests, equally diagnostically critical observations are those of the child's social behavior. Social adjustment assessment as determined by questionnaires is not only important for diagnostic reasons, but it is also the barometer of the success or failure of a treatment program.

There are many questionnaires (i.e., Werry-Weiss-Peters Activity Scale, 1968; Bell, Woldrop, and Weller Rating System, 1972). Some questionnaires have been designed for parents (i.e., Conners Parents Questionnaire, 1970), and others have been designed for teachers (Conners Teachers Rating Scale) (Conners, 1969).

MECHANISMS UNDERLYING THE HYPERACTIVE SYNDROME

The behavior of any organism is determined by an almost infinite number of independent and interdependent environmental and neuronal factors. Although there is a search for "the etiology" of the hyperactive syndrome, it is unlikely that this is a unitary disease (since "it" is not even a unitary behavioral syndrome).

Most research, unfortunately, has concentrated too prematurely on a "unitary" cause and has failed to define the population studied in clinical terms or has argued backwards from treatment success. Elegant EEG and psychophysical technology has been applied to studying a particular small "hyperactive" subgroup—sometimes so impaired that they fall outside the MBD category—and results extrapolated to the entire population. Conversely, all subtypes are mixed and when results of tests "do not differ from controls" the conclusion is reached that there is no abnormality, when in fact different abnormalities cancel each other out. For example, children with choreiform movements are very fast on motor tasks but children with "immaturity" syndrome are slow. Arguments towards unitary hypothesis, such as the catecholamine biochemical deficiency hypothesis of Wender, fail to take into account the nonspecific nature of the "successful stimulant treatment" as well as the transient and borderline nature of the "success" in many clinical subtypes.

Psychophysiological studies provide further evidence against a unitary hypothesis. Satterfield (1971), for example, has done many studies involving skin conductance and at certain times reports lower skin conductance, interpreted as low arousal but in other reports finds no difference in the arousal or even greater arousal in the so-called hyperactive subjects. It is to be noted that Satterfield's "hyperactive" subjects vary considerably in terms of IQ, in a few studies being actually retarded. More "modern" indices of CNS physiological activity such as evoked potentials and power-spectrum analysis of EEG, have yielded important and interesting results but, again, the absence of replication from one study to the other and the failure to define the nature of the populations make comparisons and conclusions particularly difficult. When careful clinical observations have been combined with evoked potentials, one comes out with studies such as that of Conners (1972) in which there are no less than seven different subgroups with different factor analytic characteristics existing before drug treatment and with allegedly different responses to treatment, suggesting that these are different disorders, all of them given a single name, "hyperactivity." The following is a brief review of some of the major theories. These theories are not mutually exclusive. Multiple factors might be implicated in any given case. Some factors may only place children "at risk," requiring other factors to cause the behavioral disorders.

Agent factors—minimal brain damage

Stills' (1902) description of the hyperactivity behavior associated with brain-damaged children has been replicated by many investigators. There have been several agents which have been incriminated as inducing this brain damage.

HYPOXIA

It has been postulated that hyperactivity is a result of hypoxia occurring either prenatally, perinatally, or postnatally (Handford, 1975). However, other studies have demonstrated that although perinatal hypoxia may induce cognitive and neurological dysfunction, hypoxia did not appear to induce hyperactivity (Graham et al.,

1962). Recently, there has been interest in maternal smoking which is also thought to induce hypoxia (Denson, Nanson, and McWatters, 1975).

LEAD POISONING

The two major sources of lead are paint and gasoline. Children who live in old houses are exposed to lead paints and children who live near heavily used roads are exposed to lead fumes and dust. Children with known lead poisoning may demonstrate hyperactivity (Wiener, 1970). David, Clark, and Voeller (1972) have provided epidemiologic evidence that lead exposure may be the major etiological agent in the hyperactive syndrome. Animal models have provided support. Not only does lead induce hyperactivity in rodents but there is symptomatic improvement with amphetamines and increased symptoms with phenobarbital (Silbergeld and Goldberg, 1974). Needleman (1978) has found neuropsychological deficits in children whose milk teeth contained higher lead levels; the nature of the deficits is strongly reminiscent of findings in studies devoted to "hyperactive" children's mental characteristics.

OTHER AGENTS

Radiation from both television and fluorescent lighting has been implicated by Ott (1974). Food allergies (Moyer, 1975) and food additives (Feingold, 1975) have also been suggested as agents which induce hyperactivity. Although there is some experimental evidence for both theories, there has been no double blind study which unequivocally supports them (Millichap, 1977).

Recently, the relationship between drugs which women have taken (e.g., alcohol, barbiturates) during pregnancy, and the hyperactive syndrome has gained the interest of investigators. Although animal models are being developed, the role of such agents in hyperactivity is at present undetermined.

Host factors

GENETIC

It has been noted that many parents of hyperactive children remember themselves as being hyperactive (Stewart and Olds, 1973). Genetic studies suggest that there is a genetic factor (Morrison and

Stewart, 1973). The exact mode of transmission has not been determined; however, Morrison and Stewart (1973) suggest a polygenetic theory.

DELAYED MATURATION ("DEVELOPMENTAL LAG")
Several investigators believe that delayed maturation caused the apparent motor, attentional, and behavioral immaturity of hyperactive children (Bax and McKeith, 1963; Laufer, Denhoff, and Solomons, 1957). Peters, Romine, and Dykman (1975) demonstrated that at a younger age, children with hyperactive syndrome showed more of a deficit when compared to normal children than they showed at older ages. However, this may depend upon which behavioral deficit is inspected at older ages. A persistent brain defect in a growing child may have changing behavioral manifestations. Oettinger et al. (1974) even demonstrated that bone age of children with hyperactivity was retarded when compared to age-matched controls; it is not yet clear whether puberty will be late in these children, so eventual adult bone length cannot be predicted.

PSYCHOGENIC
Many mothering and child-rearing techniques have been implicated in hyperactivity (Ross and Ross, 1976). However, many workers have suggested that there is a bidirectional effect. Although these children may be "difficult," parental attitudes toward these difficulties play a major role in behavioral outcome. The complexity of effects of parental interaction is increased if one considers that genetically determined hyperactive children may be raised by parents who themselves are impulsive and inattentive.

Brain Dysfunction
Although host factors besides those discussed above have been proposed, all would manifest themselves by brain dysfunction. Even proponents of some of the psychogenic theories (see above) believe that environmental and parental pressure cannot completely explain this behavior. External agents, although perhaps explaining hyperactivity in the exposed child, cannot explain hyperactivity in children not exposed to these agents.

CATECHOLAMINE HYPOTHESIS OF WENDER

Wender (1976) noted that signs and symptoms similar to those seen in MBD follow the pandemic of Von Economo's encephalitis. The causative virus induces the parkinsonian syndrome in adults by destroying the dopamine-containing neurons. Wender suggests that perhaps in children destruction of these neurons by viruses, lead, or other agents induces a hyperarousal state which is responsible for the resulting hyperactivity (Wender, 1971). In those cases where no agents exist, there is a genetic predisposition for a biochemical abnormality involving the monoaminergic neurons. As support of this hypothesis, Wender notes that MBD children respond to stimulant drugs (e.g., amphetamines) which, by a variety of mechanisms (e.g., increased release, decreased reuptake and breakdown, direct substitution) increase these neurotransmitters and increase activity in cortical inhibitory systems. Wender (1971) also notes that monoamines increase with age and with testosterone. These increases may account for the reduction of hyperactivity seen with puberty.

ATTENTIONAL AND INTENTIONAL THEORIES

There are several major problems with Wender's theory. No one has provided evidence that there are defects in monoamine metabolism in hyperactive children. The argument backwards from treatment is undermined, for it has been demonstrated that normal children may also benefit from amphetamines (Rapoport et al., 1978). Using a variety of psychophysiological measures of arousal, some investigators have demonstrated that some hyperactive children are hypoaroused rather than hyperaroused (Satterfield and Dawson, 1971) and amphetamines appear to work best on those with hypoarousal (Satterfield, Cantwell, and Satterfield, 1974).

Although hyperactivity syndrome may be associated with learning disabilities, the main defect appears to be attentional. The total amount of activity is not more than in normal children; rather, the major problem is that motor or mental activity is misdirected in hyperactive children. They are inattentive or distractable. If one looks over the hyperactive rating scales, a substantial portion of target questions refer to the child's attentional capacities. Studies of these children's vigilance (sustained attention) by techniques such as continuous performance reveal that they are inattentive (Conners, 1970; Douglas, 1976).

The neuropsychology of attention and arousal is in its infancy. There are many attentional models which have been superbly summarized by Lynn (1966). Sokolov (1963) has proposed a two-stage model where the cortex is responsible for stimulus analysis (novel vs. non-novel; significant vs. nonsignificant) and the reticular system, modulated by the cortex, is responsible for arousal (activation). It has been demonstrated that stimulation of certain cortical areas such as the frontal and inferior partietal lobes induces arousal; ablation of these areas induces inattention and hypoarousal (see Chapter 10 for a review of this literature). Lead encephalopathy as well as encephalitis lethargica involve not only the basal ganglia but also the cortex. The areas of the cortex which appear important for attention are secondary and tertiary association areas, and these areas are the last to mature and mature slower in boys than in girls. It is therefore possible that if there is brain dysfunction associated with certain forms of hyperactivity, it is these association areas which are malfunctioning.

Hyperactive children's conduct problems in part may be related to their inattention and hyperactivity; however, all of the antisocial behavior in these children cannot be explained by poor attention. As mentioned previously, some of these children appear hypoaroused. Using skin conduction and resistance, Hare (1969) and others have found reduced autonomic activity and have suggested that certain features of psychopathic behavior may be related to hypoarousal induced by cortical dysfunction. It appears that high autonomic activity is associated with anxiety. Because the psychopath has decreased anxiety and fear, his behavior is not modified by punishment.

Although an attentional defect may be responsible for the distractable behavior, it cannot completely account for the impulsive behavior seen in hyperactive children.

Still (1902), who first described hyperactive children, realized that "volition" was not an intellectual process and that volitional control was mainly "inhibitory." He noted that volition (inhibitory control) was maturationally slow to develop and varied considerably in different children. Variation, he believed, resulted from differences in both the environment and "in the innate capacity for the development of such control." Still noted that there are inattentive distractable children in whom inhibitory control is so far below standard that the question may be raised whether in such cases the defect is not the manifestation of a morbid condition. Kinsbourne (1973, 1977) has made some observations on impulsive style, which are similar to those of Still. He also notes that the position of this group on the reflectivity-impulsivity scale is far to the extreme in terms of the normal distribution. Kinsbourne suggests that as a normal person arrives at a solution to a problem cerebral activation progressively drops, approaching a "critical threshold at which point the subject will judge that uncertainty has been sufficiently reduced for a decision to be made. . . ." In the normal person, that criterion would be adaptively realistic; however, if the criterion of minimum activation would be prematurely reached, a premature decision would be made. Stimulants therefore raise the base state of activation and thus supply the impulsive individual with a higher initial level of activation.

Kennard (1939) noted that bilateral frontal-lobe lesions in animals induce hyperresponsiveness and perseverative activity. Both hyperactivity and hypokinesia have been reported in human patients with frontal-lobe lesions (see Chapter 12). Although it is not known what brain mechanisms underlie intention, because the frontal lobes have rich reciprocal connections with the reticular system (which mediates activation), the posterior neocortex (which mediates cognitive activity), the limbic system (which mediates drive states), and the motor systems, it would appear that one of the major functions of the frontal lobes is to mediate intention and volition. It is possible that in some cases, the disorder of volition first noted by Still (1902) may be related to frontal-lobe dysfunction.

TREATMENT

In 1937, Bradley prescribed benzadrine for headaches. He noted that the behavior and school performance of many hyperactive children improved when they were given the drug. Despite Bradley's observations, drug treatment for hyperactivity remains one of the most controversial topics in medicine. More recent studies, however, confirm

Bradley's observations and there is now well-documented evidence that stimulant drugs exert a beneficial effect on behavior and performance (Conners and Eisenberg, 1963; Werry and Sprague, 1970).

The major drugs used are dextroamphetamine and methylphenidate. Methylphenidate is used more frequently than amphetamines because it is more effective (Millichap and Fowler, 1967) and has fewer side effects (Gross and Wilson, 1974).

In regard to efficacy, there is a wide range of reported success. Approximately 70% of those treated respond and 10% get worse (Ross and Ross, 1976). Prior to instituting drug therapy, it is difficult to know who will improve. Although there is some research correlating catecholamine excretion with response to therapy, it appears that the best predictors are psychophysiological measures of hypoarousal such as EEG (Buchsbaum and Wender, 1973; Satterfield et al., 1973), skin conduction (Satterfield et al., 1974), and pupillary contraction (Knopp et al., 1973). Rapoport's work (1978) casts doubt on the specificity of stimulant effects.

When amphetamines or methylphenidate work, they do not decrease overall behavior but rather decrease extraneous behavior induced by distractability. In the classroom, the tasks which are most improved are those which require vigilance; however, performance on memory and intellectual tasks may also improve (Conners and Eisenberg, 1963). It is not clear if improved memory and intellectual function are independent factors or if they may be related to improved motivation and attention.

Not all children with hyperactivity are hypoaroused. Satterfield, Cantwell, and Satterfield (1974) also reported hyperactive children who were hyperaroused. These children appeared to respond less well to amphetamines. Denckla (1978) feels that hyperactive children with choreiform movements (Prechtl's choreiform syndrome) may develop serious side-effects.

The evaluation of a child's response to stimulant drugs is frequently based on casual observation by parents, teachers, and the clinician. Although in some cases, response to treatment is immediate and dramatic, this is not always the case. Even dramatic changes may represent a placebo effect (Knights and Hinton, 1969) and it is important that, when possible, prior to committing a child to long-term treatment, drug efficacy should be tested by a double-blind trial. Rather than casual reports, rating scales should be used. If a drug is proven to be efficacious, the child should be continually monitored with trial withdrawal periods. Sprague and Sleator (1976) have reported that smaller doses benefit academic attention than benefit social ratings; the higher doses needed for social improvement may adversely affect attention.

As with all medication, there are multiple potential side-effects; however, in general, side-effects with amphetamines and methylphenidate appear to be minimal. Occasionally there is temporary anorexia and insomnia. Tics may develop, particularly if choreiform movements were present (Denckla, 1976). Some children may show increased depressive emotionality and increased heart rate. Safer and Allen (1973) noted growth suppression. This may be a delay rather than a loss (Safer, Allen, and Barr, 1975). Others have failed to confirm growth retardation (Millichap, 1977). State dependency learning (that which is learned when one is taking a drug may not be retrieved in the absence of that drug) is a potential side-effect; however, it has not been found to be a major problem (Aman and Sprague, 1974).

In addition to amphetamines and methylphenidate, other stimulants have been used, including caffeine, pemoline (a CNS stimulant with reduced sympathomimetic effects), and imipramine (a tricyclic antidepressant). In general, they appear to work but not as effectively as amphetamines or methylphenidate. Very recently, each of these stimulants has been tried in adolescent and adult patients with histories or persistent signs of the hyperactive syndrome. Results are preliminarily reported to be promising.

Behavioral therapy and management principles
Most authorities agree that intervention should not be limited to drug therapy and that behavioral therapy can be effective.

Families with children who have hyperactivity frequently need counseling. The counseling may be informative and educational. If there are other members of the family who are disturbed, the members should be advised to seek the appropriate therapy.

Psychotherapy for the hyperactive child has been used, especially "brief" therapy (Weakland et al., 1974); however, as with many forms of psychotherapy, the efficacy is difficult to judge. Behavioral therapy (operant conditioning) and behavior modification have also been used successfully both in the home and at school (Ross and Ross, 1976; Willis and Lovaas, 1977.

Children of this type have not just a "book-learning" but a "life-learning" disability. Not only "b's and d's" but also "do's and dont's" constitute confusing learning challenges to them. These children are irritating. They are hard to live with. They do not "roll with the punches." They *need,* and therefore demand, more adult time and attention than adults are prepared to give them at certain "advanced" ages like five or six years. They grow up intellectually but they need the exhausting level of adult supervision more commonly dispensed to a two-year-old. They are "lopsidedly bright" but do not produce upon demand. They read today—if what there is to read interests them and nothing more attractive presents itself to entertain them—and tomorrow they do *not* read. Independent work is their downfall—unless it is very eye-catching and entertaining—and "idle hands are the devil's tool!" at home or on playground.

They become emotionally disturbed, often at a very young age, because everyone is exasperated with them. So their burden of guilt and low self-esteem is by far heavier even than that of the sweet, quiet, poor reader, and no comparison to that of their more successful peers. By the time they are teenagers, the emotional problems are often so huge that the neurologist looks almost in vain for the brain-based underpinnings, like an archaeologist poking about in rubble for a glimpse of a potsherd as evidence of what once *was* there!

Therefore, what children like this need is a *total environmental program,* in home and school, 16 hours of the waking day. There is no use whatsoever in "home vs. school" *pingpong* matches, in which the child is "hit" from home court to school court ("It's your business to get therapy." "No, it's your business to give learning disabilities help"). In this all-too-common *pingpong* "blame game," everyone—but most of all the child—is the loser.

So, the home must agree to get educated (counseled) to be a "special needs home." Intrapsychic and psychodynamic conflicts aroused by having a difficult child must of course be dealt with, but also a didactic "cookbook" of what kind of habit and character training works must be given to the parents and siblings. The home cannot wait to "feel" more healthy; the home must be instructed in how to "assume a virtue if you have it not," to be calm, repress anger in front of or toward the child, be organized and scheduled, and change into an old-fashioned home even if that's not the style. If you have a diabetic child, you may have to give up baking "goodies." If you have a hyperactive child, you may have to give up "hanging loose."

As for school, here, too, the "wide-angle lens" must move off the level (important as it is when appropriate) of modalities and methods of reading instruction and look at total supervision of the child. These children need *warm, firm, energetic, interacting, involved teachers.* The structure should be provided by a "cheerleader" approach rather than by a "police officer" approach, positive egging-onward rather than negative threats of punishment. We *do* know something from research about what does work for these children; the bitter, cold, hard truth is that it takes *people power* and not workbooks, work sheets, carrels, teaching machines, grey-painted drab rooms, etc. People power is expensive. Unfortunately for our budgets, it is what works! Because children who lack internal controls and organization need people to provide (warmly, calmly, not angrily) controls and organization.

This means that classroom teacher choice is critical, more so than issues of how much time out in a learning center, etc. It does no good to remove a child from a "regular" class into a "resource" class and hand him yet another worksheet, whatever its "approach," because without teacher supervision the child may never "approach" the worksheet! Research has shown that interchange between student and teacher rivets attention to the subject; this need not be one-to-one on a protracted time base like individual tutoring, but frequent active feedback responses from the teacher appear to be necessary for learning in such children.

Recommendations, therefore, are for class placement which affords the child the most "available" teacher in terms of *time* for him, style (warm, un-angry, energetic, responsive, organized in an explicit way); this must be a judgment made on the scene, probably independent of the issue of time out for one-to-one reading help. Carry-over of that reading help will be lost if the larger issues of work habits and social learning in the classroom are not addressed.

References

Aman, M. G. and Sprague, R. L. (1974). The state-dependent effects of methlyphenidate and dextroamphetamine. *J. Nervous Mental Dis. 158*: 268–279.

Ament, A. (1974). Treatment of hyperactive children (letter). *J.A.M.A. 230*:372.

Bax, M. and MacKeith, R. (eds) (1963). Minimal cerebral dysfunction. *Little Club Clinics in Developmental Medicine,* Vol. 10. London: Heineman.

Bradley, C. (1937). The behavior of children receiving benzedrine. *Am. J. Psychiat. 94*:577–585.

Buchsbaum, M. and Wender, P. (1973). Average evoked responses in normal and minimally brain dysfunctioned children treated with amphetamine: a preliminary report. *Arch. Gen. Psychiat. 29*:764–770.

Childers, A. T. (1935). Hyperactivity in children having behavior disorders. *Am. J. Orthopsychiat. 5*:227–243.

Connors, C. K. (1969). A teacher rating scale for use in drug studies with children. *Am. J. Psychiat. 126*:884–888.

Conners, C. K. (1970). Symptom patterns in hyperkinetic, neurotic, and normal children. *Child Dev. 41*:667–682.

Conners, C. K. (1972). Symposium: Behavior modification by drugs. II. Psychological effects of stimulant drugs in children with minimal brain dysfunction. *Pediatrics 49*:702–708.

Conners, C. K. and Eisenberg, L. (1963). The effects of methylphenidate on symptomatology and learning in disturbed children. *Am. J. Psychiat. 120*:458–464.

Conners, C. K. and Rothschild, G. H. (1973). The effect of dextroamphetamine on habituation of peripheral vascular response in children. *J. Abnormal Child Psychol. 1*:16–25.

David, O., Clark, J., and Voeller, K. L. (1972). Lead and hyperactivity. *Lancet 2*:900–903.

Denckla, M. B. (1978). Minimal brain dysfunction, in *Education and the Brain,* J. S. Chall and A. F. Mirsky (eds). The Seventy-Seventh Year Book of the National Society for the Study of Education.

Denckla, M. B. and Rudel, R. G. (1978). Anomalies of motor development in hyperactive boys. *Ann. Neurol. 3*:231–233.

Denckla, M. B., Bemporad, J., and McKay, M. (1976). Tics following methylphenidate administration: a report of twenty cases. *J.A.M.A. 235*: 1349–1351.

Denson, R., Nanson, J. L., and McWatters, M. A. (1975). Hyperkinesis and maternal smoking. *Can. Psychiat. Assoc. J. 20*:183–187.

Douglas, V. I. (1976). Perceptual and cognitive factors as determinants of learning disabilities: a review chapter with special emphasis on attentional factors, in *The Neuropsychology of Learning Disorders: Theo-*

retical Approaches, R. M. Knights, and D. J. Bakker (eds). Baltimore: University Park Press.

Feingold, B. F. (1975). Hyperkinesis and learning disabilities linked to artificial food flavors and colors. *Am. J. Nursing 75:*797–803.

Graham, F. K., Ernhart, C., Thurston, D., and Craft, M. (1962). Development three years after perinatal anoxia and other potentially damaging newborn experiences. *Psychol. Monographs 76:*1–53.

Gross, M. B. and Wilson, W. C. (1974). *Minimal Brain Dysfunction.* New York: Bruner/Mazel.

Handford, H. A. (1975). Brain hypoxia, minimal brain dysfunction, and schizophrenia. *Am. J. Psychiat. 132:*192–194.

Hare, R. D. (1969). Autonomic function in the psychopath. *J. Abnormal Psychol. Suppl. 73:*1–24, Part 2.

Hertzig, M., Bortner, M., and Birch, H. G. (1969). Neurologic findings in children educationally classified as "brain damaged." *Am. J. Orthopsychiat. 39:*437–446.

Kennard, M. A. (1939). Alterations in response to visual stimuli following lesions in the frontal lobes in monkeys. *Arch. Neurol. Psychiat. 41:*1153.

Kinsbourne, M. (1973). School problems. *Pediatrics 52:*697–710.

Kinsbourne, M. (1977). The mechanism of hyperactivity, in *Topics in Child Neurology,* M. E. Blaw, I. Rapin, and M. Kinsbourne (eds). New York: Spectrum Publications.

Knights, R. M. and Hinton, G. G. (1969). The effects of methylphenidate (Ritalin) on the motor skills and behavior of children with learning problems. *J. Nervous Mental Dis. 148:*643–653.

Knopp, W., Arnold, L. E., Andras, R. L., and Smeltzer, D. J. (1973). Predicting amphetamine response in hyperkinetic children by electric pupillography. *Pharmakopsychiatrie Neuro-Psychopharmakologie. 6:*158–166.

Laufer, M., Denhoff, E., and Solomons, G. (1957). Hyperkinetic impulse disorder in children's behavior problems. *Psychosomatic Med. 19:*38–49.

Lynn, R. (1966). *Attention, Arousal and the Orientation Reaction.* Oxford: Pergamon Press.

Millichap, J. G. and Fowler, G. W. (1967). Treatment of "minimal brain dysfunction" syndromes. *Pediatric Clinics of North America 14:*767–777.

Millichap, J. G. (1977) Growth of hyperactive children treated with methylphenidate: a possible growth stimulant effect, in *Learning Disabilities and Related Disorders: Facts and Current Issues,* J. G. Millichap (ed). Chicago: Year Book Medical Publishers.

Millichap, J. G. (1977). Panel discussions, in *Learning Disabilities and Related Disorders: Facts and Current Issues,* J. G. Millichap (ed). Chicago: Year Book Medical Publishers.

Morrison, J. R. and Stewart, M. A. (1973). Evidence for polygenetic inheritance in the hyperactive child syndrome. *Am. J. Psychiat. 130:*791–792.

Morrison, J. R. and Stewart, M. A. (1974). Bilateral inheritance as evidence for polygenicity in the hyperactive child syndrome. *J. Nervous Mental Dis. 158*:226–228.

Moyer, K. E. (1975). Allergy and aggression: the physiology of violence. *Psychology Today 9*:76–79.

Needleman, H. (1978). Personal communication.

Oettinger, L., Majovski, L. V., Limbeck, G. A., and Gauch, R. (1974). Bone age in children with minimal brain dysfunction. *Perceptual and Motor Skills 39*:1127–1131.

Ott, J. (1974). The eyes' dual function—part II. *Eye, Ear, Nose and Throat Monthly 53*:377–381.

Peters, J. E., Romine, J. S., and Dyckman, R. A. (1975). A special neurological examination of children with learning disabilities. *Dev. Med. Child Neurol. 17*:63–78.

Pope, L. (1970). Motor activity in brain-injured children. *Am. J. Orthopsychiat. 40*:783–794.

Prechtl, H. and Stemmer, C. (1935). The choreiform syndrome in children. *Dev. Med. Child Neurol. 4*:119–127.

Quay, H. C. and Peterson, D. R. (1967). *Manual for the Behavior Problem Checklist*. Champaign, Ill.: Children's Research Center, University of Illinois.

Rapoport, J. L., Buchsbaum, M. S., Zahn, J. P., Weingartner, H., Ludlow, C., and Mikkelsen, E. J. (1978). Dextroamphetamine: cognitive and behavioral effects in normal prepubertal boys. *Science 199*:560–563.

Ross, D. M. and Ross, S. A. (1976). *Hyperactivity: Research, Theory and Action*. New York: Wiley.

Safer, D. J. and Allen, R. P. (1973). Factors influencing the suppressant effects of two stimulant drugs on the growth of hyperactive children. *Pediatrics 51*:660–667.

Safer, D. J., Allen, R. P., and Barr, E. (1975). Growth rebound after termination of stimulant drugs. *J. Pediatrics 86*:113–116.

Satterfield, J. H., Atoian, G., Brashears, G. C., Burleigh, A. C., and Dawson, M. E. (1974). Electrodermal studies of minimal brain dysfunction children, in *Clinical Use of Stimulant Drugs in Children*. The Hague: Excepta Medica.

Satterfield, J. H., Cantwell, D. P., and Satterfield, B. T. (1974). Pathophysiology of the hyperactive child syndrome. *Arch. Gen. Psychiat. 31*: 839–844.

Satterfield, J. H., Cantwell, D. P., Saul, R. E., Lesser, L. I., and Podosin, R. L. (1973). Response to stimulant drug treatment in hyperactive children, prediction from EEG and neurological findings. *J. Autism Child Schizophrenia 3*:36–48.

Satterfield, J. H. and Dawson, M. E. (1971). Electrodermal correlates of hyperactivity in children. *Psychophysiology 8*:191–197.

Silbergeld, E. K. and Goldberg, A. M. (1974). Lead-induced behavioral dysfunction; an animal model of hyperactivity. *Exp. Neurol. 42*:146–157.

Sokolov, E. N. (1963). *Perception and the Conditioned Reflex,* Oxford: Pergamon Press.

Sprague, R. L., Barnes, K. R., and Werry, J. S. (1970). Methylphenidate and thioridazine: learning, activity, and behavior in emotionally disturbed boys. *Am. J. Orthopsychiat. 40*:615–628.

Sprague, R. L. and Sleator, E. K. (1976). Drugs and dosages: implications for learning disabilities, in *The Neuropsychology of Learning Disorders: Theoretical Approaches,* R. M. Knights and D. J. Bakker (eds). Baltimore: University Park Press.

Stewart, M. A. and Olds, S. W. (1973). *Raising a Hyperactive Child.* New York: Harper & Row.

Still, G. F. (1902). The Coulstonian Lectures on some abnormal physical conditions in children. *Lancet 1*:1008–1012, 1077–1082, 1163–1168.

Strauss, A. A. and Kephart, N. C. (1955). Progress in theory and clinic. *Psychopathology and Education of the Brain Injured Child,* Vol. II. New York: Grune and Stratton.

Touwen, B. C. L. and Prechtl, H. F. R. (1970). *The Neurological Examination of the Child with Minor Nervous Dysfunction.* London: Heinemann.

Tredgold, C. H. (1908). *Mental Deficiency (Amentia),* 1st ed. New York: Wook.

Weakland, J. H., Fisch, R., Watzlawick, P., and Bodin, A. M. (1974). Brief therapy: focused problem resolution. *Family Process 13*:141–168.

Weiss, G., Minde, K., Werry, J. S., Douglas, V., and Nemeth, E. (1971). Studies on the hyperactive child: VIII. Five-year follow-up. *Arch. Gen. Psychiat. 24*:409–414.

Wender, P. H. (1971). *Minimal Brain Dysfunction in Children.* New York: Wiley-Interscience.

Wender, P. H. (1976). Hypothesis for possible biochemical basis of minimal brain dysfunction in *The Neuropsychology of Learning Disorders,* R. M. Knights and D. J. Bakker (eds). Baltimore: University Park Press.

Werry, J. S. (1968) Developmental hyperactivity. *Pediatric Clinics of North America 15*:581–599.

Werry, J. S. and Sprague, R. L. (1970). Hyperactivity, in *Symptoms of Psychopathology,* C. G. Costello (ed). New York: Wiley.

Wiener, G. (1970). Varying psychological sequelae of lead ingestion in children. *Public Health Report 85*:19–24.

Willis, T. J. and Lovaas, I. (1977). A behavioral approach to treating hyperactive children: the parent's role, in *Learning Disabilities and Related Disorders: Facts and Current Issues,* J. G. Millichap (ed). Chicago: Year Book Medical Publishers.

Wolff, P. H. and Hurwitz, I. (1973). Functional implications of the minimal brain damage syndrome, in *Minimal Cerebral Dysfunction in Children,* S. Walzer and P. Wolff (eds). *Semin. Psychiatr. 5*:105.

Index of Authors Cited

599

Subject Index

615